NED KELLY
A SHORT LIFE

Here's to a very
good friend to my
late father, Sam.

Regards

Merv Ball
"Son of Sam"

NED KELLY
A SHORT LIFE

BY
IAN JONES

Lothian
BOOKS

Thomas C. Lothian Pty Ltd
11 Munro Street, Port Melbourne
Victoria 3207

First published 1995
Paperback edition published 1996

Special edition published 1996
ISBN 0 85091 836 7

National Library of Australia
Cataloguing-in-publication data:
Jones, Ian.
    Ned Kelly: a short life.

    Includes index.
    ISBN 0 85091 801 4

    1. Kelly, Ned, 1854–1880. 2. Bushrangers — Australia —
    Biography, I. Title.

364. 1552092

Cover and text design by Dennis Ogden
Maps (pages xi and xii) and Stringybark illustrations
    (photograph pages) by John Ward
Index by Russell Brooks
Typeset in Australia by Bookset Type & Image
Printed in Australia by Griffin Paperbacks

CONTENTS

Preface
and Acknowledgements

This book should begin as it ends, confronting an enigma. In her recent biography of Sir Redmond Barry, the judge who sentenced Ned Kelly to death, Ann Galbally sees Barry's approach to the trial as dominated by his privileged, Anglo-Irish past. She continues:

> Kelly too was an anachronistic figure. The last of the bushrangers, gentlemanly, polite to women, a fine bushman, he was incapable of survival in the later Victorian world of new technology and developing transport. In fact it was the telegraph and railway that had brought about his downfall.

It would be equally true to say that Ned Kelly exploited both the telegraph and the railway as key elements in the strategy of his remarkable Glenrowan campaign, and that it failed not because of his inability to cope with this technology but because his enemies used it so badly. Even then, the man often portrayed as a ruthless and cold-blooded killer might have succeeded. In the end Ned Kelly failed because he was neither ruthless nor cold-blooded; and in that failure he achieved true greatness.

I first met Ned Kelly in 1941 when an old gardener called Tom Maine lent me a battered first edition of Kenneally's *Complete Inner History of the Kelly Gang and Their Pursuers*, the ultimate portrayal of Ned Kelly as a victim and hero. It was all clear cut, but soon after, Chomley's *True Story of the Kelly Gang*, snapped up from a railway bookstall, challenged me with a darkly contrasting portrait. I had met the enigma. Now, 54 years later, I know that Kenneally's history was not 'complete' and Chomley's story was not 'true'. I hope this book is closer to being both.

In the last sixteen years of my search for Ned my wife, Bronwyn Binns, has supported me with her formidable skills as a researcher and interpreter of the past. Her contribution has amounted to a collaboration on the project.

There was a time in the early 1960s when playwright Robin Corfield and a teenage Keith McMenomy were the only others I knew who were actively pursuing the Kelly story, until Melbourne University lecturer Weston Bate and student John McQuilton joined the hunt. All have made distinguished contributions to Kelly literature and all have been generous with their knowledge and resources, as have the newer breed of Kelly scholars led by the indefatigable Dagmar Balcarek, with valued help from Noel O'Shea, Laurie Moore, Gary Dean, Kevin Passey, Rob Ogilvie, Bob Shannon, Brian McDonald, Michael Dalton and Allan Nixon (who open-handedly shared his vast Harry Power archive). Max Brown, Ned's first biographer, has inspired and encouraged my work. I am especially grateful to John Phillips, the Chief Justice of Victoria, for his friendship as much as for his contributions to our knowledge of Ned's trial. Johanna Parsons-Nicholls, Pat Kelly, Don Bennetts, John Lahey and Gary Sturgess have given many years of support; Marian Matta has prompted me to dig deeper on several topics; while Joyce Richardson's long interest in my work produced an encounter with Deborah Bird Rose's extraordinary study of Ned in Aboriginal tradition. Leonard Radic's description of Ned Kelly's Declaration of the Republic of North-Eastern Victoria was greatly valued.

Two sadly missed figures in Adult Education, Colin Cave and Jill Eastwood, prompted quantum leaps in my studies, preparing papers for their 1967 and 1993 Kelly Seminars.

Through the years, the staff of the La Trobe Library have given Bronwyn and me unstinted help — often under challenging conditions. We are specially grateful to the staff of the La Trobe Newspaper Library, Manuscripts Section and Illustrations Collection.

Gary Presland, manager of the Police Historical Unit and Police Museum, and his staff have been unfailingly helpful, as have been personnel at the Laverton and Melbourne bases of the Public Record Office. (My research stretches back to the days when Harry Nunn ran the [then] State Archives in the basement of the [then] Public Library, where he collated the five cheese boxes of documents — later to become eight boxes — which came to be called the Kelly Papers. Like all Kelly scholars, I am in Harry's debt. Because much of my work in this collection pre-dated current Public Record Office cataloguing, I have consistently used the generic term 'Kelly Papers' for this huge resource, most of it now available on microfilm.)

Long before the Minutes of Evidence of the Royal Commission of 1881 were available in a facsimile edition, bookseller Kenneth Hince sold me an original set at a generous price. Much of my delving in the Commission's 17 874 questions and answers, Appendices, Progress Reports, Tables and Supplementary Papers, was carried out in that precious original, now put out to grass. I am deeply grateful to Rupert Hammond for making available his work to date on an epic index to the Commission.

Fieldwork has played a major role in my research and through the years I have enjoyed the help of many folk in the Kelly Country. Among them are Gwen and Charlie Griffiths, Esmai and Ken Wortman — old and valued friends, generous with their time and hospitality; the Rev. Payne Croston; Janet Street; Rene, Bill and Wally Knowles; Ivy Johnson; Des Zwar and his parents, Lin and Ray; Louise Earp; Matilda and Jack Macmillan; Wilf Burrows; Walter Miller; Mr and Mrs J. Christopher; Brenda Leitch; Ted and Les Jones; Mr and Mrs Bill Gee; Mrs Stan Shelton; Mrs E. White; George Collier; George Stilley; Ernie Manton; May and Roy Harvey; Bernie Clancey; Jack Walsh; Jack Healy; Colin Crawford; Ken Embling; Len and Dulcie Griffiths; Bridget Griffiths; Wilma and Ted Wells; Margaret and Brian Gladstone; Pat and Jim White; Hubert Warner; Greg Forrest; Graeme Gray; Don Hammond; Allie and Bert Trezise; Clive and Alan Robinson; Dulcie and Len Schoer; Michael Falkenberg; Ian Shelton; Craig Burns; Brian Hayes; and Betty and Ric Shanley.

In my fieldwork I have been helped by Tony Doogood, Ron Shaw, Trevor Dawson-Grove, Albert Tucker, Peter Lawson, Geoff Richardson, John Pinkney, Bert Watts, Keith Dunstan, and consistently by my son Darren — most notably when Darren and I found the actual site of the Stringybark Creek gunfight (later confirmed in a particularly soggy expedition with Bronwyn and our daughter, Elizabeth).

I am deeply grateful to descendants of the Kelly, Hart, Byrne, Lloyd and Sherritt families for their trust. They include 'Black' Jack, Paddy and Joe Griffiths, Alma Davies and Elsie Pettifer (all nephews and nieces of Ned); Steve Hart (a nephew); and Elly Byrne, sister of Joe. An enormous contribution was made by Tom Lloyd Jr who, between 1964 and 1980, shared with me his father's reminiscences as virtually the fifth member of the Kelly Gang.

Among the many other people who have recorded and shared their family links with the Kelly story, I am specially grateful to Myra Brolan, Anne Hooper, Michael Whitty, Laurie Power, Ron White, Leigh Olver, Margot Fulton, Christina Vandenberg and Mrs W. J. Corby. I cannot adequately express my thanks to Keith Harrison who in 1969 enabled me to examine the original of Ned Kelly's and Joe Byrne's Jerilderie Letter, and Ronald Davenport who, two years earlier, provided me with a copy of Joseph Ashmead's manuscript, so often cited in this book.

For sharing their vast knowledge of colonial firearms, I am indebted to Neil Speed, Edgar Penzig and Maurie Albert.

Christine Woods in Hobart and Steven Ffeary-Smyrl in Dublin have provided expert research assistance.

With long experience of my odd ways, Veda Currie put my scribbled-over typescript onto disc, and Helen Chamberlin, my editor, was a tower of calm strength. John Ward brought his usual dedication to the endpapers, map and Stringybark Creek illustrations, and Dennis Ogden wrapped it all up with a bold and sensitive design.

To all of the above, to others acknowledged in the notes and to everyone I could not mention, my thanks.

Finally, a dedication to my great-great-grandfather, John Daly of County Cork, who was convicted of cow stealing and transported to Australia for life in 1826. Long before I knew of his existence, I'm sure he was helping my work.

Glenrowan, 1880

MORGAN'S LOOKOUT

WARBY RANGES

TO WANGARATTA

LINE BROKEN

NOT TO SCALE

KELLY TREE

PLATELAYERS TENTS

RAILWAY STATION

McDONNELL'S HOTEL

JONES'S HOTEL

STATION MASTER

REARDON'S HOUSE

POLICE STATION

CURNOW'S SCHOOL

TO BENALLA

...RTIMER'S HOUSE

1

SON OF RED

DECEMBER 1840 – DECEMBER 1866

Ned Kelly was probably born on the lower slopes of an extinct volcano within weeks or even days of a bloody battle between rebel Ballarat gold miners and the forces of Her Majesty Queen Victoria. Today, both the place and time seem appropriate to his turbulent life. Then, the years stretched ahead to modest, tranquil horizons from what seemed a fortunate beginning.

It was December 1854. Little Ned was the second surviving child and first son of John Kelly, an ex-convict from Tipperary, and his wife Ellen, who had migrated from Ireland with her family. John, nicknamed 'Red' for his carroty hair, had done well as a gold digger and horse dealer — well enough to pay £615 for a 41-acre farm here on the gentle fall of land below the Big Hill, overlooking the tiny settlement of Beveridge, 25 miles north of Melbourne. He milked a few cows, ran some horses and worked as a splitter and fencer. His business, like the town, was getting started. It would grow — or not grow — with the town.

Red never spoke of the crime for which he had been transported to Australia. This was odd. Catholic Irish saw no shame in being exiled for breaking the laws of their British rulers. One of Red's brothers-in-law, who had arrived as a free migrant, nevertheless told his children that he had been a transported convict. He saw this as a prouder way to have left Ireland. Red's silence sits even more strangely with claims that he was transported for socio-political reasons — 'the type of young Irish patriot who was prepared to make even the supreme sacrifice for his country's freedom'.

Red was a true Irishman with a profound bitterness against centuries of subjection to the English and the Anglo-Irish. He drank in with his mother's milk stories of the brutally suppressed rebellion of 1798, only 22 years before his birth, and would pass on to his son a burning pride in Ireland, a love of her traditions and a yearning for freedom from what Ned would call 'the Saxon yoke'. To this extent, like most Catholic Irish, Red was a rebel. Yet there is little to support claims that he was an activist. An activist would have railed against the law that sent him to exile, using his enemies' actions as a weapon against them. The air of mystery surrounding Red's transportation seems to deny such a role.

Many years later a newspaperman who had spoken with Ellen Kelly claimed that Red was transported because of 'a faction fight or some other affray at a fair' in which a man was killed. The journalist drily commented that no country would consider this a disgraceful crime, least of all Ireland, 'where it would have been viewed ... in a more harmless light than the permanent removal of a tyrannical and obnoxious landlord, a bailiff, a process-server, a gauger [excise man], or an informer'. Ironically, a Royal Commission would record Red's crime as 'an agrarian outrage, stated to have been shooting at a landlord with intent to murder'. (The phrase 'agrarian outrage' was usually applied to rebel activity and probably encouraged the notion that Red had been an activist.) A popular Victorian writer repeated an extraordinary yarn about Red being involved with two other men in a murder. In what sounds like pure gothic fantasy, not only does Red betray his two friends but he volunteers to act as their hangman at a public execution. On the scaffold his black mask is snatched away by one of the condemned men. Exposed, he is shipped out to Australia as a convict to save his wretched life. Interestingly, all three stories involve violent death or attempted murder, while the least likely of them introduces betrayal — elements which might have lain behind Red's curious silence.

The mystery of Red's crime seems easily solved by a small handful of Irish and Australian documents. Unarguably, Red was the John Kelly of Tipperary who, in December 1840, stole two pigs worth 'about six pounds' from a Ballysheehan farmer called James Cooney. Twenty-one-year-old John lived with his parents, Thomas and Mary Kelly, in a little cottage on ⅜ acre of bleak upland near the village of Clonbrogan. It is easy to see his crime springing from the poverty of his parents — an act of rebellion against the midwinter hardships endured by them and by his younger brothers and sisters. This may have been true. However, while tradition has the pigs taken from 'a prosperous farmer', everything suggests that Cooney was, like the Kellys, a cottier (a peasant landholder of a ½ acre or less) whose pigs were part and parcel of the potato ecology on which such battlers narrowly survived. No political shading here, not even a question of haves and have-nots. Red's crime was stock theft, pure and simple, mean and ordinary. Was this something to hide?

In Dublin Castle papers relating to Red's case were tucked away in a 'Crown Witnesses' file — identifying him as an informer, most hated of all figures in an Irish rogues' gallery. Some key documents have disappeared, but registers list their contents, sketching a story that deepens this already dark shadow across Red's departure from Ireland. Red took

Cooney's two pigs to market and was arrested in a lodging house. Though described by police as 'a notorious character' who had been involved with three men in the earlier theft of seven cows — a crime that could earn a life sentence — Red would receive the minimum term of seven years transportation. It is clear that he had struck a deal with the police and informed on his fellow cow-stealers.

There is no way of knowing what pressure, if any, was exerted on Red. To a 21-year-old who was probably the major supporter of his parents and six brothers and sisters — the oldest a teenager, the youngest a baby — a life sentence could not be thought of. A seven-year term seemed to offer Red some hope of a future — even if that future could be bought only by betraying his friends. However agonising the decision might have been, it was made and the three were arrested. In an awful, unexpected twist to a familiar-enough Irish scenario, one of Red's friends, Phillip Regan, tried to escape from custody. He was shot and killed.

Red was sentenced on 1 January 1841, shipped to Dublin and kept on a brig in the harbour until July when he joined 180 other convicts aboard the transport *Prince Regent* about to set sail for the penal colony of Van Diemen's Land. Now John Kelly steps from the mists of history into hard forensic light as surgeon Phillip Jones assesses his fitness for the voyage and records his description:

Trade, Labourer; Height, 5/8; Age, 21: Complex, Fresh: Head, Large; Hair, Reddish; Whiskers, Reddish; Visage, Long; Forehead, medium Height; Eyebrows, Brown; Eyes, Blue; Nose, Large; Mouth, Medm.; Chin, Medm.

The five-month voyage via the Cape of Good Hope was boring and conditions were harsh to modern eyes, but the ship was well managed and only three men died. Immigrants often fared worse. The *Prince Regent* sailed up the broad Derwent River to Hobart Town on 2 January 1842 and Red looked out at what an English convict called 'the savage grandeur' of ramparted Mount Wellington glowering over the port. The Englishman declared, 'I would rather be dead than be compelled to live in a savage country like this!' Red was probably prepared to make the best of it, as the Irish usually did, coming from hard lives in a hard country. He was alive and his secret was locked away, with only the memory of the dead Phillip Regan to accuse him.

Red had arrived here at a strange time. Transportation to New South Wales had just been abolished, and assignment — a convict labour system close to slavery — had been done away with. To cope with the convicts now pouring into Van Diemen's Land at the rate of some 4000 a year, a disastrous 'probation' scheme was set up by which men served a year under normal penal conditions and were then scattered over the island colony in large work gangs based at probation stations.

Classified by Surgeon Jones as 'orderly', Red was sent straight to the brand new station at Browns River south of Hobart, where monthly reports continued to show him as 'quiet and good', 'orderly', and for the sake of variety, 'quiet and orderly' — until 1 October, when he left the station without permission and was found 'in a potatoe field belong^g to Mr O'Connor'. This thoroughly Irish misdemeanour earned Red two months hard labour in leg irons. Almost as soon as they were struck off, he was officially placed on probation to start his second year as a Vandemonian.

Red had learned his lesson and gave no more trouble. From the nearby coast he could look across Storm Bay to the dwindling spine of the peninsula where Port Arthur lay — legendary penal town where serious offenders were reformed, broken or subjected to experiments as 'incorrigibles'. On the other side of Van Diemen's Land, marooned on the wild west coast, was Macquarie Harbour, abandoned eight years before as a penal station but living and growing in convict lore as the hell-on-earth where men murdered to win escape on the gallows. Red would pass on to his son stories of such 'places of tyranny and condemnation' where Irishmen were sent 'to pine their lives away in starvation and misery among tyrants worse than the promised hell itself'.

Red worked with axe and shovel, saw and hammer, accepted the close boundaries of his world and noted the occasional man whose ears and nose had been bitten off — convict punishment for informers. There were many John Kellys here, often red-headed. The affair of the seven cows and two pigs had happened in another world and Phillip Regan was becoming a strangely unreal memory, six feet under the sweet, green sod of Tipperary.

Red worked at Morven for a year and early in 1844 was sent to a station opposite Perth, on the South Esk River near Launceston. Here, on 11 July 1845, he gained a Ticket of Leave which gave him the right to travel freely within the colony and earn wages for the rest of his sentence. There was only one more blot on his record — in itself trivial but a shadow of things to come. In 1847 he was fined 5 shillings for being drunk and disorderly. Then, on 11 January 1848, seven years and ten days after his conviction, he received his Certificate of Freedom.

The labour market in Van Diemen's Land was glutted with freed convicts and within a year, as one John Kelly among many, Red joined the overflow of men streaming across Bass Strait to the Port Phillip District of New South Wales. Perhaps alone, perhaps with mates, he followed the route of the adventurers who, fourteen years before, had founded the settlement that became the river port town of Melbourne.

From there, Red could strike out and shape a new life in the broad, raw mainland of Australia.

◆

BACK IN JULY 1841, the very month that Red had sailed from Dublin, the Quinn family of ten arrived in Melbourne, straggling across its riverside hills on a grid of incredibly broad and muddy streets. The town's immediate past was clear in the rolling paddocks and fast-disappearing gum trees, the tatterdemalion shacks, the animals cropping at roadside grass, the horses, carts and bullock wagons slopping their way to and fro, and in the few dispirited Aborigines watching it all. Melbourne's future was taking shape in a surprising crop of town buildings — many of brick and stone, two storeys high — steadily blocking in the ambitious town plan centred on a regal quartet of streets running down to the Yarra River — King, William, Queen, Elizabeth. The red uniforms of soldiers guarding work parties of Sydneyside convicts, the prisoners pinioned in stocks for public abuse and a half-finished prison to be the scene of public hangings — all set the hated imperial stamp on the place. Already, James Quinn looked out to the grey billows of open bushland and the hills beyond. Here would be a better life.

The Quinns were from County Antrim at the north-eastern corner of Ireland, where the population was almost entirely of Scottish descent and Scotland was so close that Antrim Presbyterians had been known to row across there for church services. It was no place for a good Catholic family, and James Quinn was a man of energy and vision, with three sons to help make his dreams a reality, sons who would have faced unhappy lives in the developing tragedy of northern Ireland. James told his children simply that the family had migrated 'to improve their position'.

James was 37 and his wife Mary was 32. Their eldest child, Patrick, was 15; the youngest, Jimmy, a six-month-old baby. In between were Helen, Jack, Mary Anne, Ellen, Kate and Jane.

Ellen was nine, a striking, slim-faced child with keen, blue-grey eyes and black hair, enjoying to the full this yearned-for adventure. A friend would provide a romantic but probably accurate picture of Ellen's Irish childhood.

> Some said there was a wild strain in her. She loved to be free and hated restraint. She was sent to school but was often missing from her class when she would roam over the hills or in the woods after birds' nests or wild berries. She would tear her clothes hiding in some hedge when she saw someone she feared would inform on her playing truant.

Not surprisingly, like the rest of her family Ellen had learnt to read but not to write, though she is supposed to have paid closer attention to lessons about Australia, 'the great country where the law breakers of the Old Land were sent'.

The Quinns' voyage to Australia as bounty migrants on the ship *England* had been blighted by an epidemic of whooping cough that killed sixteen children and two adults. Even this had not daunted young Ellen. 'Nell soon became a favourite with all on board, and would talk to the sailors, and sing to them little Irish songs.' Sharp-eyed, sharp-tongued Ellen with the rebellious streak, Ellen who loved horses and freedom and singing, was to be the mother of Ned Kelly.

The Quinns had reached Port Phillip at a disastrous time. Falling wool prices, a punctured land boom and rampant imports brought a four-year depression. While businesses and reputations crumbled, with bankrupts paying as little as a farthing (a quarter of a penny) in the pound and spreading hardship, winter gave way to summer under a cobalt sky and the family slowly made their way in the hard-hit town. In a brick store-room, an ambitious young Anglo-Irish lawyer called Redmond Barry was given charge of a special court to handle small debt cases. Faced with a backlog of 800 litigants, he moved his court to the billiards room of a nearby hotel and founded the judicial career which would impact cruelly on the life of the Quinns, hardest of all on Ellen.

James found work as a porter 'at different commercial establishments' and saved enough to rent some land and buy 'a few milch cows and bullocks'. The family took up a small farm on Moonee Ponds Creek near the village of Brunswick, where Mary and the children milked the cows while James carted goods with the bullocks and sold firewood in Melbourne. Ellen found work at McNaughton's saddlery in Elizabeth Street for a couple of years, until James rented a bigger property out at Broadmeadows. Here Ellen's teenage brothers, Patrick and Jack, ran the bullock team, freeing their father for the farm. By now three more children had been born: Bill, Maggie and Grace.

About 1849 James was able to move further out, near the settlement of Wallan Wallan, 30 miles from Melbourne, where he rented 640 acres near Kemp's Swamp at the head of the Merri Creek.

By now Ellen was approaching 18, slim, darkly attractive and as handy on the farm as any of her brothers — good with the cattle and a superb horsewoman. That year or early the next, there was a caller at the Quinn house, a young man with a 'thick shock of . . . red hair and bush whiskers'. It was Red Kelly. He had been working his way through the district as a fencer and splitter when he met James Quinn in a Donnybrook pub. Over a few drinks, Red had talked James into a wild scheme to make some money by setting up a 'jigger still' to make *poteen*, moonshine whisky. In the hard, sober light of this new day, the scheme had lost its charm for James, and Red seemed far less appealing as a partner. Not so to Ellen. More than seventy years later she would remember the young visitor as 'six feet in his stockings ... broad shouldered, strong and active; in fact in every way a fine type of athlete'. It was probably an accurate enough memory of 30-year-old Red as he looked to a teenage girl in love.

James didn't approve of the match. He was probably suspicious of Red's curious evasiveness about his convict background, of his readiness to pursue get-rich-quick schemes and, most of all perhaps, of his weakness for grog. In later years even Ellen would admit to a friend, 'that he was a bit fond of whisky and at times took a drop too much'.

James and Mary Quinn refused Red's request to marry Ellen and, traditionally, the lovers eloped to Melbourne. In fact, Ellen became pregnant in May 1850 and, for reasons which remain unclear, another six months passed before the 'elopement'. Obviously James and Mary Quinn were no longer opposing the marriage and the formidable trio of James, Jack and Patrick Quinn would have easily persuaded Red to meet his responsibilities, if he needed persuading. Perhaps the months passed in a simple succession of initial panic on Red's part, hesitation to face the Quinns with this persuasive new argument to accept him as a son-in-law, time to let the family adjust to the situation and then give him permission to build 'a snug little hut' on their rented land and, finally, time to build it and to make and gather a few furnishings and possessions.

One other factor might have caused delay — the death of 25-year-old Patrick Quinn, accidentally drowned in the Murray River at Echuca, a numbing blow for the family.

In November, when Ellen and Red finally chose to marry in Melbourne, it's most likely that they travelled down to the city for the amazing two-week festival celebrating the independence of Port Phillip from New South Wales. No one cared that separation would not be formalised until the following year. The birth of the Colony of Victoria was hailed with thanksgiving services, feasting, processions, bonfires, sky rockets and the ceremonial opening of a huge stone bridge across the Yarra. Ten-foot balloons emblazoned 'Separation' floated inland on providential southerlies, carrying the glorious news.

Ellen and Red were probably there on Saturday 16 November, to join the crowds flocking across newly-opened Princes Bridge to a huge sports meeting at South Melbourne. On the Monday they presented themselves at handsome St Francis Church in Lonsdale Street with witnesses Patrick Kennedy and Ellen Ryan, to be married by Father Gerald Ward. Red had learnt to sign his name and traced a sloping 'John Kelly' on the register with showy loops and curlicues. Ellen signed with a cross.

They turned their backs on the dying echoes of the Separation festival and travelled back to the frugal reality of the hut at Wallan. Here, three months later, on 25 February 1851, Ellen bore a daughter.

Five days after the birth Mary Jane Kelly was baptised in Kilmore — only 12 miles northwards but a tedious climb ('very much like the ascent of a pyramid') over Pretty Sally's Hill, which marked the spine of the Great Dividing Range. This could suggest that the baby was in frail health and her parents were particularly anxious for her to receive the sacrament. It is usually assumed that Mary Jane died soon afterwards, but an incomplete and inaccurate entry in the baptism register at Kilmore is the only record of her life; the first record of her death was supplied ten years later when a brother's birth registration noted Mary Jane as 'deceased'.

While Ellen and Red lived through this shadowy tragedy, great events were reshaping the land. That year Edward Hammond Hargreaves was credited with the discovery of payable gold near Bathurst and the New South Wales gold rush was launched. As men poured out of newly pro-claimed Victoria, a reward was offered for gold discovery in the colony. It was claimed almost immediately, with strikes in the Plenty Ranges, at Clunes, Buninyong, and, in August, at Ballarat, closely followed by Bendigo, Castlemaine and soon after by Beechworth. The fickle gold seekers left the New South Wales fields and poured into Victoria by the tens of thousands. Many Victorian towns outside the goldfields were left peopled by women, children and old men; Wangaratta's adult popula-tion dwindled to six women. Ships flocked to Port Phillip Bay from Europe, America and eventually China, and the population exploded, with 3000 new arrivals a week. Within a year this was the dearest place in the world to live.

Red rarely rushed into things and let the first hysteria of the gold rushes subside before he finally decided to try his luck, probably in 1853. There was a goldfield at Kilmore, 10 miles to the north, a small, brawling, Irish diggings. Golden ambition, a desire for a more peaceful existence — or even for greater anonymity — drew him further afield to what was then 'the metropolis of the diggings of Victoria'.

Possibly with 22-year-old Jack Quinn, Red made the 70-mile trek across the Divide to Bendigo — a canvas and timber city of 40 000, straggling over an area about ten miles square among stony ridges of ironbark, yellow creeks and hills gleaming white with dug-up quartz.

Red paid his 30-shilling licence fee, staked out a claim 12-feet square and started chipping down through 20 or 30 feet of conglomerate to a bed of clayey sand, and below it to the white pipeclay where gold was to be found. A claim could yield £1000 worth of gold, sometimes £1000 per man. Or it could prove a 'shicer', a dud. Either way, everyone paid the same monthly licence fee of 30 shillings and any miner found not carrying a current licence was automatically fined £5. Goldfields police, who enforced this hated system with 'licence hunts', were often high-handed thugs who spawned the spread of a powerful anti-police culture among the diggers, one they would carry into their post-goldfields lives in city and country.

Goldfields officials included too many men who considered themselves born to rule but were incapable of maintaining discipline — let alone respect — anywhere but in a schoolroom or barracks square. Goldfields magistrates were often despotic, corrupt or both.

In the face of all this, the extraordinary Bohemia of the diggings provided a seedbed for revolt. There were early rumblings at Bendigo, even unofficial flags for a diggers' republic — a huge green banner for the Irish with harp, shamrock, pick and shovel, while an Englishman produced an amazing creation which included pick, shovel and gold cradle, the scales of justice, the Roman axe bound with rods, an emu and a kangaroo.

Red avoided trouble with the law and with those trying to overthrow it. As always, he was 'averse to quarrelling, and ever prone to act the part of peacemaker when he saw others engaged in any altercation calculated to lead to violence'. For these qualities he would be, perhaps unfairly, 'remarked as a rather timid man', a judgement never to be made of his son when Ned followed in his father's steps — hating conflict and 'frequently quelling unseemly rows at the public house'.

Red failed to make a big strike, but earned enough 'to justify his return home'. If he reached the little shack on Merri Creek in time for Christmas of 1853, it was a joyful reunion. He was greeted by Ellen and a baby daughter, Anne, born the previous month. The modest clean-up from Bendigo probably earned his acceptance by James Quinn as partner in a horse-dealing venture and, with horseflesh still at a premium in a colony of travellers, they did well — well enough for Red and Ellen to consider striking out on their own.

Ellen's older sister Helen had married red-headed Timothy Ryan the year before and the couple were settled on a 5-acre block at Beveridge, a few miles to the south. Perhaps taking baby Annie on a visit to the Ryans, Red and Ellen were charmed by the tiny settlement scattered among a parkland of banksia trees, box gum, wattles and she-oaks across the gentle southern slopes of the Big Hill — a spectacular volcanic cone that rose 'green and clear' from skirting gum trees. Just above the highest street of the town, at the knees of the hill, a farm was for sale — 41 acres 'together with buildings and etc'. Red paid £615 for the property. It was a high price, but the main Sydney road was surveyed through the town and Beveridge seemed set to thrive, like all the settlements serving this great artery of colonial and intercolonial life. Red had such confidence in Beveridge's future that later in the year he bought a half-acre town block and built a house to rent.

On this tide of optimism, Ellen became pregnant when baby Anne was only four months old. She approached full term in December, as the long, slow storm of protest against the gold licence system was about to break in Ballarat, 60 miles to the west. It had been brought to explosion point by the same volatile mix encountered by Red at Bendigo: auto-cratic gold officials, a suspect magistrate, thuggish police and what an English visitor snootily called, 'Low, red-republican foreigners ... who have no idea but of physical force, and the demolition of an existing authority'.

The rebel Ballarat gold diggers, led by a young Irish civil engineer called Peter Lalor, burnt their gold licences and built a crude stockade of mining timber on the Eureka gold-bearing lead, home of the field's 'Tipperary Mob'. They declared a republic and hoisted a magnificent Southern Cross flag which ignored the pasts of England and Ireland and looked boldly to the boundless skies of a new world. Redcoats and police attacked at dawn on 3 December 1854. There was a brief, ghastly battle in which five soldiers were killed and fifteen wounded, while thirty diggers died. Many of them were shot, bayoneted or sabred after the stockade had fallen, one man cut down by a court official called Akehurst who would make a brief appearance in Ellen Kelly's life thirteen years later. And the rebel leader, Peter Lalor, a seriously wounded fugitive with a price on his head, would play an unlikely role in the adult life of the baby Ellen was about to bear.

On an unrecorded day or night in December 1854, almost certainly at the Kelly farm below the Big Hill, Ellen gave birth to a son, helped by Mrs David Gorman from a bluestone house on the eastern flank of the hill. They called the boy Edward, after Red's closest brother, and he was baptised by a Father Charles O'Hea, possibly riding circuit from the village of Pentridge, site of a four-year-old prison stockade. Both the priest and the place would resonate in the life of Ned when he was becoming a man. And O'Hea would stand by him at his death, perhaps recalling that long-lost summer when he anointed the tiny head, promising immortality of the soul, unable to comprehend that this life would also achieve an immortality few even dream of.

The Eureka rebellion that marked Ned's birth had been a watershed of Victoria's golden years. The year had seen a rash of commercial failures in Melbourne, the per capita gold yield was falling, the populations of Melbourne and Victoria were declining.

Early in 1855, thirteen of the digger rebels stood trial for treason in Melbourne, eleven of them before Redmond Barry, the one-time billiards-room arbiter, now the senior puisne judge of the colony. Juries refused to convict them. And the rebel leader, Peter Lalor, with a wounded arm amputated and still with a reward on his head, emerged from hiding to bid for a block of land at Ballarat's first land sale. The quest for land would be the next great chapter of the Australian story as men retreated from the goldfields like an army returning to civilian life. On a high roll of reform, Victoria pioneered democratic institutions that led the world — the secret ballot, manhood suffrage and, in a brief accident in 1864, female suffrage.

Political and economic power was still wielded by the squatters, the big landholders, sheep and cattle barons. Over the coming years the squatters' grip on the land would be challenged in a series of well-intentioned but tragically unsuccessful Land Acts, seeding a struggle which rarely flared into the open violence of America's land wars. Instead, it remained a festering conflict — in Victoria's parliament and at the outermost bounds of settlement — a conflict that would embroil Ellen Kelly and help shape the destiny of her son.

Before baby Ned could walk, Red and Ellen's bright dreams were fading. The main road, which traveller William Howitt called 'a monument of engineering stupidity', approached Beveridge across a treacherous plain of 'crab holes' and 'dead men's graves' to make an interminable climb across a high shoulder of the Big Hill. Most traffic avoided these hazards and followed saner routes that bypassed Beveridge to the east and west. Neither the town nor the Kellys prospered and after only fifteen months Red had to take out a £200 mortgage on his farm.

Steadily stripped of the banksias, she-oaks, box trees and wattles, the area's low, stony rises were sun-scorched in summer and chilled by bleak southerlies in winter. More and more, the landscape came to resemble Ireland, and the 'vast numbers of parrots, paroquets and wattle birds' that had flocked to feast on the banksia flowers found other feeding grounds. A backwater air of failure settled over the place and men sought comfort at Beveridge's two pubs. (Did anyone remember that the town was named after its first publican?) Drink became a big problem, to be the ruin of many, including storekeeper John Davies — and a source of despair to a Church of England schoolteacher who wrote, 'Everything here is chaotic. Drunkenness and all its consequent evils reigns supreme.'

It is not hard to believe that grog played a major role in Red's troubles. He fell into debt, slipped behind in his mortgage payments and, before Ned was three years old, had to sell the farm. With the mortgage principal and overdue payments repaid, Red received only 252 pounds 10 shillings for the 41 acres, leaving buyer Alexander Fraser to prosper. The Big Hill would become Mount Fraser.

At the same time Red had to sell half of his town block, with the house, and the family moved into a shack he threw up on the remaining ¼-acre. Did it strike Red that this last scrap of his land was smaller than the old Kelly holding in Tipperary?

The month after this sad move, Ellen gave birth to a daughter, Margaret, of all the girls she would bear, probably the closest to her in spirit.

As the Kelly family grew, a clan took shape around the Quinns of Wallan who had now gained a stronger hold on the land — 710 acres freehold, selected and bought between 1855 and 1857. Back in 1842 two brothers, Tom and Jack Lloyd, who were descendants of a Welsh horse dealer who had settled in Ireland, had arrived in Victoria. In 1852 Ellen's sister Kate had married Jack Lloyd. This year, 1857, saw the birth of their son, Tom, who became one of Ned's soul mates, and the marriage of 'Old Tom' Lloyd to Jane Quinn.

Then, in July, there was another dramatic increase in the clan. The ship *Maldon* brought Red's brothers, Edward, James and Daniel, and his sisters, Anne and Mary, from Ireland. Some of Red's uncles would follow, to swell the roll call of Kellys, Quinns, Lloyds and Ryans towards the 50 mark.

◆

ONLY A FEW MILES from Beveridge, near Woodstock, another Irish Catholic clan was growing. Four men of the Whitty family had migrated to Port Phillip from County Wexford in 1840 and started farming between Woodstock, a few miles from Beveridge, and Darebin Vale, where a relative-to-be called Farrell managed a property. Another Farrell was working with the pioneering Faithfull brothers in the north-east of the colony. Perhaps from him the Whittys first heard of the superb King River Valley, where the Faithfulls established Edi Station, a wild domain of 45 000 acres. For James Whitty, an illiterate bounty migrant, to own such a vast tract of land became a compelling dream.

For a time the two clans were almost unaware of each other, although in some forgotten pattern of events probably involving school or church Mary Whitty, wife of Patrick, was said to have looked after the Kelly children when Ellen was ill; and young Charles Whitty, born in 1855, would be remembered as a one-time friend of Ned Kelly. The future relationships of the two clans and Charles Whitty's eventual career as a policeman lent a strange irony to these remembered links.

At last, with the support of his younger brothers or perhaps driven by the need to set them an example, Red prospered and was able to buy another ½-acre block the next year, 1858. Ned's earliest memories were probably of these sunnier days — a first climb with the Kelly uncles and aunts up the Big Hill, to marvel at its crater, 'several hundred yards in width ... overgrown with grass, as level as a bowling green, and as perfectly circular as if struck out with a compass.' Then to share their wonderment as they looked out from the summit at, 'a magnificent view, including ranges of mountains at various distances on three sides, and of level country quite down to Melbourne and the sea on the other, the great ocean of forest and another of plain filling up the area.'

This eagle's viewpoint introduced Ned to the first landscape he would learn, printing hill and gully, track and creek into his memory with a fidelity no map could ever achieve. Over this landscape he would move with his father — on foot, by cart, on horseback — watching Red fell trees, strip bark, split palings and shingles with a paling knife, adze tree trunks into posts, split rails with maul and wedges, harness the cart horse, saddle and bridle the saddle horses, milk cows, set and skim the cream. All this was part of Ned's earliest education; this and the tales told by the hearth, of Ireland and Van Diemen's Land and the goldfields, evergreen stories of Irish odyssey with the bloodline of English authority running through them.

In 1858, like a promise of better times, a handsome bluestone building with high gables, gothic windows and buttressed walls was erected on part of the town's public land to serve as a Catholic school and church. Visiting priests held services there but nearly four years elapsed before there were enough pupils for the school to be opened.

Meanwhile Red steadily made his way and in February of 1859 he was able to afford £70 for 21 acres at the south-eastern corner of town, with a couple of town blocks thrown in. Still living in the shack on the ¼-acre, he built a house on the farmland a few hundred yards from the home of Timothy and Helen Ryan.

Ned, not yet five, would have watched Red adze tree trunks into corner posts, sink the four corner holes and put up the frame of a classic Irish cottage — long, narrow and low — with a hipped roof,

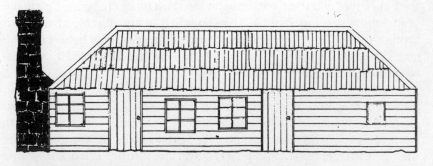

The last of the Kelly homes built by Red Kelly at Beveridge — a careful reconstruction by Keith McMenomy which clearly displays the cottage's Irish inspiration.

small-paned windows and a big, bluestone chimney taking up almost all of one end. The roof was shingled, the walls clad with split palings. A drain in the dirt floor divided the living and cooking area from the space where Red and Ellen slept with their three children. Behind this was a walled-off dairy and tack room. At the back, Red sank a deep well lined with bluestone which gave 'beautiful water ... always cool'. In this cottage three more children were born to Red and Ellen: James in 1859, Daniel in 1861 and Catherine in 1863.

It was in this period, when the Kelly family had at last achieved some security and stability, that the police began to threaten their simple world — a police force modelled closely on the hated Constabulary of Ireland and tainted with the odium of goldfield police thuggery. It had all started in 1856 when 15-year-old Jimmy Quinn had been brought before the court at Kilmore for Possession of Stolen Cattle. He was discharged. Four years later, at 19, he faced three charges: two of Assault and one of Horse Stealing. Found guilty on one of the Assault charges, he served six weeks in Kilmore Gaol. Apologists would claim that the police were 'picking on him'. If this is true, he also received the benefit of the doubt three times out of four — as he would in another Horse Stealing case almost as soon as he was released from prison. Less lucky on a charge of Illegally Using a Horse, he served a four-month sentence. Tall, darkly good-looking young Jimmy had begun a long career of crime, most of it generated by a volcanic temper that led him into a succession of brawls and sometimes murderous assaults, punctuated by a few stock thefts. Cause and effect can be debated but he emerged as a dangerous, unpredictable ratbag of a man, rarely out of trouble.

Thirty-year-old Jack Quinn had been charged with Horse Stealing in 1860 but escaped conviction — as he did that same year when he faced trial for Cattle Stealing. These brushes with the law and Jimmy's ongoing problems probably helped bring Jack into court in 1861 on the more serious charge of Robbery Under Arms. He was found not guilty. Jack or the police mended their ways and he faced no more charges for eighteen years, until the Big Trouble that engulfed them all. Meanwhile his brother-in-law, Jack Lloyd, faced the court three times between 1860 and 1862, for Assault, Drunk and Disorderly and Larceny. He was discharged each time.

In 1862 trouble came uncomfortably close to Red. His 22-year-old brother James was twice brought up before the Kilmore Police Court charged with Cattle Stealing. In both cases he was discharged. Then, in April of 1863, James faced a General Sessions trial at Kilmore for the theft of thirteen cattle from a Beveridge blacksmith. Ellen and young Ned appeared as witnesses for the defence, claiming that James had been with them in the Kelly home at the time the cattle were taken.

James and a companion-in-crime were found guilty nevertheless and sentenced to three years hard labour.

Red was shaken. Now the people of Beveridge would start prying into the background of the family. It was ironic that an ex-convict came under suspicion because of crimes committed by migrant relatives. No matter that his brother Edward would soon establish his respectability by buying land in Beveridge; Edward's town block would make no more difference than Red's 22¼ acres. Even James Quinn's hundreds of acres counted for little against the growing reputation of his sons and sons-in-law as stock thieves and brawlers. Coupled with this uncomfortable pressure, civilisation was threatening the Quinn domain with a projected road and railway through the property. Old James turned his eyes towards more distant hills and started to dispose of his land at Wallan — a piece to the Government for the railway, a block to farmer Henry Perkins for £200 . . .

Further south at Woodstock the Whitty clan were also looking to broader, more distant acres as their future expansion in the district was hampered by a cordon of small farms taken up under the new Land Acts. In the words of a descendant, they felt 'hemmed in'. The north-eastern district, 120 miles further from Melbourne, offered them room to move and space for their herds and flocks to grow, with its great patterns of rivers and ranges. By 1865 James Whitty had taken up 320 acres of rich farming and grazing land near Wangaratta on the King River, a new rallying point for the Whittys and the younger Farrells.

Two months after Uncle James Kelly's conviction there was a welcome distraction for Red. At last the Catholic School opened. Puffing steam in the icy mornings, 8-year-old Ned trudged off to school with 9-year-old Annie and 6-year-old Maggie, across the unfenced town allotments and past the reedy little swamp they called the Ponds, to the churchy grandeur of the hillside school. There Thomas and Sarah Wall started to teach the Kelly children the superb syllabus of the Irish National Schools, with virtually no corporal punishment — the result of Quaker influence on Irish teaching methods.

At the school were Gormans, Ryans, Oxleys, Barbours, Clanceys, McLeods and Hopkinses. Young Fred Hopkins gives a first glimpse of Ned Kelly, 'He was a tall and active lad and excelled all others at school games.'

Some years later an inspector would say of Tom Wall, 'Keeps [his pupils] at work; teaches with spirit and very fair skills.' In six months he taught Ned to read and write to Second Class standard — a respectable achievement for both master and pupil.

School broke up in December and the Kelly children never returned. Red's worries about police attention, the spectres of Ireland, Ellen and

Ned tainted with James's guilt — it all had gnawed at his peace of mind. He decided to make a break from everything and start all over again in the prosperous little town of Avenel, 50 miles up the main road across the Divide.

If Ellen mourned the loss of family, perhaps she hoped that a fresh start might help her husband break the destructive cycle of worry and whisky that was blighting their lives here. Red had disposed of his town blocks and in January of 1864 sold the house and farm for £80 to local farmer James Stewart. His last land deal was his most successful.

Ned saw his home stripped of its meagre furnishings, helped load everything on their cart, then probably took one of the saddle horses to drive the Kelly cows around the eastern flank of the Big Hill and up to Wallan where the family would say their goodbyes to the Quinns. To a 9-year-old it must have seemed the beginning of an epic journey to a new life. In many ways it was.

◆

NOTHING COULD HAVE BEEN less like battling, pub-born Beveridge than the hamlet of Avenel. It lay in a broad basin of summer-dry hills with stunted trees and rocks the colour of ancient bronze, gathered around a six-arched, brownstone toll bridge that carried the main road across the two channels and broad white sands of Hughes Creek. The town took its English placename from the Avenel run of pioneer English squatter Henry Kent Hughes, owned in 1864 by Lloyd Jones, who spent three months of every year 'back home' and one of whose stockmen turned out to be a baronet. A visitor described Avenel station as 'having the character of a ducal park' and the little namesake settlement within its boundaries was very much an English village with its thirty-odd houses and shops, its willow trees, its orchards, gardens, hedges and ready-made village green on the creek's small flood plain between the bridge and the Avenel Arms, one of the township's two hotels. The second pub, just before the bridge, was the high-roofed Royal Mail, run by the Shelton family. Here the red mail coaches changed six-horse teams while passengers stretched their legs and enjoyed the Sheltons' hospitality, before the driver took his lively new team across the bridge to drop a mail bag at the post office.

One of Avenel's first settlers was Cornishman William Mutton, a blacksmith and storekeeper, who had died eight years before. From his widow, Elizabeth, Red rented a 40-acre farm at the western edge of town about a mile from the bridge. With what was left from the sale of the Beveridge property — probably precious little after his debts were settled — Red started again, paying £14 a year for the use of someone else's land.

It would be recalled that, 'the family had a hard struggle to make ends meet, but every old resident spoke well of them'. This wasn't quite true. The Kellys seem to have been received less warmly by rival dairyman Michael Kelly of Limerick, who owned 88 acres, and by John and Phillip Morgan, who had bought a parcel of William Mutton's land across the creek from the Kelly block. Often called 'wealthy', the Morgans held about 300 acres, suggesting that 'comfortable' would be closer to the mark. However, the traditional picture of the Morgans as rigid, Bible-black Chapel Methodists may be accurate. Certainly, they would show little tolerance towards the Irish Catholic Kellys.

The Kellys quickly settled into the little community and Ellen won an enduring place in local memory with two of the Quinn family traits. Old-timers recalled, 'Mrs Kelly was a great horsewoman and used to ride out to help anyone in trouble or needing help.'

Ned, Annie and Maggie went off to the local Common School, a ramshackle building of slabs and palings with a bark roof and stained calico ceiling. They probably paid the lowest tuition fee of fourpence each per week to learn the three R's from teacher James Irving and his wife Henrietta. This had been a Church of England school until the previous year and Sunday services were still held in it. After the gentle Irish discipline of Tom Wall at Beveridge, Mr Irving's more English approach must have surprised the Kelly children. He was a harsh disciplinarian who frequently boxed the ears of troublesome pupils and carried a 'tawse' — a broad leather strap with its end cut into thongs like a cat o' nine tails.

The young Kellys were rarely in trouble, however, and were remembered as 'well behaved'. Michael Kelly's daughter Joanna, who sat beside Ned for a time, used to say that he was 'a very quiet boy'. Working with a squeaky slate pencil and wood-framed slate, Ned grappled with his lessons, slavishly copying words and phrases printed on cardboard 'tablets' held up by older children who acted as 'monitors', or chanting them in sing-song unison.

Irving was not a well-organised teacher and one or more of the four classes in the musty schoolroom often sat idle. The prospect of boxed ears or a cut from the 'tawse' kept workless pupils quiet and, with small, high windows offering only the sky to look at, Ned's eyes would have strayed over the array of maps on the calico-lined walls — 'Africa, Victoria, Palestine, England, Scotland, Ireland, Canada, United States', and, in a metaphor of this Anglocentric little world, 'Geology of the British Isles'.

The forty-odd children seated around him, occupied and vacant, on two long desks and rows of forms, typified the community. There was Eliza Jane Mutton, daughter of their landlady, only three years older than Ned, yet the first white child born in the town; Eliza's brother, George, a smart lad; Caroline Doxey, whose father, the local constable, conducted the momentous monotony of the Queen's business with pistol and saddle, but more often with government issue pen; Elizabeth Campion, who lived in the low stone building on the main road where her father William Campion, 'an Englishman of gentlemanly education and manners', ran a combined store, post office and library while also acting as Registrar of Births and Deaths; and there were Irvings and Bignells and Tebbles and Fords and Hodges and Smiths and Chappels and Whites — not an Irish name among them, except the Kellys.

Among the 'under sevens' were young Sarah and Richard Shelton from the Royal Mail Hotel. Their publican father, Esau Shelton, a former drover, digger and carrier, had joined his parents here, establishing an Avenel dynasty which exists to the present day — because of a dramatic incident soon to involve young Dick Shelton and Ned Kelly. The family look back on Ned with particular warmth but nevertheless recall the story of a stallion that went missing from Avenel. They tell how, after a reward was offered, young Ned appeared with the animal, telling the owner, 'I found it up in the bush'. The horse, which had disappeared weeks before, was in prime condition — well fed and superbly groomed. The owner gave Ned the benefit of the doubt *and* the modest bounty for its return. The Sheltons — who were confident that Ned had 'borrowed' the horse or had found it and kept it hidden until the reward was offered — were amused that he was too much of a horse lover to return it in the rough-fed, ungroomed condition that would have made his story more convincing.

It was probably through the Sheltons that Ned had his first significant contact with Aborigines. While droving in the Murray district some years before, Esau Shelton 'took great interest in the manners and customs of the blacks with whom he was continually brought into contact'. On his arrival in Avenel he befriended members of a tribe camped near town and encouraged the women to sell rush baskets to coach passengers during their stopovers at the Royal Mail. Perhaps Esau Shelton first took Ned to the Aboriginal camp and introduced him to the way of life of these people, helped him recognise the skills refined by thousands of years of survival in this land — including almost mystical ability to follow tracks, locate game and predict weather. Although Ned mastered some of these skills, in his fugitive years Aborigines would be the only pursuers he truly feared. In a reciprocal tribute, Aborigines would grant him a place in their mythology unrivalled by any other man, white or black.

Ned had been attending Avenel school for two months when it had a surprise visit from Board of Education inspector G. Wilson Brown. He recorded Ned's presence in Third Class and gave him passes in Reading and Writing, but failed him in Arithmetic, Grammar and Geography.

The young Cambridge graduate set tough standards. Of thirteen children in Ned's class, only George Mutton did better than him and Ned's two passes gave him second place with three other children. This was nothing to be ashamed of after only eight months of schooling.

That winter, a convoy of carts, horses and bullock drays paid their toll to cross the Beveridge bridge. It was James Quinn, for all the world like a Biblical patriarch, leading his family to a new heartland for the clan, up among the mountains of the north-east. James had sold the last of his Wallan land for a good price and was paying £2000 for the Glenmore run on the King River — a realm of 20 000 acres so wild that it could carry only 400 cattle. Ned Kelly's grandfather had become a squatter, cattle king of a 'remote and lofty monarchy'.

Less than 30 miles further down the King Valley near Moyhu, James Whitty had already established his own realm, founded on river-rich soil and to be fortified by intermarriage with the neighbouring Farrells (who were already linked with the Byrnes of Moyhu), creating a powerful, prosperous and closely-knit clan. Now as an equally formidable clan began to re-form around James Quinn, future battle lines were being drawn.

Ellen's sisters, Kate and Jane, with their husbands the Lloyd brothers and their children, had already settled in the north-east. Timothy and Helen Ryan would soon join the trek and take up land at Lake Winton outside Benalla, among a small colony of folk from the Beveridge and Wallan districts who had taken advantage of the new Land Act to select from 40 to 320 acres at a rental of 2 shillings and sixpence per acre, paying for the land in eight years.

If Ellen wanted to follow, Red persuaded her to stay where they were — in spite of the fact that the rental paid for 40 acres of Avenel land would have given them equity in 112 acres of 'selected' land. Red may have suspected that migration to the north-east would only change the location of the clan's ongoing problems with the police. Mad Jimmy Quinn was already in prison up there for Horse Stealing. Tom and Jack Lloyd would soon be under suspicion as cattle thieves and, the following year, would be convicted and sentenced to five years, leaving their wives and children to struggle along with whatever help the Quinns and Ryans could give them.

Ellen would grieve for Kate and Jane in their troubles; but the Kellys stayed in Avenel, with only Aunty Anne Kelly to threaten their peace with her sharp tongue and scratchy ways when she arrived to rent a house in the town. So the first year at Avenel passed happily and peacefully enough and in November Ellen became pregnant.

In March of 1865 Ned again faced inspector G. Wilson Brown, to manage a pass in Arithmetic as well as Reading and Writing. This time the punctilious Brown noted the lad's age as 10 years and 3 months. That minute entry in a pocket-sized notebook remains the most reliable evidence for fixing Ned's birthdate.

In late May, with Ellen six months pregnant and the 'hard struggle' made even harder by drought, Red yielded to a cruel temptation. The creek was low and one of the Morgans' heifer calves strayed across. Red killed, skinned and butchered it, put down ten pounds of meat in the brine cask and hung a hindquarter to provide a handsome meal for the family. He cut out the Morgan brand, thriftily hid the hide in the bedroom, disposed of the calf's head and lit a bonfire to destroy the bones.

Two days later Phillip Morgan (remembered as 'a hungry old bugger') brought Constable Doxey to the Kelly house, where they found the hung hindquarter and the meat in the brine cask. Red told them he had killed an unbranded stray. When Doxey found the hide with the piece missing, Red claimed that he had cut it out to make a greenhide whip and that the family's pigs had dragged away the head. Doxey found the pieces of burnt bone and arrested Red on a charge of Cattle Stealing.

Red spent the weekend in the town's lock-up, a stoutly built blockhouse of square-cut logs, and on the Monday was brought into court to face Justices of the Peace Blake and Summiss. The charge of Cattle Stealing was dismissed. Found guilty of 'having illegally in his possession one cow hyde', Red was fined £25 or six months hard labour. The Kellys were almost penniless and their friends couldn't provide the money. The two justices and Constable Doxey might have let Red start working out his time at the Avenel lock-up, while Ellen tried to scrape together the £25 that would earn her husband's freedom, rather than sending him to Kilmore Gaol, 30 miles from his pregnant wife and family.

Already tall for his years, Ned took his father's place in the home and on the farm, pushed towards maturity by the weight of work and responsibility. The months passed and in August, with only Annie to help her, Ellen gave birth to a daughter, named Grace after her youngest sister.

It was probably in this dark year that Ned made his enduring mark on Avenel and the lives of its people. One morning, 7-year-old Dick Shelton left the Royal Mail to go to school, taking his usual route across the main road and along to an old wooden footbridge beside a huge redgum, downstream of the brownstone toll bridge. Dick was wearing a brand new straw hat. As he crossed the bridge, perhaps as he leant over the rail to look down at the creek, swollen by recent rain, the hat fell or blew off and caught on a fallen tree branch. Dick climbed over the bridge railing to reach down and retrieve it, lost his footing and fell into a boil-hole of turbulent water.

Ned, on his way into town along the opposite bank, perhaps with milk to sell, saw what had happened. He sprinted down and dived in.

The Kelly house at Beveridge (see reconstruction, p.13), as it looked in 1977 after more than a century of renovations and additions and almost a decade of neglect. There was another fifteen years of decay and vandalism before its preservation became a *cause célèbre*. At the time of writing, restoration is under way.

Harry Power, Ned's mentor in bushranging and fugitive bushcraft. In spite of his dumpy build, a serious bowel complaint and crippling bunions, he was a consummate horseman and bushman who taught his 15-year-old apprentice the value of a broad sympathiser network and the use of bluff and bluster to intimidate 'clients'.

The view from Power's Lookout across the King Valley, seen in 1993. The Quinn homestead was slightly to the left of the poplar tree just visible on the near side of the modern road, bottom centre.

'Power's mate' — Ned Kelly at 15, photographed in May 1870 during his imprisonment on remand at Kyneton. He still shows signs of the sickness and gauntness commented on at the time of his arrest. It is also clear why a Kyneton reporter believed him to be '18 or 20'. Seventeen prints of this photograph were distributed by police, making it readily available eight years later to form the basis of the first published portraits of Ned.

A surprisingly accurate *Illustrated Australian News* engraving of Harry Power's capture. The artist has managed a reasonable likeness of Nicolson and shows him, correctly, in shirtsleeves, though he did not hold a revolver and gripped Harry's wrists with both hands.

He probably wasn't a good swimmer but was strong enough and determined enough to reach Dick and drag him to safety.

The arrival of the sodden pair at the Royal Mail, the emotional gratitude of the Sheltons, the two boys stripping and drying themselves by the fire, Dick's late arrival at school with the story of his adventure, Ned finishing his trip to town in some of Esau's clothing — all this has been forgotten. The shining memories are of Ned's bravery and the Sheltons' gratitude. Both were commemorated by the family presenting the 10-year-old hero with a handsome trophy, a green silk sash 7 feet long and 5 inches wide with a three-inch bullion fringe at each end. The sash would remain one of Ned's most treasured possessions, to be worn only on very special occasions. It exists to this day — faded, frayed and bloodstained — last worn by Ned on a day when all his courage was needed.

Ned's rescue of Dick Shelton — before or during his father's time in the lock-up — might have helped save Red from transfer to Kilmore Gaol. There is no record of the fine being paid and he was probably released in the first week of October with a generous remission of more than two months. He marked his freedom by registering Grace's birth at William Campion's store.

Four months without a drink had been a sore penance for Red. He now made up for lost time and on 12 December Constable Doxey hauled him into court for being Drunk and Disorderly. There was no magistrate present so the acting Clerk of Petty Sessions remanded Red to appear on 20 December with a 'recognisance' of 5 shillings — a guarantee that he would turn up. The court next sat on 19 December, not the 20th as incorrectly announced by the acting Clerk. Red's name was called three times and when he didn't appear the magistrate ruled, 'Let his recognisance be estreated.' Red lost his money. He would have been fined 5 shillings if found guilty, so the case was considered closed. Red had paid his last debt to society.

◆

IN THIS YEAR of crisis for the Kelly family bushranging in the Australian colonies reached its grand climax. As the goldfields passed their roaring days and settled into a staider, more industrial pattern, the vicious footpads of the goldrush were replaced by a new breed of bushrangers — most of them Australian-born, flashly dressed, finely mounted and shamelessly evoking the highwayman heroes of international myth who stole only from the rich and were friends to poor men. Though most of these sometimes-amiable rogues defined 'the rich' as anyone who had something worth taking, Australia-at-large embraced them as folk-heroes and men like Gardiner, Gilbert, Hall and Thunderbolt built legendary reputations.

Beechworth's conservative newspaper, the *Advertiser* saw the adulation of bushrangers as springing from the Colony's supposedly ex-convict population — a comforting argument against transportation but one that didn't fit the facts. The most respectable levels of society could show sympathy for the classic highwayman hero on stage or in literature.

The likeable Ben Hall was gunned down by eight New South Wales police and black trackers in May of 1865, without firing a shot in defence. Critically wounded, clinging to a sapling, Hall cried, 'I'm wounded — shoot me dead!' The police complied and didn't stop shooting until they had pumped nearly thirty bullets and slugs into his body. The sub-inspector in charge of the ambush admitted that his men were 'perfectly mad' and that Hall 'got a most fearful riddling'.

The *Kilmore Free Press* observed his passing in a sympathetic obituary which Ned probably read. Hall's career, the writer admitted, was 'desperate and daring' but, after summarising his early years, concluded:

> With all his crimes I believe he has never been accused of being blood-thirsty, nor did he directly kill any of the victims he robbed. It is claimed by his relatives and those who knew him best that he was affectionate and generous. It is said that the miniature found upon his person by the police after his death, is that of a favourite sister . . . and that he has constantly worn it upon his person during the last three years. Such then in brief, are some of the incidents of the early life of a most desperate bushranger, who has eluded the grasp of a strong and active police force for three years, and who was ultimately captured, but not until his body was pierced with bullets and slugs from his feet to the crown of his head.

The month before Hall died, Daniel Morgan had been shot in the back by a civilian at Peechelba in north-eastern Victoria. Even Morgan, a shaggy, sadistic runt who ranged the north-east of Victoria and the Riverina, had his apologists. As the Beechworth *Advertiser* lamented, 'Is not that blood-stained villain, Morgan, petted, feted and elevated into a hero by an entire population?' Ned might have read — in the Kilmore paper — that after Morgan's body had been taken to the Wangaratta police station,

> the apartment allotted to the corpse was converted to a human shambles — a Cawnpore [site of an Indian Mutiny massacre] on a small scale. Decapitation, hacking, skinning, fleshing and boxing up, seem to have been engaged in as a pastime or recreation.

A Dr Henry of Benalla stripped the skin from Morgan's cheeks and jaw so that Police Superintendent Cobham could have the bushranger's 'massive' beard as a souvenir. ('He pegged it out on a sheet of bark like an opposum skin to dry,' said Wangaratta's Sergeant William Montfort.) Morgan's head was then cut off to be cast in plaster. After being, 'tossed around the room like a football ... such was the eagerness of a butcher to become possessed of a lock of Morgan's hair, that the violence of the jerk to accomplish the object launched the head onto the floor, and he then, uninterrupted and unconcerned, marched off with his prize.'

Eventually, the Coroner, Dr Dobbyn, packed the head in a box for dispatch to Melbourne University's Professor of Anatomy. It was sent down by the morning coach, to pass through Avenel, where 10-year-old Ned could never imagine that his body would suffer institutional butchery on a scale little short of that inflicted on Morgan — or that he would end his career with as many wounds as Ben Hall.

Any moral provided by the deaths of Hall and Morgan was effectively obscured by the conduct of those supposedly upholding law and order. To a generation already distrustful of police after the goldfields experience, the two mangled bushranger corpses encouraged further erosion of confidence in country law enforcement, and a corresponding readiness to sympathise with those who stood against what Ned would call 'the tyrannical conduct of police in rural areas far removed from court'. The role of Victoria's police in the events surrounding the last two years of Ned's life — and the huge wave of protest against their behaviour — struck a death blow at the quasi-military force that had survived in Victoria through the 1860s and 1870s and at the born-to-rule English gentleman who led it throughout the period.

A couple of days before Christmas in this extraordinary year of 1865, a ripple of the grand bushranging drama touched peaceful Avenel and the Kelly family. Constable Doxey arrested a young fellow calling himself Allen Lowry — a pale, fair-haired six-footer with a large, crooked nose. Lowry was a Sydneysider who had overlanded to Victoria and, with an Irish mate, carried out several small hold-ups the previous year around Benalla and Glenrowan in the north-east. Armed with revolvers, the pair rode almost identical horses and strutted through their brief bushranging careers in black coats, new cabbage-tree hats and dark trousers strapped with moleskin.

The Kellys knew Lowry during his time at Avenel and Ned was clearly impressed with this bargain basement bushranger. To an 11-year-old, he was the embodiment of the Wild Colonial Boy, invested with the glamour of Gilbert, Hall and Gardiner.

For Lowry, the reality was anything but glamorous. Only 24 years old, he had already served three years for horse stealing in the north-east. Now he would receive another two years for Shooting With Intent, two years for Horse Stealing, would prove a troublesome prisoner and serve an extra eight months before being released in 1870. By then, Ned would have tasted for himself the excitement of bushranging, and some of its terror. His path and Lowry's were to cross again.

———————◆———————

NED DIDN'T RETURN to school in 1866. By now, even fourpence a week per child was a strain on the Kelly finances and the family were either too proud to throw their sons and daughters on the charity of the education system as 'free children' or simply needed every pair of hands at home, as Red fought a losing battle with the farm and with booze. His liver and heart suffered.

As the year rotted away, Ned helplessly watched his father destroy himself. There would be stories of Red's decline being caused by some poisonous rotgut he was given at a sly grog shanty and Ellen would blame 'a spirit that was served to him in mistake for brandy'. It is doubtful that Ned needed to make such excuses. He could accept what was happening without judging or blaming his father, still honouring and respecting him while swearing that grog would never claim such a hold on *him*.

In November dropsy set in and Red's body started to bloat with fluid. In years to come Ned would think of his father as he spoke of the men exiled from Ireland by their English overlords, 'all of true blood bone and beauty'. At the end, all beauty had gone from Red's body. A Dr J. T. Heeley from Seymour saw him five days before Christmas. Red clung to life until Christmas Day and died two days later. He was 45.

At 33, Ellen was a widow with seven surviving children, the oldest 13, the youngest 18 months. Ned, just 12, was the man of the family and entered on his new responsibilities the following day when he rode up past the Common School to the main road and along to William Campion's store. Here he reported his father's death, provided the details required by law and signed the register with a firm 'Edward Kelly, Son', carefully imitating the curlicues of his father's 'K'.

Next day Red was buried in the Avenel Cemetery by his family and friends. If a simple eulogy was offered by friend John Brady, who conducted the burial, it has been forgotten. Twelve years later, as Ned made a spectacular entry on the bushranging stage, he would declare, 'I'm Ned Kelly, son of Red Kelly and a finer man never stood in two shoes.' If the family raised some rough wooden marker on Red's grave, its inscription would soon weather away, leaving an anonymous piece of wood to rot into the soil. Thirteen years on, as Ned amused himself by cutting inscriptions into the woodwork of a captured police rifle, he would carefully carve, 'Ned Kelly son of Red'. That inscription survives.

Red's life could be seen as a series of failures — as a criminal, as a farmer, as a land speculator, as a provider for his family. His wife and children passed no such judgement on him as a husband and father. He was remembered with love.

2

'THIS CRIMINAL BROOD'

MAY 1867 — FEBRUARY 1870

R ed's death heralded a turbulent period for Ellen and the children. Ellen had 'a damn bad temper' at any time, but the pressures of widowhood and poverty seem to have made her even more volatile. Twice within a few months she would face the Avenel Court, presided over by Police Magistrate Arthur Akehurst. Twelve years before, when he was Clerk of Peace at Ballarat, Akehurst had demonstrated his devotion to law and order by cutting down an innocent and helpless digger called Henry Powell after the Eureka Stockade battle.

The grass had scarcely grown on Red's grave before Ellen clashed violently with her sister-in-law, Anne Kelly. They ended up in front of Akehurst, charging each other with assault and claiming £10 damages; but it was Ellen who was found guilty and ordered to pay 40 shillings damages and five shillings costs or face a week's imprisonment.

Three months later this spirited pair united against Anne's landlord, the quarrelsome Thomas Ford, who claimed they had damaged his property. Ford charged Ellen with 'abusive and threatening language'; she said he had assaulted her. Both were found guilty, but while Ellen was fined 40 shillings or seven days, Ford had to pay £5 or face six weeks in prison. It was a hollow victory for Ellen, nevertheless, because they each had to keep the peace for six months on a £50 bond.

This was the last straw. Before the onslaught of winter made a journey up the main road all but impossible, Ellen decided to leave Avenel. She sold up the goods and stock she didn't need and probably made a bonfire of those unwanted scraps of the past that were left. (Was this the first time Ned saw fire being used to cauterise painful memories?) Then they packed their few remaining belongings on Red's dray, with a cow tied behind, and headed off for the north-east to join the two grass-widow aunts at Greta whose husbands, the Lloyd brothers, were in the second year of their five-year prison sentences.

The Kellys' enemies at Avenel took a parting shot. Dairyman Michael Kelly had lost a mare on 23 May and now reported to the police his suspicion that young Ned Kelly had taken it 'to Violettown', probably the family's assumed destination. No warrant was issued and nothing ever came of the report, but the next month's *Police Gazette* described Edward Kelly as 'Charged with Horse Stealing'.

This flash of notoriety gives a first, clear glimpse of the boy who left Avenel that autumn: 'A Victorian native, 14 or 15, 5 feet 4 or 5 inches high, stout build, brown hair, light grey eyes, smooth face; wore black jumper, moleskin trousers, cloth cap and bluchers.'

Looking older than his 12 years, Ned was already as tall as his mother and strongly built. He wore calf-high leather boots — probably his dead father's — as he rode northward with the little cavalcade, across country he would travel many times, through towns marking later milestones in his life: sleepy Euroa on the Seven Creeks and busy, prosperous Benalla by the toll bridge over the Broken River.

Past here, 7 miles of level country brought the family to Winton and Seven Mile Creek, 'a chain of water holes that are dry for the greater part of summer'. A side road veered east to Eleven Mile Creek, its course dotted with deep holes that held 'a never-failing supply of water'. They took this, the wagoners' route, winding through low, timbered hills into a broad, blind valley flanked by two spurs of the Warby Ranges and barred by the main ridge. Out to the right, past the meandering creek, was a big, deeply groined hill, bare of trees like Mount Fraser back at Beveridge. Below it, close to the road, was a single house.

In a drought the previous year a young Winton lad called Joseph Ashmead had helped his father drove their cattle to water here at Eleven Mile Creek's deep holes. Young Joseph saw 'the big bald hill' and recalled:

> Almost under the shadow of this hill was the home of a solitary settler on the bank of the creek among the wattles. A number of willow trees had been planted around the house and had already grown to a good size. The walls of the house were slab and the roof stringey-bark with sapling riders to keep the bark in its place. A number of children were playing, regardless of the loneliness of the place.

The following year this became the Kellys' home. On this day, Ellen and the children passed it and climbed the last, weary slope to a gap in the Warby Ranges, guarded by grass trees with their black spears against the sky. As they crossed the ridge a breath-catching view was revealed, probably Ned's first glimpse of a central part of his world.

Below was the tiny settlement of Greta, a few shacks scattered among venerable red gums on the banks of Fifteen Mile Creek at the edge of the broad, tree-shaded Oxley flats. Beyond, across the eastern horizon, a chain of hills ran south to the ridges of the Great Divide and the blue-hazed grandeur of the Buffalo massif, with Mount Bogong and the Alps fading beyond.

At Greta the road triforked — to the left it skirted a huge swamp towards busy Wangaratta; ahead, out over the river flats towards Oxley on the King River, then on to the Ovens and Beechworth in the hills beyond; to the right, winding towards Moyhu and the Upper King.

In the roaring days of the Ovens gold rush, Greta had been on the main road to Beechworth, a watering hole for diggers and teamsters. But now the traffic could support only one hotel. A rambling, delicensed pub provided a home for Kate and Jane Lloyd and their children, and now also for Ellen and her brood.

It was a joyous reunion for the three sisters and the seventeen cousins. Perhaps 11-year-old Tom Lloyd took the Kelly children for an excited tour of their new home, with eye-widening tales of the huge tiger snakes to be found here and the bunyip that could be heard booming in the nearby Greta swamp 'Like the bellowing of bulls, or like the blowing of a bullock's horn, in short, hollow puffs'.

As soon as they were settled in they would have gone to visit Grandma and Grandpa Quinn and the uncles and aunts at Glenmore, a long day's journey out across the Oxley flats and up the King River, which wound along a broad valley, sparkling clear over its stony bed. Further south, the valley narrowed until the track snaked through open bushland between the river and a soaring escarpment to the right.

Their approach to the Quinn homestead was announced by piercing cries which echoed across the face of the range. Grandpa had a peacock tethered on his roof — a flamboyant watchdog which promised magical things of Glenmore.

Through a gateway, the homestead stood in a clearing on the banks of the King, almost at the foot of a dramatic spur, with a narrow channel of the river encircling it like a moat to form a lagoon behind.

On this superb site the house must have been a disappointment after the heraldry of the peacock. It was a wide, low, slab building with a bark roof over twin gables end-on, just two bush huts joined side-by-side without even a verandah. Only a door in the middle and a single window broke the weather-beaten monotony of the double facade. Inside, the living room was floored with slabs, the other rooms had dirt floors and the walls and roof were unlined. It had been built by a pioneer squatter battling the bush and it was now the home of a squatter who was continuing that battle and losing it.

More heartening was 'a wonderful stockyard' at the edge of the lagoon, with post-and-rail fences 6 feet high. Perhaps from here, sitting on the top rail with his uncles and admiring the Quinns' prize horses, Ned looked up the bush gullys of the escarpment face and saw a crenellated crag standing out from the rimrock cliffs like a ruined rampart. They called it 'The Rock'.

Back in the tiny community of Greta, life was busy, happy and hard. The local school was in the backyard of the shanty ('between a fowl yard and a pigsty'), and the hard-working sisters undoubtedly shooed the younger children into it. Ned probably worked with his mother and the aunts. Winter passed with crowded, boisterous nights lit by fragrant log fires, and summer brought the year of 1868. It also brought Uncle James Kelly, who had stayed out of trouble with the law since his three-year term for cattle stealing.

One chaotic summer night he turned up at the shanty, drunk and amorous. Roused from sleep by the racket, wide-eyed, giggling children watched the comings and goings as he was eventually driven out of the house with a stick after having his bottle of gin broken over his head.

Farce turned to near-tragedy when the vengeful James set the old building alight. As the three sisters and their children ran to safety, carrying what little they could, flames raced through their home, burning it to the ground.

Uncle James was arrested the next day to stand trial for Arson in Wangaratta and, later, at the autumn assizes in Beechworth. Everyone agreed that he deserved a good lesson, but the redoubtable Sir Redmond Barry, senior puisne judge of the colony, robed in red and white like some judicial Father Christmas, was not interested in reformation. Protestant Irish, son of a British general, father of Melbourne's University and Public Library, benevolent to Aborigines, he shocked the Beechworth Court as he pronounced sentence on this Irish hooligan.

Ned was undoubtedly there with his mother to hear her give evidence and had stayed for the outcome of the trial. He would not have understood why the square of black cloth was placed on Barry's grey-wigged head and probably wondered at the tremor of reaction, the catch of breath from his mother and those around him. Then those words echoed from white granite walls: 'I sentence you to be hanged by the neck until you are dead. And may the Lord have mercy on your soul'. The Lord and the law were equally merciful and eventually Uncle James's sentence was commuted to fifteen years hard labour. He would be 51 when he was released, if he lived that long.

After the burning of the old shanty at Greta, Ellen and her children had been left with little more than the nightdresses or underclothes they were sleeping in. A friend recorded:

> All she had in the world was gone. The neighbours made a collection, bought her some clothes and set her up in a little house in Wangaratta where she worked very hard, going out washing in the day and taking in dress-making at night.

The younger children went to Wangaratta with Ellen while Ned, perhaps with Annie and Jim, stayed in Greta, probably with the Lloyds in 'the Paddock hut on Fifteen Mile Creek'. Ned started to collect a mob of horses — perhaps honestly — which he ran in the bush along the Fifteen Mile. He also put together a small flock of sixteen or eighteen unbranded sheep (he would call them 'pets') which he grazed on Connolly's Myrrhee Station.

It was perhaps here that Ned learned to shear, at first 'barrowing' — practising with the spring-backed hand shears in rest breaks so that he wouldn't hold up the time-obsessed professionals — until he was ready to be trusted with a pen or 'stand' to himself. This was a key skill in the nomadic way of life that was a normal part of survival for the working man and small farmer on this huge frontier. A 400-mile ride into outback New South Wales was only the beginning of a yearly pattern for men who started shearing on the Darling in June, worked their way down through the Riverina to the 'Lower Victorian Murray', perhaps by October, then travelled across to the Broken River and finished the season in the hills around Mansfield in late November, returning home after a round trip of well over 1000 miles. In years to come, Ned would shear regularly at Gnawarra Station on the Darling. He was clearly a reliable man, putting up a tally of eighty or ninety sheep a day, earning up to 17 shillings and sixpence per 100 and walking away from three months work with a cheque for £30 or £40 and a tendency to back trouble.

This was the only sort of future Ned could imagine for himself — a cycle of hard work built on the widest possible range of frontier skills. He roamed the district with his uncles and cousins, honing his prowess as a bushman and horseman and growing tall and lean, one of a remarkable breed of first-generation Irish Australians from northeastern Victoria who caught the starry eye of English author Edwin Carton Booth:

> As a rule, the natives of this part of Victoria have a strangely, almost delicately, beautiful organization. They are almost without exception tall and straight, with those shapely and tapering extremities usually held to be indicative of high breeding. Their features are finely chiselled, and they have a delicacy of outline rarely observed in the stock from which they have sprung. They are pale, but the men have a breadth of shoulder and depth of chest indicative of a high degree of strength. Boys and girls alike have voices singularly low and soft. Their speech is characterised by a brogue decidedly Irish in its tone, but softer and smoother than any brogue found in Ireland. They are industrious and shrewd . . . and whenever practicable they devote the whole of their attention to the rearing of horse and cattle stock.

After little more than six months of what a friend called 'honest industry' in the Wangaratta cottage, Ellen had saved enough to set herself up on a farm and re-unite her family. Her brothers, Jack and Jimmy, who had moved to Greta after the fire to help their sisters, may have told her of a selection available near Greta — 88 acres on a creek, partly cleared, with a house. So Ellen and her children returned to the broad valley below the Bald Hill and to 'the home of the solitary settler' they had passed the previous year.

Among its willows on the bank of Eleven Mile Creek the house was about 50 yards from the road. Only 12 feet wide, it was built of slabs, with 'a big, bark roof' in the early style that looked like an oversize hat. This structure was made even more unwieldy by its pegged-together frame of jockey poles and riders to hold down the sheets of bark. Its interior was an empty, smoke-darkened space. The few possessions and scraps of furniture Ellen had gathered since the fire made it theirs, and she tacked rugs and blankets from the tie-beams to curtain off rooms.

After the bustle of moving in, she and Ned might have paused to consider what they had taken on. They were miles from anywhere. The only house in sight was a shepherd's hut near a big sheep fold on the lower slopes of the Bald Hill where, in the old style, the mob was turned out each morning to graze on the unfenced land, then shepherded back into the yard at night.

Here on the broad, empty bottom land of the Eleven Mile, their block had a frontage of 360 yards and stretched back 1200 yards — its 88 acres more than twice as much as they'd ever lived on before.

The previous owner had built the hut before the area was surveyed and seems to have taken up the block in 1866 under the previous year's Land Act, paying the government rental of 4 pounds 9 shillings every six months, which earned an option to purchase for £88 after three years' occupation. There were four identical blocks side-by-side along this stretch of road, all surveyed in 1866, but only this one had been taken up.

Ellen and Ned started the long battle with the land, the seasons, officialdom and the big squatters whose cattle and sheep runs were being gnawed at by selections like theirs. In June the following year, after the block had been occupied for three years, Ellen was granted a seven-year lease. Twenty-three years of struggle lay ahead: two days before Christmas 1892 the land would at last belong to Ellen, at an immeasurable price.

The 1866 survey had shown this area as 'fair agricultural land'. It has been claimed that it was, in fact, poor ground, perhaps suggesting that the Kellys were forced to crime for survival. It has also been claimed that the soil was good, implying that the Kellys would have been criminals anyway. In fact it is reasonable soil, but unsuited for wheat growing, which the architects of the land legislation had in mind when they spoke of 'cultivation'. The problem was not a question of land quality but quantity.

To clear and cultivate 20 acres was an ambitious dream. Yet, in a very good year, producing no more than ten bushels to the acre, even this area under wheat would gross less than £50, a labourer's wage. An average year, with half that yield, would earn barely £25. In bad years there would be nothing. And besides a wheatfield, there had to be a house and vegetable garden, potato patch, chook yard, milking shed, smithy and stables and enough land to graze working and saddle horses, one or two dairy cows, some pigs and a few sheep. It is unlikely that the Kellys ever cultivated more than 8 or 9 acres — just enough to satisfy the Land Act. Three years later a daughter would testify, 'None of her mother's selection was under cultivation.'

Living by a lonely stretch of road 4 miles from the nearest pub, Ellen was able to make money from travellers who wanted a bed or a meal. It was a matter of hospitality to let them have a drink if they wanted it, and not unreasonable that they should pay for this service, at the inflated rate of a shilling for a glass of brandy. This was, of course, illegal, but by bush standards it was hardly a criminal activity. Even the Chief Commissioner of Police, Captain Standish, had been a 'sly grog seller' on the Ovens goldfield back in the 1850s, though this fact was tucked away in his diary and he probably tutted with the rest to hear that the 'notorious' Mrs Kelly sold spirits without a licence.

That first winter on the Eleven Mile must have been hard, but there were enough tired, hungry and thirsty travellers, enough mutton, milk, eggs and potatoes for Ellen and the children to live, in her words, 'happily enough, if roughly'.

The year passed and in February of 1869 a minor penal incident near distant Melbourne spread ripples which would become waves to engulf the Kellys and Lloyds. Outside Pentridge Gaol, a convict gang was building a wall. A prisoner called Henry Johnstone, on light duties because of a recurrent bowel blockage, was 'picking up an odd stone here and there'. Finding a hollow in tall, dry grass, he hid in it until the party returned to the gaol for lunch, then ran off across Merri Creek and began a fateful journey towards the north-east.

The following month one of Johnstone's prison friends, Uncle Tom Lloyd, was released from Pentridge. Even before Uncle Tom's return to his family at Greta, Johnstone had probably received help from Aunty Kate and Aunty Jane. It was almost certainly through the Lloyds that Ned met the runaway convict, who, by then, had become a bushranger under his 'professional' name of Harry Power. He was the last of Australia's great highwaymen, and Ned Kelly, at 14, became his apprentice.

Harry Power was an unlikely brigand — a rumbustious, middle-aged Irishman with a greying beard, chunky build and an awkward, waddling gait caused by agonising bunions and the need to wear boots several sizes too large. One man noted that they 'turned up fully an inch and a half at the toes'.

His appearance belied a formidable set of qualities, however. A contemporary considered him 'as fearless and daring a rider as ever lived and one of the best bushmen in Australia'. Certainly he could travel from place to place through trackless bush at such bewildering speed that he baffled both pursuers and local experts, who insisted that no one man could have carried out some of his consecutive hold-ups. Covering 60 and 70 miles a day, he claimed to have held up thirty men within twenty-four hours.

He had piercing blue eyes and a booming voice which he used to great effect, easily intimidating his victims with dire threats of retribution against pursuers or betrayers. This meant that he never had to use the double-barrelled shotgun he usually carried, except for a shot at a farmer's dog which attacked him. He missed. He was full of blarney and once talked two captors into releasing him. On another memorable occasion, when a Scotsman refused to hand over any booty, Harry retired behind a tree and loudly prayed that he wouldn't have to shoot this misguided fellow. The prayer was answered.

Most importantly, perhaps, he had a broad network of friends who sheltered, helped and fed him (he never mastered the art of eating on the run) and kept him several jumps ahead of police pursuit.

According to Harry, who was often an unreliable witness, his bushranging career just happened. A friend gave him clothing, food and a firearm — probably the double-barrelled gun which remained his favourite weapon. Waddling along the road next day, he heard that troopers were after him. 'I saw I was getting into it,' said Harry. He needed transport, so bailed up a man on 'a likely looking mare', took the horse and scored £17. 'I could see I was getting into it badly,' lamented Harry. So he bailed up a station and took £70, now accepting that, 'I was in for it worse than ever and in another day or two I was in for it altogether.' Harry pilfered his way up the north-east and started blazing a trail of robberies as a classic highwayman, a mounted footpad, at a time when bushranging was becoming a thing of the past. Captain Thunderbolt, another lonely example of this old breed, was killed the following year, just twelve days before the end of Harry Power's career. By late March, when Uncle Tom Lloyd came home, Harry had probably made himself known at Glenmore and was using the Quinn property as his base for that area.

The spectacular crag, The Rock, which crowned the spur more than 1000 feet above Glenmore and commanded an eagle's view of the King Valley in both directions, became known as Power's Lookout. A couple of hundred yards below, in a gully running up the side of the spur, was a boulder-strewn shelf, a miniature plateau. Here Harry built a strange little structure which he called his 'mia-mia' — a rough bed sheltered by an A-frame of saplings covered with blankets and leafy branches. He slept with a boulder at his head and his trusty shotgun slung from the ridgepole with the trigger above his face and the twin muzzles pointing at the entrance.

Because the gully site gave Harry no clear view up and down the King, he also set up a 'watchbox' on the spur, about 300 yards further down. This was a hollow stump with spy holes drilled in it to cover a broad sweep of the valley. Branches were lopped and jammed in the holes to disguise the 'blind' when not in use.

The Quinn homestead was immediately below, reached by a bridge to the stockyard across the lagoon. Placement of the bridge meant that anyone using it had to pass close by the Quinns', where the peacock on the roof was ready to screech a warning. Glenmore was a safe retreat: remote, inaccessible and well-guarded.

It was possibly here that Ned met Harry Power. Uncle Tom Lloyd might have arranged it. If cautious Red had been alive, he might have opposed the idea, but incautious Ellen probably encouraged her son. When the world seems to offer little justice, when the law is of England, ancient enemy of the Irish, and when it can be seen to stand between you and a chance to tip the scales your way, then criminality takes on a very different perspective. And Harry Power was no ordinary criminal. He was quickly becoming a hero to many ordinary folk of the northeast, for no better reason than he made fools of the police and rarely bothered the poor. The die was cast. By late May 1869 Ned was riding with the bushranger.

The first sight of Harry must have been a disappointment. Ned was already nearly 2 inches taller and the boy's eyes would have strayed to the clown-like boots, the broad, flat feet. But as soon as Harry heaved himself into the saddle, he was transformed.

◆

EARLY THAT MONTH Harry had burst into notoriety with a day of multiple hold-ups near Bright: a mail coach and a series of travellers and passers-by. Now, in the glory of a high country late autumn, Ned joined him to ride across the ridges above the western headwaters of the King into the Wombat Ranges. These were a forbidding snarl of thickly timbered hills where Ryans Creek took its rise for the long journey to swell the Broken River and flow down past Benalla. Harry had been a gold digger in the alluvial creeks of these ranges and knew their network of ridges — past lofty Emu Swamp, down steep Toombullup ridge, across the basin below Table Top, then winding lower to more open country around Dr J. P. Rowe's Mount Battery Station near Mansfield, which they reached on Thursday 27 May.

Harry had some exploit in mind — perhaps holding up the Woods Point–Mansfield gold escort — but was clearly concerned that their horses were now too jaded for a rapid getaway if one was needed. He decided to take a couple of fresh mounts from Dr Rowe.

Harry and Ned tied their horses and sneaked down to the edge of a rocky bluff overlooking the horse paddock, where a station hand saw them and took word to Rowe in the homestead. The doctor was 'well advanced in years' (actually 59), but far from decrepit. He ordered his horse saddled, sent for one of his sons, loaded a 'long-distance rifle' and set out on foot alone.

Rowe spotted the two men 'lying full length in the sun', looking down at his horses. He managed to get within range and, without a second thought, put a bullet into the ground right in front of them, kicking gravel into their faces. It was an ugly experience for a 14-year-old. According to Harry, 'Kelly turned deathly white and wanted to surrender.' Harry dragged the boy to his feet but 'had the greatest difficulty in getting him off the ground, he was in such a fright.'

As the pair ran to their horses, Rowe's son came galloping up leading his father's mount. Harry and Ned spurred away with the Rowes hard behind, but lost them in a breakneck gallop through the bush — weaving among trees, ducking branches, bursting through scrub, hurdling fallen timber and creek beds. One spent bullet struck Harry's horse on the flank. Pursuers noted later that 'Power and his comrade' had ridden through 'the worst and most difficult part of the country'. The wild ride must have completely exhausted their jaded horses. Their northward flight became an endurance test as 'Wellington the blacktracker' and a Mansfield police party rode in pursuit, reinforced by twenty volunteers.

Harry and Ned were lucky. The weather broke and rain washed out their tracks before tracker Wellington reached the Greta district, and a pair of horsemen who had shot and skinned a sheep near Greta provided a false, rapidly fading trail off towards the Murray.

The escape from Mount Battery had shown Harry that this lad Kelly could ride, but he was disgusted at the cowardice shown by his apprentice — cowardice that jeopardised their escape. Ned said later that 'Power had such an ungovernable temper that he thought Power would shoot him.' Bitterly disappointed, probably ashamed, Ned rode back to Eleven Mile Creek. The autumn adventure was over. He returned empty-handed to the winter world of boggy tracks and swampy paddocks and the day-to-day drudgery of the 88 acres.

At first he probably worried that something might lead the police to him, but his luck held. Rowe could say only that Power's companion had been 'tall' and 'rather slight'. Only two days after the encounter it had been reported, 'Power has now got a mate named Lake who has been in gaol for illegally using a horse.' While the police hunted for young Lake, Harry rode on to loftier heights of bushranging fame in both Victoria and New South Wales. Within three months he received the accolade of a £200 reward for his capture in Victoria, matched by £200 from New South Wales.

◆

IN APRIL 1869, shortly before the ill-fated adventure with Harry, Ned's 15-year-old sister Annie had married a young Scot from Edinburgh called Alex Gunn, whose father had a property the other side of Winton. Alex, a nuggety 29-year-old with sandy hair and blue eyes, was a battler who had just lost a selection through non-payment of rent. It's easy to imagine that he had invited more trouble on his head by marrying into the Kelly–Lloyd–Quinn clan. In fact, he would prove quite capable of creating his own trouble, though a tragic chain of events spared him involvement in the Kelly outbreak.

Two months after Annie's marriage Ellen was granted her lease to the 88 acres and set about satisfying the Lands Department's ongoing requirements to 'improve' the property.

The first owner of Eleven Mile Creek had done little clearing on the block and Ned set to work felling trees, most of them heavy, hard iron-bark, with their pale, grey foliage, charcoal black trunks and gum that spilt like blood over the axe blade. There was more than the family needed for fencing and firewood, so Ned split some to sell. When he appeared in court in June on behalf of one of the Gunns, he proudly described himself as 'a splitter'.

While Ned practised one of his father's trades, his mother had found romance. Her lover was Bill Frost, a boundary rider for grazier Hector Simson of Laceby, just south of Wangaratta. He might have met Ellen on a visit to the Kelly hospice. Ellen was now 37, still slim and black haired, a striking woman. Frost was a 36-year-old Englishman, bearded and stocky. He probably cut a fine figure on a horse in his moleskins and tweed jacket — a quality which Ellen would have found attractive. He used to arrive on a Saturday and stay with her until Sunday night or Monday morning. In June Ellen became pregnant and Frost said he would marry her. After this promise of happier times, it proved a dark winter for the family.

On 24 June, up at a station on the Jamieson River outside Mansfield, cranky Uncle Jimmy Quinn turned bushranger. Armed with a revolver, he bailed up a Chinese man and took £2, but immediately gave it back. This didn't stop a warrant being issued at Mansfield and the *Police Gazette* named him as a suspected associate of Harry Power. For more than a month Jimmy remained a fugitive then, in a rare display of good sense, he walked into the Mansfield police station and gave himself up. He was committed to trial for Highway Robbery Under Arms and released on bail.

This startling news reached Greta at the same time as Uncle Jack Lloyd was released from Pentridge. The clan's reunion was brief. On 25 August Ned's grandfather died at remote Glenmore, after a six-day attack of dysentery. He was 66. The body was carried 30 miles down to Oxley cemetery and laid to rest without benefit of clergy. It was a cruel blow to Ellen and Ned only three years after Red's death, and a watershed for the family. Old James had been heavily in debt, and the wild acres and forbidding crags of Glenmore were a meagre legacy for Jack, the oldest surviving son.

Despite Jimmy's problems, old James had been, as Clune observed, 'a steadying influence'. His wealthier squatter neighbours never would have admitted this while he lived, but now acknowledged the fact in a flurry of concern.

Julius Curr, manager of Bungamero (or Degamero) across the King to the East, alerted his principal, Melbourne banker John Badcock, who referred the matter to fellow Melbourne Clubman, Chief Commissioner Standish. Curr then enlisted the support of Evan Evans — joint owner of Whitfield Station to the north. Evans was notorious for 'dummying' (using front men to select land on his run) and 'peacocking' ('picking the eyes' out of a run by selecting key areas such as waterholes), scams that exploited the Land Acts against the small farmers the legislation was designed to help.

Evans considered the Quinns 'unfit to hold a pastoral licence', declaring:

Old Quinn, the father of the family, which consists of several sons, is lately dead, and were the Government to consider the bad character which the sons bear sufficient reason for refusing them a license to occupy the run it might be the means of dispersing the fraternity that has been so long the pest of the neighbourhood.

Chief Commissioner Standish wrote to James Grant, Minister for Lands, early in September 'to protest agst [against] the renewal of Quinn's license'. But Grant was in the thick of a political crisis leading to a change of government within the month and Standish could not get the minister's ear. He wrote to banker Badcock:

> I don't know whether this criminal brood can be prevented from select-ing under the 42nd Clause. I suppose that selectors are not obliged to produce certificates of morality before getting the land they apply for.
> I'll not lose sight of the matter.

And indeed he didn't. Jack Quinn got his licence, but the following year Glenmore police station was established nearby. Men of money and influence, rarely frustrated in their exercise of power, were joining forces against the clan.

———————◆———————

IN EARLY SPRING Ellen hired a local lad called Bill Gray to help Ned with the clearing and to grub out stumps before summer baked the ground bone-hard. Ellen paid Gray £1 a week and employed him for at least a month. By mid-October of 1869 the pair were being helped by a boarder, a 29-year-old Australian-born miner from Gaffney's Creek called Bill Skilling (or Skillen). He had intended to stay with the Kellys only briefly, but lost his horse and was there 'about a fortnight off an' on'. That delay changed his life and his name.

One Thursday, a warm day, the three broke for lunch and strolled up to the house, where Annie was visiting for the day. In the peace of noon, Ah Fook, a pig and poultry hawker from the Morses Creek Chinese camp near Bright, came up across the gap from Greta and walked down into the Kelly valley. He was in shirtsleeves and carried a billy can on a bamboo over his shoulder. His pocket held a purse with ten shillings in change and he had £25 hidden in his boot. Ah Fook had good cause to honour this popular Chinese custom, since he had lost £2 10 shillings to Harry Power in a hold-up six weeks earlier. Padding along the dusty road splashed with sunlight and tree shadows, he disappears tempor-arily from historical sight.

Ah Fook would claim that, as he was passing the Kelly house, Ned emerged carrying 'a long stick' to announce, 'Me's a bushranger: me'll kill you unless money given up.' Ned, he said, looked about 20, was 5 feet 8 inches tall, clean shaven, brown-haired and wore dirty mole-skins and a straw hat with a black band. Ah Fook said that Ned forced him to walk about half a mile to a clump of trees then took the 10 shillings from his purse and struck him on the arm and leg. The follow-ing day, Sergeant Whelan of Benalla 'found the skin broken slightly on the leg and shoulder'.

The Kelly witnesses told a different story: that Ah Fook walked up to the house, where Annie sat outside sewing, and asked her for a drink. Given creek water, he abused and threatened Annie. Ned emerged and pushed him away but ran off when the Chinese man hit him three times with a bamboo. The fearsome Ah Fook left, threatening to burn the house down. With Gray and Skilling, who had seen the whole incident, Ned then returned to work until sundown.

Neither story is convincing. Much has been made of the fact that Ah Fook claimed Ned was wielding an 18-foot stick. He actually said, through an interpreter, that the stick was '2 or 3 fathoms long' and obviously one of them confused fathoms with feet. More to the point, why would a budding bushranger operate from his home, making identification absurdly easy?

The Kelly story, as presented by Gray, Skilling and Annie, is no more convincing. If we can believe that Ah Fook was an unusually assertive and volatile Chinese, the clash with Annie is credible enough, as is Ned coming to the aid of his sister. But even if we can believe that Ned would run away without making any attempt to retaliate after being beaten with a bamboo, it is hard to accept that Gray and Skilling stood limply by while this happened.

It is even harder to explain why, the following day, Ned dashed off 'at full speed' when a plainclothed Sergeant Whelan and Constable McInerny came within half a mile of the Kelly house. Whelan gave chase on horseback, evaded a couple of 'ferocious' dogs set on him as he passed the house and managed to catch Ned before he reached the selection's boundary fence. Asked twice why he ran, Ned could give no reason apart from saying that, 'If the fence was a little nearer he would have got away.'

Arrested on a charge of Highway Robbery, Ned was taken to Benalla, locked up overnight with a regulation dinner of bread and water and brought into court next day. Whelan asked for a remand to allow time to find an interpreter — even though he had readily found one the previous day to translate Ah Fook's story. The bench remanded Ned until the following Tuesday, four days off, and accepted Whelan's arguable advice that, 'The law did not allow bail to prisoners of this description'. Ned had one consolation: as a longer term remand prisoner he was now given 10 ounces of meat a day.

On Tuesday Whelan antagonised the bench by again failing to produce an interpreter. Eventually, after eleven days in the Benalla lockup, Ned faced the court on 26 October with Superintendent Nicolas prosecuting.

Police Magistrate Wills listened to both versions of the incident and, in the face of three witnesses contradicting an uncorroborated story, dismissed the charge with apparent reluctance. He restrained his cynicism to the mild but telling comment: 'You must be a very quiet lot out there — three of you and to allow your friend to be beaten like that is most extraordinary.'

The Benalla Ensign, which reported this remark, obviously believed Ah Fook, and the following year made the bald statement, 'The cunning of himself [Ned] and his mates got him off.' Beechworth's *Advertiser* declared however, 'It is impossible to avoid coming to any other conclusion than that the charge of robbery has been trumped up by the Chinaman to be revenged on Kelly, who had evidently assaulted him.' This may well have been true, though it means that the Kelly witnesses also lied.

It seems most likely that Ah Fook took offence at being given creek water, as described in the Kelly version, and flew at Annie, bringing Ned on the scene. Ah Fook probably defended himself with the bamboo — a popular Chinese weapon — but Ned snatched it from him and sent him on his way with a caning.

In years ahead men who knew Ned well would call him a 'rather impulsive young fellow'. The Ah Fook clash is our first glimpse of this quality. It foreshadows a similar reaction to a similar event nine years later, and much more.

Sergeant James Whelan, the loser in this legal contest, removed the white gloves he had worn for his court appearance and returned bareknuckled to his desk at the Benalla police station. Whelan was bearded and pale-skinned, with calm, penetrating eyes and the lofty brow of a scholar — a man who combined machine-like efficiency with high intelligence. If needed, meticulous notes jogged his memory that only three months before he had prosecuted a farmer called Yeaman Gunn (probably a relative of Alex) for possession of stolen mutton. Young Kelly claimed to have sold Gunn a couple of sheep the very day the meat was found. The bench had been unimpressed and, in a controversial judgement, fined Gunn £10.

From now on, Sergeant Whelan would keep a careful eye on Ned Kelly and his relations, eventually to become 'a perfect encyclopedia of useful knowledge' about them. An officer commented, 'His diligence, his fidelity, his wisdom in council ... were amazing.' Young Ned had made a formidable enemy.

◆

BY THE MIDSUMMER of 1870 Ellen's pregnancy was approaching full term and it seemed that Bill Frost was changing his mind about marriage. Then, in mid-February, Frost narrowly survived a murder attempt, shot by a man he knew only as 'Harry'. It's tempting to imagine one of the clan avenging Frost's betrayal of Ellen; but tall, thirtyish,

English 'Harry', with his 'sandy beard of Yankee cut' and his sheep dog, resembled no one in the family circle and disappeared into New South Wales. Frost spent several weeks recovering in the Beechworth hospital.

The prospect of another mouth to feed in the Kelly family, and the imminent loss of Bill Frost as a provider, may have prompted Ned to seek or accept another chance with Harry Power. Certainly, Harry believed that he had missed thousands of pounds in booty by operating alone: 'I only wanted a mate to help me make a big haul, and then I meant to go to America and live an honest man.'

Ned and Harry wiped the slate clean, settled for the best qualities in each other and rode off together in the brutally dry autumn of 1870, both buoyed up by grand dreams. Ned was determined that he would not let Harry down again. This time, it was Harry who would blunder, fatally, in their very first exploit.

3

POWER'S MATE

MARCH – JUNE 1870

Robert McBean of Kilfera Station, with its 44 000 acres and 11 000 sheep, was a man of wealth and power in the Benalla district — a burly, bearded Scot who dispensed justice as an honorary magistrate with more fairness than many fellow squatters. Nevertheless he battled as hard as any against the encroachments of selectors, was a declared enemy of the Quinns and openly admitted his interest in buying Mrs Kelly off what he saw as his land.

Significantly, McBean was a member of the Melbourne Club and a respected friend of fellow clubman, Chief Commissioner Frederick Charles Standish, who often listened to McBean rather than following the advice of senior police officers.

While Harry Power had been in Pentridge, one of the Lloyds had received a letter from his wife telling how McBean had impounded some of their stock. Harry swore that McBean would, in his words, 'pay the piper' for this, but his rage was hard to maintain when another letter told how McBean's wife had given Mrs Lloyd 'a few pounds to redeem her cattle'.

Not only was McBean spared a visit from Harry but the bushranger actually tried to avoid a confrontation — unsuccessfully, as it turned out.

On Wednesday 16 March 1870 McBean had been checking some fencing work on Kilfera. He was riding across his straw-dry paddocks at noon when he saw two horsemen: a nuggety, bearded man in tweed jacket and moleskins and 'a lad'. The Kelly selection was on the edge of his property and he thought he recognised Bill Frost, just out of hospital, and young Ned.

As he approached, the horsemen swung away, but McBean rode after them with a cheery, 'Good day, Bill!' He quickly realised his mistake. The 'lad' dismounted, 'turning his face away', while the bearded man wheeled with an indignant, 'Confound your impertinence. I'll teach you how to speak to a gentleman. Fancy calling me "Bill!"' Told to dismount,

McBean stared blankly at Harry Power until the bushranger drew a large revolver.

McBean swung to the ground and Harry demanded his watch. While the squatter tied it to his bridle as ordered, Harry said that he had 'heard at Lloyd's hut that Mr McBean was a decent man', and he had avoided taking one of his horses, until now. When McBean asked for the return of his watch, a valuable heirloom, Harry said he could have it back for £10 'at a future time', and rode off southwards with his young companion, leading McBean's mare.

The disgruntled squatter tramped 2¾ miles to his homestead, rode into Benalla in a lather of fury and raised the alarm.

In that single hold-up, Harry had antagonised a very powerful, very determined man and admitted what everyone suspected, that he was intimate with the Lloyds.

McBean 'never caught a glimpse of his mate's face' but must have recognised Ned. If he told the police of his suspicions, they bided their time. The official report of the robbery merely noted that Power was 'accompanied by a lad who rode a brown horse and carried a swag in front'. McBean theorised that he was 'a pilot' for Power.

Early that afternoon a horseman of Harry Power's description was seen between Kilfera and Greta, driving two horses. One of them was a saddled and bridled roan, apparently the horse ridden by the bushranger when he held up McBean. Yet at almost the same time, Harry, with Ned under cover, bailed up a man called Charles Dickens on the fringe of the Wombat Ranges almost 20 miles to the east. There could be no mistake. Dickens knew Harry, who was now riding McBean's superb brown mare.

An early theory identified the man driving the two horses as 'the pilot present during Power's escapade with Mr McBean'. The police must have realised very quickly that the theory didn't work. 'The lad' described by McBean could hardly be mistaken for a bearded, middle-aged man of Harry's build. Obviously one of Harry's friends had been called on to take the bushranger's discarded roan and perhaps provide a fresh horse for his young 'pilot'. Clearly, the friend resembled Harry. It could have been Bill Frost. But then, Harry had mentioned chatting with the Lloyds ...

Deep in the Strathbogie Ranges that night, as Harry unrolled his possum-skin rug and Ned spread his blue blanket, they probably congratulated themselves on the day's takings: a mare, saddle and new Pelham bridle, worth about £40 altogether; the handsome gold watch with enamelled face, valued by McBean at £45; and Charles Dickens's '£3 odd'. Not the 'big haul' but a good start. They would continue their careers as highwaymen with McBean's watch ticking away the remaining weeks of freedom, like a small, gold bomb.

◆

RIDING WITH HARRY through those halcyon days, Ned got to know the old rogue better. Perhaps, like journalist James Stanley, Ned found in him 'a fund of good, a greatness of heart and soul . . .' without having to add the hasty and unconvincing qualification for respectable consumption, 'perverted by vicious training and mode of life'. Perhaps, as they travelled the parched ranges and hunted for water, Harry rhapsodised to Ned as he would to Stanley:

> It's grand to be in the ranges, and to breathe the beautiful, pure air, and to see Mount Feathertop far above ye, and down below, for miles and miles, the beautiful country. There's water all the year round, and it's always cool and pleasant. That's the place for a man to live . . .

In bewildering switchbacks they travelled down past Merton — avoiding a police contingent at Nolan's pub — through the Puzzle Ranges and across to Tallarook, then up to Jamieson, down to Longwood . . .

The brutal three-month drought broke on 29 March, Easter Sunday, and the north-east was lashed with rainstorms. Almost grassless country turned to a quagmire, creeks brimmed and flooded. What the *Benalla Ensign* called 'the wild bull mountains in which Power can rest in peace', became a treacherous tangle of slippery slopes and cascading gullies.

Harry and Ned headed more determinedly south and were said to have visited Melbourne, Geelong, Ballan, Daylesford and even Gippsland. Rumours flew as 'Power and his mate' became highwaymen hydras, multiplying and dividing, while the police careered around in baffled pursuit to the embarrassment of that darling of Melbourne society, Chief Commissioner Standish.

Beechworth's *Advertiser* recited the litany of police failure and quoted 'Mr Longmore, a tribune of the people and ex-minister of the crown', who blamed the lack of success on 'Captain Standish's love for metropolitan life'. The staunch *Benalla Ensign*, however, laid the blame squarely on 'a niggard Government' which 'cuts down the police force to a state of inefficiency', a situation the paper called 'a national disgrace'.

Coming events — which would embroil the Victoria Police, Ned Kelly, another 'niggard' government, Standish and even Longmore — were casting their shadows, while more immediate shadows caught the eye on all sides.

In May Beechworth's *Advertiser* published a much-repeated story about Ned and Power. 'A poundkeeper' is riding 'in the vicinity of Moyhu Common' when he sees Ned rounding up some cattle. After an exchange of words the gentleman hauls Ned from his mare and gives him 'what he was sorely in need of — a sound thrashing'. 'Some time after' this encounter, the poundkeeper, 'again riding out in the same neighbourhood', is bailed up by Ned and Harry, both with pistols. They take him to 'a deserted hut' and Ned warns the victim that he has 'only a few minutes to live', Harry intervenes, threatens to disarm Ned and turns the man loose, telling him that he can live three months longer before being shot 'for ill treating the boy'.

A week later the *Advertiser* had to say that, because of 'some doubt having been thrown on the authenticity' of their story, they would reveal its source — 'the illustrous captive himself', who had told the yarn 'in the hearing of three witnesses of undoubted veracity'. While the 'veracity' of the man telling the story seems rather more to the point, the *Advertiser* simply tells us he had been a politician. Despite this unimpressive provenance, the tale is usually quoted as fact, with various embellishments. The most that can be offered in support of the story is the later claim by a senior policeman that Ned 'showed such great ferocity of character and displayed such readiness to shoot that Power feared he might hang for a murder committed by "his youthful ally".'

 No reliably recorded statement by Harry Power justifies this claim and it was probably inspired by the very news item it seems to support. Against the poundkeeper's story of the apparent ease with which he unhorsed Ned and thrashed him, it is worth noting that exactly twelve months later a 16-stone trooper who dragged Ned from his horse was able to subdue him only after several labourers came to the trooper's aid. Even then, he had to beat Ned into submission with a revolver.

The celebrated story of 'the Moyhu poundkeeper' is probably a furphy, one of many that helped obscure Harry's and Ned's movements in April and May. Along with 'copycat crimes' and the pair's extraordinary ability to cover amazing distances in remarkably short times, these false alarms gave rise to theories that 'there was more than one highwayman' carrying out robberies and that 'the two men are working in concert to baffle the police'.

Ever since the Power look-alike was seen with the two horses after McBean's hold-up, a web of evidence had been forming. In early April a warrant was issued at Kilmore for the arrest of Jack Lloyd, 'he being now considered the actual perpatrator' of eight robberies previously attributed to Power, including the hold-ups of McBean and Charles Dickens. The description of Uncle Jack on the back of the warrant was uncannily like that of Harry: 'A Tipperary man, labourer, aged 47, 5 feet 6 inches high, fresh complexion, grey hair and eyes, several scars on forehead, nose broken, scar left side of head, left fourth finger injured.'

It would not have escaped the notice of the police that Jack had a son, Tom Lloyd, who might have been the 'lad' with the pseudo Power'.

Less than two weeks after Jack's arrest two men, supposed to be Power and Ned, bailed up a woolsorter called Joseph Balwoski on the main Sydney road a few miles from Seymour. In two accounts Harry and Ned both hold normal bushranging weapons, pistols or revolvers. In a third version, Ned covers Balwoski with 'a firelock' — an intriguing description from a man familiar with firearms who lost a pistol to Harry. Could this 'firelock' have been the antique-looking, sawn-off carbine that was to play a key role in Ned's later career?

While there were some doubts about the Balwoski hold-up, it seemed possible that the police had arrested the wrong man. Proof came five days later when a herdsman called Murray was bailed up by Harry near Lauriston. After taking £5 and sending Murray on his way, Harry called for Ned to 'bring up the horses'. It emerged that this was the herdsman's second encounter with the pair. The previous week, Murray and a companion called O'Leary had stumbled on Harry and Ned, who were spelling their horses in a grassy gully and letting them feed. Here Harry made another mistake. Instead of releasing the empty-pocketed, poorly mounted men as soon as he had sworn them to secrecy, Harry kept them waiting 'for several hours' while the horses grazed and rested. Murray had plenty of time to study the bushranger's mysterious 'mate' and after the second hold-up gave a detailed description: 'Aged 20, 5 feet 9 or 10 inches high, light build, sallow complexion, smooth face, surly appearance; wore dark coat and hat, and dirty moleskin or tweed trousers.'

The description was published in the *Police Gazette* of 2 May (with a curious addendum that Power's mate 'is now stated to have the appearance of a half-caste'). It would not have escaped Sergeant Whelan's notice that the age of the younger bushranger tallied with Ah Fook's overestimation of Ned's age.

Meanwhile Jack Lloyd, in police custody as the suspected perpetrator of the Power robberies, was trying to prove his innocence and save his son from arrest as 'Power's mate'. He could achieve both by incriminating Ned. There were other pressures on Jack. Late one night in the Melbourne Club, Robert McBean urged Standish to increase the money on Harry's head. He believed that 'a sufficient reward' would help persuade Jack to lead police to Harry's 'retreat' on the pretext of buying back McBean's heirloom watch.

Standish duly recommended an increase to £500, prompting a barbed note from the Chief Secretary that this might encourage 'real energy' in the police. Standish bridled and said that the intention was to encourage 'private individuals' or to 'induce members of the criminal classes to give information'.

The reward of £500 was gazetted on 29 April. This was a fortune, close to ten years' pay for a labouring man. It was a cruel carrot to dangle in front of a battler like Jack Lloyd. Yet if Jack was persuaded to reveal Ned's involvement, it would only confirm what the police already knew.

The *Benalla Ensign* had already incriminated Ned while defending the police force against its critics. Stressing the difficulty of the country and 'the fact of his being harboured by villains only a shade better than himself', the paper declared, 'The effect of his example has already been to draw one young fellow into the open vortex of crime, and unless his career is speedily cut short, YOUNG KELLY will blossom into a declared enemy of society.' It was an extraordinary outburst. Obviously the source was McBean, or the Benalla police leaking McBean's evidence.

◆

NOT LONG AFTER the Murray hold-ups, Ned and Harry split up for a second time. Ned said that, 'When they were riding in the mountains, Power swore at him to such an extent, without giving him any provocation, that he put spurs to his horse and galloped away home.' It was a miserable, wet autumn and Harry was as bad as ever at finding food. (Soon afterwards he took a post boy's cut lunch, and, on another occasion, a farmer's wife found that Harry 'had been making free with her bread and butter'.)

For a cold, tired, wet, half-starved 15-year-old, bushranging had simply lost its glamour. He arrived at Eleven Mile Creek to find his mother with a new baby daughter, Ellen, born a week after the McBean hold-up. Ned, who may have ridden 180 miles in some three days, was in a wretched state — dirty, gaunt, exhausted and ill — prompting Mrs Kelly's bitter denunciation of Harry as 'a brown-paper bushranger who could not make tucker either for himself or for his friends.' Ned arrived empty-handed, and with an expensive habit. He had 'learned to smoke while out at night with Power'. He collapsed into bed unwashed, to be shocked awake at dawn when a heavily armed police party crashed into the house.

Superintendent Nicolas, Sergeant Whelan and constables Arthur and Mullane had surrounded the Kelly shanty during the night. Noting two horses tethered outside, they waited to see if Harry and Ned — 'the old fox' and 'the cub' — would leave before daylight. With dawn breaking, Nicolas sprang his trap and caught 'the cub'. He reported that Ned was 'much worn, jaded and altered from his former appearance and complains of being very sick'.

'The entrance of the escort into Benalla was quite imposing,' the *Benalla Ensign* reported, 'the prisoner being surrounded by his captors, and every now and then a smile passed over his face as he recognised some one he knew.' Once in the lock-up, Ned became 'moody'. The paper noted that he had grown since his last Benalla stint and 'appeared quite exhausted' and 'very pale'.

Bread and water and a good night's sleep did wonders. Next morning he sang in his cell 'like a bird' and managed 'a jaunty air' in court. Charged with Robbery in Company and Highway Robbery Under Arms of Balwoski near Seymour, he was remanded for a week.

Immediately Ned was a focus of keen interest among senior police. From information supplied by Nicolas, Captain Standish memoed Superintendent Winch on 7 May 1870 that Ned was 'evidently fresh from a long and fatiguing journey ... the young man seen with Power in the Kyneton district is described to have the appearance of a half-caste. Kelly certainly does not ... but he has the peculiarity of never washing himself and is said to be one of the distinct looking young men in the Colony'.

(Standish's comment on Ned's 'never washing' was clearly based on Superintendent Nicolas's report of his condition when arrested. Cleanliness — as demonstrated by Harry Power and later by Ned — was a mark of sound bushmanship. There is little doubt that Ned quickly resumed his usual clean habits as his health and spirits improved.)

Two days before Ned's next court appearance, Superintendents Hare and Nicolson and Detective Mainwaring arrived by buggy from Melbourne on a mysterious mission. The two superintendents cut striking figures in their trim, blue, silver-corded uniforms but apart from that, they were an odd couple.

Charles Hope Nicolson was a Scot — stern-faced, with thinning hair and a spade beard, not strong on humour. Francis Hare was 6 feet 3 inches, 'remarkably tall' for the times, big-framed, hearty and handsome, with a carefully groomed mane of hair and full beard enhancing his resemblance to Lord Tennyson. He was South African-born, the son of a British army officer, a tally-ho enthusiast for almost everything. Both officers were men of great physical courage and both were impulsive, but Nicolson coupled these qualities with a doggedness and shrewdness honed by fourteen years as head of the detective force.

The previous year his health had broken down under the city-bound stress of the job and he had been placed in charge of the beautiful Kyneton district, scene of Harry's and Ned's last joint exploits. It was rumoured that Nicolson's appointment foreshadowed his being given 'the comparatively light duties of a police magistrate'. Health notwithstanding, Nicolson was now hard on the trail of Power, commenting dourly, 'I had information that he had passed through a portion of my district, and on that I acted.' He had interrupted Melbourne sick leave to take up the pursuit.

Nicolson may have been tempted to ask why Hare, a 'junior super-intendent' in charge of the Richmond Police Depot, had been appointed with him to the Power pursuit 'over the heads of at least eleven senior officers', including Superintendent Nicolas. Nicholson knew the answer. It sprang from Captain Standish's great regard for the dashing, engaging Hare, described by a colleague as 'like the love of Jonathan for David'. In coming years this regard became an obsession.

Such were the two officers who, on the morning of Tuesday 10 May 1870, confronted 15-year-old Ned Kelly in a room of the Benalla police station. Their three lives would interweave.

Hare, who loathed dealing with criminals, thought Ned 'a flash, ill-looking, young blackguard'. Nicolson, on the other hand, was 'taken with his appearance' and, with characteristic 'skill and patience', easily established an effective level of dialogue with the lad. Nicolson con-vinced Ned that there was no use pretending he knew nothing about Harry Power and Ned admitted to the two officers that he was 'Power's mate'. He spoke of Harry's 'ungovernable temper' and described how he had left the scratchy old rogue after his last unjustified outburst.

Still wounded and embittered by the break-up and physically at a low ebb, Ned was unusually vulnerable to Nicolson's expertise, especially given the uncomfortable news that when he appeared in court in two days time he would face additional charges: the McBean robbery and the hold-ups of herdsman Murray and his mate, O'Leary.

The next day Standish would memo Winch:

> From what Kelly has said since his apprehension it is not at all unlikely that Power has worked his way back from when he and Kelly departed to Glenlyon ... and is not unlikely to seek medical attendance, as his stricture will not allow him to lead the rough and roving life he has been [following] of late with impunity.

Within two days Standish would alert the Inspector-General in Sydney that Power 'may be making his way to Eden where he is likely to take ship', also advising, 'He is well acquainted with the country about Kiandra and Snowy River and may be working his way to the coast either by Kiandra or by Bendock in the North Gipps Land.'

The same day the officer-in-charge at Seymour was told: 'It appears that Power contemplated robbing the bank at Seymour saying it could easily be done in the day time, though unlikely that attempt will now be made.'

With this valuable crop of information drawn from Ned, Nicolson and Hare drove out to see McBean at Kilfera. Jack Lloyd had just been released from Kilmore and McBean had already spoken to him. Worn down by his arrest and interrogation and tempted by the

£500 reward, Jack broke. He told the squatter he would betray Harry.

At dusk that evening McBean introduced the two superintendents to Jack. The interview was almost a disaster. Hare refused to trust 'a Pentridge bird' and had aborted negotiations when Nicolson stepped in, quickly gaining an undertaking from Jack to find Power's hideout and come back to McBean 'within a month'.

On Thursday 12 May, when Ned again faced the Benalla court, his condition had improved 'greatly', his manner was now 'flash' and his language 'hideous' (which in that period might have meant a few 'bloodys' and 'damns').

Ned first stood trial on the McBean robbery. Superintendent Nicolas — obviously taken into the confidence of Hare and Nicolson and ordered by Standish to 'give them every assistance' — said simply that 'Prisoner could not be identified as having taken part in that robbery'. A deal had been struck with McBean — probably part and parcel of the negotiations with Jack Lloyd — and Ned was discharged.

On the second charge, of robbing Balwoski near Seymour, Nicolas said that the police had 'made every exertion to find the principal witness . . . but he could not be discovered'. This second case could not proceed and Ned was again discharged. It all seemed too easy, but he wasn't free yet.

He was next charged with the Robbery Under Arms of the herdsman Murray at Lauriston, near Kyneton. At this point, manipulation of the trial by Nicolson and Hare became blatant. Murray and his mate O'Leary had been summonsed to appear and had reached Benalla the previous day. It would be reported that 'they failed to identify Kelly as one of their molestors', but they would return to Kyneton from Benalla, insisting that 'they were not confronted with him'. Totally ignoring the fact that the crown's two witnesses were waiting in the wings, Superintendent Nicolas told the court that he had 'that morning received a warrant from Kyneton, and that prisoner answered the description contained in the warrant'. Nicolas applied for a remand to Kyneton which the Bench granted.

Ned would have expected to travel to Kyneton by coach, via Kilmore. Instead, he was sent to Melbourne by coach and train and taken to the lock-up in the Police Depot at Richmond. There he passed Saturday, probably subjected to further questioning by Nicolson and Hare.

On the Sunday morning he had an unexpected visitor — Captain Standish, who was at the depot for almost three hours of 'consultations' with Nicolson and Hare. For Standish, the call on Ned may have sprung from little more than idle curiosity to see this interesting young specimen in his cage, a minor criminal celebrity to chat about at the Club.

The urbane, almost foppish Standish was a most unlikely policeman and in fact he had no training for the job. From a distinguished English Catholic family, he had fled a fortune in gambling debts and migrated to Australia under an assumed name. A brief stint in the army had given him his rank; renunciation of the Catholic faith now gave him easier entrée into the Melbourne establishment.

For the post of Chief Commissioner his major qualifications were some minor goldfields appointments, administrative ability, a keen political sense and an impressive façade. After eleven years in the job his official duties were taking second place to an aimless social round and the awful compulsion of the race track and gambling table. On a single night he lost more than £600, half his annual salary.

The highlight of Standish's career had been the recent visit to Australia of Queen Victoria's son, the Duke of Edinburgh, and Standish appears to have acted as procurer for His Royal Highness while in Melbourne. Though Standish's own sex life seems ambiguous, he was professionally familiar with the city's brothels and had been known to stage dubious entertainments for a close circle of Melbourne's gentry. He was once said to have provided naked women, seated on black-velvet-covered chairs, as dinner companions for his guests.

An entry in Standish's diary — normally a recital of trivia — records the conference with Hare and Nicolson and the brief encounter with Ned, highlighting the degree to which the Power pursuit had begun to impact on the reputations both of the force and its Chief Commissioner.

On the Monday evening Ned and Nicolson travelled north to Kyneton by train. A local reporter thought Ned 'a fine, active, athletic young fellow of by no means unprepossessing personal appearance. He gives his age as 15 but he is probably between 18 and 20'.

Ned was taken to the bluestone lock-up of the bluestone police station, within spitting distance of the bluestone courthouse. This stolid and sombre complex would be his world for the next three weeks. Showing that Ned was no ordinary remand prisoner, they sat him on a chair to be photographed. He brushed his long, dark hair back from his forehead but didn't bother to open the lapels of his jacket, which were folded across his collarless shirt against the cold. He stared defiantly past the camera at something, his lazy left eye lending a dangerous edge.

Not all the police at Kyneton proved to be enemies. The sergeant was James Babington, a very different figure from Sergeant Whelan of Benalla. Babington, a warm, fatherly man, became almost a friend to Ned, someone he would turn to in trouble. This and the relationship being cultivated by Nicolson meant that Ned's time in Kyneton was at worst boring and at best a glimpse of a justice system which could treat him with some dignity and fairness, even kindness.

Nicolson's careful interrogation of Ned continued. There is no record of what else the boy told him, apart from describing 'Power's watchbox', as he called it — the lookout stump with branches stuck in its spyholes. Because he had not divulged the location of the 'blind', it seemed harmless information.

On Friday 20 May Sergeant Babington donned his white gloves and Ned was taken into court to face an imposing four-man bench: a police magistrate, the Shire President and two justices of the peace. Babington applied for a week's remand, explaining that 'the case was a difficult and complicated one, and the police had been unable as yet to get all the evidence together'.

This was nonsense. The essential evidence was Murray's account of the robbery and his identification of Ned as one of the two men involved. Obviously aware of this, the magistrate asked if the prisoner had been identified. Babington said that 'the witness had not yet been confronted with the prisoner with a view to any formal identification'. It would have been reasonable to ask why. Ned had been at Kyneton for three days and four nights and Murray worked at Lauriston, only five miles away. Instead, the bench merely asked Ned 'whether he had anything to say why he should not be remanded'. Ned, who had now spent more than two weeks in custody, raised no objection.

In the week before Ned's next day in court events moved fast. McBean informed Standish that Jack Lloyd was ready to 'point out the exact hiding place of Power'. Nicolson first learnt of this when he received two letters: one from Standish telling him he was obviously too ill to join the expedition to capture Power; the other from Hare, announcing, 'My dear fellow, I am so sorry to be off without you.'

Nicolson's Scots blood was up. He raced to Melbourne, obtained a medical certificate and insisted that he was taking charge.

At 6 a.m. on Friday 27 May Nicolson and Hare set out by buggy for McBean's Kilfera Station. That morning Ned appeared again in Kyneton court. Acting on previous instructions from Nicolson, Sergeant Babington told the Bench that 'in a week he should be prepared to bring forward such evidence as, if published now, might defeat the ends of justice.' Ned was remanded for *another* seven days. It was noted that 'the youth Kelly offered no objection to this course, and in fact appeared to contemplate the entire proceedings with great indifference'.

Nicolson and Hare reached Kilfera on Sunday evening. Hare's clerk, Sergeant Montfort, had been in the north-east for a week and had arranged for a blacktracker called Donald to join them. A day or two later, when Jack Lloyd arrived, McBean provided him with £15 in notes to buy back the watch from Power, who had returned to his hideout near Quinns'. Hare initialled the notes.

On Wednesday morning the party started off — Nicolson, Hare, Montfort, Donald and Jack Lloyd. They struck out from Ryans Creek across the ranges to the headwaters of the Fifteen Mile, 'carefully avoiding all roads and tracks'. For some reason, they carried only 'two meals per man' and a single rug between the five of them.

They camped in the ranges on Wednesday night and on Thursday pushed on to a lonely hut. They broke in ('We put the blackfellow down the chimney') and stole some tea and sugar. Next morning, before they set off, Hare killed an unfortunate chook roosting on the roof and hid it in a sack on the blacktracker's saddle.

At ten that morning, while this badly organised and dubiously conducted expedition was riding deeper into the ranges towards Glenmore, Ned made his third appearance in the distant Kyneton court. This time Babington surprised the Bench and the local press by asking for the boy's discharge. 'He was accordingly set at liberty', recorded the *Observer*, with the comment, 'It seems strange that not a particle of evidence should have been produced against him but no doubt the police had good reasons for all that they did in the matter.'

Ned was free, but in a strange town 120 miles from home. Babington arranged a room for the boy at Murphys' Hotel in Mollison Street. Both Babington and Nicolson later suggested that this was Ned's idea, but admitted that it was desirable. Significantly Nicolson said that, while on the Power expedition, he left Ned '*under the care* of the police at Kyneton'. [my italics]

The name of 'Power's mate' was by now well known in the town and Ned was booked in as 'Dan Kelly'. It is not clear whether this was a police initiative or Ned's.

That evening, while 'Dan Kelly' joined the other guests at Jane Murphy's generous table, Nicolson, Hare, Montfort and Donald 'made a meal off the fowl . . . the poorest creature four men ever dined off'. While Ned settled into the unaccustomed comfort of mattress, pillow and freshly laundered sheets, the policemen and the tracker spent the night sitting in pouring rain, holding their horses, as Jack Lloyd headed for the Quinn house some 6 miles off. He carried McBean's £15 to buy back the watch from Harry.

The police waited all Saturday in steady rain. Jack Lloyd came riding back at about four in the afternoon. 'What luck have you had?' asked Nicolson. Jack said nothing but took a tied-up handkerchief from his pocket, undid the knot and revealed McBean's watch and chain. He had seen Power.

Jack now tried to avoid leading the police back to the bushranger's hiding place, making every excuse to delay the expedition. But Hare and Nicolson — soaked, frozen and starving — would not be deterred. The

Edward Hall in later life. As a 33-year-old senior constable he set out to arrest the teenage Ned Kelly *on suspicion* that he was riding a stolen horse. Hall tried to shoot Ned, beat him about the head with a revolver and committed perjury to 'prove' he knew the horse was stolen. (*Police Museum*)

(Below left) Claimed to be a portrait of Annie Gunn, this photograph shows a strong resemblance to Ned as a teenager but the hair style and dress are more typical of the 1880s than the late 1860s or 1870s. Annie's death, after an affair with a policeman, proved a powerful influence in the Kelly outbreak. (*Dagma Balcarek*)

(Below right) The gaol photograph of Ned taken shortly before his release from Pentridge in 1874. After Ned's outlawry this unflattering portrait quickly replaced the Kyneton photograph as the 'standard' likeness.

Believed to be George King, the young Californian who married Ned's mother in 1874. He was an expert horse thief and probably encouraged Ned to give up his career as a timberman. *(Elsie Pettifer/Leigh Olver)*

James Whitty, who arrived in Victoria as a penniless, illiterate Irish Catholic and an assisted migrant, became a successful squatter — and arch enemy of Ned Kelly. As his face suggests, he was a man of great determination. *(Burke Museum, Beechworth)*

Myrrhee Homestead, home of James Whitty from April 1877, represented the peak of his steady climb to wealth and power. This photograph was taken in 1993 before the homestead was rebuilt. The section to the right of the chimney was added after Whitty's time.

party set out at dusk as the rain continued, aiming to pass the Quinn house after midnight when everyone was asleep.

It was a wretched journey. Jack was terrified and managed to get them lost, probably deliberately. Montfort took over and found the track to Glenmore.

That evening Harry was at the Quinn house. It later emerged that at least one of the Quinns was involved in his betrayal. Six years later, when he knew or suspected this, he recalled:

> I mind well I was sitting in the hut and the old woman was peeling per-taters for supper. 'Harry,' says she, 'I dreamt as ye was took last night.' I thought nothing of it, and she went on afterwards, 'Harry, I dreamt as ye were taken; it might be tomorrow.' If I hadn't been a born fool, I'd have known she meant to warn me, but I rode off.

Harry crossed the bridge behind the house, headed up the gully to his camping place and tethered his horse. He carried his saddle and gun to the mia-mia, slung the gun from the ridgepole, took off his boots and rolled himself in his blankets. He was dry and warm on his bed of fresh straw 'in a spot where I thought no one would ever find out'. A soft rain was still falling, pattering on the leafy branches that sheltered and disguised his blanket roof. He fell asleep almost at once but later recalled, 'It was a beautiful night, the last I ever saw as a free man.'

In the early hours of the morning the dismounted police party, led by an increasingly frightened Jack Lloyd, prepared to pass within 20 yards of the Quinn house to reach the bridge over the lagoon. A sudden downpour drove the Quinn dogs to shelter, the peacock put its head under its wing and the five men crept past.

Jack, near panic now, claimed he couldn't pick which gully to follow. A drizzling daybreak was strengthening as the party spread out to search.

Nicolson, on a timbered slope just above the flat, saw a tree stump sprouting dead branches. He recalled Ned's story of 'Harry's watchbox', ran up to it and found the disguised spyholes with the nest of grass inside the 'blind'. Nicolson turned to Jack Lloyd, who made a hopeless gesture and, said Nicolson, 'disappeared'.

The superintendent scanned the ranges above. Mist was rising from the gullies in smoke-like wraiths but Donald pointed to one wisp among the many. 'Moke! Moke!'

Signalling to Montfort and Hare, Nicolson ran straight up the slip-pery hillside and saw the little plateau, a campfire and billy, then a 'small thicket of leafy green scrub' with 'a foot in a clean worsted stocking pro-jecting from the end next to the fire'. Nicolson stripped off his bulky, rain-soaked pea-jacket as he ran, signalled again to Hare and Montfort and dived through the low entrance to the mia-mia, straight under the muzzle of the shotgun. He grabbed Harry's wrists, Hare and Montfort caught his ankles, and they hauled the shocked bushranger out into the open.

Harry Power was caught at 7.30 a.m., Nicolson recorded in a telegram he sent to Standish from Wangaratta that night. Harry was in the lock-up and Hare was under treatment from a local doctor for 'the effects of cold and exposure'. Nicolson found it amusing and satisfying that Hare was now the invalid 'and I stronger than ever'.

Harry was taken to Beechworth the next day to await trial, and the news of his capture spread through Victoria. It's hard to imagine what Ned thought when he heard, perhaps from Babington. Had he accepted that it was inevitable? Had he hoped that Harry would escape or feared he would be killed?

Ned's family had been notified that he was free and Babington was told that 'some of his friends were to come for him'. Meanwhile, Ned continued to stay at Murphys' Hotel while rumours began to circulate that he had been involved in Harry's capture — even a strange fantasy that he had been disguised as a blacktracker to lead the police to the hideout. The *Kyneton Guardian* quickly reminded its readers that Ned had been seen in town throughout the week, though the local *Observer* was unaware of this and was anxious only to point out that, even if such an act of betrayal had brought about Harry's capture, great credit was still due to Kyneton's own Superintendent Nicolson and his two colleagues.

Eventually, on the Sunday, Alex Gunn arrived in town to pick up Ned, with a highly plausible tale of losing all his money on the journey. Sergeant Babington paid for Ned's ten days accommodation at Murphys' and lent the pair 25 shillings for the return trip, a total of 3 pounds 5 shillings, which, according to Babington, Ned 'promised faithfully to pay as soon as he returned home'.

Ned's intentions may have been good but, once he was back at Eleven Mile, the money owed to Babington took a low priority compared with the family's needs. The loan remained unpaid for two months and the sergeant applied for reimbursement from the department.

Supporting Babington's claim for reimbursement, Nicolson wrote to Standish in October:

> I quite concur with the serjeant in the advisability of enabling Kelly to remain in Kyneton during the period referred to until the result of my expedition with Supt. Hare in search of power was known, *least Kelly should have returned to that offender's neighbourhood and have given him warning of the information we had collected (from Kelly himself) about Power.* [my italics]

Nicolson is quite specific that Ned had provided information that posed some threat to Harry. Yet he also makes it clear that Ned showed enough loyalty to his old mate to warn him, if possible, which suggests that Nicolson may have tricked Ned into telling more than he intended.

One immutable fact remained. In the eyes of the law, Jack Lloyd qualified for the entire £500 reward and specified that it should be paid to him via Jimmy Quinn. Before or after the fact, at least one of the Quinns shared Jack's guilt, and probably some of the money.

Yet it was Ned who was publicised as Power's betrayer — a tale which even Harry believed. Seven years later he told James Stanley: 'Young Kelly ... was no good, and helped to sell me at last. They say that he or one of the Quinns was dressed up as a blacktracker to deceive me. God will judge them for taking blood money.'

Ned returned to a world of alienation. Though unconvicted — not even tried — he was on the one hand 'a junior highwayman', on the other the betrayer of Harry Power; a disreputable young criminal or a Judas to a highwayman hero. For the first time he experienced what would become a pattern in his life — a recurrent state in which his sense of himself was distorted, threatened by the polarised attitudes of a divided society. At least, in later years, vilification would be balanced by equally distorted adulation. Back at Greta in the wretched winter of 1870, he was almost totally alone; even his family was touched by the doubt and guilt of betrayal. For Jack Lloyd and Jimmy Quinn — and probably others — Ned became a God-given scapegoat, whispered about, pointed at, slighted and ignored.

He toughed it out for six weeks then scratched out a letter to Sergeant Babington.

James Babington 28th July

I write these lines hoping
to find you and Mis^tr Nickilson
in good health as I am myself
at present I have arrived safe
and I would like you would see
what you and Mstr. Nickelson
could do for me I have done
all circumstances would
allow me which you now [know]
try what you con do answer
letter as soon as posabel
direct your letter to Daniel

Kelly gretta post office
that is my name no more at presa[nt]

Edward Kelly

every one looks on me like
A black snake send me
an answer me as soon
posable

It is a pathetic document on more than one level. As John Lahey wrote, on its first publication, 115 years later:

> Some of us who love his memory will look a little sadly on his one letter that has come to light. This sadness is not about his tortured spelling, his misshapen characters or his ignorance of punctuation, but rather what these things denote. We see Ned as a teenager, struggling against poverty and a system he cannot respect . . . He was probably bewildered. He may also have been frightened . . .

The letter might have prompted a last gesture of sympathy from Nicolson. It was later reported that the superintendent put forward 'a proposal [for Ned] to leave the bad company he was in and go to a station in New South Wales'. It has been suggested that Mrs Kelly dissuaded Ned from accepting. Only one thing is certain. If the 'proposal' was made, for one reason or another nothing came of it.

Creeks flooded, subsided, frosts struck, the sun shone, the weeks and months slipped by and the darkness of those days passed, leaving Ned with a rich legacy of memory and experience from his time with Harry.

Many years later Ned called at a Wangaratta newspaper office.

> Our representative asking . . . who his visitor was, he replied that he was Kelly from Greta. On the representative asking if he was at one time Power's mate, a smile lit up his countenance when he said he was . . .

James Babington 28th July

I write you those lines hopeing
to find you and Mrs Nickelson
in good health as I am my self
at present I have arrived safe
and I would like you would see
what you and Mrs Nickelson
could do for me I have done
all circomstances would
alow me which you now
try what you con do answer
this letter as soon as prosabel
direct your letter to Daniel
Kelly gretta post office
that is my name no more at present

Edward Kelly

every one looks on me like
a black snake send me
an answer me as soon
posible

The letter written by 15-year-old Ned Kelly to Sergeant Babington at Kyneton — the only example of his writing, apart from signatures, yet discovered. (*Public Record Office*)

4

THREE YEARS HARD

JUNE 1870 – FEBRUARY 1874

While Ned was at Kyneton a police station had opened at Greta, in the main street which ran down to the bridge over Fifteen Mile Creek. It was a long, low, brick building with a shingle roof and picket-fenced verandah. An arched, wooden sign board emblazoned with the cipher of Victoria Regina affirmed her authority over the surrounding sprawl of muddy tracks, scattered shacks and ancient, spreading red gums.

The policeman who was given charge of this challenging post was an Irish-born Protestant, Senior Constable Edward Hall, all 16 stone of him, a man so big that he had a constant problem finding horses with the stamina to carry him on bush work. Hall had been 'specially selected' for the post by Nicolson and Hare. This was odd, for Hall was fresh from two unsavoury incidents.

At Eldorado he had become involved in a dispute at a hotel and while taking a man (an ex-policeman) to the lock-up 'fell on the prisoner with his knees' and bashed his head against a verandah post. He was subsequently charged with assault and perjury. Police Magistrate H. C. Wills of Wangaratta 'strongly recommended the removal of Sen. Const. Hall from Eldorado on the ground that *he was too hot tempered to deal with the class of people who are met with there*' (my italics), an opinion shared by Sub-inspector Dobson.

Hall was transferred to Broadford, where he found himself as senior to an unfortunate constable called Tighe who had allowed himself to be disarmed by Harry Power. Hall announced his intention of getting Tighe dismissed at all costs and achieved his aim after barrelling into another pub dispute between drunks. Hall charged Tighe with insubordination; he was found guilty and dismissed. There was uproar from the people of Broadford. A newspaper considered that the senior constable's evidence in the case 'proved that Hall did not have the strongest regard for adherence to the truth'. Again Hall was transferred.

For the Greta station Hare and Nicolson had hand-picked a

policeman who had shown a propensity for violence, extraordinary vindictiveness and a readiness to lie. He would display the same traits in his latest posting.

At a time when everyone looked on Ned 'like a black snake', Hall emerged as an unlikely ally, offering the boy some degree of friendship, some promise of the relationship he had formed with kindly James Babington back in Kyneton. He may have given Ned the odd job around the station, perhaps helping with the horses or cutting firewood. Hall was interested in recruiting 'fizgigs' — criminal informants and *agents provocateurs*. To Ned, the policeman's apparent amiability blurred the already confused line between friends and enemies.

On 2 August at Beechworth General Sessions the saga of Harry Power came to a theatrical end. Harry had pleaded guilty but throughout his trial was concerned to show that he had conducted himself as a highwayman hero should. Back in June, when a witness could not say if the shotgun pointed at him was cocked, Harry told the Bench firmly, 'The gun was cocked,' and explained how he had refused to take money from a coach driver 'as he knew that drivers earned their money hardly, as he did himself'. The revelation that when he was captured the trusty shotgun slung above him in the mia-mia had been loaded but uncapped, so couldn't be fired, was a minor embarrassment.

The likeable old rogue was spared a further appearance at October's Circuit Court and sentenced to fifteen years hard labour (after warning the judge to be lenient in case they should meet when Harry was again free). He tried to make a farewell speech to the folk of Beechworth but was bundled into a coach and driven off. The show was over.

It was a dark month in a miserable winter for Ned — a time when his apparently good relationship with the local police offered an uncertain but available path towards the future. Then on 26 August mad Uncle Jimmy Quinn and his equally cranky brother-in-law, Pat Quinn, turned up in Greta with a young friend called Kenny. Their shenanigans, drunk and sober, fell just short of disorderly, just short of disturbing Her Majesty's peace; but they were a thorn in Senior Constable Hall's plump side. He said quietly to Ned in his North-of-Ireland accent, 'I wish you would get up a row,' suggesting that Ned 'insult the Quinns and Kenny'.

Did Ned know that Uncle Jimmy was one of Harry Power's betrayers? Was Uncle Jimmy hiding his guilt by taking part in ostracising Ned? Or was it just a chance to unleash some of the resentment built up in the two months he had been home? Certainly Ned seems to have tackled the assignment with some enthusiasm. The two Quinns and Kenny were outside O'Brien's hotel at dusk. Ned reported, 'I run my horse up against James Quinn and nearly knocked him over. He asked why I did so? I said, "Find Out".'

Uncle Jimmy dragged Ned from his horse but he beat him off and leapt back into the saddle. 'Young Kenny' grabbed at the horse and Ned hit him then swung away. Kenny and Pat dived for their horses, Uncle Jimmy scrambled into his saddle and charged in pursuit. Hearing the ruckus, Hall pulled on his shako and loomed from the lit doorway of the police station as Ned, pursued by the enraged trio, came galloping up from the hotel. Hall reported, 'Kelly threw himself off the horse. He broke the gate open. He said, "He is going to kill me".'

Hall sent Ned out to the back for safety and, with foul language starting to fly, called for Constable Archdeacon before he barged through the picket gate on to the street. The looked-for 'row' quickly became ugly. Hall pulled 6-foot Jimmy off his horse and was on his knees, handcuffing him, when Pat Quinn unbuckled a stirrup iron, swung it on the end of its leather as a 'skull cracker' and smashed it down on Hall's head. The blow knocked off his shako and he slumped into the mud as Constable Archdeacon dived at Jimmy. Hall was struggling to his feet when he received a second blow from the iron on his bare head. He blacked out for a moment then, with blood pouring from a 3-inch gash, saw Pat Quinn, holding the stirrup iron, walking towards Archdeacon, who was still trying to handcuff Jimmy. As Jimmy yelled, 'Stave his skull in!' Hall ordered Archdeacon to release his prisoner and the two policemen retreated into the police station to collect their revolvers.

The two Quinns and young Kenny rode off, leaving Greta's guardians of law and order covered in mud, blood and some sort of glory. After all, they had been outnumbered, defending a local lad against a pack of rowdies. Despite losing this skirmish, Hall had achieved his aim: Jimmy and Pat Quinn were in serious trouble.

The case against Kenny was less clear-cut. Hall persuaded Ned to lay a complaint against him and swear 'an information' before Alex Tone, a Justice of the Peace from Wangaratta. The following Thursday, 1 September, Jimmy and Pat faced several charges and Kenny joined them, charged with Using Obscene Language With Intent to Provoke a Breach of the Peace. Ned was the Crown's prime witness.

In a move that displayed considerable courage, the boy made a clean breast of the whole messy affair and described how Hall had used him to stir up the fracas. Ned then told the court, 'Constable Hall came with me to Wangaratta and advised me to swear an information against Kenny . . . Wish to withdraw the charge. Would not have sworn an information against the defendant but for Constable Hall'. Kenny was discharged and Ned resumed his seat under the baleful glare of Hall.

Eventually Pat Quinn received three years and Jimmy Quinn three months hard labour over the affair. Hall's tactics had been successful and he had escaped censure, but Ned would not be forgiven for this betrayal. After Ned had given his evidence Hall commented, 'Kelly is not a particular friend of mine'. The senior constable would bide his time.

The next month Ned was involved in a silly squabble between some hawkers — a Euroa man named Ben Gould who employed 11-year-old Jim Kelly, and a couple called McCormick, correctly identified by Ned as a former convict constable and a female convict from Tasmania.

Usually seen as a simple case of rivalry between hawkers operating in the same district, the affair cut much deeper. Even though the police seemed unaware of it, Ben Gould had also been a convict in Tasmania — a Nottingham pickpocket transported from England in 1851. A tiny, wildly rebellious man, his convict record showed him 'guilty of gross violence to officers, ever ready to join in Riot and disorder'. Convicts loathed turncoats like Jeremiah McCormick, who joined the 'field police', and fiery little Ben Gould would have carried this hostility into his free life. Mrs McCormick was doubly tainted. Her previous husband, a court-martialled soldier, had also been a convict constable in Tasmania.

The setting for this conflict was a cataclysmic spring. Melting snow and torrential rain turned north-eastern Victoria into a huge swamp. After 'an incessant downpour' on Saturday 29 October, Benalla was 'literally submerged . . . the greater number of the houses were deserted . . . the country for miles in every direction was one sheet of water'.

On the upper reaches of the Eleven Mile the Kellys were spared serious flooding but, in Ned's words, 'The ground was so rotten it would bog a duck in places'. Ben Gould became impossibly stuck on the road nearby. He unharnessed his horses and stayed with the family, waiting for the rain to pass. The McCormicks were stranded 4 miles away at Greta.

Early on Sunday 30 October, the day after the deluge, Gould saw the McCormicks' horse which, supposedly, had been enticed away from their camp by a rogue gelding. Gould retrieved the horse and Jim Kelly took it back to the McCormicks.

Some time later the couple turned up at the Kellys', roundly abusing Gould for having 'worked' their horse. When Ned said drily to Gould, 'That's for your good nature!' Mrs McCormick flew at him, accusing him of taking the horse from Greta to try to pull Gould's wagon out of the bog. Ned commented, 'I did not say much as my mother was present.'

Later that day, when Ned and Uncle Jack Lloyd were castrating and branding some calves, Gould wrote a note, wrapped it up with a pair of calf's testicles and asked Ned to give the parcel to Mrs McCormick. Ned obviously knew that the note suggested to Mrs McCormick that her husband should take the testicles and 'tie them to his own cock [so] he might shag her better the next time'. It was a tacky exercise and Ned hesitated to become involved. Eventually he gave the package to his cousin, young Tom Lloyd, for delivery to McCormick.

It is impossible to say what happened next. McCormick alleged that Ned rode up to him and swore, with no apparent motivation, 'I will ride my horse over you and kill the whole bloody lot of you, you bloody wretches'. After these unlikely threats, McCormick claimed that Ned, 'jumped the horse upon me and knocked me down. I fell against John Lloyd and knocked him down'.

Ben Gould said that McCormick, armed with a stick, threatened Ned and that Ned knocked the hawker down as he spurred his horse forward to get past on a narrow track.

According to Ned, the hawker declared that he would 'welt' him 'or any of his breed'. As Ned dismounted to accept McCormick's challenge, Mrs McCormick hit his horse with 'a bullocks shin'. 'It jumped forward and my fist came in collision with McCormack's nose and caused him to lose his equilibrium and fall prostrate.' This tongue-in-cheek description is unconvincing. It seems most likely that when Mrs McCormick struck at Ned's horse with the bullock's shinbone (the 'stick' of other accounts), the animal plunged forward and cannoned into her husband. As Ned was tethering his horse 'to finish the battle', the hawker ran off to fetch Senior Constable Hall. Ned's fighting spirit was up. On his own account, he told Hall that, 'I hit him and would do the same if he [Hall] challenged me', admitting both to assault and his readiness to resist arrest.

At the trial in Wangaratta on 10 November Uncle Jack Lloyd testified that, while he saw Mrs McCormick 'throw a stick at Kelly', he 'saw Kelly try to ride over McCormick'. Coming from Ned's uncle, this testimony of a deliberate assault was damning. It is possible that Uncle Jack told the truth, valuing it above family loyalty. More likely Hall had found a new collaborator — someone already embroiled in a shadowy family feud that had developed over Jack's betrayal of Power and his probable readiness to divert suspicion to Ned. Although Ned protested to the court, 'It wasn't me wrote 'em nor yet sent it,' Hall claimed that Ned had admitted sending the package of calf's testicles and the note.

Ned was sentenced to three months hard labour for Violent Assault and a £10 fine or three months hard labour for Sending Indecent Letters, etc., to a Female; with an additional twelve months unless he could provide a personal surety of £20 and two other sureties of £20 each 'to keep the peace towards McCormick and his wife'.

By the time they had covered the £60 in sureties, the £10 fine was beyond the family and Ned faced a six-month sentence. This was clear proof that the Kellys received none of the £500 Power reward and that, for whatever reason, Uncle Jack would not spare £10 of the reward money to save his nephew from three months extra hard labour.

While Hall received a £2 reward for this arrest and successful prosecution, Ned was taken off to serve his time in Beechworth Gaol, a handsome white granite fortress which crowned the far end of the town's main street.

Beechworth's *Advertiser* gave Ned a chilling welcome. Two days before, the paper had provided an appalling description of fifty lashes being administered to an unfortunate sodomist convicted at the town's last Circuit Court. After unhesitatingly identifying Ned as 'the young man ... who for a time acted as mate and bush telegraph of Power', the paper declared, 'It seems a pity that the lower courts have not the power to award similar punishment to that inflicted on Morrison ... Twenty-five or fifty lashes would be more efficacious in deterring such as Kelly from crime than a sentence of two or even four years imprisonment'.

On the night of Friday 11 November 1870, ten years to the day before his death, Ned disappeared behind the prison's massive wooden gates and round-turreted walls. In the dimly lit reception area he was stripped, bathed, cropped, measured and issued with a dark prison jacket and waistcoat and broad-arrowed moleskins. Then a warder marched him to his cell through the echoing hallways and daunting two-storey cell blocks with their iron-railed galleries.

By day the prison was a place of clattering iron staircases and walkways, high-barred windows, hard work, suppressed violence and boredom. The stigma of having betrayed Harry Power hung over Ned here, tainting his status as Power's mate. Everything suggests he could look after himself. If he couldn't, he would have learned quickly, his muscles hardened by the daily round of quarrying and carting granite or breaking it for road metal in the labour yard.

Ned was entered in the prison register as being 5ft 10ins; he was already tall for the times and not yet 16 — at least not until December. He passed the first three months of 1871 here and was released in late March with five weeks remission, to make his way home, down from the ranges and over the Oxley Flats to Greta, the gap and the Eleven Mile. His return was undoubtedly noticed by Hall or drawn to his attention by one of his toadies.

Ned arrived home to find that Annie and Alex Gunn were living with the family. A daughter, Ellen, had been born to them in December, but she had lived only thirteen weeks. Ned probably visited the tiny grave of his first niece in the Greta Cemetery and shared his sister's tears.

On 14 April, in the third week of Ned's freedom, Alex Gunn had a visitor: a young farmer and horsebreaker from Mansfield known as 'Wild' Wright. Hardly anyone but the police used his Christian name, Isaiah. Wild had earned his nickname for good reasons. 'He could fight like a threshing machine. And mad with it. Mad as a tiger snake that's been run over by a mob of sheep,' one man said. Wild's favourite 'joke' was to walk into a bar and push drinkers out of the way with a loud 'Men first, dogs last!' It usually provoked a fight, which was the idea. He had a deaf mute brother called 'Dummy' who 'couldn't speak but made a lot of noise'. Wild was devoted to him and it was a foolish man who treated Dummy with anything but respect. A Wombat Ranges farmer recalled accidentally bumping Dummy in a Mansfield pub. Dummy whirled, making ferocious noises and drawing his hand across his throat, then Wild loomed beside his brother — 'a great bony man with a great bony face'. A quick, sincere apology and a couple of whiskies solved the problem.

Such was Alex Gunn's visitor. Wild was tall and fierce-eyed, with a fair beard and moustache. He wore a wrap-around moleskin cloak and a broad-brimmed, low-crowned hat, a 'wideawake'. His horse was no less out-of-the-ordinary and Ned recalled every detail: 'She was a chestnut mare, white faced, docked tail, very remarkable, branded M [in a circle] as plain as the hands on the town clock.'

Wild stayed the night at Kellys' and next morning found that his handsome mare had disappeared — perhaps herded off by the rogue gelding. Wild 'was in a hurry to get back to Mansfield' so, after searching for most of the day, Ned lent him a horse 'and he told me if I found his mare to keep her until he brought mine back'.

Wild and Alex neglected to tell Ned one vital detail. A few weeks before, while Ned was still in prison, Wild had 'borrowed' the mare from the Mansfield postmaster. (Alex had taken a schoolmaster's horse from a nearby paddock shortly before.) Wild had 'borrowed' the horse before and the postmaster seems to have been tolerant or perhaps just a little scared of this formidable young character. As the fourth week of his latest 'borrowing' started to pass, however, even Wild should have realised that he had been stretching his luck — and now Ned's.

Only two hours after Wild rode off on one of Ned's horses, his cloak billowing splendidly, Alex Gunn and a friend of the Kellys called Brickey Williamson found the strayed mare and brought her back to Ned. It was Saturday afternoon and, fancying the idea of 'cutting a flash' on this 'rather remarkable' horse, Ned decided to treat himself to a stay in Wangaratta before resuming work. He decked himself out with jacket, waistcoat and spurs and rode away from Eleven Mile Creek. It would be almost three years before he returned.

Ned stayed at the Star Hotel in Wangaratta for the next four days and let the publican's daughters ride the mare around town. 'All the police and Detective Birrell seen her,' Ned offered, as proof that he didn't know the horse was stolen.

On Thursday 20 April, Senior Constable Hall intercepted Ned as he rode the mare across the bridge into Greta on his way home, again a clear indication that he had nothing to hide. Rather than accuse Ned of horse stealing, with the risk of his galloping off (Ned admitted, 'I would have rode quietly away'), Hall told him there were papers to sign at the police station, connected with the sureties to keep the peace.

Hall (who wrote about himself in the third person in his reports), claimed that, as the boy went to dismount at the station, he [Hall] said, 'You are my prisoner for horse stealing and made a jump and caught him by the neck, but coat, waistcoat and shirt all gave way so he gave another spring and pulled him right off the horse but could not hold him by the flesh . . .'

'Hall made a mistake,' said Ned, 'and came on the broad of his back himself in the dust the mare galloped away and instead of me putting my foot on Halls neck and taking his revolver and putting him in the lock up I tried to catch the mare.' Claiming that Ned was escaping, running towards scrub across the road, Hall drew his revolver and called, 'Stand!' On the policeman's evidence, Ned 'immediately turned round to show fight' with a cry of, 'Shoot and be damned!' Harry would have been proud of 'the cub'.

Hall reported that he 'presented the revolver straight at his [Ned's] face', and pulled the trigger. There was a sharp crack and a spurt of smoke but no shot. The first cap on the cylinder of Hall's percussion Colt had failed to fire the first charge. Moving closer, Hall cocked his revolver twice more and tried to shoot Ned in the head. Twice more, as Ned put it, 'the Colts patent refused'. Ned might have run, but instead he faced Hall and the revolver muzzle. 'He had me covered and was shaking with fear, and I knew he would pull the trigger before he would be game to put his hand on me.'

There were three shots left, three more chances for Hall to kill him in this game of Russian roulette. 'So I duped and jumped at him, caught the revolver with one hand and Hall by the collar with the other. I dare not strike him or my sureties would lose the bond money I used to trip him and let him take a mouthful of dust now and again as he was as helpless as a big guano [goanna] after leaving a dead bullock or a horse.'

Hall admitted only that Ned 'rushed at him to try and take the revolver from him and in the struggle succeeded in catching it by the muzzle and barrel.'

Ned continues:

I kept throwing him in the dust until I got him across the street the very spot where Mrs O'Briens Hotel stands now the cellar was just dug then there was some brush fencing where the post and rail was taking down and on this I threw big cowardly Hall on his belly I straddled him and rooted both spurs into his thighs he roared like a big calf attacked by dogs and shifted several yards of the fence I got his hands at the back of his neck and tried to make him let the revolver go but he stuck to it like grim death to a dead volunteer he called for assistance to a man named Cohen and Barnett, Lewis, Thompson, Jewitt and two blacksmiths who was looking on. [Elsewhere, Ned twice claimed there were fourteen men involved.] I dare not strike any of them as I was bound to keep the peace or I could have spread those curs like dung in a paddock they got ropes tied my hands and feet and Hall beat me over the head with his six chambered Colts revolver.

Hall made no mention of the spur-raking, nor of binding Ned, but described how 'the Senr. Const. wrenched it [the revolver] from his hand, Hall had it by the stock all the time and he struck Kelly with all his might 4 or 5 times on the head but could not stun him and the only effect the blows had although they were given ... with all his might was simply to leave that part of his head a mass of raw and bleeding flesh.'

Ned was dragged to the lock-up, leaving a trail of blood across the street. That night Hall reported, 'a dozen of the prisoner's confederates ... came shouting about the place like wild savages saying they would take him out of the camp'. Hall got 'the servant girl' to light 'a large fire before the lock up door' and scrawled a hasty note to Sub-inspector Montfort. By now he was so thoroughly rattled that he addressed it to Castlemaine instead of Wangaratta.

I have arrested Young Kelly after a desperate row with him for horse stealing, I struck him on the head with the revolver in self defence while arresting him, he is now in the lock up, please send a doctor and two constables I cannot open the lock up until the latter come you will oblige me if you telegraph the occurrence to Supt Barclay
E Hall 569 S.C.
Let the doctor come at once E.H.

Montfort sent Constable Arthur with Dr James Hester of Wangaratta and telegraphed Benalla for Constable Thom to attend. Arriving at Greta, Dr Hester put nine stitches in the boy's scalp and upper forehead and, after two hours, managed to stop the bleeding. This was the first of three attendances which, with travel, would cost the government eight guineas, prompting a note to Standish from the Chief Medical Officer, Dr McRea: 'If the Chief Commissioner concurs I shall feel obliged if he will caution Hall about recklessly causing medical expenditure the next time he breaks the head of an Irishman.'

Next morning, in view of the explosive situation at Greta, Ned was taken to Wangaratta in a cart under mounted escort. He claimed, 'I was handcuffed a rope tied from them to my legs and to the seat of the cart ... Hall was frightened I would throw him out of the cart.' According to Ned, the escorting trooper, Constable Arthur, 'laughed at his cowardice'.

On the way to Wangaratta, Hall questioned Ned about the mare, reporting, 'He said he did not steal the horse but would not split.' Ned was adamant that he would serve another prison term 'before he would put anybody else into it'. The boy accused of betraying Harry Power was determined not to incriminate his new 'friend' Wild Wright. He would even try to avoid implicating Alex Gunn and Brickey Williamson, claiming that he found the mare himself on his way to Wangaratta.

Hall saw his battered prisoner locked up then prepared to justify his extraordinary behaviour to his superior, Superintendent Barclay. Ned's account of the clash with Hall is undeniably colourful, a classic of its kind, but it is confirmed on essential points by Hall's report to Barclay, written two days later. The policeman had tried to shoot an unarmed 16-year-old in the head before he had made any threatening move. Hall had then given the boy a severe pistol-whipping which might have caused death or permanent injury. Hall's justification was, of course, that Ned was riding a stolen horse. But how did he know this?

When he had seen Ned riding the horse on a previous occasion, Hall said that, 'I had reason to believe that the horse was a stolen one, but I did not know who the mare belonged to.' Hall did not explain the grounds for this belief but swore in the Wangaratta Police Court, 'I arrested him after I had seen the criminal offence notice', claiming to have sighted a Criminal Offence Report which confirmed his suspicion before the encounter on the Greta bridge.

At the General Sessions trial, Hall was even more specific, swearing that he had 'seen the *Police Gazette* containing an intimation that the horse was stolen about an hour before the arrest'. Once again Senior Constable Hall had perjured himself. The theft of the postmaster's mare was reported in the *Police Gazette* of 25 April, five days after he had arrested Ned. The entry was based on information dated two days after the arrest.

Hall had tried to kill Ned Kelly on the basis of mere suspicion that he was riding a stolen horse and his superiors cannot have failed to notice that he had acted without a scrap of evidence. The belated *Police Gazette* entry might be seen as a first hasty move on their part to obscure this fact — complete with an inaccurate dating of the theft to 3 April — a week after Ned's release from prison. Standish, already wary of what he had called Hall's 'hasty and injudicious conduct', wrote to Barclay, 'I think it is a very fortunate occurrence that Senr Const Hall's revolver did not fire.' Beyond this, he chose not to comment on Hall's conduct, 'as it appears to me somewhat extraordinary'. It now became essential for the Crown to gain a conviction in the case to provide the justification for Hall's actions. In the end his conduct would be tacitly approved and officially rewarded.

Babington had shown Ned the scales of justice; Hall had wielded the sword, it remained for the courts to employ the blindfold.

Wild (who had probably been involved in the police station siege) was arrested at the Kelly homestead two weeks later, after a 160-mile pursuit in which Hall and another trooper fired at least four shots at him. After another couple of weeks Alex Gunn was hauled in.

Ned had three-and-a-half months in police cells where he could brood over his treatment before eventually facing trial at Beechworth on 2 August. The original charge against him had been Horse Stealing but this was untenable: the Mansfield postmaster swore that his mare had disappeared on 16 March; the Beechworth gaol governor testified that Ned had been in his custody until 27 March. The charge was amended to Receiving.

Although it was clear that Ned had not known the horse was stolen, he was found guilty and sentenced to three years hard labour. Alex Gunn also received three years hard labour for stealing the school-master's horse. Wild was found guilty of Illegally Using the postmaster's horse and sentenced to only eighteen months hard labour — as McQuil-ton comments, 'a curious paradox'. Ned had been convicted of 'receiv-ing' a horse that had not legally been stolen, never mind the discrepancy between Ned's sentence and Wild's.

On several levels, the case reflected little credit on the police or the courts. The battered, embittered youth who was taken up the street to the granite fortress he had left four months before seemed an unlikely subject for reform. He had shown considerable courage and formidable physical powers in his clash with Hall, dangerous qualities for a criminal.

In this midwinter of 1871, as Ned was again stripped and cropped for the ritual of admission to gaol, the recording warder must have noted the muscles developing in this near-adult body; he recorded the four recent scars on his stubbled head — one on the top, two on the crown, one in front. Not surprisingly, Ned became a troublesome prisoner and a list of misdemeanours whittled away his remission time.

Back at Greta, Senior Constable Hall applied for a transfer and received it — the more gratefully since the posting had been down-graded to a one-man station and Hall feared the vengeance of Ned's friends and relatives. Easy-going Constable Montgomery had taken over when Sub-inspector Montfort — promoted for his role in the capture of Harry Power — inspected the station. He noted that there had been no arrests or prosecutions and Montgomery was removed. In his place came Constable Ernest Flood. Montfort considered him 'active', the sort of policeman to keep the Kellys, Lloyds and Quinns 'continually under pressure'. Flood would soon bring tragedy to the Kellys.

Meanwhile blows continued to fall on the family. Ellen's daughter by

Bill Frost was a little more than four months old when Ned entered prison. Frost, now working as a butcher, occasionally provided presents of money and clothing for the child and promised to support her. Then on 4 June he married an Irish-born housekeeper called Bridget Cotter. In response to a solicitor's letter Frost called on Ellen and offered her '£5 or £10 and the horse he was riding'. Ellen refused and took what was for those times the courageous step of suing Frost for their daughter's maintenance. Two adjournments headlined in the local press as 'Support of an Illegitimate Child' guaranteed that maximum attention was focused on the case when it came to the Benalla Police Court in October. The story of the couple's weekends together at the Eleven Mile was told by several witnesses. Frost suggested that Ellen had other lovers, but all evidence refuted this. In finding against Frost, Police Magistrate Butler said that he had been 'foolish' but that Ellen was also 'in fault in allowing it'. She was awarded maintenance of 5 shillings a week for two years, with 7 pounds 2 shillings against Frost in costs and two sureties of £20 'to ensure fulfillment'.

It was a victory tainted with humiliation. Ellen reacted against the stares and whispers of Benalla's respectable citizens in a characteristic way. With her witnesses, Annie Gunn, Bill Skilling and James and Anne Murdoch, she mounted her horse and led the little party in a series of wild gallops through the streets of Benalla 'in the most reckless manner to the danger of young and old'. These 'equestrian feats' continued 'for the greater part of three days'.

The next Tuesday Ellen and her supporters faced the court charged with Furious Riding in a Public Place. The evidence seemed unanswerable until their counsel, the talented Mr McDonnell, asked Sergeant Whelan whether or not Benalla had been gazetted as a township. The sergeant didn't know. With the prosecution unable to prove that the streets of Benalla were legally a Public Place, Police Magistrate Butler dismissed the charges. A reporter noted, 'the offenders left rejoicing' while the civic fathers of Benalla faced the awful possibility that 'the hundreds of people fined for similar offences for the last ten or twelve years' could 'apply for a refund of their money'.

Early in 1872 baby Ellen, only fourteen months old, contracted diarrhoea — rife in the summer months and a dangerous frontier disease. Ellen, with her father's death as a warning, sent for Dr Nicholson of Benalla. He arrived on the third day of the illness but was unable to save the child and she died that day. Frost had supported his daughter for the last three months of her life.

The death was registered by Maggie Kelly. Ellen's oldest daughter, 18-year-old Annie, may not have been home. With her husband in lock-ups and prison these past eight months, she had embarked on a shadowy, doomed relationship with Constable Ernest Flood, the new trooper at Greta. Flood was 29, tallish, with black hair and beard and large, hazel eyes outlined by dark lashes. He was Protestant Irish, married a couple of years with a seven-month-old son.

The relationship first drew attention — in fact it may have begun — on Tuesday, 2 January 1872. That day Annie attended the Benalla police court where three men were on trial for stealing a horse from her. Flood had escorted her to Benalla, supposedly fearing that friends of the accused would 'tamper with her'. When one of the three men was acquitted, Flood 'proposed to ride home with her', again for protection. At the constable's suggestion, Annie had left her horse in a paddock opposite the police station, next to the home of tailor James Short and his wife. The Shorts, both drunk, later made wild and demonstrably inaccurate allegations about Flood's behaviour with Annie at their home, also claiming that Annie had stolen a watch and chain from them. A police inquiry suggested that the Shorts, knowing Flood was married, had tried to blackmail him. The fact remained that Annie gave the tailor's wife a note:

Mrs Short

Please give the bearer any dress that she requires and charge the same to me

Ernest Flood

(Public Records Office)

While the Shorts' evidence is dubious, it is equally clear that the police inquiry was an exercise in damage control, with Standish concluding, 'No doubt he [Flood] was shepherding her to give evidence and to obtain information from her which he would doubtless have to pay for in some way — and he did by ordering a dress.'

To Standish, Flood's error was in associating with 'a notorious woman', even though Annie's major claim to notoriety seems to have been her association with Flood — a relationship that became a matter of gossip in the district after Flood 'boasted' of his conquest.

Standish urged Flood's transfer, commenting, 'Though active enough I am afraid he is greatly wanting in discretion and stability.' District Superintendent Barclay agreed that Flood had been indiscreet but suggested that such exploitation of Kelly womenfolk was acceptable police conduct: 'Unless a Const. who is stationed at Greta familiarises himself with the female portion of this gang he has but little chance of learning what is going on amongst them.' The following month Annie became pregnant. Flood was not transferred and his record was unblemished by the incident with the Shorts or its aftermath. Annie's husband and brother passed autumn and winter rock-breaking and in late spring a baby girl was born.

The day after, poor Annie was gripped by convulsions. A Dr Henry gave her what treatment he could but the convulsions continued and she died the next day. Ellen's youngest brother, Bill, buried 18-year-old Annie on the banks of Eleven Mile Creek, under the coolness of the willow trees, and that very day Constable Flood prosecuted Ellen and her friend, Jane Graham, for the theft of a saddle. Nothing came of the charge.

Maggie made a trip to Greta to register the death and birth, defiantly identifying the father of Annie's child as Alex Gunn, even though he had been gaoled fifteen months before. If Ellen was aware of the father's true identity, she kept her peace, loved baby Anna and set out to raise her as a daughter. Only thirteen months later little Anna would be struck down by diphtheria. She died, like Red, two days after Christmas, and was buried beside her mother under the willows, the twin graves within sight of the house as a daily reminder of Ernest Flood's diligence.

At last, after this wretched year, there was a breath of happiness in Ellen's life. In full summer a traveller came riding down the dusty gap road, called at the Kelly shanty and stayed. He was a Californian called George King, a tall, brown-haired and lightly whiskered 23-year-old. He had a shadowy background. There were suggestions that he had fought in the Civil War as a sixteen-year-old and that he had been a trick horse-man with a circus. Eventually he would slip back into the mists of rumour from which he had appeared, but for the time being he shared one of the few tranquil periods of Ellen Kelly's life. By the end of the summer Ellen was pregnant and George prepared to fend for her and the new baby as best he could, without the help of 14-year-old Jim Kelly.

That February, Jim was involved in an inept piece of cattle theft with 17-year-old Tom Williams who was working for Ellen. In another harsh summer many cattle were grazing 'the long paddock' along the road-sides. The boys rounded up five head and sold them along the way to Wangaratta.

They were arrested in town and finally tried at Beechworth General Sessions in April. In spite of Jim's youth, the jury's recommendation for mercy and the fact that Tom Williams said he had 'led Kelly into it', the judge gave each of them five years hard labour and regretted that he could not order a flogging. Jim entered Beechworth Gaol to find that Ned had left two months before. Still four months short of 15, he began five years of rock-breaking.

In the third week of February 1873, with half his sentence completed, Ned had been sent from Beechworth to Pentridge Gaol near Melbourne. He travelled by coach as far as Longwood, the newest station on the north-eastern railway line to the Murray which was being built at that time.

Young Joseph Ashmead happened to be here with his father on business. He recorded many years later, 'I saw the coach arrive, surrounded by a strong escort of police, saw Kelly taken off the coach, and saw him placed in a railway carriage ... I saw this fair youth manacled to an old man. By the degraded look on his [the old man's] face it was plain his life had been steeped in sin'. To Joseph, self-confessed 'son of puritan parents', Ned was doomed by further contact with 'hardened criminals'. Yet the transfer to Pentridge marked a potential turning point in his life.

If Beechworth was a fortress, Pentridge was a walled city, with a bluestone perimeter 2½ miles long. Passing through the main gateway, which was flanked by battlemented towers, Ned was taken to the unfinished 'A' Division where he spent a month for each year of his sentence under the 'model' or 'solitary' system. This meant total silence and separation from other convicts and only one hour a day, for exercise, outside his badly ventilated cell.

In a bizarre refinement of isolation Ned, as a 'probationary' prisoner, was given a hood — a pointed canvas cowl with two eye slits — which he had to wear while being marched to his exercise yard. In this narrow, bluestone-walled space he was left alone to prowl backwards and forwards for an hour, then marched back to his cell, one masked figure among many, 'with naught visible of their faces save a twinkle of their eyes peeping through the eyelet holes — moving noiselessly about like so many ghouls'.

Apart from this hour, his days were eked out with meals (hominy and brown bread for breakfast, meat and potatoes for dinner, bread and water for supper) and sleep. There was no bed, just a coconut mat on the floor with a rug and blanket.

This lasted for six weeks. Then he moved to 'B' Division and gaol life as he knew it — the now-welcome routine of mustering in the yard and being marched off in gangs. Ned probably worked in the quarry gang, cutting bluestone from the prison quarry in its huge paddock, and in the stoneyard, where he passed the day chipping and facing bluestone blocks. He may have worked in the gangs continuing to build 'A' Division with slow, rigorous craftsmanship. Each day he attended an hour's school (11.30 to 12.30) in a vast, church-like hall. He ate all meals in his cell and had a day-and-a-half to himself at the weekend when there was virtually nothing to do but read the Douay Bible and books from the prison library. He might also receive 'a short visit from the Chaplain of his Church'. The Catholic Chaplain was Dean Charles O'Hea, who had held the post for twenty years. His Church, St Paul's was next door to the prison and his parish included Beveridge. O'Hea had known Ned's parents; his curate had baptised Jim and Maggie; O'Hea himself had baptised Dan and Ned. O'Hea, from Cork's Augustinian Monastery, was a true Irishman, but one who accommodated English rule with dignity and, as Chaplain of Victoria's military forces, would wear the Queen's uniform as proudly as any man. God and Caesar, Ireland and England, convict and gaoler — all were given appropriate loyalty.

O'Hea must be seen as the greatest single influence on Ned in his convict years. The Chaplain's philosophy of life, conveyed with the presence and humour of a born storyteller, provided the perfect antidote for the bitterness left by Ned's encounter with Hall. Just as importantly, it would arm him for the coming encounter with Flood and his crimes against the Kelly family.

Ned spent no more than three months in 'B' Division before being transferred to the prison hulk *Sacramento* at Williamstown. A few years before, this would have been a punishment, but now it represented recognition of his ability as a stonemason and the chance to live and work under conditions at least as good as those in 'C' Division, next rung on the ladder to release.

On Wednesday 25 June 1873 Ned left Pentridge and was carried into another penal world which echoed his father's stories of the convict ships. Ned and his 116 fellow convicts were herded below decks into twin rows of whitewashed wooden cells, cosier than the stone coops at Pentridge, to be well fed and issued with small clay pipes and one-sixth of a plug of tobacco per day.

Each day the gangs were rowed ashore to build sea walls along the foreshore and fortify the artillery batteries guarding the Bay. While here Ned had only one blot on his record, when he was caught giving a fellow prisoner two tobacco rations. Could it have been Alex Gunn, sharing his life on the hulk? The gesture cost seven days off his remission.

After three months of hard winter work, Ned was sent ashore to accommodation at one of the batteries. He was now a 'first-class prisoner', earning a shilling a day and with tea and sugar added to his daily rations.

Ned returned to Pentridge after Christmas, to be lodged in 'C' Division with cells symbolically opening onto the yard or the gallery overlooking the yard — a further step towards the outside world. Then, unexpectedly, the news came in January that he would be released next month, exactly six months before the end of a three-year sentence. In his time at Beechworth, Ned had lost almost three months of the maximum remission for good conduct. At Pentridge, under the influence of Dean O'Hea, he had lost only seven days.

Soon after he received news of his coming release he was photographed, probably on 24 January. It is an unflattering portrait. His prison crop has started to lengthen and he has been allowed to stop shaving. A dark stubble sketches the line of moustache and beard around his thin, determined mouth. His face is fuller after the good food and healthy life at Williamstown, his eyebrows dark, almost forbidding in the flat light, the lazy left eye lending coldness to an expression that conveys vulnerability as well as the impression that this is a young man to be reckoned with.

On Monday 2 February 1874 Ned Kelly walked out of Pentridge. He was 19, almost 6 foot, had been growing his hair and beard for several weeks and would never shave again. With the 2 pounds 10 shillings and elevenpence he had earned as a stonemason he headed home by train, looking out at the sweeping parade of his life's landscape. Past Beveridge, Wallan and Avenel, the journey became a faster replay of his northward ride seven years before. Across the Seymour hills he had ranged with Harry, passing the Strathbogies at Euroa, then through Benalla and the steady climb to his destination, the infant settlement of Glenrowan where the railway crossed the Warby Ranges through a gap below Morgan's Lookout. At Eleven Mile Creek he faced a world that had changed.

Ellen, in her happiness, probably looked almost younger than when Ned had last seen her. She had a two-month-old baby (another Ellen) at her breast. Ned shared with his mother the pain of the graves of Annie and her baby under the willows and the loss of Jim, locked away for five years. At 16, Maggie was the mother of a baby girl not yet four months old (yet another Ellen!). She had married Bill Skilling six weeks before the birth. Kate was a sparkling 10-year-old and baby Grace was now 8. Dan was almost 13, every inch a Quinn with his lean face, black hair and blue eyes, not big for his age but a sharp, spirited boy.

And there was George. How did Ned react to this stranger sharing his mother's bed — this young American only five years older than himself? Ned might have resented him, but didn't. Only one comment about his youthful stepfather is recorded and that would suggest a degree of admiration and affinity. Ellen loved George and she was happy. Because Ned truly loved his mother there was no room for petty, complex jealousies.

Two weeks later, on Thursday 19 February, Ellen and George were married at the Benalla home of the Reverend William Gould of the Prim-

itive Methodist Church. Ned and Bill Skilling were witnesses. The
homely service provided two telling glimpses of George King. On the
certificate, Ellen (who had fibbed about her age, reducing it from 42 to
36) listed no 'rank or profession', while George called himself a
'labourer', not wishing to claim the role of farmer on his wife's land.
Because Ellen was illiterate, George, too, chose to sign his name with a
cross. That same day in Benalla he registered baby Ellen's birth and
wrote his signature with a flourish.

When Ned went to round up his horses — 'over thirty head of the
very best horses the land could produce' — he could find only one. Ned
claimed that 'Constable Flood stole and sold most of them to the navvies
on the railway line. One bay cobb he stole and sold four different times.'

This may have been true (Flood was later found guilty of 'assisting' in
a horse theft) but the line was completed, the navvies scattered and, as
Ned tellingly comments, 'Flood was shifted to Oxley'. There is some
suggestion that this prevented a confrontation over the horses, and
perhaps over his treatment of Annie. Yet Oxley was only 9 miles across
the flats from Greta. Ned bit hard on his hatred of Flood. This was one
of the lessons gained from Beechworth, Pentridge, the *Sacramento* and,
most of all, from Dean O'Hea.

Ned's first test came very soon. He was enjoying a drink at Laurence
O'Brien's Victoria Hotel in Greta, a two-storey brick building with
a handsome balcony now gracing the site of his battle with Hall.
Constable Flood walked in and noted that Ned 'pretended to be drunk'.
Flood claimed, 'He made use of some insulting words to me, and I said
to him, "You had better look out, Ned. Now you are out you had better
keep yourself as straight as you can." I said, "If I ever have to lay my
hands on you it is not Hall you will have to deal with." '

Brave words from Ernest Flood. A famous surgeon would observe
that Ned Kelly 'had a rare type of eyes — "alexandrite" eyes that sometimes glowed a startling crimson when he became excited'. That day in
the Victoria Hotel Ned's eyes must have burnt like coals, but he let Flood
go his way. Ned had passed his first, exacting test.

5

A QUIET MAN

1874–77

Within a few weeks of leaving Pentridge, Ned found work as a 'faller' (a tree-feller) at a sawmill run by partners James Saunders and Richard Rule in the ranges near Moyhu.

He learnt to cut a slot in a tree trunk with a few axe strokes, deep enough to hold a plank; to spring up on to the plank and balance there while he chopped through the trunk above the 'spurs' spreading to the roots, or cut deep wedges for felling with a cross-cut saw. Bullock teams yoked in pairs hauled the felled logs on jinkers and whims or dragged them through trackless scrub with chains, the bullock driver cracking his long-handled whip, bawling instructions to the lead bullocks and encouragement to the team. Each animal had a name and a personality. Handling them was an art — another timberland skill which Ned mastered. Soon his abilities won the notice of his bosses.

On a visit to Beechworth one Saturday early in August, Ned had a drink at the Imperial Hotel in High Street — a Protestant pub with a bust of Queen Victoria mounted on its sign. Perhaps this had attracted the Protestant Wild Wright to the place. It would have been an uncomfortable meeting, probably their first encounter outside prison since the affair of the Mansfield postmaster's horse. Words flew, but before any punches were thrown, publican Edward Rogers would have stepped in. He didn't like ugly brawls in his pub but a boxing match was very much in his line — along with wrestling bouts and cricket matches, as well as 'quoits, skittles, and other good old classic or English games'. He was well known as a 'caterer for the public' and had established a small sports ground below the hillside fruit and hop garden of the Imperial on the grassy banks of Spring Creek.

Rogers probably outfitted the combatants. A photo of Ned taken to commemorate the occasion shows him wearing silk shorts over long underpants and undershirt with lightweight shoes. His beard had been growing for eight months — dark reddish brown with a lighter moustache — bringing maturity and unexpected strength to the strong line of his brows above the fierce but calm eyes. Long, almost-black hair hid the scars of the beating from Hall's revolver. Wild's failure to tell him the postmaster's horse was stolen had brought Ned that beating and two-and-a-half years of hard labour, while Wild had paid only eighteen months for the crime. This fight aimed to even the score.

They fought bare-knuckle to the old London Prize Ring rules already illegal for professional fights. Ignoring the niceties of the gentlemanly Marquis of Queensberry code, they simply came up to 'the scratch' — a line drawn on the ground — and hammered at each other until a man was felled or blood was drawn or, in the jargon, 'claret was tapped'. This marked the end of a round and each man's 'picker up' had thirty seconds to revive him for the next, with an additional eight seconds for him to reach the scratch without help (an innovation aimed at preventing over-zealous supporters from carrying a semi-conscious man to the scratch where he could be beaten to death).

Wild was a notorious and experienced fighter. The following month it would be reported that, 'He is rather given to commit assaults [and] is quite indifferent whether it is the police or a civilian he lets drive at.' At 25 he was perhaps an inch taller and a stone heavier than his lean, 19-year-old opponent. But Ned brought to the fight his legacy of stone-breaking and tree-felling, his balance refined by swinging an axe on a springy plank, his eye sharpened by the hair's-breadth judgement that placed every axe blow to gain maximum effect. He was driven by a fierce anger but he was containing it, using his head and conserving his strength — another hard-learnt lesson.

Four years later Wild said, 'Ned Kelly is mad' — a strange comment from a man who was by then totally dedicated to Ned. After another two years the world saw Ned Kelly wage a battle against impossible odds, crippled by serious wounds, weakened by loss of blood to the point of death, but still fighting. Ned simply didn't know when he had had enough. Perhaps Wild was right and it was a sort of madness, but it made him almost unbeatable.

The fight lasted for twenty bloody rounds, perhaps for hours, until at last Wild conceded defeat. Many years later, as a boxer in a travelling tent show, he admitted to legendary spruiker Charlie Fredricksen, 'He gave me the hiding of my life.'

In the early, midwinter dusk of this highland gully, steaming with feral sweat, Ned Kelly tasted his first real victory, won the allegiance of Wild Wright and with it the respect, fear and envy of other men. 'The notorious young Kelly,' as Beechworth's *Advertiser* had described him when he faced trial for horse stealing, was now a man, and unofficial boxing champion of the district. Notoriety had bled into a sort of local fame. Everything suggests that Ned didn't like it and, with almost a year of honest work behind him, he moved on.

———————◆———————

IN 1875 Wangaratta was struggling to recover from 'the gigantic failure' of 1874 when James Dixon, a Canadian miller, general merchant and twice former mayor of the borough, became bankrupt with unsecured debts of some £20 000 in Wangaratta alone, much of it owed to farmers who had given him their harvests in return for 'bills' promising above-market prices. Dixon, it was said, '. . . had as much paper floating as would cover the walls of a moderate sized room'. To Dixon, the banks were the villains for cutting his line of credit before he could trade out of his problems. In his words, 'They screwed me up and when I tumbled, the town fell with me.'

A man who held £300 in Dixon's 'bills' suicided, and a high propor-tion of the district's farmers and traders, still adjusting to the mixed blessings of the railway, faced receiving only 5 shillings of every pound Dixon owed them. Many were ruined and property values plummeted. Prominent in the settlement of Dixon's affairs were grazier and cattle dealer Frank Heach, who became a trustee for local creditors, and sawmiller Christopher Dockendorff, who bought up Dixon's assets. The pair were thrown together in the fire sales of everything from groceries, ironmongery and wine to saddlery, timber and agricultural equipment, and became business partners.

They also became Ned's new bosses. Dockendorff had been refused a 237-acre selection at Killawarra, 9 miles north-west of Wangaratta, 'as the ground was valuable on account of its timber'. The energetic duo re-applied for a timber lease and became partners in a sawmill on the gentle fall of land between Mount Killawarra at the northern end of the Warbys and the Ovens River. The country offered handsome stands of ironbark on the slopes and red gum along the river flats which would supply railway sleepers for the first section of the Wangaratta–Beechworth branch line. With four steam engines driving saws to cut logs hauled to the mill by sixty working bullocks, it was an ambitious operation — perhaps too ambitious. The mill filled its railway contract and had 100 000 feet of red gum timber left over.

Ned had worked for 2 pounds 10 shillings a week with Saunders and Rule and probably earned more with Heach and Dockendorff. Three years later some of his workmates recalled him as, 'quiet, very unobtrusive and an excellent axeman'. They also had found him, 'a warm-hearted but rather impulsive young fellow', who 'would almost do anything to serve a friend'.

He made one close friend at the Killawarra mill: a Ballarat timber worker called Walter Power who had moved to the north-east with his parents. Walter was 25, Australian-born of Irish Catholic parents, a couple of inches shorter than Ned but 'immensely powerful'. He found Ned, 'a quiet, brooding type not given to mixing much with the other men'. He even said that Ned sometimes seemed 'in a world of his own'. They shared a sleeping hut and would sometimes talk 'late into the night'.

One day at the Killawarra races everything changed. A visitor seems to have recognised Ned as the bare-knuckle conqueror of Wild Wright and tried to pick a fight. Ned avoided two punches and 'warned him not to do so again, or else he would make it a caution to him'. The man threw a third punch and Ned 'gave his assailant such a mauling that his nearest and dearest friend scarcely knew him'. Fame, it seemed, was as hard to escape as notoriety.

Again Ned moved on. Walter Power was going down to Gippsland, probably drawn by news that old friends from Ballarat, the Wrights, had selected there — more especially that their 21-year-old daughter Eureka had accompanied them. So Ned joined Walter on the 200-mile ride to the south, past the headwaters of the King, up the ribs of the Great Divide, across its spine then down the long ridge above the Thompson River. It was an easy ride, perhaps through some early snow, along a well-worn track with pubs and shanties every 4 or 5 miles.

Beyond the valley of the Latrobe they reached Flynn's Creek, where the Wrights had settled. Ned (and probably Walter) did some fencing on a neighbouring dairy farm owned by the Grahams, friends of the Wrights from the Ballarat district. In Graham family lore it would be remembered that 'Ned and Dan Kelly [sic] split fiddle-back posts and rails on the property' and were 'good honest hard-working boys'.

Ned and Walter found jobs at a local sawmill which exploited the open red gum forest and easy terrain of the district. It was unchallenging work in this cheery, tightly knit community and Ned probably spent some time further afield among the 300-foot gums of Southern Gippsland, some of which sent trunks up 200 feet without a branch. The place was a timberman's dream. But it was the heart of winter, often under a second sky of gum crowns laced together with supplejack creeper, a sunless, vertical world. Even back at Flynn's Creek Ned found the damp chill of a Gippsland winter depressing after the crisp, dry cold of the north-east. At least that was the reason he gave Walter Power when he decided to go, and Walter knew him well enough to leave it at that. Ned said goodbye to his mate and rode north to the country he knew and loved.

Harry Power, born in Ireland and raised in the slums of Manchester, had loved the ranges of the north-east and learned them as a man learns a new language. For Ned, these ranges came to represent a mother tongue — key to the mystic art of true bushmanship in which navigation and tracking were not just a matter of what you saw, but what you felt and sensed, what the landscape told you.

Walter Power married Eureka Wright the following year and became a farmer, sometime prospector and long-serving member of the Alberton Shire Council. Until his death in 1932 he expressed 'great respect' for Ned Kelly.

Back at Eleven Mile Creek Ned spent some time with his new half-brother John King, born in March, who would grow up as John Kelly, doubly honouring the memory of Ellen's first husband. Then Ned began his second year of honest work. Beechworth's *Advertiser*, a newspaper which became one of Ned's harshest critics, would nevertheless admit; 'No man could work harder or better than he when he chose.'

Ned did some hillside ploughing for grazier John Evans of Whitfield Station. Evans treated him well and four years later would receive an unusual measure of his gratitude. Ned earned money as a bullock driver, probably with his own team, and did some shearing, though it was too late for the winter odyssey to Gnawarra Station on the Darling. He took fencing jobs, among them Baileys' vineyard at Glenrowan. (He never became a heavy drinker, but it was perhaps here that he developed a taste for claret with his favourite meal of roast lamb and green peas.) He also worked as a horsebreaker. Joseph Ashmead of Winton recalled Ned breaking a horse for his father:

> At that time a great part of the country was still open and young horses were allowed to roam about in the bush. I shall never forget the wild gallop we had after those horses. They had not been yarded for many months and were determined they were not going to be. We chased them over the hills and through swamps. I could not help thinking what a dashing, fearless fellow Ned Kelly was, and a companion he had with him who was known as Bricky [Brickey Williamson], was if possible more reckless. At length the horses were yarded, and Ned was on the back of the one he had to break in. He took it away and returned it in due course, but he had been in gaol and a great many people avoided him and he was seen less and less on the creek.

'A great many people' were wary of this formidable young man, even intimidated by him, and the police continued to regard him and his family with open suspicion and hostility, seeming to show little regard for Police Regulation 183:

> In keeping under as close surveillance as practicable all discharged prisoners . . . the police are to act with caution and consideration. They must not interfere unnecessarily with such members of the community, and must particularly avoid a harassing and vexatious course of conduct

towards them, lest they do more harm by placing difficulties in the way of those who are desirous of earning an honest living than they will do good by obtaining information of the movements of those who are resolved to persevere in a criminal career.

A Greta storekeeper recalled Ned in this period as 'very industrious … very quiet … frequently quelling unseemly rows at the public house.' Yet he also reported,

> He bitterly complained of not being allowed to get an honest living. To use his own expression, he was 'hounded down'. If anyone lost a bullock the police would visit his mother's place at Greta, and frequently rouse its inmates in the middle of the night, without assigning any reason for the action.

Police harassment would be an ongoing problem for the family, but it was like the confrontation at the Killawarra races. The first punch didn't get him fighting; nor the second.

◆

SEVEN MILES north-west of the Kelly home was Winton Swamp, a huge expanse of superb old swamp gum growing from a shallow lake which often sprouted with weed, green and level as a rice paddy. The exciting ride after the Ashmead horses had taken place along its shores. On a low, man-made hill on the lake's northern shore, Ned contracted to build a granite house. Probably helped by Brickey Williamson and 14-year-old Dan, he quarried pink granite in the Warby Ranges behind Glenrowan and hauled it to the site with his bullock team. Some of the blocks were 6 feet by 3 by 3. When the house was finished, looking out across the lake to the Warbys, the Buffalo Ranges and the Mansfield hills, Ned carved '1875' in one of the granite blocks at the back, marking a year he could be proud of.

That year Ned's first bosses, Saunders and Rule, were running one of the James Dixon properties, Burkes Holes sawmill, 4 miles north-east of Greta on the banks of Burkes Holes Creek. The partners hired Ned as their overseer — a man of proven ability in the trade and an excellent worker, well known in the district and able to handle the most belligerent timberman. He proved, in the words of one of his men, 'a natural-born leader'. With its 13-horsepower steam engine, vertical and crosscut saws, travelling rack benches and a 'substantial' timber shed, the mill was supplying timber for the second section of the Wangaratta–Beechworth railway — a lucrative though short-term contract.

On a visit to Beechworth Ned posed for a portrait at photographer James Bray's studio in Camp Street, scarcely recognisable as the boxer photographed the previous year. He wears a suit and double-breasted waistcoat, every inch the solid, sober man-about-town. Further along Camp Street was the shop of bookseller and stationer James Ingram, where Ned was a frequent visitor. A description by the Scots Baptist Ingram confirms the impression created by the photo. 'He was in his usual manner, of a quiet, unassuming disposition — a polite and gentle-manly man.'

Now, when Ned seemed at last to have escaped both youthful notori-ety and unwanted fame, a trivial incident triggered a chain of events that eventually brought his honest years to an end. On a Saturday afternoon in January 1876, Ned and Tom Lloyd rode up the King Valley towards Glenmore. Ned cut quite a different figure from the polite young gentle-man seen in Beechworth — wearing light-coloured riding pants and waistcoat, lace-up boots and an old cabbage tree hat with a red fly veil.

Passing Henry Lydecker's farm at King Flats, Ned and Tom noticed a chestnut mare and her filly. They saw that the mare carried the JQ brand of the Quinns and assumed that she had strayed from nearby Glenmore or had been 'borrowed' by Lydecker. That night they took the two horses for return to Jack and Jimmy Quinn who, if they had been home, would have told their nephews that Lydecker had bought the mare from them. It was a simple misunderstanding that should have been easily cleared up, but it wasn't. Lydecker had seen Ned and Tom either taking his horses or showing undue interest in them. He reported the theft at the Glenmore Police Station and on the Tuesday warrants were sworn at Oxley for the arrest of Ned and Tom on charges of Horse Stealing.

Already a chapter of accidents, the case quickly became a shambles. The mare and filly disappeared, and while Ned was back with the sawmill, Tom negotiated with Lydecker and persuaded him to accept a horse and calf 'in lieu of the one stolen'. Lydecker withdrew the charge and Tom's warrant was burnt but, inexplicably, Ned's was not. Mean-while, the Glenmore Police Station was closed down and, for the time being, the case lapsed.

◆

THE BRANCH RAILWAY reached Beechworth in July 1876 and Ned's mill lost its mainstay. These were harder times, with bad seasons and dwindling gold production. Beechworth, the colony's largest gold dis-trict, produced the second lowest yield in both quartz and washdirt. At the end of 1875 the *Wangaratta Dispatch* had lamented: 'That which was in fact the industry of the colony has collapsed, it was but is not.'

An uneasy sense of change blighted the north-east. Travelling up the main Sydney Road, you passed through a succession of dying towns and villages presenting 'a ruinous and desolate appearance' — hit by the loss of passenger and freight traffic to the railway. New towns were springing up beside the railway stations, but to the ordinary country traveller only the decay was evident. Bankruptcy and embezzlement became increasingly common, with pillars of local society starting to crumble. In this economic climate, stock theft — both for sale and to provide food — was becoming more widespread. Squatters were more determined in their efforts to discourage selectors in the land war that followed government attempts to encourage farming after the gold rushes. Big graziers lobbied more vigorously with the police and there were cases of 'arrest on request'.

While Ned kept out of trouble, he must have worried for his brothers. Jim was released from prison in August with more than eighteen months remission, a sinewy 6-footer, good-looking and volatile. Overshadowed by both his brothers, wiry little Dan, now 15, was overassertive both in and out of their company. A couple of years before, Joseph Ashmead had met Dan while watering stock on the Eleven Mile:

> He was riding a smart black pony, and proudly told us it was a galloper and could clear any fence in the north east. The boy was alert and active with piercing black eyes that took in everything at a glance. He wore strapped trousers, a red shirt and straw hat tilted forward, secured by a strap under his nose. The back of his head was broad and covered with close cropped hair as black and shiny as a crow; his jaw was heavy, his lips thin, and when closed tightly, there seemed to be something cruel in them, but when they relaxed into a smile, he appeared to be a jovial, good-natured fellow. His name was Dan Kelly and he was a great lover of horses. I was the only one of the boys who had a horse. A bay pony. She had belonged to a clergyman and was an honest goer. Dan ran his eye over my horse and proposed that we should have a race, a challenge that I gladly accepted. When Dan found that he could not shake me off, he developed a great respect for me, and declared there was not a kangaroo in the whole of the country who could get away from us, so we went kangaroo hunting, not once, but many times. I left my cows to look after themselves, or bribed some of the boys to look after them for me, with the promises of some sinews out of the kangaroo's tail to make whip crackers with.

Racing the local boys and chasing kangaroos were becoming less exciting pastimes to Dan. He galloped around the countryside with a band of lads who wore brightly coloured waist sashes and adopted Dan's quirky fashion of hat tilted over eyes and chin strap under nose. They called themselves the Greta Mob. Dan was increasingly likely to try to prove himself a big man in his mates' eyes by stealing a showy horse.

It would emerge that Ned's stepfather, George King, was an expert horse thief and probably urged Ned and the lads to join him in that trade. George had never been charged with the theft of a horse, and never would be. But could Dan and Jim hope to be so lucky? Ned was reminded of the accusation of horse stealing hanging over his own head and, with things quiet at the mill, set out to clear up the Lydecker mess.

Ned presented himself at the Oxley Police Station on Wednesday 19 July and appeared in Oxley Court the next day. He was remanded for a week and applied for a further week's remand to prepare his defence. On 3 August 'a number of witnesses' testified for him and the case was dismissed. The Bench 'passed a severe censure' on Lydecker and a newspaper correspondent considered that his action in accepting the horse and calf from Tom Lloyd had been 'very like' Compounding a Felony. It is clear that the police, rather than Lydecker, had pursued the case against Ned after this initial settlement with Tom.

At about that time Ned's sawmill bosses had good news for their men. With little work available in the district, Saunders and Rule had managed to secure a contract supplying timber for the main Gippsland railway. The mill would make a two-stage move to Gippsland — the sawmill plant with half the men, followed by the rest of the team when the mill was set up. The fates seemed kind to Ned. Just when old enmities, old troubles were re-emerging, here was a chance for another fresh, clean start.

Then, on 30 September, Dan was charged with stealing a saddle. He may have been innocent. Back in May a saddle had disappeared from the kitchen of a Benalla hotel. The owner later recognised it on Dan's horse and he was arrested. The lad had a plausible explanation of having swapped saddles with 'a man named Roberts' and, in the Benalla Police Court on 16 October, produced witnesses Jack Lloyd, Bill Skilling and Ned to confirm his story. He had a receipt signed by Roberts for the transaction which also had involved Dan paying £1. The Benalla Bench was unconvinced nevertheless, and Dan was committed for trial at Beechworth General Sessions in February.

It was probably Dan's trouble that first prompted a change in Ned's sawmill plans. If he had intended to travel to Gippsland with the first group, he now arranged that his leading hand, a friend of Brickey Williamson's called Jack McMonigle, would go ahead with the plant and set-up team. Ned would follow later with the rest of the men. This proved a fateful decision.

Dan's trial was in February and Ned determined to see that Dan and Jim kept out of trouble in the intervening four months. With two of his sawmill men, brothers Oakley and Peter Martin, he took the boys up to Bullock Creek, one of the little alluvial streams draining the Wombat Ranges. There had been a small rush here in the 1860s and abandoned gold claims were dotted along the creeks and gullies, almost swallowed by the bush.

Jim Kelly a month before he turned 18, as he began three years hard labour for horse stealing. Jim's dejection is obvious, yet this prison sentence prevented him becoming a member of the Kelly Gang and almost certainly saved his life.

Tom Lloyd, Ned's and Dan's cousin, was a kindred spirit who became virtually a fifth member of the Kelly Gang. From Stringybark Creek to Glenrowan, he devoted himself to their safety and survival.

Ned Kelly at 19, unofficial boxing champion of the north-east, a remarkable study by Melbourne photographer Chidley which captures something of Ned's daunting physical impact.

Constable Alexander Fitzpatrick, photographed in Beechworth soon after he joined the police force in 1877. He displays the newly issued 'Bobby' helmet, still with his old district number. A sometime friend of Ned and suitor of Kate, Fitzpatrick tried to exploit his relationship with the family in saving a shaky police career. (*Police Museum*)

The *Police Gazette* entry, 'Horses and Cattle', read by Constable Fitzpatrick on 15 April 1878. It prompted his visit to the Kelly homestead and the arrest of Dan Kelly, which triggered the Kelly outbreak.

See *Police Gazette*, 1875, pp. 22 and 32.

PATRICK QUINN, charged with obtaining money by false pretences from James Kennedy, has been arrested for horse-stealing by the Menindie police, N.S.W. See also *Police Gazette*, 1868, p. 326.—O.6338. 9th April 1878.

See *Police Gazette*, 1878, p. 67.

NEIL SMITH, charged with imposing on Jane Murray, has been arrested by the Geelong police.—O.1602. 9th April 1878.

STEALING OTHERWISE THAN FROM THE PERSON OR FROM DWELLINGS.

See *Police Gazette*, 1877, pp. 305 and 336.

JOHN DUNBAR, charged with Hector and Norman Wilson's larceny, was seen in the parish of Minyip about ten days ago, in charge of a flock of sheep said to belong to Mr. Williams. The offender's brother-in-law, Joseph Branfield, and his sister, have selections in the vicinity of Minyip.—O.6982. 7th April 1878.

See *Police Gazette*, 1878, pp. 44 and 50.

JOHN CONNELL, charged with larceny as a bailee on David Graham and William Smith, has been arrested by the Inglewood police.—O.881 and 1007. 9th April 1878.

WILLIAM DAVIS is charged, on warrant from the Richmond Bench, with stealing a pair of trousers (recovered) belonging to Elisha Henderson, on the 19th of February last. Description:—A bootmaker, 17 or 18 years of age, about 5 feet 5 or 6 inches high, stout, dark complexion and hair; wore dark coat, light tweed trousers and vest, lace-up boots, and black hat with narrow stitched rim.—O.2160. 9th April 1878.

HORSES AND CATTLE.

See *Police Gazette*, 1878, p. 78 and *ante*.

COMPLAINANTS, John C. Farrell, James Whitty, James A. Whitty, and Robert Jeffrey.—Daniel Kelly and John Lloyd are charged, on warrants from the Chiltern Bench, with these offences. For Kelly's description, see list of *Prisoners discharged*, week ended 21st January 1878. Lloyd is about 20 years of age, 5 feet 6 inches high, stout, 12 stone weight, has dark complexion, round full face, no beard or moustache.—O.5959. 8th April 1878.

See *Police Gazette*, 1878, p. 68.

— RISDON, charged with James Ross's larceny, left the horse and buggy at the City Arms Hotel, Elizabeth street, Melbourne, on the 4th instant. The warrant has been cancelled.—O.1598. 9th April 1878.

Ned and Harry had operated through here in 1869 and Ned knew that there was a derelict hut built from crossed logs by Bullock Creek, a tiny, forgotten fortress in this remote amphitheatre. The little party started to repair the hut, holding down new bark for the roof with jockey poles and riders, cutting a forked prop to hold up a sagging southern wall, clearing, building a dog-leg fence for a horse paddock . . . then Dan and Jim could set to work digging out washdirt and cradling or panning it in the icy water of the tiny creek.

There may have been two other members of this band — a couple of lads from Beechworth whose lives had crossed Ned's at some lost place on some forgotten day — perhaps at the fight with Wild Wright, perhaps through Kate Kelly who often stayed at Beechworth with a girl who knew one or both of the lads. They were Joe Byrne and Aaron Sherritt, fresh from Beechworth Gaol after a six-month sentence for what was effectively cow stealing. Like Red Kelly all those years before, they'd been convicted for possessing meat and a hide with the brand cut out. They were inseparable mates who would become engaged to each other's sisters. Joe — no relation to the prosperous Byrnes of Moyhu — was a handsome 19-year-old, pale-blue-eyed, with reddish, fair hair, considered tall at 5 ft 10 ins, soberly dressed and outwardly quiet. Aaron was 21, equally handsome, a slim 6-footer, olive-skinned, dark-haired, brown-eyed, flashly dressed and outwardly an amiable larrikin. In other ways too, they were chalk and cheese. Joe was from Irish Catholic rebel stock while Aaron's parents were Irish Protestant Loyalists, his father a former member of the hated Irish Constabulary. This all seemed no bar to their friendship and was certainly not a problem for Ned, whose Protestant circle included Wild Wright (now or soon to be a loyal friend), Ben Gould, Bill Skilling and George King.

Ned and the others probably left Dan and Jim at the Bullock Creek mine and headed back towards Beechworth, through the Wombat Ranges and down into the King Valley. This was still a special haunt of Ned's — a boyhood domain that may have gained new magic with his reading of *Lorna Doone*, R. D. Blackmore's classic adventure set against the wilds of Exmoor. It would be remembered as his favourite book. How that story must have resonated for him — the formidable young hero, Jan Ridd, fighter, farmer and horseman, with a sister called Annie, living with his widowed mother on a farm by a creek, helper to a famous highwayman. Most of all perhaps, the fabulous Doone Valley with its sheer, rocky slopes, stronghold of the outlaw Doone family, prompted memories of the remarkable Quinns, firelit in their prime, brief masters of the valley below The Rock,

Ned loved the King Valley and shared it for a time with his new friends in these pre-Christmas days of early summer when a blanket, a gun, a quartpot and a saddle were all you needed, wanting only a jarful of tea and a quid of tobacco to live like a king.

One day they saw a wild bull in the open bush and natural pasture of the valley. Ned spurred after it and 'ran it in', chasing it until it tired, dodged his horse from the lunges of its horns, then perhaps roped it between two horses with a couple of halters and took it down the valley. At King Flats, Ned dropped by Henry Lydecker's farm and left the bull with him — perhaps as a gesture of gratitude, certainly an acknowledgement that Lydecker had played no willing part in the recent prosecution.

When the Martin brothers left for Gippsland, Ned didn't accompany them. The reason remains a mystery. Dan's appearance at Beechworth's General Sessions in February provided an excuse rather than a reason: it would have been comparatively easy to come back from Gippsland for the trial. Something else intervened — another series of misadventures that dominoed from his dealings with Henry Lydecker and, if Ned is to be believed, plunged him into the very heart of the land war between the squatters and selectors of the north-east.

According to Ned, Lydecker sold the wild bull to a local butcher and publican called Carr, 'who killed him for beef'. At about this time, Moyhu grazier James Whitty lost a bull. It was suggested that the sides of beef hanging in Carr's premises were from the missing beast. 'Some time afterwards,' says Ned, 'I was told I was blamed for stealing this bull from James Whitty of Boggy Creek.'

This was the James Whitty who had first settled a few miles from Beveridge all those years before, whose cousin's wife was said to have looked after the Kelly children when Ellen was ill and who was related to Ned's old friend, Charles Whitty. Whitty was now a man of substance, living in prestigious Red Camp homestead on a hillside above Boggy Creek, which wound down a rich valley to join the King River near Moyhu. Choosing to remain a background figure, a grey eminence among the powerful squatters of the district, Whitty wielded considerable power through his holdings of land and stock, through family influence on the Oxley Shire Council and through complex personal and business interrelationships among the Byrnes and Farrells, who, with the Whittys, dominated the lower King Valley. Whatever his origins, James Whitty had become one of the enemy.

Ned brooded over the accusation that he had stolen Whitty's bull and might have been reluctant to set off for Gippsland leaving this piece of unfinished business behind him. Then came another crisis in his circle of close friends. While Dan and Jim managed to stay out of trouble through this increasingly harsh summer of 1876–7, Joe Byrne and Aaron Sherritt were less lucky. One hot afternoon they stripped and went for a swim in a Chinese dam near the Byrne house. Joe — who spoke Cantonese, was an opium addict and virtually a member of Beechworth's Chinese community — was on bad terms with three Chinese miners who lived in a hut by the dam and seem to have been outcasts among their fellow countrymen. There was an argument, the Chinese produced bamboos and Aaron threw a stick or stone which struck one man in the face, shattering a bone. Aaron and Joe were committed to face a General Sessions trial at Beechworth — the same circuit court at which Dan's case was to be heard.

Wednesday 28 February was oppressively hot and Ned took his place with Jack Lloyd and Bill Skilling, in the pew-like benches of the Beechworth Court House while Dan, Aaron and Joe sweated in the badly ventilated holding cell. Late in the morning Dan was called. His defence was conducted impressively by Frederick Brown, former Shire President, and Dan's three witnesses told a persuasive story of exchanging the saddles, paying the £1 and writing the receipt. Ned, in suit and waistcoat, must have cut a particularly impressive figure in the witness box as he swore that he knew the man Roberts involved, and 'had tried to find him for the purpose of this trial'.

In charging the jury Judge Hackett said, 'He did not see why the prisoner was there at all.' Dan was promptly found not guilty and the court was adjourned. Joe's and Aaron's case was postponed until the next morning and, perhaps on an impulse, Ned rode off across the Oxley Flats to attend that afternoon's Moyhu races.

There a 'T. Lloyd', probably Tom, was riding a horse called Wildspie in the Maiden Plate and a grey mare, Chance, in the Hurdle; but this wasn't what drew Ned. Moyhu was the very heart of Whitty territory. Charles Whitty was Clerk of the Course, John Whitty and the Byrne brothers were stewards and James Whitty's son Mark was running a refreshment booth. James Whitty, lover of horseflesh, would be there; he could not miss his local racing club's annual meeting. In the afternoon's fierce and sultry heat, Ned threaded among the 500-odd racegoers, past 'a negro minstrel ... dressed in appropriate style', strumming a banjo, past the lady spinning her Wheel of Fortune, until he found his man.

James Whitty — now 62, a Dickensian figure of stern authority with his starched collar, rawboned face and grey sidewhiskers — found himself facing the equally authoritative figure of Ned Kelly. A threat of thunder hung in the still, stifling air and a strange haze closed in across the ranges from the north-west — not rain, not the smoke of bushfire. A storm was coming, 'one of the most curious ... we have ever seen,' said a correspondent. The stage seemed set for an explosive confrontation.

There was probably a touch of fire in Ned's 'alexandrite' eyes as he asked Whitty why he had been blamed for stealing the bull. Yet, as

reported by Ned, the squatter's response was reasonable, even conciliatory. 'He said he had found his bull . . . and *he* never blamed me for
stealing him . . . but his son-in-law Farrell . . . told him I stole the bull . . .
[and] sold the bull to Carr.'

So that was it. Ned could redirect his anger against Farrell or enjoy
what was left of the meeting, congratulate Tom on a brilliant win over
the hurdles and commiserate with him over a narrow defeat in the
Consolation Handicap. After this last race, the storm broke — a wild
swirl of wind and dust lashing the trees and a cloudburst to soak the
racegoers as they scattered for home.

On Ned's ride back to Beechworth he could enjoy the malty smell of
rain on hot earth and dry grass as he weighed the exchange with Whitty.
After the chapter of accidents that had started more than a year before
when he and Tom took the JQ mare and foal from Lydecker, the accu-
sation over the bull seemed to have emerged as just one more accident.
If this was the problem that had stopped him following the mill to
Gippsland, nothing now stood in his way; only the outcome of Joe's and
Aaron's trial. He could leave as soon as it was over.

In court next morning the police case against Joe and Aaron was
pressed home with vigour. There was no dispute that Chinese miner Ah
On had been seriously injured by Aaron — according to the prosecution
by a rock thrown in an unprovoked attack, according to the defence by
a stick hurled in self-defence when Ah On and his mates attacked Aaron
and Joe with bamboos. Ned might have been reminded of his clash with
Ah Fook, and perhaps he smiled when a trooper said that the two lads
'belonged to the class of rural larrikins'. After some confusion on the
jury's part, Joe and Aaron were found not guilty. The local *Advertiser*
clearly disapproved of the pair and pointed to the fate of two young
locals called Smith and Brady, 'who commenced life like them and
ended it on the gallows'.

Ned didn't go to Gippsland. 'Some time' after the encounter with
James Whitty he heard another rumour started by the Whitty clan:

> I heard again I was blamed for stealing a mob of calves from Whitty and
> Farrell which I never had anything to do with and along with this and
> other talk I began to think they wanted me to give them something to talk
> about. Therefore I started wholesale and retail cattle and horse dealing.

'Wholesale and retail cattle and horse dealing' was Ned's euphemism
for stock theft. This latest accusation against him had been the third
punch, a justification to give up the mill, his career, his honest life.
There was also the provocation by Flood, the harassment of his family,
the jobs he failed to get, the 'great many people' who avoided him, the
unrecorded hurts and injustices, perhaps minor in themselves, that had

accumulated during his three years of honest work ... all this might have contributed to Ned's decision not to rejoin the mill in Gippsland. Or perhaps there was no decision. Perhaps there was always something to justify him postponing his departure — not least the worsening economic conditions in the north-east, the continuing drought and the escalating land war between the big graziers and the struggling selectors — the squatters and the cockies. Ned's account of his dispute with Whitty over the bull blends with an indictment of Whitty and fellow squatters for their treatment of small farmers.

> Whitty and Burns not being satisfied with all the picked land on King River and Boggy Creek and the run of their stock on the certificate ground free and no one interfering with them, paid heavy rent for all the open ground so a poor man could not keep his stock and [they] impounded every beast they could catch even off government roads.

Six unfenced roads ran through Whitty's land and, on the face of it, for him to impound any animals that strayed from these roads on to his grass seems high-handed. Yet to Whitty, as to graziers throughout the north-east, it was a question of survival. As the drought of 1876-7 approached crisis proportions, even the more benevolent squatters like the Dockers of Bontherambo took a tougher line on stock grazing at the roadside while crossing their land and tried, unsuccessfully, to close some roads through their property for a five-year period.

Ned's former boss, grazier and wheeler-dealer Frank Heach, made an arrangement with squatter Hector Simson to impound stray stock found on the Laceby run. He attacked the task with such vigour that one local farmer claimed impoundings had cost him £20 'in a very short time'. Some of Heach's victims petitioned the local Land Board to set up a Laceby Common, while one man took a more direct approach. An uninsured stack of oats, valued by Heach at £300, was put to the torch. The drought was giving the land war an ugly edge.

In mid-February, with 'permanent' wells drying up and many graziers cutting down saplings to feed their animals, James Whitty, John Byrne and Andrew Byrne had published notices that, as lessees of the Union Bank's land in Moyhu, Laceby and Oxley, they would:

> impound all cattle and other animals found trespassing thereon or sue the owners thereof for trespass, on or after the 20th of February, Inst.

It was not a hollow threat. Ned records:

> If a poor man happened to leave his horse or a bit of poddy calf outside his paddock they would be impounded. I have known 60 head of horses impounded in one day by Whitty and Burns all belonging to poor farmers. They would have to leave their ploughing or harvest or other

employment to go to Oxley. When they would get there perhaps they would not have money to release them and have to give a bill of sale or borrow money which is no easy matter.

In speaking on behalf of the 'poor farmers' whose horses were impounded by 'Whitty and Burns', Ned neglects to mention that, scarcely a fortnight after the race-course confrontation with Whitty, he was a victim of this harassment. On 12 March 'Messrs Byrne and Whitty' impounded fifteen horses with Oxley poundkeeper George Kennedy (probably the man who claimed to have given Ned 'a good thrashing' during his time with Harry Power). If the horses were not claimed and their expenses paid, they would be sold on 7 April. Among the fifteen were a pair of bay mares, each with a filly, owned by 'Mr Edward Kelly, of Greta' and 'Thos. Lloyd, of Greta'.

Ned and Tom acted promptly. The night after their horses were impounded they broke the lock on the Oxley pound yards and rescued them. It would have been a grand gesture to release all the other horses at the same time — and a smarter thing to do. But Ned and Tom took only their two mares and fillies. They clearly wanted Whitty and Byrne to know who had hit back at them, while unable to prove it.

Ned had now joined the fight in which his friends and relations were heavily involved. If stock theft provided any measure of that fight, 1876-7 was Armageddon, with losses in both horses and cattle at record levels. Ned Kelly, on his own admission, would make a significant contribution to the total.

Like all young men who see themselves as fighters for a cause, Ned was aware of the philosophy behind the land war, embodied in his picture of 'poor farmers' and the 'poor man' oppressed by land-rich graziers. Ned's allegiance was clear, yet, as in any other war this allegiance sanctioned crime and elevated adventure into patriotism or its regional equivalent. Add to this the mystic symbol of the horse — in Ireland a measure of wealth, power and authority; here, a mark of new freedom, an assertion of equality.

There was one other factor which might have influenced Ned's decision — George King. Ned must have seemed a highly desirable 'business' partner whose stature, abilities and knowledge of the country would complement George's considerable talent as a horse thief. The influence of Ned's stepfather cannot be measured or exaggerated — perhaps even as far as introducing a tang of shrewd Irish-American republicanism into what was, in essence, a fight between haves and have-nots. One thing is certain. George King would inspire the exploit that marked the climax of Ned's horse-stealing career and, at the same time, brought on the Big Trouble.

6

'THE WHITTY LARCENY'

1877–78

Through much of 1877 Ned Kelly and George King led a well-organised gang in an ambitious two-colony stock-stealing operation. A detective commented, 'They had ample paddock space — indeed all their arrangements were as perfect as any properly conducted business.' And Beechworth's *Advertiser*, fairly quivering with disapproval, conceded that Ned was 'head centre of the most perfect horse stealing organization that has ever existed in Australia, which is saying a good deal'.

The team included Joe Byrne, Aaron Sherritt, Wild Wright, Brickey Williamson, a young fellow called Big Mick Woodyard who had lived with the Kellys for a couple of years, and Ned's boyhood, local hero of the bushranging days, Allen Lowry, now known as Billy Cook.

Aliases were the order of the day. Big Mick Woodyard (whose real name was Albert Laxon) was now called Mick Miller, Joe Byrne became Billy King, Lowry changed his name yet again to Johnny Mack and Ned called himself 'J. Thompson', an outwardly respectable *nom de guerre* which might have represented a couple of private jokes — echoing the names of Joe Thompson, a well-known bookmaker, and John Thompson, a sparring partner of the legendary boxer, Jem Mace. George King called himself George Stuckey.

They made an impressive group, with four of them — Ned, Aaron, Big Mick and Lowry — standing 6 foot or more. Not only their appearance was impressive; all were fine horsemen and bushmen, riding behind an unchallenged 'natural-born leader'.

Ned later admitted that in his 'wholesale and retail horse and cattle dealing', he had 'sold horses and cattle innumerable' and would boast that he had stolen 280 horses. On the face of it the claim seems exaggerated, as it would account for virtually all the horses stolen in the north-east over two record years, but Ned and the Gang probably stole at least as many horses in New South Wales as in Victoria.

It would be wrong to imagine that all the horses stolen by the Gang belonged to wealthy squatters. It might have been true, as the Moyhu correspondent of Wangaratta's *Dispatch* claimed, that, 'In some cases the ruffians have taken the only pair of draught horses a farmer has, in some cases four . . .' But there is clear evidence that at least some of these thefts represented the settling of old scores within 'the selector class' — as when Bill Frost, Ellen's former lover, twice had horses stolen — and that references to 'respectable' farmers as victims often indicated that these men had aligned themselves with the police and squatters.

The plan of operation was simplicity itself. Horses stolen in Victoria were driven up across the drought-dwindled Murray River into New South Wales and sold from Albury to as far north as Wagga and as far west as Jerilderie. Horses lifted in New South Wales were taken across the border and sold as far south as Melbourne. Brands were changed by plucking hair in the desired pattern and tattooing the horse's skin with iodine to change, say, an H into an 'HB conjoined'. For several months this produced the effect of an old brand.

There was an extra problem in New South Wales, where 'No man can legally ride another man's horse without either a permit or some notification in his pocket that the horse belongs to another man.' The Gang devised a method of 'proving' ownership of the horses they stole. The Gang would split into two groups, one probably led by Ned and the other by Joe Byrne. Superintendent Hare described both Ned and Joe as 'good looking, well dressed men' — they could easily pass for young squatters. One team, with the stolen horses, would arrive at a station, make themselves known to the owner and camp for the night. The team leader, masquerading as a grazier, might even share the host's table while his men ate with the station hands. That day or the next, the second team — apparently another grazier with one or two stockmen — would arrive and pretend to negotiate a deal to buy the first team's horses. The station owner would be happy to witness the transaction — probably recorded on his stationery — and the two groups would ride off, apparently in different directions, with what appeared to be legal bills of sale for their stolen horses. In a variation of this scheme, stolen horses with altered brands would be impounded in the other colony and subsequently bought at low, ex-pound prices — the receipts again providing 'legal' documentation.

This operation, which thrived during the drought of 1877, required considerable nerve, the ability to find and quickly round up small mobs of good quality horses, knowledge of obscure stock routes to minimise the chance of recognition and the 'side' to carry off the scheme without attracting suspicion.

That April the dogged Nicolson, now Inspecting Superintendent, visited Greta and was dissatisfied with the senior policeman, Constable

Hugh Thom, suspecting that he was not 'active' enough to keep the Kellys and their relatives under 'pressure', quite apart from which he had dirty breeches, dirty firearms and an untrimmed beard. During his time at Greta Nicolson made a point of visiting the Kelly homestead. His frequently quoted report to Captain Standish gives a vivid picture both of the Kelly family's situation and of the police attitude to the clan.

> I visited the notorious Mrs Kelly's on the road from hence to Benalla. She lived on a piece of cleared and partly cultivated land on the road-side in an old wooden hut, with a large bark roof. The dwelling was divided into five apartments by partitions of blanketing, rags, &c. There were no men in the house, only children and two girls of about fourteen years of age, said to be her daughters. They all appeared to be living in poverty and squalor. She said her sons were out at work, but did not indicate where, and that their relatives seldom came near them. However, their communications with each other are known to the police. Until the gang referred to is *rooted out of the neighbourhood* one of the most *experienced and successful* mounted constables in the district will be required in charge of Greta. I do not think the present arrangements are sufficient. Second-class Sergeant Steele, of Wangaratta, keeps the offenders referred to under as good surveillance as the distance and means at his disposal will permit. But I submit that Constable Thom would hardly be able to cope with these men; at the same time some of these offenders may commit themselves foolishly some day, and may be apprehended and convicted in a very ordinary manner. (my italics)

In a subsequent interview with Inspector Brooke Smith at Beechworth, Nicolson expressed the opinion:

> That without oppressing the people, or worrying them in any way, that he should endeavour, whenever they commit any paltry crime, to bring them to justice, *and send them to Pentridge even on a paltry sentence*, the object being to take their prestige away from them, which has as good an affect as being sent into prison with very heavy sentences, because the prestige these men get up there from what is termed their flashness helped to keep them together, and that is a very good way of taking the flashness out of them. (my italics)

This 'opinion' — which seems suspiciously like a directive — is often quoted as proof that there was an official policy of 'persecuting' the clan. Certainly Nicolson's qualification, 'without oppressing the people, or worrying them in any way', is hard to square with the tone of his advice and seems to pay mere lip service to Police Regulation 183.

Universally ignored is Nicolson's apparent admission that the police have such a degree of influence with the magistracy and judiciary that conviction and sentencing also can be seen as a matter of police policy. (Ned's three years for receiving and Jim's five years for cattle theft would emerge more clearly as sentences imposed to satisfy police requirements rather than as responses to the evidence placed before the court, or even, in Jim's case, the recommendation of the jury.) Any such merging of police and judicial powers defied a basic principle of British justice. Nicolson's admittedly ambiguous statement would be accepted without query by a Royal Commission.

In April 1877, the same month that Nicolson noted the 'poverty and squalor' of Eleven Mile Creek, James Whitty drove his buggy along an undulating driveway lined with young elms, oaks and chestnuts, up to a broad-verandahed homestead of apricot-coloured bricks, sited on a high, cliff-like bank of the King River near Moyhu. He strode through empty rooms that had housed the Dockers and Clarkes, legendary squatting families, and from the front verandah looked out past a dark sentry line of fashionable bunya pines to sunlit miles of paddocks stretching to the Fifteen Mile Creek and Greta. They were his. James Whitty had taken possession of Myrrhee Station, bought at auction three months earlier.

Whitty's pleasure was diminished by the fact that his beloved wife Catherine had died three years before, almost to the day. In a measure of his grief, the normally thrifty grazier had donated a superb stained-glass rose window of Madonna and child to Moyhu's new Catholic church, a few miles down the road.

The widower and his younger children moved into the homestead with its detached kitchen and servants' quarters, bath house, overseer's cottage, store and office, stables, 20-pen woolshed and 1¼-acre garden, 'well stocked with vines and fruit trees of all descriptions'. From this handsome seat Whitty now controlled the 12 000 'certificated' acres and 3000 sheep of the Myrrhee run, a crown jewel for his already substantial pastoral empire which included the 12 000 acres of Union Bank land he rented with the Byrne brothers.

It had been a long, hard journey for the then-illiterate Irish labourer, who had arrived in the colony on an assisted passage thirty-seven years before. Whitty's achievements spoke of great energy and determination, and he brought the same spirit to his inevitable clashes with the battling selectors who surrounded him. Ned, in determining that he would give Whitty and his friends 'something to talk about', must have realised that he was taking on a dangerous enemy.

In June came another warning for Ned. Up at Wagga, Jim Kelly and a young Scot called Tom Manly stole a couple of horses and sold them on the way to the Snowy Mountains. Hot-headed young Jim tried to fight his way out of an arrest at Kiandra but was brought to trial and sentenced, with Manly, to four years hard labour under the name James Wilson. Jim and young Manly were carted off to spend their first nine months 'probationary' term in the notorious dungeons of Berrima Gaol. After that Manly went to Parramatta and Jim to Darlinghurst Gaol in Sydney.

If Ellen Kelly tried to persuade her husband and eldest son to go more carefully, they paid little heed. By now Joe Byrne was living with the Kellys. Joe's quiet, 'respectable' exterior masked a larrikin adventurer who loved the excitement of horse stealing. He and his flamboyant mate Aaron Sherritt had been 'borrowers' of horses for much of their lives. With Joe on one hand and George King on the other, Ned had plenty of encouragement to enjoy what he called, 'this successful trade' to the full.

◆

ON 2 AUGUST, after his visit to Hedi Police Station in the King Valley, Nicolson wrote in the Crime Report Book:

> About six cases [of stock theft] to date in 1877, mostly horse-stealing, which horses were ultimately recovered, impounded in New South Wales. This is a form of crime which is said to be common here, when the Murray River is low. The animals are said to be impounded with the object of buying them out cheap. They are frequently recovered but the offenders, said to be New South Wales men, are never convicted. I can see no difficulty in bringing the offenders to justice, if the Ovens District police make systematic arrangements, with the co-operation of the well-known Mr Singleton, who is in command of the New South Wales Police, Albury District.

This directive filtered through to Inspector Brooke Smith at Beechworth and he and Inspector Singleton were in communication six weeks later. Singleton wrote:

> I beg to report that I believe that a regular system of horse-stealing is carried on by Victorian thieves and that the animals are brought across the Murray ... Very many horses stolen from Victoria have, I believe, been impounded at Quat Quatta, near Howlong. I would suggest that on a report of horse-stealing being made within a reasonable distance of the border, that you give instructions to [your men that] the police in Albury, Howlong and Corowa be informed as soon as possible.

Before Brooke Smith read Singleton's letter, news of a major robbery shook the King Valley. Eleven horses had vanished from Myrrhee — six of them owned by James Whitty, one by his nephew (also James), three by Whitty's son-in-law John Farrell and one by his neighbour Robert Jeffrey. The mob had been taken by Ned, George and their gang, supposedly to hit back at Whitty and Farrell for their injustices against Ned and his people — including one injustice suffered by George King. After describing his problems with the Whitty clan, Ned claims that:

Farrell the policeman stole a horse from George King and had him in
Whitty and Farrells paddocks until he left the force. All this was the
cause of me and my stepfather George King taking their horses . . .

'Farrell the policeman' was Constable Michael Farrell, brother of
Whitty's son-in-law. He had left the force two years before with a clean
record. Did he in fact steal a horse from George and keep it on his relatives' land? George had not reported any such loss. If it was a stolen
horse his reticence was understandable. But this means that the animal
was on record as stolen, and, even if George had altered its brands, it
could have been 'recognised' in Whitty and Farrell's paddocks, and
George could have reported it, perhaps anonymously. Of course, it
would have been returned to the original owner, but the Whittys and
Farrells would have been exposed or even prosecuted in the process.

It is tempting to believe that this 'injustice' was invented by George to
help win Ned as a partner. As we shall see, Ned's trust in his fellow man
was almost boundless. He would never have doubted his young stepfather's word, least of all when George's grievance helped to vindicate
Ned's decision to abandon his honest life. Certainly, the theft of Whitty's
horses seems to have taken on an almost obsessive significance for Ned.
Like Harry Power taking Robert McBean's horse and watch all those
years before, he was inviting retribution.

Although Ned claimed that only he and George carried out the
Myrrhee raid, there is clear evidence that four or five men were
involved, including Allen Lowry, who would play a prominent role in
disposing of the horses. It was probably about Monday 20 August, during the full moon in a dry midwinter, when the Gang rode along one of
the six roads into Whitty's land and rounded up the mob from the handsome, unfenced paddocks of Myrrhee. The eleven horses were worth
£170 — more than $30000 in modern Australian currency. Ned had
indeed given the Whitty clan 'something to talk about'. At any time
Whitty would have been galled by the loss of eleven horses from his
land, but the theft came at a particularly bad time. Whitty's daughter
Mary — John Farrell's wife — was seriously ill and would die in November. Already as close as father and son (Farrell used the Whitty W brand
on his stock), the two graziers were drawn even closer together in their
concern and grief for Mary and in their desire to hit back at the thieves
who had disrupted their lives in this tragic period.

The Whitty raid conjures up images of the Gang galloping across the
ranges with echoing stockwhip cracks at the heels of a mob of thor-
oughbreds, but the reality was less colourful. At least four of the mob —
the most valuable — were heavy draught horses and one was a mare
about to drop a foal. The Gang drove them northwards at a steady jog,
along the gullies running up to the broad Murray Valley.

Just across the river in New South Wales, between Albury and Corowa, was the little settlement of Howlong, conveniently isolated, without bridge or telegraph to link it with Victoria. Allen Lowry scouted ahead and on Saturday 25 August arranged with German farmer Andrew Petersen to graze some horses on his farm over the weekend. The Gang drove the eleven horses into Petersen's paddock and set to work altering the brands.

One Whitty and Farrell W was cleverly changed to 'KY conjoined', another to AN, several to WB or AB. At least one brand was given a hurried, cosmetic job — the Robert Jeffrey 'HJ, the J reversed' changed to HB. Some time later, to the surprise of the buyer, the alteration would wash or wear off, leaving the original brand exposed.

Three horses which Ned considered the pick of the mob were, in his words, 'taken to a good market' and sold. On the Sunday a Howlong farmer called Samuel Kennedy bought two of 'the culls' from 'George Stuckey' for £26. The remaining six were driven out of Petersen's paddock on the Monday night and sold three days later to William Baumgarten, who had a property near Barnawartha, 9 miles away on the Victorian side of the Murray.

Ned claimed that Kennedy and Baumgarten were 'strangers to me and I believe honest men'. He seems to have been protecting them. Kennedy had previously been implicated in horse theft but William Baumgarten and his brother Gustav, who also became involved in the sale of the Myrrhee horses, seemed unlikely 'fences'. 'They were regarded as respectable, well-to-do farmers, in fact as small squatters, and they both married well.' Nevertheless, suspicions of stock theft had hung over them the previous year and the police would note their kinship with the Margerys, a family who had helped Harry Power. They would also note that they were neighbours of John Tanner, whose brother William had married Mary Lloyd, daughter of old Jack. Such was the fineness of the net which eventually closed around anyone connected with 'the Whitty larceny', as the police called it.

If Baumgarten was an honest man, it is very odd that he was prepared to buy several horses which carried his own WB or his father's AB brand, and equally odd that Ned would try to sell them to him. Although Baumgarten later admitted that 'the brands were wrong', he readily paid £44 for the horses — £26 in cash and a cheque for £18 made out to 'J. Thompson'. The cheque and the receipts witnessed by Gustav Baumgarten were dated 20 August, even though it was now the 30th, presumably an attempt to dissociate the transaction from the Myrrhee theft.

The Gang rode off and Baumgarten's cheque was cashed at Benalla's Bank of New South Wales the following Monday, then the Gang divided the proceeds and split up. Ned, Joe and George quietly returned to the Eleven Mile where they picked up their normal lives, waiting for the storm to come.

Whitty had missed the horses soon after the theft but didn't report his loss to untidy Constable Thom at the Greta police station for more than a week, first making sure that they hadn't strayed, then getting the approval of the other owners. The eleven horses were listed as stolen in the *Police Gazette* of 26 September, with a full description of each animal and the brands they had carried when last seen. By then, Ned had been briefly imprisoned.

On Monday 17 September Ned rode into Benalla. He might have passed some time there with a new, and very unlikely, friend — a young mounted constable called Alex Fitzpatrick who had arrived at the Benalla police station from the Richmond Depot on 1 August. Fitzpatrick was 21, tall, 'stalwart', good looking, a fine horseman ('I could ride like a centaur,' he said) and a larrikin at heart, fond of girls and grog.

In the month-and-a-half of their friendship Ned had recognised worthwhile qualities in Fitzpatrick, and even Tom Lloyd, with much to turn him against the policeman, conceded, 'he wasn't a bad fellow, just irresponsible'. Yet, just over a year later, Ned would say of Fitzpatrick:

> He looks a young, strapping, rather genteel man more fit to be a starcher to a laundress than a policeman for to the keen observer he has the wrong appearance . . . to have anything like a clear conscience or a manly heart . . . The deceit and cowardice is too plain to be seen in the puny cabbage hearted looking face.

By then, Ned had good reason to look back on the relationship with bitterness, perhaps even with pain. Slow to make a true friend but ever ready to trust a man, Ned recalled, 'He said we were good friends and even swore it.' At the time Fitzpatrick might have believed this to be true, since he admired Ned's qualities and seems to have liked him. More than thirty years later he told a journalist:

> Ned Kelly rises before me as I speak. Considering his environment, he was a superior man. He possessed great natural ability, and under favourable circumstances would probably have become a leader of men in good society, instead of the head of a Gang of outlaws.

Fitzpatrick may have found it amusing that his four colleagues at the Benalla police station regarded this imposing young man with suspicion and some degree of awe. Undoubtedly Sergeant Whelan disapproved of his newest constable consorting with the Kellys, perhaps recalling Flood's disastrous association with Annie Gunn. Yet it must have struck him that Fitzpatrick was in a unique position to catch out Ned in some 'paltry crime', help take the 'flashness' out of him and damage his local 'prestige'. In a time of police cut-backs, an unimpressive recruit like Fitzpatrick was certainly vulnerable to a suggestion that he could strengthen his rather shaky position in the force by exploiting his friendship with Ned Kelly.

That Monday in Benalla Ned became drunk, which was unusual. He did not 'care about grog' and was never seen drunk on any other occasion. In an interesting coincidence, when Ned rode his horse across a footpath Alex Fitzpatrick was on hand to arrest his friend, claiming, 'I looked after him in the lock-up and treated him kindly.' If this helped make Ned a compliant prisoner overnight, it was a different story in the morning when he woke up, 'still dazed', and weighed the strange events of the previous day. He reached an almost inevitable conclusion. 'I think I was drugged.'

When it was time to bring Ned from the lock-up to face the Bench at the Police Court a few hundred yards away, Sergeant Whelan took unusual precautions. Leaving only one man to mind the station, he prepared to escort Ned, assisted by Fitzpatrick, Mounted Constable Lonigan and the watchhouse keeper, Constable Day. Ned was clearly in a dangerous mood and, in spite of the four-man escort, Fitzpatrick suggested that his prisoner should be handcuffed. This odd behaviour by his 'friend' must have suggested to Ned that Fitzpatrick had been involved in drugging his drink. In a surge of anger, he broke away and charged around the corner from the police station into a bootmaker's shop almost opposite the court, pursued by the policemen.

The four police and the bootmaker hurled themselves onto Ned in a continuing struggle to manacle him and the six bodies crashed around the small, weatherboard shop, between the counter, walls and workbench, in a prolonged shambles. Three years later solicitor and parliamentarian David Gaunson gave Ned's account of the battle:

> In the course of this attempted arrest Fitzpatrick endeavoured to catch hold of me by the foot, and in the struggle he tore the sole and heel of my boot clean off. With one well directed blow I sent him sprawling against the wall . . .

Earlier Ned claimed, 'Fitzpatrick is the only one out of the five I hit in Benalla, this shows my feelings towards him . . .' and suggested that the punch knocked Fitzpatrick unconscious, commenting drily, 'He is very subject to fainting.' In the course of the struggle Ned's trousers had been 'almost torn off' and Constable Lonigan used an old English police tactic to subdue a particularly violent prisoner: he 'blackballed' Ned — that is, grabbed him by the testicles. 'He inflicted terrible pain on me: but still I would not surrender . . .'

In a widely quoted piece of apocrypha, Ned is supposed to have roared, 'Well, Lonigan, I never shot a man yet; but if ever I do, so help me God, you will be the first!' Ned goes on to describe the extraordinary finale to this epic brawl.

> While the struggle was still going on a miller [Justice of the Peace, William Magennis] came in, and, seeing how I was being ill-treated, said the police should be ashamed of themselves, and he endeavoured to pacify them and induce me to be handcuffed. I allowed this man to put the handcuffs on me, though I refused to submit to the police.

After this supreme gesture of contempt for his police enemies and of respect for justice, Ned accompanied Magennis across the street to the court house to stand his trial. Ned's symbolic surrender to due process of law seems to have impressed the Bench. He pleaded guilty to being Drunk and Disorderly and was fined only 1 shilling or four hours imprisonment. He also cheerfully admitted to assaulting the Police in the Execution of their Duty and was fined £2 or one month, with 5 shillings 'for damage to Constable Fitzpatrick's clothing'. He was then found guilty of Resisting the Police in the Execution of their Duty and fined an additional £2 or one month.

Ned paid his debt of 4 pounds 6 shillings to society and walked from the court, convicted of a 'paltry crime' but with his 'flashness' undiminished and his local 'prestige' greater than ever. If Fitzpatrick did contrive Ned's arrest, with or without Whelan's influence, the plan had backfired.

Just over a week later the family were in trouble again. On the evening of Thursday 27 September Dan and his cousins, Tom and Jack Lloyd, became involved in a mysterious fracas with Mrs Amelia Goodman while her husband, Winton storekeeper and hawker Davis Goodman, was away. Mrs Goodman had asked Dan to bring her some meat and the three cousins arrived at the house, allegedly drunk and rowdy. They punched in a door panel, threw some furniture around and broke windows. A visiting Jewish hawker, Moris or Moses Solomon, became involved and Dan supposedly knocked him down. Mrs Goodman described him lying on the floor, saying 'his brains were out'. When Goodman returned two days later he spun a fantastic tale to the police. The Benalla Bench issued warrants charging the cousins with Breaking and Entering the Goodman dwelling and stealing an incredible array of goods valued at £133, including a case of boots, six coats, fourteen pairs of trousers and several watches. Goodman capped it all off with an allegation that Tom Lloyd had attempted to rape his wife. Dan was also charged with assaulting Moris Solomon. The three lads went bush, probably to the hut on Bullock Creek.

Under the headline 'BUSHRANGING AND BURGLARY', Beechworth's *Advertiser* trumpeted its indignation.

> In the neighbourhood of Greta for many years there has lived a regular Gang of young ruffians, who from their infancy were brought up as rogues and vagabonds, and who have been constantly in trouble, and on Sunday we learnt that, though it is but a short time since some of them have been released from gaol, where they have been serving sentences for horse stealing, a little game with which they are thoroughly *au fait*, they have again indulged in their pranks.

After giving Goodman's version of the 'burglary' by the 'young wretches', the upright *Advertiser* declared: 'The matter is in the hands of the police, and we trust the rascals will soon be brought to justice.'

Ned called at the Wangaratta office of the paper and, after asking to see the piece, told the *Advertiser*'s 'representative' that, 'It was too bad to publish paragraphs so far apart from the truth ... he knew the circumstances of the case, and the paragraph was very much exaggerated.'

Ned refused an approach from Inspector Brooke Smith to 'give the boys up'. The next week he was riding out of Benalla when he met Constable Fitzpatrick on the road. The brawl with the police that had followed Ned's highly suspicious drunkenness was, literally, a painful memory: he still suffered 'excruciating pain and inconvenience' from the injury to his testicles — and would endure it for over a year. Despite this, three weeks after that bitter clash, Fitzpatrick managed to persuade Ned that the boys should surrender to face trial. The trooper reported:

> I told him I did not think there was anything serious against them, so accordingly the following morning he brought them into Benalla, came galloping up to the police station and told me he wanted me, so I went down the street with him. He said that the three of them had ridden in that morning from their own place, or wherever they had been hiding ... so I arrested the three of them, read the charges to them and brought them to the lock-up.

On 19 October Dan, Tom and Jack stood trial. They were promptly found not guilty of Breaking and Entering and Stealing, but Police Magistrate Butler was quite undeterred by the fact that the prosecution case had been exposed as an elaborate fabrication. (Goodman eventually received three years for perjury, his wife escaped a similar charge on a technicality and Moris Solomon had disappeared.) Butler now found the three boys guilty of Damaging Property to the value of £10, ordered each of them to pay 5 pounds 10 shillings damages *and* serve three months hard labour. Tom was remanded on the Assault with Intent to Rape charge and, five months later, received an additional four months hard labour for Common Assault. Ned's second gesture of respect for the process of law had gained nothing — except to provide further evidence that the scales of justice were weighted against his family. One other thing was clear: Alex Fitzpatrick had used up his last chance with Ned, having thrown the second punch. His next blow at Ned or his family would invite disaster.

The fate of Dan and his cousins probably put an end to a spring-time romance. Kate Kelly, a striking 14-year-old, had caught the eye of Fitzpatrick almost immediately after his arrival in Benalla. Joseph Ashmead, now 18, witnessed or was told of one of their meetings near Eleven Mile Creek in September that year.

> Under the shade of a big box tree a young man is seated on a horse. He is tall and dark; there is something striking about his face; you would not call it handsome as there is something about his eyes that is hard to understand. Every few minutes he looked up the valley as if expecting someone. Now let us look at the horse. It is a lovely dappled bay. It tosses its head and paws the ground with its front feet. It is well shod and well groomed. By appearance we would say it was a trooper's horse. We look closely and see by the brands that it is. The horse lifts up its head and gives a loud neigh. We hear the sound of horses hoofs and see a horse-man coming down the creek, but when the rider draws near we see it is not a man, but a woman riding astride. This is an uncommon sight, for in those days, riding astride was regarded as an offence against decency, but this is a girl only in her teens, and a girl of bewitching beauty. Her features are well rounded, her eyes are large and dark and her long, black, wavy hair is glossy and the flush of health is in her face. She looks a perfect picture. By the way they meet we see they are not perfect strangers. Their horses are drawn up close together. The man places his hand on her horse's bridle and whispers in her ear the old, old story of love, and the girl draws back with a long, harsh laugh. Her eyes then fill with tears . . .

Ashmead imagines a brief conversation between the pair about the futil-ity of their relationship. He then describes how Kate broke off a small switch of wattle, flicked it at Fitzpatrick as he pleaded for a kiss, then touched her horse 'and was gone like a flash'.

According to Ashmead, Kate saw the relationship as 'impossible'. But Alex Fitzpatrick was not easily deterred and, as he had demonstrated with Ned, was also a highly persuasive young man. His infatuation with Kate continued and proved to be a dangerous factor in the coming Trouble.

———————◆———————

IN OCTOBER £170 worth of horses disappeared in a single night from a number of properties between Greta and Moyhu. The job was as big as 'the Whitty larceny' but attracted no special attention. Ned might have been involved or it might have been George King settling a few local scores, a farewell performance by the horse-stealing maestro before he vanished from Ellen's life, leaving her three months pregnant.

Stung by this latest blow, and with no apparent progress in police pursuit of the Myrrhee thieves, the gentlemen of Moyhu took the matter into their own hands and met to discuss the formation of 'a league for the prevention of sheep, cattle and horse stealing'. Similar organisations in New South Wales and other parts of Victoria had proved effective and 'all the chief farmers of the locality' supported the idea. Whitty, as usual, adopted a low profile, but the subsequent inaugural meeting of the North Eastern Stock Protection League was held in his son's hotel, while he and John Byrne became the committee members for Moyhu and Andrew Byrne was elected president. The League would offer 'substantial rewards' for the conviction of anyone taking subscribers' stock: 'and otherwise ... assist the owner to regain his property and prosecute the thief'. Without even waiting for the official formation of the League, Whitty took his own steps to encourage pursuit of the Myrrhee raiders. On 24 October he had advertised a £20 reward — several thousand dollars today — 'on conviction of the thief', at the same time betraying the total lack of evidence by adding, 'and £1 per head if strayed'. The police investigation swung into high gear over the next week, perhaps by coincidence.

Two months before the Whitty robbery Allen Lowry had taken a horse from James Whitty's son, Mark. Ingratiating himself with Whitty, Uncle Pat Quinn informed on Lowry and suggested that the horse could be found at Howlong — already highlighted in the combined New South Wales–Victoria investigation. Here, the police found the German Petersen able and anxious to help in their investigations. By 4 November, New South Wales police were questioning Samuel Kennedy, who had bought two of the Myrrhee horses from 'George Stuckey', and over the next five days they caught up with William Everitt and John Studders, each of whom had bought two horses from Baumgarten.

On 10 November a plainclothed Victorian constable turned up at the Baumgartens' with a story that his father 'had bought a station near Hay' and was 'badly in want of draught horses'. Baumgarten offered to sell the undercover policeman his two remaining Whitty draught horses. He was arrested and, with Kennedy and Studders, charged with the Myrrhee theft. It is illuminating that William Everitt was not arrested although, like Studders, he had bought two horses from Baumgarten. Studders had a prior conviction for horse theft — as a boy of 14!

Soon after, a warrant was issued for Wild Wright. James Whitty had offered a £2 reward for his arrest before he was found to be in the Jamieson lock-up, serving one month for Assault. Big Mick Woodyard was the next member of the Gang to be hunted — at first for the theft of three horses from Ned's uncle, Jack Quinn, and by 4 December a warrant was out for Allen Lowry. He was arrested four days later by Detective Brown, who had been sent up from Melbourne to help wrap up this high-profile case.

On a bend of the Murray between Barnawartha and Wodonga, two of the horses taken from Greta the previous month were found floating in the river with their heads cut off and brands sliced out — an ugly symptom of panic among thieves or fences. Ned and Joe Byrne, however, kept their nerve and remained around Greta, moving between there and the King River, where Joe showed his coolness by lifting a chestnut worth £20. They might even have shared a drink at O'Brien's hotel with scruffy Constable Thom, whose easy way with the locals annoyed Sergeant Arthur Steele.

Steele, a haughty, dark-bearded Englishman with the eyes and nose of a hawk, had been promoted to Second-Class Sergeant and put in charge of Wangaratta the previous November. The son of a high-ranking army officer, he displayed a tweedy charm to people of what he considered his own class. A hawker Steele moved on when he tried to camp under a local bridge thought the sergeant had 'more side than a billiard ball'; a priest considered him 'a very dour man'. Steele's 'strenuous efforts' to break up what the local *Dispatch* called a 'ring' of horse thieves in the district quickly earned the approval of squatters and the disapproval of others, marked by a brick shattering his window one night in March.

Steele's efforts had paid off in July when Steve Hart, a mate of Dan Kelly, was charged with Horse Stealing and convicted of Illegally Using. Steve, a small, dark, bow-legged 16-year-old, lived with his Irish parents on the Three Mile Creek between Wangaratta and the Warby Ranges. He was a sometime jockey and brilliant horseman, a decent, slow-speaking boy whose size, abilities and temperament made him a perfect companion for the horse-loving, more assertive Dan. One of the Hart girls would claim that Sergeant Steele 'had a down on Steve' ever since the lad had tied the tail of Steele's horse to a fence one night. The sergeant went to ride off and couldn't move.

Steve had barely left the dock after being sentenced to four months in Beechworth Gaol when he was arrested on another Horse Stealing charge. He would end up with a twelve-month sentence on thirteen counts of Illegally Using, a small triumph for Sergeant Steele and yet another warning for Ned and Dan.

Since the arrest of Baumgarten, Steele had been pursuing the mysterious 'J. Thompson'. He suspected Ned and combed the district with Detective Brown, making inquiries. The sergeant was always superbly mounted and rode like a cavalryman. He was easily recognised, even in plain clothes, and constantly irritated by children dashing off across the paddocks to warn of his approach. For the moment Steele's suspicions of Ned were unsupported by evidence, but as the Gang members and their associates were rounded up it must be only a matter of time before someone talked.

◆

IN THIS UNEASY SUMMER of 1877–8 Ned carried out his last building job: a new home for his mother. Joe Byrne, Brickey Williamson and Bill Skilling probably helped him to build a neat cottage on the far bank of Eleven Mile Creek, opposite the old hut — its walls of split and adzed ironbark slabs (each inch-thick slab weighing a daunting 40 to 50 lbs), with interior walls of bark sheets and a roof of stringybark. There were two main rooms — a living/dining room/kitchen to the left, a bedroom to the right — and a short passage leading to the back door with a bedroom to either side under a sloping skillion roof. Ned gave the house a broad, unfloored verandah with nicely chamfered posts and a chimney of slabs and split palings lined with tin, built around a roomy, stone fireplace. It was a classic Australian homestead — a small palace compared to every other home Ellen had lived in, and something to cheer her in the last few months of her last pregnancy.

Then, with pegs driven through auger holes to hold the roof's jockey poles and riders firm, the doors carpentered and the bought, twelve-paned windows fitted, Ned and Joe quietly prepared to leave the Eleven Mile.

Ned probably waited for Dan's return home from Beechworth Gaol in late January of 1878 before he and Joe rode off with a last string of horses to sell. Soon after the Myrrhee mob had been traced by the police, Ned had written to a Lake Rowan auctioneer to arrange the sale of his remaining horses. He recorded: 'I bought some of them to that place [Lake Rowan] but did not sell. I sold some of them in Benalla, Melbourne and other places and left the colony and became a rambling gambler.'

Perhaps, as Superintendent Hare believed, Ned meant that he and Joe headed up into New South Wales, literally gambling their way from town to town with the proceeds of the sale. More likely, as writer Frank Clune suggests, 'rambling gambler' was just a whimsical piece of rhyming slang for a few footloose months of vagabonding — across the Riverina, up to the Murrumbidgee valley and Wagga Wagga where one of Joe's uncles had settled, then on to the Darling.

◆

THE FORCES that eventually destroyed Ned and Joe were quickly gathering strength. On 15 March 1878 a warrant for Ned was sworn at Chiltern, charging him with the Myrrhee thefts. Three weeks later there was an unexpected turn. Back in August 1877 two lads had been seen near Chiltern, driving some horses towards the Murray. Now, after eight months, it was decided that the horses *resembled* some of those taken in 'the Whitty Larceny' and that the boys *resembled* Dan Kelly and Jack Lloyd. On 5 April warrants were issued, commanding 'in Her Majesty's name' Senior Constable James Lynch of Chiltern and 'all other peace officers' in the colony to bring the boys before C. G. Darvall J.P. of Chiltern 'or some other of Her Majesty's Justices of the Peace … to answer to the said information and to be further dealt with according to law'.

Within the month Jack Lloyd was arrested, to face the Chiltern Bench on 25 April and be discharged, 'as his accusers failed to identify him'. Dan, too, was arrested and there can be little doubt that, if he had stood trial, he would have walked from the court a free man, like his cousin. But this simple process of law was interrupted by a mysterious incident.

7

THE FITZPATRICK MYSTERY

15 APRIL 1878

I n the late afternoon of Monday 15 April 1878, Constable Alexander Fitzpatrick rode his dappled bay along the road from Winton and entered the broad valley that ran by Eleven Mile Creek towards Greta. Aglow with autumn sunshine and brandy, Alex passed the Skillings' hut, then Brickey Williamson's place, and came in sight of the two Kelly houses squatted on either bank of the meandering creek.

Since leaving Benalla three hours earlier on his way to Greta police station, Alex had planned a visit to the Kellys — confident that Ned was still away, hoping to find Dan home and always eager to see Kate. Her feelings towards him would have cooled even further if she had heard rumours of his involvement with two other girls — a lass from Meredith he had left with a baby, and his fiancée in Frankston who was four months pregnant. These personal problems would soon reach the desk of the Chief Commissioner, and Alex was again in trouble with Sergeant Whelan, but if everything went according to plan, this visit to the Kellys would change everything and put his police career back on the rails.

With alcoholic optimism and more than a dash of fatalism, Alex swung his horse from the road on the track that dipped across the creek towards the new Kelly homestead. Unnoticed under the creekside willows were the graves of Annie Gunn and her baby, which would influence the events of this dying day.

In the brutal summer of 1877–8 Victoria had yet again found itself in a state of crisis. The colony's economic troubles were deepening as gold yields continued to dwindle and bad seasons wrought havoc with farmers and graziers alike, who were overcropping and overstocking to combat falling prices. Embezzlement, bankruptcy and suicide became increasingly common, while paranoia over the activities of a Russian naval force, 'the flying squadron', demanded £350 000 to fortify Port Phillip Bay.

Now came a new political flashpoint in a colony that had seen ten governments in as many years. The doleful-looking English radical,

Graham Berry, who had been premier for two months in 1875, was a key figure. Returned to power in 1877 and, allied with the equally radical David Syme of the *Age* newspaper, he locked horns with the squatter-dominated Upper House over the payment of members of parliament. The House fought back and refused to grant his government supply.

In a bizarre attempt to eke out government finances and rid himself of some conservative stalwarts, Berry sacked hundreds of public servants, including all County Court judges, Police Magistrates, Coroners and Crown Prosecutors. The axe first fell on Wednesday 8 January 1878, immortalised as 'Black Wednesday'. The colony's financial problems, now seen as the 'Berry Blight', deepened.

Berry's most outlandish plan was to disband the Police Department. Superintendent Sadleir claimed that the department was saved only because Chief Commissioner Standish had helped to hush up a scandal involving 'a high official' of the colony, 'a man notoriously of unclean life', who had been found in a gentleman's home at night in what were called 'ambiguous circumstances'. When the schedule for disbanding the Police Department came before this official, he used his power to veto it, with or without prompting from Standish. The force narrowly survived but continued to be weakened by attrition and retrenchment. As Sadleir commented, 'The shadow of Black Wednesday was still over the service, no officer felt secure in his position under the Berry regime.'

Few would have felt less secure than Constable Fitzpatrick, whose first year in the force had been a chapter of unreliability, bad company, narrow scrapes and a fondness for liquor. Now, in mid-April, he was in hot water again.

When Inspector Brooke Smith in Beechworth gave Senior Constable Strahan six days leave from Greta to look for Ned Kelly in New South Wales, he scanned his remaining men to find a replacement, like a chess player nearing defeat. Constable Fitzpatrick was due back at Benalla on Saturday 13 April, after duty at the two-day Cashel race meeting. He would do. On the Thursday, Sergeant Whelan in Benalla received a telegram:

> As soon as M.C. Fitzpatrick returns send him to Greta. S.C. Strahan will have left.
>
> *A. Brooke Smith Inspr.*

However, young Alex Fitzpatrick found his own pressing reasons to spend Saturday night at Cashel. When he had failed to return by 2 p.m. on Sunday, an exasperated Whelan sent Constable Healy 'on patrol' to Greta with orders to return tomorrow.

Only two hours after Healy left, Fitzpatrick turned up at Benalla, full of implausible excuses. Conscious of his shaky position in these difficult times and anxious to convince Whelan that he was really a diligent policeman, Alex set about reading the 10 April issue of the *Police Gazette* and noticed an item reporting the issue of warrants for Dan Kelly and Jack Lloyd over the Whitty case. He had seen the two lads at the Cashel races and his route to the Greta police station passed the Kelly homestead. Here was a god-given chance to redeem himself.

According to Fitzpatrick, Whelan agreed to a suggestion that he should try to arrest Dan, 'and told me to be careful'. When a Royal Commission suggested that Fitzpatrick had disobeyed orders by calling at the Kelly house instead of going straight to Greta, Whelan strongly defended the constable's actions. Whether or not the sergeant actually gave Fitzpatrick permission to arrest Dan, he certainly condoned the attempt.

At 1 p.m. on Monday 15 April, Constable Healy returned to Benalla and at 2 p.m. Fitzpatrick set off for Greta. A relieved Whelan took Brooke Smith's four-day-old telegram, folded it diagonally and scrawled across the back the information that Trooper Fitzpatrick was at last on his way to take over the unmanned station.

At 2 a.m. the next morning, Whelan was awakened by a pounding on the door of his married quarters. It was Fitzpatrick — pale, shaken, smelling of brandy, with a bandaged wrist, a damaged helmet and a story 'that he had been shot at by Ned Kelly and wounded in the arm'. Whelan sent for Dr Nicholson and took Fitzpatrick's statement. It is a strange tale.

On his way to Greta he has 'some brandy and lemonade' at Lindsay's shanty at Winton and reaches the Kelly homestead 'at 4 or 5'. Mrs Kelly is there with 'three children' (actually her two-day-old baby, Alice King, three-year-old John, 4-year-old Ellen, 12-year-old Grace and 14-year-old Kate). After spending 'about an hour' with Mrs Kelly and Kate 'to see if there was any chance of Dan putting in an appearance', Fitzpatrick investigates a sound of chopping and finds Brickey Williamson splitting fence rails on a hill near the Kellys'. By now the sun is setting. As Fitzpatrick turns back towards the road he sees two horsemen arrive at the Kelly homestead.

By the time Fitzpatrick has ridden over, only one man is at the yards with the horses, a man he swears to be Bill Skilling. Recognising Dan Kelly's horse, Fitzpatrick asks where he is. Skilling tells him, 'Up at the house'. Dan answers the door holding a knife and fork and submits to arrest on a charge of Horse Stealing with a calm, 'Very well ... I suppose you'll let me have something to eat. I've been out riding all day.' The two go inside. Dan sits at the table and Mrs Kelly calls Fitzpatrick 'a deceitful little bugger', declaring, 'you won't take him out of this tonight!' Dan continues to be a docile prisoner and tells her, 'Shut up, Mother, that's all right.'

Fitzpatrick sees Skilling pass the front door leading a horse. Suddenly, Ned Kelly appears in the doorway and, at a range of 1½ yards, fires a revolver at Fitzpatrick. He misses. As Ned says, 'Out of this, you bugger!' Mrs Kelly hits Fitzpatrick on the side of his helmet with the fire shovel ('like a contractor's shovel worn down') and when the trooper raises his arm to ward off another blow, a second shot fired by Ned strikes his left wrist. Dan has snatched the revolver from Fitzpatrick's holster. The trooper grapples with Ned and the revolver goes off a third time. By now Skilling has appeared behind Ned in the doorway and Brickey Williamson has emerged from the bedroom, both armed with revolvers.

There follows some extraordinary dialogue in which Ned turns angrily on Skilling. 'You bugger, why did you not tell me who was here? If I had known it was Fitzpatrick I would not have fired a bloody shot.' Ned examines Fitzpatrick's wrist and says, 'Here's a bullet here. We must have it out of that,' wanting to perform the operation with a rusty razor. Fitzpatrick hastily offers to remove the bullet himself and cuts it out with his own penknife. It is 'a small, pointed ball'. Mrs Kelly bandages the wound.

Ned urges Fitzpatrick to fabricate a story in which he is ambushed 'by two big men, one like me, and they will think it is my brother Jem. Say that was the man who stole Jackson and Frost's horses and altered the brands from G to OO, one a little chestnut horse with a bad back, which he sold to Kennedy on the other side of the Murray.' Ned makes Fitzpatrick write this odd tale in his notebook and promises him 'a few hundred [pounds] which I will have after the Baumgarten case is over' if he doesn't mention 'this case'.

Fitzpatrick is released about 10 p.m. Pursued by Skilling and Williamson, he gallops to Lindsay's shanty. Lindsay rebandages the wound, gives him some food and brandy and escorts him to Benalla.

Questioned on details of his statement, Fitzpatrick subsequently admitted, 'Miss Kelly [Kate] was in the house when the firing was going on.' Asked what she did, he said simply, 'she sat down and cried'. On the strength of Fitzpatrick's story, Ned and Dan Kelly, Mrs Kelly, Skilling and Williamson were charged with Attempted Murder.

Fitzpatrick's evidence has been widely discredited through the years, most often for the ridiculous claim that Ned Kelly could 'miss a man three times at a yard-and-a-half'. This, of course, is not what Fitzpatrick said, though Ned's missing him *once* at such short range seems unlikely. Ned's supposed friendliness towards Fitzpatrick is preposterous. The constable told the Royal Commission, 'I was on friendly terms with him in this respect, that I had arrested Ned Kelly for being drunk *and I never pressed the charge against him; and he said I was the only man up in the district any good.*' [my italics] Most preposterous of all is the claim that Ned tried to incriminate his brother for the shooting and on horse-stealing charges — even ignoring the fact that Jim was serving four years hard labour at the time.

Fitzpatrick's wound has always been seriously suspect, largely because of Dr John Nicholson's frequently quoted trial evidence:

> Examined his left wrist. Found two wounds, one a jagged one, and the other a clean incision. They were about an inch and a half apart; one was on the outside of the wrist, and the other near the centre. They *might* have been produced by a bullet, that is the outside wound. [my italics]

The unusual nature of the wound and Dr Nicholson's apparent reluctance to say that it had been caused by a bullet would lead to suspicions that Fitzpatrick had created the wound with his penknife or enlarged some slight injury.

There was difficulty in confirming that three shots had been fired in the Kelly homestead. Fitzpatrick claimed to have seen 'a bullet mark' in the bark partition behind him, but when he returned to the house some days later he alleged that two sheets of bark had been removed from the partition. Subsequently, on 13 May Constable Flood would find a bullet mould in the homestead and cast two bullets from it — one of which would be claimed to match the 'small, pointed ball' which wounded Fitzpatrick.

When police went to the Kelly homestead the day after the 'incident', Ned and Dan had disappeared. That night and before dawn next morning Williamson, Skilling and Mrs Kelly (with her three-day-old baby) were arrested, to face almost six months of committal and remand before trial for Attempted Murder.

Their defence was organised and orchestrated by Ned. He based it almost entirely on the greatest single flaw in Fitzpatrick's evidence. Skilling had not been present at the 'row'. It would be confirmed, many years later, that, in the dusk and firelight, Fitzpatrick had mistaken Joe Byrne for Skilling. Knowing this, it seemed that 'if one part of the evidence of the Crown is proved false, the jury cannot believe the rest'. As a secondary plank of the defence, it was claimed that Ned Kelly, too, had been absent from the Kelly house and therefore could not have shot Fitzpatrick.

Apart from Fitzpatrick, no eye witness of the fracas was called. Ned and Dan were fugitives; Joe Byrne was by now wanted for horse stealing and, if he came forward he would simply have had to join his friends in the dock as one of the accused. Of the two other competent eye witnesses, Kate and Grace, neither was called by the defence in spite of an invitation to do so by the Crown Prosecutor. This seems odd, but Ned had decided that the true story should not be told. His version, which underlay the defence of the three accused, remained untold until three months after the trial when he described the 'row' in a letter to parliamentarian Donald Cameron.

> The man who the trooper swore was Skillion [Skilling] can prove Williamson's innocence ... The trooper after speaking to this man rode to the house and Dan came out. He asked Dan to go to Greta with him ... They both went inside and Dan was having something to eat ... Mrs Kelly said he need not go unless he liked without a warrant. She told the trooper he had no business on her premises without some authority beside his own word. He pulled out his revolver and said he would blow her brains out if she interfered in the arrest. Mrs Kelly said that if Ned was here he would ram the revolver down his throat. To frighten the trooper Dan said Ned is coming now. The trooper looked around to see if it was true. Dan dropped the knife and fork which showed he had no murderous intention, clapped Heenan's Hug [a wrestling hold] on him took his revolver and threw him and part of the door outside and kept him there until Skillion and Ryan came with horses which Dan sold that night. The trooper left and invented some scheme to say he got shot when any man can see it was impossible for him to have been shot.

Ned went on to claim, 'I knew nothing of this transaction until very close on the trial I *then* being over 400 miles from Greta.' [my italics]

So much for Ned's account of what happened. Even his greatest supporters and apologists would come to accept that his version of the 'brawl' — like Fitzpatrick's — was far from the truth. Ned's scenario set out to contradict Fitzpatrick's evidence and, in trying to clear his mother, brother-in-law and friend, he reduced the clash to a bloodless, shotless scuffle, seeing his absence as the ultimate contradiction of Fitzpatrick's story.

Tom Lloyd was not an eye witness, but no one would prove more loyal to Ned, or to his memory. Tom's version of the brawl, which was published by the writer J. J. Kenneally in 1929, must be taken very seriously. Kenneally's account broadly follows Fitzpatrick's evidence until his return to the Kelly house (though omitting all mention of Skilling or Williamson). Fitzpatrick is seated, waiting for Dan to eat his dinner, when Kate passes him 'in the exercise of her domestic duties'. According to Kenneally, Fitzpatrick 'seized her and pulled her on to his knee. Kate resented this and Dan, in defence of his sister, sprang at the constable ... and threw [him] to the floor. Fitzpatrick, on regaining his feet, drew his revolver just as Ned appeared at the door. The constable levelled his revolver at Ned Kelly, but Dan Kelly struck him a violent blow as he fired, and the bullet lodged in the roof. The two brothers then seized the constable, and disarmed him.' Fitzpatrick's wound is caused when he strikes his left wrist 'against the projecting part of the door lock'.

This account departs from Ned's on four points: The 'row' is triggered by Fitzpatrick making an advance to Kate; a shot is fired; Fitzpatrick's wrist is injured; and, most importantly, Ned is present. In following Tom Lloyd's narrative, Kenneally not only ignored Ned's version but deleted it from the text of the Cameron letter published in his book, dropping with it all references to Ned being 400 miles from Greta when he heard of 'this transaction'.

Tom Lloyd wasn't the only member of the Kelly circle to contradict Ned's revamping of the Fitzpatrick brawl. In 1911, more than ten years before Kenneally spoke to Tom Lloyd, Mrs Kelly had given a brief description of the clash in a unique interview with Sydney journalist, B. W. Cookson. She, too, departed from Ned's version of events and admitted that he was present:

> Fitzpatrick started the trouble. He had no business there at all, they tell me — no warrant or anything. If he had he should have done his business and gone. He tried to kiss my daughter Kate. She was a fine, good-looking girl, Kate; and the boys tried to stop him. He was a fool. They were only trying to protect their sister. He was drunk and they were sober.

Even Ned, while continuing to deny that he was there, may have confirmed that the ruckus had been triggered by Fitzpatrick's advances to Kate. At Jerilderie in February 1879 he is supposed to have told a captive audience:

> I swear I was 400 miles away from home when I heard of how he treated my sister. I hurried home and found I had been accused of shooting Fitzpatrick, I don't like to present a revolver at any man, as it naturally makes him tremble, unless I am compelled to do so, and what must have been the feelings of my sister — a mere child — when she had a revolver put to her head, demanding her to submit her virtue, or be shot by Fitzpatrick. I don't deny having stolen horses and sold them, but shooting Fitzpatrick I am entirely innocent. When outlawed I was only three weeks married.

A fantastic detail — Ned's marriage — discredits this story, but there is a ring of genuine Kelly rhetoric in his remarks about Kate and Fitzpatrick.

Jim Kelly was to take the story a step further. He learnt what had happened when he was released from prison in 1880 and he gave his version in 1909. It was reported twenty-one years later. While Mrs Kelly is 'in another part of the house', Kate and Fitzpatrick are alone.

He tried to put his arm around her and she gave him a punch that sent him reeling ... he told her that if she would consent to certain suggestions, he would go back and say that Dan was away, and could not be got. He did not know my sister for she hurled herself on him in a wicked temper, and it was then that the struggle began in which he attempted to assault her.

Hearing the scuffle, Ellen Kelly enters the room.

There was a heavy spade standing in one corner, and my mother seized it, and with a mighty swing of it struck the officer to the ground. Almost at the same moment a shot rang out and *I saw* Ned standing in the doorway. He had fired his shot just at the same moment as my mother had swung at the policeman with the spade. (my italics)

Allowing for embroidery by Jim and lapse of memory by the recorder (Fitzpatrick is 'killed outright' by the shot) here is a second account of Kate's and Ned's involvement. Many years later Jim also admitted to a relative that Ned shot Fitzpatrick after he had made an advance to Kate. Kate herself seems to have made similar admissions only ten months after the events of 15 April. A group of travellers who had met Kate previously called at the Kelly homestead in February 1879 to buy 'some milk and other refreshments' and found her willing to discuss 'the outrages alleged to have been committed on herself by members of the police force'. This conversation was reported in Melbourne's *Herald*. The story might be dismissed as a flight of fancy by the travellers or the journalist, but some details prove that the interview did take place, including Kate's bitterness at the recent disappearance of a chestnut pony, a theft documented in the *Police Gazette* three months later. Here, third hand, is Kate's story.

She was in the house alone when Fitzpatrick came, and he commenced in a violent manner to behave improperly. Just then her brother Ned came to the door, and caught Fitzpatrick in the act of attempting an outrage, whereupon he, with the natural instinct of a brother in such circumstances, rushed for his revolver. Fitzpatrick ... immediately bethought himself of the warrant which he pulled out and held up to Ned, saying at the same time, 'I've got this for you'. At this moment Ned Kelly, having seized the revolver, fired, and this was how it came that Fitzpatrick was shot in the wrist.

Despite the inaccurate detail about the warrant, the tone of the piece is sympathetic to Kate — at that time an 'unfashionable' position — and there is no reason to doubt that at least the main thrust of her account has been preserved.

On the day after the incident Brickey Williamson told police that 'he heard no shots fired' at the Kelly house. However, in 1881 while trying to gain a remission of his prison sentence, Brickey gave a highly detailed account of what had happened, claiming that he was present at the beginning of the heated argument between Mrs Kelly and Fitzpatrick. The trooper had drawn his revolver and Mrs Kelly was about to hit him with a spade when Williamson stepped between them and took it from her.

> Two of Mrs Kelly's children, two and four years of age, were screaming. I took them in my arms and went out of the house to quiet them. Soon after this Ned Kelly rushed around the corner of the house to the door and fired two shots.

Williamson later added the words 'at Fitzpatrick'. It is clear that he was telling the authorities what they wanted to believe. But this part of his story retains a ring of truth.

The misty events of 15 April are now taking sharper focus. Everyone admits that a brawl took place. Fitzpatrick's advances to Kate provide a credible and well-attested starting point. The involvement of Dan is admitted by most parties. Williamson says he was there. Joe Byrne, mistaken for Skilling, was also present. Two key areas of doubt remain.

First, was Ned involved? The accounts from Tom Lloyd, Mrs Kelly, Jim Kelly, Kate Kelly and Williamson suggest that Ned was present. At Mrs Kelly's trial, one of Ned's witnesses would testify that Ned was not at the house, *though he was in the Greta district the day of the brawl*. Ned subsequently let slip to a policeman that he was present during or immediately after the incident. ('I almost swore after letting him [Fitzpatrick] go that I would never let another go.') Did he then shoot Fitzpatrick? There is sworn evidence from two policemen that, after his capture two years later, he admitted to the shooting. ('Yes, it was I that fired at him.') This confession may be discredited as another example of police perjury about the Kellys, but it supports stories told by Kate, Jim and Brickey Williamson (even though, as we have seen, none of their stories can be accepted as reliable).

One more scrap of evidence was found buried in police files — an apparently trivial document which throws new light on the events of 15 April. On 24 May Fitzpatrick wrote a memo to the Officer in Charge at Beechworth where he was on transfer:

Application of Constable Fitzpatrick for the cost of a new uniform jumper [tunic].

> I respectfully request the Officer in Charge, would be good enough to recommend me to the favourable consideration of the Chief Commissioner of Police, for reimbursement of the cost of a new uniform jumper as the one I wore on the occasion of the affray with the Kellys at

Greta was destroyed *haveing been shot through the sleeve* and otherwise damaged and has to be kept for evidence against them. [my italics]

A. Fitzpatrick
Mtd. Const 2867

The Chief Commissioner approved the application two weeks later and 25 shillings was supplied for a new jumper. The damaged uniform would be produced as an exhibit at the subsequent trial, though little attention would be paid to it, then or in the years to come. It disappeared. A slight wrist injury suffered by Fitzpatrick during the scuffle could have been enlarged to suggest a bullet wound, but it is less believable that he also would have faked a bullet hole in the sleeve of his uniform. The wound was 'just on the edge of the knucklebone' of his wrist, a point exposed in the action of 'throwing up' his arm, so there would have been no need to destroy the sleeve to make this injury believable. It is also significant that the memo is the only time the bullet-holed sleeve was mentioned by Fitzpatrick. If he had manufactured it to support his story, he would have made rather better use of it and at least referred to it in his evidence.

The case for a genuine bullet wound is strengthening. Why then did Dr John Nicholson express doubts that a bullet had caused the constable's wrist injury? The answer lies in the doctor's original deposition of 17 May 1878, sworn before three Justices of the Peace.

I examined the left wrist there appeared to be a bullet wound — the bullet had apparently entered at the ['left' crossed out] out side of the wrist in the end of the bone that curved upwards in a slanting direction & lodged in the back of the wrist under the skin the entrance wound was slightly elongated in the course of the bullet. At the exit end there was a clean incision a little more than half-an-inch in length — the incision was not in a direct line but slightly cut to the left — wound was quite fresh — none of the deep structures were injured I dressed the wound & attended to ['him' crossed out] it for a few days it went on satisfactorily and healed — It could not have been produced by the first bullet produced the second one could have caused it.

Cross-examined, Nicholson said, 'Could not swear it was a bullet wound.' However, as the Bench went to prepare the deposition for his signature, he saw fit to add, *'but it had all the appearance of one'*. (my italics) So what reads as doubt in the press report of Nicholson's evidence emerges in the deposition as professional caution. The original wound appears to have been consistent with one produced by a projectile that had travelled under the skin for about 1½ inches (the distance given in the trial evidence), was clearly visible at its point of lodgement and could be removed by making a simple, short incision across the skin

A studio portrait of Kate Kelly, still in mourning for her brothers, two years after Fitzpatrick became infatuated with her. A quiet teenager, Kate was a brilliant horsewoman who preferred to ride astride, at that time an affront to prudery.

Maggie Skilling, Ned's formidable sister who headed the family during her brothers' outlawry and their mother's imprisonment. An expert bush horsewoman, she baffled police pursuit while carrying supplies to the Gang and created much of the legend attached to her younger sister, Kate. *(Elsie Pettifer/Leigh Olver)*

Steve Hart, Dan's mate, was a superb horseman and sometime jockey. Shown this photograph in December, 1878 — about a year after it was taken — Constable McIntyre commented 'Hart is now fuller in the face, stouter and somewhat older'.

Dan Kelly, Ned's younger brother, when he was about 16. The boy's over-large clothes symbolise his problem in following two older, bigger brothers. He tried too hard to match them, but on the last day of his life, at 19, proved himself a man of courage and decency. (*Police Museum*)

Aaron Sherritt, a phenomenally tough bushman, regarded Ned Kelly as 'superhuman'. Damned in folklore as the betrayer of the Kellys, he actually played a complex and dangerous double-agent role. Here he displays the 'badge' of the Kelly sympathiser, wearing his chinstrap under his nose.

stretched over the projectile. As Dr Nicholson said at the trial, in a neglected comment, 'The wounds are consistent with Fitzpatrick's statement', meaning that, in his opinion, the entry wound was caused by a bullet and the exit wound by a knife.

If the weight of evidence suggests that Ned fired at least one shot at Fitzpatrick, this does not mean that all of Fitzpatrick's story is true — only that it appears to be closer to the truth than Ned's version.

Fitzpatrick obviously spent longer at Lindsay's shanty than he cared to admit. He claims to have left Benalla at 2.30 p.m. while Whelan gives 2 p.m. as his departure time. Fitzpatrick says he reached Kellys' 'at 4 or 5'. Skilling saw Fitzpatrick ride past his house at about 5 p.m., meaning that he arrived at Kellys', half-a-mile away, some five minutes later.

The encounter with Williamson seems to be reported accurately, except for his later claim that Brickey was carrying a revolver. The meeting with Skilling was, of course, an encounter with Joe Byrne who, like Williamson, was probably unarmed.

The 'arrest' of Dan and the early exchange with Mrs Kelly may be described accurately, though Fitzpatrick fails to mention drawing his revolver.

Brickey Williamson confirmed that 'He drew his revolver and threatened to shoot her.' According to Ned, at this moment his mother 'was putting some fire on the oven in which she was baking bread' — using a shovel to pile hot coals on a camp oven. In Williamson's 1881 statement, 'She then took a spade and was going to hit him with it when I stepped between them and took it from her and threw it behind the fire.'

Immediately after, Brickey takes the crying children outside. Does this mean that he missed seeing Fitzpatrick making his advances to Kate? The flare-up he has described hardly sets the scene for dalliance. It seems most likely that, with his eye firmly set on gaining freedom from prison, Brickey, like Fitzpatrick, simply edited this inconvenient detail from his story.

If Dan was home — and everyone seems to agree with Fitzpatrick that he was — the constable would not have let his prisoner out of his sight. This means that the sexual overture to Kate must have been far more subtle than the attempted 'outrage' described in the more colourful versions. It may have occurred while Mrs Kelly was out of the room feeding baby Alice. Whatever Fitzpatrick attempted, Kate objected vigorously, perhaps violently, and both Dan and Mrs Kelly may have come to her aid.

At this point Ned entered, alerted by Williamson or Joe. He drew or held a small, pocket revolver. Already, knowing only that Dan was being arrested, his temper was at flashpoint, fuelled by Fitzpatrick's betrayals of the previous year. The third punch had been thrown. A policeman insulting his sister summoned the spectre of Flood and Annie; the graves under the willows. Only five months later the editor of Beechworth's *Advertiser* would state that Ned rushed into the house 'imagining that the constable was a man against whom he had a special hatred'. It seems unlikely that Ned actually mistook Fitzpatrick for Flood. More likely long-suppressed anger against one policeman fed his anger against the other, detonating all the impotence of the past.

In such moments men kill, but Ned Kelly did not. A deadly marksman, he put two bullets past Fitzpatrick's head. If the constable spoke the truth, Ned's 'Out of this, you bugger!' makes it clear that this was no murder attempt. As Ned is supposed to have told the police two years later, 'I ... shot *at* him.' (my italics) In an explosion of anger he was lashing out, hitting back — like kicking a chair or cracking a whip. Fitzpatrick threw up his arm, either against the threat of Ned's fury or to ward off Ellen's attack with the shovel, swinging his wrist into the path of the second bullet.

It's tempting to imagine that the shot came from Fitzpatrick's own revolver, drawn and knocked aside in the struggle, as suggested by the Mansfield newspaper owner–editor G. Wilson Hall. But a round-nosed, .45-calibre bullet from a police Webley cartridge revolver, fired at such close range, would have smashed Fitzpatrick's wrist or gouged a bloody trough across it. A small-calibre, percussion revolver, however, could have lodged a small, conical bullet under the skin of his wrist without causing serious damage. If Ned Kelly shot Fitzpatrick, this is the most feasible scenario.

Subsequent events prove that Ned was not disposed to lie, though he would do so — even incriminating himself — to protect others. If Ned had admitted that he shot Fitzpatrick, he would also have given credence to the rest of the trooper's evidence and implicated his mother, Skilling and Williamson. So he lied.

Nine years before, in the Ah Fook case, Ned had first faced a court over his 'impulsive' reaction at an insult to a sister. Now an equally impulsive reaction in defence of another sister had spawned the Kelly Outbreak.

8

'THERE WOULD BE MURDER NOW'

15 APRIL – 12 OCTOBER 1878

Almost as soon as the ruckus with Fitzpatrick had subsided, it was hard to believe the few moments of violence. The huge shadows thrown across the firelit walls were again tranquil; the tang of gunsmoke was lost in the homely smells of burning eucalypt and baking bread; the children had stopped crying. Ned convinced himself that Fitzpatrick might prove true to his one-time promise of friendship and protect the family from retribution. When they released the police-man, Ned rode with him a little way on the road back to Benalla and, as he returned, met Brickey Williamson heading next door. Ned told Brickey, 'He had made it all right with him. Fitzpatrick had promised to say nothing about being shot, if he could help it.' Nevertheless Ned farewelled Brickey and rode after Dan and Joe, who had started off already, with food and swags and spare horses. In the hills they split up. Dan rode off to warn Jack Lloyd that he was wanted for horse stealing while Ned and Joe headed for Stricklands' shanty in the King Valley. It is clear that Ned never considered that anyone but himself, Dan and, possibly, Joe would be implicated by Fitzpatrick.

As soon as the Benalla Telegraph Office opened at 8 a.m., Sergeant Whelan sent off a barrage of telegrams describing Ned's shooting of Fitzpatrick. He predicted, 'The offenders will likely make for New South Wales,' and advised, 'warrants will issue at once.' The warrants were for the arrests of Ned, Dan, Ellen Kelly, Skilling and Williamson for Attempted Murder.

In Wangaratta Sergeant Steele received his telegram at 9 a.m. and showed it to Superintendent Nicolson, who was on an inspection tour. Nicolson offered no advice or orders and left for Bright — hardly the actions of a man who, according to one theory, stage-managed the Fitzpatrick affair.

Sergeant Steele waited around for three hours, expecting some instructions from Benalla. When none came he rode off to Eleven Mile

Creek with Detective Brown and spent the rest of the day watching the Kelly house from a nearby hill.

At 9 that evening, reinforced by Senior Constable Strahan (who seems to have returned from leave almost as Fitzpatrick was on his way to take over Greta), Steele at last rode down to the Kelly homestead. Ellen told the police that Fitzpatrick hadn't been at her house for a month, 'And as for seeing my son Ned I have not seen him for the last four months.' Kate bore out her mother's story, but when Steele later told Ellen that Fitzpatrick 'accused her of rushing him with a shovel', she said, 'I know I've got a damn bad temper. You would not like to see a son of your own taken away. If they got him into gaol there's no telling what those bloody wretches would swear against him. He got into it innocently before.' According to Steele, 'Kate Kelly admitted that only for her they would have finished Fitzpatrick off.'

Steele and Strahan arrested Williamson next door and, failing to find Skilling at home two blocks further on, they took Brickey to Greta. They returned to the Kelly house at about 1 a.m. and found Jimmy Quinn, just out of Beechworth Gaol, and his sister, passing a sleepless night. On their second try they arrested Bill Skilling at his home and, on their way back with him, they finally arrested Ellen and three-day-old Alice. The three prisoners spent the rest of the night at Greta, to be driven into Benalla the next afternoon.

Before hearing of the arrests, Dan Kelly and Jack Lloyd rode across to Stricklands' shanty on the King to alert Ned and Joe to the flurry of police activity. Dan now rode off to the hut at Bullock Creek in the Wombat Ranges while Ned and Joe, as predicted by Whelan, headed up across the Murray into New South Wales. Jack Lloyd wisely decided to return home to face arrest and trial on the horse-stealing charges.

In 24 hours characterised by false starts and misjudgements on both sides, Ned, Dan and Joe had set out on a 26-month career as fugitives from the law; the police were launched on 26 months of futile and, at times, disastrous pursuits.

For Ned, it all represented an unpromising debut to a bushranging career. Exactly two weeks after the shooting, a £100 reward would be placed on his head, with notices proclaiming, 'Attempt to Murder at Greta'. Ned had blundered into a capital crime. He had incriminated his mother, a brother-in-law and a friend and had apparently run away, leaving them to face possible death sentences.

Ellen, Skilling and Williamson were taken to Beechworth Gaol for a week then carted back to Benalla for trial, to be remanded, locked up in Beechworth for another three weeks, tried again at the police court on 17 May and committed 'to stand trial on the capital charge at the court of Assize to be holden at Beechworth'.

The autumn Assizes had just finished, the spring Assizes would be held in October. Winter lay between and snow had already fallen in the ranges around Beechworth. The three justices of the peace of the Bench granted bail for Ellen — 'herself in £100 and two sureties of £50 each'. But no friends of the Kellys could produce the money. Ellen and her baby joined Skilling and Williamson on the now-familiar journey back to Beechworth Gaol.

That night it poured. Driving back home from Benalla in a dray loaded with supplies, Kate and Maggie became bogged and were rescued by a police party led by Strahan and Detective Ward, who were on their way to watch the Kelly house in case Ned and Dan came home to learn the results of the trial. Ward and Strahan rode ahead to take up watch while two troopers helped the girls home. The Kelly girls didn't always fare as well from police forays to Eleven Mile Creek. Ned described:

> ... how the police used to be blowing that they would not ask me to stand; they would shoot me first and then cry surrender. And how they used to rush into the house ... when there was no-one there but women ... and upset all the milk dishes, break tins of eggs, empty the flour out of the bags on to the ground and even the meat out of the cask and destroy all the provisions and shove the girls in front of them into the rooms like dogs so if anyone was there they would shoot the girls first. But they knew well I was not there, or I would have scattered their blood and brains like rain. I would manure the Eleven Mile with their bloated carcases, and yet remember there is not one drop of murderous blood in my veins.
>
> Superintendent [Brooke] Smith used to say to my sisters 'See all the men I have out today? I will have as many more tomorrow and we will blow him into pieces as small as the paper that is in our guns.' Detective Ward and Constable Hayes took out their revolvers and threatened to shoot the girls and children in Mrs Skillions absence. The greatest ruffians and murderers no matter how depraved would not be guilty of such a cowardly action.

In this wild, almost unpunctuated flow of words Ned told the tale as he heard it in New South Wales or on his return. The details may be coloured but the fact remains that Inspector Brooke Smith would worry himself to the point of a nervous breakdown in dread of Ned Kelly's revenge.

◆

BEECHWORTH was in the grip of its coldest, wettest winter for years and on 16 June the *Advertiser* reported:

> Mrs Kelly: A day or two since, Mr W. H. Foster [the town's newly rein-
> stated Police Magistrate] attended at the Beechworth Gaol and admitted
> to bail this woman ... It was an act of charity, as the poor woman,
> though not of the most reputable of characters, had a babe in arms, and
> in the cold gaol without a fire, it is a wonder that the poor little child
> lived so long during this bitter wintry weather.

As the historian McMenomy has commented, this was hardly charity.
Two respectable Greta farmers, William Dinning and Robert Graham,
had come forward, each prepared to lose his £50 if Ellen did not present
herself for trial on 9 October. The only concession seemed to be that
Ellen's personal surety was reduced from £100 to £50. So Ellen and
baby Alice returned to the Eleven Mile Creek for slightly less than four
months.

That week Dan Kelly's mate, Steve Hart, also walked out of Beechworth Gaol, having served eleven months of his one-year sentence for
Illegal Use. Steve returned to the Hart selection on Three Mile Creek
outside Wangaratta, and heard all the local gossip about Ned and Dan
'making a rise'. When Sergeant Steele dropped by the Hart place to see
how the lad was adjusting to freedom, Steve 'promised he would work'.
But as he helped his father grub stumps on the rich, creekside flats, the
nearby Warby Ranges running south to meet the ranks of ridges that
rose into the Wombat Ranges would have caught his eye. Steve would
have learned from fellow members of the Greta Mob that Dan was up
there on Bullock Creek, digging for gold and clearing and fencing horse
paddocks that were safe from the hawk nose and hawk eyes of Sergeant
Steele. Steve kept his promise to work; but not on the Three Mile. Steele
later reported, 'It appears he threw down the axe they were grubbing
with, and said, "A short life and a merry one," and he got on his horse
and rode away.'

Joe Byrne's mate, Aaron Sherritt, also threw in his lot with the Kelly
boys — though in a far subtler way, foreshadowing the dangerous role
he would play for the next two years. Fitzpatrick, while still officially
stationed at Benalla, was given temporary duty at Beechworth to keep
him safe from Kelly supporters until the trial was over. Aaron — another
horsy larrikin fond of girls and grog — struck up an acquaintance with
Fitzpatrick and told him that 'he could lead me to the Kellys in a very
short time. He told me that several times ... that the Kellys were in that
locality.' Aaron claimed that he was trusting Fitzpatrick with this information because he had a 'down' on the Beechworth police.

Fitzpatrick believed Aaron, never suspecting that this was an attempt
to lure him into a trap, but Senior Detective Kennedy scoffed at the idea
of Aaron betraying his friends. Fitzpatrick didn't take up the offer, later
quoting this as a missed chance to catch the Kellys.

Aaron's information was correct in one respect. As the trial approached, Ned, Dan and Joe were in hiding near Beechworth. The plan to capture Fitzpatrick had failed. Ned now had to rely on proving in court that Fitzpatrick had concocted the whole affair, as Skilling was 4 miles away when the brawl took place.

Everything promised that the Beechworth spring Assizes of 1878 would be a momentous affair. The *Advertiser* commented, 'The calendar is decidedly the heaviest and most serious that we have had in the north-eastern district for years' — a symptom of the deepening recession. There were twenty prisoners for trial and, out of 166 jurors on the rolls, 140 had been summoned. As well as the trials of Ellen, Skilling and Williamson for Attempted Murder, William Baumgarten and Samuel Kennedy were to face judgment in the final act of the 'Whitty larceny' courtroom saga, another case in which Ned's name dominated the evidence.

In the most forbidding detail of all, the judge would be Sir Redmond Barry, who had sentenced Uncle Jim Kelly to death for arson and whose views on horse stealing were well known. 'By a firm adherence to just severity, the crime was repressed,' he had said seven years before. Now he was to sit in judgment in an area where, in his words, 'the offenders oppress the inhabitants and enjoy almost an immunity'. Here, there was no room for what he called 'mistaken, misdirected lenity'. Clearly such 'lenity' had enabled horse thieves to thrive in the north-east and progress to the Attempted Murder of police trying to apprehend them. This *must* be stopped.

Ellen Kelly surrendered herself on Wednesday 9 October and at 10 a.m. stood in the dock of Beechworth court house with her son-in-law and neighbour, as the senior judge of the British Empire, the Great Man of the colony, took his seat at the austere bench, red-robed and grey-wigged beneath the dark, wooden canopy. Fitzpatrick told his story again. Mr Bowman for the defence cross-examined him; Dr Nicholson gave what seemed to be ambiguous evidence about the wound; and storekeeper Lindsay claimed that Fitzpatrick was sober when he left for Greta. Now Mr Bowman played his only cards. Ned had provided Frank Harty and Joe Ryan, who swore that Skilling was with them when Fitzpatrick swore that he was at the Eleven Mile.

Frank Harty, a proud-eyed, decent man, had once declared, 'Ned Kelly is the best bloody man that has ever been in Benalla, I would fight up to my knees in blood for him, I have known him for years, I would take his word sooner than any other man's oath.' Crown Prosecutor Chomley had on his table a report from Fitzpatrick quoting this extraordinary expression of Harty's allegiances. However, coming from a man like Harty, it might prove altogether too effective a testimonial for Ned

Kelly. Chomley merely led Harty to admit, 'I offered to go bail for Mrs Kelly,' and 'I told the police they wronged Skillion.'

Joe Ryan told the same story as Harty — being with Skilling, 4 miles from the Kelly homestead, between 5.30 and 6.40 p.m. Joe also swore, 'I bought a horse from Ned Kelly on the 15th, and gave £17 for it.' He produced a receipt. Chomley simply argued that 'the facts had been proved and that the alibi set up was worthless, accusing the witnesses Harty and Ryan of perjury'.

The jury retired for two hours and returned to announce that all three prisoners were guilty. Barry remanded them for sentence.

Three days later, on Saturday 12 October, Ellen was sentenced to three years hard labour and Skilling and Williamson each to six years hard labour. Baumgarten and Kennedy were found not guilty of Horse Stealing but guilty of Receiving. Baumgarten received four years, Kennedy six.

> His honour . . . hoped that this would lead to the disbanding of the gang of lawless persons, who have for years banded themselves together in that neighbourhood against the police.

The *Advertiser* thought the sentences 'severe' (an opinion shared even by the Chief Commissioner of Police) but considered that Sir Redmond 'acted throughout in a most impartial manner'.

It has been claimed that Barry 'intimated' that if Ned Kelly 'had . . . stood beside his mother in the dock, he would have received a sentence of 21 years.' If the learned judge were so outspoken a unanimously anti-Kelly press hesitated to record his indiscretion; though the following year one pro-Kelly editor would imply that such a statement had been made.

Taken back to her cell in the Beechworth Gaol, Ellen Kelly saw Brickey Williamson in the yard outside her window. Williamson claimed she said to him, 'that they would play up, that there would be murder now.'

♣
———

9

STRINGYBARK

12 – 26 OCTOBER 1878

Ellen's sentence of three years hard labour was a cruel blow to Ned. His bitterness towards Fitzpatrick now became obsessive. He told a friend 'that he would rush through a hundred bayonets to get at him'. Yet he knew that, directly or indirectly, he was also to blame. Fitzpatrick had been arresting Dan for a crime that Ned had committed. He had wounded Fitzpatrick, then let him ride back to Benalla. He had ridden away from Eleven Mile Creek, never believing that the law would strike at his mother and the others. He had clung naively to the desperate conviction that one pebble of truth — Skilling's absence from the brawl — would knock down Fitzpatrick's unsteady structure of fact and fiction. Now he made a gallant effort to undo all these mistakes.

Police Magistrate Alfred Wyatt of Benalla was a delightful character who rode circuit around the district in a velveteen suit, wearing goggles against the dust and 'a towering pyramid of a hat', swathed in a massive white puggaree with long tails floating behind. He always led with him an unsaddled horse 'as company' for his mount. In north-eastern legal circles the trio were known as 'Wyatt, Webb and A'Beckett'.

Eccentricity aside, Wyatt was known as a fair man — an 'old English gentleman' of strong convictions and kindly heart who made no secret of the fact that he considered Ellen Kelly's sentence 'very severe'. An approach was made to Wyatt through Uncle Pat Quinn — 'a proposition that, if the Kellys' mother was liberated, some promise or some arrangement would be made by which the Kellys, Ned and Dan . . . would give themselves up'. It was a remarkable offer — two men willing to surrender on a capital charge if a prisoner sentenced to three years was released.

'I made answer thus,' said Wyatt. 'That I could not make a shadow of a stipulation on behalf of the Government, but if such efforts were made, and were successful, I would use my most strenuous endeavours to carry out the condition they wished to impose.' If Uncle Pat knew what on earth Mr Wyatt was talking about, he reported back that Ned's offer had not been accepted; but if he and Dan surrendered, Wyatt would *then* do his best to have Ellen freed — though he was unable to promise anything.

It was hardly an attractive counter-offer. The two brothers would face very long gaol terms or death sentences, with no guarantee of their mother's release. They did not accept.

Meanwhile Wyatt told 'the police authorities' of the proposition. Three years later he could not recall who he had spoken to, but 'most probably ... the person was Sergeant Whelan'. A Royal Commission, like the officer concerned, proved totally uninterested in the Kelly brothers' surrender offer. This was not the way things were handled in the self-governing colony of Victoria.

Ned had another plan. He and Joe rode back with Dan to the log hut at Bullock Creek in the Wombat Ranges, where the gold sluicing enterprise had been making 'good wages'. Now, Ned explained, 'I came back with the full intention of working a still to make whisky, as it was the greatest means to obtain money to procure a new trial for my mother. We had ... 2 miles of fencing, 20 acres of ground cleared for the purpose of growing mangle wursels [mangold wurzel, a kind of beet] and barley for the purpose of distilling whisky.' The barley had been sown in winter, the mangolds the previous month. On the banks of the creek, about 150 yards from the hut, Ned set up a still with a massive cast iron pot, 2 feet 6 inches in diameter.

He took precautions against discovery:

> We had a place excavated close to the house for the purpose of erecting a small distill, so if anyone informed on us they would not get the most valuable or main distill that was further down the creek with the sugar and other requisites.

The fortress-like hut with its log walls and small, loophole windows, was made truly impregnable by building a new door of stout slabs armoured with sheets of iron cut from a ship's ballast tank. All around the hut the scrub was cleared and the timber ringbarked, the foliage stacked ready for burning. For hundreds of yards on all sides of the clearing, targets were drawn with charcoal on white gum trunks, or cut into the ridged bark of the peppermints. Then, at ranges of 20 to 400 yards, countless hundreds of shots were fired — five into one target, 50 into another — all the bullets cut out and melted down to be re-cast in bullet moulds.

Ned used a remarkable old weapon he might have carried when he rode with Harry Power — a muzzle-loading Enfield carbine of .577 calibre with the barrel sawn off to about 14 inches and the butt to about 5 inches — making an ungainly, elongated pistol. Capping off its strange appearance, the barrel was held on at an angle by three or four inches of tightly bound string covered with wax — in Ned's words, looking as if it would 'shoot round the corner'. But once loaded with powder, wadding and ball, with a percussion cap fitted on the nipple (an operation that could take 15 or 20 seconds) this was a deadly firearm in Ned's hands. He was to say, 'I will back it against any firearm in the country — I can shoot a kangaroo at 100 yds [with] every shot fired.'

Dan probably practised with his old shotgun: 'a single-barrelled fowling piece — a cheap gun — common bore'. It would be claimed that Steve Hart had a double-barrelled shotgun here and that Joe Byrne was armed with 'a very old-fashioned gun, with a very large bore, more than an ordinary large bore'. Yet, when the lives of these four men depended on every firearm they could find, neither of these guns were seen. Almost certainly the defence of Bullock Creek had to depend on the rickety old carbine, a cheap shotgun and a pocket revolver.

Long after the last shots had reverberated in this lonely basin, a journalist walked from tree to tree, silently studying the mangled targets. He recorded:

> On one small tree a circle of charcoal 6 in. in diameter had been traced, and into this two or three revolver bullets had been fired, one striking the black dot meant to represent the bulls-eye in the centre, and the other two being close to it.

These shots were almost certainly from the revolver Ned had fired at Fitzpatrick.

Ned and Joe had been back at Bullock Creek for scarcely a week when word came from Greta that there were plans to send a four-man police party into the ranges to hunt them out. The party would be led by their old enemy Sergeant Steele. Almost immediately, they heard that a second party was to be led by Senior Constable Strahan who, according to Ned, 'said he would not ask me to stand but would shoot me like a dog', a threat later confirmed by police sources. Ned was told that Flood would join one of the police parties.

The following week work on the whisky-distilling project must have become more frenzied, uninterrupted by target practice. No more shots could be allowed to betray the location of the hidden valley to the police advancing south from Greta. Then in that second-last week of October came the news that a third police party was about to ride northwards from Mansfield, its imminent departure betrayed by hobbled horses in the police paddock. They were being accustomed to hobbles for an extended stay in the bush.

The horses had disappeared by daybreak on Friday 25 October. That day, probably with Joe, Ned rode south over steep Toombullup ridge, the watershed between Ryans and Hollands Creeks. Past the bogs beyond Hollands was a broad basin rimmed to the south by the Tabletop ridge. Here Johnny Byrne, a distant relative of Joe, had taken up a selection and built a beautiful little slab hut where he lived with his wife and young family. Johnny was an expert blacksmith and had probably helped the lads set up the still and armour the hut's door. Ned found the tracks of four mounts and a packhorse shod with government-issue shoes, leading across the hollow towards Hollands Creek and Toombullup.

That evening Ned rode back up the eastern end of Toombullup ridge near lofty Emu Swamp and struck west towards Bullock Creek. He came across more tracks of police horses, suggesting that a second, south-bound police party had looped around the headwaters of Ryans Creek. They were heading down towards some gold diggings near an old shingle hut on Stringybark Creek, less than a mile from the Kelly clearing.

As night closed in on the hut at Bullock Creek, the lads would not have risked a cooking fire — only tinned sardines for dinner, with a drink of creek water. There would be little rest that night. If Dan, Joe and Steve slept at all, Ned stood guard on a rise above the dark hut, leaving a pattern of tracks. Even before the dawn chorus had hushed, Ned and Dan slipped through the bush to Stringybark Creek and found the police camp in a clearing on the far bank, near the shingle hut. There were four police in plain clothes. Ned recognised the loud-mouthed Strahan and his enemy, Flood. The other two were strangers. Five horses were hobbled on the creekside flat.

> We saw they carried long firearms and we knew our doom was sealed if we could not beat those before the others would come. I knew the other party of police would soon join them and if they came on us at our camp they would shoot us down like dogs at our work as we only had two guns.

Ned and Dan returned to Bullock Creek to tell Joe and Steve what they had found. It was a Saturday and Tom Lloyd was due. Wild Wright was away shearing on the Murray but perhaps Aaron Sherritt or members of the Mob would join them. The morning passed and no one had arrived. In the afternoon, shotgun blasts rattled among the gullies in echoes from Stringybark Creek. Why would the police advertise their presence so blatantly? Perhaps in the hope that Ned and Dan would try and escape — into the jaws of a trap between the other two parties, to surrender or face a gunfight, poorly armed. 'We thought our country was woven with police,' Ned said. They could choose to wait here until the police reached Bullock Creek and laid siege to the hut. Instead, Ned took the initiative.

First he pulled the chinstrap of his hat under his nose and borrowed from Dan or Steve a sash of bright red silk to bind around his waist. He would face the police as a member of the Greta Mob — as a rebel. This afternoon, even 'respectable' Joe would wear his hat 'Greta fashion' to stand with his mate, Ned, just as Steve stood with Dan.

Perhaps Ned thought of leaving Joe and Steve at the hut, but they were unarmed, so the four of them headed up through the bush, over the low ridge behind their hut, across Germans Creek then down towards Stringybark.

Their direct line of approach led into a treacherous little swamp of speargrass and rushes, just downstream of the police camp, to its north. On their right, an open-timbered slope fell almost to the creek, directly opposite the clearing, offering little cover. So they circled further south, struck through dense gully scrub and crossed the tiny creek a little way upstream of the camp, to take cover in a thicket of tall speargrass behind a fallen log.

It was a cheerless place, an acre or so of bush half-destroyed by a party of gold diggers who had quarrelled and split up. Several big gums on a low rise had been felled to clear a safe, dry site for a hut. Others were ringbarked and left to die. Along the creek, white gums rose in sombre colonnades among black-plumed speargrass, mossy fallen logs and dense thickets of dead wattle shedding bark. Forty yards across clear ground, in the centre of the open space, a camp fire was blazing among some fallen timber, set in an angle formed by two big logs. Flood and Strahan were nearby. Fifteen or 20 yards past them, a tent had been pitched beside a couple of fire-blackened posts — all that remained of the diggers' hut burnt down some six months before.

Suddenly Flood picked up a double-barrelled shotgun. Ned tensed, but Flood walked to the far side of the clearing and led a horse back. He hobbled it near the tent then returned to the fire, leaned the shotgun against a stump and stood with his back to them. Strahan was 10 or 12 feet further off on the other side of the fire, sitting on a log.

'We could have shot these men without speaking but not wishing to take their lives we waited.' Ned knew he couldn't wait long. As the shadows deepened among the tall timber of the gully, the camp fire was blazing like a beacon — a bigger fire than was needed to boil a billy — guiding other police to this place. 'We thought it best to try and bail these two up, take their firearms and ammunition and horses and we could stand a chance with the rest.'

Dan was to Ned's right in the speargrass, 2 or 3 yards off, and Joe and Steve were the same distance beyond him. With guerilla instinct the four were in open skirmishing order, wary of the spreading pattern of a shotgun blast at this range. Telling Dan to cover Strahan, Ned cocked his faithful old carbine then lunged to his feet with a cry of 'Bail up, throw up your hands!'

Flood swung around to face him across the clearing as the cry was repeated by the others, echoing in the gully for several seconds. Ned's carbine was aimed at Flood, his finger on the trigger. Flood raised his arms to shoulder height but Strahan turned aside and ran towards a log several yards away, snatching his revolver from its holster behind his hip. Dan didn't fire. Strahan dived behind the log as Dan stood there, his gun aimed. Strahan came up to fire and in that second Ned swung the carbine from Flood to Strahan, a tiny shift of angle to the right, and squeezed the trigger. His target was momentarily obliterated by a blast of flame and smoke, then Strahan staggered to his feet, shot through the right eye, raising his arms in surrender. He blundered forward, falling across the log with a cry of 'Oh Christ, I'm shot!' then 'lunging and plunging' in the grass.

Ned tossed the carbine into his left hand, drew the revolver from the back of his waistband and yelled, 'Keep your hands up! Keep your hands up!' as he ran towards Flood, who stood with his arms raised, glancing around at the dying man still struggling in the grass.

As Ned ran closer a strange thing happened. The helpless policeman with his hands raised had Flood's dark beard and Flood's large dark eyes, but he was taller. It was a stranger. And the dying man wasn't Strahan. Ned would find that it was Lonigan, who had 'blackballed' him in the bootmaker's shop brawl, who may have wrung from him that cry, 'If ever I kill a man, Lonigan, you'll be the first!'

Perhaps the confusion of identities lent another dimension of unreality to what had happened in this scarred tract of bush. Ned had spared the life of one policeman, believing him to be a man he hated. He had taken the life of another, not knowing that he was a man he may have threatened to kill. The ironies changed nothing, however. A policeman was dead; Ned Kelly was his killer.

◆

THE POLICE PLAN to capture Ned and Dan Kelly had been masterminded by Superintendent John Sadleir, who took charge of the reorganised north-eastern police district in July. Sadleir, a grey-bearded Irishman of aristocratic descent, tackled the problem in a characteristically unhurried way. As early as 7 May Detective Michael Ward — an old enemy of Joe Byrne and Aaron Sherritt — had received information that Ned and/or Dan were at 'Bullocky Gully or at the head of Ryans Creek', also described as 'the old diggings place'. With Senior Constable Strahan and constables Mooney, Hayes and Whitty (Ned's former friend), Ward searched the area but failed to find Dan and his mates.

In mid-October came another report that Dan was 'on the Fifteen Mile Creek, working with a man there'. Ward suggested that two parties should search the Fifteen Mile, the western branch of the King 'and thence on to Mansfield'.

Two months before this Sadleir had been corresponding independently with Sergeant Michael Kennedy of Mansfield, with the idea of forming a party to start north from Mansfield while a second party struck south from Greta. Kennedy, in his first memo to Sadleir on 16 August, suggested Stringybark Creek as a depot from which the Mansfield party could scour the ranges while the Greta men moved along 'the flat country' to meet them in a pincer movement by which Ned Kelly 'would soon be disturbed if not captured'. Kennedy nominated for his party a fine bushman, Constable Michael Scanlon (he and Kennedy had once shared a reward for arresting Wild Wright), and one of his own Mansfield constables, Thomas McIntyre, 'a zealous, conscientious man'. Sadleir would bring Constable Thomas Lonigan from Violet Town to join Sergeant Kennedy's party, because he could recognise Ned and Dan Kelly. If Lonigan didn't arrive in time the party would start without him.

Sergeant Steele was to lead the Greta party and Sadleir arranged a meeting in Benalla between the two sergeants. Because this was planned as a clandestine operation and Kennedy usually rode 'a very remarkable white horse', Sadleir arranged for the sergeant to bring a saddle to Benalla and ride back to Mansfield with a less noticeable mount, a 'quiet, handy horse' that had two unusual traits. If jabbed with spurs it reared, and to lean forward on its neck set it off at a gallop.

Steele's party was to consist of Senior Constable Strahan and Constables Thom and Ryan, but at the last minute Steele was subpoenaed to attend the Equity Court and the Greta party was led by Senior Constable Shoebridge from Bright. Due to clerical errors, the final orders did not include this change and listed an additional man, Constable Baird. Ned's bush telegraph seems to have been confused by this 'strictly confidential' police correspondence and gave him the inaccurate information that *two* parties were leaving from the Greta end — a five-man party led by Steele and four men under Strahan. Flood was said to be riding with one of these groups. The Greta and Mansfield parties set out before daylight on Friday 25 October, planning to meet at Hedi Station in the King Valley.

Meanwhile Detective Ward headed for the area, on his own initiative, armed only with a pocket revolver. He disbelieved Fitzpatrick's story of being shot by Ned. 'I thought they would fight,' Ward said, 'but I never had the remotest idea they would shoot.'

Whether or not they believed Fitzpatrick's story, other members of the two parties were ready to use their guns. Ned heard later that Lonigan had 'blowed before he left Violet Town that if Ned Kelly was to be shot he was the man who would shoot him'. Strahan spoke of shooting Ned down 'like a dog'. McIntyre readily admitted that he was prepared to gun down the Kelly boys and recorded that, during the Mansfield party's ride up into the Wombat Ranges, he killed a tiger snake and chortled, 'First blood, Lonigan!' The Mansfield saddler, Boles, revealed that the party carried two long straps, specially made to sling a pair of bodies on either side of their packhorse. They also carried extra armaments. Sergeant Kennedy had borrowed a double-barrelled shotgun from the Mansfield vicar, Mr Sandiford, and a Spencer repeating carbine from the Woods Point gold escort. The Spencer, which loaded seven .52-calibre rounds in a tube through the butt, was operated by an unusual combined trigger guard and loading lever. Beside these 'long firearms', each man carried a Webley revolver and eighteen rounds of ammunition.

Rather than riding straight up the face of Toombullup ridge, leading a packhorse loaded with a tent, bedding for four men and eight days supplies, it is possible that Kennedy veered across the slope to the east before turning back westwards, producing what Ned misread as a second set of tracks.

The police reached the old hut site on Stringybark Creek about 3 p.m. on Friday, pitched their tent and made camp. McIntyre was the party's cook and Kennedy told him to take a shot at some kangaroos to provide variety in their menu over the coming days — giving the lie to claims that the sergeant knew the Kellys were in the vicinity.

They rose at 5 next morning and at 6 Kennedy and Scanlon rode off on patrol to the north, leaving McIntyre and Lonigan to look after the camp. After they had tended the horses and spread brush on the floor of the tent, Lonigan read *The Vagabond Papers*, which included journalist James Stanley's revealing interview with Harry Power — and Harry's poor opinion of the young Ned. McIntyre baked 'soda bread' and tried to shoot some parrots — another try for dinner-time variety. Towards 5 o'clock McIntyre built up the fire to help guide Kennedy and Scanlon back to camp and he had just made a billy of tea when the sharp cry shocked him. 'Bail up, throw up your hands!'

McIntyre turned to see four men emerging from the speargrass at the southern edge of the clearing. He would claim that all were aiming rifles or guns. He was holding a fork — probably to stir the tea. He dropped it and raised his arms. Then Lonigan made his break for cover.

McIntyre's version of what happened next is confused. He would claim once that Lonigan was shot as soon as he put his hand to his revolver; many times that the constable ran four or five paces towards a tree before being shot; and once that he reached cover behind a log and was shot as he came up to fire.

He later drew a diagram trying to show that Lonigan was killed as he ran *away* from Ned. Yet Lonigan was shot through the right eye, suggesting that he was facing his killer and, at a range of 40 yards, not even an expert marksman would choose to shoot at the head of a running man. On the other hand, if the man was not running but about to fire from behind a log, his head offered the only possible target.

McIntyre eventually admitted that he was facing Ned Kelly and saw him fire the fatal shot. He had his back to Lonigan when the bullet struck him, admitting, 'I heard him fall, I did not see him fall.' To say — as he once did to Sadleir — that Lonigan was under cover and preparing to fire at the Kellys when killed, provided Ned Kelly with the justification of self-defence. To say — as he did on every other occasion — that Lonigan was shot as he went to draw his revolver or as he ran *towards* cover portrayed the killing as a cold-blooded murder. Or, if McIntyre had been driven by a more admirable motive he might have been trying to depict the killing as Ned's immediate response to an impulsive reaction on Lonigan's part, thus minimising the extent to which Lonigan's actions brought about his own death.

Some thirty seconds after Ned Kelly's bullet lodged in Lonigan's brain the visible mechanisms of life had stopped. By then Ned had run across the clearing, followed by the other three, covering McIntyre and demanding, 'Have you got any firearms?' McIntyre said 'no' and, while Dan kept the policeman covered, Ned jumped the log and crossed to Lonigan's body. As he bent to pick up the fallen revolver, he confronted the appalling detail of the man's death and failed to recognise him. He came back to McIntyre, clearly shaken. 'What a pity; what made the fool run?'

Then Ned crossed to the tent, returned with McIntyre's revolver and signalled that the constable could put his hands down, telling him: 'I thought you were Flood and it is a good job for you that you are not, because if you had [been] I would not have shot you but roasted you upon the fire.'

This remark was widely reported, encouraging the spread of rumours that Flood had seduced Annie and eventually promoting the view that the Stringybark tragedy was an act of revenge for police ill-treatment of Kelly womenfolk.

A bizarre 15-minute conversation began, reconstructed in great detail by McIntyre. Told that he had killed Lonigan, Ned responded, 'No, that is not Lonigan, I know Lonigan well,' though eventually accepting the fact and commenting, 'well, I'm glad of that for the bugger gave me a hiding in Benalla one day.'

McIntyre studied his four captors, carefully remembering their descriptions to provide the first portrait of what had become, with Lonigan's death, the Kelly Gang.

He thought Ned looked older than his 23 years, with 'sallow complexion, dark-brown hair, full beard and moustache of a dirty, dark red colour, moustache cut square across the mouth, hazel eyes with a greenish tint; wore dark tweed clothes, red silk sash, dark low hat'. McIntyre estimated Ned at 6 foot, noted that his jacket was 'very short' and that his 'Sydney soft crown hat' had a black velvet band.

Dan, at 17, also looked older. He was '5 feet 5 or 6 inches high, very dark hair and complexion, small dark piercing eyes, beard not grown'. He was 'nervously excited and laughing with a short laugh, almost hysterical. There was something grotesque about his appearance. All his clothing, including his hat, was much too large for him, and when he turned his back on me . . . there was very little of the inhabitant of the clothing visible.' Apart from size, Dan's suit was 'light and stylish' and he wore a billycock hat.

McIntyre had no idea who Joe and Steve could be and was particularly unimpressed by Steve in his 'light clothes and flat hat', recalling him to be, '19 or 20 years of age, 5 feet 8 inches high, fairish complexion, rather stout, straggling hairs over face, hooked nose, sinister [elsewhere 'cruel'] expression'. Joe, on the other hand, made a very favourable impression on McIntyre who thought he lacked 'the villainous expression of the others'. He would record Joe as '21 years of age, 5 feet 9 inches high, very fair complexion, fair moustache and long beard on chin, very fine like first growth, respectable looking,' also describing him as of 'slight build' and 'thin'.

Without realising its significance, he also noted what would become the trademark of the Kelly Gang and a symbol of allegiance to its supporters: 'A string from the hat under the nose was indulged in by all four bushrangers, and the hat was worn tipped well over the eyes.'

While McIntyre, Dan, Steve and Joe shared the policemen's tea, ham and freshly baked bread, Ned busied himself unloading the police shotgun, removing the shot pellets from its cartridges and loading each with a single bullet. It was an unusual weapon for a police party to carry. 'You buggers came here to shoot me, I suppose.'

McIntyre pretended he didn't know he was speaking to Ned Kelly but admitted, 'No, we came to apprehend you,' claiming that the fowling piece was 'to shoot kangaroos'. Ned was not convinced, later commenting:

They had eighteen rounds of revolver cartridges each, three dozen for the fowling piece and twenty-one Spencer rifle cartridges and God knows how many away with the rifle this looked as if they meant not only to shoot me but to riddle me . . .

McIntyre admitted that the two absent police were armed with revolvers and a breech-loading repeater and that Sergeant Steele was leading a second party from the north. McIntyre claims to have protested that he would rather die than contribute to the death of his companions. 'I'm no coward,' Ned replied. 'I would shoot no man if he gave up his arms . . . and promised to leave the force.' McIntyre promptly promised to leave the force, and he would . . . eventually.

Ned stressed that he had no wish to kill McIntyre ('I could have shot you half an hour ago when you were sitting on that log . . .') and that he would spare Kennedy and Scanlon if McIntyre persuaded them to surrender ('We don't want their lives, only their horses and firearms'). McIntyre never doubted this to be true, an opinion which would be shared by the Royal Commission and even by Captain Standish.

Suddenly Ned heard horses approaching from down the creek and called, 'Hist lads! Here they come!' Dan and Joe took cover in the spear-grass again, Steve ducked into the tent and Ned dropped down by a log near the fire, telling McIntyre, 'You go and sit down upon that log and mind you give no alarm or I'll put a hole in you.'

Almost as McIntyre settled on the log, Kennedy and Scanlon rode into view 40 or 50 yards off, with Kennedy in the lead and Scanlon 10 or 12 yards behind. Kennedy had his revolver holstered on his hip; Scanlon carried the Spencer on a strap over his shoulder with the butt upwards and the muzzle behind his right arm.

McIntyre stood and moved forward. When he was 5 or 6 yards from Kennedy, he called loudly, so Ned could hear, 'Oh sergeant, you had better dismount and surrender for you are surrounded.' To Kennedy, this greeting had all the earmarks of a practical joke put together by a couple of bored policemen. McIntyre recalled, 'Kennedy smiled and playfully put his hand upon his revolver — which was in the case buckled up [actually, fastened with a brass stud].'

Ned rose from behind the log and called, 'Bail up! Hold your hands up!' Kennedy's smile vanished. He jerked at the holster flap and Ned fired a warning shot. Dan, Joe and Steve all left their cover, ran forward and yelled for the police to bail up, making it clear that they did not intend to kill anyone.

Scanlon tried to wheel away to the right but the clamour of noise and the shot had frightened his horse. It fought bit and rein, breasting forward a couple of lengths. 'Quick as thought,' Scanlon turned back, swung the barrel of the Spencer under his arm, levelled the carbine across his body, still slung, and fired at Ned. The half-aimed shot missed.

I then fired at Scanlon and he fell forward on his horse's neck I still kept him covered thinking he was shamming — when the horse moved and he rolled off . . .

Helpless, McIntyre was watching Kennedy a few yards in front of him. The sergeant ducked forward in the saddle, swung his legs to the ground on the off-side and fired across his horse's rump. The bullet grazed Dan's shoulder as he and Joe moved forward across the open ground between the speargrass and the logs. McIntyre hadn't noticed Ned's shot at Scanlon and was unaware that he was badly wounded, but he saw the trooper slip from his horse, recording:

He fell upon his knees in dismounting — he caught at his rifle as if to take it off his shoulder out of the strap — and endeavoured to get upon his feet. He again fell upon his hands and knees and in that position was shot under the right arm . . . I saw him fall — I saw the blood spurt out from the right side as he fell.

(McIntyre first said that Scanlon was shot while making for a tree and, even though he had sworn a deposition to this effect at Scanlon's inquest, later tried to claim that he had been misreported by journalists.) Although he noted 'three or four shots fired at the same time', McIntyre assumed that Ned had shot Scanlon. Ned was 30 yards off, engaging Kennedy; Steve was 40 yards away, with Ned, Kennedy and McIntyre between him and Scanlon; Dan had just been wounded; Joe was no more than 12 or 14 yards to Scanlon's right. He probably fired the fatal shot straight into the wounded trooper's exposed right side as he raised his arm to try and unsling the Spencer.

Kennedy's riderless horse was prancing in front of McIntyre, frightened by the firing. On an impulse, McIntyre caught it, swung into the saddle and clapped spurs to its flanks. This was the 'quiet, handy, horse' with the two unusual tricks. It reared. Losing a stirrup, the trooper fell forward on its neck and it plunged forward into a flat gallop back along the creek. McIntyre heard several shots. Sometimes he claimed they were fired at him; sometimes he claimed that Kennedy had surrendered; sometimes he suggested that Kennedy had already fallen.

Firing with his revolver, Kennedy moved to cover behind a tree then doubled back to another tree. At some stage he loaded another six cartridges, roughly following the track taken by McIntyre.

Ned ran across to Scanlon's body and dragged the Spencer free, but he didn't understand the unusual loading action and abandoned it on the run, starting off after Kennedy with the double-barrelled shotgun. The delay meant that Kennedy had made good distance ahead of him. Now the sergeant could afford to move more slowly and quietly. If Ned hurried through the bush, he advertised his approach. Moving from tree to tree, over the creek and across the low ridge to the north-west, it must have struck Ned that Kennedy was heading straight for the hut on Bullock Creek — where Tom Lloyd was due to arrive. Perhaps his cousin was already heading down through the bush towards them, investigating the gunfire.

Ned knew that Kennedy had fired four shots since reloading his revolver — he had two more shots to fire before loading his last six bullets. Ned crossed Germans Creek and started up the flank of its gully — now scarcely half a mile from the hut. The gentle slope ahead was almost free of undergrowth but well timbered. There was no sign of movement. The sun was below the ridge, the light was failing.

Suddenly Kennedy appeared from behind a tree, his revolver levelled at Ned.

I thought I was done for as he fired and the ball grazed my ribs, I immediately fired ... I shot him in the armpit ... Kennedy then ran and I followed him when he wheeled around ... raising his arm as if to fire ... and I fired and shot him ... the bullet passed through the right side of his chest and he could not live ...

Kennedy fell in a small, bark-strewn clearing, about 6 yards past a huge, white gum. Running up to him, Ned made an awful discovery. Kennedy's Webley lay on the ground some distance back, by the tree where he had been shot in the armpit.

When I shot him ... he must have dropped his revolver and the blood running down his arm formed a clot in his hand which I took for his revolver knowing he had one shot left.

Kennedy had been turning to surrender when Ned shot him the second time.

Joined by Dan, Steve and Joe, Ned tried to make the sergeant comfortable and Dan brought some water from Germans Creek. Wounded in the temple, chest and side, Kennedy was slowly dying.

In his accounts of Stringybark Ned never gave a detailed description of Kennedy's death, but 'some time later', told sympathiser Henry Perkins what followed. Perkins's version of Ned's account was recorded by Mansfield editor G. Wilson Hall and widely published. Minus Hall's more obvious embroideries, the narrative is probably close to the truth, though not in Ned's words.

The sergeant never moved from the spot where he fell, but complained of the pain from the bullet wound ... He ... endeavoured to turn the conversation in the direction of his domestic affairs, his home, his wife and family, and very frequently of the little one he had recently buried in the Mansfield cemetery [11-month-old John Thomas Kennedy had died on 1 April 1877], to whom he seemed very much attached, evidently knowing he would soon be by his side. I could not help being very much touched at his pitiable condition, and after a little I said, 'Well, Kennedy, I am sorry that I shot you. Here, take my gun and shoot me.' Kennedy replied, 'No, I forgive you, and may God forgive you too.' He then wrote as much on some slips in his note-book as his fast-failing strength would allow him. After he had written what he could with his pencil, he handed the paper to me, and asked if I would give it to his wife. I took the paper and promised that when I had a safe opportunity I would do so. The sergeant then appeared to be suffering very much and in great agony. I could not look upon him so, and did not wish to leave him alone to linger out in such pain, so I suddenly, without letting him see what I intended, I put the muzzle of my gun to within a few inches of Kennedy's breast . . . When he saw that I was going to shoot him he begged of me to leave him alive, saying, 'Let me alone to live, if I can, for the sake of my poor wife and family. You surely have shed blood enough.' I fired, and he died instantly, without a groan.

After his capture Ned was to tell police that Kennedy said, 'God forgive you,' and sent his love to his wife, but he denied that he had been given any note for delivery to Mrs Kennedy, despite the fact that searchers subsequently found near Kennedy's body 'some sheets of writing paper, fastened together with a small paper binder, with three leaves torn from it'. Later that year Ned confirmed that 'Kennedy asked him to let him live'.

G. Wilson Hall went on to note dispassionately:

The Kellys then turned out the dead man's pockets, retaining all that was worth securing, including a valuable gold watch, a small sum of money, and two excellent photos of themselves [actually, a photo of Ned only] . . . The report that the corpse was mutilated by the cutting off of an ear, is like many other rumours in connection with the affair, altogether without foundation. On the contrary, the Kellys were full of admiration at the bravery of the deceased, in recognition of which they laid him out, and covered him carefully up in his regulation cloak [a waterproof cape], which they went to the tent for on purpose.

Ned said that Kennedy was 'The bravest man he ever heard of,' commenting:

I put his cloak over him and left him as well as I could and were they my own brothers I could not have been more sorry for them. This cannot be called wilful murder for I was compelled to shoot them or lie down and let them shoot me. It would not be wilful murder if they packed our remains in, shattered into an animated mass of gore to Mansfield. They would have got great praise and credit as well as promotion . . . Certainly their wives and children are to be pitied, but they must remember those men came into the bush with the intention of scattering pieces of me and my brother all over the bush . . .

It was almost dark when they returned to the police camp, four young men now bound in a terrible brotherhood. With no concern for appearances, only the brutal facts of survival, they searched the bodies of Lonigan and Scanlon, took money and a watch and left their pockets turned inside out. As though this was some terrible sacrament, Joe took rings from Scanlon and Lonigan and slipped them on to his own fingers. He wore them until his death.

During the gunfight in the clearing, the bodies of Lonigan and Scanlon had been struck by two or three bullets. This would lead to the ugly claim that 'Ned Kelly insisted on each of his companions discharging their weapons into the dead bodies of the three police, thus fully implicating, as he thought, each and all in the crime that had been committed.' Ned's subsequent behaviour made nonsense of the story. In every account of the killings, he would take all blame on his own shoulders, claiming that Joe and Steve were not even present.

With the clearing in near darkness they caught Scanlon's horse, untied and unhobbled the other three, then gathered all the provisions and equipment from the tent and set it alight. They rode off to Bullock Creek with their plunder, leaving the flames to advertise a victory in which they could find little glory.

The burning tent — another beacon to attract attention — suggests that Ned had no intention of staying nearby. Almost immediately after their return to the hut at Bullock Creek, Tom Lloyd arrived with supplies and money from the sale of their gold. The police horses — some marked with the crown brand — and the police revolvers holstered at their waists would have told Tom what had happened before anything was said. Tom picked up the Spencer and remarked that it was a heavy weapon. 'Yes, and very deadly,' Ned replied. Tom understood what he meant.

All day, cloud had been banking up to the south — heavy spring rains were coming. Perhaps this encouraged Ned to risk a few hours badly needed sleep while Tom stood guard over them, prowling across the same hillock Ned had paced the previous night, his tracks blending with his cousin's. Before dawn they saddled up, packed and mounted, leaving three of their rundown horses in the paddock and driving two spare mounts and the four police horses ahead of them through the creek and up the northern slope across the gap towards Greta.

Again, Ned took a curious risk for the sake of a symbol. He fired the hut before setting out, as though this act could wipe out a phase of his life. The rain fell in sheets and the building was left almost intact with its detritus of 'empty jam and sardine tins, old powder flasks, cap boxes, broken shovels, old billy-cans, glass bottles, door hinges . . .' Outside the hut Ned had left 'a good axe and other tools'. He would have no further use for them.

10

FUGITIVES

26 OCTOBER – 3 NOVEMBER 1878

McIntyre galloped out of the clearing on Kennedy's horse, his memory printed with a last glimpse of the doomed sergeant's face. 'Kennedy was quite close to me when I rode away and made no remark on my leaving.' The terrified constable heard 'a great number of shots' and imagined that each must mean a bullet in his back. Neither he nor his horse were hit, which suggests that Ned made no attempt to kill him. Joe said later that he fired one shot after the fleeing policeman.

McIntyre gave the horse its head in a wild gallop for a couple of hundred yards to the north, through the speargrass bog and into thick scrub, then swung to the left across the creek and spurred westwards through the gully of Germans Creek and up towards the head of Bullock Creek, heading for the setting sun, hoping eventually to cross the telegraph line between Mansfield and Benalla.

After a desperate half-mile ride with branches ripping his clothes and flesh, his luck ran out. 'I was torn off the horse by the timber and severely hurt.' Winded and badly bruised, he remounted, but soon found that the horse was exhausted and took off saddle and bridle before shooing it away towards the south, hoping to confuse his pursuers. He hid the saddlery then ran towards the sunset. After about a mile he came to a gully which cut down towards Hollands Creek. Nearby was a large wombat hole. McIntyre squirmed into it, feet first, for about 3 yards and lay there, hardly able to breathe, watching the daylight vanish, listening for the sounds of pursuit. In pitch darkness he climbed out, scribbled in his notebook a brief account of what had happened, then removed his boots to avoid leaving tracks and headed off again. At 3 p.m. on Sunday he reached McColls' homestead, only a couple of miles from Mansfield. The McColls' neighbour, Matthew Byrne, provided a buggy and Byrne's son Ned drove McIntyre into town. Ned Byrne, like his brother Johnny, was a distant relative of Joe. One

Byrne — directly or indirectly — had warned the Kellys of Kennedy's party; another Byrne helped bring the news of its fate.

McIntyre walked into the Mansfield police station at 4 p.m., wet, muddy and feverish, covered in cuts and bruises, his clothes in tatters. His first words were, 'This is hell.' By 5.40 p.m. he had dictated the earliest detailed account of the shootings and was preparing to join a hastily organised posse of eight or nine townsmen led by newly promoted Sub-inspector Pewtress, a stolid product of the London Metropolitan Police who had spent years as sergeant-in-charge at Melbourne Town Hall. He was 'unacquainted ... with bush work', intent solely on recovering the bodies of the dead police. McIntyre had to be lifted into his saddle and the party faced a dark, wet journey to Stringybark Creek. Failing to find Kennedy's body in the camp, they roped the rain-soaked corpses of Lonigan and Scanlon on a blindfolded packhorse and headed back to Mansfield with little thought of searching further afield for the sergeant — let alone pursuing the Kelly brothers and their two unknown accomplices.

Since the colony's telegraph offices would not open until Monday morning, Constable Meehan had meanwhile set out from Mansfield on horseback, carrying McIntyre's report to Superintendent Sadleir at Benalla. Meehan saw 'two suspicious-looking men' and panicked. His revolver — the only firearm left at the station — had been taken by McIntyre. 'I said to myself, "I must do something. I must use my head ..."' He dismounted, turned his horse loose and, like McIntyre, removed his boots to baffle pursuit. By the time poor Meehan reached Benalla, news of the killings had been telegraphed all over the colony — along with a report of his disappearance.

Ned could not know that the hue and cry raised by McIntyre would produce such a tardy and timorous response; that the gang would have a thirty-hour start on their pursuers. They rode off from Bullock Creek late on Saturday night, dogged by images of the dead police and the last sight of McIntyre galloping for help.

With Tom Lloyd scouting for them the Gang covered more than 30 miles, riding down through the ranges in drenching rain, driving the six horses through a late, slow dawn, along the high bridle track above Ryans Creek. At Greta they got dry clothes and hot food from the Lloyds and Tanners. As the rain continued that night they mounted, rounded up the four spare saddle horses and the two packs and struck out across the Oxley Flats to cross a succession of swollen creeks and rivers. They were looping to the east by Beechworth, then north, following their old horse-disposal route, which offered safe passage for men and horses to the thinly populated outback of New South Wales. They were no longer running scared, because Ned had formed a plan in these first, fugitive hours. His actions — to some extent, his mistakes — had led the other three into this mess. He would claim sole responsibility for the police killings but he knew that all four would be branded equally as murderers. There was no escape within the law, so the four of them must live *outside* the law. To do this they needed money. Tom Lloyd would claim that Ned was already planning to rob a bank — at Howlong just across the Murray. Yet, even in this first day of the Kelly Gang's life, the plan went much further than just a bank hold-up.

Ned had decided that they would not behave like ordinary bushrangers, scooping up whatever loot they could find from homesteads, travellers, hotels, mail coaches and stores ... They had plundered the bodies of the dead police and left their pockets turned inside out to advertise the fact. They needed the money, as they needed the horses, guns and ammunition; and they needed the watches because time was now vital. These were spoils of war, claimed from enemies killed in battle. From this day on, Ned was determined to show that he had not chosen this path. He and Dan had offered to give themselves up; he had tried to disarm his enemies and spare their lives; the choice to kill had not been his. Now that the fight had been joined, he would wage his war in a way that transcended even the highwayman code honoured by Harry Power and Thunderbolt. His enemies would be the police and the banks. Even though the idea was half-formed at this early stage, Ned saw himself as leading a band of men who were no enemies to ordinary folk — not even to prosperous squatters.

Soon after 2 a.m. on Monday 28 October, as they approached the Ovens River, Ned gave the first signal that there was something different about the Kelly Gang.

Beside the first of nine bridges over the Ovens and its anabranches was Moon's Pioneer Hotel. The Gang reined in at the bridge, which provided a ready-made yard for the driven horses, while Joe knocked up the landlord at the hotel and bought a bottle of brandy, probably for Dan, whose shoulder wound was troubling him. They rode across the bridge towards Everton but found their way blocked by a sheet of fast-flowing water almost half a mile wide. The next series of bridges had been engulfed by the Ovens and its eight channels. To turn left, they faced worse floods and the town of Wangaratta. They turned right and headed up to the south-east towards the river's headwaters, in search of a crossing place. They had to ride almost 8 miles more before finding a ford near Taylors Gap. It was still several hours before Morse code keys would rap out word of Stringybark, and it was by a stroke of luck — good or bad — that they were sighted here by Constable Hugh Bracken. He had been stationed at Greta and recognised the four of them, knowing only that Ned and Dan were wanted over the Fitzpatrick affair. As they swung left, back along the far bank of the Ovens in this costly 16-mile detour, Bracken went on to raise the alarm, eventually bringing fourteen troopers there, led by Sergeant Steele, days after the Gang's passing. In the foothills at Everton, almost opposite the Pioneer Hotel they had left some three hours earlier, they halted at Coulson's Store near the railway station and bought several boxes of tinned sardines and some oats to give their horses stamina, then struck up towards Beechworth.

Twice within three hours the Kelly Gang had paid for their needs, signalling that they were no ordinary bushrangers. A hotelier and a storekeeper offered the first testimony, published in the press within days of these events, that something unusual was happening.

As day broke the Gang rode up into the ranges west of Beechworth and, at the highest corner of the tableland above Sheepstation Creek, risked firing eight shots to attract Aaron Sherritt. Joe's lifelong mate and a phenomenally tough bushman who regarded Ned with awe, Aaron accompanied them to a magnificent cave below the rim of the rocky, thickly timbered escarpment forming the southern flank of the Woolshed Valley. A random structure of giant boulders stacked together like an ancient Irish *dolmen*, the cave provided roomy, dry shelter with a commanding view over the sheer, bush-covered slope that dropped away to the floor of the valley and the meanderings of Reedy Creek. Down to the left was Joe's home and the Chinese miners' camp where he bought his opium.

Aaron guarded the four while they slept and rested. Perhaps this magnificent site reminded Ned of the Rock from which he and Harry Power had looked down on the King Valley all those years ago. Perhaps, too, Ned looked at Aaron standing guard over them — too tough to worry about jackets, eternally shirtsleeved in the bush in all weather — Aaron who cared little for guns, perhaps on this one occasion armed with one of the police weapons, open-handedly accepting this symbol of guilt.

Only hours after the first news of the killings had spread through the colony's telegraph network on Monday 28 October, Graham Berry had announced an £800 reward — £200 a head for Ned, Dan and 'two men names unknown'. The size of the reward and the government's extraordinarily quick response made it clear that this was being treated as an extraordinary crime.

Superintendent Nicolson was immediately placed in charge of the Kelly pursuit with 'authority to take any steps he thought proper, and to incur any expenditure he thought necessary'. Nicolson, now 49, was a patriarchal figure with his balding dome and grey-streaked, spade beard. He left for Benalla at 4.30 p.m. with the first of the seventy-nine men who would be transferred to the north-east in the next few weeks, almost doubling the district's strength. Extra firearms were sent and the government approved the purchase of twenty-four double-barrelled shotguns for issue to men engaged in the pursuit.

As Nicolson picked up the reins a freakish thunderstorm hit the ranges. A huge fireball rolled across Beechworth and branches of lightning lit the countryside as the Gang struck north through torrential rain. Aaron Sherritt scouted for them on the start of this last leg of the ride to the Murray, made more critical by the hue and cry and by the flooding creeks and rivers that turned their route into a treacherous maze. They had to find safe passage for their ten horses while at the same time avoiding all those ordinary folk who saw any four horsemen as the dreaded 'Mansfield Murderers'.

Daylight meant easier travel and easier recognition. It was a tedious journey, its slow pace increasing their tension and encouraging them to choose hurriedly, to strike out along higher ground that dwindled to a neck of land surrounded by floodwater. They must have made many such wrong choices, picking their way through the network of lagoons and anabranches, before they confronted the spectacle of a vast, brown flood swirling down the Murray Valley, turning hills into islands and rolling huge, waterlogged trees down the river bed, their branches ready to claw any living creature from the surface. In the words of Superintendent Nicolson, they faced 'the greatest flood that had taken place for a very long time'. It seemed impossible to consider swimming horses across this torrent, but even as they made this decision the rising backwaters cut off their retreat.

It was Wednesday morning, 30 October. They encountered a Murray Flats farmer with the Dickensian name of Gideon Margery who saw them only as four young men in trouble. He gave them some bread and cheese, fetched a couple of bottles of wine and drank with them. They lit a fire in a hollow log and Ned told Margery he was 'Ned Kelly the bushranger' and that he intended calling on a man named Whitty at Moyhu about some horse-stealing case. The fact that Ned said this in such a situation is a good measure of his obsession with Whitty.

Margery proved unhelpful to the police. A detective reported two days later, 'Margery cannot or will not describe the men but says one of them had a face like a Chinaman'. He also said that one had been 'winged'. Police disbelieved another local called Neil Christian who claimed the Gang 'stuck up' his house, even though he reported that 'one of the bushranging party must be wounded . . . as he could not sit upright'.

The rest of Wednesday and Thursday were lost in attempts to cross from island to island. Ned must have become increasingly desperate — so desperate that he rode up out of the lagoons on Friday afternoon barely 2 miles from Margery's and called at the home of William Baumgarten, now serving his four-year sentence over the disposal of Whitty's horses. The embittered Mrs Baumgarten offered no help and watched the four camp forlornly about 200 yards from her house until sunset, then drive their horses off across one of the Murray's flood channels. Only 'a very few minutes' after their departure, a police party, led by the formidable duo of Sergeant Harkin and Senior Detective Kennedy, came riding up to Baumgartens'.

Pushing through a patch of scrub, the Gang found their way blocked by floodwater. As they turned back they saw Mrs Baumgarten pointing out their route to the police. There was only one way of avoiding a gun battle and Ned took it. They left the horses in the scrub and waded into a clump of reeds for cover as the police party spurred in pursuit.

From the reeds Ned and the others watched, ready to fight, but the muddy water began to swirl higher at such an alarming rate that they would have to move out of the reeds to keep their guns dry. The police rode into the anabranch only minutes after the Gang, yet the floodwater had risen so rapidly that they found it impossible to cross. Harkin led the party to a shallower ford he knew of.

Superintendent Sadleir recorded, 'Standing up to their necks in water were the four bushrangers concealed by the reeds ... Their weapons under water, and they themselves benumbed with cold, the gang could have offered no resistance whatever had it been the fortune of the police to see them, but they did not'.

As soon as Harkin, Kennedy and their men were out of sight the Gang emerged, retrieved their horses from the scrub and made off in the opposite direction from the police. By the time Harkin had circled around to find the tracks of men and horses which told of this near miss, the Gang were safe from pursuit in the quickly changing maze of channels under a darkening sky. In that miserable dusk they took the chance of lighting a fire to warm themselves briefly, dry their guns, then re-load them with dry ammunition from the packs.

There was one last chance. Ned cut across to a punt at Bungowannah wharf but found it dragged underwater by its moorings. By dark on Friday 1 November, he had abandoned the attempt to cross the Murray and prepared to double back southwards. By Saturday evening they had reached the tableland above the Woolshed and called briefly at the Sherritt farm on Sheepstation Creek. The Sherritts had grim news. On Wednesday the reward on the Gang's heads had been increased to £2000 — £500 for each of them. It was too dangerous to stay long and they prepared to move on, but a bark stripper had already seen them, noting, 'men and horses pretty well worn out'. As they headed off towards Everton, the bark stripper rode to alert the police in Beechworth. Fortunately for the Gang, he was thoroughly shaken by the encounter and decided to stiffen his nerves with a couple of drinks. He arrived at the police station 'in a speechless state of drunkenness' and was carried to a cell to sober up.

Opposite the Everton Railway Station was the Victoria Hotel and Dining Rooms run by young Henry Vandenberg and his wife Mary. This Saturday night Henry was away, working on the railway. Scots-born Mary had closed up for the night and was going to bed when she heard 'the rattle of a whip on the door'. She took a lamp and unlocked the door. A tall, bearded bushman stood there with a coiled stock whip in his hand and a rifle slung across his shoulder. Three others stood on the verandah behind him — all of them soaked to the skin. Ned touched the brim of his hat and said simply, 'My men are in rags and must be fed.'

Mary knew immediately that they were the Kelly Gang; their call at Coulson's Store the previous Monday had caused a sensation in the tiny railway town. Heart pounding, she ushered them inside. Dan, Steve and Joe filed past her without a word but Ned stayed on the verandah.

'What of you?' she asked.

'I'll keep watch.'

Mary sat the three lads in the dining room, re-kindled the fire, then woke a young Irish maid and told her the Kelly Gang was here. The girl was terrified and started to cry. Mary told her, 'Get a bucket of potatoes and get them peeled.'

'I'll not do it,' the girl sobbed.

'You'll do it, or where will you go!'

'Shivering and crying', the child set to work and eventually, Mary gave the three young men their plates of stew and took one out to Ned on the verandah. He thanked her and apologised that he couldn't pay for the meals. Mary was happy to see it as an act of charity, even happier to see the three finish their stew and trail out to join Ned. They retrieved their horses from the hotel's accommodation paddock and rode off.

'Of all the sorrowful sights I saw, it was those poor men,' Mary recalled. She remembered Ned as 'a gentleman, nicely spoken, not bold'. Not wishing to worry her husband, she didn't mention the incident to him when he returned. 'One wild night', weeks later, there was a rap at the door and Henry investigated. He returned, mystified, with 8 shillings for Mary from a tall, bearded bushman. As the man turned to leave, a gust of wind had caught his coat, revealing a revolver in his belt.

Mary laughed. 'It's Ned Kelly, Dad.'

'Damn Ned Kelly!' Henry exploded. 'What's he doing here?' Two more people were left to wonder at the ways of these most unusual bushrangers.

AFTER LEAVING EVERTON, the Gang again faced the flooded Ovens River. Aaron Sherritt would have told them that it had risen even higher since they had been forced 8 miles upstream to Taylors Gap five days ago. Now the first crossing place was at Bright, 30 miles south-east. The only other possibility was at Wangaratta, less than 15 miles in the opposite direction. This was a town of some 2000 people, with its six police on the lookout for the Gang *and* a railway line to cross at the far side of town before they could reach the safety of the Warby Ranges. Railway lines were a formidable barrier to mounted fugitives, guarded on both sides by fences with chunky wooden posts, solid top rails and four strands of wire. There was rarely suitable ground to make the double jump a possibility, even for single horsemen. It was out of the question for the packs and driven horses. Railway crossings were easy to watch and many were supervised by resident gatekeepers. Unmanned gates were often locked.

Steve, however, had a way around the problem of the railway so, in a bold gamble, Ned struck out towards Wangaratta. He had no way of knowing that a special party of twenty-two troopers had been stationed there to pursue the Gang.

◆

THE DELANEYS, 'respectable people', lived in a brick house at the far north-western edge of Wangaratta, between the railway station and a railway bridge over One Mile Creek. At 4 a.m. 'just at grey in the morning', Mrs Delaney heard 'horses galloping and chains rattling, coming towards the house'. The family had horses grazing on the flat and she feared horse thieves.

> I got up to the window to see who they were, and saw four young men riding four horses, two pack horses in front with two heavy packs on each horse, and four others running bare-back in front of them. The horses seemed exhausted and the men were forcing the horses from the township before daylight as well as they could.

Two of the Delaney boys were up early and saw the four horsemen drive their packs and spare mounts along to the nearby railway bridge over One Mile Creek, which was running bank-high. They saw Steve Hart, who they knew, urge his horse into the flooded creek and pick his way along an underwater ledge which ran along the bank under the bridge beside the first set of brick pylons. The six loose horses followed him, deftly herded by the other three riders. On the other side of the bridge, on the far side of the line, Steve plunged his horse up out of the floodwater in a wild scramble. The others followed and they headed north, away from town. A little way on they swung left, galloped over a

The Kellys' fortified hut on Bullock Creek. After the Stringybark Creek killings Ned tried to burn it down, but the building was only damaged, saved by a downpour. The place was in ruins by 1884, the last vestige destroyed in 1930 when a sawmill set up its log yard on the site. (*Keith McMenomy*)

Constable Scanlon, a fine bushman, was a former partner of Sergeant Kennedy's and had shared a reward with him for the arrest of Wild Wright. Kennedy chose Scanlon as his right-hand man for the pursuit of the Kelly boys. (*Police Museum*)

Sergeant Kennedy of Mansfield was a fine policeman, loving husband and father, deeply religious and a teetotaller. Nevertheless he seemed fully prepared to kill the Kelly brothers and blundered fatally in dividing his party because he believed he was 10 miles from the Kellys' haunts. He made camp less than a mile from their hideout.

The author's reconstruction of the gunfight at Stringybark Creek, illustrated by John Ward. The clearing is shown in its actual proportions, correcting the drastic foreshortening of contemporary photographs, though for greater clarity the figures are larger than scale. The creek runs across the centre background, almost obscured by speargrass and scrub.

In the first phase, Constable Lonigan has run from the campfire to take cover behind the fallen log and, as he comes up to fire, is shot by Ned Kelly, the right-hand figure of the group emerging from the speargrass. McIntyre stands with his back to Lonigan. He heard but did not see the impact of the bullet.

The second phase, with the Kellys and police in their approximate positions just before the death of Constable Scanlon, who is on his knees in the centre of the picture. He is trying to unsling his rifle, after being wounded on horseback by Ned, who stands, aiming his shotgun. Steve Hart, with a revolver, has left the tent. Sergeant Kennedy, taking cover behind his horse, is about to wound Dan Kelly who has advanced with Joe Byrne from the speargrass. Joe is perfectly placed to fire the fatal shot into Scanlon's exposed right side. McIntyre escaped out to the right, to the north, on Kennedy's horse and Kennedy later followed on foot, to be killed by Ned several hundred metres away, after a running gunfight.

Joe Byrne, Ned's best friend, hangs on a lock-up door at Benalla, dead for some 30 hours. As lieutenant of the Kelly Gang his good looks won him a pop star following among the girls of the north-east, while Beechworth folk remembered the 'quiet' and 'respectable' son of a widowed dairywoman. The crocheted scarf may be a frayed memento of his youth. (*Police Museum*)

Constable Lonigan, an enemy of Ned Kelly after a brawl in a Benalla bootshop. He was attached to the Stringybark Creek party only because he could recognise Ned and Dan. This portrait is an early reproduction from a lost original photograph.

Constable McIntyre, seated, was the sole survivor of the Stringybark Creek party. With him is Edward Monk, a Wombat Ranges sawmill proprietor, who helped recover the bodies of McIntyre's dead comrades. (*Police Museum*)

wooden bridge behind the town's hospital and spurred towards the Warby Ranges.

The Gang had negotiated the floodwaters on the eastern side of Wangaratta then crossed the bridge at the end of the town's main street, just below the junction of the Ovens and King Rivers. They had ridden through the empty streets, within a stone's throw of the police station, past the railway station and, rather than using the nearby level crossing which might be watched, they had carried out the precarious manoeuvre under the One Mile Creek bridge.

After a last desperate gallop the Gang continued to push their horses as hard as they could, away from town, across 5 miles of flats to the Warbys. Just past the steep eastern face of Mount Warby, gentler spurs and gullies led to a saddle. In among the timber they climbed doggedly to gain a view across Wangaratta to the creeks, rivers and flood-plains they had crossed in the night and fore-dawn, now shining under a cloudy sunrise. Despite boggy ground, flooded creeks and rivers and the days lost among the lagoons of the Murray, they and their ten horses had travelled more than 200 miles in one week — a bravura display of horsemanship. It was only by sheer fluke that one policeman had seen them, even before the alarm was raised.

From these eastern slopes they could see the Hart house on Three Mile Creek. Beyond the crest of the range, they would come in sight of the undulating, green hogback of the Bald Hills, marking the Eleven Mile. This was the country and the people they knew best.

They could not afford to become careless and over-confident. They would not recross the railway line past Glenrowan and make for Greta, the centre of their strongest support, since it was also their most obvious destination. They would ride down the far side of the Warbys, by Briens' orange grove at Morgans Gap, and make for Uncle Timothy Ryan's farm at Lake Rowan, about 10 miles away. There they could have hot food and drink without a tell-tale fire in the bush and discard one of the packs and the spare saddle horses. When the police pursuit had run itself out, they would head back to the ranges and make their way south to Greta.

In a last scramble across the spine of the Warbys, Scanlon's horse broke down. They unsaddled it, left it to graze on the range and pushed on towards Lake Rowan. This was Sunday. Three days would be wasted before the Wangaratta police started their pursuit.

11

PURSUERS?

OCTOBER – NOVEMBER 1878

The news of Stringybark sent a shock wave through the colony and paralysed whole communities. Riding to Mansfield on 29 October, Sadleir found, 'So great was the alarm on every side that carriers on the roads halted their journey, fearing lest they should run up against the Kellys: and each man I met was astonished that I should ride through the country without an escort, some of them imploring me to turn back.' Sadleir readily admitted that his bravery sprang from a belief that the Gang would be 100 miles away by then.

Even normally courageous policemen were unnerved by the three deaths. Detective Michael Ward had been searching near the headwaters of the King River the day of the killings. He had returned to Moyhu when he received a note from Senior Constable Strahan telling him of the murders and asking him to ride back to the Upper King.

> I said 'No' to myself . . . I am not going to return as long as there are three police shot, and me only with a little revolver; they are well armed; I am not well armed. I will make my way to head-quarters for proper arms and accoutrements.

Back at Wangaratta by 30 October, Ward was 'hemmed in by the floods' for 'two or three days'. He was still there when the Gang passed through the town. The next morning, Monday 4 November, he rode across to Oxley and began to piece together the Kellys' route up to the Murray — a week behind them.

It is significant that Ward remained 'hemmed in' a full twenty-four hours after the Gang and their ten horses had negotiated the floods around the town. Already Sergeant Steele, another prominent policeman of the district, had shown apparent reluctance to pursue the fugitives.

At 12.45 a.m. that Monday morning Steele had passed through Wangaratta on a special train taking fourteen men and horses to Beechworth. He had heard rumours in Benalla of the Gang riding under the One Mile

Creek bridge the previous morning. Now, Constable Twomey met Steele at the railway station and confirmed the rumour. Twomey had interviewed young Delaney and followed the Gang's tracks a little way. Steele told Twomey 'that it was undoubtedly the outlaws . . and it was evidently Steve Hart who had piloted them under the bridge . . . I told him my opinion was the outlaws would make for the Warby Ranges . . .' Steele told Twomey to 'report the matter to Mr [Brooke] Smith' and headed for Beechworth with his men on what he knew to be a wild goose chase.

A Royal Commission considered his action 'highly censurable', commenting, 'had he exhibited judgement and promptitude on that occasion, he would have been the means of capturing the Gang'. They went on to say, 'No one knew better than Sergeant Steele the personal peculiarities and unsuitability of Mr Brooke Smith for the work, and to have referred his informant [Constable Twomey] to that officer was simply an attempt to evade responsibility.'

Inspector Alexander Brooke Smith was the officer accused by Ned Kelly of bullying, braggart behaviour towards the Kelly girls and women during raids on the homestead at Eleven Mile Creek. He was 44, a policeman since he was 17. Although senior to Nicolson in years of service his career was undistinguished, apart from some notoriety eight years before when he was imprisoned briefly for debt. Since then he had moved from post to post with such regularity that Beechworth's *Advertiser* noted drily, 'He seems to be under a chronic state of marching orders.' Brooke Smith himself would comment, 'I have been appointed acting superintendent four times over, and never got the district afterwards.'

Superintendent Nicolson considered Smith 'natty in his person'. To Ned he was 'that article that reminds me of a poodle dog half clipped in the lion fashion', reserving for the inspector some of his most colourful invective.

> He knows as much about commanding police as Captain Standish does about mustering mosquitoes and boiling them down for their fat on the back blocks of the Lachlan, for he has a head like a turnip, a stiff neck as big as his shoulders, narrow hipped and pointed towards the feet like a vine stake. If there is anyone to be called a murderer regarding Kennedy, Scanlon and Lonigan it is that misplaced poodle . . . it takes three or four police to keep sentry while he sleeps in Wangaratta for fear of body snatchers.

Already, as Ned obviously knew, Brooke Smith was showing signs of paranoia. The Inspector was to comment, 'I did not keep any books at all at that time [the first week of the Kelly pursuit] — I thought it was too dangerous.' He would advise Nicolson not to use a notebook, 'because . . . the outlaws might get hold of it'. A year from now, Nicolson would find him, 'A wreck both in body and mind ... He seems to go about muttering and speaking incoherently about the Kellys etc.' The possibility of suicide would be suggested, prompting Nicolson's icy comment, 'I do not think Brookes has the courage for that remedy.'

Such was the man woken by Constable Twomey, at 2 a.m. on 4 November, to be told that the Kelly Gang had ridden through Wangaratta 22 hours before. The inspector was stationed at Ketts' Royal Hotel with twenty-two men detailed for pursuit of the Kellys.

Brooke Smith told Twomey to interview Mrs Delaney and her sons. When the constable returned at 5.45 a.m. the inspector 'said something about sending a telegram about half-past eight, about the office being open then'. Nothing happened that day or the next, and Twomey was 'disgusted'. After midday on 6 November, nearly 60 hours after being told of the Kellys passing through the town, Brooke Smith led his twenty-two men to Peechelba Station, some 13 miles north of Wangaratta. Here he split his party, sending thirteen men, under Senior Detective Kennedy, past the northern end of the Warbys to Lake Rowan, while he led the rest another 17 miles up to Yarrawonga on the Murray, where they stayed the night. Ironically the Gang probably left Timothy Ryan's place that day and rode back into the Warby Ranges. If Brooke Smith had led his men straight to the Warbys, they might have found a trail only hours old or even encountered the Gang.

Next morning, 50 miles away at Sheepstation Creek outside Beechworth, a force of some thirty police swooped on the Sherritt house at dawn — acting on the information of the drunk bark stripper who had seen the Kellys there *five days earlier*. Captain Standish, attended by two Melbourne reporters, rode with the party which was led by either Sadleir or Nicolson. No one seemed sure at the time and Nicolson later denied responsibility. Each officer headed a small group galloping up to the house and Nicolson dead-heated to the front door with Constable Bracken. The irritable Scot pushed Bracken aside and his shotgun went off, causing a general charge by the twenty remaining horsemen.

Finding no one there but a rudely awakened Sherritt family, the party proceeded to Aaron's hut on his selection, a mile away at the edge of the tableland. This, too, was empty. Undaunted, the horsemen rode down into the Woolshed Valley and charged up to the Byrne house at Sebastopol, where they interrupted Mrs Byrne's milking and earned a tongue lashing from that formidable lady.

As full daylight revealed the dramatic dawn raid as a fiasco and neighbours and gold miners gathered to watch the police have a picnic breakfast, Aaron Sherritt strolled up with an axe over his shoulder. He had slept the night at the Byrne house, as he often did, and had been chopping wood for Mrs Byrne while she and the children did the milking.

Senior Constable Strahan introduced Aaron to Nicolson and Sadleir as an intimate of the Kellys, but Aaron would speak only to the Chief Commissioner. Asked to betray the Gang, Aaron said he would — on one condition: that Joe Byrne's life was spared. Standish promised to use his influence with the government.

This inept operation was immortalised as the Charge of Sebastopol, the Great Sebastopol Raid and, most popularly, as the Rats Castle Fiasco. (Steele and his men had been on the way to Rats Castle, 18 miles away, when they were diverted to Taylors Gap then called back to take part in the raid on Sherritts'. Because reporters and later writers liked the name 'Rats Castle' it survived the two changes of venue.)

It was Thursday 7 November. Up at Yarrawonga on the Murray, Brooke Smith was roused at an unrecorded hour — probably late — and led his party down to Lake Rowan, travelling so slowly that the men complained. On Friday morning, they started on the return journey to Wangaratta and had called at Timothy Ryan's farm where Senior Constable Charles Johnston, an able, zealous policeman, rode across and checked the stockyard. He saw the tracks of several horses — some shod and some unshod — tracks no more than 48 hours old.

Brooke Smith was unimpressed and led the party on its way while Johnston hung back, looking for more tracks. He found the hoof marks of five horses within a quarter of a mile, 'three of them riding singly, and there was evidently a packhorse beside one of the others'. Johnston gave a 'coo-ee' and called Smith back. The Inspector had to agree that these could be the tracks of the Gang. Also with the party was a civilian volunteer, Jim Dixon, son of the bankrupt entrepreneur. He was, like Johnston, a first-class bushman and tracker. They found where the horses had crossed a brush fence and one had left some white hairs. Johnston recalled from descriptions in the *Police Gazette* that one of the police horses from Stringybark Creek, a chestnut gelding branded M42, had a white face and legs.

Now sure that they were on the trail of the Kellys, Johnston and Dixon followed the tracks across the rain-softened ground of the flat country then, with greater difficulty, up into the Warby Ranges by Morgans Gap.

Here, near Brien's orange grove, Johnston found a quantity of fresh orange peel and orchardist Brien admitted to Brooke Smith that 'the outlaws used to come to his house and get tea and oranges', but would not say how recently. 'He was too experienced a man of that kind,' said the redoubtable inspector.

While Brooke Smith stayed talking with Brien, his party continued following the tracks. When the inspector started off fifteen minutes later, his men were out of sight, and he fired a shot to bring them back

— an undisciplined action for a policeman in pursuit of bushrangers. According to Brooke Smith, the men became 'nervous and excited' — he believed because 'the firing of a shot was what led to the murders on the Wombat'. It never occurred to Brooke Smith that his shot could warn the Gang.

Two years later Ned Kelly told Johnston 'that he did not sleep any that night; that he knew they were on to them; that they held their horses in their hand all night'.

Ned's caution was unnecessary. By the time Brooke Smith had rejoined his men and explained why he had fired the shot, it was approaching dusk. He announced that they would return to Wangaratta for the night, 'get the black trackers and be able to run the tracks to-morrow'. They reached Ketts' Hotel at 9 p.m. and, after talking with Nicolson, Brooke Smith said they would set out at 4 the next morning.

Woken at 4 and advised that men and horses were ready to leave, Brooke Smith told Johnston 'he would get up immediately'. Called at 5, Brooke Smith again said 'he would get up immediately'. He appeared two hours later, directed Johnston to take the men back to Brien's orange grove, and said he would follow.

When the inspector hadn't arrived by 1 p.m., Johnston 'suggested the advisability of going on and picking up the tracks and fighting the outlaws'.

Three hours later Johnston and his seven men had followed the tracks to a place on the crest of the range where the Gang had camped while their horses grazed. After an hour of trying to pick up a trail from the wandering hoof prints, they sighted a bay gelding among the trees, cropping peacefully at the scant native grass. As they rode closer, Johnston saw the brand — a crown over B87. It was Scanlon's horse.

At dusk the triumphant party had reached the foot of the range, planning to send to Wangaratta for food and to camp out overnight, when Brooke Smith came riding up.

'Halt; form up!'

The surprised police formed a line.

'Any applications or complaints?'

Johnston told the inspector of their find.

'Right,' said Brooke Smith, 'proceed to Wangaratta.'

Next morning, Sunday 10 November, poor Johnston went through the usual routine of rousing the inspector; a call at 4, another at 6. Brooke Smith appeared at 8.30. Eventually Johnston and his men started off without their intrepid leader and he caught them up after a couple of hours because he had been turned out of the hotel by Nicolson.

Brooke Smith refused to continue following the tracks where Johnston had left them the previous day, so the disgruntled party rode back 10 miles, picked up the tracks, followed them for 10 miles to the point they had reached the day before, then started off again 'and ran them in the direction of Taminick Station'. After camping overnight at the station, by the western edge of the Warbys, they started out again at daylight on Monday — for once with Brooke Smith — and found the tracks leading south to Glenrowan. Here the trail was suddenly warmer.

The previous Friday evening three horsemen had met a train, waiting on the main road a couple of hundred yards uphill from the line. A man got off the train and walked up to them. From this point, horse tracks headed up around the eastern shoulder of Morgans Lookout, a broad, bush-clad pyramid that rose behind the town. A chestnut with white face and legs had been seen loose near the railway line. A man had walked down from the bush, caught it and disappeared 'on to the range'.

After Brooke Smith's party had stumbled on to their tracks the previous Friday, the Gang had ridden to Glenrowan for their evening rendezvous with the mysterious train traveller — possibly Tom Lloyd or Joe Ryan checking on police movements.

The Gang had spent a tense night on the range, holding their horses, but it seemed that the police had lost their tracks. Ned's confidence was shaken nevertheless. Perhaps his first instinct had been right; perhaps they would be safer in the New South Wales outback.

They split up, two riding across the railway line to 'the neighbour-hood of Greta' while the other two cut back along the Warbys to 'within a few miles of Yarrawonga', almost certainly to check on the possibility of crossing the Murray now that the rain had passed. They planned to join up again, here on the Warbys, probably on the Tuesday morning.

Meanwhile, by Monday afternoon, Brooke Smith had found three-day-old tracks from the train rendezvous and had a nearby sighting of what was probably a second police horse from Stringybark. Even though he was within a few hundred yards of a hotel, he again ordered his men 10 miles back to Wangaratta for the night. By now it was clear to Nicolson that 'the men ... were very much dissatisfied' and that the inspector 'was quite unfit for that work, as he had abandoned the pursuit while on what he believed was a genuine track'.

Nicolson professed to believe 'that the outlaws were 100 miles away at the time' and claimed that, purely 'to soothe the men', he organised a major expedition for the following morning. He and Brooke Smith rode to Glenrowan with Sergeant Steele's search party and Johnston's. There they met Superintendent Sadleir and, with two Aboriginal trackers, sup-posedly set out to follow the trail of the horses that had ridden around Morgans Lookout the previous Friday. It was now daybreak on Tuesday, four days later. On the face of it, the operation promised little hope of success, except as a morale booster for Brooke Smith's sorely tried men.

Nicolson wasn't being completely honest when he said that the expedition had been mounted, 'to soothe the men'. He and Sadleir had reliable information that two Gang members had been 'near', 'in the neighbourhood of Greta' on Monday morning. They also knew that a platelayer called McEvoy had seen horsemen, believed to be members of the Gang, who had galloped through the railway crossing at Glenrowan in the late afternoon or early evening of Monday 'and ridden in towards the Warby Ranges, riding from Greta to the Warby side'.

Sadleir's official report on 'Appearances of the Kelly Gang' and 'Action Taken by the Police' would show this large-scale foray as a pursuit based on that Glenrowan sighting — now scarcely more than twelve hours old. Evidence to the Royal Commission by Nicolson and Sadleir, and their behaviour on the expedition, would give little hint of this.

Not surprisingly the hoof-marks leading out of Glenrowan were 'perfectly plain' and the trackers — an old man called Doctor and his young 'pupil', Jimmy — led the twenty-strong party across a spur of Morgans Lookout then along the eastern flank of the Warbys. After about 2 miles the tracks took them, in Sadleir's words, 'into within a short distance of cover, where an ambush might be'. Johnston agreed that 'the tracks led into some thick scrub'.

'The tracks were still visible,' said Sadleir, 'but those trackers took us clean away from them; they left the tracks . . . and took us to a swampy ground, where there were thousands of tracks, where all the cattle of the neighbourhood came to water . . . I am perfectly satisfied that they were simply misleading us.' Sadleir hastened to add, 'I do not blame them . . . they were actuated by the spirit of self-preservation, because they would be the first to be shot.'

Johnston confirmed that the trackers 'did not appear to like to go into the scrub at all'.

Obviously, the two Aborigines recognised fresh tracks that had been made far more recently than the previous Friday and believed they were close on the heels of some of the Kelly Gang. Nicolson refused to acknowledge this. He even refused to admit that the tracks had led into scrub. He was to tell the Royal Commission:

> The tracks led to a dry swamp with low tussocks of grass and a few swamp trees with clear stems for 5 feet of their height. There was no scrub or other cover whatever . . . it is perfectly untrue as asserted by Johnston that there was scrub in front of us.

Surprisingly, the Royal Commission seemed content with this straight contradiction, ignoring or forgetting the fact that Johnston's evidence had been borne out by Sadleir's.

Nicolson was describing the dead-end reached by the party: the swamp with the maze of cattle tracks into which the Aborigines had led them *after* veering away from the possible ambush site described by Johnston and Sadleir.

The two trackers, Johnston and Sadleir had all recognised the danger of following the tracks into threatening scrub. If Nicolson was speaking the truth, he had failed to notice the scrub, the danger it posed or the Aborigines' resulting detour. This is very hard to believe, even given his alleged belief that the Gang were 100 miles away. It is equally hard to understand Sadleir's acceptance of the situation and his readiness to abandon the pursuit, especially when he subsequently admitted, 'With a good party of blacks we would have had a very good show.' On Sadleir's evidence, 'the tracks were still visible' approaching the scrub. It would have been a simple matter to pick up the trail at this point, using Johnston and Dixon.

Certainly Johnston was mystified when, as he put it, 'the track of the outlaws was completely given up'. He and the other men 'were all very anxious indeed to follow on', but were told by Brooke Smith, 'we must obey the orders we got'. Yet Nicolson would claim that he did not interfere until 'Johnston gave up the job'. He would tell the Commission, on oath, 'When they could do nothing further, I turned back along with them.' As with the Great Sebastopol Raid, he would portray himself as a mere bystander, reluctantly involved in a fiasco created by others.

It seemed to Johnston and his comrades that Superintendents Sadleir and Nicolson had deliberately avoided a possible encounter with the Kelly Gang only seventeen days after the killings at Stringybark Creek. Their behaviour remains inexplicable.

As a finale to this aborted pursuit, 'through some mistake of orders' Nicholson left Sergeant Steele and a small party to 'scour the Warby Ranges to the end'. They started without a proper briefing and seem to have ridden straight past the Gang. Ned was almost certainly watching, probably incredulously, as Nicolson, Sadleir and their men sat down to a picnic lunch beside a spring, then packed up and rode back to Glenrowan before returning to Wangaratta. Here Nicolson sent Brooke Smith off to Beechworth 'with orders not to interfere in the Kelly business any more'.

Like Nicolson, Sadleir would play down suggestions that they had been close to the Gang, though he testified,

I heard it reported afterwards as coming from Ned Kelly, that he saw us and could have shot Mr Nicolson and myself if he liked, of which I do not believe a word; but he must have heard we were there, for he described that we sat in a little open place where there was water; and ... that he saw the brands on the horses — recognized different men in the party.

A frustrated Johnston had planned to follow the tracks himself after the hillside picnic but was ordered back to Wangaratta. 'I was dissatisfied,' he said, 'and the following day applied [to be transferred] and left for Benalla with three men.' The astonishing retreat from the Warbys on 12 November marked the end of a black eight days for the police.

The Royal Commission would severely censure Brooke Smith and Steele for their failure to follow up the One Mile Creek sighting of 3 November, while virtually ignoring the fact that, on 12 November, Nicolson and Sadleir had abandoned an even fresher trail. Nevertheless, the Commission's judgment on the eight days remains valid. 'Upon no other occasion throughout the pursuit, from the murders at the Wombat to the final affray at Glenrowan, was there presented a more favourable prospect of capturing the Gang.'

The handful of men in the force who, like Johnston, were capable of posing any significant threat to the Kellys, would continue to be hampered by a police hierarchy totally unfitted for the unique demands of this problem. In months to come, when some of the most formidable Aboriginal trackers in Australia had joined the Kelly chase, they would have no more success than old Doctor and young Jimmy, blocked by an amalgam of inefficiency, inappropriate policies, stubbornly held convictions, clumsy tactics and racism.

Until the events of 12 November, Ned clearly had grave doubts about remaining here among the friendly hills the four of them had known since boyhood. Any such doubts must have been dispelled by the spectacle of Nicolson, Sadleir and at least a dozen heavily armed police, within gunshot, sitting down to an alfresco lunch before trailing back the way they had come.

Below and beyond the Gang's position on the eastern flanks of the Warbys, the sunlit Oxley Flats were drying out, offering faster, safer travel to the huge spine of ranges that defined the heart of their world, dappled by clouds driven from the south by spring winds, while the shadow of Morgans Lookout moved steadily out across the flats and the Fifteen Mile and Burkes Holes towards the King and the Ovens, claiming it all. If any single day could be seen to mark a turning point in the fortunes of the Kelly Gang, this had been the day. The sun was setting on the north-eastern police district of Victoria. It would rise tomorrow on the Kelly Country.

12

'THE COUNTRY BELONGS TO US'

15 NOVEMBER – 10 DECEMBER 1878

Three days after the debacle near Morgans Lookout, Ned, Dan, Joe and Steve were declared outlaws. It had been a weighty process. A Felons Apprehension Bill had been introduced on 30 October, passed the following day and given vice-regal assent on 1 November. Three days later notices were published all over Victoria under the royal coat of arms calling on Ned, Dan and Two Men Whose Names are Unknown (but whose persons are described as follows . . .) to surrender at Mansfield by 12 November.

While Nicolson, Sadleir and Brooke Smith played out the last act of the Warby Ranges fiasco, the Mansfield court house stayed open all day, with Sub-inspector Pewtress and a constable symbolically ready to receive the surrender of the Gang. When the court house door was shut and the key turned, the ponderous mechanism of the law proceeded three days later to the Declaration of Outlawry by the Chief Justice and immediately to the Proclamation of Outlawry . . .

> By his excellency Sir George Ferguson Bowen Knight Grand Cross of the most distinguished order of Saint Michael and Saint George Governor and Commander in Chief in and over the colony of Victoria and its Dependencies and Vice Admiral of the same &c &c

The four documents — one for each member of the Gang — with their handsome calligraphy and seals, look thoroughly mediaeval and they were. They echoed the same ancient procedure by which Robin Hood would have been declared an outlaw — a 'wolf's head' — a being deprived of all rights as a human, to be killed on sight by men-of-law or civilians, with a handsome prize for the killer.

The fine print offered a member of the Kelly Gang a slightly better deal than is sometimes claimed. He could be killed without challenge, 'if . . . found at large armed or there being reasonable ground to believe that he is armed'. This was cold comfort, however, since the fact that he was an outlaw probably provided 'reasonable ground' in itself to assume that he was carrying a gun.

Any person harbouring, concealing or assisting the Gang, giving them information or withholding information from the police, could receive up to fifteen years imprisonment 'with or without hard labour'. It was, as J. J. Kenneally put it, 'a declaration of war'.

This draconian measure had little impact. Ned's loyal supporters remained loyal and his enemies found the outlaw just as elusive as the mere fugitive had been. Perhaps the Outlawry Act's main effect was to place an added pressure on Ned to live outside the law and try to depend less on friends and relatives for food and supplies.

By mid-November Maggie Skilling had emerged as a tower of strength for Ned and the Gang. Already, the police were aware that she was baking bread 'in such quantities that it could not have been for the ordinary family'. Each night, in these first weeks, she rode off, usually on her horse White-foot, and arrived back 'a couple of hours after day-break' with White-foot exhausted.

The police tried to follow but found it 'impossible'. By galloping in short bursts then stopping to listen for the sound of horses following her, Maggie forced her pursuers to come within sight or lose her.

There were two traitors in the Kelly circle — one of them a man called Donnelly, then boarding with the family. He was in regular contact with Sadleir and Nicolson and alerted them to Maggie's activities. Through Donnelly the two superintendents knew that the Gang was 'near' — except on 12 November when it had seemed more convenient for them to be 100 miles away. The police lost their ace of spies when he resigned because he feared that he was suspected and his life was at risk. No other agent would ever be as close to the family.

Accepting north-eastern Victoria as his operating base, Ned returned to his first plan, aborted by the flooded Murray: a bank robbery. Now the Gang needed a large sum of money if they were to fulfil Ned's plan and show that they were not ordinary bushrangers who simply had chosen to live by the gun. A bank robbery would provide both the money and a public platform — a chance to display themselves as high-wayman heroes such as Australia never had seen.

The bank robbery itself must be worthy of this ambitious design. Joe Byrne, as the best educated member of the Gang and 'for a bushman rather clever with his pen', worked with Ned, putting the developing plan to paper, refining details and searching for loopholes.

Seymour, where Ned and Harry had considered robbing a bank, was an early thought but Nicolson and Hare had known of those plans. Oxley and Milawa were also possibilities, but too obvious as targets and already taking precautions. Beechworth, Benalla and Wangaratta were too ambitious. Down the line between Benalla and Seymour was Euroa, a prosperous 'sleepy hollow' with a branch of the National Bank in the new part of town that had sprung up beside the railway, a quarter of a mile from the main road and the old town. The bank was almost opposite the railway station so the operation demanded a 'cover' for the Gang members carrying out the robbery. This, of course, fitted Ned's broader plans. The Kelly Gang would not look like bushrangers.

An essential detail of the strategy was a depot where the Gang could rendezvous, collect hostages, rest the horses and change from bush clothing into town clothes and where they could bring the bank staff after the robbery, before heading back to their home ranges.

Ned's widowed Aunt Grace and Grandma Quinn lived in the district and Ned was familiar with Faithfull's Creek homestead, almost perfectly placed 3½ miles from Euroa, half a mile west of the main road and fairly close to spurs of the Strathbogie Ranges. Faithfull's Creek may also have appealed to Ned on philosophical grounds. It was an out-station of the 80 000-acre Euroa run, one of nine properties in the area which had been scooped up by Isaac Younghusband and Andrew Lyell MLA over the last eight years, creating a half-million-acre conglomerate. These absent tycoons could afford a little hospitality. Although the north-eastern railway ran past the homestead only 150 yards to the west, it was flanked by the government and railway telegraph lines which could be broken immediately before the strike at the bank, neutralising this threat.

Ned had friends at Faithfull's Creek who would make it possible to introduce other friends as casual workers before the chosen date. Posing as prisoners of the Gang, these undercover allies could help monitor the real prisoners who would be held until the robbery was over. Among them would be Andrew Morton, black sheep of a respectable Beechworth family who had befriended Ned in Pentridge, and 'John Carson', a trusted sympathiser who would help Joe guard the prisoners then disappear after the robbery.

The cleverest detail of Ned's and Joe's plan was the delivery of their new outfits to the homestead. Ned's old friend, the hawker Ben Gould, lived near Seymour and was currently staying at a Euroa store. His relationship with the Kelly family was well known to the police and his direct involvement would have invited prosecution under the Outlawry Act. (Even without such involvement, Ben's unconcealed enthusiasm for the project led to his arrest soon after the robbery.) Probably through Ben they recruited another Seymour hawker, James Gloster, possibly an old friend from Ben's Tasmanian days. Gloster would arrive with his cart during the hold-up and become a 'prisoner'. His stock would include a new outfit for each Gang member — complete from boots to hat.

Gloster's white-hooded cart, boldly painted with his name, was well known in Euroa and a perfect vehicle to carry the bank robbers into town then bring the bank staff back to the homestead after the robbery.

◆

ON 14 NOVEMBER, the day before the Gang were proclaimed outlaws, Mr Donald Cameron MLA, member for West Bourke, had asked a question in parliament concerning the origin of 'the Kelly outbreak' and the 'scandalous' conduct of the pursuit. Premier Graham Berry calmly promised 'a searching inquiry' if provided with appropriate evidence. Ned and Joe were avid readers of metropolitan and local newspapers and Ned was excited by Cameron's question, failing to recognise it as a routine attempt to embarrass the government. As historian and writer McMenomy shrewdly commented, they 'mistook the political football for a genuine opportunity to state their case'.

Ned set out to write a long letter to Cameron. More accurately, Ned dictated it while Joe hurriedly scrawled out a rough draft, bibbing and tucking here and there, prompting, sometimes editing. Their voices blended. The resulting letter is vivid, undisciplined and in part bombastic, but mostly restrained.

Ned set out to 'state a few remarks concerning the case of Trooper Fitzpatrick' and in tracing the genesis of the trouble back to Lydecker's bull, immediately digressed to an attack on James Whitty and the conduct of 'Whitty and Burns' towards 'poor men of the district'. He gave his version of the clash with Fitzpatrick and his vivid account of Brooke Smith's raids on the Kelly homestead:

> This sort of cruelty and disgraceful conduct to my brothers and sisters who had no protection coupled with the conviction of my Mother and those innocent men certainly made my blood boil as I dont think there is a man born could have the patience to suffer what I did.

In the most remarkable passages of the letter, Ned gave a detailed account of the killings at Stringybark Creek, taking all blame, claiming that the unnamed Joe and Steve were not even present and denying the cruel lies that he had mutilated Kennedy's body or fired 'into the bodies of the troopers after death'. He readily admitted his bitterness towards Lonigan and described the bootmaker's shop brawl in Benalla. This reminded him of the fight with Hall in Greta and this led to the tacky affair over the calf's testicles — even to Dan's involvement in the case of Goodman, the hawker. In a sonorous finale, Ned threatened that if Fitzpatrick's 'falsehood' were not exposed,

> ... horrible disaster shall follow. Fitzpatrick shall be the cause of great slaughter to the rising generation than St Patrick was to the snakes and

toads of Ireland. Had I robbed plundered ravished and murdered everything I met my character could not be painted blacker than it is at present but thank God my conscience is as clear as the snow in Peru.

As Joe was contributing a few lines of lighthearted verse to tag the letter, Ned included the ringing declaration, 'If I get the justice I will cry a go.' Some would try to see this as a plea for a pardon, but it was not Ned's style to plead for himself. Justice, for Ned, would be served by the release of his mother, Skilling and Williamson. He would then 'cry a go' — give up bushranging. Surrender? Probably not. He had made that offer once. Perhaps he and the lads would simply ride away from it all, as they could at any time, perhaps with the money from Euroa, and set sail for America as old Harry had planned . . .

Ned must have known, nevertheless, that he could receive justice only in terms of British law, which could offer him but two alternatives: death by bullet or rope. The only future for any of the Gang lay outside the law of Britain and her colonies.

For now the scribbled draft was folded away. When they rode to Euroa Joe carried a bottle of red ink and a thick sheaf of notepaper. Fine copies would be made and sent to parliamentarian Cameron and to Superintendent Sadleir, who at least was an Irishman. When the letter was read in parliament and published in the press — all 3500 words of it — many more questions would be asked and the Mansfield Murderers would be seen in a very different light. Ned prepared for Euroa with growing optimism.

◆

SCARCELY MORE than two weeks before Christmas 1878, 12-year-old Bill Gouge of Euroa was galloping along the Sheans Creek road, bareheaded, ducking under branches, enjoying the warm wind around him. His flying hair caught in a branch and snapped his head back, dragging him from his horse and killing him. Young Bill's father was 'an old resident' of Euroa and the boy's funeral, set for the afternoon of Tuesday 10 December, was attended by most of the townsfolk, apart from those at a sitting of the Licensing Court late the same afternoon.

On Sunday 8 December Joe Byrne rode into Euroa and met Ben Gould. Joe was unknown in the town and still not yet officially identified as a member of the Gang. Checking final details for the hold-up and lunching at De Boos's hotel near the bank, he heard of the two events which would occupy the people of Euroa on Tuesday afternoon. It seemed a perfect time for the bank robbery.

At about 12.30 p.m. on Monday the Gang quietly rode up to the Faithfull's Creek homestead — a 'comfortable, well-built' brick house with a few slab outbuildings, drowsing in a corner between the gums and weeping willows of the creek and the nearby railway embankment. Ned was riding his favourite mare, Mirth, a superb bright bay with white hind feet. Joe was mounted on his mare, Music, a handsome grey who had recently foaled and was not yet back to her top condition, but still able to carry Joe 65 miles in a day. Dan and Steve rode a pair of bays. All the horses were shod, all were described as 'magnificent', 'very valuable' and 'far superior to anything in the district'.

Despite their striking horses, the men's weather-beaten hats, old tweed jackets and riding trousers, dark-stained with horse sweat, made them look almost commonplace, if it were not for the holstered revolver on each belt and the barrel or butt protruding from the small swag strapped at the front of each saddle.

With a pipe between his teeth, Ned strolled over towards the house and announced their arrival to the cook, Mrs Fitzgerald, who was at the clothesline. She was probably one of their friends. Her husband, one of the 'knockabout hands', took Ned down to the stable where 'John Carson' was repairing his hat in the harness room while he yarned with station groom, George Stephens, a keen-eyed ex-policeman.

'Do you know who I am?' Ned asked.

Stephens shrugged. 'Perhaps you're Ned Kelly.'

The alexandrite eyes lit, just a spark. 'You're a damned good guesser.' Ned quietly drew his revolver, told Stephens to get some oats and signalled the lads to bring up the horses.

The other station hand, a shadowy fellow called Peter Chivers, and a few casual harvest workers who were never identified by the police were bailed up as they trailed in from haymaking. All were locked in a slab shed across the yard from the homestead, to be joined by a couple of locals unlucky enough to drop by and the overseer, Macaulay, who returned about 4.30.

There was a total lack of drama until hawker James Gloster came driving up in his wagon at sunset with his 18-year-old assistant, Frank Beecroft. Gloster took no notice when told the place had been held up. After Ned's stirring declaration, 'I am Ned Kelly the son of Red Kelly and a better man never stood in two shoes,' Gloster tried to get a revolver from his wagon and there was much shouting, with Ned threatening to shoot him, until Macaulay intervened and persuaded Gloster to surrender. ('Macaulay ... told me I was foolish & that any one else who put himself in my position would have been shot.') Despite being overplayed the scene convinced its audience and no-one suspected that Gloster was an ally of the Gang.

That night, the fourteen male prisoners — real and sham — settled down among the stores and tools in the 20 ft by 15 ft shed, where Ned joined them. For hours he yarned with them, answered their questions and told them the story of his family's problems with the police.

He said that his mother had seen better days and had struggled up with a large family and he felt very keenly her being sent to gaol with a baby at the breast by the perjured statements of Fitzpatrick.

Among shadows of the past, a shadow of the future flickered briefly: 'He said that if his mother did not get justice and were not released, he would overturn the train.' (This remark was reported and produced a brief spate of patrols along the north-eastern line. Then, two days after Christmas, 'between forty and fifty half-pound tins of gunpowder' were found hidden beside the line within 500 yards of the Benalla railway station. Little was made of this discovery. There was no sense in alarming train travellers unnecessarily . . .)

The prisoners in the lamplit shed were Ned's first audience — literally a captive one — and he enthralled them. He also left the clear impression, 'that he took the talking on himself about the shooting of the police as though he wished to screen the others'. '. . . I did all the shooting in the ranges, none of the others did any shooting . . . the people and papers call me a murderer but I never murdered anyone in my life.' Of Kennedy he said, 'I killed him in fair fight. Fair stand up fight . . . I was sorry afterwards that he did not surrender.'

Some of the men went to sleep and some sat up, sharing Ned's memories of that terrible day. Some offered him money, which he declined.

At dawn Ned returned to the homestead where Joe was sitting at the overseer's desk writing the fine copy of the letter to Cameron. Perhaps they went over the last details of their plans for the day until the sun rose, promising heat.

The morning passed quietly with Joe writing out the second copy of the letter for Sadleir, resting, chatting with Mrs Fitzgerald, reading a magazine and playing the accordion. The job finished, he sealed Cameron's copy in a square envelope, asked Mrs Fitzgerald for two stamps, then tucked the precious letter in his pocket.

After lunch, while Dan guarded the prisoners, Ned, Steve and Joe took a tomahawk and broke the telegraph lines — four government wires to one side of the railway, with a railway telegraph line on the other. They not only cut them, but twisted, looped and plaited them into a repairman's nightmare, taking a skein of wires from one side of the line, through a culvert, and joining them to the broken railway wire on the other side. Several wooden poles were chopped down, iron poles bent to the ground and porcelain insulators smashed. Before the job was finished Ned rode back to the homestead. He had dismounted and was with Macaulay in the yard when he noticed that a large group was gathering down near the railway gate, about 200 yards from the homestead. There was a horseman, a man on foot, three men in a spring cart and four men on a railway trolley . . .

'Here's a go!' Ned crowed. 'Here's nine traps!' He vaulted into the saddle and spurred off towards the threat in true highwayman hero style. Perhaps he believed for a moment that the men were police, but it is more likely that he was enjoying his role.

Two elderly gentlemen from Melbourne — a splendidly John Bullish Englishman called Dudley and a dour Scot named Macdougall — had been kangaroo hunting in the Strathbogie Ranges with two locals, Tennant and Casement. They had enjoyed a few beers at a hotel on the main road and, as they were 'some distance from another house', Dudley had bought a soda water bottle of whisky. With a double-barrelled shotgun, a superb 'needle rifle', 80 or 90 cartridges, plus 'three tails and the hindpart of a kangaroo', the hunters were halted in Casement's spring cart while Tennant rode ahead to open the railway gates. He was intercepted by Joe just as four railway gangers happened to arrive on their trolley.

As Dudley and Macdougall were discussing the coming feast of kangaroo haunch and kangaroo tail soup, Ned galloped up with drawn revolver declaring, 'Turn the horse around, the station is stuck up!' The three men noticed a pair of handcuffs hanging on his belt and assumed he was a policeman. When Dudley demanded to know his authority for this high-handed behaviour, Ned realised their mistake and rose to the occasion splendidly. He pointed at Casement.

'You're Ned Kelly! Where did you shake this horse and cart?'

In his own words Dudley was, 'a rather touchy customer' and started blustering at Ned, who threatened to handcuff him unless he kept quiet.

'I'll report you to your superior officer!' Dudley barked.

Tennant, another Scot, came riding back and asked what was happening. When Dudley told him, 'The Kellys are about,' he clambered up into the cart, announcing that they would load their guns — presumably to help these officious, plainclothed police.

The joke was wearing thin and Ned exploded, 'Good God! Will you get down!'

'Mind what you're about,' Tennant warned as he prepared to load one of the guns, 'Or it'll be the worse for you.'

Ned shoved the revolver in his belt and raised clenched fists. 'My knuckles are as hard as any man's here . . .'

Wisely, Tennant put down the gun and climbed off the cart. With their guns commandeered, Dudley still clung to the notion that Ned was a policeman and admitted, 'I gave him a good deal of impudence,' as they were herded back to the homestead. Macdougall agreed that Dudley 'was giving tremendous cheek . . . he was getting outrageous'.

As Ned arrived with the troublesome hunting party and Joe brought in the four railway gangers, the groom, Stephens, was by the gate.

'These gentlemen don't seem to understand or comprehend who I am,' Ned told him.

Stephens smiled. 'Gentlemen, allow me to introduce Mr Edward Kelly and his party.'

While Macdougall commented dourly, 'the sensation created by the information did not tend to reassure us ...' the irrepressible Dudley found something to be grateful for. 'The glory of it was that, before we met Kelly, a gentleman had taken a fancy to my gun and I sold it to him, so I did not lose,' though he later noted with some regret that he never saw his whisky again. So another eight men joined the fourteen prisoners in the store shed. They had arrived just in time for the great transformation.

Ned and the lads changed into the new clothes Gloster had brought for them. Ned's suit was characteristically sober — a blue sack coat, brown tweed trousers and vest, elastic-sided boots, grey-striped flannel shirt, brown felt hat and a single dash of colour in a magenta tie. Each member of the Gang finished off his outfit with a white handkerchief in the breast pocket and a splash of perfume from Gloster's stock.

Ned, who loved symbols, and especially the cleansing symbol of fire, piled up the four suits of old bush clothes and set them alight. Dan's outsized, once-stylish suit, his own dark tweeds, the dark, low hat with the black velvet band — these were the clothes of the murderers and fugitives. The four outlaw phoenixes were now ready for Euroa.

Gloster's lad Beecroft was, like his boss, an undercover ally. He drove the hawker's wagon with Ned beside him, Dan drove the hunters' spring cart and Steve rode a station horse. Joe stayed behind guarding the prisoners, assisted by 'John Carson'.

It was just after four when the party reached Euroa and drove down empty, drowsy Binney Street to the National Bank — a brick corner building rented from the local blacksmith. Young Beecroft drove the cart into the back yard, followed by Dan in the spring cart and Steve on his stock horse. While Dan and Steve stayed at the back Ned went to the front door, knocked and said that he had a cheque to cash. With the door ajar, the accountant, Bradley, told him the bank was closed. Ned shoved the door open, sent Bradley staggering and bailed him up. A clerk, Booth, also raised his hands and Ned took a bank revolver from the counter where it was lying ready for return to the manager for the night.

Meanwhile Steve had come in the back door and found one of his Wangaratta school friends, a lass called Fanny Shaw, doing some ironing in the kitchen. She was the family's maid. After brief hellos, Steve told her, 'I have a little business to do with the boss.'

'The boss' was manager Robert Scott, a balding, bespectacled and stubborn middle-aged man. Ned walked into Scott's office, caught up a second bank revolver from the manager's table and told him to bail up. About to leave for young Bill Gouge's funeral with his sons, Scott was thoroughly irritated and stared defiantly at this intruder. Steve had entered beside Ned, armed with two revolvers. Again ordered to bail up, Scott raised his hands, though only 'to the armpits of my vest'. He said later, '. . . I tried to bustle them about to gain time.' Ned found only £300 or £400 in cash and was about to go into the adjoining residence when Scott declared, 'Kelly, if you go in there I'll strike you, whatever the consequences may be.' Steve cocked two revolvers at his head and Scott reconsidered his position.

Mrs Susy Scott was a spirited, youngish matron from a well-known Western District family, the Calverts. She had seven children, the oldest 13, the youngest a baby of five months. She found life at Euroa rather boring, but suddenly all that changed. Confronted by Ned as she and her old family nanny were dressing the baby for a walk, she later told Superintendent Hare that she 'began chaffing Kelly' and told him 'he was a much more handsome and well dressed man than she had expected and by no means the ferocious ruffian she imagined him to be'.

Finding her husband stonewalling Ned in his attempt to find the keys of the safe and strong room, Mrs Scott went hunting and found them on a hook in a drawer of Scott's table. This enabled Ned to gather up another £1500-odd in notes, sovereigns and silver, and a 31-oz gold ingot lodged with the bank by a Dry Creek gold mine. The total haul of some £2260 was scooped into a sugar bag with a collection of bills and securities held against bank loans.

Mrs Scott's mother was staying with the family. She, too, was charmed by Ned, recalling his first words, 'Don't be frightened, nothing will happen to you, I have a mother of my own.'

Scott noted all this with a rather tight-lipped, 'My wife and family, contrary to my expectations, took the visit very calmly . . .' Indeed, Mrs Scott entered so thoroughly into the spirit of the occasion that, for the trip back to Faithfull's Creek, she changed into a costume worthy of the Melbourne Cup:

> . . . the French muslin she had just got up from Robertson and Moffats . . . with all its lace and ribbons . . . with a shearers hat all covered with tulle and flowers, and a pair of long, white driving gloves.

Everyone, including Robert Scott, 'looked rather surprised' at her entrance. Perhaps this explained the odd little exchange that followed. Ned, finding that he had to transport a bank contingent of fourteen, asked the manager if he would harness his buggy for their use.

'No, I won't,' Scott grumped. 'And my groom is away. Do it yourself.'

The words hung for a moment in the dimly lit room, its blinds drawn against the heat. No anger lit Ned's eyes. He smiled. 'Well, I *will* do it myself.'

Perhaps, as one theory has it, he was simply charmed by Mrs Scott. Or perhaps he respected a man in an impossible position, potentially humiliated in front of his wife and children, showing more spirit than most men did when they faced Ned Kelly. It was a turning point. After Ned had harnessed the buggy Scott offered Ned, Dan and Steve a whisky. They accepted, but waited for him to drink first, just in case . . .

Out in the back yard they all prepared to leave. Dan drove the hawker's wagon carrying Beecroft (whose enjoyment of the occasion had been a trifle too obvious), the two bank staff and a couple of the older boys. Mrs Scott was at the reins of the buggy with her mother, nanny, baby and younger children, and Ned drove the hunters' spring cart with the loot at his feet, Scott beside him and maid Fanny in the back. Steve rode along behind.

Just before they climbed aboard, Susy Scott gave her 13-year-old son 'a parcel consisting of things for the baby and, wrapped in a shawl, a large cake baked as usual for the children that morning'. Characteristically the boy put the parcel down in the yard and forgot it. Characteristically Ned noticed the bundle and put it in the buggy.

This odd procession rattled out of the yard and headed briskly towards Faithfull's Creek, noticed by the stationmaster's wife who told her husband that 'she had seen the bank people with a lot of friends going off for a picnic'.

The journey back to the homestead was marked by two incidents. It was a strange moment when they jogged past the cemetery where the funeral was taking place. 'The mother of the lad . . . was horrified that Mrs Scott would drive past at such a pace when the poor boy was being laid in his grave.' Then Ned and Scott took a short cut across a creek and while Ned was driving up the bank the horse fell, nearly overturning the spring cart. Scott held the horse's head while Ned gallantly lifted Fanny clear. They unharnessed the horse, got it up and continued on their way with Scott driving. They got on famously. Ned spoke of the gunfight at Stringybark Creek. All Scott would tell police of this conversation was that Ned admitted to shooting Lonigan. (At Ned's trial for murder Scott commented, 'The prisoner treated me personally very well,' and 'did not use a single rude word to Mrs Scott'; altogether a most unsatisfactory witness for the prosecution.)

Back at Faithfull's Creek Ned found that Joe had collected one more prisoner. A luggage train to Melbourne had dropped a telegraph line repairer called Watt, who scanned the chaos of wires and posts then strolled across to the homestead. There Joe bailed him up and put him in the store shed. They couldn't know that the train had also been carrying the 'old English gentleman', Police Magistrate Wyatt, who noted the damage to the telegraph lines without any fallen trees or branches to suggest that they had been struck by a storm. Wyatt got off at Euroa, conducted the brief business of the Licensing Court then, still pondering the mystery of the fallen posts and wires, hired a buggy and drove out towards Faithfull's Creek.

On the way he encountered a rude young man on horseback also looking for the homestead. It was Steve, who had doubled back to trace Ned's and Scott's short cut. (Later, Steve spoke of meeting the 'old buffer with the sheet round his hat'.) Running out of time, Wyatt drove back to town and waited (oddly enough, with the Kellys' hawker friend Ben Gould) for the evening train from Melbourne that would take him back to Benalla. There was no sign of Watt, the line repairer, and by now Wyatt was sure that the telegraph line had been broken by the Kelly Gang.

At Faithfull's Creek the Gang ate dinner. The male prisoners — allowed to walk free after the heat of the day — were hurried back into the store shed at 7 p.m. when a train approached from the south and stopped opposite the house. The Gang watched Wyatt get down from the train and collect some pieces of broken wire. Then he climbed back on board and the train boomed off towards Benalla.

The male prisoners were again released from the shed, and, after another hour or so the Gang prepared to leave. First, partly to entertain their captives and partly from pure high spirits and bravado, they staged a brief exhibition of trick riding.

Ned, it was noted, 'quite excited the admiration of the station hands' as he 'performed a number of clever acts on a magnificent animal'. Hunter Dudley recalled, 'The horsemanship displayed by Ned Kelly is something surprising. He maintains his seat in the saddle in any position, sometimes resting his legs at full length along the horse's neck, and at others extending his whole body till his toes rested on the tail, dashing along at full speed.'

With the loot from the bank on Mirth's saddle Ned delivered a brief speech to the prisoners, warning them to wait for three hours after he and his men had left and adding dire threats against betrayal. At 8.30 p.m., with a full moon well up in the sky, the Gang spurred away 'at full gallop . . . in a perfect cloud of dust', soaring over a fence like four night birds and off across the moonlit paddocks towards Duck Ponds Creek and the ranges beyond.

This exit, watched by an audience of thirty-seven, was as dramatic as the entrance had been unremarkable. It was hard to believe that these dashing outlaws were the same earth-coloured bushmen who had ridden into the dusty yard the previous day, and harder still to believe that these were the feared Mansfield Murderers. The haul from the robbery was a fraction of the £10 000 Ned had hoped for, but this remarkable piece of theatre was certainly an artistic triumph, if not a runaway financial success.

The spirited Scots huntsman, Mr Macdougall, told a reporter:

> With regard to the conduct of the Gang ... although domineering in giving their orders, no attempt at violence or roughness was made on any of us.

Mrs Fitzgerald said, 'They were perfect gentlemen,' and the *Weekly Times* reported that the Gang's behaviour had been:

> ... of a character polite in the extreme; everyone was more or less 'mastered', and 'thank-yous' and 'much-obliged's' were frequent in their conversation.

The Melbourne *Herald* noted that '... The bushrangers played with the children and boys and treated everyone with the greatest civility.' They also recorded that, on Ned's return from the bank, he told the prisoners he was sorry he hadn't passed a pub or he would have bought them a drink.

The *Age* hailed the operation as 'daring and skilfully planned', describing the 'proceedings of the bushrangers' as 'most cool and audacious'. The *Argus* spoke of the 'four cool, determined men' who had displayed such 'cool impudence and daring effrontery'. The *Herald* considered the hold-up, 'more like romance than a narration of an actual occurrence', calling it, 'daring' and 'skilful' and declaring 'Nothing could have been better designed or carried out'. The impact created by Ned was striking. The prisoners testified to his good looks, charm, impressive bearing and prodigious horsemanship. Bank manager Scott described him as, 'a splendid specimen of the human kind, tall, active, rather handsome ...' and told an *Argus* reporter, 'He did not seem a bit afraid of the police, but on the contrary, laughed at them.' When Scott had asked where they were going when they left Faithfull's Creek Ned told him, 'Oh, the country belongs to us. We can go where we like.'

The newspapers would note that Euroa was protected by a solitary policeman who 'was standing only 100 yards away when the outrage was perpetrated', while '16 well mounted troopers and two very competent blacktrackers' were based at Mansfield, still beating around the hills the Gang had left six weeks before. Within two days of its first report of the hold-up the *Argus* was saying, 'There is something radically wrong in the operation of the police force.' Beechworth's *Advertiser* had already recorded 'a great outcry about police mismanagement', while the *Herald* had noted that Sydney considered the affair 'an awful disgrace on the Victoria police system'.

These cracks had appeared in the facade of police credibility long before it was known that, while the Gang were still at Faithfull's Creek, Police Magistrate Wyatt was on the Benalla railway station only 27 miles to the north, telling Nicolson and Sadleir that the Kellys had struck at Euroa. Wyatt carried pieces of cut wire and broken insulators.

Nicolson and Sadleir duly boarded their train and headed off in pursuit of the Gang — but in the wrong direction. They had what Standish called 'some strange evidence' — a piece of misinformation, contrived by Ned and Joe, that the Kellys were going to cross the Murray. Although Sadleir admitted, 'There was no pressing reason why Nicolson and I should both proceed to Albury,' the two left on their 70-mile wild goose chase in a train that had been within a couple of hundred yards of the Gang not an hour before. They left a 'nonplussed' Wyatt standing on the platform clutching a handful of wires and insulators like a bunch of flowers. It was not yet 8 p.m. Back at Faithfull's Creek, only 27 miles to the south, the Gang was more than half an hour from leaving. If an alert had been raised from Benalla, if every available policeman in the district had converged on Euroa, if even a couple of patrols had been sent to investigate, the outcome could have been very different.

The Gang's professionalism was being thrown into high relief by a bumbling police pursuit. Ned Kelly's mastery of men and events was providing a startling contrast to the leadership of the police force — even of the colony, as Graham Berry prepared to go to London with demands for a new constitution. Within nine days of the Euroa robbery the *Herald* would suggest, seriously, that Ned Kelly provided the perfect model for the sort of policeman to solve the problems of stock theft and bushranging. The same day a *Melbourne Punch* cartoonist showed Ned occupying the vacant premier's chair. The tide was turning.

13

STATE OF WAR

DECEMBER 1878 – FEBRUARY 1879

The colony of Victoria, which had seen itself as 'a country' threatened by invasion from the sea, now went into a state of war against an enemy striking from within. Professional soldiers of the Garrison Corps, who manned coastal batteries and forts (as well as providing sentries for the Treasury and Government House), were rushed up to the Kelly Country to mount guard on the district's banks. In scenes reminiscent of troops leaving for the front in wartime, another fifty-eight policemen converged from all over Victoria to bring the north-eastern police strength to 217 men equipped with an additional 217 Adams revolvers, 20 Colts, 62 Martini Henry rifles and 32 shotguns.

The government quickly acknowledged the stature of its enemy. Three days after the Euroa robbery the money on Ned Kelly's head was doubled to £1000, bringing the total reward for the gang to £2500. This was advertised throughout the north-east on '700 or 800 calico posters'.

By then, a new man was leading the Kelly pursuit. Poor Nicolson had hurried back from his fool's errand to Albury. About 12 hours after the gang had left Faithfull's Creek, he met a seven-man party there, led by Senior Constable Johnston and Detective Ward, and headed off in pursuit. In the best part of a day's galloping in fierce heat they supposedly followed the gang's trail in a strange course that looped northwards then swung all the way back to the railway line between Faithfull's Creek and Euroa. They rode into town for a late dinner and the men fell asleep 'in all sorts of attitudes, not drinking a drop or anything of the kind'. Johnston, 'the strongest and most energetic of the party', was sprawled on a sofa, 'so dead asleep that he was not awakened, though they poured water over him'.

The party continued their search throughout the night and returned to Euroa at 6 the next morning. Nicolson was exhausted, 'heart-broken' and almost blind from ingrowing eyelashes. At 10 a.m. Captain Standish arrived in town. He found Nicolson 'quite knocked up', ordered him back to Melbourne to take temporary charge of the department and telegraphed his longtime protégé, Superintendent Frank Hare, to come up and lead the Kelly pursuit.

The towering Hare unfolded himself from the afternoon train with shotgun, greyhound, white sun helmet and less than his usual self-confidence. For once in his career he chose not to charge off immediately in pursuit of bushrangers, announcing, 'I knew nothing of the circumstances of the robbery, except what I had seen in the papers.'

And that was not encouraging. 'Reliable' reports of the gang's movements had them all over Victoria as four men on their 'three bays and a grey', or careering around in pairs — even two of them crossing into New South Wales. Soon Hare was receiving his own 'reliable' reports — from a squatter outside Benalla 'that the Gang were shooting parrots near his garden'; from 'the late Chief Justice' that 'the gang had been in Mrs Rowe's garden cutting cabbages, near Euroa'.

In fact Ned and the Gang had ridden straight back to the familiar hills near Greta. 'About a mile from Faithfull's Creek' (probably at Duck Ponds Creek) they had met Tom Lloyd, Dinny McAuliffe and two other sympathisers riding 'three bays and a grey', ready to act as decoys. The changeover was probably made in the creek. The four sympathisers continued the bank robbers' apparent course, up the opposite bank and off to the north, while the gang turned along the creek bed a little way towards the Strathbogies then struck out for home, leaving Tom and the others to bamboozle pursuers with their false trail.

There would be laughter in the hills with the happy homecomings of the Gang, followed by the mock gang. The jollity spread as Ned began to distribute Euroa money among friends and relatives who had helped them or simply believed in them through those dark days after Stringy-bark. The Benalla correspondent of the *Herald* reported: 'People who were without money a short time back have been noticed to be rather flush with cash during the week.' One of Ned's friends was seen in a Benalla pub buying drinks with 15 shillings worth of sixpences; Maggie Skilling went on a shopping expedition to Benalla, spending sovereigns; Joe Byrne's mother settled a £65 bill the family had run up with a Beechworth storekeeper; Aaron Sherritt escaped losing his precious selection by paying the Lands Department £36 (plus agent's and solicitor's fees); and hawker James Gloster of Seymour, who had been in debt before the robbery, was noted by a policeman now to have 'plenty of money'. National Bank notes smelling of earth began to appear all over the Kelly Country — briefly deposited for safe keeping in the bosom of Vinegar Hill between Greta and Winton.

In the meanwhile, Standish moved quickly to prevent publication of Ned's and Joe's letter when it reached Mr Cameron on 17 December. Standish had already seen the copy sent to Sadleir and claimed 'it contains a tissue of falsehoods & makes various threats'. He telegraphed Premier Berry: 'I think it inadvisable that publicity should be given to such a production.' Cameron was duly 'advised' not to let the letter be published, although reporters were allowed to read the twenty-two pages of red copperplate produced by Joe in those tedious sessions at Macaulay's desk.

The next morning's papers were dismissive. To the *Argus* it was the work of 'a clever illiterate person' and 'evidently composed with the object of obtaining public sympathy'. The *Daily Telegraph* ranted at 'Kelly's morbid vanity' and alleged that he had made 'frightful threats . . . unless a free pardon be granted to himself and his fellow-miscreants'. That afternoon the *Herald* went as far as it dared without actually publishing the letter. It quoted Ned's claims that he and his family were 'continually dogged by the police' and spoke of 'the outrages committed on his sister and the unmerited punishment of his mother'. Most disturbingly for Standish, the paper summarised Ned's account of Stringybark, including his insistence that 'neither himself nor his comrades intended to commit murder' and that Lonigan 'got behind a log and fired at him. Ned Kelly then fired in return, and Lonigan fell dead.' The *Herald* argued Ned's case more strongly than he had. He had never mentioned 'outrages' on his sister, nor did he claim that Lonigan actually fired — only that he was about to. The *Herald* refuted the claim that Ned had sought a free pardon, but went on to say that the letter 'does not make any proposition to the government'.

Ned's 'If I get justice I will cry a go,' had been mis-read by the *Telegraph* and missed by the *Herald*, but Ned must have felt some satisfaction as he read,

> The writer does not ask for mercy for himself, and admits that he knows he is outside the pale of mercy. He, however, asks that the grievous wrongs inflicted on his sisters may be righted, and that justice may be done to his mother, brother-in-law and another man convicted with them, all of whom he declares to have been improperly imprisoned on perjured evidence.

Concluding, the *Herald* noted that the letter was signed, 'Edward Kelly, enforced outlaw'. This highly sympathetic summary, which was run in Beechworth's *Advertiser* the following day, eased the frustration of not having the Cameron Letter published; but already Ned had suffered another, more serious blow.

It was emerging that, apart from the persona and abilities of Ned Kelly himself, the Gang's greatest source of strength lay in its core of support in the north-eastern district — a small army of allies, built on the eighty-odd members of the clan and spreading through its close friends and their friends and relatives to form a network of operatives reaching every town and settlement. Until Euroa there had been a strong, vocal anti-Kelly faction. Some of this group had been moved to revise their attitudes by the constant talk of Fitzpatrick's perjury and of 'outrages' against Kelly womenfolk; by the very different picture that was emerging of the Stringybark fight; and by the Gang's clear failure to fit the mould of ruthless bushrangers. More of them had been persuaded simply to step back from the conflict, avoiding involvement on either side. They may not have given the Gang active support, but in failing to help the police they became tacit sympathisers. An unusually well-informed correspondent from Yea wrote to the *Herald*,

> There is a great deal of sympathy for them all over these districts among certain classes. I know for a fact that there are hundreds of confederates of the Gang between Mansfield and Benalla. No doubt their horses are taken at convenient places, and paddocked in some secret place till required, and they [the Gang] are hidden in some quiet spot among their friends and confederates. They don't do much roughing. My opinion is that they will be found not very far from their own home, but I think a large number of people will have to be locked up before the gang can be had.

In spite of clear and widely publicised evidence that Kelly sympathisers had been salted among the prisoners at Faithfull's Creek, only one accomplice had been arrested. This was Ben Gould, who was picked up on 14 December, hauled before the court at Benalla and imprisoned in Beechworth Gaol on remand. Ben had been talking and drinking very freely during and after the robbery. 'While suffering a recovery', he was arrested by Detective Ward, much spoken of in the press as an intrepid pursuer of the gang. In the parade of fumbled opportunities which characterised the police pursuit to date, Ward had emerged as a danger. Such a blow at the sympathisers drove home the Outlawry Act's threat of fifteen years imprisonment for accomplices and struck at the heart of the gang's strength. Ward was one of only a handful of men in the force who knew the country and its people well enough to pose any serious problem for the gang. He was an old enemy of Joe Byrne and Aaron Sherritt, too — he had arrested them for butchering a stolen cow and was said to have seduced Joe's sister. Joe was reported as saying, 'that he would swing easily if he could shoot Ward and put his body in a hollow log and burn it'.

Ned and Joe laid a plan to rid themselves of Detective Ward.

◆

THE YEAR WENT OUT in a cloud of economic gloom, with a thunderclap as Premier Berry left Melbourne for London, threatening open revolution — 'broken heads and houses in flames' — unless the Imperial government restricted the powers of Victoria's Governor and Legislative Council.

In Benalla Captain Standish celebrated the passing of 1878 with a gathering of,

all responsible men in charge of different stations ... constables and officers and detectives. They ... all went into a room, and were asked the names of the persons in the district whom they considered to be sympathisers.

Those named would be arrested and charged under the Outlawry Act. Sadleir tried to dissuade Standish from this 'unwise step'. Hare, who recorded a list of some twenty men, admitted,

The police ... had no evidence against these persons beyond the fact that they were known to be associates, relatives and friends of the outlaws.

All would have to be arrested the same day 'because if we had not done so, it would have been just as much difficulty in catching them as the Kellys'. Warrants were issued on Wednesday 2 January, and the police swooped on the Friday. News of the first four arrests in Mansfield were telegraphed to Melbourne with the dramatic announcement that Steve Hart had been captured. It turned out to be John Hart, no relation of Steve, who had been arrested on the strength of his name. He, Robert Miller, Wild Wright and Henry Perkins were all arrested 'at various occupations in the harvest field, getting in the crops'. Jack Lloyd and Daniel Delaney soon joined them. Remanded for eight days to Beechworth, they were handcuffed in pairs, packed on a coach and sent to Benalla, guarded by six troopers.

At Wangaratta Jack Quinn, Richard Strickland, William Woods and the Clancey brothers were charged, remanded and sent off to Beechworth. In Benalla Tom Lloyd, John McElroy, Jimmy Quinn, Frank Harty, Jack McMonigle, Michael Haney and Joe Ryan were brought before the bench and also remanded to Beechworth. The Benalla operation was far from perfect. The police arrested Tom Lloyd Senior instead of his nephew of the same name and cagey old Tom got permission to send a telegram home, 'Turn the four bullocks out of the paddock' — a warning for the gang.

Benalla troopers set out to arrest Joe Ryan but picked up his brother Jack by mistake. Discovering they had the wrong man, they released him, but when he immediately galloped off to warn Joe they had to arrest him all over again before he could raise the alarm. Eventually, only Joe was brought in.

The arrest of Jack McMonigle was their worst blunder. Jack, Ned's leading hand from the Burkes Holes sawmill, had returned from Gippsland before the killings at Stringybark Creek. The police deaths appalled him and 'he had sent word to the family that he wanted nothing further to do with them & they had kept scrupulously out of his way, not out of fear'. Yet Jack found himself handcuffed to the others, 'innocent and guilty alike ... and marched publicly up the Benalla [railway station] platform'.

The sight of farmers dragged from their harvests and manacled together as a public spectacle was disturbing. The *Herald* reported, 'A great crowd was assembled at the station to look at the men, and a few uncomplimentary remarks were passed at the police for their action.' In spite of this, the paper's same issue claimed that the arrests had 'given universal satisfaction throughout the district'. In weeks and months to come, the 'uncomplimentary remarks' would become more frequent, to be heard even from the newspapers who had urged this step and applauded it being taken.

On the Friday a sergeant and twelve men of the Garrison Corps arrived in Beechworth and were quartered at the gaol, ready to mount a guard with rifles and bayonets when the first of the sympathisers were brought from Benalla by train the next morning. Next day twenty-one men were marched to a court convened in Beechworth Gaol. Only one was represented by counsel and no evidence was given. Ben Gould was remanded to Euroa; the rest were remanded to appear in seven days then marched back to their cells.

This scene was repeated weekly for the next 3½ months, with the same failure to produce evidence, seven- or eight-day remands and imprisonment without trial.

Sadleir denounced the tactic as 'unlawful'. It was an ill-advised move which advertised the police force's inability to cope with the Kelly phenomenon. It provided further impetus to the swing of sympathy away from the police. And it further united the pro-Kelly forces in their co-operative efforts to harvest the crops of the gaoled men.

After the first shock of the mass arrests Ned and the Gang moved to pay for the defence of their friends and supposed friends. In their coming court appearances the talented Messrs Zincke of Beechworth and Reade of Melbourne would appear for the sympathisers, launching increasingly bitter attacks on this flagrant abuse of the law, eventually earning the police and government an almost universally hostile press.

Meanwhile Ned and Joe badly needed a second robbery as a source of funds and as a hitback. And there was still the problem of the devious, amoral Detective Ward. In a characteristic ploy Ned and Joe decided to kill two birds with one stone.

The week after the first sympathiser trials Ward had an accident. While tom-catting across a Beechworth backyard in the early hours of the morning, 'the virtuous detective' fell down a pit, breaking some ribs and injuring his leg. He was admitted to the Ovens and Murray Hospital and, two weeks later, had a most unexpected visitor — Aaron Sherritt.

Aaron told Ward that Joe Byrne and Dan Kelly had called to see him the previous day, with an invitation to join the Gang on an expedition into New South Wales. If Ward went with Aaron, they 'should be able to get them before they crossed the river'. It was a replay of Aaron's attempt to lure Fitzpatrick into Ned's hands before his mother's trial, but Ward was less gullible than Fitzpatrick and hardly in a condition for a ride to the Murray. Aaron, however, refused to take anyone else. Stalemated, he agreed to Ward's suggestion that he give his information to Captain Standish in Benalla. This was the second prong of the plan.

Aaron strolled into the Benalla police station the following evening to be told that Standish was away overnight. He agreed to see Superintendent Hare, the one senior officer in the Kelly pursuit he hadn't met on the Great Sebastopol Raid. The tall Hare and the rangy bushman sized each other up and each decided that the other was a prize target for his manipulative talent: Hare saw himself as a person of enormous charisma; Aaron recognised Hare's great weakness — his ego.

With the help of a few drinks Hare eventually persuaded Aaron to divulge the information he had come to give — that the Kelly Gang were about to cross the Murray on the way to Goulburn. Convinced that he had completely won over this 'head centre of the district' — the Gang's key agent — Hare recruited him on the spot, gave him £2 and, eventually, a trio of code names: 'Moses', 'Tommy' and 'Sheck'. Aaron went on his way, chuckling, while Hare legged off to Sadleir, bursting with his momentous tip-off. Scanning the wall map, they found the chain of hills that crossed the Upper Murray and ran towards Goulburn: this would be the Kellys' crossing place! Parties of troopers galloped eastwards to intercept the gang.

Ned and Joe had come up with an audacious variation of the strategy they had used to divert attention from Euroa. While Aaron's 'information' decoyed the police to watch for a crossing of the Murray above Corryong, the Gang quietly prepared to cross the river 160 miles to the west.

Everyone had been impressed with the planning of the Euroa hold-up, but if Euroa had seemed 'more like romance ... than an actual occurrence', this exploit was to border on fantasy. The gang would travel some 40 miles across the border, move into a town of 300 people on a Saturday night, bail up the two police and use the police station as their base. They would then put on police uniform, occupy the town throughout Sunday while they checked final details of the robbery, then on the Monday quietly gather hostages and rob the bank.

A contingent of sympathisers crossed the Murray — now shallow in another drought — to establish themselves as swagmen, itinerant workers and stockmen enjoying a weekend in town.

The editor of the local paper had complained in his column that the town didn't have enough police to protect it. He was about to note the arrival of four reinforcements, impressive young men, 'the sort to catch the Kellys'. He set out to write that story, but never finished it.

A metal bas-relief of the Kelly armour on 'The Kelly Tree' at Stringybark Creek, supposedly marking the site of the police killings. It is on the wrong side of the creek, several hundred metres from the actual location.

The actual site of the fatal gunfight at Stringybark Creek was identified in 1993 by the author and his son, Darren, here seen near the position of the fallen tree and speargrass thicket which screened the Gang as they prepared to bail up the police.

Superintendent Hare, centre, at 6ft 3 in and 20 stone, looms over a typically plain-clothed party of police setting out from Benalla on 20 June 1879. Standing, from left, constables O'Loughlin, Kirkham, Mills, Mayes, (Hare), Canny, Falkiner, Lawless; kneeling, Barry and tracker Moses.

The Bank of New South Wales at Jerilderie. At the time of the hold-up, the hotel verandah at right had been continued along the façade of the bank. The staff are from left, clerk Mackie, accountant Living and manager Tarleton. The dog caused a scare some months after the robbery when a voice was heard from the bank, 'I'm bailed up!' The dog was protecting the premises by holding a customer at bay, a role it had neglected during the Gang's visit.

Superintendent Nicolson was arch-rival of the towering Hare. Impetuous and brave like Hare, he was a far shrewder tactician. Aaron Sherritt called him a 'cranky Scotchman'. Many, including Chief Commissioner Standish, agreed. (*Police Museum*)

14

A LONG WEEKEND

7–10 FEBRUARY 1879

On the night of Friday 7 February 1879 Senior Constable George Devine of Jerilderie was awoken by his pregnant wife. She had dreamt 'that the moon was like day; you could read a newspaper by it and the Kelly gang was here'. He calmed her and they went back to sleep.

Saturday passed quietly for Devine and Probationary Constable Henry Richards, except that Devine suffered 'a severe rupture' from the pommel of his saddle and looked forward to a restful Sunday. During the afternoon they picked up an elderly drunk and put him in the log lock-up beside the police station, a primitive slab building that stood in the middle of the police paddock at the edge of town.

It was bath night. The two Devine children played and splashed late and, after they were all in bed, Mrs Devine remembered that she hadn't emptied the bath water from the big tin tub in the kitchen. She'd do it in the morning before she went across to put flowers in the court house and prepare it for the Roman Catholic Mass.

At midnight the Devines were woken by a clatter of hooves and shouting from the street — a man was calling Devine's name. The senior constable pulled on his trousers and socks, hurried through his parlour to the front door and stepped out onto the verandah. It struck him that the moon was as bright as day; he could have read a newspaper by it. A man on a frisky, black horse had come through the front gate into the police paddock, and was yelling of trouble at Davidsons' Hotel, 2 miles out of town. 'There's a row going on . . . they're fighting . . . If they're not stopped, there'll be murder before the morning . . . a lot of drunken fellows . . . where's Richards?'

Richards emerged from the office on Devine's right: 'I'm here. What's up?'

The horseman gestured wildly. 'Aren't there more than two of you to come and stop the row? The men are mad with drink.'

Devine told the stranger that there were only the two of them, and suddenly, the man's horse was still. He drew a revolver and spoke very calmly, after all the yelling.

'Move and I'll shoot you. I'm Kelly. Put up your hands.'

Joe appeared at the end of the verandah to their left, Dan and Steve to their right. Senior Constable Devine and Probationary Constable Richards, in undershirts, uniform riding breeches and stockinged feet, glumly raised their hands.

The Gang quietly occupied the police station, gathering up two revolvers, two carbines and ammunition. Mrs Devine appeared, hastily dressed, and pleaded with Ned not to harm her husband 'for her sake and that of her little children'. Aiming his reply at Devine and Richards, Ned assured her that the two police were safe unless he saw 'signs of hanky panky work' when he would 'shoot them without a moment's hesitation', adding, 'So long as they remain quiet, you and the children will be safe'.

Ned sent Dan and Steve to stable and feed the Gang's horses then asked Mrs Devine for some supper. Lighting the lamps in the kitchen, she was embarrassed to notice the tub of dirty bath water and was going to empty it when Ned stopped her and said she shouldn't attempt such a thing 'in her condition'. He carried it outside and emptied it for her, the first of several small gestures that led Mrs Devine to speak of him, within the family, as 'the kindest man I ever met'.

As Ned and Joe were putting the two police in their lock-up with the drunk, Devine pleaded with Ned not to 'interfere with his wife'. Ned was genuinely offended, protesting that 'No female could say otherwise than that he and his mates had treated women with the greatest respect and courtesy ... more than could be said about many of the Victorian Police ...' Ned assured the policeman that 'Mrs Devine and her children would have every respect shown them.'

At about 2 a.m. the Gang settled down in the parlour, taking turns to mount guard while the others slept. Ned took the first watch. It had been a well-orchestrated start to one of the great set-pieces of Australian bushranging.

The gang had crossed the Murray on the Friday afternoon between Mulwala and Tocumwal, wading their horses through the few feet of water, then ridden north for 20-odd miles and camped in what was then the Riverina forest. On Saturday morning they struck out past Wunnamurra Station and Mairjimmy Swamp, entering saltbush plain scribbled with myall, boree and a few native pines on the sandy ridges.

In the afternoon they camped among the pines until the sun was almost down, then they rode on to Davidsons' Woolpack Inn, a couple of miles from Jerilderie. There they said they were squatters from the Lachlan on their way to Melbourne, and chatted with the publican's daughters and a fabled barmaid, Mary the Larrikin, fondly remembered by Ned from a previous visit. The girls told them all they needed to know about Jerilderie's two policemen and, warmed by a few whiskies, they rode on to a good supper and a few hours sleep on the floor of the policeman's parlour.

The night was 'excessively hot' and it was easy to rise early. Ned and Dan put on police uniforms — Richards's was a good fit for Ned and Devine's not too big on Dan.

Ned invited the two police to join the gang for breakfast in the parlour-cum-dining room while the recovered drunk ate in the lock-up. Mrs Devine mentioned the mass in the court house and Ned laughed. 'You'll have to do without Mass for once, Ma'am.' When she explained that it was her job to clean the court room, decorate it with flowers, and prepare the altar, Ned realised that her failure to appear would attract attention. He sent Dan across with her to make the preparations and, to speed things along, Dan helped.

The Gang was in luck. The priest best known to the townsfolk, Father Slattery, took mass on alternate months and would have come across to the police station to have a chat and see why Mrs Devine hadn't joined the flock. Today's celebrant, Father Kiely, had been to Jerilderie only once before. When he saw strange police moving about at 'the barracks' he assumed, like the rest of the congregation, that these were 'more police going to the border in quest of the Kelly Gang' and that this had meant 'extra household duties' for Mrs Devine.

The butcher's cart pulled up during the morning and the butcher gave Mrs Devine her meat for the Sunday dinner, watched 'narrowly' by Ned from the bedroom window. After 11 a.m. mass the Catholic congregation drifted away from the court house and the combined Protestant congregation left the nearby Assembly Hall, where Congregational minister John Gribble preached. Jerilderie's main street was again almost empty.

The Gang spent the morning grooming and exercising their horses, emptying, cleaning and re-loading their weapons and occasionally giving their three prisoners a breather from the stuffy little lock-up. During the afternoon Richards was released and forced to take Joe and Steve around the town in police uniform, with orders 'in case anyone came up and spoke to him, to introduce them as new constables about to be stationed here'.

Joe checked the position of the Bank of New South Wales — a converted assembly hall under the large iron roof of the sprawling Royal Mail Hotel — and the Post and Telegraph Office, a poky little brick building down near Billabong Creek, an artery of the southern Riverina.

After the reconnaissance, Ned and Joe plotted the following day's robbery, using a photolithographed plan of the town mounted on cardboard. To amuse Ned, the Devine children or himself, Joe wrote a riddle on its back:

> Q. Why are the Kellys the greatest matchmakers in the country?
> A. Because they brought loads of ladies to Younghusbands (station), Euroa, Victoria.

The drowsy Sunday afternoon passed and the police station settled down for the night. Joe rode back to the Woolpack Inn to see Mary the Larrikin.

Chatting with Mrs Devine, Ned produced a thick wad of paper and read her 'several pages'. It was a letter he planned to get printed tomorrow — an 8300-word autobiography-cum-manifesto he had dictated to Joe. It was based on the original draft of the Cameron letter and would be known to history as the Jerilderie letter.

In some of its passages we hear Ned clearly. In others, Joe's admiration of his mate colours the language and the tone. Ned speaks as Joe believes he should speak — how Joe would speak if he were such a formidable man. The two voices blend, creating a composite portrait which baffles attempts to build a psychological portrait of Ned from the document.

The Jerilderie Letter covered more ground in greater detail than the Cameron Letter, and showed a significant development from Ned's attitude of just two months before. It acknowledged the state of war that now existed between Ned and the government, with the first hints that there was much more to this war than exposing the injustices committed against himself and his family and vindicating his actions at Stringybark. True, there were the same pleas for justice on behalf of his mother and the others (almost word for word), the same denunciation of 'Whitty and Burns' and their high-handed treatment of 'poor men', the same self-incriminating account of Stringybark and the same tirades against Fitzpatrick and the others. But in this new letter Ned's anger reached out past the squatters and police to the government itself — even to the British Crown and the grey armies of men who sat at government desks and deliberated over baize-covered tables 12 000 miles away.

In the Cameron letter Ned had warned that, without justice for his people, 'Fitzpatrick shall be the cause of greater slaughter to the rising generation than St Patrick was to the snakes and toads of Ireland.' In the Jerilderie Letter the threat was given new weight and a startling new direction:

> It will pay the government to give those people who are suffering innocence justice and liberty if not *I will be compelled to show some colonial*

stratagem which will open the eyes of not only the Victorian Police and inhabitants but also the whole British army. No doubt they will acknowledge their hounds were barking at the wrong stump, and that Fitzpatrick will be the cause of greater slaughter *to the Union Jack* than St Patrick was to the snakes and toads in Ireland. [my italics]

Ned declared that, 'The Queen of England was as guilty as Baumgarten and Kennedy, Williamson and Skillion ...' and proclaimed, 'There never was such a thing as justice in the English laws, but any amount of injustice to be had.'

He spoke of Ireland's Troubles under the British overlords and the agony of the convicts, 'all of true blood bone and beauty', sent to Australia where:

many a blooming Irishman rather than subdue to the Saxon yoke, were flogged to death and bravely died in servile chains but true to the shamrock and a credit to Paddy's Land.

Perhaps the voice of Ned's American stepfather, George King, chimed with his and Joe's, when they wrote:

What would England do if America declared war and hoisted a green flag as it is all Irishmen that has got command of her forts and batteries? Even her very life guards and beef tasters [beefeaters] are Irish. Would they not slew round and fight with their own arms for the sake of the colour they dare not wear for years and to reinstate it and rise old Erins Isle once more from the pressure of tyrranism of the English yoke which has kept it in poverty and starvation and caused them to wear the enemy's coat? What else can England expect ...

Worried for her husband and children, good Mrs Devine listened to Ned reading from the fifty-six pages but 'could not remember anything about it' two days later.

Joe didn't get back until after midnight. Ned probably waited for him while Dan and Steve slept — long after Mrs Devine had gone to bed — thinking of tomorrow and looking at the uniform he would wear: a dashing blue tunic with polished pewter buttons, skin-tight white breeches, V-cut Napoleon boots and a blue cap. William Elliott, the Jerilderie schoolteacher, saw him in that uniform and would recall, 'In appearance and gait he resembled a military man ...' and, after reading Ned's letter, mused that he, '... would seemingly have liked to have been at the head of a hundred followers or so to upset the existing government or bring them to terms.' In Ned he would see 'a lot of the Don Quixote ... also a bit of a fanatic, or rather, a dreamer in his own way'. Yet the next day another of Ned's dreams was about to touch reality.

◆

THE EVENTS of Monday 10 February in Jerilderie are like some comi-cal pageant performed on several stages at once. In police uniforms, Joe and Dan took their horses to the blacksmith and had them re-shod. They then checked the telegraph wires which ran from the nearby post office to meet the main line, across the creek to the north. Unless they cut the wires as they left the post office — which would be too obvious — posts would have to be felled. Surprisingly they left the line unbro-ken and the telegraph key operating and returned to the police station.

Joe changed back into his bush clothes and Ned donned the uniform then, a little after 10 a.m., they walked into town with Constable Richards. Uniformed Dan and plainclothed Steve followed on horseback.

Richards introduced his fellow 'policeman' to the publican of the Royal Mail Hotel, Charlie Cox, and Charlie became the first hostage. Meanwhile Dan and Steve left their horses in the Royal Mail's stables and rounded up a number of hotel employees. Dan, stationed in the bar, continued to gather prisoners. Steve would guard them in the parlour.

As the crop of hostages grew Ned and Joe proceeded with the robbery of the bank next door. Instead of walking in the front entrance and bail-ing it up, Joe went through the charade of pretending to be a drunk who had wandered along the pub's back verandah and entered the bank's back door by mistake, something that happened quite often. The bank accountant, Edwin Living, was irritated when a bushman staggered into the banking chamber. Living — a tall, athletic man, a fine horseman and expert cricketer — was about to tell him to 'clear out' when Joe aban-doned his drunk act, drew a revolver and said, 'I am Kelly.'

Mackie, the junior clerk, had been waiting out the front for the arrival of the manager. He came in and was bailed up as Ned appeared in his police uniform. The teller's safe yielded only £691; it was Euroa all over again — except that this time *two* keys were needed to open the inner compartment. Living had one and the manager, Mr Tarleton, who had been away and was expected back this morning, had the other.

As Ned and Joe took the two bank men around to the hotel, the man-ager entered by the back door and ran a bath. He was just starting to enjoy a luxurious soak after his ride when the bathroom door opened and Living entered, announcing with his slight stammer that the bank was held up. Tarleton was in no mood for a silly joke and asked his accountant what on earth he meant by such 'damned nonsense'.

'There's no nonsense about it,' said Steve, appearing in the doorway with his revolver in hand. 'We want your key to the safe.'

Tarleton, a large and determined man, decided he would finish his bath first, giving Steve time to notice a watch and chain in the pocket of his vest, which hung in the bathroom. Disgusted that it wasn't gold, Steve took the 'tin pot' article all the same.

Joe and Living returned to the bank in time to bail up the school-master, Elliott, who had released his pupils for lunch and dropped in to deposit the collection from Reverend Gribble's service. Ned re-entered with Tarleton and, while Joe and Elliott held a sugar sack open, Tarleton was forced to take the bags of coins and notes from the inner safe and drop them in the sack — another £1450. Ned also retrieved some deeds, mortgages, bills and jewellery from the safe. Most of the papers were destroyed, with Ned denouncing 'all financial institutions as "slavers" and "poor-man crushers"'.

The low-key nature of the robbery was making Ned careless. On their way through the residence back to the hotel, Ned asked Tarleton for the bank's revolver and let him walk ahead to fetch it from his bedroom. Realising his mistake he lunged after the manager and Joe instantly dropped the bag of plunder, whipped a second revolver from his belt and covered Elliott and Living. Tarleton picked up the revolver from his dressing table as Ned sprang into the doorway and took aim at his head. 'It isn't loaded,' Tarleton said, calmly handing Ned the weapon. Just as calmly, Ned took the three prisoners into the bar and slapped a 2-shilling piece on the counter to buy them a drink.

◆

JERILDERIE'S NEWSPAPER editor, Mr Gill, was on the trail of a story. Notebook in pocket, he went to the police station to interview Devine about the four new policemen everyone was talking about. When a panicky Mrs Devine told him, 'Run, for your life is in danger!' He did just that, all the way into town, and told storekeeper Rankin J.P. what had happened. They both told the next-door storekeeper, Mr Harkin J.P., that something strange was going on. The three of them decided to warn bank manager Tarleton, one door further along.

Finding the bank empty, which was decidedly odd, Rankin knocked on the counter. Ned, who had just changed into civilian clothes in the residence, called, 'Just a minute,' and ran towards the banking chamber. The three musketeers — now sure that the bank was being bailed up — made a dive for the front door. Gill and Harkin escaped (Harkin to be recaptured later) but 20-stone Rankin fell and was scrambling to his feet as Ned hurdled the counter and thrust a revolver at his head.

Meanwhile editor Gill scurried through the town like Henny Penny, spreading news of the hold-up, and didn't stop until he reached Carrah homestead, 6 miles away. This was the man Ned wanted to print the Jerilderie Letter. He was genuinely angry when he found out who the escapee was and stormed back into the bar parlour to confront his large prisoner.

'His aspect was perfectly demoniacal,' said a man from Ballarat who happened to be in town that day, 'his face became distorted with the violence of his passion, and the veins in his forehead stood out in strong relief until he looked horribly ferocious.' Editor Gill would be told that 'his eyes were in a frenzy rolling'.

Ned shoved Rankin into the passage. 'Get out there you fat bugger! I'm going to shoot you! . . . you and those other two went into the bank and try and cop us.'

Steve, who had been playing the bushranger to the hilt, followed up with a bloodcurdling, 'Put the bugger on his knees and I'll put a bullet into him!' As Rankin protested that he and his comrades had merely intended 'to see the manager on business', prisoners crowded to the parlour door, pleading for the merchant's life.

Having tightened his grip on the reins effectively, Ned quickly 'relented' and went off with Rankin to hunt for Harkin and Gill. A few of the townsfolk genuinely believed that Rankin had narrowly escaped death at the hands of two bloodthirsty killers. Schoolteacher Elliott, a shrewd observer and eventually a chronicler of the Jerilderie hold-up, was not deceived, commenting, 'It was only a matter of bluff . . . from first to last.'

Joe had missed the drama. Again in police uniform, he had ridden down to the Telegraph Office, quietly bailed up postmaster Jefferson and made him dismantle the Morse key. He then read the file of telegrams transmitted that day, supposedly to make sure that no news of the robbery had reached nearby towns. Ned arrived and recruited some townsmen to start chopping down telegraph poles, announcing that if anyone touched those wires before the next morning, he would 'shoot him like a bloody dog' on his way back from robbing the Urana bank.

Postmaster Jefferson was not bluffed and started running telegraph wires along a fence that night; but the men chopping down the poles kept hard at it even after the Gang had left town, eventually felling all the telegraph posts for a third-of-a-mile.

The disappearance of Gill was a major setback for Ned. Constable Richards and bank accountant Living took him to the newspaper office, where Ned told Mrs Gill that he wished her husband no harm. Producing the Jerilderie Letter, he told her, 'I want to get him to set this up and run me off some printed copies of it,' also assuring her, 'I intend to pay him well for it.'

Mrs Gill's only response was that she had no idea where her husband had gone. At this point Living offered to take the letter and arrange for Gill to print it. Ned hesitated, but perhaps because he had done Living a favour — letting him rescue an insurance policy from among the bank papers — he decided to trust the accountant. It was his way to trust people; he was a man of his word and expected others to be like him. Nevertheless he warned Living as he handed over the precious fifty-six pages, 'Mind that you keep your promise and see that they are printed, or you will have me to reckon with next time we meet.'

The day was losing its shine and Ned decided to cheer himself up. With Richards and Living, he went to the Albion Hotel where an admired racehorse, a black mare called Minnie, was stabled. As she was brought out of her loose box, bridled but unsaddled, Ned commented that she was 'small and rather too fine for his work, but he would take her away with him'. He stuck the revolver in his belt and vaulted on to the back of the horse, which fidgeted and pranced.

'Richards,' Ned asked, 'can this mare jump?'

'I know she can gallop, she's one of the millionaire stock, but I've never seen her jump.'

Ned took Minnie to the far side of the stableyard, turned and raced her at the high fence. She baulked. If she had fallen or thrown her rider, Ned could have been injured — certainly an easier mark to be overpowered by the strapping young constable and the sportsman accountant. To Ned, with supreme confidence in his mastery of horses and men, the possibility had seemed so slight that it hardly represented a risk; to Richards, he was 'the gamest man I ever saw'.

◆

THE HOLD-UP had run its course. There was nothing to keep the gang in Jerilderie and Ned went back to the Royal Mail to arrange their departure. Joe took the bag of money and headed back with Dan to the police station.

With about thirty prisoners now packing the bar and parlour, Ned gave a farewell speech. Tarleton recollected that he spoke quietly and a rowdy drunk made him hard to hear. People came up with wildly varied accounts of what he said, including that he had been married three weeks when outlawed! He damned Flood and Fitzpatrick, damned the persecutors of his family 'who were constantly formulating charges against them' until 'he was goaded into retaliation'. Again, he described Stringybark and tried to take all blame on his own shoulders.

As he spoke he looked across the half-door between the bar and parlour and saw Constable Richards at the back of the crowd, poor Richards with his empty revolver holstered behind his hip, after a day of humiliation trailing around after the Gang. Ned gave the policeman back his dignity in a remarkable way. He announced, 'Now, I'm going to shoot Constable Richards before I leave.'

He ordered Richards to come forward and the trooper pushed

through the shocked crush of prisoners to the half-door. Ned knew that Richards had been one of a police party who had seen four men crossing the Murray in a punt near Tocumwal and, believing them to be the Kellys, opened fire. The four men turned out to be Victorian Police. No one was hurt.

'You were one of those who fired?'

'Yes, I fired across the river at them.'

'You did your best to bring us down?'

'Yes, I did my best.'

'You did not know me, and yet you tried to kill a man you never saw before, or who never did you any harm?'

Richards met those fierce eyes squarely. 'I was doing my duty; you were outlawed at the time.'

'You would have taken my life if you could, so you now cannot blame me for shooting you?'

'Yes, I can,' said Richards. Probably unaware of what Ned was doing, he rose to the occasion splendidly. 'We were both armed then and had an equal chance in a fight. If you shoot me now, you shoot an unarmed man who has no chance of his life ... give me a loaded revolver and I'll fight you now, and if you shoot me, it will be a fair fight.'

Ned paused for effect in the hushed bar, then his face softened. 'You can go now, for I'm damned if I don't like your pluck; but if we ever meet again, I'll shoot you.'

Richards had the bit between his teeth. 'That's all right, so long as the two of us are armed; it will be you and me for it.'

Elliott, who recorded this exchange, knew that it was 'another piece of bluff', but the sub-text escaped him. The bar and parlour relaxed. No one would scorn Henry Richards: he had stood up to Ned Kelly. And Senior Constable Devine had been locked away since Saturday, a dangerous man in the Kellys' eyes, whom Ned Kelly had also threatened to kill. Only his wife's pleading saved his life. Ned Kelly had said so! Jerilderie had no reason to be ashamed of its two policemen.

Ned told the prisoners they could 'go when they liked', then went back to the police station with Richards. If Richards's account of their conversation, recorded 50 years later, is to be believed, Ned said, 'I like you Richards,' and invited him to 'throw in your lot with us and come along now.' Certainly Ned made it clear that he admired Richards's style. The lapse of time and a clear memory of the curious affinity they had achieved probably did the rest.

Meanwhile, on Ned's instructions, Steve had fetched Living's hunting saddle from the bank, saddled Minnie the racehorse at the Albion's stables, and rode her along to the police station. He was closely followed by Living, who asked Ned if he could have his saddle back. Ned agreed,

telling Steve to unsaddle Minnie and get another one from the local saddler. Irritated, Steve removed the saddle and dumped it on the ground.
A supposedly grateful Living headed back to town, planning to ride for
help and carrying the Jerilderie Letter.

While Living was returning with his saddle, bank manager Tarleton
sent Mackie, the junior clerk, to fetch his horse from a nearby paddock
behind the parson's house. He, too, planned to ride for help. The
Reverend John Gribble was reading in the passage of the parsonage,
with the front and back doors open to catch any breeze, when he saw
Mackie dash through the back gate carrying a saddle and tell his wife
that the Kellys had held up the bank.

While Mackie caught and saddled Tarleton's horse, Gribble strode
across the paddocks, furled umbrella in hand, towards the backyards of
the main street's buildings, where he saw Living 'on horseback, sneaking
away under cover of the Royal [Mail] Hotel'. Concluding that 'it would
be rather dangerous to intercept him', Gribble walked on and Tarleton
emerged from the hotel, telling the clergyman as he passed, 'If I can once
get on my horse, they shall never catch me.'

The manager and the accountant would both ride the 60-odd
miles to Deniliquin, then travel by train to the bank's head office in
Melbourne, which, Gribble drily noted, they 'reached in safety'.

In the main street Gribble found a large group of the Gang's former
prisoners, 'laughing and talking over their amusing adventures'. Asked
what they were going to do, they replied, 'Do? Do nothing of course.
Why should we interfere with the men, unless they interfere with [us]?
They came to stick up the bank and they have stuck it up, and that is all
they want to do.'

Gribble, an enthusiastic duck hunter and owner of a double-
barrelled shotgun, argued that it was the 'honest duty' of them all 'to
protect the town and, if possible, capture such desperate outlaws', suggesting that they collect arms and ammunition for the purpose. When
the townsfolk 'simply laughed at the idea', Gribble said, 'We shall be
branded by the whole country as a set of cowards', as indeed they were.

The human chemistry of the hold-up displayed a significant aspect of
the Kelly phenomenon in microcosm. The vivid self-portrayal of the
Gang as men who were dangerous only when crossed, coupled with the
townspeople's justified suspicion of undercover supporters, increased
the reluctance of ordinary citizens to become involved. Ned's message
was that his only fight lay with the police. In accepting that message,
albeit as an excuse for inactivity, these people of Jerilderie became sympathisers by default, like so many folk in the north-east.

Gribble proceeded to demonstrate the moral and physical courage
which would characterise his future career as a champion of the

Aboriginal people. During this exchange he had learnt of the Gang taking Minnie from the Albion's stables. He knew that the owner was Miss Macdougall, the publican's daughter, and 'at once conceived the idea of getting it back'.

Raising his umbrella against the sun, Gribble strode towards the police station. Here the gang had burnt some discarded clothes (Dan was still wearing police breeches and boots, Ned had taken a pair of riding pants from Tarleton), and released Saturday's drunk from the lock-up so it could accommodate the two policemen, postmaster Jefferson and his assistant.

Ned gave the lock-up key to Mrs Devine with strict orders that no one should be released until 7.30 that night. In following this instruction to the letter, Mrs Devine later claimed that Ned had threatened to burn the house down if she disobeyed. She gave her family a more likely explanation. 'She didn't want her husband chasing Ned Kelly.' In fact she persuaded him to take to his bed for several days and leave the police force soon after.

Ned had noticed that Devine's horse, a big grey, carried the brand of John Evans of Whitfield, a 'decent squatter' who had been a good boss to him. Confident that it had been 'commandeered' by the police, he planned to return it. Steve would ride it back to the north-east and the horse he had ridden here would carry the bag of bank money, led by Joe. Dan would lead a second police mount — which Ned believed to be another Evans horse with an altered brand — as a spare saddler. One detail remained, another saddle for Steve. He would pick one up while Ned had a farewell drink with sympathisers and amenable townsfolk at the Albion before coming back to collect Minnie on his way out of town.

As they took the horses out through the gate of the police paddock on to the main road, Ned noticed a black figure advancing towards them, black umbrella hovering overhead like a bat. Marching as to war along the footpath, Gribble saw Dan and Joe mount flashily and ride off, leading the packhorse and spare saddler.

Ned and Steve Hart remained for a few moments longer, and then mounting, they came in my direction.

Hart was riding a large grey police horse without a saddle; Ned was riding the horse I was desirous of obtaining [actually, the bigger black horse he had arrived on]. Just before I met them Hart gave his horse the spurs and dashed past. But Ned Kelly, never having once taken his eyes off me, came straight along the footpath. He was a fine, noble-looking fellow, tall and well-proportioned, with long, flowing brown beard. Round his waist he wore a strong leather belt, upon which hung a number of revolvers. I saw this formidable array of weapons, but never for a moment thought he had a revolver in his right hand, which was hid from view by the horse's mane.

Introductions over, Gribble announced that he had come 'to have a little talk' about Miss Macdougall's horse.

Ned sprang to the ground and walked up to the bespectacled parson. 'I'll tell you, sir, why this horse has not been returned to the owner. If Macdougall had come to me and asked me for his daughter's horse he should have had it; but he went to one of my chaps and got him to say that the horse should be left in the police paddock.' This annoyed Ned and he 'swore that the horse should never be returned'. Conceding that it was not 'gentlemanly' to take a young lady's horse, Ned agreed to see Macdougall about it. He 'vaulted into the saddle' and rode off to the Albion Hotel.

Gribble decided to follow, and on the way he saw publican Macdougall walking back to the Albion with Steve and carrying a new saddle on his head. The parson blithely announced to Macdougall that he had spoken with Ned about Minnie, whereupon Steve raised his revolver and said, 'Up with that watch!'

'I think it is very mean of you to take a parson's watch,' said Gribble, watched by Macdougall from under the saddle, 'as motionless as a statue and as pale as a whitewashed wall'.

'A parson's no more to me than any other man,' Steve announced in his best bushranging style. 'Up with that watch!' Gribble handed over the watch 'after a purposed delay' then continued into the Albion. His entrance coincided with one of Ned's finest touches.

Standing at the bar, he placed his revolver beside his glass and announced, 'There's my revolver. Anyone here may take it and shoot me dead, but if I'm shot, Jerilderie shall swim in its own blood.' This brought a cheer from the pub's patrons, just as Gribble placed his hand on Ned's shoulder. In a single movement Ned caught up the revolver, whirled and covered Gribble. He relaxed and listened to the parson's urgent, whispered request to speak to him privately. It was about the watch . . .

'One of my men has stuck you up!' Ned boomed. 'Come and show me the man that took your watch.'

Steve was girthing the new saddle on Devine's grey when Gribble pointed him out. Ned asked for the watch and glanced at it with the dry comment, 'If you're going to stick up a man for a watch, why can't you stick him up for a first class one?' About to hand it to Gribble, he paused and then thrust it at Steve. 'You take it and give it back to him yourself like a man.' And so Steve did, in Gribble's words, 'looking daggers'.

Joe and Dan had ridden off. Now Steve mounted grumpily and rode after them. Ned went back into the Albion for a last drink with his audience — including several of the 'strangers' who had been seen earlier in the Royal Mail — then mounted and rode off, cheered by this well-primed gallery as he flourished his hat in farewell.

Joe and Dan had been waiting outside Jerilderie in the shade of a boree tree, where they were joined by Steve, probably still complaining at his treatment. And at last Ned came riding out of town with angry news. The gang's agents had told him that Tarleton and Living had ridden for help and that it was Mackie who had gone to fetch Tarleton's horse.

They spurred off to Wunnamurra homestead where Mackie's brother was manager. Eventually convinced that none of the bank men were there, they gave up any further idea of pursuing them and rode off towards the Murray to the south-east as thunderheads towered in the late afternoon sunlight, signalling the end of the drought.

It rained for four hours that night, refreshing the horses and washing out tracks. They had probably crossed the rain-stippled river before dawn — hours before parties of police embarked on the hopeless task of watching 'every crossing place'; a week before the gallant Sergeant Walker, the 'Man Who Shot Captain Thunderbolt', came riding in pursuit of them; and seventeen months before they would be seen again.

◆

JERILDERIE HAD been a farce — a superbly conceived but sometimes carelessly executed farce — in which the highwayman heroes emerged as caricatures of themselves. People recalled Joe as nervous and even 'effeminate' in his good looks; Dan would receive a better press for his role as Trooper Dan, with mention of a 'pleasing' look when he smiled; Steve had now taken over the role of surly, would-be killer, narrowly curbed from bloodshed by his leader. And over them all, Ned would tower as 'commander-in-chief' (Gribble's term) of the band, 'prepossessing' in appearance, terrible in his rage, total master of every situation — except one: he had failed to get the letter printed. That passionate, almost unpunctuated torrent of words would be read by only a handful of people — bankers, policemen, a schoolteacher, a publican and one government clerk in Melbourne who was required to make a copy.

Living did not keep his promise to give the letter to editor Gill and it disappeared for ninety years. The government copy re-surfaced and was published after fifty-one years but, for every hour of that time, the words and ideas of the letter lived and smouldered, warning of the firestorm to come.

♣
_____

15

'LIKE A WANDERING WIND IN THE NIGHT'

FEBRUARY – JUNE 1879

For almost all of 1879 Ned Kelly was to be a shadowy figure, moving from place to place through a series of hiding places which the police struggled to catalogue: 'Hedi Ranges, Gum Flat, Hurdle Creek Ranges, Woolshed, Barrambogie, Pilot Ranges and vicinity, Rats Castle, Wooragee, and Hurdle Creek'. One could add the Black Range, Eleven Mile Creek, Greta and Winton Swamps, all of the King Valley, the Buckland, the Buffalo, Emerald, Melbourne ... and huge, uncharted areas of the public imagination.

Ned was recognised getting on a horse-drawn bus in Bourke Street, Melbourne; Steve may have appeared at a St Kilda doctor's surgery to be treated for syphilis; Dan was seen being rowed across the Goulburn River near Seymour, swimming his horse behind the boat; Joe continued visiting his mother's house with impunity, once literally stepping over Superintendent Hare to get there. The entire Gang appeared at the home of an Emerald farmer less than 30 miles from Melbourne and spent several hours looking for a strayed horse.

It was a restless, sometimes boring existence which encouraged the very things they could not afford: carelessness and complacency. Once a random police search party almost ran into them, and they supposedly hid in the crown of a fallen tree. On another occasion Ned claimed that he amused himself by riding along with a police party for two hours.

All this time the Gang's stature increased — partly as a result of Ned's continued campaign to have them seen as 'police-made criminals', champions of the poor farmer and his family, enemies of corrupt police and a corrupt, unjust system. Even more, Ned and his followers were transformed by their pursuers' acknowledgement of the great threat posed by this outlaw band. Ned Kelly was growing beyond the role he had set out to play. The process had started at Euroa, then the events at Jerilderie achieved results out of all proportion to anything Ned and Joe could have imagined. In crossing the Murray they had ridden boldly into the circus ring of inter-colonial politics.

New South Wales had been more or less secretly enjoying Victoria's embarrassment over the exploits of the gang. Because the Riverina was geographically and economically part of Victoria, Sydney *Punch* actually managed to hail Jerilderie as yet another slap-in-the-eye for the southern colony. Melbourne *Punch* bounced back promptly.

> Compare the different fate that met
> Our gallant Mansfield three
> With that absurd, degrading act
> Up at Jerilderie
> Where bobbies were in their own 'logs'
> Locked up for several hours;
> *Now* whose police have proved the best
> The New South Welsh or ours?

The leonine Sir Henry Parkes, premier of New South Wales, had no doubts as to who had been embarrassed by the hold-up. Parliament was in session and Parkes gained prompt support for his proposal that the government contribute £3000 to the Kelly reward, with another £1000 from 'the banks in Sydney chiefly concerned in the border trade'. Sir Henry wrote to Sir Bryan O'Loghlen only four days after the robbery, 'If a like sum was raised in Melbourne, the joint reward would amount to £8000, or £2000 for each of the outlaws'. Sir Bryan telegrammed Parkes, 'We cordially reciprocate your offer', and the combined £8000 reward was announced in a special *Government Gazette* on Tuesday 18 February.

This almost unparalleled display of unity by the rival colonies and the huge reward it had produced — equivalent to about two million dollars in modern Australian currency — provided a startling measure of the status the gang had achieved in its four-month career.

While both colonies were poised for further robberies, with the usual shuffling of police reinforcements from place to place and the usual crop of 'sightings' (the Riverina had a plague of Kelly Gangs for weeks), the first sign of the Gang was the Bank of New South Wales notes, again smelling of earth, which began to appear in north-eastern Victoria within a fortnight of the hold-up. Those who fondly believed that the Kellys had been blocked from re-crossing the Murray desperately hoped that this money had been smuggled south.

Months later the two police horses taken from Jerilderie were found grazing in the King Valley near John Evans's station. Evans had sold them to the New South Wales police and they were duly returned.

Slowly the ripples settled and all along the Murray men began to recall 'that night the dogs barked furiously' and how 'there were hoof-marks on the sand-bank where the boat had lain moored the night before', to be found 'stranded up against a snag some half-mile down the stream'. At least the endings of these stories were true. 'The Gang had passed like a wandering wind in the night, and were safe among their own hills again.'

Troops continued to guard major Kelly Country banks while, in smaller towns, security was maintained with complex arrangements.

> In our bank ... the manager had a string attached to a peg at his foot, beneath the table at which he sat. The string was fastened to a cord which held up a curtain on the outside verandah. If the Kellys stuck up the bank, all the manager had to do was to kick over the peg, down fell the curtain, and in a few minutes the bank would be surrounded by the gallant 'specials', and the Kelly gang captured. But one day, as time went on, the cord, exposed to wind and weather, gave way, and the curtain fell. No one took the slightest notice, and it was never replaced.

On 22 January 1879 a handful of British redcoats at Rorke's Drift in Natal forged a legend as they defended a military hospital against thousands of Zulus. That very day a true gentleman of the law, John Bowman, defended the integrity of Victoria's courts against the attacks being launched on them by Standish.

The previous Saturday (when the trials of the remaining sympathisers were first moved from Beechworth Gaol to the court house) Bowman, the Crown Prosecutor, had promised that he would either withdraw the charges or 'prosecute to an issue' on the following Saturday if the defence agreed to one more remand of the prisoners. There would be no more remands without evidence being given.

On Wednesday 22 January Bowman telegrammed the colony's Attorney-General, Sir Bryan O'Loghlen, asking if he was to prosecute the sympathisers on Saturday. 'If evidence to be taken', he said, 'have received no information from police since Saturday last'.

This was an ultimatum. No evidence, no prosecution, therefore prisoners discharged. O'Loghlen forwarded the telegram to Standish in Benalla with the note, 'I believe this matter entirely in your hands'. He had washed *his* hands of the grubby affair. Standish's response to O'Loghlen was prompt and characteristically arrogant. He was sacking Bowman and the prosecution would be taken over by Superintendent Hare. Standish informed the Attorney-General, 'Remands will be applied for in all cases where we are not prepared to proceed & I have every hope that the Police Magistrate will grant them.'

Standish congratulated himself on neatly disposing of a troublesome prosecutor who dared to demand evidence, but his self-satisfaction lasted only three days.

Ned immediately hired the sacked Bowman as a member of the

defence team and when poor Hare arrived in Beechworth Court on Saturday, he faced a devastating barrage from Zincke and the disgruntled Crown Prosecutor.

Bowman challenged Hare's right to appear, then told the story of his telegram to the Attorney-General — how Superintendent Sadleir had instructed him to make the pledge of the previous week — and Sadleir was now absent. He pointed at the increasingly uncomfortable Hare. 'They have imported Mr Hare into the case because Mr Sadleir dare not appear to falsify his pledged word.' He gestured dramatically at Wild Wright, who happened to be in the dock at the time. 'What reasonable cause can possibly be shown why this man should be kept in custody?' Bowman smote his breast. 'They might as well arrest *me!*'

Zincke leapt into the fight, sympathising with Police Magistrate Foster for having to preside over this travesty in which Sadleir and Hare were mere puppets operated by a 'wire puller'. When one had done what was required of him, 'another puppet was sent to ask for a further remand, utterly ignoring what had been agreed upon before'. Zincke played outrageously to the gallery. He described how one of the sympathisers objected to his photograph 'being hawked about the country just as if he were a common member of Parliament', and had asked Zincke if he were obliged to let 'the photographer cove' take his photo. Zincke had advised the sympathiser, 'Tell him to photograph the reverse side of your medal.'

Wild Wright had his usual parting shot. Remanded for another week, he tossed at Magistrate Foster, 'You may as well remand us for life, the police only stick to the main roads.' Another eleven sympathisers followed, to be remanded, 'none of them having anything to say'.

Three weeks before, Standish had written to O'Loghlen of his strategy, 'It is possible that I may have gone a little too far, but . . . I feel sure that the Government will support me in what I have done.'

It was an odd situation. Standish had initiated the sympathiser prosecutions and was the shadowy 'wire puller' behind them — so shadowy that even Bowman believed he had been dismissed by the Attorney-General. Both he and Zincke made sarcastic, thinly-veiled references to Sir Bryan's role in the affair.

Whether or not he knew it, Bowman was in the hands of another 'wire puller', Ned Kelly. It was common gossip in Beechworth that, in the very week Bowman changed sides, Kate Kelly had tethered her horse outside Zincke's office while she paid the fees for the sympathisers' defence.

Ned Kelly was fighting Captain Standish on the Chief Commissioner's chosen battlefield and steadily gaining ground on his opponent. Standish had created a situation in which their puppet battle, now in a highly public arena, could be seen all too easily as a metaphor of the broader conflict as defined by Ned: a fight for justice against exploitation of the process of law. The Chief Commissioner of Police had surrendered the high moral ground, and the respectable legal ground, to an outlaw.

As week followed week and remand followed remand, the immorality and ultimate futility of the process drew stronger, more strident criticism from the press, fuelled by an indiscreet remark from relieving magistrate Wyatt to Wild Wright, 'I would give you fair play if I could.' Wyatt claimed he had been 'misunderstood'.

Two *causes célèbres* leapt to prominence. The police had suspected Ned's cousin, Mary Miller, of helping the gang, probably with good reason. A superb horsewoman who easily evaded pursuit, she could not be found on 3 January and the police had arrested her father instead — hard-working, sad-faced Robert Miller, widowed husband of Mary Ann Quinn who had died two years before. In a master stroke of media manipulation, the *Herald* was supplied with a letter Mary had written to her father in Beechworth Gaol — a portrait of a bush heroine left to complete the harvest from which her father had been dragged by the police.

> My dear Father — I embrace this opportunity of writing these few lines, in hopes it will find you in good health, as this leaves all here — thank God for it. Dear Father, I am glad to say we got in all the crops. Dear Father, I would like to know what arrangement you made with ——— with the horses, as he has served us a very bad trick. When we wanted them to cart the crops in, he would not give them to us. Dear Father, Mr ——— and Mr ——— is doing their best for you, and I think you will soon be home again, Dear Father, write soon and let me know if you want anything up here. I think this is all at present from your ever affectionate daughter,
>
> *Mary Miller*
>
> P.S. There is a stamp in this for you. If you know when you are coming out some one would go to Benalla and meet you with a horse if you send word up.

The letter merited a *Herald* editorial, 'The Liberty of the Subject', a scarifying attack on the sympathiser debacle, pointing out that while ordinary criminals were brought into court by policemen armed with batons, 'those suspected men now lying in Beechworth Gaol ... are brought up between rows of soldiers with loaded guns and bayonets fixed. Was ever so sorry a farce enacted?' From the outset the *Herald* had hoped that the police would use 'the utmost discretion' before resorting to the Outlawry Act. 'Now,' the paper declared, 'we regret to say, we have not a particle of confidence in their prudence and judgement ... We sincerely hope that the magistracy will allow no further remands to take place.' In fact the *Herald* and its readers were to see another three months of remands, although Robert Miller had been released nine days before Mary's letter was published.

In a more sophisticated development a writ of *habeas corpus* on sympathiser John McElroy was heard in Melbourne by Sir Redmond Barry in what Zincke pointedly called, 'an untramelled court'. Counsel for McElroy asked Sir Redmond, 'Could a magistrate remand a prisoner from time to time without evidence, and so keep him in gaol for life?'

Barry avoided the question, eventually tried to postpone the case and, when pushed into a corner, found that McElroy's petition for a writ 'was not attested by two witnesses' as required by an act of Charles II. Learned counsel calmly announced that he would apply again the following week.

The police wisely had McElroy discharged the following Tuesday, along with Jack McMonigle and Michael Haney. Joe Ryan had broken his leg 'while larking in the prison yard with some of his mates' and he, too, would be discharged.

Nine men remained, including Wild, who snarled at the magistrate as he left the box, 'If I ever get out of this I'll make my name a terror to you!'

At last Tom Lloyd Junior joined the band in Beechworth Gaol. He and Bill Tanner had been in Benalla on the night of Tuesday 11 March, when headstrong Senior Constable Johnston, with Constable Bell, recognised Tom and caught his arm. Tom whirled, giving one trooper 'a left rip to the chest' and the other, 'a crucifying right to the face'. Bill Tanner joined in and both lads ended up in front of Captain Standish J.P. to receive a week for Assault and 5 shillings for damage to uniforms. Tom claimed, straight faced, that he didn't know the two men were police until he heard a police helmet hit the ground. He was belatedly charged as a sympathiser and, of course, remanded for seven days.

The loss of Tom, most active and loyal of the sympathisers and virtually a fifth member of the Gang, was a blow to Ned. Perhaps as a gesture of bravado, he and Joe attended the Larry Foley/Abe Hicken prize fight near Echuca on Thursday 20 March. This was doubly remarkable because the event was illegal and a force of twenty mounted police tried to prevent it. When it seemed that the fight would be barred it was reported that Ned had written to the legendary Jem Mace, Foley's mentor, expressing his regret and saying that 'if the party would come to the Strathbogie Ranges he would take care the police were not within twenty miles of the scene of the fight ... and, after Foley and Hicken had done, show "Jem" how they box in the ranges'.

The match eventually took place on the New South Wales bank of the Murray at dawn, in front of 150 enthusiasts who had gathered during the night. The only policeman able to reach the venue in time, Senior Constable O'Meara of the Victoria Police, declared the fight an unlawful act, was told he had no authority here and stayed to watch. With Ned and Joe, O'Meara saw a first round that lasted 22 minutes; the remaining fifteen rounds took an hour. English Hicken was defeated by the younger, Australian-born Foley, a never-to-be-beaten champion.

Amid cries of, 'You've shown 'em what Australia can do, old man,' Ned and Joe slipped away among the river redgums into the sunrise. One legend in the making had honoured another, and homage had been paid to the image Ned and Joe were fostering in a carefully organised campaign.

Suppression of the Jerilderie and Cameron letters had been a bitter blow. The published summaries had told some of the story, though the more even-handed *Herald* had stressed in its brief précis, 'The parts most unfavourable to the police are suppressed from the synopsis.'

Even before Jerilderie Ned and Joe had begun to use the ageless methods of the rebel Irish, telling their story in balladry and poetry, the true 'seeds of fire' of Gaelic — weapons of a people whose rich oral tradition had been used against the British invader for hundreds of years. Before Jerilderie Joe had composed a 'Ballad of Kelly's Gang', which, appropriately, had started its life as a parody of 'The Wearing of the Green'.

> Sure Paddy dear and did you hear the news that's going round
> On the head of bold Ned Kelly they have placed two thousand pounds
> For his brother Dan, Joe Byrne, Steve Hart, a similar sum they'll give,
> But if they doubled that amount, the Kelly gang would live.

New verses were added after Jerilderie and the song became one of the Gang's anthems — what a sympathiser editor called 'hymns of triumph', sung to a clapping of hands and stamping of feet.

At Jerilderie Mary the Larrikin had sung another of these ballads, 'The Kellys Have Made Another Escape'. Joe Ryan wrote out Joe's (or perhaps his?) parody of a song called 'Such Lies', lampooning a police informer who:

> . . . came riding across the Pitchibaw [Peechelba] Flat
> With a saddle made of sheepskin
> And three miles of puggery [puggaree] slung to his hat.

Caricatures and cartoons, rewards for the capture of Standish and his officers, a drawing of a coffin and a piece of black crêpe sent to Detective Ward — all played their part.

Schoolteacher James Wallace, a schoolmate of Joe and Aaron and another double agent, wrote a satirical serial, 'Christmas in Kelly Land' for a local paper. Sympathiser editor G. Wilson Hall serialised *The Book of Keli* in the *Benalla Standard* (later published in pamphlet form), an often hilarious account of the police pursuit told in mock-Biblical language, in which 'Captain Dishstand' with his 'chief officers, named Nickelsilver and Harus' led the bumbling 'hosts of King Georgius' from disaster to disaster against 'the men of Keli'.

A sympathiser wrote a sixteen-page letter to the *Herald* which clearly drew on the draft used by Ned and Joe for the Cameron and Jerilderie letters. Large slabs of the document were quoted in the paper and reprinted by Beechworth's *Advertiser*, saying of the gang, 'Their actions are more like those of four sisters of charity than four outlaws ... their robberies are confined to banks, the police and the Government.'

Increasingly the Kellys were summoning up images of Michael Dwyer who, after the brutal suppression of the great Irish rebellion of 1798, had led a band of green-cockaded cavaliers through the Wicklow Hills in a five-year guerilla campaign, defying a 500-guinea reward on Dwyer's head. In Irish minds they had created 'an imperishable idea of outlaw heroes who were friends to ordinary folk and enemies to their oppressors'.

The spectacle of a sick, penniless woman suddenly able to employ men to do fencing, to buy a sidesaddle and bring a daughter back from domestic service in Tasmania made bank robbery seem a noble exploit. The police who were 'allowed to threaten to shoot respectable men, women and even children ... and ransacking the house; yelling and roaring and galloping through the crops, shouting at the trees ...' — such men diminished the authority of the Queen whose cipher they no longer wore, as they abandoned their uniforms and 'dressed like bushrangers'. The eloquence of Bowman and Zincke, directed against abuse of British law, resonated in many ears as the voice of the Kelly cause — increasingly the voice of justice.

Chief Commissioner Standish seemed oblivious of this. To the end, he failed to recognise that his cynical campaign against the sympathisers was strengthening Ned Kelly's hand and, at the same time, damaging what Standish held most dear: his status as Melbourne's best-known citizen. When the 'remand' policy was eventually discarded on 22 April, it was against his wishes.

The discreditable farce came to an end when Magistrate Foster simply refused to continue remanding the last eleven sympathisers and discharged them, with a firm word to Wild Wright that he had been sailing close to the wind with all his parting shots.

Standish, who had been given no warning of the move when he spoke with Foster the previous night, reported grumpily to the Attorney-General: 'As soon as prisoners were discharged they ran away as fast as they could in every direction & in less than five minutes had left Beechworth.'

The Royal Commission of 1881 wrote the epitaph of Standish's disastrous strategy, describing the endless remands as 'arbitrary proceedings' and commenting,

> They did violence to people's ideas of the liberty of the subject; they irritated and estranged probably many who might have been of service to the police; they failed to allay apprehensions of further outrages on the part of the gang, or to prevent them from obtaining the requisite supplies; they crippled the usefulness of officers who had been called away from active duty ... to attend the Petty Sessions at Beechworth ... and what was of more significance, the failure of the prosecutions led the public to believe that the conduct of affairs was mismanaged.

What of the 'active duty' interrupted by this three-month fiasco? In March another prize opportunity had been fumbled. Back in December 1878, the Queensland government had offered 'native trackers' to help catch the Kellys. The offer was declined because Standish did not approve but, after Jerilderie, the matter was taken out of his hands. On Saturday 8 March Sub-inspector Stanhope O'Connor of the Queensland Police arrived in Benalla — 'a fine, smart, dashing-looking young man' with 'the appearance of one who would care very little whether he met one or a half-dozen Kellys. He carried a belt around his waist in which are about a dozen sockets, which are filled with rifle and revolver cartridges.'

The following Monday six Aboriginal Mounted Police reached Benalla 'and were the cause of much speculation'. The people of Victoria had already been told that 'Lieut O'Connor ... denies them the perquisite of eating the vanquished bushrangers, although most of the natives of Northern Queensland, to which these men belong, are cannibals to the extent of eating enemies slain in battle'.

Benalla saw six slim, bright-looking Aboriginals, aged between 17 and 20, smartly turned out in blue uniforms and caps with red facings, armed with revolvers and Snider carbines. They had been recruited from the Mackay district and Fraser Island, signing on for a five-year term at £3 a month. With colonial wisdom they had been allotted demeaning 'official' names — Hero, Johnny, Jimmy, Jack, Barney and Sambo — which tended to give them 'tracker' status rather than their proper standing as mounted police. O'Connor, however, always referred to them as 'troopers'. They called him, like all their officers, 'Marmie', an Aboriginal word for 'Mister'.

At last Standish had at his disposal a squad of men who posed a real threat to the Gang. Brilliant horsemen and fearless fighters, they could follow tracks which were invisible to the average eye. They could see where a man had touched a sliprail by the specks of salt crystals left by a sweaty hand. They could identify a track on the sand of a creek bed by the mark of a spur's under-strap. They were formidable, and appallingly misused.

O'Connor was a pleasant surprise to Standish — not only a handsome young man with fine, dark mustachios, but a retired lieutenant whose well-bred family in County Westmeath, Ireland, was related to Sir Hercules Robinson, retiring Governor of New South Wales and another representative of the Westmeath gentry.

The foundation was laid for an exciting new phase of the Kelly pursuit. Hare, Standish and O'Connor lived together 'like brothers' at Craven's Hotel, until the Sub-inspector met the beautiful young Louisa Smith, sister-in-law of Superintendent Nicolson. They immediately became lovers and were secretly married. For reasons which Standish never quite explained, this made O'Connor totally unacceptable.

O'Connor's position was at best awkward. The Royal Commission would call it 'anomalous'. While he had the nominal rank of Sub-inspector he was given 'no authority over white constables . . . none over any white policemen or officers whatever'. Though under his direction, his men were at the whim of Standish who, on 21 April, called them back from one of their few active pursuits of the Gang to join Hare on one of his cumbersome mounted safaris through the Warby Ranges. According to Sadleir, Hare 'showed no interest in their work and failed altogether to appreciate their useful qualities'. Hare himself commented, 'I did not see anything particularly striking about them.'

Ned, on the other hand, recognised in the Aboriginal troopers his most potentially dangerous pursuers. Perhaps from his brief contact with tribal Aborigines all those years before at Avenel, he understood something of their abilities and their indefinable affinity with a land they had inhabited for tens of thousands of years — where even the move from tropical Queensland to alpine Victoria affected only the things they remembered and none of the things to be read and interpreted and 'felt' in this new field of experience. In the coming winter, the Gang moved to a hut above the snowline to evade them. (Ned recalled having to get up in the night and clear snow from the roof to save it from collapse.) The Queenslanders suffered in the cold and one of them, Corporal Sambo, died from 'congestion of the lungs' soon after arrival and was buried in a pauper's grave. Moses, a Queensland tracker living in Victoria, was sworn in to take his place.

Ned was reassured when he realised that the Queenslanders were being wasted, but he knew that they alone were a match for him in his own country. At the very end he hoped to destroy them, showing near-obsession with the threat they posed. For his part, Standish would refuse to address a police victory parade until the Aboriginal troopers had been removed.

While Standish was, in the words of the Royal Commission, 'rusticating peacefully' in Benalla, reading novels, eating chocolates and being 'discourteous' to O'Connor, Hare put all his eggs in two baskets — search parties galloping around virtually at random and his trump card, Aaron Sherritt.

Detective Ward, who knew Aaron as well as any policeman could, warned Hare that Aaron would never betray his lifelong mate, Joe Byrne. And Aaron himself told Hare of his great regard for Ned Kelly:

> Ned Kelly would beat me into fits . . . I can beat all the others; I am a better man than Joe Byrne, and I am a better man than Dan Kelly, and I am a better man than Steve Hart. I can lick those two youngsters into fits; I have always beaten Joe, but I look upon Ned Kelly as an extraordinary man; there is no man in the world like him, he is superhuman . . . I look upon him as invulnerable.

In spite of this, and in spite of Aaron diverting the police to Towong to give the Gang clear passage to Jerilderie, Hare was convinced that he had won the young man's loyalty. He now let himself be led by Aaron into a bizarre, month-long exercise in which a party of police camped in the Woolshed ranges by day then crept down and spent each night watching the Byrne homestead, waiting for the Kelly Gang to arrive.

This was the first so-called 'cave party'. Hare slept in a cave while most of his men lay around beside boulders, under trees, wherever they could spread a rug. Aaron spent each night with Hare and his men, entertaining the gullible superintendent with stories of his adventures with Ned and Joe. He made sure that the police watched only from positions where they couldn't possibly see Joe as he crept up to his mother's house behind the high bank of a Chinese miners' water race.

Aaron was paid 7 shillings a day, in itself enough to justify this rather obvious hoax in his eyes. Quite apart from that, the cave party took up all Hare's time for weeks and tied up a large party of police. Perhaps most importantly from Aaron's viewpoint, his apparent energy in helping to catch the Kellys kept alive the deal he had struck with Standish the day of the Great Sebastopol Raid, when he had agreed to betray the Kellys if Standish used his influence to save Joe Byrne's life.

It is true that standard police orders were for Joe to be taken prisoner if possible. But what then? Aaron would die unaware that Standish had never intended to try to save Joe from the gallows. Telling the Attorney General that a deal had been proposed by which Joe might betray the gang 'were his life assured', Standish commented, 'That . . . is a course which I should be unwilling to recommend.' So much for the word of a gentleman.

Aaron Sherritt built his dangerous career as a double agent on this false hope of saving his friend's life. His old enemy, Detective Mick Ward, was forced to take part in the farcical strategy contrived by Aaron and Hare with full knowledge of the game Aaron was playing. Ward bit his tongue and bided his time.

Aaron had made critical errors of judgement. He had not told Mrs Byrne of his double-dealing with the police, nor had he confided in his family, who seem to have believed that he was genuinely acting as a police agent. These miscalculations, which could easily have been corrected in the early stages of Aaron's career as a double agent, would prove fatal. Both were exploited by Detective Ward in a patient and ruthless campaign to make this remarkable young man a dupe in his own scheme to trap the Gang.

Meanwhile Ned and Joe laughed with Aaron at the success of his role as their betrayer and sent him £100 of the Jerilderie money through Joe's brother, Paddy. By then Mrs Byrne had become suspicious of Aaron, however. His engagement to Joe's sister was broken off and the £100 never reached Aaron. He stole a horse from the Byrnes which replaced one he had given Kate Byrne as an engagement present and, almost unbelievably, he sold it to Ned's sister, Maggie Skilling, in the course of a hurried and ill-fated courtship of Kate Kelly.

When this complex squabble hit the Beechworth court — a case involving a police agent, the mother of a member of the Kelly Gang and the sister of Ned Kelly himself — local and metropolitan newspapermen gathered. From the witness box, Margret Byrne — slim and strong-faced, with pale blue eyes — looked across at Aaron, flashly dressed as ever, as reporters' pencils were poised. 'We had a falling out about his giving the police assistance . . . I thought that Sherritt was giving assistance to the police in the pursuit of the bushrangers.'

The magistrate dismissed the case against Aaron, but that was a mere detail. Aaron Sherritt was officially a traitor. Already distrusted by many sympathisers because he was a Protestant *and* the son of a former member of the hated Irish Constabulary, Aaron became a strange, lonely, defiant figure. He was still loyal to the gang and still trusted by Ned and Joe, but that trust was being steadily eroded by an increasing chorus of hostility from their closest friends and relatives. Detective Ward watched and waited.

Before this Celtic brew of suspicion and ancient prejudice had been brought to boiling point by Margret Byrne's denunciation, the police party left the safe, well-fed boredom of the cave party to rejoin Hare's wild, cross-country gallops, looking like a chorus of brigands from some comic opera. An enterprising photographer persuaded Hare to pose one of his parties in the Benalla police paddock as he prepared to set off for the Strathbogies on 20 June. Cut gum branches were stacked against the post and rail fence and a burnt stump was carried in for Hare to plant his foot on as he gazed stolidly into the distance while his favourite tracker, Moses, knelt by him, supposedly examining tracks. The photo taken, the party rode off. Then it was Standish's turn, decked out in a pair of strapped riding pants and a broad, pork-pie hat, posing unconvincingly against another wonderfully spurious background of cut gum branches, complete with tent, campfire and dog.

Standish had actually spent one night with Hare and his men watching the Byrne house but, apart from this, he lounged around Craven's Hotel and the Benalla police station and waited anxiously for Hare's safe return. This appears to have been a source of great strain to him. He told the Royal Commission, 'I lost upwards of a stone weight.' Superintendent Sadleir recalled,

> It was almost pathetic to see, during the months Captain Standish spent at Benalla ... how restless and uneasy he became were Hare out of his company. I have seen Standish on the top rail of a fence watching anxiously for Hare's return from a short ride of a mile or two. He said to me that he was in constant fear lest some accident should happen to him ... I think I see in this exaggerated affection another symptom of that mental trouble under which he quite broke down a very few years later.

The sympathisers remained a gall to Standish and Hare. Two weeks after the collapse of his 'remand' policy, Standish considered:

> that the Gang were secure of the good will of a great proportion of the inhabitants of these regions, a poor but semi-criminal class whom they never annoy and frequently assist, and who supply them with food and information of the movements of the police. Indeed, the outlaws are considered heroes by a large proportion of the population of the North Eastern district who ... look upon the police as their natural enemies.

One strategy against the sympathisers had actually swelled their ranks. Already, a second strategy was foreshadowed by Standish, described by him as 'remedial measures contemplated by the Honble the Minister of Lands'.

When the Benalla sympathisers had been arrested they were noted as 'all of the labouring class but ... described as farmers and selectors'. This is precisely what many of the Kellys' staunchest sympathisers were: farmers without land, young fellows engaged in seasonal work as farm labourers, harvest hands, shearers and the like, yet to take up their own selections. Now, in a plan to strike at this group and at sympathiser farmers trying to increase their holdings beyond bare subsistence level, lists of applicants for land who were due to appear before Land Boards were circulated to key police officers and sub-officers of the district.

These were the very men who had nominated the sympathisers to be arrested.

Any friends and relatives of the Gang who appeared on the lists were noted and their names supplied to Sadleir, who then informed the relevant Land Board that the police objected to these men taking up land in the north-east. Their applications would be refused. The Royal Commission noted that, 'In the North-Eastern district ... a very large number of names are in the hands of the Lands Department who will be refused land on applying for it in that particular district.'

The plan was in full swing by late May. On 9 June Bill Tanner, who had been Tom Lloyd's ally in the night fight with Johnston and his fellow constable in Benalla, wrote to ask why his application for 44 acres at Myrrhee had been refused. The Secretary for Lands wrote to him on 16 June, advising, 'I have the honour to inform you that the land in question was refused on the recommendation of the Police Department.'

A Lake Rowan bullock driver, William Jacks, was put on the black list by Sergeant Whelan because he came from Wallan, hometown of the Quinns fourteen years before, and 'having come from there he is likely to be a friend of the outlaws': Owen Trainor of Devenish was blacklisted because his father was a brother-in-law of Jack Quinn and he was said to have been a friend of the Kelly family when 'a carrier on the Greta Road'. Sub-inspector Montfort would say of Jack Quinn, 'He was on my mind, for though he was never convicted, yet at the same time he is a most undesirable man to be allowed to select, more especially on the verge of civilization.'

As in the previous sympathiser trials, mere suspicion convicted a man, and he now faced a far more insidious penalty than a few months imprisonment without trial. He was denied the right to take up land in the country he knew, among his friends and relatives, denied the only future he could see for himself. This 'lever' had 'more potency than an army of police'. It tipped the Kelly Outbreak into full-scale rebellion.

At this critical phase, Hare led one of his beloved search parties (the very one photographed in the police paddock) down to the Strathbogies near Euroa. He was jumping his horse over a fence when, he wrote, 'something gave way in my back, just above the right hip'. Hare travelled back to Benalla by buggy and told Standish, 'that the hardships I had gone through had affected my constitution and that I wished him to relieve me.'

Hare had simply run himself to a standstill. Standish was forced to ask Nicolson to take charge again — a bitter pill. He wound down the strength of the force Nicolson would have at his disposal, removing seventeen mounted constables and fourteen foot police, as well as most of the garrison artillerymen guarding banks, so placing further demands on depleted police strength. He also put an end to the *carte blanche* expenditure enjoyed by Hare, leaving Nicolson without an extra penny to spend on the pursuit.

Nicolson was understandably bitter when he took over from Hare in Benalla on 3 July:

> When he (with the assistance of Captain Standish) spent eight months in pursuit of the Kellys with the largest body of police that ever was in the district, and with the artillery forces at his command to watch the townships, so that he had full benefit of the police, and when he spent more money per month than was spent on the pursuit at any other time; and with all these advantages, when I relieved him in July 1879, *he did not know if the Kellys were in Victoria*. [my italics — and probably Nicolson's, too]

Still fuming, Nicolson hurled himself into a canny economy campaign. He bought a horse for £15 instead of paying a £15 hire bill run up by Hare. He expanded the police spy network, paying new agents out of his own pocket, while letting his depleted forces and beggared bankroll suggest a less rigorous pursuit. He hoped that this would lead the Gang to become over-confident, so they would be tempted into some exploit he could control, and he refrained from sending parties galloping off at every report that the Gang had been sighted. They would not draw him out; he would draw *them* out.

Nicolson's expertise in criminal espionage and knowledge of the criminal mind made him a formidable opponent, but he failed to understand the profound change taking place among the Gang and sympathisers. He was unaware that this baffling outbreak had run full-circle, now driven by the same undefined force that operated below the surface of the north-east in the days before Stringybark. Again, it was about land.

16

A REPUBLIC

JUNE 1879 – JUNE 1880

By the winter of 1879 the Kelly Country was a mixture of many volatile and combustible elements. The failure of the Selection Acts had been seminal. The economic problems of the district and colony had pushed the conflict between squatters and selectors to the level of war, and stock theft had come to be seen as a weapon. Political brawling had further damaged the economy and created a climate in which class bitterness became a political tool — a climate in which the premier could openly tout revolution and civil war in his ongoing battle with the squattocracy, a common enemy to the Kellys and their supporters. There were six months of drought in the year; business was considered to be 'in a state of unexampled depression'; in the winter there were bank failures and deputations of unemployed to the premier.

The timing of the sympathiser arrests in the heart of harvest had been a blow at small farmers, a particularly cruel blow as they battled to make up for the previous year's 'almost total failure'. Now, in barring Kelly sympathisers from the land itself, the blacklists were creating a hard-core group of people who were pushed to the point of having nothing to lose. Because Ned Kelly blamed himself for their plight, this 'remedial measure' challenged him to help them.

Ned's first instinct was his usual response to the third punch — to hit back — in this case with another bank robbery. But the banks were now security-conscious and more heavily armed. They were guarded by the last of the Garrison Artillery standing on sentry duty, by plainclothed police and by special constables, civilian volunteers 'of the right sort' recruited by Nicolson in another move to eke out his outrageously reduced resources. Some bank precautions against robbery, like the collapsing blind, were primitive and ineffective. Others, like those operating in Beechworth, were impressive — a telegraphic network connecting the town's banks to the police station.

Ned considered the possibility of robbing government premises which handled money and Joe asked his brother, Paddy, to find out how much money was carried in the nearby Eldorado Post Office. Paddy enlisted the help of Aaron Sherritt's brother Jack, who had been recruited by Nicolson as a police spy. Through Jack, Nicolson made sure the message went back that 'even £20 would not be found in the Eldorado or any other small post office'. Joe turned his attention to the Eldorado Savings Bank and received another discouraging report from Jack Sherritt.

A bank robbery with the near certainty of bloodshed was not what Ned wanted, but the dashing summertime robberies would never be repeated.

In mid-June Maggie Skilling and Tom Lloyd went to Melbourne by train and bought 'a large parcel of ammunition' from Rosier, the well-known gunsmith. Unable to obtain as much as they wanted for 'a certain rifle', they left a deposit, saying they would return tomorrow. Rosier was suspicious of both the quantity and class of ammunition. He contacted the police and they staked out his shop the next day. When it became obvious that the suspicious customers weren't going to reappear, the police telegraphed Benalla and Sadleir's men met that night's train from Melbourne. Maggie and Tom were aboard and their bags were searched — as was the luggage of an innocent first-class passenger, Bridget O'Brien of the Greta hotel. No ammunition was found. It had been brought up on the previous night's train by an undetected sympathiser. The deposit left with Rosier had been Maggie's and Tom's clever ploy to divert police attention from their courier. The Gang now had a new reserve of ammunition for whatever lay ahead.

As the storm slowly continued to gather, Ned appeared at the Sherritt house near Beechworth with an offer for Aaron to join the Gang — a demonstration of his faith in Joe's mate; but neither Aaron nor his parents were home. The time Ned passed with the Sherritt girls gives an unusually intimate glimpse of him in this darkening period.

> He took the baby, a child of four or five months, in his arms and said that he was hungry. And there was some bread in the oven baking, and there was some dough in the dish, and he took some of the dough up, and he flattened it on the table and pulled out the fire with his foot and baked two or three pieces ... and all the time he was inside he kept the baby in his arms.

In the last month of winter when travel in the ranges was hardest and tracks were easiest to follow, the Gang could no longer afford their overnight dashes of 60 and 70 miles and their fugitive lives became a bleak pattern of survival.

Ned's plans took a new and startling shape. Perhaps he was re-reading his favourite book, *Lorna Doone*. Or perhaps it was just a vivid memory of the hero's first glimpse of those fabulous outlaws, the Doones of Bagworthy, riding with their plunder back to the valley stronghold across dark, misty moorland lit by a hilltop beacon: 'Heavy men and large of stature, reckless how they bore their guns or how they sate their horses, with leather jerkins and long boots, *and iron plates on breast and head*'. [my italics]

Ned decided that the Kelly Gang would have armour. His reasoning was simple: 'Without armour I could never have possibly robbed a guarded bank and disarmed police without taking life.' Joe opposed the idea and in the last hours of his life, would remind his mate, 'I always said this bloody armour would bring us to grief'. Ned would not be swayed. The gang would be equipped with armour — armour that was a symbol of the new direction his rebellion was taking. 'Farmers had been denied land; the idle plough was to become a weapon.'

Ned chose plough mouldboards for his armour — the broad, slightly twisted steel blades that turned back the sod from the furrow after the soil had been sliced by the ploughshare. The Gang started collecting the necessary mouldboards; many were donated by sympathisers; others were gathered by men like the double agent, Hurdle Creek school-teacher James Wallace. In the late winter or early spring of 1879, Wallace travelled around in his buggy offering to buy mouldboards, claiming that 'his father was a dealer in old metals and he was purchasing for him'.

The armour was designed primarily for close-range, dismounted action, although it was able to be worn on horseback — a combination of mounted infantry tactics and heavy-armoured firepower.

As in the Gang's two earlier hold-ups sympathisers would play vital roles, but now it would not be possible to plant them in advance. The hold-ups were now planned as sudden-strike operations, with the result that the sympathisers became members of an extended gang in which the four armoured Kellys would act as storm troopers to confront and disarm any defenders of the bank within a screen provided by well-armed and fast-moving scouts.

In planning a bank robbery on military lines, involving men who had not been openly involved in the gang's crimes until now, Ned had to take them with him, outside the law. To do that he had to challenge the law itself and — as he stated and re-stated in the Jerilderie Letter — the authority of Her Sovereign Majesty.

The dream of a republic, as a symbol of freedom from British rule, was common to many peoples — accomplished in America, yearned for in Ireland and about to be realised in South Africa, now on the brink of the first Boer War of 1880. 'Boer' was Dutch for 'farmer'. Armies of men on their stock horses, carrying their own rifles, were about to defeat the

The five surviving Queensland Aboriginal troopers photographed at Benalla with, at left, Senior Constable King and Sub-inspector Stanhope O'Connor, and at right, Superintendent Sadleir and Chief Commissioner Standish (in highly uncharacteristic and probably borrowed bush gear).

Thomas Curnow, the crippled schoolteacher who thwarted Ned's plans at Glenrowan. He was a brave man who deserved the praise he received, but he tended to trade on his exploit, even after successfully campaigning to increase his share of the reward to £1000 (about $250 000 in present-day value). (*Noel O'Shea*)

The Glenrowan Inn, a detail from a photo taken late in the siege. Visible on the verandah are the stool where young Jack Jones had played his concertina and the table carried out of the dining room to make room for dancing. The slab-and-bark kitchen at rear is separated from the white, weatherboard inn by a 2-metre breezeway.

This group includes six of the seven Benalla police who followed Hare in the first attack on the Glenrowan Inn (missing is Constable Kirkham). From left, Barry, Bracken (the Glenrowan constable), Phillips, Arthur — one of the best shots in the force and the first policeman Ned encountered in his Last Stand — and Kelly, who played a key role in Ned's capture. Second from right, Gascoigne, who seriously wounded Ned in the first exchange of shots, and Canny. The group was photographed at Glenrowan in the failing light of 28 June.

A remarkable collection of relics, including Dan's and Steve's armour, photographed at Glenrowan by Bray of Beechworth on the day of the siege. Ned's Colt revolving rifle is in the foreground with his padded cap and one of his shoulder pieces, shot off in an exchange with Constable Gascoigne. The two headpieces disprove the tedious claim that only Ned wore a helmet.

Sergeant Steele, kneeling with his shotgun for all the world like a gentleman hunter, photographed with his men from Wangaratta. The eccentric Constable Dwyer poses dejectedly at right.

British and win a republic in the Transvaal as a prelude to the devastating Boer War of 19 years later. The war was won by England at enormous cost, yet in the end it was a political and moral victory for the Boers.

The Kellys and their supporters were in many ways like the South African farmer soldiers, with the same potential to baffle colonial militias and Imperial troops. The greatest difference between them lay in the fact that the Boer leaders included men who were politically sophisticated, capable of envisaging and realising the republic they fought for. To these men freedom from English rule was a beginning. To Ned and his mates, it was an end.

Ned's idea of the republic was naive, not properly thought through and seemingly doomed to failure — qualities it shared with many Irish rebellions. And it is easy to mock the idea of a bushranger turned political visionary, until — as historian McQuilton points out — one considers Garibaldi, a man of Ned's lifetime who had filled the roles of 'guerilla soldier and emotional political symbol'. To the Victorians of 1879 there was a more parochial example of renegade turned politician in Peter Lalor. In the month of Ned's birth he had led the Eureka rebels against the forces of the Queen, under the Southern Cross flag of a brutally aborted republic. Now Peter Lalor — one-armed from that battle — was Commissioner of Trade and Customs in the Berry government, soon to become Speaker of the Assembly.

It is doubtful if such thoughts had occurred to artist Thomas Carrington of *Melbourne Punch* when, after Euroa, he had shown Ned Kelly occupying the premier's vacant chair. It was a piece of whimsy from this member of the Athenaeum Club, foundation member of the Yorick Club and drama critic of the *Australasian*, 'the clubman's paper'. Nevertheless, in a darker moment he summoned up Ned Kelly, Graham Berry and a tiny, bonneted, booted lady labelled *The Age*, dancing hand-in-hand around a flagpole carrying a skull and crossbones banner emblazoned, 'Communism'. He captioned his picture, 'OUR RULERS'. Carrington, the professional mocker, would be hurled into the battle which decided the fate of Ned Kelly's republican dream; he would glimpse and record the stature of the man who brought this unimaginable concept so close to reality.

As the darkness of that winter passed, the image of the armour and the shadowy republic still pervaded the gang's plans. Joe — grandson of a transported Irish rebel and joint author of the Jerilderie Letter — clearly embraced the idea of a republic and, as 'confidential' of the gang, wrote in exercise books the 'records of meetings' as the Gang discussed their plans with the inner circle of sympathisers.

Still opposing the armour strategy, Joe came up with an alternative

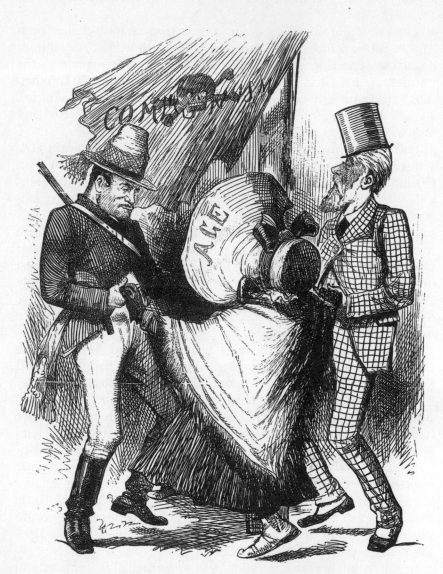

OUR RULERS.

scheme to rob a Beechworth bank. Aaron and Jack Sherritt were to join the Gang in bailing up the manager at night and forcing him to unlock the safe. Joe called at the Sherritt farm to tell the Sherritt brothers of the plan and they agreed to take part.

Aaron said nothing to the police of this meeting with Joe, but Jack reported it. When Nicolson urged him to play along with the scheme, Jack was appalled, envisaging himself caught in the crossfire of a gun battle between Kellys and police. Disgusted at what he called Jack's cowardice, Nicolson turned to Aaron, who was now courting a 15-year-old Woolshed girl, Ellen Barry. When Nicolson established another 'cave party' to spy on the Byrne homestead, Aaron resumed his strange role as pretend betrayer of the gang and again spent each night with the watching police.

One evening, before the police joined him, he appeared at a nearby Chinese store with Joe. Another night, as the police watched from positions carefully chosen by Aaron, Joe visited the homestead, picked up some clothing and left. Informed of this by Jack Sherritt, Ward protested that it couldn't have happened, knowing in his heart that it had. By now Detective Ward had devised a way to exploit Aaron Sherritt's precarious double-agent role. If Aaron was only pretending to help the police, Ward would make him look like a real traitor and encourage the gang to kill him. To do this they would have to break cover. It was a ruthless, amoral plan — in every way worthy of Detective Mick Ward.

Nicolson had his own agenda, at the very least suspecting Ward's use of Aaron. Nicolson was highly cynical about Aaron's fidelity to the police, distrusting him 'in everything' and telling the Royal Commission, 'What did Aaron ever do for the police? Nothing.' Yet he refused to sack Aaron, against Standish's orders, and paid him out of his own pocket to remain an agent months after the supposedly secret cave party had been exposed as a farce, its existence virtually common knowledge to the Byrnes and the other people of the Woolshed. Like Ward, Nicolson saw a particular value in Aaron; perhaps as potential bait to draw the Kelly Gang into the open.

The barrage of warnings that Aaron Sherritt was a traitor, the formidable enmity of Mrs Byrne, the clumsy, faint-hearted operation of Jack Sherritt as a double-agent and the open hostility of many key sympathisers to Aaron — all were gradually wearing down Joe Byrne's belief in his friend.

◆

IN NOVEMBER 1879 a strange group blundered on to the bushranging stage. A partially crippled, probably homosexual ex-convict and ex-preacher called Andrew Scott led a sad little retinue of youths, all looking for work as they tramped through Victoria on their way to Sydney. Scott had achieved notoriety seven years before as 'Captain Moonlite' when convicted of a bank robbery at Mount Egerton in Victoria. The Victoria Police watched the northward progress of the party, who professed to be on 'a possum-hunting picnic'. Sadleir claims that, on his trek, 'Scott sent word to Ned Kelly that he wished to join forces with him. Kelly sent back word threatening that if Scott or his band approached him he would shoot them down.' Although the offer and the threat are equally unlikely, the destinies of this odd band would soon interact with those of the Gang.

Refused a hand-out at Wantabadgery Station in New South Wales, Scott and his young followers took their revenge in a clumsy and point-less hold-up of the homestead. After a clash with a small, timid, police party, the 'amateur bushrangers' muddled into a pitched battle with a larger, more determined group of policemen. A trooper was critically wounded and two of the youths were killed, one of them probably Scott's lover. The 'Captain' and the three survivors of his 'gang' surrendered.

This sorry affair was immediately portrayed as the heroic defeat of a band of desperate Victorian criminals; Jerilderie had been avenged. When the wounded trooper died, wily Sir Henry Parkes received a political windfall in the drought-stricken, strife-torn colony — a martyr in the cause of law and order *and* four bloodthirsty enemies of society to be made examples of. Tried with indecent haste, all were sentenced to death, though eventually only one lad — who had spent the entire gun battle hiding under a bed — accompanied poor half-mad Scott to the gallows in Sydney's Darlinghurst Gaol on 20 January 1880.

Jim Kelly was completing his term in Darlinghurst when the four occupied the gaol's condemned cells and was released the week the ex-ecutions took place. He began a secret journey to meet his brothers and their mates, a very different man from the teenager who had entered prison three years before. He was almost 21, a lean, handsome 6-footer, now with the trade of bootmaker. He had changed in other more impor-tant ways: he was less pugnacious, less headstrong and the fate facing Ned and Dan had been driven home to him.

The Victoria Police were worried that Jim would try to join the Gang and circulated copies of his latest prison photo to stations all along the Murray, but he easily crossed into Victoria without being seen and arranged a meeting with Ned. Jim urged his brother to break up the Gang and advanced or supported a plan to replace its members one by one: 'Say, Steve would leave and be replaced by Wild. Then Dan would be replaced by Tom, and so on. Eventually, the Gang would disappear.' Travelling singly, the Gang members would journey to another colony or leave Australia.

It was a sound plan which offered escape from inevitable death by gun or rope. One can imagine Joe's enthusiasm for a scheme which had the twin advantages of avoiding the problem with Aaron and obviating the need for armour. Like the escape of the Anzacs from Gallipoli only 35 years later, it was a retreat that outsmarted the enemy.

'But,' reported Tom Lloyd, 'Ned was committed to the rebellion.'

Jim disappeared again, ready to emerge among the sympathisers when the great day came, but haunted by the image of a triangular balcony in an angle of honey-coloured sandstone walls, overlooking a garden shaded by poplar and loquat trees — the gallows of Darlinghurst Gaol.

Aaron Sherritt had married Ellen Barry on Boxing Day 1879 and gone to live with his in-laws in the Woolshed Valley. As the absurd cave parties continued into 1880, Detective Ward persuaded Jack Sherritt to steal a saddle from Aaron's bride and plant it in the Byrne homestead. On information provided by the Sherritt family, Joe's brother, Paddy, and Mrs Byrne would be arrested for theft. The charges hung over them for the rest of 1880.

Someone, perhaps Ward or a vengeful Byrne family, spread stories of threats supposedly made by Aaron against Joe, including the ugly and unbelievable, 'I'll shoot Joe Byrne and I'll fuck him before his body gets cold!' Joe probably never heard this product of some vindictive mind, but he heard enough. Worn away by the constant whispers of betrayal, the corrosive months of fugitive life and Ward's cold-blooded campaign of incrimination, the last strands of doubt snapped. Joe decided that Aaron must die.

Ned seems to have opposed the murder. Always ready to trust a man — especially a friend — he could not believe that Aaron had betrayed them voluntarily and he clung to an idea that Aaron had been tortured by the police. In the end, however, he reluctantly accepted Joe's decision to kill his mate.

For Joe to emerge from hiding to murder Aaron threatened the plan they were developing. Every available policeman would converge on the scene and the calm that had settled over the Kelly Country would be destroyed. They would have to wait for the hue and cry to subside or use the police activity as part of their plan. They could let the killing of Aaron decoy police from the place where the gang planned to strike, just as they had been decoyed from Euroa and Jerilderie.

For the time Ned used this as an excuse to make Joe stay his hand. Aaron must live until the great exploit was completely planned. Ned may have hoped that this postponement would give Joe time to change his mind, and apparently it did. In May 1880 Joe appeared near the Sherritt farm and told Aaron's mother that he intended to kill her son.

This was, of course, a warning, a chance for Aaron to leave the Kelly Country. It was a chance to escape which he didn't take.

In late summer and autumn the gang's plan gathered impetus. Joseph Ashmead recalled,

> One morning when a number of the farmers in Greta went out to plough they found that the mouldboard had been stolen. Brown, Smith and Jones all met in Wangaratta. They had all come in for the same purpose. It was most annoying that their ploughing should be delayed and they were hard in their condemnation of the silly practical joke of some brainless hooligans. Most likely their boards were laying at the bottom of some dam in the district and would not be found until the next drought came, and not a few of the men swore about it.

Still short of the thirty-odd mouldboards needed for the four suits, the Gang had made up the number with these thefts from 'two or three different farms', the first of them from a Glenrowan farmer called Sinclair on 22 March. A Greta selector called Kearney also lost a side of bacon. All the stripped ploughs were in the neighbourhood of Greta and Oxley, within a radius of about 8 miles.

Senior Constable Kelly led an investigating party including two Queensland Native Police who found tracks, 'one of them ... the footsteps of a man with a very small boot, with what is called a "larrikin" heel upon it'. Nicolson's suspicions were confirmed when an agent reported, 'The Kelly gang were the offenders.'

Over the next two months four sets of armour were made. Even though Joe didn't like the idea he may have helped design the suits — basing the body armour, with breast and back plates, aprons and shoulder guards — on a set of ancient Chinese armour imported for the Beechworth carnival of 1874 and preserved in the town's Burke Museum.

Two mouldboards were straightened, cut to shape and riveted together to form a breastplate, with another two or three forming a backplate. These would be hung over the shoulders on straps and joined at the sides by straps or iron plates bolted between back and front. One or more of the suits would have curved guards to protect the shoulders and upper arms. An apron piece, slung by straps from the bottom of the breastplate, would protect the loins. Ned's suit, at least, would have a similar piece hung at the back. The legs would be unprotected, to minimise weight and give maximum mobility, and because leg armour seemed unnecessary for close-quarter work in a bank hold-up.

Helped by Tom Lloyd, the Gang set up a bush forge by a creek 'on the far side of the Bald Hill'. While the first set of mouldboards were buried in the coals and made red hot, they laid a freshly cut and stripped red box log across the creek with both ends butted into the banks and the underside dipping into the water. This would be the Gang's 'anvil' — the sappy wood resisted fire and the water helped to carry away the sound of the hammer blows. Lifted from the fire with tongs and laid on the stripped log, the mouldboards were hammered and chiselled into the two halves of a breastplate. They were then riveted together and rested against a stump.

Using a police Martini Henry rifle dropped near the Kelly homestead one night by a member of a panicky watch party, they fired a test shot into the concave, inner side of the breastplate at 10 yards range. The .45 bullet, with an effective range of some 800 yards, drove a deep dent but failed to split the steel. The forging had not made the mouldboards brittle. Work proceeded on backplate, aprons and shoulder guards, then the helmet.

It has been claimed that the gang found its inspiration for the armour in 'an illustrated edition of one of Sir Walter Scott's novels'. Fanciful as this sounds, the Kelly helmet closely resembled the massive *heaume* of the Crusades period — a cylindrical head-piece with a square-cut gap for the face, covered by a broad mask plate attached by two or more bolts, leaving a horizontal slit for the eyes. Small holes were punched in pairs around the upper rim of the helmet so a quilted lining could be laced inside.

The prototype suit was for Ned. As it was finally strapped and bolted on to him, even Joe must have marvelled at this forbidding, almost awesome figure, bigger than a man, the voice ringing harshly behind the steel mask plate, the eyes glittering behind the eye slit.

As he first lowered the helmet on to his shoulders, completing the hundredweight burden of armour, Ned saw the familiar world confined within the harsh, black frame of his vision. Behind him and to either side, there was nothing; he could only look ahead.

Three other suits and helmets were made for Dan, Steve and Joe in other parts of the Kelly Country. Oxley blacksmith William Culph was involved, with Patrick Delaney of Benalla, Beechworth smith Charles Knight and Tom Straughair of the Woolshed. All these men — and the other men, women and even children who had a part in the work — would be protected by the gang's propaganda machine, which spread misinformation about the forging of the armour. Joseph Ashmead, an old acquaintance of Dan and Ned, recorded the story he heard in nearby Winton North.

The Kelly gang secured the services of a blacksmith to make the stolen mould-boards into suits of armour. The man was a foreigner who had been working in the district. No-one would suspect him. He was a good man and never failed to attend church. He always stayed for the prayer meetings and was deeply grieved at the dishonesty of the mean theft of the persons who stole the farmers' mould-boards. The blacksmith disappeared shortly after the mould-boards were taken and was never seen again. It was thought he had been well paid and betook himself to green fields and pastures new.

There was much talk as to where and how the armour was made ... There is a place in the ranges, only known to a few who call it 'The Devil's Basin'. It was accessible from one point and that was so overgrown with scrub and undergrowth as to make the entrance hard to find. It was thought that this was the safe retreat where the blacksmith worked with hammer and tongs ... At the time of the capture of Ned Kelly at Glenrowan, I had the novel experience of trying on the armour and I saw distinctly the stain of sap from a green tree. This proved it had been made in the bush, and turned into shape on logs cut for the purpose.

Within months detectives Ward and Considine would follow the trail of the armour's makers to dead end after dead end. Only 31 years later the Sydney journalist E.W. Cookson also tried.

During the course of a few casual inquiries, we found that the armour was made, solely and individually, by each of eleven blacksmiths, living in all parts of the territory; that the man who really made it was dead; that this man had never existed, but that it was his brother who had fashioned the plates; that the armour was made by a government farrier that time the outlaws stood over him with pistols and threats ... The armour business is a popular subject for discussion. It is a sort of eternal guessing competition without prizes.

Over the years many people would marvel at the long-term secrecy surrounding the armour makers, not realising that there was much more to this than simply being a Kelly sympathiser. They had been involved in the bid to set up a republic, high treason against Her Sovereign Majesty and a hanging matter.

One police agent broke the inner circle of sympathisers and heard about the armour being made, though he failed to learn of the republic. His codename was 'Denny' but he was often referred to as the Diseased Stock Agent, or DSA, because he used the code phrase 'diseased stock' to identify the Gang.

Back in 1874 Laurence O'Brien of Greta's Victoria Hotel had been thrown from his horse and killed one night when riding back from an Oxley Council meeting. His widow, Bridget, continued running the hotel with the help of her brother-in-law, Daniel Kennedy, a former schoolteacher at Greta. This man, who may have taught Dan Kelly briefly, was the Diseased Stock Agent. No one can be sure why he chose to betray the Gang. It is possible that members of the Kelly circle supported a petition to stop him taking up some public land in the little town. Certainly, he was involved in a bitter dispute over a piece of land needed for water access by the McAuliffes, staunch supporters of the

Kellys. On top of this Kennedy, like many people in Greta, needed money badly. Whatever motivated him, he quickly became Nicolson's most effective agent.

Usually calling himself 'B. Charles Williams' or 'B.C.W.', he wrote to Nicolson on 20 May 1880, addressing him, 'William Charles Balfour (the B.C.W. initials reversed!).

> Dear Sir, — Nothing definite re. the diseased stock of this locality. I have made careful inspection but did [not] find exact source of disease ... Missing portions of cultivators described as jackets are now being worked and fit splendidly. Tested previous to using and proof at 10 yards ...

Nicolson, in his single-minded pursuit of criminals, noted a comment by the DSA that 'a break out may be expected as feed is getting scarce' but did not immediately take the report of armour seriously. And Sadleir would say, after it was all over, 'I had been informed for months ... that the armour was preparing; I never thoroughly believed it, I looked upon it as an impossibility.'

Nicolson had good reason for single-mindedness. He had been told on 3 May that he was being replaced as leader of the Kelly pursuit. Increasingly aware of the ground swell among the sympathisers, knowing that something was brewing, confident that 'matters were drawing to a close', he 'made urgent representations' to stay in charge and saw the move to replace him as 'simply a second attempt ... to deprive me of the credit of the work'.

Nicolson won a month's extension and launched out in a last, obsessive attempt to catch the gang. Against his usual 'no pursuit' policy he arranged for Aaron Sherritt to join a party of fourteen police and Aboriginal troopers who were investigating a furphy that Joe had been sighted in a gully near the Byrne house. Knowing that this was another charade, Aaron went along with the exercise and was with the police party when the family's nextdoor neighbour, a well-known sympathiser, stumbled on them and saw Aaron with the police.

Many, including Jack Sherritt, believed that this incident doomed Aaron. Three days later, on 2 June, Nicolson again handed over leadership to Hare. In fairness, Hare had protested against the change; Sadleir had written to him, urging him not to accept. However, the new government wanted, as Chief Secretary Ramsay put it, 'a change of bowlers', and Standish — enemy of Nicolson and champion of Hare — did nothing to dissuade them.

Whether or not Ned realised it, a major threat to his plans had been removed. Nicolson had been closing his net around the Gang. Now that net was broken and some agents were dismissed, alienated or ignored.

With the remains of Nicolson's spy network, Hare had inherited Ward's plan to set up Aaron as bait to lure the Kellys into an 'outrage'. The detective had one last trick up his sleeve to make sure that the gang could have no doubts as to Aaron's 'betrayal'.

Ward arranged for another police party to watch the Byrnes', but this group would not operate from caves. With Hare's approval and despite strong opposition from Sadleir, they would hide in the hut Aaron had moved into with his young bride. It was a few yards from the main road along the Woolshed Valley, within sight of the Byrne homestead and surrounded by Kelly sympathisers. Joe's younger brother Denny passed the front door twice a day, going to and from school. As if all this were not enough, Ward arranged for the party to wear a sort of uniform — long, blue diggers' smocks — and ordered them not to post a sentry, a standard precaution on the cave parties.

It is not clear whether Hare had an inkling of Ward's real purpose in this inept exercise, but his own strategies aligned very closely with Ward's.

When both the Queensland Government and O'Connor grew impatient with the ongoing misuse of the Aboriginal troopers, Hare welcomed the idea of their returning to Queensland (and in fact would claim that it was his initiative). Perhaps picking up an idea from the *Benalla Standard* ('Let the trackers be withdrawn and the Kellys will be heard of very soon'), he suggested that the departure of the Aboriginals would encourage the Gang to break cover, 'and I was anxious they should do something as it would give us a better opportunity of falling across them.'

This was the heart of Ward's plan. Hare intended to leave the police in Aaron's hut until they *were* discovered. As the Royal Commission was to comment, this would have been enough, in itself, to establish Aaron's guilt in the eyes of the gang and 'seal his doom'.

So Aaron continued his strange, self-destructive course. With four police sharing the small, roadside hut with him and his bride, he slept by day and crept out each night to watch the Byrne house. Young Denny Byrne tracked the party to and from the Byrne house while Paddy Byrne hung around, watching.

Autumn was past and winter deepened. On the creek, ice formed a waxy crust among the reeds on still pools and froze into knobs where water splashed over rocks. Still Aaron passed each night with the watching police in his white cotton shirt, curled up asleep like a dog in the frosty grass, while they wrapped themselves in coats and possum rugs and wondered at his toughness, his fearlessness, at the strange game he was playing. Before dawn each morning Aaron woke and led them back to his hut. There he would sleep a few hours with his wife while the four police lay by the fire in the next room, hurrying to take turns in the warm bed when the young couple rose. It was a strange life for all of them.

All this time the Kelly plans were sharpening focus. Aaron's murder must become part of the great plan. To decoy the police from the place where the gang would strike? There was a darker alternative: to let Aaron's murder lead the police into a trap. Ned had spoken in the Jerilderie Letter of 'wholesale and retail slaughter'. In the Cameron letter he had railed against the police with wild talk that he would have 'scattered blood and brains like rain'. It may have been nothing but intimidating rhetoric — Harry Power bluff — or a flight of bushranging fantasy by Joe. Or perhaps it had been seen always as one fork of the path they had followed since Stringybark.

When Aaron died at Beechworth a few local police would ride to the scene while the major search party travelled by train from Benalla. Nicolson, the men and horses he had been holding in reserve for this very moment and the Queensland Native Police would all come hurtling along the main line, up through Glenrowan then down through the Gap high above the Oxley Flats, swinging to the left around the lower slopes of Morgans Lookout, out onto the sweeping curve of rails carried on a steep embankment across a gully . . . That was where he would strike.

Ned had threatened railways three times: in a casual remark at Euroa; a warning, 'remember your railways' in the Cameron letter; and in a planted rumour that he would blow up the Beechworth train 'out of revenge' for locking up the sympathisers. Were there memories tangled in these threats — of Old Country stories telling how smoke from steam trains had blighted the potato crop, causing Ireland's great famine? Memories of all the attempts to de-rail trains when they first appeared in the north-east? Images of the dying towns along the main coach road?

To break the railway line on the high curve past Glenrowan, sending the police train and its men and animals down to their destruction in the gully bed behind the locomotive, plunging like a comet, was perhaps another symbol. If it was, it was also an act of war. It had to be or it would be simply mass murder. If nothing else had brought Ned to the idea of declaring a republic, and everything suggests he had been developing the idea for more than a year, the decision to wreck the police train demanded it.

Ned and Joe drew up a Declaration of the Republic of North-eastern Victoria — a manifesto foreshadowed in the Jerilderie Letter and probably incorporating some of its wild rhetoric.

> Any person aiding or harbouring or assisting the police in any way whatever, or employing any person whom they know to be a detective or cad or those who would be so depraved as to take blood money will be

outlawed and declared unfit to be allowed human burial. Their property either consumed or confiscated and them theirs and all belonging to them exterminated off the face of the earth. The enemy I cannot catch myself I shall give a payable reward for . . .

I wish those men who joined the Stock Protection Society to withdraw their money and give it and as much more to the widows and orphans and poor of Greta district where I spent and will again spend many a happy day fearless free and bold . . .

I give fair warning to all those who has reason to fear me to sell out and give £10 out of every hundred towards the widow and orphan fund and do not attempt to reside in Victoria but as short a time as possible after reading this notice, neglect this and abide by the consequences, which shall be worse than the rust in the wheat in Victoria or the druth of a dry season to the grasshoppers in New South Wales.

I do not wish to give the order full force without giving timely warning but I am a widows son outlawed and my orders *must be obeyed.*

Some copies of the Declaration were printed in the form of handbills. At least one survives, seen by Leonard Radic, a highly reputable witness, in 1962. He retains a vivid memory of its 'old fashioned block type' and 'quaint, mock legalistic language'. Another handwritten copy is hidden away with 'some letters from a girl and a handkerchief'. The letters were probably written to Ned during his last imprisonment, the handkerchief one he wore as a scarf until the day before his death.

The last plans were made. The best of the gang's guns — the Spencer repeating rifle from Stringybark, the Callisher and Terry carbines from Jerilderie, Ned's favourite rifle 'Betty', taken from the hunters at Euroa, the Martini Henry that had tested the armour — all these and more were distributed among the sympathisers. The gang, safe in their armour to work at close range, would use the old-fashioned, shorter range firearms — percussion revolvers, shotguns, inferior repeaters (like a Colt revolving carbine with a nasty trick of firing all six chambers at once) — even the old, sawn-off carbine that had killed Lonigan. Their only up-to-date weapons would be Webley cartridge-loading revolvers.

Dan and Joe planned to kill Aaron at night, a Saturday night. Ned and Steve would break the railway line on the curve past Glenrowan after the last train had gone through. No regular trains ran on Sunday. The line would be empty, except for the police special. Joined by Joe and Dan, they would bail up the town and wait for the train. When it had crashed over the embankment and they had shot any survivors or taken them prisoner, Chinese signal rockets would be fired to summon the sympathisers. Then, with the tiny army gathered, Ned would lead his men down to Benalla, blow up the railway line on the other side of the town with a huge bomb made from a drum of blasting powder and move on the Bank of New South Wales.

Ned claimed that there was an alternative plan:

> to capture the leaders of the Police and take them into the bush and allow the superintendent to write to the head department and inform them if they sent any more Police after me or try to rescue him, I would shoot him and that I intended to keep them prisoners until the release of my mother, Skillion and Williamson.

In another statement of the plan: 'I was determined to capture Superintendent Hare, O'Connor and the blacks for the purpose of exchange of prisoners.'

Tom Lloyd claimed that after 'lifting the rails, they would compel the stationmaster to stop the train at the platform, where it would be captured.'

These 'cover' stories demand great gullibility. Why break the line half a mile past Glenrowan, on an embankment, when the police train could be stopped by closing the level-crossing gates just before the station and showing a red flag or signal light? As a failsafe measure, rails could be lifted on the straight, level stretch of line just past the station, de-railing the train without wrecking it.

Breaking the line past the town on the curving embankment over the gully, opening the crossing gates and forbidding the use of a 'stop' signal as they did, shows that the Gang intended a decisive first strike. It was an act which would catapult the Kelly Country into open guerilla warfare with the authorities — warfare joined by the 'disaffected' farmers of the north-east who were threatened by the blacklists. The Glenrowan campaign is inexplicable without the central, carefully obscured fact of the republic.

During autumn and early winter there were many warnings that something out-of-the-ordinary was about to happen. There had been strange goings-on at the Glenrowan Inn — rowdy celebrations by sympathisers who usually drank on the other side of the railway line at the Railway Tavern run by sympathiser Paddy McDonnell. It seemed that they were diverting attention from their usual watering hole or accustoming the police and uncommitted locals to the presence of groups of sympathisers on the northern side of the line.

In another strange diversionary tactic, Tom Lloyd was seen with Tom, Dan and Mick Nolan, riding north through Glenrowan, supposedly going shearing. The four were very flashly dressed, as though to attract attention. When the others reached Yarrawonga Tom Lloyd had disappeared. He had doubled back to Lake Winton and, when found by police, proceeded to give them cheek.

Hare continued to watch the developing pattern with unseeing eyes. During their outlawry the gang had made a point of buying and borrowing horses. Suddenly, Hare noted, 'horses were reported as being stolen in several directions, all supposed to be by the gang'. Two of these were taken from Michael and James Ryan of Dookie between 17 and 20 June — a magnificent thoroughbred bay mare of 16 hands, 'a fine jumper and hunter', and a handsome chestnut only half a hand shorter. The mare would become one of Ned's mounts and the chestnut would be ridden by Joe.

Rumours reached Hare from every quarter,

> that the sympathisers were very active, that something was going to happen. Old Mrs Byrne was very jubilant, and she told a person — who repeated it to me — that the gang were about to do something that would astonish not only the colony, but the world.

Another agent brought word 'that the Kellys were still in the country, that they were going to do something good, that Mrs Byrne's people were in great joy.' Jack Sherritt was urging that Paddy Byrne should be watched closely, 'as this is a particular time', warning, 'I am certain before long they are going to make another raid; I have not yet heard what it is.'

In response to this heightened activity, four police were stationed in the Glenrowan police station. They crept out singly to watch the Kelly homestead each night. A similar party went out nightly from Wangaratta to watch the Hart home on nearby Three Mile Creek. On Friday 25 June O'Connor and his five Aboriginal troopers left the Kelly pursuit and travelled down to Melbourne on their return journey to Queensland. That afternoon, the Diseased Stock Agent arrived at Benalla police head-quarters. Expecting to see Nicolson, 'he was somewhat put out at find-ing Hare, whom he did not know.' In Sadleir's presence, the DSA told Hare,

> 'that the Kellys were now entirely out of funds . . . and a fresh exploit was to be expected immediately. The Kellys had provided themselves with bullet-proof armour . . . and part of their plan was to effect something that would cause the ears of the Australian world to tingle.

Sadleir wrote,

Hare treated him with scorn, dismissed him from all further service, and, turning to me, remarked; 'If this is the sort of person Nicolson and you have been depending on, it is no wonder you have not caught the Kellys.'

In 1879 Hare had noted a pattern in the Gang's exploits:

that their depredations were committed at full moon, because they had to ride through the night — generally two days after the full moon, and also generally about Saturday and Sunday and Monday — those were their lucky days.

Hare scorned the DSA's warning on 25 June. The following day was a Saturday and the moon was full. The Kelly Gang would be riding.

17

TO GLENROWAN

25 – 27 JUNE 1880

On Friday 25 June everything was ready for the Glenrowan campaign. Aaron would be killed on Saturday night by Joe and Dan, while Ned and Steve tore up the railway line at Glenrowan. Some time on Sunday — probably in the morning — the special train carrying police to Beechworth would be wrecked. Signal rockets would rally the sympathisers and they would join the Gang in their move on Benalla to blow up the railway line west of the town, plunder the Bank of New South Wales and declare the republic. And then? Half-glimpsed images of the day of triumph and of others to come. Winter days of sunlight and a proud south wind to flaunt a green banner over Benalla, proclaiming that the law of Queen Victoria no longer held sway in the north-east. A wild, vague dream of justice for all. A dream obscured for the moment by the scaffolding of detail needed to realise the grand design.

The Gang prepared at least ten horses. They would ride four, take four spare mounts and carry packs on the other two. In a curious detail, the packs would be strapped or tied on Lonigan's and Scanlon's saddles. Joe's and Dan's packhorse probably carried their armour, in case of a pitched battle with the police at Aaron's hut. The other pack, to go with Ned and Steve to Glenrowan, carried the bomb — an oil drum packed with 56 pounds of blasting powder — with two coils of fuse, shoeing equipment, extra firearms and ammunition. Because of this already-heavy load, Ned's and Steve's armour was padded with sacks and packed in a buggy with the back seat removed. To be driven by Jack Lloyd, it would also carry the two Chinese rockets and probably more ammunition.

In preparation for the great day, Ned and Joe — and probably Dan and Steve — had short haircuts. The four would dress almost identically in long, grey oilskin coats, with their hats worn in a 'flat' pork-pie style. Their individual taste would be expressed in strapped riding pants, Crimean flannel shirts, waistcoats and jackets.

Ned's costume matched the importance of the event. He wore a pair of high-heeled mounted police boots with the lining removed to make them more supple. The V-cut, concertinaed tops were hidden under buff whipcord trousers with grey strapping patterned in a slate-grey check. A waistcoat matched the trousers and a jacket matched the check strapping. His Crimean shirt was white with black spots, a popular bush fashion. In a detail which underlined the unusual significance of the occasion, he bound around his waist the green silk sash with its gold fringe — the 'sash of honour' he had been given all those years before at Avenel for saving young Dick Shelton from drowning. An odd piece of Ned's outfit was a skull cap of waterproof tartan silk quilted with cotton wool, designed to be worn under the open-topped helmet. With the quilting laced inside the head-piece, it completed a protective shield to encase the head.

Joe, with his assassin's role to play, dressed more sombrely in dark jacket, dark-striped Crimean shirt and dark, strapped trousers. An old crocheted scarf which he tied around his neck may have been a frayed memento of his youth. He wore Lonigan's and Scanlon's rings and carried a Catholic prayer book in one pocket and a brown-paper packet of poison in the other. It is impossible to imagine his state of mind.

Probably on the Friday night Joe and Dan rode off across the Oxley flats on their grim mission. They would camp all Saturday in the ranges near the Woolshed and move down into the valley at dusk to kill Aaron and trigger the plan, while Ned and Steve rode to Glenrowan.

How did Ned fill in that Saturday? There would have been last-minute meetings with the key sympathisers — the McAuliffes, Tanners, Tom and Jack Lloyd, Wild Wright, the Delaneys, the Ryans and the rest — all of whom had roles to play at Glenrowan. Brother Jim was almost certainly there, and Maggie Skilling, who had prepared a special outfit to mark the great days when the fighting was over.

Ned may have had time for himself — it would be claimed that, early on the Saturday evening, he was with 'a young woman . . . to whom he is understood to have been deeply attached'. Ned had perhaps gained from Harry Power a courtly attitude to women. ('No woman was ever the worse for knowing me,' Harry had said.) Ned, with his love of babies, must have dreamt of marrying and being a father, until the day of Stringybark. After that, what life could he offer a woman; what legacy could he offer a child? But now that his dream of the republic was about to become reality, there was a future, and someone willing to share it: his cousin, Kate Lloyd, daughter of old Tom.

Other girls had caught Ned's eye. Steve's sister Ettie; a lass called Julie Martin; another cousin, the gallant Mary Miller; and how many like Mary the Larrikin? But it was Kate Lloyd he truly loved — one of the

Clan, already bonded with him by the blood of the Quinns and the race memory of another landscape still green in straw-dry summers.

Kate was not yet 17, with long, dark hair and classic beauty. She loved Ned and shared his dreams. Like Maggie, she seems to have prepared a special costume for the triumph to come — a flamboyantly plumed hat and handsome, ankle-length coat. If the more-than-cousins met on this eve of great and terrible events, it must have been a strange parting, lit by their hopes for the coming days and at the same time shadowed by dark possibilities and the darker certainty of what Joe and Dan were about.

Over in the Woolshed Aaron Sherritt passed his last day mysteriously. His Catholic wife, Ellen, was pregnant and on the Friday night Protestant Aaron, who claimed he was 'nothing', had told her he would turn Catholic. 'He said he would get the horses next day and come up to the Catholic Chapel at Beechworth.' On the Saturday he was away from home for three hours, supposedly 'to look for some cattle of his mother-in-law's in pound'.

He was often away, telling the police he had horses up on the Sugarloaf — a round granite hill behind the hut. There were no horses there, but on the far side of the hill was a cave said to be used by the Gang. On this last day did he try to meet his old friends and repair the rift which he was now aware of? Whatever he did that Saturday it was more important to him than embracing a religion with which he 'seemed well satisfied'.

Aaron's mother-in-law, genial, red-headed Mrs Barry, joined the couple for dinner before Aaron and the four police prepared to set out for the night's surveillance of the Byrne house. Seated around a candle-lit table top resting on a packing case, they lived out the last vestiges of a normal life while three of the police — Constables Armstrong, Dowling and Alexander — sprawled around the partitioned-off bedroom and Constable Duross finished his meal by the roaring log fire.

A hundred yards down the road that ran past Aaron's hut, Joe and Dan bailed up a German miner and market gardener called Anton Wick who had known Joe and Aaron most of their lives. They handcuffed him and told him he was to knock at Aaron Sherritt's door. It was approaching 6.30. While Dan covered the front of the hut, Joe took Wick around to the back door beside the big slab chimney. Joe held the double-barrelled shotgun Sergeant Kennedy had borrowed from the Mansfield vicar for the expedition to Stringybark. Each cartridge had been reloaded with a huge slug.

Joe gestured with the gun. 'Knock.' Wick rapped at the door.

'Call Aaron.' Wick called feebly.

'Call loud.' His louder call brought a response from Aaron. 'What do you want?'

'Say, "I have lost myself".' Wick, a few yards from the main road and less than a mile from his home, obeyed the order. Perhaps Joe heard Aaron's laugh. There was the sound of a prop being removed from the door and it started to scrape open.

Joe drew back behind the chimney as Aaron stood in the doorway silhouetted against the fire-lit room. Failing to notice the handcuffs, Aaron was still amused at Wick being lost.

'See that sapling?' He was about to tell the old German to climb up it and see his house. Then he broke off, seeing the shadowed figure near the chimney, and went to step back. 'Who's there?'

Joe moved forward, almost beside Wick, with his shotgun raised. One of the twin muzzles exploded in Aaron's face and he staggered back with a one-inch hole blown in his throat. The second barrel blasted a huge slug through his body and he fell, his head slamming against the packing case table. Joe stood in the doorway and looked down at his dying mate as blood from the two massive wounds flooded over his white shirt and obliterated his face. Wick heard Joe say, 'That's all. That is the man that I want.'

Frantic, young Ellen Sherritt asked Joe why he had shot Aaron. 'If I had not shot him, he would have shot me if he could get the chance.' To a similar question from Mrs Barry Joe said, 'The bastard will never put me away again.'

Joe had heard Constable Duross hurry into the bedroom after Wick's knock. He asked who was in there and was told it was a man staying the night who was looking for work. Joe ordered Mrs Barry to open the front door and Dan Kelly walked in, bidding the women a polite 'Good evening' and smiling as he saw Aaron's bloody corpse.

In the bedroom behind the calico-curtained doorway the four police were fumbling with their guns. Joe heard a shotgun hammer being cocked. He challenged the police to come out and fired shots through the partition. Twice he sent young Ellen in to bring them out and, the second time, the police held her in the room and pushed her under the bed. Joe and Dan threatened to burn the place down. Mrs Barry pleaded with them and went in to bring out the police. She, too, was kept in the bedroom.

Joe and Dan made a half-hearted attempt to kindle a fire against the outside wall (a log from the fire would have set the calico door-curtain blazing in seconds) and, after a bizarre two-hour stand-off, they released Anton Wick and rode away, leaving the four police and the two women huddled in the bedroom. Aaron's corpse was still sprawled by the table while his dog, chained outside, howled an awful lament.

Detective Ward's plan was working: by incriminating Aaron he had brought the Gang out of hiding. Yet Aaron's murder was also the trigger of Ned's strategy. Both plans depended on a rapid police response. As Joe and Dan rode towards Glenrowan, the four police in the Sherritt bedroom dithered, convincing each other that it would be suicidal to venture outside. Poor Harry Armstrong, nominally in charge, was a brave policeman, credited with valorous behaviour among the larrikin pushes in Melbourne. His description of the earlier councils of war in the bedroom conveys the situation:

> I said, 'Men, have you got anything else to suggest; our conduct will be severely commented upon if we don't do something.' I said, 'If I rushed them will you be game to follow?' I asked each separately and they all said 'Yes.' We then determined to wait for a better opportunity.

They would not leave the hut until daylight, 12 hours after the murder. (The Sherritt inquest erupted in laughter when Ellen described how 'when it was daylight they went out and looked round the house to see if the gang were about'.) They then wasted hours unsuccessfully sending off various locals to carry news of the killing to Beechworth. No one could have foreseen such a flabby response to the murder.

Another serious flaw had already appeared in Ned's and Joe's plan. Sympathisers hung around the murder hut, talking until dawn, encouraging the police to stay indoors, then, at daylight, Paddy Byrne would patrol the valley, turning back messengers or discouraging them from setting out. This ill-advised tactic compounded the inefficiency of the police response, throwing out the timing of the Glenrowan campaign even further.

Before Joe and Dan had left the murder scene, Ned and Steve reached Glenrowan and put on body armour under their oilskin coats. They left the four spare saddle horses and the packhorse with the drum of explosive up in the hillside bush behind McDonnell's Railway Tavern, on the southern side of the line.

Below them, scattered in open bushland across the starlit saddle of the Gap, was the 'insignificant collection of buildings' to be immortalised by the events of the next two days. Directly opposite McDonnell's across the railway line was the lit railway station. Past it, up to the left, was Ann Jones's Glenrowan Inn, a neat little shanty of whitewashed weatherboard with a corrugated iron roof, a bark-and-slab kitchen behind and a makeshift stable at the top of a narrow accommodation paddock. Someone was playing a concertina on the front verandah. Between the inn and the station, lanterns were glimmering among a group of railway labourers' tents pitched among straggling gum trees just outside the railway reserve. Behind the little settlement the squat, bush-clad pyramid of Morgans Lookout brooded above a gentle slope of open bushland cut by the main Sydney Road, which formed the township's High Street, a couple of hundred yards above the Glenrowan Inn. Down that road to the left, just under a mile towards Benalla, was the town proper, with post office, police station and school.

At nine o'clock the last train passed through the town, labouring up the long slope from Benalla and disappearing across the Gap towards Wangaratta, gathering speed. John Stanistreet, the stationmaster, extinguished the lamps in his office, closed up the station and sent the big white railway gates clattering open across the line. Glenrowan was ready for its day of rest. The lights went out one by one until there were only the front lamps of the two pubs, proclaiming their feeble rivalry across the railway. With no sign yet of Joe and Dan, Ned decided to move. He and Steve rode down through the level crossing, opened the iron gate of the road to the station, and headed up along the fenced railway reserve where the labourers had been burning off grass, creating a black lawn on either side of the line. Out through the Gap and around the bend was the curving embankment where the line was to be broken, 30 feet above the gully bed. Ned and Steve had brought tools but could not shift the nuts on the 'fish plates' joining the rails.

As the full moon was rising behind them out across the Oxley flats, they rode back to Glenrowan and roused seven labourers from the four railway tents. There was some noise and Ned was concerned that it had been heard at the nearby Glenrowan Inn. He went across to the prim little building and banged at its front door. He distrusted publican Ann Jones and when there was no answer he hurried around to the back.

Mrs Jones, 'rising 40', was an Irish-born battler, dogged by bad luck. An earlier venture of hers, roadside refreshment rooms near Wangaratta, had been doomed by the coming of the railway and the drop in highway traffic. Her English husband Owen became a bankrupt 'paying ten pounds in the hundred' and had to take a railway job in Gippsland. Mrs Jones had opened the Glenrowan Inn some 18 months before — a courageous project. On a £6 block of land she had put up a weatherboard shell with interior walls of hessian and paper and ceilings of calico. It would be called 'a pitiable shelter' but 'very nicely furnished' — the furnishings had been sold to a Wangaratta businessman and rented back at two shillings and sixpence a week. A £100 mortgage paid back the man who had lent money for building materials and left Mrs Jones £30 to invest in the business.

A daughter had been killed by a falling tree the previous year. Now, just as the family's fortunes were beginning to turn the corner and the Inn was making a profit of £30 a month. Mrs Jones was bed-ridden with neuralgia and the fist of Ned Kelly was pounding on her doors, shaking the paper walls and calico ceilings.

When she asked who it was, Ned called, 'Never mind.'

'If you are a policeman, go to the men's tents to look for whom you want.'

'If I was one, you would like me better.'

Perhaps Mrs Jones realised then who her after-midnight visitor might be. She knew Mrs Kelly (her husband had buried baby Ellen, Bill Frost's daughter) and she was on good terms with the Hart family. Perhaps because of this, Mrs Jones tried to avoid being tagged as a sympathiser ('sampythaiser' as she called it) by offering the police warmer hospitality than they could find at Paddy McDonnell's pub. Her attempts to be all things to all men in this polarised community eventually earned only suspicion from both sides.

The Kelly girls had a 'down' on her; Tom and Jack Lloyd thought her 'too much of a traps' woman'; and Ned believed that Detective Ward had helped her get the inn's licence. He probably didn't know that Mrs Jones had known Sergeant Kennedy 'very well'. Only a month before his death the sergeant had invited her to stay with his family and she kept a photo of him in her album. Her maiden name was Kennedy.

When 14-year-old Jane Jones eventually opened the back door to Ned, he grumpily ordered Jane and her mother to dress and took them down to the railwaymen's tents, even though Mrs Jones protested that she was 'staggering with sickness'. Ned left her four young sons asleep, locked in the separate kitchen.

Now came another setback — the railway labourers had no tools. In an increasingly bad mood, Ned strode off with Mrs Jones to get the stationmaster. It was well after 1 a.m. When there was no immediate response to his knocking and 'impertinent talk . . . to open up quickly' he burst the door open while Stanistreet was still dressing.

Satisfied that only Mrs Stanistreet, two little girls and a baby were in the house, Ned took the stationmaster out to the workmen and told him, 'Now, direct these men how to raise some of the rails, as we expect a special train very soon.' Stanistreet professed to know nothing about lifting rails and told Ned he would need the platelayers, James Reardon and Dennis Sullivan, who lived down the line, nearer the town. While Ned rode off to fetch them, Steve made one of the workmen break open a shed in the railway yard and bring out the tool chests.

Ned returned with Reardon and his wife, Margaret, their eight children, their lodger, Benalla labourer John Larkins, and the second plate-layer, Reardon's mate Sullivan. Now nothing stood in the way of his plan. Joe and Dan had arrived at last, riding across from McDonnell's pub where Joe had helped lay the ghosts of The Woolshed valley with a quick drink.

Ned had told Reardon that there had been a clash with police at Beechworth the previous night and that 'a lot of them' had been shot.

When he heard that only Aaron had died, was he relieved or, with the bloodbath to come, had he ceased to care?

The safe arrival of Joe and Dan improved his mood. When Reardon revealed that he needed a crowbar from his home, Ned simply sent Steve to fetch it. Steve then headed off to break the line with the plate-layers and the labourers, taking young Jane Jones with him. Steve had met her before (though he misremembered her name as Kate) and this frail, sad-eyed girl would comfort the last day of his life. As the men were at work on the rails, Steve rested his head on Jane's knee and 'said he was sick'. Ned arrived to hurry things along and Reardon — hoping the train would jump the gap — convinced him that one length of rails was enough. He eventually lifted a pair of them, with nine sleepers still attached, and dumped them down the embankment. They had spent 1½ hours on a 5-minute job. When they trailed back to the railway crossing, where the prisoners waited in the icy fore-dawn, they found that Mrs Jones had brightened considerably. She sent young Jane up to kindle a fire at the inn then turned to Ned.

'Come on up, Ned, have breakfast and a wash — you've been up all night, it'll refresh you.'

When Ned refused this invitation she followed Jane up to the hotel, but soon returned to ask him again. Line repairer Denis Sullivan noted that this time Ned looked across to McDonnell's pub then up to the inn before he said, 'Let ye all walk up here to Mrs Jones's.'

Perhaps it changed nothing, using Jones's as a base instead of McDonnell's. But Joe, Dan and Steve would die inside the walls of the inn, five civilians would be wounded there — three mortally, another to die not long afterwards — and Mrs Jones would lose two of her children and everything she owned. Nearby, Ned would lose his freedom.

While most of the women and children stayed at the stationmaster's house, guarded by Steve, the rest of the Gang's prisoners trooped up the gentle slope to the Glenrowan Inn where kitchen smoke drifted into the dawn sky, promising comfort, and young Jack Jones's concertina still lay on the front verandah stool where he had been playing it last night. Jane brought it in and played a tune, brightening the arrival.

The inn's main room was the dining room, opening off the verandah to the right. At the far left was a tiny parlour. Between was a small bar room with a counter, a shelf of bottles, glasses and 'pewter pints', a 10-gallon keg of brandy and several cases of brandy, gin and wine stacked in the corner. From a doorway by the end of the bar counter, a short passage led to the back door between two skillion bedrooms. Separated from the hotel by a 6-foot breezeway was the slab kitchen.

Now fires were blazing in the dining room and parlour fireplaces as the Gang's prisoners spread between the kitchen, dining room, parlour and bar. The Gang occupied the two skillion bedrooms. Ned and Steve stripped off their armour and locked it in 'the best room', to the right, with their extra firearms and ammunition. Dan's and Joe's suits were carried in from their packhorse and also put in the armoury.

At some stage, a couple of lads — probably McAuliffes — brought the Gang's spare horses down from the hillside on the other side of the line and put them in the stable at McDonnell's. The packhorse with the drum of explosive was left tied to a fence. Sharp-eyed James Reardon noticed all this but would mention only the packhorse to police. Like most of the prisoners, he stood in that strange borderland between sympathiser and neutral. The next 24 hours nudged him closer to sympathy.

For the sake of appearances, sympathiser publican Paddy McDonnell and his wife and children were brought across to join the prisoners. They would tell quite different stories of how and when they were bailed up, though admitting that Ned had gone in to say 'hello' to 'Mrs Mac', as he called her, while she was still in bed.

Other sympathisers arrived to be made 'prisoners' — the McAuliffes, three of the Delaneys and red-bearded James Kershaw, who had married Mrs Kelly's great friend Jane Graham (the 'loose woman' who rode astride). Tom and Jack Lloyd, Dick Hart, Wild Wright and probably Jim Kelly were all nearby but keeping in the background. The other sympathisers would rally when Jack Lloyd fired the signal rockets to announce the wrecking of the train.

Surprisingly, Ned made no attempt to bring in the Glenrowan policeman, Constable Bracken, even though the trip to Reardons' had taken him within a stone's throw of the police station. Normally four police were stationed at the Glenrowan barracks, sneaking out each night to watch the Kelly homestead 6 miles away. They had been withdrawn the previous day after their health broke down under the mid-winter ordeal: Bracken was in bed with gastric flu. Postmaster Hillmorton Reynolds lived next door and in fact rented the police station premises to the government. Ned would pay a visit to Reynolds that night without taking him prisoner. It seems likely that Reynolds was keeping an eye on Bracken for the Gang. Certainly, Mrs Jones would comment, 'He [Ned] left Mr Reynolds at holme because he would not tell on him.' When she asked Ned, 'Where is that bloody old Reynolds?' he told her, 'He was as right as if he was locked up.'

As the Gang's harvest of prisoners steadily grew some of the captives began to enjoy the occasion. Ned and Joe were on horseback, stopping anyone who came along the road to cross the railway. At first Ned wouldn't say who he was and passers-by would be reluctant to accept his invitation to come up to the inn. Then, when Ned announced, 'Well, boys, I am Ned Kelly; you must come,' the gallery of prisoners would roar with laughter, 'seeing how quick they would come when they found they had Ned there'.

A little after 11 a.m. Ned was on horseback at the railway crossing talking to 19-year-old John Delaney, whose family had helped in making the armour. Behind him, down the broad track that wound among the trees from the High Street, came a buggy carrying a man and two women — one of them nursing a baby — accompanied by a horseman with a greyhound loping beside him. As Ned heard the rattle of wheels and the clop of hooves, did he feel any prickle of warning, any sense of threat? He didn't turn in the saddle to look, perhaps because young Delaney was telling him that the new arrivals were unknown quantities — people of the town whose allegiances were unclear.

The buggy's driver was Thomas Curnow, the local schoolteacher, a tallish 25-year-old with large, keen eyes and a downy beard. Although he had been in Glenrowan for four years and had married a local girl, Jean Mortimer, he remained something of an outsider, carefully keeping himself aloof from the little community's active or tacit sympathy for the Gang. Outside his family, stationmaster Stanistreet was the only local he trusted.

Curnow's sister, Catherine, a rather delicate 23-year-old, had arrived from Ballarat two days before. This morning, wearing a red llama scarf, she was being taken on a drive in the family buggy towards Greta, escorted by Curnow's brother-in-law, Dave Mortimer. As Curnow saw the groups around the railway crossing and the Glenrowan Inn, his first thought was, 'Mrs Jones must be dead: she has been very ill.' Even when his friend Stanistreet told him, 'The Kellys are here; you can't go through,' Curnow thought the stationmaster was pulling his leg until the bearded horseman who was blocking the crossing wheeled his horse and came over to the buggy. Curnow noticed the array of revolvers in his belt and saw this was no joke. Ned identified the schoolteacher and his party then said, 'I am sorry, but I must detain you.'

Curnow climbed down from the buggy, helped his wife and sister to the ground and saw them ushered off to the Stanistreet house. Then Ned started blustering at young Delaney, threatening to shoot him — supposedly because he had obliged the police on some occasion and tried to join the force two years before. This was clearly for Curnow's benefit and the teacher later recognised it as 'a ruse on Kelly's part', but Delaney was 'in a state of extreme terror' at the outburst. Joe, who had been riding between the crossing and the inn, produced a bottle of brandy and gave the lad 'three-quarters of a tumbler', offering the grog 'to all adults there'. Then a couple of boys took Curnow's horse and buggy to the inn's paddock and the teacher and his brother-in-law walked up to Mrs Jones's.

Perhaps Ned noticed that Curnow limped, crippled by a hip deformity;

perhaps he felt a pang of sympathy for this young man with his wife and baby. This response would be the first chink in his armour. On the verandah of the pub, Curnow gave Reardon a smoke of his pipe and the platelayer told him how the railway line had been broken. Soon after, Dan Kelly asked Curnow to have a drink at the bar, admitting that there had been 'some shooting' near Beechworth and 'they had burned the buggers out'. Joe noticed Dan's glass as he walked past and said, 'Be careful, old man.' Dan added water to his brandy and Joe stayed to chat, telling Curnow, 'They had come to Glenrowan in order to wreck a special train of inspectors, police and black trackers, which would pass through Glenrowan for Beechworth, to take up their trail from there.' Joe acknowledged freely that, 'they ... were going to send the train and its occupants to hell'.

It was close to midday. Aaron had been shot nearly 18 hours before and there was still no sign of the police train. Ned organised some dancing in the dining room, the inn's biggest room, and Mrs Jones had the table moved out onto the verandah. It was one of her prize pieces, a rectangular, pine-topped table with turned cedar legs.

While Dave Mortimer, with his faithful greyhound at his feet, played little Jack Jones's concertina, Mrs Jones and Jane danced with Ned and Dan. Because the rest of the women were down at Stanistreets', Joe danced with male prisoners who formed buck sets. Later, perhaps while Joe was dancing with Jane or her mother, Dan invited Curnow to join him.

The schoolteacher was forming a plan: 'The intention to do something to baffle the murderous designs of the Gang grew on me, and I resolved to do my utmost to gain the confidence of the outlaws, and to make them believe me to be a sympathizer with them.' In a first attempt Curnow had asked Ned to come with him while he fetched a pair of dancing shoes from his residence behind the school at the far edge of town. They would have to pass the police station and Curnow knew that Constable Bracken could recognise Ned, having been stationed at Greta. Ned had agreed to accompany the teacher until someone reminded him that the school was near the police barracks. So Curnow continued to bide his time, ingratiating himself with the Gang.

By mid-afternoon, Ned was organising athletic contests in the paddock behind the kitchen, competing in the 'hop, step and jump' with a revolver in each hand. In Mrs Jones's words, 'the inn was a house of sport'.

Curnow strayed down to Stanistreets' to see his wife and sister. Noticing Catherine's red llama scarf, it suddenly struck him, 'What a splendid danger signal that would make.' He continued in his role as sympathiser, advising Steve Hart on treatment for his sore feet and helping Dan look for a mysterious 'parcel in a small bag which he had lost'. In his most calculating move, the young Cornishman (whose very name meant 'Cornwal' in the ancient language) told Ned that Stanistreet 'possessed a loaded revolver from the Railway Department', and said 'he was worried that someone might get it and do them an injury'. Ned was grateful. Always too ready to trust people, he was easily deceived by the teacher's careful campaign. He had trusted Fitzpatrick; he had trusted Living at Jerilderie. This was a third critical misplacement of trust. It was ironic that Ned's inherent honesty would be his undoing.

18

'In the Very Jaws of Death'

27 – 28 June 1880

By late Sunday afternoon sixty-two 'prisoners' were scattered in and around the Glenrowan Inn and Stanistreets'. There was more dancing. As it grew dark and frosty, some of the men gathered around a big bonfire in the paddock behind the kitchen. Ned and Joe passed some time playing cards with Mrs Jones in the parlour, and prisoners noted that Jane Jones helped stand guard, counting heads with a revolver. If she heard anyone speaking of escape, she threatened to tell Ned.

Tom Cameron, who was 15 and a former schoolmate of Jane's, would write to his brother: 'Jenny Jones was making very free with them getting on their knees and dancing with them and kissing them. I think 6 months in gaol would do her no harm.'

Ned had spoken of bailing up a circus to entertain the prisoners and considered butchering a bullock to feed them. (Earlier, when Mrs Jones asked him what they would eat for tea, he laughed and said 'there were some nice fat dogs about'.) Mrs Jones worried at the amount of grog the 'Glenrowaners' were getting through and the size of the fires they had built up in the parlour and dining room, threatening to catch the wooden mantelpieces.

Ned had more profound concerns. His Grand Strategy was crumbling, eroded by the lapse of time. He and his men were frayed by lack of sleep, and the inexplicable delay in the arrival of the police special was becoming a threat. It was now almost 24 hours since Aaron's murder. Somewhere out in the darkness beyond the lamp-lit shell of the inn and the gatehouse, the police must be moving towards him. But were they advancing into a trap or had the Gang trapped itself, waiting immobile for all these hours?

A Beechworth journalist would note that: 'The ironclads placed themselves in the very jaws of death.' It was a shrewd comment. Trading on the invincibility of the armour, Ned had stationed the Gang between two major police centres on the very route by which attacking parties could converge. He was gambling everything on a decisive first strike at the special train. But why hadn't it arrived hours ago? Had the police departed from their usual methods? Were they approaching on horseback, or even on foot, led by the Queensland Aboriginal troopers, described by Ned as 'those six little demons'? Ned should have abandoned the plan and ridden away. But something in him wouldn't allow that.

During the late afternoon and evening Ned released twenty-one 'prisoners', the McDonnells among them, all of them locals he could trust implicitly. Those who remained were people he was less certain of, or staunch sympathisers with roles to play: the Delaneys, McAuliffes and James Kershaw. Thomas Curnow was still here, still bent on 'checkmating the outlaws'.

When Curnow heard that Ned was at last going to pick up Constable Bracken, he asked if he and his family could accompany Ned and then go on home. 'I assured him that he had no case for fearing me, as I was with him heart and soul.'

Ned looked into the teacher's large, bright eyes. 'I know that, and can see it,' he said. Yes, the Curnows could go with him. Curnow fetched his wife, baby daughter and sister from Stanistreets' and they waited in the kitchen behind the inn. Another two or three hours crawled by before Ned told the teacher to put his horse in the buggy.

Ned and Joe buckled on their body armour and, with helmets slung at the front of their saddles, rode off with the Curnows and other locals. Dave Mortimer was mounted, young Alec Reynolds, the postmaster's son, rode in the Curnow buggy, while Reynolds's brother Edward and a friend, Robert Gibbins, walked.

Almost a mile down the High Street the party halted near the long, low police barracks with its broad verandah and, covered by Ned's rifle, Dave Mortimer knocked at the door and called Constable Bracken. When there was no answer Ned took Gibbins with the postmaster's brother and son and disappeared into the yard of the post office, nextdoor to the police station.

Ned had a long chat with postmaster Reynolds then left his son with him and took Gibbins and Edward Reynolds around to the back of the police station. After further knocking and calling, the ailing Constable Bracken opened the door.

> As I did so, a tall man, whose face was hidden behind what seemed to be a nail can turned upside down, stepped into the doorway, and pointing a revolver at my head, said, 'I'm Ned Kelly; put up your hands.'

Bracken's response was unexpected. 'You be damned; you are only someone sent here from Benalla to try my pluck!'

Perhaps Ned was amused. He told Bracken to bail up again; but when the trooper raised only one hand, still thinking this was a joke, Ned snapped angrily, 'Throw up *both* hands; we will have no bloody nonsense!'

Hugh Bracken was at last convinced. The policeman's wife was still in bed with their young son and Ned shook the lad's hand, telling him, 'I may be worth £2000 to you yet, my child.'

After an interminable wait out in High Street, guarded by Joe, the Curnows were joined by Ned, Reynolds and Gibbins, with Bracken leading his horse. The trooper mounted and Joe took the reins from him. At last, Ned turned to Curnow.

'Go quietly to bed, and don't dream too loud.' The teacher drove off towards the schoolhouse a couple of hundred yards further along the road as Ned and Joe rode back to the inn with their prisoners.

With every turn of the buggy wheels, Curnow's excitement grew. He told his wife and sister he was going to warn the police at Benalla. They were appalled, fearing that Ned might have sympathisers watching, but Curnow wouldn't be swayed. He drove the two women to his mother-in-law's home a few hundred yards from the school. When Jean Curnow became hysterical and refused to stay, Curnow took her back home, promising to abandon his plan. As soon as he and his sister had calmed

Curnow's school and residence at Glenrowan. Note the railway embankment in the background. Curnow stopped the police train a few hundred metres down to the right. (*Sketcher*)

Jean and put her to bed, he gathered up a candle and matches with Catherine's red scarf, and hurried out to re-harness his horse. He planned to drive as close as possible to the railway line in case he met the train before reaching Benalla. Then, in the clear, frosty air, he heard the rhythmic beat of a speeding locomotive. He scrambled down across the gully behind the little schoolhouse and up the steep embankment of the railway line. He had started to run down the slope towards Benalla when he saw the approaching headlamp beyond a cutting.

Standing by the line he lit the candle, which wavered brightly in the still air. The train came closer and he held the red scarf in front of the flame. The locomotive started to slacken speed and loomed past, with only a tender and guard's van coupled behind it. As the van drew abreast, the guard called, 'What's the matter?'

'The Kellys!' Curnow yelled.

Half a mile or so behind this pilot locomotive the special train was heading up the slope. The first engine driver blew his whistle in a series of short blasts to warn it. More than a mile away in Glenrowan, the danger signal sounded like a cock crowing. It was shortly after 2.30 a.m. on the morning of Monday 28 June.

◆

THE EVENTS of the preceding 31 hours had conspired to defeat Ned's bold plan just as surely as Tom Curnow had set about his campaign to gain Ned's confidence then betray him. It had started with the timid police in Aaron's hut and continued with Paddy Byrne intercepting messengers sent to Beechworth with news of the killing. When Constable Armstrong eventually arrived there to tell Detective Ward of Aaron's murder, it was after 1 p.m. on the Sunday. The Beechworth telegraph operator couldn't raise Benalla then, and word eventually reached Hare via Melbourne and Wangaratta after 2.30 p.m. Hare now telegraphed Standish, who had left the Melbourne Club shortly before the telegram arrived and did not return to find it until 4.30 p.m.

Meanwhile Hare dithered. He had ample men and horses in Benalla, ready to set out at a moment's notice. He had two expert Aboriginal trackers, Moses and Spider. From mid-afternoon there was a locomotive under steam at Benalla, of the type needed to make the steady climb to Beechworth, with trucks to carry horses. Yet Hare waited for more than 2½ hours until he heard from Standish, waited further while Standish ate humble pie and asked O'Connor and his men to rejoin the hunt, then prolonged the delay with the idea of sending the Queensland contingent up by an early train on Monday morning.

Why did Hare have to wait for a train from Melbourne — whose only purpose was to bring the Aboriginal troopers he had dispensed with three days before and for whom he had little regard? The question was never put to him and there seems no satisfactory answer.

On the initiative of Chief Secretary Ramsay a special train was readied for despatch from Melbourne on Sunday night. Meanwhile Queensland permission for O'Connor and his men to rejoin the hunt was initially refused, then granted.

The special train — a locomotive, one carriage and a brake van — left Melbourne at 9.57 p.m., carrying four journalists: Thomas Carrington of the *Sketcher* and *Australasian*, Joe Melvin of the *Argus*, George Allen of the *Daily Telegraph* and John McWhirter of the *Age*. It picked up O'Connor and the five Aboriginal troopers at Essendon at 10.15 and the game was, rather tardily, afoot, lent colour by the fact that O'Connor was accompanied by his wife and her sister. They both wore the handsome gowns they had worn at the dinner where Standish's message (carried by a hansom cab driver) had eventually reached O'Connor. The ladies thought that this dramatic late-night train journey presented a charming opportunity to see Beechworth.

The party had scarcely settled down for the journey when there was 'a crack, like a bullet striking the carriage'. Just beyond Craigieburn the train had crashed through a railway gate, tearing away the locomotive's brake and shattering the carriage's footbridge and the lamp on the guard's van. After a brief halt, when it was decided that the train could rely on the guard's brake, the damaged special continued on its way 'at a rattling pace . . . through the bright, clear, frosty night'. Joe Melvin noted 'the great speed we were going at caused the carriage to oscillate'.

The train reached Benalla at 1.30 a.m. and a new round of dithering took place. When a pilot engine was suggested, Hare had telegraphed Standish for approval. There was now a notion of tying a constable to the boiler of the first locomotive as a lookout (one journalist insisted he had heard rumours in Benalla that the line had been torn up or that logs had been placed on the line). Eventually, without a lookout, but with the original, damaged loco travelling ahead as a pilot, the special train pulled out of Benalla at about 2 a.m. with Hare, seven troopers (plus seventeen horses) and a civilian volunteer, bringing the total complement to twenty-four.

Across the flat approaching the Glenrowan Gap, the trains reached 40 m.p.h., expecting to accelerate to 60 m.p.h. down through the Gap and around the bend towards Wangaratta — the bend where the line was broken. Then, about 1¼ miles before Glenrowan, a feeble red light appeared ahead. At first taking it for a burning log beside the line, the guard realised it was a signal. He pulled off the old hat he was wearing, donned his uniform cap and wound on the brake. The pilot engine dragged to a halt.

This rare study of the Last Stand by a 'special artist' of the *Sydney Mail* is the most impressive press drawing of the time. It accurately records the setting — the fallen tree, Morgans Lookout through the scrub — and captures the daunting impact of the Kelly figure.

A second *Sydney Mail* artist has a valiant try at Ned's collapse and shows him toppling like a falling tree. Actually, Ned crumpled straight down to his knees, weakened by massive blood loss and borne to the ground by his hundredweight of armour.

Ned fell on the far side of this huge fallen tree, out of frame to the right. In the background is the small clump of trees where he rested during his Last Stand and where he had left his cap and rifle early in the battle (see page 252). The Glenrowan Inn is about 100 metres to the left. Late in the siege, police and civilians are still wary of moving from cover.

A previously unpublished photo of the Glenrowan Inn's ruins photographed the following day. The remains of the inn sign have been placed inside the burnt-out building. In the foreground, one of the whitewashed rails from the slip panel of the accommodation paddock, thrown aside by Ned and Joe just before the start of the siege. *(Benalla and District Historical Society)*

A rare lantern slide shows Dan's and Steve's coffins, on the way to Eleven Mile Creek, left outside McDonnell's pub at Glenrowan while undertaker Grant and a group of journalists take some refreshment.

The guard jumped down and Curnow gasped out his story 'of the line being torn up beyond the station, and of the Kelly Gang lying in wait at the station for the special train of police'. The guard said he would go back and warn the special, asked Curnow who he was and invited him to climb aboard. Curnow declined, anxious to get back to his wife and sister, and hurried off, asking the guard not to say who had stopped the train, 'as I was doing it at the risk of my life'.

When Hare heard this extraordinary story he ordered all the carriages unlocked and lights extinguished. Then the two locomotives were coupled together and, with Hare and three constables on the footplate of the pilot engine and his other four men on the tender of the second engine, the train started off, slowly climbing up the long slope into Glenrowan.

As the train passed the little schoolhouse, it was in darkness. Curnow had hidden his wet clothes and the red scarf and put out all the lights. He heard the twin locomotives huffing away, the rattle of train wheels fading slowly, and listened in the crowded darkness, waiting.

◆

WHEN NED AND JOE brought Bracken back to the inn, what old Glenrowan folk would refer to as 'The Party' was in full swing. It was a night Ann Jones would never forget.

> Ned Kelly asked the people all about to sing and one young man sang two songs, and he then looked at me and said, 'Are you not going to sing?' I said I could not and he said 'Try' and I said I had a little boy who could sing a little but he was delicate, and I called the boy and he sang 'The Wild Colonial Boy' and *Colleen das cruitha na mo* ['The Pretty Girl Milking the Cow'].

Jack Jones was a frail lad, small for his 13 years, with a bony forehead, deep-set eyes and thin cheeks. He was singing for the last time in his life, singing the tale of the 16-year-old bushranger who went down fighting three troopers. The members of the Gang and their friends must have joined in this song many times, to the rebellious air 'The Wearing of the Green'. Then came the sweet, curiously poignant song in Gaelic. When it was finished, no one else sang.

Ned spent some time with Constable Bracken. Did Ned know that this was the man who had spotted them at Taylors Gap on their ride up to the Murray after Stringybark? A former policeman who had been working at the Beechworth Asylum when the police were shot and who volunteered to take part in the chase, equipping himself and going six months without pay?

Bracken had been at Glenrowan for only a month, but was popular with the locals. That morning Paddy McDonnell had told Ned that

Bracken was 'a decent fellow'. Ned replied, 'They are all decent fellows until you get into their clutches.' Nevertheless he chatted amiably with the trooper, telling him, 'There was one bugger in Parliament he would like to kill: Mr Graves ... because he suggested in Parliament that the water in the Kelly Country should be poisoned, and that the grass should be burnt.' It was Bracken who recorded Ned's clearest reference to his vision for the north-east: 'They are all damned fools to bother their heads about Parliament for this is our country.'

The women and children from Stanistreets' had been brought up to the inn and Dave Mortimer's return meant that the dancing could start again. Ned joined in 'a set of quadrilles' but became confused by the dance sequence. Mrs Jones described the scene in an unusually revealing letter.

> Ned could not go through the walces [waltzes] he was laughing and amused all around him he said he would have to nock off as he was no dancer David Mortimer ... said he would be M.C. and put them through it the people did not think about the special [train] it took up their attention watching the gang as they were noble looking men ... the divel was in us we had to ... be looking at the darling men but sure Ned was a darling man.

As Mortimer called the quadrilles like a square dance, Ned romped happily around the room with young Jane and Dan partnered Mrs Jones.

In her 'red stuff dress' Mrs Jones was a new woman, her illness forgotten as she enjoyed to the full this exciting holiday from the ordinary. She was also enjoying the discomfort of some locals who had treated her 'like a bloody blackfellow', telling John Delaney, 'revenge is sweet'. Perhaps most of all she was excited by her curious intimacy with these handsome, engaging outlaws — seen 'against a fence' with Ned in the moonlight, and trying to pull a ring from Joe's finger while he tugged playfully at her hair. She was heard to say, 'She would be pleased if Kelly and his Gang stopped for a week'.

The dining-room clock was chiming the first hour of Monday morning and the jollity was wearing thin as overtired children were getting weepy. After a time Ned announced that the women and younger children could go home. These bush wives were reluctant to leave their menfolk drinking, however, and chose to stay on.

When Joe Byrne came in the front door, locking it behind him and removing the key, Bracken noticed that 'he laid it carelessly near the chimney'. The trooper moved casually over, picked it up and, folding a cuff on his trousers, slipped the key into it.

After two o'clock on the Monday morning Ned arrived at the decision he should have reached hours before. All the civilians could leave. Now, only moments before the forty-odd men, women and children were to stream out of the hotel, Mrs Jones told them that Ned was going to give 'a lecture'. Though she subsequently denied it, the 'lecture' seems to have been her idea — a very costly one.

Everyone packed into the dining room and bar, with an open door between them, and Ned, after a piece of light-hearted business — climbing onto a chair and getting down again — started some by-play with a couple of the prisoners and Bracken.

There was no hint of the revolutionary here, no attempt to present his case. It seems as though a load has slipped from his shoulders; almost as though he is glad to abandon his plan, 'such thought of slaughter, such preparations for a feast of blood', as a Beechworth journalist would see it. Significantly Ned fastened on the platelayers who had played the major role in breaking the line, telling James Reardon, 'Do not be too fond of getting out of bed till you are called out of it.'

Ned then asked Denis Sullivan if he had ever been in New Zealand and told him, 'If you were Sullivan the murderer [who had turned Queen's evidence against fellow killers] I would give a thousand pounds for you,' spinning a preposterous yarn that they had held up Glenrowan hoping to find this hated stool-pigeon. This prompted Ned's usual threat that, if anyone gave information to the police, he would shoot them down like dogs. His eye caught Bracken's. 'I do not mind a police-man doing his duty so long as he does not overdo it.'

Bracken replied that police were only earning an honest living and asked Ned 'how he, if he was an honest man, could get on without them?'

'And am I not an honest man?' Ned challenged.

'I'm damned if you are!' said Bracken, bringing a roar of laughter from the audience, and probably from Ned.

The mood was broken by a clatter of high-heeled boots in the passage from the back door. It was Joe.

'The train's coming!'

Ned snapped, 'All stop here!' and hurried into Mrs Jones's 'best room', followed by Joe, Dan and Steve. The prisoners heard the clang of metal as James Kershaw helped the Gang into their armour for the coming battle. Bracken waited his chance. If he made his break from the hotel too early the Gang would simply come in pursuit and shoot him down. If he waited too long the special train would speed through Glenrowan to its destruction.

Ned and Joe were ready first. With coats pulled on over their armour they went out the back to their mares, still saddled from the Bracken expedition, led them down the side of the inn and tossed the white-washed sliprails aside from the paddock entrance at the right hand end of the verandah.

Ned rode down the line and saw the train halted at the cutting. Curnow had probably left the scene before he arrived — he was perhaps already at home in the darkened schoolhouse. Ned saw the train's lights being extinguished, then rode back to the inn.

He ordered the lights out and Mrs Jones hurried around, blowing out the lamps, glad to douse the fires with jugs of water. The 'house of sport' became a nightmarish place, sinking into steamy, kerosene-reeking darkness behind drawn window blinds as the four ironclad outlaws moved around like automatons with men, women and children trailing after them, frightened and confused.

Ned mounted and rode down towards the line again. The train was approaching too slowly — it had been warned of the broken line. But had the police been told the Gang were in Glenrowan? Ned clung to a hope that the train wouldn't stop. The coupled-together locomotives rumbled through the crossing, drawing the horse trucks along to the station platform, and clanked to a halt.

Hare jumped down to the platform, where he saw his civilian volunteer, Charles Rawlins, a local grazier and former cattle-dealer.

'What had we better do?' Hare asked.

Rawlins pointed out and named the two hotels and the 'station house' where he had seen a light burning. 'We are sure to hear of the Kellys at the railway gate, because of the horses having to cross. We will go down and see Stanistreet.'

Hare gave Rawlins a revolver and, with a couple of troopers, they hurried over to the gatehouse. Mrs Stanistreet was huddled in bed with her children, 'the bedclothes up to her eyes'. In tears, she told the two men that the Kellys had taken her husband to Jones's hotel. When Rawlins asked how many there were, she said, 'Forty.'

In the silent, darkened inn Bracken was choosing his moment, going from room to room and quietly telling the prisoners, 'Lie down as flat as you possibly can on the floor, it is the only chance you have got.' Moments later he would slip out the front door, the discovery of his escape prompting one last pun from Joe: 'Let me but catch him, and I will make a Bracken of him.' *Bracken* is Gaelic for a tartan rug.

Hare and Rawlins ran back to the station and the police started to unload the horses. O'Connor recalled, 'The noise was terrific, the horses coming out, half rearing and plunging through the van.' Standing at the end of the platform, Rawlins had seen a horseman riding around the back of Jones's Inn. Soon after, a figure came running down from the building, a man without hat or coat, jumping the railway fence, stumbling and running to the station. It was Bracken.

He gasped out, 'Over there — the Kellys — not five minutes ago — stuck us all up — the four of them — quick, quick!'

Hare turned to his men. 'Let go the horses! Come on boys! They are at Jones's!'

With men scrambling for their guns in a welter of horses clattering around the platform, Hare started running towards the inn, followed by O'Connor, Rawlins, several Benalla policemen and one or two of the Aboriginal troopers. *Argus* reporter Joe Melvin was close behind, with the train driver and guard in the rear.

This was a brave but foolish piece of leadership by Hare. Scarcely half his men were behind him, since some had heard neither Bracken's warning nor Hare's order in the noise. Some continued saddling their mounts while others were still trying to wrestle horses out of the trucks.

The moon was high in the sky behind Morgans Lookout, throwing the front of the inn into deep shadow and shining straight onto the small group of police running up the gravel path from the station. The Gang had come down from the back of the hotel and spread along the front of the building, three on the verandah, unseen in the shadows, Ned standing at the left corner.

Recognising Hare in the lead, head and shoulders above the rest of the party, Ned raised his Colt revolving rifle. The helmet made it hard to aim properly but, in brilliant moonlight at short range, he couldn't miss.

It was an extraordinary moment. After all these months there was nothing between the two men but a small, revolving iron gate in the railway fence, perhaps 30 yards from the inn. Hare barged through it, shotgun held high, swerving slightly, and Ned fired. The bullet smashed through Hare's left wrist and fanned past his body. A following trooper heard him say, 'Good gracious! I am hit the very first shot!'

The other three members of the Gang opened fire and the flashes lit the verandah, momentarily revealing the four unearthly figures. Some police charged through the gate after Hare; others jumped the fence to either side and threw themselves to the ground, taking cover behind fence posts or trees; O'Connor dived into a deep drain. The police unleashed a ragged volley.

A voice echoed strangely from a steel helmet, 'Fire away you bloody dogs, you can't hurt us!' Constable Gascoigne called, 'That is Ned Kelly's voice!'

Ned moved out into the moonlight and took aim, but Gascoigne fired. A Martini Henry bullet smashed through Ned's bent left arm, inflicting four wounds, two below the elbow, two above. Ned went to turn back and, as he moved, a bullet ripped into his right foot by the big toe and burst out from the sole near his heel. He was almost totally disabled.

In the first minute about sixty police bullets had cut through the flimsy walls of the inn behind the Gang. Its dark interior had become a nightmare of splintering wood and glass. Dave Mortimer was on the floor of the bar. 'The women and children were screaming with terror, and every man was saying his prayers. Poor little Jack Jones was shot almost at once.'

A bullet hit the frail 13-year-old near the hip and drove up into his prone body. He lay, shrieking in pain, bleeding from the mouth. Mortimer was helpless. 'I put my hands in my ears so as not to hear his screams of agony.' At almost the same time a bullet had grazed Jane Jones's forehead. She and her frantic mother took Jack out to the kitchen and laid him near the brick chimney for protection until labourer Neil McHugh bravely carried the boy out through the police barrage and along to the Reardon house. Little Jack reached the Wangaratta Hospital nine hours later and died soon after midnight.

Two other civilians were fatally wounded by police fire: quarryman George Metcalf, whose eye was injured when a bullet ricocheted from a chimney he was sheltering in, and an old local called Martin Cherry, a line repairer, 'an Irishman of the old school, a merry old soul'. When he had heard that the Kellys were at Jones's, he had said, 'I don't believe it. I will go and see.' Now he lay on the floor of the separate kitchen, terrified, 'his limbs . . . cramped and numbed from lying on the hard boards'. In a pause between volleys he climbed onto one of the Jones boys' beds, where a bullet ripped into his groin. John Larkins, the Reardons' lodger, left his cover among some sacks of grain and was trying to staunch the flow of blood with a strip of sheet when a bullet grazed the back of his head and clipped his ear. Larkins dragged a mattress over Cherry to give him some protection and dived back to cover. 'The bullets,' said Larkins, 'came thick and fast like showers of hail.'

Across the railway line in front of McDonnell's, Jack Lloyd had been waiting with the rockets. He hesitated as the storm of gunfire reverberated across the Gap. His orders were to fire the signal when the train was wrecked. At the second police volley he made his impossible decision and sent the two rockets streaking up into the sky, scattering falling stars with dull, delayed thumps.

Two policemen, Arthur and Gascoigne, saw the rocket bursts and wondered what they meant. Ned saw them and knew. The sympathisers would start on their way to the meeting place. For the moment, shocked by his wounds, he may not have grasped the consequences.

Outside the inn someone called, 'Don't fire. The place is full of women and children; stop firing!' Eventually there was an uneasy lull. The Gang had fired forty or fifty shots, the police eighty or 100. Under cover of their own gunsmoke the Gang moved down the side of the building to the back door.

In the lull all the women and most of the children left the inn, led by the wounded Jane Jones with a lighted candle. Mrs Jones was with them, wandering dementedly, abusing the Gang, calling the police 'murdering dogs', turning back to the inn, wandering out again . . .

The Reardons had been delayed. One of the girls was suffering cramp. Mrs Reardon with her baby, James Reardon, two older boys and two youngsters were on the moonlit road in front of the inn, approaching the crossing, when a voice called, 'Who comes there?' The whole family called, 'Women and children!' and the male voices prompted a volley of shots. 'They were right across our faces,' said Margaret Reardon. 'I shut my eyes at once with the fire and smoke.' Three of the Reardon children had reached safety with the other women. The rest of the family turned and ran back into the inn.

The police had scattered into a rough crescent across the front of the building, reinforced by the remaining constables and the other Aboriginal troopers, who doubled forward to join O'Connor in the drain immediately in front of the building. Crouched out to the left of the inn, opposite the breezeway, Constable Phillips heard a remarkable conversation between Ned and Joe.

'Is that you, Joe?'

'Yes, is that you, Ned? Come here.'

'Come here be damned. What are you doing there? Come with me and load my rifle. I'm cooked.'

'So am I. I think my leg is broke.'

'Leg be damned. You got the use of your arms. Come on. Load for me. I'll pink the buggers.'

'Don't be so excited; the boys'll hear us and it'll dishearten them.' Joe's words sobered Ned and for a moment he seemed defeated by the collapse of his plan, by his wounds . . .

'I'm afraid it's a case with us this time.'

'Well, it's your fault; I always said this bloody armour would bring us to grief.'

And it had. Because of the armour they had sat here for 24 hours, waiting at the inn for an attack rather than taking the initiative and picking off the police as they milled around the station. Yet criticism of the armour sparked Ned's fighting spirit again.

'Don't you believe it. Old Hare is cooked and we'll soon finish the rest.'

Still angry, Joe limped back into the inn where, Dave Mortimer recalled, he 'cursed and swore at the police. He seemed perfectly reckless of his life.'

Ned, his rifle re-loaded, hobbled down the Benalla side of the building and out into the open above the railway crossing. He fired a shot and drew three shots in reply.

Smoke still hung between the police and the hotel, screening Ned

PICNICING UNDER THE "KELLY TREE"

The tree and group of saplings where Ned left his cap and rifle early in the siege and where he rested during his Last Stand, sketched by Thomas Carrington the following year during a school picnic. (*Sketcher*)

from men looking towards the moon. From across the road to the side, Constable Gascoigne could see Ned clearly as he fired at three men on 'the closed road' in the railway reserve. Then Ned turned to face Gascoigne and the trooper fired. Ned returned his fire, twice hitting the 'small sapling post' sheltering the policeman. Gascoigne put another two or three shots into the strange figure and Ned yelled, 'You bloody cocktails, you can't hurt me. I am in iron,' before turning and walking back towards the top corner of the hotel paddock until the trooper lost sight of him in a drift of moonlit smoke.

Ned had left his mare in the bush beyond the far side of the paddock. He limped along the back fence past the stables and reached the clump of three small trees where she was tethered, about 100 yards east of the inn, screened from the railway station directly below by a huge, white fallen tree.

Before Ned could mount he sank to the ground and realised that blood was pouring from his shattered left arm, leaving a dark trail on the pale, moonlit ground. He removed his helmet, took off the padded waterproof silk cap and set it under his elbow to catch the blood. When the cap was almost filled, he got to his feet, somehow struggled into the saddle and rode east towards the Gap. He met Tom Lloyd and realised he had left his rifle with the cap. Tom went back and found the Colt, but felt it was sticky with blood. He struck a match and saw that blood was clogging some of the nipples on the back of the cylinder. The weapon was useless and he left it with the cap.

As Tom started back towards Ned two police approached and moved to cover between the three trees he had just left. Tom watched only a few yards away as they found the cap of blood and the rifle. He heard their excited conversation, waited for them to move away, then returned to Ned.

By now Ned had formed a plan: he would turn the sympathisers away from the fight then go back, alone, to rescue Joe, Dan and Steve. It was a remarkable yet characteristic decision. A true revolutionary would always be prepared to sacrifice lives, but Ned lacked the ruthlessness to follow such a path, even if it led to victory.

For a time his cause and the cause of the selector sympathisers had blurred together in the shadowy outlines of the republic. Now, as the dreams and the rhetoric disintegrated in hailstorms of lead, all those 'decent hard-working men' clutching Kelly guns and riding their farm horses, summoned here by the falling rocket stars — they had no part in this ugly reality.

At the meeting place, probably beyond the Gap on the far side of a spur that ran down towards the break in the line, the sympathisers were waiting. One man thought there seemed to be 150 men gathered in the shadowy, moonlit bush, another no more than thirty. Even if only a dozen men had ridden here, they could have carried the day at Glenrowan. But Ned ordered them to stay out of the battle.

'This is our fight,' he told them. It would be remembered that he also said, 'I am prepared to die.' As the tiny army broke up, confused and disbelieving, Ned moved off a little way with Tom and rested before returning to the inn in an attempt to rescue the other three. It was perhaps 4.30 a.m. There remained little more than two hours of darkness.

The two policemen who had stumbled on Ned's cap and rifle were Senior Constable Kelly and Constable Arthur. Kelly was now in charge of the siege, since Superintendent Hare was back in Benalla. Hare had returned to the railway station soon after the start of the fight and *Sketcher* artist Thomas Carrington had bandaged his wrist with a silk handkerchief — supposedly on the wrong side of the wound, an allegation hotly denied by Carrington. Hare had then returned briefly to the firing line and come staggering back to the station a second time. One of his men commented, 'Here comes Hare as drunk as possible.' Hare then collapsed onto a pile of sacks with a faint, 'Catch me please.' Arrangements were made to evacuate him by the pilot locomotive but it left without him in the confusion. Eventually Hare headed off on the footplate of the second engine, chilled with shock and trying to warm himself at the open firebox. He left O'Connor's wife and sister-in-law marooned at the station with a bodyguard of armed journalists.

Stanhope O'Connor and his five Aboriginal troopers were still in the drain opposite the front of the hotel. The other seven police formed a broken half-circle from the far side of the roadway on the Benalla side of the building to the open bush on the Wangaratta side. Stationmaster Stanistreet had walked calmly out of the inn during the first lull in firing and explained that there was a large number of civilians in the kitchen and front rooms. This message was imperfectly communicated and O'Connor went through the siege believing that all the prisoners were in the kitchen. 'I took that as Gospel,' he said. He and his men poured almost constant fire into the front rooms, their Snider bullets ripping straight through the weatherboards and paper, fanning across the prone civilians and creating a danger zone across the top of the paddock, so no police could safely take position. This offered a line of escape for men in armour almost until daylight, and Ned was gathering strength for his attempt to rescue the other three.

◆

AFTER WARNING Hare and his men that the Gang were in Jones's, Bracken had grabbed one of the saddled police horses and galloped off along the sleepers between the railway lines to Wangaratta, where Sergeant Steele was already alerted by the sound of gunfire from Glenrowan and a telegram from Benalla. While Steele readied a party of five men, including Bracken, to set out for Glenrowan on horseback and two foot police to travel on a special train, Bracken sent telegrams all over the district, spreading word of the battle. Meanwhile Superintendent Sadleir prepared to bring thirteen reinforcements from Benalla by train (equipping himself with a rope to pull down the inn's brick chimneys!).

◆

FOR NED time meant nothing, but for the police it became critical in their attempts to justify their own actions or gain recognition or reward for their parts in the drama, and in the disputes which developed about what really happened.

Sergeant Steele came galloping up with his five troopers: Mountiford,

Cawsey, Healy, Moore and Bracken. He claimed it was 5 a.m., but it was probably at least half an hour later. Dismounting in sight of the inn and moving down from the Gap, Steele and his men passed within a yard or two of Ned and a movement of his armour attracted their attention. Mountiford suggested it was a hobble chain on one of their horses.

Steele sported a double-barrelled shotgun and was dressed like a gentleman hunter in a tweed jacket, tweed hat and long waterproof leggings — ready to shoot at anything that moved. He zig-zagged his way to a tree opposite the breezeway between the inn and the kitchen, with his men on either side.

There had been a long lull in the firing and Margaret Reardon made another attempt to escape with her baby, her 17-year-old son Michael and two young daughters. Her husband followed.

> I put the little girl out in the yard, and she screamed, and I came out myself next. One of the outlaws (by the voice I took it to be Dan Kelly) said, 'If you escape' — and I said, 'What shall I do?' and he said, 'See Hare, and tell him to keep his men from shooting till daylight, and to allow all these people to go out, and that we shall fight for ourselves.' I came out into the yard and I screamed for the police to have mercy on me. I said, 'I am only a woman, allow me to escape with my children;' and I added, 'the outlaws will not interfere with us — do not you.'
>
> A voice said, 'Put up your hands and come this way or I will shoot you like bloody dogs.' . . . It was Sergeant Steele . . . I put my baby under my arm and held up my hand, and my son let go one hand and held the other child by it, and we went straight on. The man commenced firing and he kept on firing at us . . . I then turned and went down along the fence towards the railway station, and two shots went directly after me, and two went through the shawl that was covering the baby. I felt my arm shaking, and I said 'Oh, you have shot my child.'
>
> My son was close behind me . . . and he said, 'Mother, come back; you will be shot' and I said, 'I will not go back; I might as well be shot outside as inside;' but I said, 'I do not think the coward can shoot me.' My son turned away and walked back towards the house, pulling the little child by the left hand, and with the right hand up. I looked round and saw him going, and that was the last I saw of him.

Margaret Reardon was lifted over the railway fence and taken to the station by a Benalla railway guard who had just arrived. He was Jesse Dowsett, one of the battle's few heroes. A slug had lightly grazed baby Bridget's forehead.

After Steele had fired at the mother and baby Constable Arthur called, 'If you fire at that woman again, I'm damned if I don't shoot you!'

Steele re-loaded and turned his attention to Michael Reardon, who was retreating to the inn's back door with one hand raised, the other hauling his little sister behind him. Steele called on him to halt then fired both barrels at the lad's back. A slug glanced off Michael's shoulder blade and lodged near the breast bone. Michael fell in the doorway and his father helped him inside.

As this took place, Ned was making his way down to the back of the inn, masked by the stable and then the kitchen.

Joe was in the bar room, daunted by the arrival of Steele's party on horseback and Sadleir's train from Benalla soon afterwards (its official arrival time put back at least half an hour). Joe called to the McAuliffes to come and help and one of them replied, but no help came. Joe fired two shots from the bar window and limped back to the counter. As he removed his helmet and stood at the corner of the bar, pouring a glass of whisky, Ned appeared in the doorway at the end of the short passage. Looking down into the dark room, Ned probably couldn't recognise his friend, but Joe knew the giant armoured shape which filled the back-door frame.

Joe raised the glass, suddenly defiant. 'Many more years in the bush for the Kelly Gang!'

Ned then knew it was Joe but, before he could reply, a volley of bullets splintered through the walls of the pub. Joe twisted and fell to the floor with a crash of armour, fatally shot through the groin. Lying nearby in the darkness, James Reardon could hear blood gushing from the wound. The same volley had hit the dining room clock and it began chiming, on and on.

Joe was dead at 23 — Joe the punster, the maker of songs, the lover of women and whisky, the true friend who had said he would die at Ned's side before betraying him, who had helped build the legend that already enclosed them.

Dan and Steve were left. Ned said later, 'When I saw my best friend dead, I had no more faith in them.' Then he summoned the extraordinary spirit that had brought him back here. He told Dan, 'My best friend is dead. I'll go out in the verandah and challenge them.' Ned said 'he went outside and called a challenge to the police but there was no reply. I went back to the house. My brother and Steve Hart had gone outside or into one of the rooms. I thought they had cleared. I said, "I'll challenge the lot myself" and walked out past seven or eight police. "I could have shot them easily, and could have got away if I wished."'

From his position on the Benalla side of the inn, Gascoigne, who had exchanged shots with Ned early in the battle, saw him 'with a loose cloak on', moving up the paddock to a small stockyard beside the stable. 'I saw him go among the horses; and I saw the horse rear up in the yard, and the man could not get on, and she broke through the sliprail through the fence of the hotel away on the Benalla side, and turned into Morgans Creek out into the ranges.'

According to Gascoigne it was about 6 a.m. He called out to the police on the other side of the inn that the Kellys were trying to escape and they started shooting the remaining horses in the paddock and yard.

Ned struggled up the slope towards the Gap and was met by Tom, whose first words were: 'Where are the others?' Ned realised that Dan and Steve had not 'cleared', they were still in the hotel. He fainted. By now he had been bleeding from serious wounds for about three hours, dragging himself for hundreds of yards through the bush in a hundred-weight of armour. He had already done more than anyone could expect in terms both of courage and physical endurance. Yet he readied himself for one last, impossible attempt to rescue 'the boys', as the clear sky began to lighten out across the Oxley flats and beyond the jagged spine of Buffalo.

Tom helped Ned prepare three revolvers — each a symbol of the strange sequence of events that had led him here. A neat little .31 calibre pocket Colt was probably the weapon that had wounded Fitzpatrick; a .45 Webley was the revolver Lonigan had been aiming when Ned shot him; a superb, long-barrelled Colt Navy had come from Senior Constable Devine at Jerilderie. Of the three handguns, only the cartridge-firing Webley could be re-loaded, with some difficulty, by a one-handed man. The other two revolvers were old-fashioned percussion firearms in which each of the six chambers were charged separately, like a muzzle loader, and the nipples were fitted with percussion caps.

At some stage, Tom had helped remove Ned's oilskin coat, probably to tend his wounded arm. As Ned prepared for battle, Tom draped the garment over his shoulders like a long cloak, held in position by the helmet as it was lowered over his head on to its shoulder pads. Everything was ready. Ned started to limp back across the Gap towards the inn and the thirty-four policemen now scattered around it. Behind him the sun was about to rise. He lurched on, down into the shadows, into the realm of legend.

19

THE LAST STAND

28 JUNE 1880

The inn squatted in its clearing with its windows shattered and its weatherboard walls a lattice-work of bullet holes. A dawn ground-mist lay across the freezing grass and skeins of gun-smoke faded among the gum trees. Everything was numb with cold, quiet and waiting for sunrise.

The scratch and flare of a match was startlingly loud. Constable James Arthur, who had found Ned's cap and rifle and challenged Steele when he fired at Mrs Reardon, squatted with his rifle across his knee to light a morning pipe. After the clash with Steele he had moved back to a position about 100 yards from the inn because he was worried that the bullets from his Martini Henry could go straight through the building and hit a policeman on the other side. His line of fire was now slightly downwards — a safer position for the other police.

As Arthur sucked the match flame down into the bowl of his pipe he heard a faint sound behind him. 'I turned round and saw . . . I could not make out what it was . . . a tremendous size.'

Something unearthly was moving across the slope of the Gap, something bigger than a man lurching among the trees, with a strange, square head and shoulders hunched under the heavy folds of a long, grey cloak that trailed down into the mist. It was coming out of the sunrise straight towards him. The pipe dropped from Arthur's mouth.

From a less threatened position at the railway station, artist Thomas Carrington watched in disbelief.

There was no head visible, and in the dim light of morning, with the steam rising from the ground, it looked for all the world like the ghost of Hamlet's father with no head, only a very long, thick neck.

Reporter George Allen, who was also reminded of 'the sepulchral form of Hamlet's avenging father', felt that 'some unknown demon was let loose for evil purposes amongst us'.

Constable Arthur, however, believed the thing to be human. 'I thought at first it was some madman in the horrors who had put some nail can on his head … I told him to keep back or he would be shot … he made some rumbling noise.'

Ned called, 'I could shoot you, sonny,' and swept back the folds of the oilskin to raise a revolver in his right hand, awkwardly supported by his bloodied left.

Arthur quickly aimed and fired. The rifle bullet resounded on Ned's helmet with dizzying force and he staggered back, then summoned the strength to raise his revolver and squeeze the trigger. The barrel sagged as he fired and the bullet kicked up the earth a yard or two in front of Arthur, who realised, 'he could not raise his arm properly … he seemed to be crippled'.

Arthur re-loaded his rifle and fired a second shot. Again the monstrous figure was thrown off-balance, 'but it had no other effect on him'. James Arthur was one of the best shots in the force. He knelt and took careful aim at just below the eye slit as Ned lumbered slowly to within 20 yards. A third bullet sent him staggering. Arthur went to run forward but Ned had recovered and fired another shot from his revolver. Arthur yelled a warning, 'It's no good firing at him!'

Others among the watching police thought the figure was 'a madman … or a ghost … some said it was the devil'. Senior Constable Kelly, down near the station, seemed to yell, 'He's the bunyip, boys!' (but later insisted that he had actually said, 'He's bullet-proof, boys!').

Constable Phillips, who was firing from near Arthur, heard Ned call, 'Good shots, boys. Fire away you buggers. You cannot hurt me!'

Healy and Mountiford, two of Steele's men, came running up to within 10 yards and fired both barrels of their shotguns. 'But Ned only laughed,' Phillips said.

Healy drew his revolver but it jammed or misfired and he was forced back by the monster's slow advance as Mountiford, too, veered out of its path.

Over at his tree near the inn's breezeway, Sergeant Steele couldn't see what his men were firing at. Then, through the trees, he saw that their target seemed to be 'a tall, black man' wrapped in a blanket or possum rug, with an old top hat on his head. It struck him that it must be a local Aborigine called Tommy Reid. Steele called out, 'Steady firing … it's a blackfellow!', an odd display of scruples after his pre-dawn shooting spree with the Reardons.

Ned had been beating his revolver butt against his breastplate, calling, 'Come out, come out, boys, and we'll whip the beggars!' Dan and Steve, who had been heard calling for Ned before daylight, appeared at the back door and opened fire from the breezeway. Their bullets scattered splinters from Steele's tree and he retreated — towards the advancing 'Aborigine'.

Two more of Steele's men, Cawsey and Moore, had begun shooting from their positions out in the bush opposite the inn's stable. Caught in a cross-fire between them and Ned, Healy moved up the slope to Ned's right. Phillips retreated ahead of him to join Moore behind a large tree and Arthur and Mountiford edged down towards the railway fence on Ned's left, where Senior Constable Kelly, railway guard Dowsett and Constable Bracken were edging closer from tree to tree.

The way to the inn was opening up, but Ned found himself advancing into a broad half-circle of gunfire, with bullets hitting him 'like blows from a man's fist'. Arthur's shots had hurt and blackened both his eyes. The unpadded face plate of his helmet was smashed back against his cheeks, its top edge chopping skin from the bridge of his nose and a bolt-end ripping the side of his face. Somehow he stayed on his feet and kept stumbling forward, his weakened legs and smashed right foot supporting the fantastic weight of his armour.

George Allen thought he moved, 'like someone in a trance'. To artist Carrington, 'he seemed to be drunk from the way he was staggering about'. Constable Arthur said simply, 'he was more dead than alive'. After four hours of sporadic bleeding from major wounds, Ned's body was trying to ration a dwindling reserve of blood, limiting circulation to arms and legs to keep the brain and vital organs supplied. In spite of this there wasn't enough for all his brain functions and it was becoming increasingly hard to co-ordinate his movements, even to remain standing.

Ned had only covered about 50 yards since the start of the gun battle and the inn was still 100 yards away. He was outflanked on both sides and Arthur and Senior Constable Kelly were now behind him, to his left. He had reached the clump of three small trees where he had rested after first leaving the inn. Did he imagine the Colt revolving rifle was still there? In this inadequate cover he sank to his knees.

Now came a moment of such unreality that few men even recalled it. Music, the grey mare, had appeared among the misty trees of the hillside. Ned called her 'my grey mare', but she was really Joe's, ridden by both men and loyal to both. As Ned knelt among the trees Music came towards him, saddled and bridled. It was as if Joe were offering his mate one last gesture of help, a chance to escape.

'We fully expected to see him make a rush and mount it,' said an onlooker. 'But he allowed it to pass.' As Music started to gallop away, Constable Moore took careful aim, fired twice and she fell.

Ned had emptied the pocket Colt and perhaps the Webley. Unable to carry out the Colt's complex re-loading operation, he tossed it aside. If he re-loaded the Webley, it was with cartridges probably cut to size by Tom Lloyd. The proper ammunition was still in the hotel. Before he could fire, however, a bullet knocked the Webley — Lonigan's revolver — out of his hand, badly damaging it. He drew his third and last revolver, Devine's Colt Navy, from its holster.

Dan and Steve were still shooting from the breezeway and Sergeant Steele, 50 yards away, faced the prospect of being caught between two fires. He gambled that Ned was re-loading and broke from cover, running towards the three saplings where Ned had gone to earth.

Ned saw him coming, rested the heavy, long-barrelled Colt against a tree and fired. Steele threw himself to the ground and clutched at his eye. Standing among the saplings, Ned was again a target. Healy fired from up the slope and hit Ned's hand, splattering one of the trunks with blood. Another bullet from downhill chopped the tip from his little finger and knocked away the edge of the Colt's walnut grip.

He swayed out into the open, still 100 yards from the inn, and defiantly struck the revolver barrel against his helmet, 'which sounded like a cracked bell', as he called, 'You bloody dogs, you can't shoot me!' But he knew very well that they could shoot him — in the arms and legs and hands and feet.

Between him and the railway station a huge, dead-white, fallen tree offered cover 25 yards away. Ned limped down towards it, turning away from the inn. Tunnel-visioned behind the helmet's eye-slit, he did not see that Steele was watching him, unhurt. As the sergeant had dived to avoid Ned's shot, dirt had been kicked into his eye. A moment's pain and 'a few minutes' of unclear vision and Ned's old enemy was there, half-behind him, waiting his chance.

As Ned approached 'the lying tree', Dowsett, the courageous little railway guard, crouched behind its massive trunk and took aim with his departmental Colt revolver.

> When he was within 12 or 15 yards of me, I fired five or six charges straight at him ... and hearing almost seeing them jump off his body I felt very queer ... I then cried out to the others, 'This man must be the devil.'

Mountiford closed in from Ned's right, Senior Constable Kelly from the left, and Dwyer — an unlikely figure in red shirt, watch chain and smoking cap — sprinted forward from the station as Ned reached the fallen tree's fork of bare, broken branches, lying along the edge of a tiny creek running down from the ranges.

Dowsett, crouched by the butt of the tree, saw Ned sag, exhausted, against an arm of the fork. The railwayman called out, 'You had better surrender.'

'Never, while I have a shot left.'

Dowsett aimed carefully and fired at Ned's head, 'but it went off like a parched pea'. Nevertheless, he managed a perky, 'How do you like that, old man?'

Ned straightened. 'How do you like *this*?' He put a bullet past Dowsett's head, 'very close singing as it passed'.

This exchange gave Sergeant Steele his chance. Now that he was closer he realised how he had mistaken Ned for an Aborigine: the effect of thin, black legs had been created by bands of dark strapping on light-coloured riding trousers. Steele recognised the vulnerability of those unprotected legs and ran forward. Ned was still turned away.

The wounded Music had regained her feet, and plunged forward between Ned and the advancing sergeant. The movement caught Ned's eye and he may have started to turn. Steele dropped to his knee behind a small stump about 15 yards off and fired. A charge of buckshot bit deep into Ned's right knee. He staggered, legs spread to save himself from falling.

Steele ran closer and fired the second barrel. A second blast of shot splintered through the branches into Ned's hip and thigh, and behind the steel apron into his groin. Ned swayed and his strength drained. He said later, 'that . . . he fell from loss of blood, that he was unable to stand from weakness, that the helmet he wore was choking him, and the rifle bullets completely stunned him'.

He managed a despairing cry, 'I'm done, I'm done!' as his legs buckled and the weight of his armour brought him crashing straight down like an unstrung puppet on the creek bank against the tree. But the revolver was still in his hand.

Steele ran forward and grabbed Ned's wrist from behind. As blood 'shot out' from several wounds in his clenched hand, Ned forced the revolver back over his shoulder with a last surge of strength.

Dowsett and Kelly had leapt across the fallen tree and hurled them-selves on Ned and Steele. Dowsett grabbed at Ned's revolver, perhaps helping to pull the trigger. The Colt went off beside Steele's face, blow-ing off his tweed hat and blackening his cheek, just as Senior Constable Kelly's burly frame cannoned into the three of them and bore them to the ground with a crash of armour. In a wild scrimmage, Dowsett twisted the revolver from Ned's hand, nearly breaking his finger in the trigger guard, and Steele found himself under Ned with a piece of armour stabbing into his groin.

Volunteer Charles Rawlins grabbed Ned's wounded arm to haul him aside and Kelly lifted the helmet off his shoulders from behind.

'By God!' Steele exclaimed. 'It's Ned!'

Hardly aware of his injury, the sergeant caught the helmet from Kelly and held it aloft like a hunter's trophy, declaiming, 'You bloody wretch, I swore I would be in at your death, and I am!'

Determined to make the oath true, Steele drew his revolver and prepared to shoot Ned as he sprawled there against the dead branches, pinioned between Dowsett and Rawlins. It was a momentary tableau. Driven by some battle frenzy that fed on revenge, fear and the hunting instinct, this guardian of the law was about to execute a man who had shown far less eagerness to kill.

George Allen witnessed the moment and had no doubt that Steele 'meant to blow the outlaw's brains out'. To Doctor John Nicholson, Ned was 'a wild beast brought to bay and evidently expecting to be roughly used'. He was 'shivering with cold and ghastly white', his face covered with bruises, both eyes swollen and discoloured, blood trickling from his nose and cheek injuries and from more than twenty-eight shot wounds in arms, legs, hands, feet and groins. With a 'wild ... wasted look' he stared up into the muzzle of Steele's revolver.

Years before, Ned had shouted at the thuggish Hall, 'Shoot and be damned!' All he said now was, 'That's enough: I have got my gruel.'

The eccentric Constable Dwyer ran up 'with something like a war whoop' and made a kick at Ned. He bashed his shin on the armour and hopped painfully away. Dowsett protested, 'Take the man alive — take him alive!' And the tableau was abruptly transformed. Constable Bracken, Ned's prisoner of the previous night, stepped across the fallen outlaw with his shotgun ready and declared, 'I'll shoot any bloody man that dares touch him.'

More police, reporters, a clerk-of-courts and a doctor had reached the group and the moments following Ned's fall would be lost in a con-fusing pastiche of straight-out error, glory seeking and perjury.

Steele, in describing Ned's capture, put himself in the same heroic spotlight that transformed his account of Mrs Reardon's escape, ('I told her to run on quickly and she would not be molested ... and called on the police not to fire'), and the wounding of her son. ('From the sounds of the shots upon the man I was convinced that he wore armour.' Steele told Sadleir that he believed he had shot Joe Byrne.)

In Steele's version of the capture Ned turned and was taking aim at the sergeant before the first shot hit his legs, and was raising the revolver again when the second charge of shot struck him. Ned's helmet fell off as he collapsed and Steele took the revolver from his hand then held him until the others arrived — thus accomplishing, single-handed, the shooting, unmasking and disarming of the outlaw. Steele also said, on oath, 'one of the constables asked me to take my hand away that he might shoot the prisoner, who then said, "Don't kill me, I never did you any harm." '

The Last Stand had lasted for half an hour and suddenly the glen was quiet as the first sunlight struck through the Gap and across the slopes of Morgans Lookout, leaving the tree-shaded hollow in shadow.

For a moment Dan and Steve were stunned by Ned's fall. Then Dan 'shouted with rage ... and rushed outside shooting at everyone he could see'. He left the cover of the breezeway and directed 'some very vicious shooting' at the group around Ned — probably at Ned himself, perhaps to honour some pact the Gang had made before the battle. Bullets flew around Steele, Kelly and Dr Nicholson as they tried to remove Ned's armour, one hitting the ground between Kelly and the doctor.

'Keep watch! Keep watch!' yelled reporter Joe Melvin. Constables Arthur and Mountiford ran to cover nearer the inn and opened fire. Kelly and Dr Nicholson gathered up the armour and Ned hobbled towards the railway station, supported by Steele and Bracken.

As the police fire grew heavier, Dan was forced back to the inn. Dwyer, hurrying to tell Sadleir that Ned was captured, saw the armoured figure retreating into the breezeway 'in a shower of bullets' and saw 'the bark shot off the side of the kitchen door where he was standing'. Dan called, 'Fire away, you buggers, you cannot kill me!' A bullet struck his leg and he limped inside.

Ned was lifted across the railway fence by police and reporters and taken to the guard's van of the latest train. When bullets from the inn started to strike the van in what seemed to be further attempts to kill him, he was evacuated to Stanistreet's office at the railway station, where he was placed on a stretcher with his hands loosely tied.

Dr Nicholson thought Ned was dying and did what he could to make him comfortable. *Age* reporter McWhirter cut off both Ned's boots, a pillow was put under his head and cotton waste was piled to support his left arm.

Thomas Carrington observed, 'He fainted once or twice, but uttered no word of complaint about his wounds.' Ned did complain, however, at the coldness of his feet (a symptom of his massive blood loss) and told the doctor 'they would never get warm again'. Some reporters heated a kerosene tin of water and placed it against Ned's feet while they interviewed him.

Sadleir, summoned by Dwyer, was struck by Ned's 'gentle expression', commenting, 'It was hard to think that he was a callous and cruel murderer.'

When Ned gratefully drank some brandy offered by Dwyer and asked for bread, Sadleir sent the constable to bring some scones and a bottle of brandy from McDonnell's. As Sadleir helped him sip the liquor, Ned thanked the superintendent for his kindness.

'You shall have every care and attention, Ned,' Sadleir told him. 'Do not irritate yourself; keep yourself quiet.'

Asked by Sadleir if he could get the other members of the Gang to surrender, Ned mentioned Joe being killed and said he 'had no more faith' in Dan and Steve, speaking of them as 'cowards'. He was clearly bitter that he had received so little support from them in his extraordinary rescue bid.

This was a harsh judgement. Dan and Steve were left in the bullet-riddled inn with the remaining thirty-odd civilians. Their position was hopeless. At about 10 a.m., Sadleir called a cease fire and offered safe passage for the civilians. The ubiquitous Rawlins, who had 'a voice like a bull', bawled out, 'All those inside there had better surrender at once; we will give you 10 minutes to do so; after that time we shall fire volleys into the house.'

Sadleir recorded, 'the prisoners came buzzing out like bees; running out from the front door in great confusion'.

Rounded up by reporters McWhirter and Melvin, both armed with revolvers, the terrified group were herded across to Sadleir in the paddock to the right of the inn. Their fear was well justified. As they appeared, 'one of the constables came jumping over the fence, and he said, "Let us polish off this lot . . ." '

The prisoners were forced to lie on the cold, damp grass, checked by police to make sure that Dan and Steve were not among them, then released — except for the two McAuliffes, who were briefly handcuffed and held. Michael Reardon was taken to Dr Nicholson for treatment of the wound he had received from Steele four hours earlier. His condition was considered critical but he would survive.

Sadleir noted that Dan and Steve made no attempt to shoot at him or at other police who stood in the open during the release of the prisoners. The boys were now alone in the hotel, except for poor old Martin Cherry, who still lay out in the kitchen. As the prisoners prepared to leave they had seen Dan and Steve standing together in the breezeway, 'for all the world like two condemned prisoners on the drop'.

James Reardon had heard Steve ask, 'What will we do?' Dan replied, 'I'll tell you presently.' Reardon believed they intended to commit suicide.

The sun was grey-blanketed by cloud and 'a grisly winter's day' settled over Glenrowan. The broken line on the Wangaratta side of the Gap had been repaired by 7 a.m. and, as the morning passed, police reinforcements and onlookers in their hundreds continued to arrive.

An *Illustrated Australian News* artist, on his way from covering Aaron Sherritt's murder at Beechworth, had his trip to Melbourne interrupted and produced a splendidly gothic study of Ned looming from the mist-shrouded bush to confront a recognisable Steele and Dowsett.

The Beechworth postmaster had tapped into the telegraph line near the railway station and set up a small Morse key. Melbourne and

Australia began to receive communiqués on the capture of Ned, the astonishing fact that he had been wearing armour and the progress of the siege.

More reporters and artists were on their way. An enterprising Wangaratta photographer called Madeley had arrived soon after Ned's capture and started taking photographs of the besieged inn from behind the railway station with his unwieldy 'wet plate' equipment. Two other photographers were there before the end of the day.

In Melbourne, 'business appeared to be suspended' and traffic halted as crowds blocked streets outside the offices of the city's four daily newspapers. 'Extraordinaries' were on the streets by 11 a.m. News of the action reached London in only 5 hours and, by a trick of the international dateline, was published on 28 June, the day of the siege.

The badly wounded man lying in the station, the dead man on the floor of the inn and the two boys wandering hopelessly through its shattered rooms had become a media event of a scale never before seen in Australia. Yet the thousands of words sparking through the telegraph (90 000 to Sydney alone) and the tons of paper making up the press coverage of the siege would miss the real significance of what had happened.

There were clues: the rockets, followed by 'constant galloping between Greta and Glenrowan'. As he left on the locomotive, the wounded Hare had warned about assistance reaching the Kellys from 'the Greta side of the line'. Someone had been interrupted trying to drive away the police horses. A constable had warned reporters of 'a bad nest of them at the back ... a bad lot in that hotel over the road, keep a lookout!'

Hare was to say, 'There is no doubt that at Glenrowan they had parties of scouts, both in the hotel and outside of it; most of them no doubt were their own relations, and their name was legion.'

Three months later, in an account of the battle, The *Illustrated London News* would number the 'Kelly Gang' at 'about thirty', commenting, 'but few of them kept inside the house'. Apart from vague stories of armed men being seen in the bush outside the police positions, there was no sign of the sympathisers. For the moment they remained a phantom army.

◆

SOON AFTER MIDDAY Catholic priest Dean Matthew Gibney arrived in Glenrowan. He had been going to Albury on a fund-raising tour for a Western Australian orphanage that had been struck by lightning, when his train stopped at the town. Hearing that Ned was lying seriously wounded in the stationmaster's office, he broke his journey. He could not get through the clamour of reporters and onlookers until Dr Nicholson made way for him and eventually emptied the room. Ned, said Gibney, 'at once asked him to do anything he could towards preparing him for death'. After almost an hour's conversation, during which he heard Ned's confession, Gibney was 'satisfied as to his penitential disposition' and anointed him in the last sacraments of penance and extreme unction. It struck Gibney that 'although he was evidently suffering the most intense agony and pain from the wounds on his hands and feet, he never uttered a strong or impatient word'.

Gibney recalled that when he said, 'My son, say, "Oh Jesus have mercy on me, and pray for forgiveness."' Ned replied, 'It's not now I'm beginning to say that: I've done it long before today.'

While Gibney was with Ned several police volleys were fired into the hotel. Gibney suggested that Dan and Steve might surrender to a priest. Ned stared at him 'for some time' before replying. 'Don't you go. Your cloth won't save you ... they may take you for a policeman in disguise.'

Leaving Ned in some kind of peace, Gibney met a Church of England clergyman over at McDonnell's. As they strolled along to see the place where the line had been broken, Gibney told his colleague that Ned's advice had only 'partly deterred' him from trying to gain the surrender of the two boys. The Anglican gentleman made it clear that, in his view, it was the job of policemen, not men of the cloth, to take such risks.

As the day wore on several men volunteered to rush the hotel — including poor Harry Armstrong who would be branded a coward over his poor showing after Aaron's murder two nights before. 'I had the same answer for all,' said Sadleir. 'It is not time to rush yet; stand back and keep your ground.' He was determined that no more lives would be lost, and a strange languor settled over the siege as he moved around, chatting with his men and smoking his pipe. He would be widely criticised for this approach and, in later years, would concede that 'a sudden rush in upon the two men might have been effected without serious loss'. If all else failed, this was Sadleir's intention and he actually selected the men he would lead in a surprise attack — but only as a last resort.

In a much-lampooned move, Sadleir contacted Melbourne and Chief Secretary Ramsay arranged for a party of artillerymen to bring a field gun to Glenrowan (they left at 2.30 p.m. and would reach Seymour before receiving word that the siege was over). Ramsay had telegraphed to Sadleir his idea of storming the hotel with a bullet-proof shield mounted on a dray — a primitive tank. The livewire Chief Secretary also contacted the Government Astronomer, the local expert on electricity, and suggested that he supply electric lights in case the siege lasted into the night. When the astronomer foresaw technical difficulties Ramsay promptly suggested a circle of bonfires to guard against the escape of the last two outlaws.

Two of Ramsay's initiatives were carried through. He 'directed' Standish to attend the siege and arranged for Dr Charles Ryan, who was experienced in the treatment of gunshot wounds after recent adventures in the Russo-Turkish war, to accompany him.

One of the last police arrivals in Glenrowan was Senior Constable Charles Johnston from Violet Town, an enthusiastic and notoriously impetuous veteran of the Kelly pursuit. Sadleir knew Johnston well (his wife had been in service with the family) and on his arrival told him, 'Johnston, you will have to keep quiet and not irritate the men.' As soon as Johnston heard that a cannon was being sent to blow up the inn he suggested that he could simply set fire to the building instead. Sadleir liked the idea but considered using a younger, unmarried man. Johnston persisted and Sadleir eventually agreed to let him do it. The Senior Constable hurried off to find some straw and a bottle of kerosene.

At about this time Maggie Skilling appeared on horseback — a striking figure in the outfit she had chosen for a very different occasion: 'a black riding habit with a red underskirt, and white [plumed] Gainsborough hat'. She rode up to the fence of the railway reserve, near a group of four police who were watching the inn from cover — Mountiford, Dwyer, Armstrong and Dixon. Mountiford ordered her to go back and Maggie swore at him. The constable 'threatened to fire on her if she did not retreat'. Maggie wheeled her horse and rode off towards McDonnell's.

Meanwhile, out on the Benalla side of Glenrowan, 'far outside the police lines', Johnston encountered four armed men, 'not police'. He was unarmed and, after answering 'a few simple questions', was allowed to continue. As Sadleir put it the four were, 'men . . . who were waiting to join the Kellys in further raids'. The phantom army was beginning to emerge.

Undeterred by this encounter, Johnston found the straw and kerosene and returned to check final details with Sadleir. He circled to the west again to make a covered approach along the little creek that ran across the front of the battlefield — the 'drain' where O'Connor and his men were stationed. This time he was spotted by Dick Hart and Tom Lloyd.

Seeing an unarmed policeman carrying a sheaf of straw and a bottle, Dick realised what he was about and went to raise his rifle. Tom pushed it aside. 'There's been enough killing.' Ned had ordered them to stay out of the fight. They would obey his orders for a little longer.

Towards 3 p.m. Sadleir briefed a firing party to cover Johnston's approach to the inn and established a cordon of police to keep back the crowd. The Herald reported that by now 'there were considerably over a thousand spectators present'.

In a coincidence of timing typical of the Glenrowan saga Maggie, Kate and Grace Kelly and Wild Wright appeared on foot, crossing the railway line from McDonnell's. They had almost certainly been alerted by Dick Hart and Tom Lloyd that something was astir. Both arrived at about the same time.

Senior Constable Kelly asked Maggie if she would go to the inn and advise her brother to surrender. She told him 'she would sooner see them burned first'. Kelly then asked Dean Gibney to repeat the request to Maggie. Again Maggie refused but said, 'she would like to have an interview with her brother before he died'. Kelly took her to see Sadleir.

Someone pointed out Kate Kelly to Gibney and he told her he had spoken with Ned, who 'was not in any imminent danger at present'. As they were speaking there was 'a sharp rattle of gunfire' covering Johnston as he 'walked quite coolly' to the blank Benalla end of the inn, placed a bundle of straw against the wall, doused it with kerosene, splashed some on the weatherboards and struck a match. It 'missed fire'. A second match lit the straw and Johnston came back to the police lines with most of the onlookers near the station unaware of what had happened on the far side of the building.

Perhaps prompted by the last volley, Gibney asked Kate if she would ask the boys to surrender. Her reaction was very different from Maggie's. 'Of course I'll go and see my brother,' she said excitedly, and ran towards the building, but the police turned her back. Kate returned to Gibney, distressed, and they set off to find Sadleir.

Maggie was already pushing through the huge crowd towards the superintendent, who had watched 'the small blue tongue of flame' flicker and vanish against the wall of the inn as the straw burnt away. 'I thought it had failed to catch the building,' said Sadleir. Maggie must have realised what was happening, and broke towards the hotel, but was stopped at gunpoint on Sadleir's orders. Joined by Kate, she stood near the railway gates, urged by some onlookers to make another attempt.

Then smoke began to drift from under the roof. Driven by a light breeze from the south-west, the flames had licked under the wall, run up the paper lining and caught the calico ceiling. Flames appeared through the shattered parlour window. Kate screamed, 'Oh, my poor, poor brother!'

Gibney had been approaching Sadleir. Now, the priest turned and walked deliberately towards the burning inn. Sadleir called on him to stop and Gibney hesitated, about to speak when he remembered Ned's warning. If anyone inside the building saw him talking with the super-intendent, 'they would conclude at once that he was in the service of the police'. He called to Sadleir, 'There is no time to lose!'

By now the fire had swept across under the iron roof and 'small jets of flame issued from innumerable bullet holes' as smoke billowed from under the verandah. Sadleir saw Gibney 'make the religious sign of the cross on his face' and stride towards the inferno, bareheaded. As the thousand onlookers burst into applause, Sadleir ran forward, caught up with the priest on the verandah and was about to follow him through the right-hand door 'when a great sheet of flame fell between us'.

The calico ceiling of the dining room had collapsed across the doorway, bringing 'a cloud of fire and smoke down close to the floor . . . there was no getting into the building'. Wild Wright thought the whole inn was about to 'tumble down' on Gibney.

Hidden from view by the dangling curtains of flame, the priest found himself in the empty dining room, starred with bullet holes which shone through the smoke. He moved into the bar, its walls ablaze, and saw Joe lying across the doorway into the passage, half on his side, with his eyes open, legs flexed, arms raised from the elbows, almost as though he was about to move. Gibney touched him and found the body quite stiff. He stood and called loudly, 'For God's sake men, allow me to speak to you: I am a Roman Catholic priest!'

The only way to the back of the inn was through the burning doorway of the passage. Gibney stepped over Joe's body and 'rushed through a sheet of flame'. A cry of horror came from outside as 'he was plainly seen in the midst of the blaze'. He reached the little skillion bedroom on the left of the passage and registered a startling image. Two 'beardless boys' lay on the floor, 'full length on their backs', their heads pillowed on sacking, suits of armour and a dead dog — Dave Mortimer's greyhound — beside them. The walls and ceiling were blazing but the priest knelt quickly and felt the hand of the nearest boy. It was 'quite lifeless' and his eyes 'showed unmistakeable signs that he was dead for some time'. Satisfying himself that the second youth was also dead, Gibney walked through the back door and called, 'They are all dead.'

Some policemen ran towards the door and Gibney walked around to the front of the inn, cheered by the huge audience as he appeared. He saw a constable in the burning bar room, revolver raised as if to fire at Joe's body. Gibney called, 'Don't shoot: the man is dead.'

The constable was Harry Armstrong, who had crouched in the Sherritt bedroom a few feet from Joe only two nights before. He started to drag the armoured figure by the legs, out of the flames which had just reached him. Constable Dwyer grabbed the shoulders and they lugged Joe on to the verandah, his helmet dragged by a thong or wire.

When Gibney told them that 'the other two men' were in a bedroom, Armstrong and Dwyer dropped Joe and ran back into the blazing passage, shielding their faces with raised arms. Dwyer reached the doorway of the skillion room. Twelve months later his memories of the feverish moment would be confused. But his momentary picture of the bodies rings true.

Steve Hart had his feet up on the bed. He was burning down to here — [the waist] — and his feet were on the bed, and his hands were in that position — [folded?] and his face all burnt and his blood was passing and frizzling like steak in a pan. Looking again to the left of us, the north [west?] end near the chimney, Dan Kelly was lying in this position. The left knee was crippled and his hand was outstretched. His helmet was off: he had the armour on — the breast-plate; and on his neck and thighs and hand there was blood. I knew him to be Dan Kelly from the low forehead, and the description of them, and the other must be Steve Hart.

Armstrong yelled, 'Come out Dwyer, we can't take them!' As the two constables turned to the back door, the calico ceiling of the bedroom fell away, dropping a blazing shroud over the bodies.

Before the flames could reach the separate kitchen, Martin Cherry was lifted clear. All he said was, 'Don't hurt me,' and, to a man who called him by name, 'oh, you know me.' He died in a few minutes, just after Gibney had given him the last sacraments.

In minutes the fire destroyed the flimsy structure, made an inflammable brazier by the hundreds of bullet holes: The western wall was burnt out and the inner walls quickly fell away.

The crowd flocked along the side to peer into the blazing shell of the skillion. Johnston, apparently proud of his handiwork, pointed out to Sadleir the corpses of Dan and Steve. Artist Thomas Carrington recorded that they 'could now be plainly seen amongst the flames, lying nearly at right angles to each other, their arms drawn up and their knees bent'. He preserved the moment in a striking sketch, a last glimpse before the two bodies started 'roasting and shrivelling up in a horrifying manner'.

Soon after the inn had collapsed into a smoking shambles of burnt wood and twisted sheets of iron between the two brick chimneys, the police started trying to recover what was left of the two men, raking at the remains with a long pole. Eventually, they were lifted clear as Maggie and Kate 'howled loudly and lustily over the blackened bones'. Someone had kept poor young Grace away from this horror. The crowd pressed forward for a glimpse of 'those two charred stumps' and one was photographed, laid on a sheet of bark beside Mrs Jones's dining room table, which had been rescued from the verandah. Someone sat on the table, dangling his legs near the head — a mosaic of skull fragments clinging to a mass of crusted black tissue.

As the crowd jostled around the spectacle, Constable Gascoigne worried that his Martini Henry was still loaded. He had just ejected the cartridge when someone near him said, 'Do not be so smart unloading your rifle, young man, look what is coming before you.' Out of the sad winter afternoon, the phantom army was materialising. Gascoigne said simply, 'I saw some of their friends coming up.'

The four corpses were carried down to the railway platform — Dan, Steve, Joe and Martin Cherry. Sadleir reported, 'The friends ... they all began to come up at this moment.' According to Mrs McDonnell, 'The people came up in hundreds to the station.'

Silently the sympathisers emerged from the crowd, from the bush, from across the railway, and converged on the platform where Kate and Maggie knelt by the bodies. The sisters were, the *Herald* reported, 'terribly affected. They cried bitterly, and repeatedly kissed the burnt bones of Dan. Mrs Skillian divided her time between Dan's remains and ministering to the comfort of Ned. She was very violent, and fiercely cursed and abused the police, calling upon God to visit them with vengeance for their bloodthirsty and cruel murders.'

Sadleir was facing an ugly situation. He had fifty heavily armed police on the field, but a show of force at this stage could trigger a pitched battle. The railway between Benalla and Glenrowan had been blocked for about two hours by a mysterious 'encumbrance'. It would be an easy matter for the sympathisers to break the telegraph line. And Ned Kelly was still alive and becoming stronger. If the growing anger of the sympathisers generated an attempt to rescue Ned Kelly, how could anyone know what would happen?

The police had glimpsed a superhuman monster that morning. Now the monster lay in pieces — so much battered plough steel, a bullet-riddled oilskin coat and an almost helpless man. But Sadleir knew that their war with the monster was not yet over. He made the decision that a final victory in this war was more important than a skirmish over two burnt corpses. In what seemed a capitulation, he handed over Dan's and Steve's bodies to Dick Hart, Wild Wright and the Kelly girls, reporting, 'This seemed to please them very much, as an unexpected favour.' He did not mention an inquest on the bodies but may have said that 'they were not to be buried without a magisterial order'.

Later Sadleir was anxious to avoid any suggestion that he had been intimidated by the sympathisers. 'I was gratified at getting this trouble over that we had had on our hands for two or three years, and I was inclined to act liberally, *and I know the effect has been most beneficial to the public peace*.' [my italics]

The crisis was defused but, before the bodies had been wrapped in blankets and taken away, a train pulled into the station and Captain Standish alighted. He had left Melbourne at 10 a.m., to be delayed at Benalla by the mysterious line blockage. Now it was well after 5 p.m. and a ragged peace was settling over the battlefield. Sadleir was determined that nothing would disturb it.

I told Captain Standish what I had done about the bodies. I said, 'Please do not interfere now; leave the matter as it stands,' and he never interfered — never said another word about it. He did not interfere at all. I was afraid he would.

Sadleir's fear was well founded. Standish would tell the Royal Commission, without a blush:

I instructed Mr Sadleir not to hand over the charred remains of the outlaws. It is just possible that he may have misunderstood me, but I certainly did say that to him, but it seems possible that there was a misapprehension.

Sadleir would comment drily, 'It must be a misapprehension on Captain Standish's part.' However much Standish resented seeing the two blanket-swathed corpses carried off to McDonnell's by the contingent of family and friends, he was wise enough to let it happen and try to save face later. The fact remained that the victory was his. Ned Kelly was his prisoner, loaded into a train with the body of Joe Byrne and taken to Benalla that evening.

Under normal procedure, Ned would have been sent to Beechworth Gaol and held there for trial, but Standish had brought a special six-man squad to escort Ned back to Melbourne. That night he would telegraph the Chief Secretary from Benalla, 'Please inform if there is any objection to his being taken to Melbourne instead of to Beechworth Gaol *former preferable for many reasons.*' [my italics]

These reasons were never specified, except for Ned's need for expert medical attention (a suggestion that infuriated the resident surgeon and staff of the Beechworth hospital). The real reasons would emerge later. The Chief Commissioner wanted to get Ned Kelly out of the Kelly Country as soon as possible — back to Melbourne, the centre of government and his power base, back to Standish territory. Standish, too, feared the monster.

20

'A DEAL OF ILL BLOOD STIRRING'

28 JUNE – 5 JULY 1880

Still between life and death, Ned passed a haunted and sleepless night in the Benalla lock-up, with Joe's corpse in the next-door cell. On the pretext of giving his prisoner a drink, Senior Constable Kelly confronted Ned with Constable McIntyre. At first Ned thought he was Flood, in an echo of Stringybark Creek. The two policemen wrung from their critically ill charge an admission that he had shot Fitzpatrick. When Ned asked McIntyre if he had seen Lonigan dive for cover behind a log then come up to fire, McIntyre declared, 'Oh, that's nonsense.'

In spite of protests from defence counsel, this conversation was admitted in evidence at Ned's trial for murder. After this, Kelly let a *Daily Telegraph* reporter called Gale interview Ned about Kennedy's death. Gale's story, too, became part of the prosecution brief.

Across the hills the two charred bodies now lay in Maggie's home, mourned by the two families and friends, while Dick Hart made arrangements with Wangaratta undertaker John Grant for 'coffins of a first class description, the cost being a matter of no consequence'. Good Mr Grant would work through the night to finish a pair of coffins handsomely ornamented with brass fittings and name plates.

The Benalla police station was astir at 6.30 a.m. with preparations to send Ned to Melbourne. During the night a young English artist, Julian Ashton, had been allowed to make a drawing of Joe's body for the *Illustrated Australian News*. Now Melbourne photographers Burman and Lindt persuaded the police to hang his stiffened corpse on a door of the lock-up. Dead for more than 24 hours, Joe's calm, handsome, young face looked out at the cameras, police, blacktrackers and gawkers with a wistful half-smile, an eternal echo of the optimism of his last conscious moment.

While Benalla woke to its day of police triumph, Glenrowan stirred into a strange, new life, a life it would never escape. Visitors and locals wandered the battlefield and surrounded the still-smouldering ruins of the inn, starting to rake souvenirs from the ashes, 'burnt knives, forks, cartridge cases . . .' Someone found a charred foot. Over in the clump of saplings where Ned had rested, people collected bloodstained leaves and, when these were gone, scooped up blood-soaked soil.

Eight horses lay dead in the paddock behind the inn, at least half of them owned by prisoners of the Gang who would claim compensation from the government. Some bridles and saddles were souvenired (one or two replaced with inferior articles) and someone hacked the shod feet from the horse believed to be Dan's.

The Kelly horses at Glenrowan were already enveloped in mystery. While the inn was still burning, James Reardon had pointed out Ned's and Steve's packhorse tied to the fence at McDonnell's. Constable McHugh retrieved the horse and most of its pack but left the heavy drum, contents unknown, hidden under a nearby log. The Stanistreet children later stumbled on the drum, which became another minor press sensation as 'a rude infernal machine'.

Unaccountably, the Gang's four horses stabled at McDonnell's would stay there until found, late in the day, by Detective Ward. The McDonnells and the other sympathisers obviously knew they were there but probably suspected a police trap and didn't go near them. These four horses supposedly included the two superb animals taken from the Ryans a couple of weeks before, yet the Ryan chestnut ridden by Joe had been caught (and photographed) the previous day. And the Ryan bay mare Ned had been seen riding would be found on her way home to Dookie. All this can be explained by press and police muddle, but the mystery surrounding the most famous of the Kelly horses at Glenrowan is less easily solved.

What had happened to the grey, Music? After being wounded during the Last Stand, had she gone off to die in the ranges? Had she been found by sympathisers, to be nursed back to health? The police found a 'mongrel', flea-bitten, grey 'pony horse' which broke away from them on the way to Benalla and was recaptured weeks later. Had this unlikely animal been planted by sympathisers to cloud the issue after they had spirited Music away?

Sergeant Steele was uneasy at the disappearance of the grey mare — so remarkable an animal that she had faced gunfire to be near a master and, after being shot by one of the sergeant's men, could still intervene in the closing moments of the Last Stand. Perhaps she suggested to Steele some legend-in-the-making; some half-recognised symbol, defying bullets and evading capture to remain a free spirit in the ranges that lay around the rim of his well-ordered world. Steele's solution was simply to deny that Music had ever existed. Every time Ned Kelly had referred to 'my grey mare' he had actually said 'my *bay* mare', Steele claimed.

Nevertheless reporter George Allen searched for her in the bush around Glenrowan, Carrington sketched her from memory after witnessing the Last Stand and the Royal Commission would twice seek information about her, without success. Music had disappeared. The subsequent appearance of 'Ned Kelly's grey mare' with Jim and Kate Kelly in the so-called 'Kelly Show' represents one more complication of the mystery — or perhaps its solution.

In mid-morning the undertaker, John Grant, in a top hat fluttering with black ribbons, drove down past the ruins of the inn and across to McDonnell's hotel with two coffins in his buggy. Reporters flocked around the vehicle and posed for photographer Madeley, hamming it up with pencils and notebooks, before Grant continued to Eleven Mile Creek. This was probably as close as any reporter ever got to the wake being held at Maggie's home. This would not stop them producing 'eye witness' accounts of wild scenes as Maggie kept order with a shotgun, a crowd of 'some of the worst looking people ... I ever saw in my life' drank themselves into a dangerous state, and Tom Lloyd, 'lifting his right arm to heaven', swore to exact vengeance. In fact, as Wild Wright put it, 'Everything went off quietly.'

Mrs McDonnell, who may have given a *Herald* reporter a more sober picture of the wake, also told him that Ned's cousin, Kate Lloyd, 'who was very fond of him', had gone to Benalla. Mrs Mac added, 'She will break her heart, poor girl, if he is hanged.' Kate was waiting on the platform of the Benalla station at 9 a.m., 'the only relative present', when Ned was brought to board the train for Melbourne. She wore the tailored coat and ostrich-plumed hat chosen to celebrate Ned's triumph. Now, 'crying bitterly', she saw him wheeled onto the platform in an unharnessed spring cart escorted by eight armed police. He was swathed in a blanket, 'very calm and pale'. To James Ingram Junior, son of the Beechworth bookseller, 'He looked like a wild horse brought in from the hills.' Kate had already been at the Benalla lock-up with one of the McElroy girls to see Joe's body and bid 'an affectionate farewell' to Ned. At the station Kate moved towards Ned as a large crowd crushed forward for a glimpse of the fabled outlaw.

Several reporters witnessed this encounter without understanding what they had seen and one man recorded it. He had been at Glenrowan, drawing the ruins of the inn for the *Australian Pictorial Weekly*, a struggling magazine that was halfway through its 8-week life (it produced a Glenrowan issue without a drawing of Ned in armour and with a cover picture, 'Distribution of Medals by the Victorian Humane Society'). This anonymous artist, who had heard that Kate was 'Ned Kelly's favourite cousin', recorded their farewell.

Smoke pours from the Glenrowan Inn as the siege nears its end. One of the Wangaratta police still watches from cover, wary of a last suicidal sortie by Dan Kelly and Steve Hart. Both are dead. This is one of a series by the Wangaratta photographer Madeley, showing the burning of the inn. They are so remarkable for their time that, when shown them in the early 1950s, photographic expert Jack Cato thought they were stills from an early Kelly film.

Thomas Carrington's dramatic eye-witness sketch of the bodies of Dan and
Steve after the western wall of the Glenrowan Inn had burnt away (see
pp.270–1). Constable Dwyer, who earlier had run into the blazing building
to try and retrieve the two bodies, recalled that Dan Kelly was still wearing
his breastplate and 'the hand was outstretched' — both details matching the
left-hand body in Carrington's drawing. (*Sketcher*)

One of the bodies taken from the smouldering ruins of the Glenrowan Inn and laid on a sheet of
bark near Mrs Jones's table, rescued from the verandah of the burning inn. Two of the table's legs are
visible and an onlooker sits on it, dangling his feet at extreme right.

PARTING OF NED KELLY AND HIS COUSIN, MISS LLOYD.

AT BENALLA RAILWAY STATION.

Ned's farewell to Kate Lloyd at Benalla, the morning after his capture, recorded by an artist from the short-lived *Australian Pictorial Weekly*. The artist has done some justice to Kate's classical beauty, has managed to capture Ned's compassion for his beloved cousin and shows Hare towering in the background, self-satisfied despite a serious wrist wound.

When she went forward the crowd made way for her, and she went up to the bed and took leave of her doomed relative. 'One touch of nature makes the whole world kin;' and the spectators, by their sympathetic looks, showed that they completely forgot the crime of the one cousin in the grief of the other.

While the *Age* correspondent noted simply that Kate 'appeared terribly agitated', the *Pictorial Weekly* man watched the beautiful 16-year-old holding a handkerchief to her eyes as she bent over Ned. He saw a moment of restrained grief. He also saw the tenderness and compassion in Ned's face as he looked up at her; and the lack of compassion from Superintendent Hare as he watched the farewell. Ned was lifted into the guard's van, to be joined by Hare, the special six-man escort and Dr Charles Ryan. The train drew away and Kate 'cried without restraint', standing there in her sad finery.

As the train drummed towards Melbourne, with crowds flocking to see Ned at each station, Dr Ryan gave his arm and leg wounds expert attention.

He spoke very little, and seemed like a man in a trance, and glared at any strangers he saw. He had had no sleep the previous night. Most men wounded as he was would have been far more prostrated than he was but he had a splendid constitution ... I expected to find him, after the life he had been leading, very dirty; but his skin was as clean as if he had just come out of a Turkish bath. I attended to his wounds and now and then gave him some brandy and water. He seemed grateful but gave me the idea that he wished to die. Of course, in attending to his wounds, I gave him temporary pain, but he never complained in the least.

In spite of a high fever, Dr Ryan thought Ned would live, but qualified his opinion by pointing out that 'the prisoner is ... suffering from a severe mental shock, and moreover wants to die.'

In Melbourne several thousand people gathered at Spencer Street station behind the barricades used to control Melbourne Cup crowds. They saw only the arrival of Superintendent Hare. Ned had been taken off the train at North Melbourne and driven to the Melbourne Gaol in a wagonette with a strong police escort. As the vehicle arrived 'at a brisk pace' and disappeared through the Gaol's massive bluestone gateway, a crowd of 600 or 700 responded 'mildly' to a call for three cheers. The *Argus* was unsure whether the gesture was 'a recognition of the success of the police officers' or a display of sympathy for Ned and 'recognition of the prisoner's reckless daring'.

Passed into the hands of the gaol governor, J. B. Castieau, Ned was transferred to a water bed in the prison hospital, under the care of Dr Shields, who proceeded to issue the sort of bulletins we associate with royalty.

Ned was also visited by Father Aylward of St Patrick's, who had been alerted by Dean Gibney. After a brief meeting with Ned, the priest accepted the duty of seeing Mrs Kelly and breaking to her the news of Dan's death and Ned's capture. When Ellen was brought from the prison laundry to see the priest, she probably expected bad news. On the Sunday night she had dreamt of a clash between the Gang and the police, but it was still a cruel blow. She took it well, and was spared work for the rest of the day; but when Castieau visited her she cried uncontrollably and pleaded to see Ned. The governor promised she could visit her son as soon as his condition permitted.

Castieau was a decent, just man. He would soon find that ordinary standards did not apply to his latest inmate. On the one hand, treatment of him would be exemplary; he must be nursed back to health as soon as possible to face trial and execution. On the other hand, nothing must stand in the way of that confidently predicted outcome; no opportunity given for escape by force of arms, suicide or legal loophole. Every scrap of paper concerning Ned that passed over Castieau's desk would be subjected to scrutiny by the Chief Secretary (whoever he may be after the imminent election) and the Sheriff, the redoubtable Colonel Rede, who had presided over the government camp during the Eureka Stockade rebellion and had been an architect of the massacre that destroyed it.

The monster had been captured and brought to this bastion of British civilisation. Decency and justice would prevail, even if a thoroughly indecent conspiracy of injustice must be mobilised to guarantee that end. Ned Kelly was presumed guilty and must not be proved innocent.

◆

WITH NED AND HARE gone, the Benalla police station remained a focus of great tensions. Standish had brought a telegram from the Governor congratulating only Hare on the destruction of the Gang. Sadleir objected and Standish accused him of being 'mad with jealousy'. Eventually, the Governor's secretary produced a more diplomatic message.

Sadleir suggested that Standish address a victory parade of all the police. When they were formed up, Standish refused to say a word until the Aboriginal troopers had been removed.

The slate-coloured clouds rolling up from the ranges that day threatened much more than rain. With the chill winds came stories of threats against Steele, Dowsett, Senior Constable Kelly, Curnow, Bracken, Johnston, the Sherritt family, the volunteer Charles Rawlins ... The threats were taken seriously. Curnow, who had already been brought to Benalla, was ordered to Melbourne; Dowsett was transferred to Queenscliff; a party of police were stationed at Glenrowan to protect Bracken; and Aaron Sherritt's brothers were taken into the police force. Steele's greyhound was poisoned and a rumour spread that Kate Kelly had killed the sergeant — a rumour so quickly and widely believed that Sadleir had to deny it in a telegram to Standish. A furphy that Charles Rawlins had been shot by sympathisers would produce the revelation that he had been forced to leave his property and seek compensation in Melbourne.

The eye of the hurricane was Maggie's hut on Eleven Mile Creek and the pair of handsome coffins. Sadleir could protest, truthfully enough, that the stories of the wake had been wildly exaggerated, but there was no exaggeration in the story that the families were refusing to surrender the two bodies for an inquest. During the day Tom Lloyd left the wake and rode into Benalla to ask for Joe's body. He was told it could not be handed over for burial until after an inquest, which was scheduled for the following day, the third day after his death.

When Senior Constable Kelly advised him, 'Keep out of the way and behave yourself,' Tom replied, 'Oh, for God's sake don't interfere with us; we have done you no harm. Be satisfied with the work you have already done and leave us and the poor girls in peace; our load is hard to bear.' A *Herald* reporter noted scornfully that there were tears in his eyes.

Standish was still in Benalla, likely to inflame the sympathisers as effectively as he inflamed almost everyone else. That evening, while 'friends of the deceased' continued to beg for Joe's body, Standish pre-empted the inquest and, with Robert McBean J.P., conducted a hurried, semi-secret 'inquiry' into Joe's death. Standish then ordered immediate burial. The body was stripped, wrapped in canvas and smuggled into a pauper's grave without priest or mourners. It was 'a great disappoint-ment' to the sympathisers — a provocative action unlikely to encourage the surrender of the two charred corpses for an inquest. Dick Hart announced, 'We have got the bodies and we intend sticking to them.'

While Ned lay on the prison water bed, enjoying his first sleep in at least three nights, the phantom army and the forces of the Queen prepared for a confrontation. Dan's and Steve's funeral was set for the following afternoon, Wednesday.

Overnight the oil drum of blasting powder and the coils of fuse arrived at the Benalla police station. For Sadleir this was a disturbing metaphor of the situation at Greta, yet, with Standish at his elbow, he must proceed with the inquest. The coroner, Mr Bickerton J.P. and his clerk, Mr Eli, would leave for Greta at 9 next morning.

That night, despite cold and rain, pro-Kelly and anti-Kelly groups staged several clashes in Benalla, three of them in the main street and one pitched battle in a paddock near the telegraph office lasting for three hours. At McDonnell's hotel Wild Wright and Mrs Mac were seen in whispered conversation until late into the night as Wild covered the backs of more than a dozen telegram forms with notes. About thirty mourners stayed at Maggie's overnight in preparation for the funeral. They found what shelter they could outside the house and 'lay on sacks until the day'.

Wednesday dawned grey and wet. Senior Constable Kelly and five troopers left Benalla for Glenrowan, to be joined by three men from Wangaratta, ready to move to Greta. At 9 a.m. Coroner Bickerton and his clerk prepared to leave for Eleven Mile Creek to claim the bodies of Dan and Steve. Sadleir had not provided 'a conveyance' for them and incredibly, the two gentlemen could not find a suitable vehicle any-where in town. While the *Argus* would say bluntly that they 'altogether seemed disinclined to undertake the duty', it is obvious that Sadleir was doing nothing to encourage their departure, now that Standish had returned to Melbourne.

The situation at Eleven Mile was becoming critical as scores of horse-men converged on Maggie's hut. Dick Hart was reported as saying that, 'If the police came for the bodies of Dan and Hart, they would have to fight for them.'

At 11.30 Benalla stationmaster Clement Stephens telegraphed the Melbourne traffic manager.

It is reported that Hart's brother and others about fifty armed men are at Greta intending to resist the holding of inquest there today. A body of police armed left by the morning train & also a detachment from Wan-garatta. As there is likely to be bloodshed & other special trains run will you please send me a good operator with sounder instrument so that I may open an office at Glenrowan if I find it necessary. Great excitement prevails everywhere & other necessary precautions you would wish me to take please advise.

Meanwhile, preparations for the funeral continued at Maggie's home.

Large numbers of persons arrived on horseback from all parts of the district, the most of them with bundles on their arms, these contained their Sunday suits of clothes; and they nearly one and all retired to a creek near the hut, where they conducted their toilet and changed their garments.

For a time, Sadleir considered the possibility of Mr Bickerton con-ducting an inquest at Glenrowan and issuing permission for the burial from there. Then, at last, he received approval from the Crown Law Office to waive the inquest. It had been decided, said the *Argus*, 'that the game was not worth the candle'. Alex Tone J.P. drew up 'a curious cer-tificate' — a magisterial order of interment — for each body, and these were despatched to Eleven Mile Creek. It is unclear when or if they arrived.

In the early afternoon Dan's and Steve's funeral procession left Maggie's house — eighty horsemen and eight vehicles in a sad cavalcade up through the Gap and out along the Moyhu road on a 9-mile journey across the Oxley flats to the Greta cemetery. There, on a low rise by the Kilfera crossroad, the coffins were placed in a single grave, 8 feet square. There was no priest: the service was conducted by Michael Bryan, a Greta farmer and Rate Collector for the Oxley Shire.

Between the muddy flats and the leaden sky, an icy wind blew from the south, promising the first snow of winter on the surrounding ranges and sleet on lower land. The hundred mourners lingered in silence, all eyes on the tallest man at the grave-side. It was Jim Kelly, at last emerging from the shadows of the last five months to share with Dick Hart the rite of shovelling the first soil onto their brothers' coffins. The two men waited, still and windswept, for what seemed a long time. Suspecting a change of heart by the authorities, were they leaving the grave open as a gesture of defiance or to avoid the possibility of exhumation? The long, straight roads from Benalla and Wangaratta remained empty, however, and the symbolic clod of earth eventually drummed on each coffin. The mourners straggled off to their homes and the grave was filled in.

At 3 p.m., while the funeral was in progress, Melbourne Gaol governor Castieau came to see Ned in the hospital and told him that his mother was on her way, urging him, 'Keep calm and be quiet.' Perhaps not appreciating that the advice was in the interests of his health, Ned retorted, 'Yes, and tell her to be quiet, too.'

When the slight, grey-clad figure was brought into the ward and approached her son's bed, both fought against the emotion of the moment, watched as they were by prison officials, a doctor, two other patients and a wardsman. One of these witnesses later described, with proper Victorian stiffness, this extraordinary reunion. It was the first meeting between Ellen and her son since she had surrendered for trial 20 months before.

> Ned, though not demonstrative towards his mother, or exhibiting very much emotion, nevertheless showed that he was sensible of the painfulness of the meeting. He exhibited a proper filial affection according to his own rude nature; and she, on her part, though of that class known as bushwomen, hardened by a rough and almost savage life, exhibited that maternal instinct and solicitude which is hardly ever absent. She is described as a woman who on a farm would probably be agreeable in her way, and useful.

Their conversation was considered 'general but unimportant', apart from Ellen's expression of 'deep regret' at the deaths of Dan, Steve and Joe ('my brave fellows' Ned called them), and Ned's explanation of how he came to be captured: 'My grey mare would have carried me away, armour and all, if I had chosen to go, and I could have escaped, but I decided to see it out.'

It was starchy and impersonal on the surface, but this was the mother who had wept uncontrollably the previous day. This was the son who had offered to surrender on a capital charge if his mother was released. Their behaviour at this meeting was a question of dignity, an unexpected quality in a woman who had led an 'almost savage' life and in a man with a 'rude nature' — unexpected, that is, to those who knew little of the bush and its people. It was perhaps Castieau who commented, 'The interview . . . was of a very affecting character to those who witnessed it.'

After about 20 minutes Ellen was taken back to the prison laundry, assured by Castieau that she would see her son again — though the gaol governor did not put it so baldly — before his execution.

That evening's *Herald* carried what were, for the place and time, banner headlines: 'FIFTY SYMPATHISERS ARMED' and 'ANOTHER OUTBREAK THREATENED', and a Benalla correspondent wrote, 'Dick Hart swears that he will head another and stronger Gang than that of Ned Kelly and take to the bush.' This story was largely inspired by that morning's telegram from the Benalla stationmaster. The Railways traffic manager had referred it to Standish, who immediately released its contents to the *Herald*.

Sadleir continued to hose down both sympathiser unrest and press speculation, though in his telegram to Standish denying that Kate had killed Sergeant Steele, he admitted, 'There is a deal of ill blood stirring, and I cannot at present reduce the strength of the force stationed here.' (In fact, he was calling in men from outlying districts to reinforce Benalla, Wangaratta and Beechworth.) Standish also showed this telegram to reporters. Unlike Sadleir he was keen to advertise the explosive condition of the north-east. Recognition of the scale of the threat — by the public and, more importantly, by the government — would help to justify police behaviour at Glenrowan and guarantee that Ned Kelly was regarded as an establishment-threatening monster. Perhaps most importantly, it would help win police immunity from the government economy campaign demanded by the huge cost of the coming International Exhibition and the vast building created in Melbourne to house it.

Standish's campaign was well-timed. Press euphoria at the destruction of the Gang ('A disgrace is removed from Victoria . . . the men-wolves have perished') was already giving way to a strengthening wave of criticism in editorial columns and letters from readers. Even the previous day's *Age*, which had rejoiced at the passing of the 'men-wolves', also started to count the cost. That evening's *Herald* had strong words on police readiness to fire into a hotel packed with civilians, and the following day published a letter which proclaimed, 'In place of sending messages of congratulation upon the gallant deed — Heaven save the mark! — let us appoint a day of prayer.' The *Herald* called for an inquiry and the *Age* quickly followed with the firm comment, 'The moral pointed out by the police operation seems to be that the constabulary force requires reorganization.'

The rot had set in. The *Argus* fought a rearguard action with an apologia for the police, while also urging 'a searching inquiry'. Before the month was out even Beechworth's staunch *Advertiser* would concede, 'the tone of the force has deteriorated', specifying 'inefficiency' and 'poor organization and discipline'.

Perhaps the most remarkable statement of disillusionment came from the journalist James Stanley, the famous 'Vagabond'. In a scarifying attack on the police he declared, 'The want of judgement displayed by them was criminal. The indiscriminate firing into a house filled with women and children was a most disgraceful act.' By contrast, he found the exploits of the Gang 'more startling than anything in the most thrilling of Reynolds' stories of highwaymen and robbers ... Bushrangers clad in armour, attacking a train and standing a siege of many hours, this is more wonderful than the wildest dreams of fancy indulged in by the authors of boys' novels. Truth is indeed stranger than fiction.'

Sadleir made an early, ill-grounded attempt to fight the tide. The day after the burial of Dan and Steve he released to the press a story that old Martin Cherry had *not* been mortally wounded by police fire. Cherry had been deliberately shot by Ned Kelly, Sadleir alleged, for refusing to hold back a window blind at the beginning of the battle. Sadleir claimed to have written statements to this effect from three of the Gang's prisoners.

One of the three was probably Louis Piazzi, who also came up with a story that George Metcalf had been shot accidentally by Ned Kelly, not, as Metcalf himself claimed, by police fire. Piazzi had been the only civilian witness at the undercover inquiry into Joe's death. His undue eagerness to say what the police wanted to hear may have been related to a compensation claim for horses shot by the police at Glenrowan. Piazzi and a fellow contractor claimed £40, which was approved without query.

Sadleir's ill-advised claim that Ned had shot Cherry quickly backfired. Within a day the *Age* was saying, 'The statement that Kelly shot the unfortunate man Cherry is generally discredited.' It remained for the *Benalla Standard* to publish eyewitness John Larkins's account of how Cherry was mortally wounded by a police bullet. Larkins concluded with a disturbing allegation.

> I wish to observe that some members of the police force have visited me since the Glenrowan tragedy, and have implied by indirect threats to keep my mouth shut respecting how Cherry came by his death. But

thinking it best to let the public know the truth is my only excuse for trespassing on your space.

Standish, ever the political animal, sniffed the changing wind and, within a week of Glenrowan, wrote to the Chief Secretary urging 'an inquiry ... into the whole proceedings and management of the police force, from the perpetration of the murders to the present date'. Standish suggested only that the inquiry be 'full and impartial' and open to everyone but the press.

Within a month the radical Graham Berry would again be premier of the colony. The next month Standish would 'retire' after twenty-two years as Chief Commissioner. Six months later a Royal Commission would begin its inquiry into the Kelly Outbreak, open to the press and chaired by Francis Longmore, vitriolic critic of Standish and the police during the reign of Harry Power.

For the present, Ned Kelly's body continued to fight off infection and the numbed, unco-ordinated body of the sympathisers also began to gather strength. On Monday 5 July, exactly one week after Ned's capture and the very day that Standish wrote his letter requesting an inquiry, Maggie Skilling, Tom Lloyd and Jim McElroy arrived in Melbourne to be 'triumphantly escorted' from Spencer Street station by a large crowd of supporters. Whatever might happen in the Kelly Country, the fight for Ned's life would be waged in the courts.

21

A LAST FIGHT IN BEECHWORTH

8 JULY – 12 AUGUST 1880

The Kelly Outbreak continued to claim victims for months, even years, after the destruction of the Gang. George Metcalf, wounded in the eye at Glenrowan, died four months later; Jane Jones, always a frail child, never regained her health completely and succumbed to a lung disorder after less than two years, before she had turned 18. The most unusual casualty was the wife of Constable McGuirk of Euroa. Knowing he was collecting evidence for the Kelly trial, she developed an obsessive fear 'that her husband would meet with violence from the hands of the Kelly sympathisers'. Her death, barely two months after Glenrowan, was said to have been 'caused from the anxiety occasioned by this impression'.

McGuirk was only one member of a police team working under the direction of Detective Sub-inspector Kennedy, a leader of the party that almost caught the Gang in the Murray floodwaters. This time Kennedy was determined that he wouldn't miss his man as he pieced together a body of evidence that would give Ned no chance of escape from the gallows. Even Captain Standish played a part, personally writing a list of questions to be put to the Jerilderie bank manager Tarleton, now working in New Zealand. The search for more elusive witnesses included quaint 'Missing Friends' entries in the *Police Gazette*.

While the Crown marshalled its forces against him, Ned was carefully isolated from any source of support. Ramsay, the Chief Secretary, refused all applications to visit the prisoner — from Maggie, Tom and Jim, and even from the Sisters of Mercy. By 8 August 100 requests had been rejected. Kate Kelly appeared at the gaol in deep mourning, black-clad, black-veiled, and asked to see her brother. She too was refused and sadly slipped away, dodging a crowd of gawkers.

Detectives dogged the steps of Tom, Maggie and the others in their increasingly forlorn expeditions from the Robert Burns Hotel in Lonsdale Street to the gaol, the government offices in the Treasury, even

to St Francis Church and the waxworks, while application after application passed from Gaol Governor Castieau to the Sheriff to the Chief
Secretary, back to the Sheriff, back to Castieau ... with a comment, signature and date to record each handling and demonstrate that it was all
properly done. Defeated, Ned's people returned home.

This policy of keeping Ned in isolation — to be described as 'a monstrous tyranny' — sprang in part from the belief that friends or relatives
would give him the means to kill himself and cheat the hangman. In the
darkest corners of the official conscience this passively brutal treatment
of an untried, unconvicted remand prisoner also represented fear and a
desire for revenge. The more sinister reason for Ned's solitary confine-
ment was to deny him, for as long as possible, the means to prepare an
effective defence.

The Crown was going to remarkable lengths to secure 'justice' in this
case. One particularly shabby ploy would be revealed when Maggie
tried to obtain money for Ned's defence by taking out a mortgage on her
mother's 88 acres. Ellen Kelly had borrowed money from the Land
Credit Bank of Collins Street with the fully-paid-up, seven-year lease on
her selection as collateral. Maggie discharged her mother's debt and had
negotiated a new mortgage on the property when she was told that the
Lands Department had refused to grant title, 'on the application of the
police'. The Crown was trying to prevent the family from raising money
on its major asset: the £62 equity in Eleven Mile Creek.

When this tactic was exposed in an affidavit before the Central
Criminal Court the more liberal papers, the *Herald* and *Age*, accurately
reported the contents of the affidavit, while the conservative *Daily
Telegraph* and *Argus* omitted all reference to police intervention, clearly
concerned that justice was not appearing to be done.

Despite a recurrence of fever, Ned's health steadily improved under
the care of Dr Shields and his nurse, prisoner David Henry, 'the erst-
while celebrated financier of Collins Street'. After a series of remands,
his committal hearing was set for Monday 2 August in the City Police
Court. Ned did not speak to his solicitor — William Zincke of
Beechworth — until the Thursday before the hearing, nine days after
he had first sought the means to arrange his defence. Through the years
Zincke had defended Joe Byrne, Aaron Sherritt, Mrs Kelly and the sympathisers. He was a small man with an impish face, a balding pate and a
shock of grey curls, who thoroughly looked the part when he played his
cello in a Beechworth string ensemble. Nevertheless he had shown in
the sympathiser trials that he was a talented advocate, with the added
stature of a newly-elected MLA, 'the junior member for the Ovens'.
During his election campaign a heckler had asked what he was going to
do with the Chinese and Germans and Zincke had countered:

What are you going to do with *me*? My father was a Hungarian, my mother was an English woman, I was born in Jamaica; I was suckled by a yellow gal: I was educated in Great Britain; and I was transported — so to speak — to Australia (great laughter).

Zincke had been approached by Tom and Maggie and, after a formal written request from Ned on the Wednesday, agreed to defend him. In the gaol hospital next morning Ned, in pyjamas and canvas slippers, greeted the man of law with a wary, 'You are a member of Parliament, and I suppose if I say anything to you it will be used for the benefit of the Government.'

On Zincke's assurance 'that he would not make public anything he heard', Ned immediately relaxed and spoke freely, claiming, 'in consequence of the tyranny of the police he had been compelled to take up arms to protect his sisters' (which could be read as another admission that he had shot Fitzpatrick). Zincke agreed to deliver a letter to Kate on his way back to Beechworth and, before leaving, urged Ned 'not to show his hand until the trial took place'. In Beechworth the following day, he was nonetheless prepared to tell an *Advertiser* journalist,

He ... justified his actions, and that of his three associates in shooting the police, by stating that the latter had pursued the gang with the intention of taking the lives of its members, who had simply acted on the defensive. He also blamed Constable Fitzpatrick as being the primary cause of the bushranging outbreak.

A credible defence was taking shape: a blackguard constable as the cause of the police pursuit which threatened the lives of Ned and Dan, doubly justifying their decision to defend themselves.

Zincke also gave the reporter an interesting portrait of Ned.

He is ... an extremely well and powerfully made young man, whose features are well formed, with dark brown whiskers and black hair and eyebrows. His demeanour was throughout the interview calm and self-possessed, and his address was rather that of an educated man than otherwise. [Tom Lloyd said that he 'spoke more like a priest than a man'.] He is perfectly resigned to his impending fate ...

The next day, Friday, Tom and Maggie returned to Melbourne in readiness for Monday's trial in the City Police Court. In a surprise move, at 5 on the Saturday afternoon Ned was taken to a hurriedly convened court in the hospital kitchen and Monday's hearing was secretly transferred to Beechworth, foreshadowing a further remand to Beechworth on the Friday.

A press engraving by an unusually trusted artist shows Gaol Governor Castieau and a magistrate with whiskers like a cocker spaniel's ears, both seated at a scrubbed kitchen table while the formidable team of Crown Prosecutor Smyth and Crown Solicitor Gurner face them to apply for the change of venue. A rather smug-looking Constable McIntyre poises in the background, ready to officially identify the prisoner. Incongruous in pyjamas and slippers, Ned hunches glumly on a form beside the table, elbows on knees, hands clasped.

A startlingly different figure limped out into the gaol courtyard at 8.30 the next morning under heavy escort. Despite the crippling pain of his foot and leg wounds (it was barely more than four weeks since his capture), Ned managed 'an impudent bearing' in a stylish new outfit: blue serge jacket, check waistcoat, Bedford cord trousers and a white hat (which he disliked) slouched rakishly over one ear. His boots were new, the right one cut to the shape of a slipper. He was helped into a hansom cab beside Sergeant Steele and driven out through the massive gateway of the prison into the empty, Sunday morning streets. A wagonette carrying three plainclothed troopers — McIntyre, Bracken and Falkiner — followed.

At the same time a mysterious special train was leaving Spencer Street — a light, speedy locomotive which drew the ministerial saloon carriage carrying two senior railway officials behind drawn blinds, with a guard's van fore and aft. Even the driver did not know the train's purpose or destination, told only that he would stop at Newmarket 3 miles on. At Newmarket station, Ned hobbled aboard the forward van with Steele and the escort — now reinforced to six. The party settled on platform chairs by the van's windows and the train accelerated northwards.

Leaving prison and boarding the train had wrought an extraordinary change in Ned, perhaps echoing release from Pentridge and the journey home six years before. It was as though he was being carried back to sunnier days in the landscape and among the people he loved. He was in high spirits, poking his head out of the window to exchange banter with jockeys exercising horses on Flemington Racecourse, pointing out his birthplace at Beveridge and showing easy familiarity with the stations along the line. Then, as they came in sight of the Strathbogie Ranges towards Euroa, he became shadowed and said quietly, 'There they are. Will I ever be there again?' The troopers exchanged glances and some smiled.

The steady climb towards Glenrowan brought another darkening of his mood as he approached the site of the grand dream that was also the place of death and capture, with Steele sitting beside him in a tweed hat and jacket like those he had worn during the Last Stand. As the train passed through the railway crossing and came in sight of the ruins of the inn, Ned murmured, 'A good man fell there.'

Steele couldn't resist a jibe. 'You weren't such good shots as you thought you were.' Ned's emotion exploded in anger. He lunged to his feet, tore off his coat and, as the six troopers moved to restrain him, hurled it at Steele ('whom he advised to go to India for safety'). This emotion discharged, he quickly regained his good humour for the rest of the journey.

At Beechworth there was another flash of anger while Sadleir and a police contingent supervised his transfer to a cab. Constable Alexander, one of the men from the Sherritt hut, let his horse venture threateningly close. Ned tried to kick it away but was held back and lifted into the cab.

As the cab and its mounted police escort entered the bottom of Camp Street and turned into High Street, Ned saw Zincke standing with two women on the balcony of the corner's Empire Hotel and waved his hat in greeting. He probably didn't realise that the women with Zincke were Aaron Sherritt's widow and her mother.

That night Ned settled into a roomy cell at the rear of Beechworth Gaol near the governor's quarters. It was unheated and bitterly cold, but no great hardship for Ned. Constable McIntyre, guarding him that night, came down with bronchitis which eventually developed into pleurisy.

At a special hearing in the gaol on Monday morning, Ned was remanded until the Friday. Before returning to Beechworth Zincke had at last gained permission from the Chief Secretary for Maggie to visit her brother, but when she reached Beechworth on the Wednesday, only two days before the start of the trial, the gaol authorities refused to let her see him. This was a turning point.

Tom and Maggie had decided that their position was weakened by Zincke being a member of the Opposition. If there was also a member of the Government on the defence team, surely this would give them a better chance of gaining permission to see Ned and prepare the strongest possible case. And who could be better for the job than solicitor David Gaunson, member for Ararat, a restless tilter at windmills?

They had spoken informally with Gaunson before leaving Melbourne and he had clearly shown interest. They told Ned this in a letter on the Thursday morning and he immediately telegraphed Gaunson, who went straight to the Chief Secretary, obtained permission to see Ned that night and prepared to catch the 3 p.m. train to Beechworth with his brother and partner, William.

Meanwhile there was a bombshell: Zincke flatly refused to work with Gaunson and resigned from the case. More than a week's preparation was wasted. Ned would face trial at 10 the next morning, defended by a man who had arrived in Beechworth less than eleven hours earlier, knowing nothing about the case.

The gaol governor met David Gaunson at the train and took him straight to see Ned, who was roused from sleep after midnight for the interview. Gaunson later described their conversation to an *Age* reporter:

> On [his] entering the cell, Ned Kelly gave Mr Gaunson a keen and searching glance, and said 'Good evening' in an abstracted manner. He was evidently taking stock of his legal visitor; the reserve in his demeanour was only momentary; the doubt of strangeness passed away almost at once. When Mr Gaunson confidently took his seat on the prisoner's bed, he at once became cordial, communicative and unreserved.

The man now thrown together with Ned in this last fight was — and remains — an enigma. Gaunson was 36, tall and spare, his long, handsome face given gravity by a sombre moustache and closely trimmed beard. Sydney-born, he had completed his education in Victoria and entered the law at 16 as an articled clerk to his brother-in-law, James McPherson Grant, who had won deserved fame as unpaid defender of the Eureka rebels and undeserved notoriety as an architect of Victoria's Land Acts. An attorney at 23, David Gaunson set out to follow in Grant's footsteps as a hard-drinking, radical politician and reformer and, in 1875, on his fourth attempt, won a seat in parliament. To Gaunson the end justified the means, and he pursued his goals with a ruthless energy and self-confidence that made him fight against the harness of party politics taking hold in Victoria ahead of the other colonies. Alfred Deakin, a rare combination of political animal and idealist, left a candid portrait of his colleague:

> Endowed with a musical voice, good presence, fine flow of language, great quickness of mind, readiness of retort and a good deal of industry, ability and humour, he was only disqualified from marked success by his utter instability, egregious egotism, want of consistency and violence of temper.

When Gaunson died in 1909, the *Labor Call* had no cause to admire him (he had won his last seat in parliament as a Labor candidate then deserted the party) but would concede: 'Mr Gaunson was a decidedly able lawyer, and there was probably truth in his boast that he had cheated Pentridge out of more deserving tenants than any other practitioner in Victoria.'

James McPherson Grant, Gaunson's legal and political mentor, was a republican — so rabid that 'he was accustomed to say [probably when drunk] that his proper period was the French Revolution when he could have seen the heads of the aristocrats rolling on the scaffold'. No doubt this extremism made a part of Gaunson's political coat-of-many-colours. Grant had helped rescue Eureka's digger revolutionaries from the scaffold. Did Gaunson glimpse in Ned Kelly a similar challenge to the old regime of landed wealth and imperial puppetry? In any case the man considered 'as unstable as water' would wage a three-month battle to save Ned Kelly, with a zeal that set his political career back several years and damaged his standing in the legal profession. Those three months of his life may well have been David Gaunson's finest hour — effectively obscured by his involvement with such controversial figures as Tommy Bent and John Wren. Ned had a champion.

In a 45-minute conversation the two men agreed that a further remand was essential to prepare an adequate defence. Ned told Gaunson:

All I want is a full and fair trial, and a chance to make my side heard. Until now, the police have had all the say, and have had it all their own way. If I get a full and fair trial, I don't care how it goes; but I know this — the public will see that I was hunted and hounded on from step to step; they will see that I am not the monster I have been made out. What I have done has been under strong provocation.

He also complained bitterly at the repeated refusals to allow a visit by Maggie:

I have been kept here like a wild beast. If they were afraid to let anyone come near me they might have kept at a distance and watched; but it seems to me to be unjust when I am on trial for my life, to refuse to allow those I put confidence in to come within cooey of me; why they won't so much as let me have a change of clothes brought in . . .

This encouraging conversation ended at 1.15 and resumed at 8 a.m. after a police escort smuggled Ned into the prisoners' room of the Beechworth court house by a back door, two hours before the trial was due to start. The upstairs gallery of the court, reserved for women, was filled by 9.15. The *Age* noted that 'many . . . were very young — many mere girls'. Just before 10 the doors to the body of the court were opened and 'the place was instantly rushed, and every available space of standing room occupied'. Beechworth's *Advertiser* regretted that the crowd included 'a large number of boys' who clearly saw Ned 'in the light of a hero of romance'.

Apart from a formidable police presence, the fact that this was no ordinary committal hearing was made clear from the start. Captain Standish entered with Police Magistrate Foster and sat beside him on the Bench. Foster would insist that 'he was sitting alone, and that Captain Standish simply took a seat on the bench by courtesy'. Almost immediately a side door opened and Ned was escorted into court by a group of police, including Steele and Senior Constable Kelly.

He was unhandcuffed and unrestrained in his movements; but as he appeared weak, and hopped on one leg, there was little fear of his making any attempt to escape. Kelly looked somewhat thinner and paler than when taken prisoner at Glenrowan. He appeared to have suffered a good deal; and although his manner was more impudent and indifferent, he was evidently much changed ... On entering the dock he placed his back against the wall and scanned the crowd assembled in the body of the court with evident interest and pleasure, occasionally smiling and nodding to friends he saw among the throng, including Mrs Skillion, Hart, and two Lloyds, and a number of others ...

Ned was formally charged with the murder of Lonigan and Scanlon at Stringybark Creek and all eyes were on Gaunson. He asked for Ned to be allowed to sit as he was 'lame and maimed' and immediately applied for a remand to give him time to prepare the defence, his request vigorously opposed by Smyth, the Crown Prosecutor. Gaunson quickly swung to the attack, castigating the Crown over denial of visiting rights to his client:

It has been said that it is dangerous to let [his friends and relatives] see him. What nonsense! Could his relatives not have been allowed to speak through a grating? Could they not have been allowed to ask who do you wish to defend you? What possible objection could be raised to such a course? What danger was there in it? There was none. To deny him that right is a monstrous tyranny and I should fail in my duty if I did not denounce it.

Gaunson was in fine form and the disapproving Crown Solicitor leant across to Smyth, muttering, 'He has no right to be here.'

Gaunson pointed accusingly, and boomed, 'The Crown Solicitor says I have no right to be here!'

Smyth flashed back, 'You had no right to hear that; it was said to me!'

Gaunson turned to the court with a derisive half-smile. 'I venture to say that if this is to be the style of the prosecution the prisoner will be acquitted.'

Magistrate Foster quickly granted a remand — though only until 2 p.m. — and the court was adjourned.

Maggie and Tom pushed forward through the crowd towards the dock, and, as police moved to block them, reached out to catch Ned's hand. Their fingers locked briefly. 'I've tried hard to see you,' Maggie told him. 'But they would not let me.'

Ned half-smiled. 'It looks as if they will not let me see you now even — goodbye.'

'Never mind, Ned,' Maggie called as constables pushed between them, 'They are only a lot of curs.'

Ned's reply was for the police as much as his sister. 'There's one native that's no cur, and he will show them that yet.'

During the adjournment Gaunson read through a pile of *Arguses* and began to familiarise himself with the sequence of events at Stringybark. When the court resumed at 2 p.m. he applied for a week's remand 'in view of the immense mass of facts which had been collected by *The Argus*'. Foster refused, and the question of visitors to the prisoners was outside his jurisdiction. The case would proceed.

Police reinforcements had been arriving in Beechworth all day, 'in small bodies from all parts of the country'. As a crowd of several hundred onlookers jostled outside the doors of the packed court, Smyth outlined the prosecution case and called his star witness, Constable McIntyre, who took the stand to give a lengthy description of the Stringybark Creek expedition and his often-told and often-varied story of the death of Lonigan. Describing how four men 'each holding a gun' appeared from spear grass and ordered Lonigan and himself to bail up, McIntyre told the court:

> I noticed the right-hand man of the party particularly, and saw his gun pointed directly towards my breast. I immediately held out my arms horizontally. As soon as I did so, I saw the same man remove the gun a little towards his right hand and fire it, at Lonigan, who had started to run. Lonigan was standing on the opposite side of the fire to me at a distance of ten or twelve feet. He was running towards a tree and was about forty yards distant from the man who fired at him. I heard him falling immediately after the gun was fired. He had taken about four or five steps before he fell. Did not see him fall, but heard him breathing heavily and stertorously. The prisoner, Edward Kelly, was the man I alluded to as the 'man on the right'.

This time, McIntyre had made no mention of Lonigan drawing or even trying to draw his revolver, but later quoted a remark from Dan Kelly: 'He was a plucky fellow, did you see how he caught at his revolver?'

McIntyre was still describing his long conversation with Ned before the return of Kennedy and Scanlon when Magistrate Foster adjourned the court until 10 on the Saturday morning. As Ned was being driven back to the gaol, a pack of boys ran behind the cab. Ned smiled and pretended to shoot at them.

The next day, as wind rumbled in the court's chimney and rain slashed against the high windows, McIntyre continued and concluded his evidence. There were seventy-seven closely written foolscap pages of it which would take an hour and a half to read back for his confirmation.

That day artist Julian Ashton began a watercolour of Ned in the dock with Steele standing guard. Suspicious that the portrait was 'for legal purposes', Ned asked for 'something to keep the cold air off'. Given a scarlet-lined, possum-skin rug, he drew it around him and raised it across one arm to screen his face from 'the gentleman with the brush and pencil' — a gesture which one unsympathetic reporter interpreted as an attempt to assume 'the bearing and appearance of a true brigand'.

In spite of Ned's attempt to thwart him, Ashton completed his paint-ing — an accurate portrait which featured as a full-page cover engraving for the *Illustrated Australian News* later that month. Ashton's portrayal of Ned in the handsome serge jacket — with his wounded left arm sup-ported by gripping a lapel and his crippled right fist resting confidently on the rail of the dock — evokes the image of him as a boxer. Ashton had captured the same defiant physical power, the same air of confi-dence. Ned was still a fighter, and no longer fighting alone.

When Gaunson moved to his cross-examination of McIntyre, he went for the jugular and forced the policeman into a number of damag-ing admissions. Some of these were perhaps more damaging than Gaun-son could realise, given his all-too-short time to study the events of Stringybark, but their significance was not lost on McIntyre or Ned. A reporter noted Ned 'smiling and looking towards his friends whenever a point is made'.

Gaunson pressed McIntyre on the party's unusually heavy armament and asked with heavy sarcasm, 'You did not take a cannon with you?'

'No,' McIntyre replied, hastening to add, 'we expected resistance', eventually admitting, 'we had about twenty spare cartridges each. *It is not usual to carry so much ammunition.*' [my italics]

McIntyre seemed to admit that Scanlon was already wounded when he fell to his knees after dismounting, tending to confirm Ned's version that he shot Scanlon while he was mounted. 'I will swear Scanlon did not fire a shot *and he was incapable afterwards as he fell on his knees.*' [my italics] He confidently stated, 'Prisoner fired the shot that took affect on Scanlon's right [side], yet admitted, 'I will not swear he [Ned] fired at Scanlon.'

Gaunson pressed McIntyre hard for having escaped on Kennedy's horse. 'Is it true that the instant Kennedy got off his horse you seized it and left him in the lurch?' This line of questioning would goad McIntyre into his once-ever admission that Kennedy was firing at Ned. 'The horse was restive and came towards me. *No horse could stand still between two men firing at each other.*' [my italics]

Before Gaunson had finished with the Crown's prime witness, McIntyre was 'suffering from such serious nervous excitement that he was several times nearly hysterical and during the adjournment had to be prescribed for.' Gaunson's closing remarks to the badly shaken policeman were scathing. 'I will leave you in the hands of a man better able to deal with you and turn you inside out in the Supreme Court.'

On one vital point, however, McIntyre had not been shaken. He con-tinued to deny that Lonigan had dived behind a log and was coming up to fire at Ned when he was killed. In his evidence he quoted the controversial interview with Ned in the Benalla lock-up, on the night of his capture.

> I said, 'When I held up my hands you shot Lonigan'. He said, 'No; Lonigan got behind some logs and pointed his revolver at me. Did you not see that?' I said, 'No; that is only nonsense.'

Apart from Ned there was another man who knew that McIntyre had committed perjury. Superintendent Sadleir, seated in the body of the court, knew what McIntyre had told him three days after Stringybark and he held a transcript of that statement.

> Lonigan was sitting on a log, and on hearing the call to throw up his hands, he put his hands to his revolver, at the same time slipping down for cover behind the log on which he had been sitting. Lonigan had his head above the level of the log and was about to use his revolver when he was shot through the head.

Yet John Sadleir, a thoroughly decent, 'austere and dignified' man of ancient Irish aristocracy, remained silent. Was it just that he saw his commitment to the Police Force taking precedence over justice? Or was it an acknowledgement that Ned Kelly was not really being tried for the murder of two policemen? Decent men like Sadleir knew that the British social-legal system which sought to indict Ned was deeply flawed, but — because they were decent — they believed in the ideals that *justified* it all, and those ideals must not be jeopardised by giving an inch to a man like Ned Kelly — a dangerous figurehead and focus of everything the decent man hated and feared.

Sitting on a pew-like bench, John Sadleir listened to McIntyre's evidence and kept his peace. Perhaps as balm to his conscience he published the text of McIntyre's statement thirty-three years later in his *Recollections of a Victorian Police Officer*. He might have breathed a long sigh of relief when no-one noticed that he had withheld this vital piece of evidence for all that time — or, if they had noticed, they too were thoroughly decent men, and understood.

The only other witness on the Saturday was Dr Reynolds of Mansfield, who described his examination of the police bodies and would eventually give his opinion that a wildcat had chewed off Kennedy's ear, scotching the slow-dying furphy that the sergeant had been mutilated by Ned.

On the Sunday, probably as a result of the sympathetic *Age* coverage of Gaunson's first meeting with Ned in Beechworth Gaol, Gaunson interviewed his client on behalf of the *Age* reporter and brought back some excellent copy, including what is perhaps the most famous statement of Ned's case.

I do not pretend that I have led a blameless life, or that one fault justifies another, but the public in judging a case like mine should remember that the darkest life may have a bright side, and that after the worst has been said against a man, he may, if he is heard, tell a story in his own rough way that will perhaps lead them to intimate the harshness of their thoughts against him, and find as many excuses for him as he would plead for himself. For my own part I do not care one straw about my life now for the result of the trial. I know very well from the stories I have been told of how I am spoken of, that the public at large execrate my name; the newspapers cannot speak of me with that patient toleration generally extended to men awaiting trial, and who are assumed according to the best of British justice, to be innocent until they are proved to be guilty; but I do not mind for I have outlived that care that curries public favor or denies the public frown. Let the hand of the law strike me down if it will, but I ask that my story might be heard and considered; not that I wish to avert any decree the law may deem necessary to vindicate justice, or win a word of pity from anyone. If my life teaches the public that men are made mad by bad treatment, and if the police are taught that they may not exasperate to madness men they persecute and illtreat, my life will not be entirely thrown away. People who live in large towns have no idea of the tyrannical conduct of the police in country places far removed from court; they have no idea of the harsh and over-bearing manner in which they execute their duty or how they neglect their duty and abuse their powers.

This statement was attacked by Beechworth's anti-Kelly *Advertiser* which claimed to recognise in it, 'too much of the big language used in parliament'. There is certainly some paraphrasing by Gaunson but, in the context of the whole interview and particularly in the light of widely reported statements to be made by Ned at his next trial, this testament deserves to be treated as a genuine expression of his views and at least as accurate as any other material drawn from him in interviews after his capture.

On monday morning Kate Lloyd appeared in the court house gallery and Ned 'boldly kissed his hand to her'. Kate 'immediately returned the salute'. A *Daily Telegraph* reporter, who did not know her name but had heard she was Ned's 'sweetheart', thought her 'good-looking, elegant in her manner, quietly but still well attired'.

That day and the next saw a parade of witnesses reporting Ned's version of the police shootings: bank manager Scott, the Faithfull's Creek groom Stephens, hawker Gloster and his lad Beecroft, the kangaroo hunters Macdougall and Dudley — all from Euroa; and bank accountant Living from Jerilderie.

Stephens took a mauling from Gaunson. He described himself as 'a groom out of employment' but under relentless cross-examination was forced to admit that, until recently, he had been engaged as a detective (at Glenrowan, helping Bracken to watch Maggie's house) and hoped to be re-employed by the police.

Some of Gaunson's toughest questioning was reserved for Senior Constable Kelly, who had taken McIntyre to see Ned the night of his capture and badger him about Stringybark and the Fitzpatrick incident. Kelly was forced to admit that he had failed to caution Ned that this material might be used in evidence, in spite of the fact that it was 'a general rule' to provide such a warning. The implication was that normal standards of justice did not apply to Ned Kelly. When the Senior Constable described the siege of Glenrowan, Gaunson again swung to the attack and asked Kelly if he 'fired into a house where there were innocent people'. Mr Smyth suddenly decided that this line of evidence about Glenrowan 'had nothing to do with the murder of Lonigan'.

Gaunson retaliated. The Crown had presented evidence that Ned pointed guns at people 'to show that he was a man capable of shooting Lonigan'. Now he wanted to show what the police were capable of. 'In Superintendent Sadleir's report, Ned Kelly was charged with murdering Martin Cherry. Such was not the case. It was the police who murdered Cherry.'

Magistrate Foster, who had been giving the Crown Prosecutor a virtually free hand, ruled that this evidence was 'irrelevant' and went on to declare that the Crown had established a *prima facie* case. Ned was committed to stand trial for the murder of Lonigan, the case to be heard at the next Beechworth Assize Court on 14 October.

The prisoner at the bar was now charged with the murder of Scanlon and the Crown had started to re-cycle its evidence as Tuesday's proceedings, the fourth day of the trial, limped to a close. With a continuing air of anti-climax and *déjà vu* the remaining witnesses were heard on the fifth day, which was, enlivened by the arrival of Kate Kelly, escorted by Dick Hart.

Gaunson's closing remarks were succinct, based on Senior Constable Kelly's admission that he had not followed 'the ordinary course of the law' in questioning Ned the night of his capture. Claiming that 'there was manifest injustice and illegality in preventing the access of prisoner's friends and relatives', Gaunson accused the police of 'pushing the case to an extremity', seeking 'vengeance rather than justice'.

In a wintry dusk Ned was committed to stand trial for the murder of Scanlon and that night Gaunson appeared by invitation at a Beechworth charity concert, singing, appropriately, 'I Fear No Foe'.

Next morning the police's neuroses about rescue, poison, assassination and riot resulted in Ned being whisked out of gaol in a wagonette with three armed constables, picking up a waiting mounted police escort on the outskirts of town and rattling away through the hills, down to Wangaratta, while a decoy locomotive was under steam at Beechworth.

In spite of the secrecy, a crowd of 500 or 600 people on the Wangaratta station watched Ned being taken aboard a guard's van which carried special signalling facilities and equipment to replace torn-up rails. Ned looked out at the crowd with the amused comment, 'There's a lot of colonials,' but, as the train drew away he was heard to murmur, 'Goodbye ladies, I shall never see you again'. He 'appeared for the moment very downcast, and tears could almost be discerned in his eyes'.

As Engine No. 68, 'one of the swiftest on the line', drummed towards Melbourne, Ned looked out across the Oxley Flats to Mount Buffalo, majestic under heavy snow, watched until it was almost hidden by a slope of the Glenrowan Gap, then crossed the van to say his goodbyes to Morgans Lookout, the huge white tree where he had fallen and the scree of charcoal between the two brick chimneys of the inn, memorial to Joe, Dan and Steve.

The train raced on, not stopping for water at Benalla, and ploughed through a mob of sheep that had blocked the track. A policeman who looked back saw a dozen or more of them, dead and maimed, 'rolling like balls along the line' as Engine No. 68 carried Ned headlong towards Melbourne.

♣

22

'THEY WILL ONLY BE SATISFIED WITH MY LIFE'

12 AUGUST – 11 NOVEMBER 1880

B ack in Melbourne Gaol Ned was 'tired and depressed' and complained of considerable pain from his wounds. A bullet was removed from muscles in the sole of his left foot, but many of Steele's slugs remained near his right knee, there was a rifle bullet still embedded in his left leg and his shattered left arm was almost useless. (Two months later it was reported 'that the wounds in the left arm have caused that member to shrivel up and his left hand has a wasted and crushed appearance'.) His right hand remained crippled and he would never write again.

In spite of all this, by 26 August he was fit enough to be removed from the gaol hospital to a cell, where his isolation was even more complete and Beechworth's *Advertiser* would report, perhaps with some satisfaction, that 'the premier bushranger . . . is exceedingly low-spirited. I suppose the prisoner sees what the end will be, and wishes it was all over.'

That spring the vast dome of the Exhibition Building towered above Melbourne's modest skyline and the visitors flocking to the city for the Exhibition promised to make the coming spring horse-racing carnival a dazzling event. The new Berry government weeded out the public service in a desperate economy campaign (the *Herald* said they were being 'Black Wednesdayed'), yet passed the Payment of Members Bill in three minutes — a £25 000 drain on the budget. The Yarra River's worst floods for almost twenty years swirled through riverside suburbs and turned Princes Bridge into a huge spillway. A towering wooden pole winched into place at the corner of Queen and Collins Streets heralded the arrival of the city's telephone system. The troubled 1870s watched the dawn of the 1880s with hope; the slow-dying nineteenth century watched the arrival of the twentieth with wariness.

Unemployment remained a huge problem and a public works programme set out to help solve the problem, employing 1200 men at 6 shillings a day. The desperate nature of this remedy was revealed when the Minister for Public Works sacked 100 of the men so he could replace them with 100 unemployed. Rural unemployment was immeasurable and many selectors were in desperate plight, living on 'boiled wheat and wild rabbits'. Graham Berry, who had predicted 'broken heads and houses in flames' less than two years before, now found himself facing deputations of unemployed and discontented people talking of 'riot and revolution'. And he might have noted that the now-frequent land war hitbacks — stock killing, the burning of haystacks and barns — had been described in the north-east as 'agrarian outrages', the term applied to Irish rebel activity.

In this climate of threat and change the spectre of the Kelly trial hung like a thundercloud. It was too dangerous to stage it in Beechworth. A summons for a change of venue to Melbourne was heard before Sir Redmond Barry in chambers on Saturday 18 September. Crown Prosecutor Smyth pointed out that the intimidation of only one juror could prevent him 'finding a verdict in accordance with the evidence', thus aborting the trial; while a guilty verdict could produce reprisals against jurors and their families. Gaunson, on the other hand, protested that the change would 'prejudice the fair trial of the prisoner', who had 'a clear right' to be tried where he was known. 'It would be a farce for the prisoner to challenge jurors called to try him in Melbourne.'

Barry found the decision 'very simple'. In his view, Smyth's argument — that a conviction would be difficult in Beechworth — not only justified the change but *demanded* it. Told that he would be tried in Melbourne, Ned 'did not show any concern', though he must have known that the already-slim hope of an acquittal had dwindled. Nevertheless, a powerful groundswell of support for him was developing. During the Beechworth hearing, the *Daily Telegraph* reported:

> Nor do the expressions of sympathy for 'poor Ned' emanate only from the larrikin and criminal classes, but many men and women who ... are designated 'enlightened citizens', freely express their commiseration ... We go further than that to say that a petition for his reprieve would be widely signed. We believe that money would be readily forthcoming for his defence.

It was almost three months before such a petition was circulated; the question of financing the defence was a more pressing problem.

Under the new Chief Secretary and Premier Graham Berry, there was some relaxation of the brutal 'no visitors' policy. Ned had a second interview with his mother and was at last allowed to see Maggie. The popular rumour that he would be able to direct her to a cache of money from the bank robberies was quickly revealed to be false. The *Benalla Standard* reported accurately, 'The Kellys and their relatives ... have not even as much as will pay for the defence of the prisoner Ned Kelly.' Gaunson was unpaid and would continue to be, but he could not appear as a barrister in the Supreme Court. This role would be filled by the formidable Hickman Molesworth, son of a Supreme Court judge, sixteen years a barrister. His fee, Molesworth told Gaunson, would be 50 guineas for the first two days and a 10-guinea 'refresher' for each subsequent day.

Sittings of the Central Criminal Court would begin on Friday 15 October. By the Wednesday it was tipped that Ned's trial would begin on the second day, Monday. Sir Redmond Barry would preside. Molesworth applied to have the trial postponed and, on the Friday, presented Barry with an affidavit from Gaunson detailing how the family's attempt to raise money on Mrs Kelly's land had been thwarted by the police. Barry refused adjournment. Ned would face trial on Monday.

Molesworth and Gaunson decided on a time-honoured tactic to gain the needed postponement. It is described by John Phillips:

> A junior barrister, who could truthfully tell the judge that he knew nothing about the case, would be sent to make a last-minute application for an adjournment. The judge's hands were effectively tied. He either granted the adjournment or accepted a situation where the prisoner could not be properly defended. Invariably the adjournment was granted.

Molesworth's 'young friend', Henry Bindon, was the perfect man for the job. He had practised as a barrister for less than ten months and had never appeared in the Supreme Court.

William Gaunson spoke with Ned at the gaol early on Monday and told him the plan for that morning's appearance. When Ned expressed concern that his jacket was looking 'shabby' after two months continuous wear, William lent him his overcoat to wear in court.

By 9 a.m. several thousand people had gathered at the corner of Russell and La Trobe Streets, outside the rather scrappy collection of buildings that then comprised the Supreme Court. Maggie, in the same black dress she had worn at Beechworth, had been allowed into the courtroom at an early hour, accompanied by Kate Lloyd.

The old court was a sombre, church-like place of dark, carved and polished woodwork with rows of pews, a fitting background for its cast in quasi-ecclesiastical costume — the barristers in their black gowns, white 'bands' and short, grey wigs, Barry presided over it all in long wig, sumptuous red robe and cape trimmed with white fur, enthroned behind the Bench like a high priest under a handsome, gothic canopy.

Ned was escorted into the dock and looked down at the bar table for Bindon, the young, dark-bearded man described by William Gaunson.

Grey-bearded Smyth and grey-moustached Arthur Chomley, the prosecuting barristers, looked coldly up at him. Bindon was not there. Ned was so shaken that, when being arraigned by the judge's associate, he had to be asked three times to raise his right hand. He had been charged with the murder of Lonigan, pleaded 'Not guilty', almost inaudibly, and the second charge was being read before Bindon at last entered with apologetic bows to Barry and applied for a remand, pointing out that Ned was to be defended at the expense of the Crown and there had been insufficient time to 'instruct' counsel.

Smyth rose to his feet, daunting the court with his pale, deep-set eyes. There was, he said, no valid basis for the application *but* he wished to avoid any suggestion that the prisoner had been 'improperly prosecuted or harshly treated' and would agree to 'four or five days' postponement. When Barry announced that he would be at the Castlemaine Assizes until 27 October, Smyth agreed to an adjournment until Thursday week, 28 October.

'It is very becoming on the part of the Crown', Barry said.

The day after the hearing Tom and Maggie visited Bill Skilling in Pentridge. Maggie probably discussed with her husband the possibility of raising money on their selection to help finance Ned's defence. The three went on to discuss what were called 'private matters' — perhaps the fact that Maggie and Tom, devoted cousins drawn even closer together by the tragedy of Glenrowan, had fallen in love. Certainly Skilling accepted the relationship on his release three years later, and left the couple to raise a family.

In the week before the trial Gaunson battled for more money. The Crown was providing a paltry 7 guineas for counsel and 7 guineas for a solicitor, amounts described even by the anti-Kelly *Ovens and Murray Advertiser* as 'wholly inadequate'. The Attorney-General refused to provide more, though the fee *might* be increased *after* the trial if 'sufficient grounds' could be shown. Molesworth and Barry were both involved in a case until Saturday. (A Mr McIntyre was suing the *Age* for libel, claiming £3000 damages. He would win and be awarded £150.) On the following Monday, told that only 7 guineas was available for his fee, Molesworth declined to defend Ned.

It is hard to believe that neither Gaunson nor Ned's family could raise the additional 43 guineas that would have secured Molesworth for two days — the top-up reduced to 36 guineas if Gaunson contributed his fee to the cause — yet by Monday not one additional penny had been found for Ned's defence.

The failure to find more money seems inexplicable, as does Gaunson's next move. Late on Monday night, two days before the trial, Gaunson gave the eighty-five-page brief to Henry Bindon. Apart from being 'the most inexperienced barrister in the colony', Bindon had not even been in Victoria at the time of the Stringybark killings (nor, in fact, for most of the Kelly Outbreak) and therefore knew less about the case than almost every man, woman and child in the colony.

Gaunson had probably decided that his only hope of success lay in a further adjournment, giving him more time to raise the money to lure back Molesworth or find an adequate replacement. His best hope of securing an adjournment was to present Sir Redmond with a barrister who could not only plead the now-well-worn excuse of inadequate preparation time, but also a lack of background knowledge.

If this was Gaunson's strategy — and there seems no other explanation for his selection of Bindon — it represented a desperate gamble. If it worked, he had won precious time to mount an effective defence; if it failed, Ned Kelly would face the Supreme Court defended by a man almost uniquely ill-equipped for the job. It is a matter of history that this gamble failed.

On Thursday 28 October 1880 Ned Kelly stood trial for his life in the Supreme Court defended by Henry Bindon, whose one strong point seems to have been a powerful, though ill-founded, belief in his own ability.

Sir Redmond Barry's attitude was very plain. As the *Herald* had reported two weeks before, 'The trial of Ned Kelly . . . will be disposed of as soon as possible, arrangements having been made for lighting the court with gas after dusk.' On the day of the trial the *Herald* would claim that Barry was willing to sit until midnight. He was keen to wrap up the wretched business in a single day's sitting, a possibility strengthened by the Crown having stripped the case down to a single charge — the murder of Lonigan. This was a wise move in view of McIntyre's damaging admission that he could not swear Ned had shot Scanlon.

Henry Bindon launched into the trial by describing the negotiations with Molesworth, the time-consuming chain of correspondence about the fee with the Sheriff, Crown Law Office and the Attorney-General. He then pleaded ignorance of the case and lack of preparation time, fumbling and bumbling so badly that Barry had to ask, 'What is your motive?' Told that Bindon was seeking a further remand, Barry asked Smyth's opinion on the matter. No one was surprised when the remand application was refused and the trial proceeded.

The fact that Ned Kelly was on trial, not for the murder of a policeman but as an enemy of society, was made very clear at the outset by the Crown Prosecutor's outline of evidence. Smyth claimed that he would put before the jury 'such facts as directly bore on the case' and proceeded to deal with the Fitzpatrick incident, Stringybark, the bank robberies, the murder of Aaron Sherritt, the siege of Glenrowan and

Ned's Last Stand. Bindon would try, ineffectually, to restrict evidence to 'what had taken place at the killing of Lonigan'. The parade of witnesses — sixteen in all — plodded through a replay of the two hearings at Beechworth with new faces — Constable Richards and bank manager Tarleton from Jerilderie, Detective Ward and Sergeant Steele.

The great contrast between this trial proper and the lower court hearing lay in the ineffectual cross-examination by Bindon. Even when firing shots loaded by Gaunson, he missed the mark. Since he didn't fully understand the questions he asked, he could not make capital from the answers, however inadequate they might be. He would even confuse the deaths of Lonigan and Scanlon, claiming that Lonigan 'met his death in a fusilade'.

There were a few minor shocks for the Crown. Jerilderie bank manager Tarleton proved to be an embarrassing prosecution witness when he presented a splendid summary of the defence while quoting Ned:

'It is all very well to say that we shot the police in cold blood. We had to do it in self defence.' He also said that he had been driven to become an outlaw.

Bank manager Scott from Euroa would also irritate the prosecution by pointing out that 'Mr Kelly had been a thorough gentleman' and 'had not used a single rude word' in front of Mrs Scott, prompting Ned to wink at the jury. Gloster, the Gang's undercover ally from Euroa, gave Ned's version of the police killings in fine style, but McIntyre had presented his by-now carefully orchestrated account of Stringybark virtually without challenge, even reverting to his claim that Ned had shot Scanlon. Senior Constable Kelly would take his Glenrowan evidence further again, producing Ned's armour and even donning his helmet, while Steele would manage to give his testimony without a single reference to the death of Lonigan.

It all dragged on until 6.05 p.m., when Barry asked Smyth if the case could be completed that night. 'I am prepared to sit until midnight to clear it,' he offered hopefully, confirming the *Herald* story already being read in the streets and homes of Melbourne. Told there were eight witnesses still to give evidence, Barry was philosophical and adjourned until 9 a.m. the next morning. Ned was returned to his cell and the jury was conducted across the way to spend the night under lock and key at the Supreme Court Hotel.

◆

FRIDAY 29 OCTOBER was unseasonably warm. An unsettling spring wind blew and 'the city was enveloped in dust'. While a smaller crowd gathered outside the court, Maggie and Kate Lloyd occupied the same seats, today accompanied by Tom Lloyd, Dinny McAuliffe and his sister. Ned, it was noted, looked 'somewhat paler' though he chose to stand in the dock during the earlier part of the day. He wore 'a light but elaborately flowered silk handkerchief' knotted at his throat.

Bindon's major blunder of the day — perhaps of the entire trial — came when assistant prosecutor Chomley tendered the government clerk's copy of Ned's Jerilderie Letter as evidence. Bindon objected on the technical grounds that the document was not in Ned's handwriting. Though reluctant to give Bindon an inch, Barry conceded, 'I think the objection *could* be sustained' and Smyth demurred.

Bindon, with or without Gaunson's agreement, had lost sight of the vital point that 'if the prosecution tenders a declaration in evidence then "it becomes evidence for the prisoner as well as as against him".' Baron Parke in *King and Higgins* 1829. If the Jerilderie Letter had been read in court, Ned's case would have been pleaded in his own words, with the voice of dead Joe joining his in unison. The death of Lonigan would have been described as it happened:

> He had just got to the logs and put his head up to take aim when I shot him that instant or he would have shot me as I took him for Strahan the man who said he would not ask me to stand he would shoot me first like a dog.

The plea of self-defence would have been delivered first-hand, with persuasive effect.

> This cannot be called wilful murder for I was compelled to shoot them or lie down and let them shoot me ... Remember these men came into the bush with the intention of scattering pieces of me and my brother all over the bush. And yet they know and acknowledge I have been wronged and my mother and four or five men lagged innocent.

The rebellious Irish-Australian rhetoric of the letter would have helped define the real nature of the Kelly Outbreak and salved the consciences of decent men like Sadleir, who may have had some qualms over the need to see Ned Kelly hang at any cost. To many other decent men less disposed to the idea of 'noble falsehoods', this extraordinary document might have provided a manifesto of great power, a text to inspire the many ordinary folk in the colony who had lost faith in the police as instruments of justice and saw them as a weapon of oppression.

The Jerilderie Letter lay on the table in front of Chomley, unread. Ned and Joe remained silent, this time gagged not by the police or the Crown but by Henry Bindon and, perhaps, David Gaunson. In the eyes of the public the man in the dock continued to stand trial as a criminal, not as a rebel.

After the luncheon adjournment Bindon asked Barry if he would refer to the Full Court — a panel of three Supreme Court judges — his objection that all evidence concerning 'transactions that took place after the death of Lonigan' should not have been admitted. In effect Bindon was asking the Senior Puisne Judge to admit that he might have erred. Barry's response was predictable. He 'had no doubt that the whole of the evidence . . . was admissible and refused to receive the point for the consideration of the Full Court'. To modern eyes, such judicial self-regulation seems outrageous, but Bindon had exhausted the only avenue of appeal then available. He went on to say that the defence would call no witnesses. This meant that Ned would not give an unsworn statement from the dock. Several times during the trial Ned had been seen to raise one arm and spit across it in a gesture of derision; if this was not one of those moments, he must have been sorely tempted.

Smyth summed up for the Crown and Bindon then rose to address the jury, 'the sole speech in defence', a dubious advantage that had been gained by not allowing Ned to speak.

Bindon pointed out that the Crown had 'brought forward a number of things foreign to the present case' and, rather forlornly in the light of Barry's ruling, urged the jury to ignore evidence of 'the shooting of Kennedy and the proceedings at Euroa, Glenrowan and Jerilderie'. Bindon made a hash of the death of Lonigan — the central issue, trying to claim that the constable had died 'in an unfortunate fracas' and that 'who shot the man no-one could tell'. McIntyre said that he saw the prisoner fire at Lonigan, *but there were shots fired by others at the same time*, and to tell which was the fatal bullet is a matter of impossibility.' [my italics]

Bindon was simply unfamiliar with the evidence. No one had ever claimed that others had fired when Lonigan was killed. It was Scanlon who had died during a volley of shots. However, Bindon touched on a core truth: 'The story of McIntyre is too good to be true. It showed the signs of deliberate and careful preparation and of being afterwards carefully studied.' But he lost the impact of that truth in continuing confusion: '*Lonigan evidently met his death in a fusilade* and the fact of Ned Kelly being singled out as the murderer points to a desire to do away with him.' [my italics]

Sir Redmond now delivered his summing-up. In the opinion of Supreme Court Judge John Phillips — formerly a distinguished criminal barrister and later to be Chief Justice of Victoria — Barry misdirected the jury on a vital point of law 'in terms that were conclusive in favour of the Prosecution'.

Barry gave a rambling discourse on murder, then proceeded to demolish the scrappily stated argument of self-defence by telling the jury that the police party 'had a double protection: that of the ordinary citizen and that of being ministers of the law charged with the administration of the peace of the country'. Their plain clothes and armament were not issues. 'What right had four other armed men to stop them and ask them to surrender, to put up their hands? I repeat, they were executive officers of the law and no person had any right to stop them or question them.'

John Phillips's verdict is unequivocal. 'Sir Redmond should have told the jury that it was for them to decide whether the police were acting as ministers of justice or summary executioners and then reviewed for the jurors the evidence relevant to this issue.' To John Phillips, 'the conclusion is inescapable that Edward Kelly was not afforded a trial according to law'.

The jury retired at 5.10 p.m. and returned after only half an hour. The inevitability of their decision was all too clear. Maggie, Tom Lloyd and Dinny McAuliffe had left the court, unable to face hearing the verdict and sentence. Only Kate Lloyd remained, with Dinny's sister supporting her.

The foreman of the jury, Samuel Lazarus, dairyman, pronounced a verdict of guilty. Ned was standing with his hand on the rail of the dock. Perhaps he recoiled slightly. There was a gasp, little more than a catch of breath, from Kate. Reciting the routine formula, the Clerk of the Court asked if Ned had anything to say. In a momentous hush, he leant forward slightly.

> Well, it is rather too late for me to speak now. I thought of speaking this morning, but I thought afterwards that I had better not. There was little use, and there is little use blaming anyone now. Nobody knows about my case except myself — and I almost wish now that I had spoken — and I wish I had insisted on being allowed to examine the witnesses myself. I am confident I would have thrown a different light on the case. On the evidence that has been given, no doubt, the jury or any other jury could not give any other verdict.
>
> It is not that I fear death; I fear it as little as to drink a cup of tea. But it is on account of the witnesses and with their evidence no different verdict could be given. That is my opinion, because no man understands my case as I do myself. I do not blame anybody — neither Mr Bindon nor Mr Gaunson: but Mr Bindon knew nothing about my case. I lay blame on myself that I did not get up yesterday and examine the witnesses, but I thought that if I did so, it would look like bravado and flashness, and people might have said that I thought myself cleverer than Counsel. So I let it go as it was.

Silence was called, the black square of cloth was placed on Barry's grey-wigged head and, with all the weight and majesty of the law, he

David Gaunson MLA, Ned's solicitor, a baffling and complex man of enormous potential which remained largely unrealised. He seems to have taken up Ned's case with genuine idealism, mistaken by some as a cynical bid for the Irish Catholic vote. This portrait is an early reproduction from a lost original.

Sir Redmond Barry, Irish-born son of a Major-General, brought to the young colony of Victoria all the neuroses of the privileged Anglo-Irish — and several of his own. Considered a severe judge even in his own time, some of his sentences today seem almost demented.

Kate Lloyd, Ned's cousin, here seen in the late 1880s, was the great love of his life. She was the only relative who stayed in the court when Ned was sentenced to death. (*Myra Brolan*)

Julian Ashton's watercolour of Ned in the dock at Beechworth (see pp.294–5) was the basis of this superb, front-page engraving for the *Illustrated Australian News*. Ned tried to stop Ashton finishing the painting by screening his face with a possum rug.

Three drawings were made of Ned as he lay near death at Glenrowan. Curiously, all three distort the size of his head. This rarest version, from the *Sydney Mail*, shows Ned's features battered, bruised and swollen from the impact of the bullets on the face-piece of his helmet.

turned to face the man standing in the dock. It was a remarkable moment. Irish-born Barry, son of a British general, had sprung from and still belonged to a class 'who feared and detested the bog-Irish'. To Barry and his kind Ned Kelly represented, in Kelly authority John McQuilton's words, 'the epitome of the Anglo-Irish nightmare'.

The contrast between the two men — the two faces of Ireland and the two faces of Australia — was in historian Paul de Serville's phrase, 'almost too symmetrical for comfort'. It tempted Barry into dialogue with the man he was about to sentence. 'Edward Kelly, the verdict pronounced by the jury is one which you must have fully expected.'

Ned leant towards Barry, his elbows on the rail of the dock. He 'appeared, calm and collected' and replied 'in a mild undertone'.

Ned: 'Under the circumstances, I did expect this verdict.'

Barry: 'No circumstances that I can conceive could have altered the result of your trial.'

Ned: 'Perhaps if you had heard me examine the witnesses, you might understand. I could do it.'

Barry: 'I will even give you credit for the skill which you desire to assume.'

Ned: 'No, I don't wish to assume anything! I don't say this out of flashness. I do not recognize myself as a great man, but it is quite possible for me to clear myself of this charge if I liked to do so. If I desired to do it, I could have done so in spite of anything attempted against me.'

Barry: 'The facts against you are so numerous and so conclusive, not only as regards the offence which you are now charged with, but also for a long series of criminal acts which you have committed during the last eighteen months, that I do not think any rational person could have arrived at any other conclusion. The verdict of the jury is irresistible, and there could not be any doubt about its being the *right* verdict. I have no right or wish to inflict upon you any personal remarks. It is painful in the extreme to perform the duty which I have now to discharge, and I will confine myself strictly to it. I do not think that anything I can say would aggravate the pain you must be suffering.'

Ned: 'No! I declare before you, God and man that my mind is as easy and clear as it possibly can be.'

Barry: 'It is blasphemous of you to say so. You appear to revel in the idea of having put men to death.'

Ned: 'More men than me have put men to death. No man abhors murder more than I do. I do not fear death, and I am the last man in the world to take a man's life away. I believe that two years ago, before this thing happened, if a man pointed a gun at me to shoot me, I should not have stopped him, so careful was I of taking life. I am not a murderer, but if there is an innocent life at stake, then I say I must take some action. If I see innocent life taken, I should certainly shoot if I were forced to do so, but I should first want to know whether this could not be prevented but

I should have to do it if it could not be stopped in any other way.'

Barry: 'Your statement involves wicked and criminal reflection of untruth upon the witnesses who have given evidence.'

Ned: 'I dare say. But the day will come when we shall all have to go to a bigger court than this. Then we will see who is right and who is wrong. No matter how long a man lives, he is bound to come to judgement somewhere, and as well here as anywhere. It will be different the next time they have a Kelly trial, for they are not all killed. It would have been for the good of the Crown had I examined the witnesses, and I would have stopped a lot of reward, I can assure you, and I do not know but I will do it yet if allowed. As regards anything about myself, all I care for is that my mother, who is now in prison, shall not have it to say that she reared a son who could not have altered this charge if he had liked to do so.'

Barry: '*An offence of the kind which you stand accused of is not of an ordinary character. There are many murders which have been discovered in this colony under different circumstances, but none show greater atrocity than those you committed.* These crimes proceed from different motives. Some arise from a sordid desire to take from others the property which they acquired or inherited — some from jealousy, some from a base desire to thieve, *but this crime was of an enormity out of all proportion. A party of men took up arms against society, organised as it was for mutual protection and regard for the law.*' [my italics. Barry, too, seems to admit that Ned has been tried for something more than murder.]

Ned: 'Yes, that is the way the evidence brought it out. It appeared that I deliberately took up arms of my own accord, and induced the other three men to join me for the purpose of doing nothing but shooting down the police . . .'

Barry: 'Unfortunately, in a new community, where society is not bound together so closely as it should be, there is a class which disregards the consequences of crime and looks upon the perpetrators of these crimes as heroes. But these unfortunate, in-considerate, ill-educated, ill-conducted, un-principled and ill-prompted youths must be taught to consider the value of human life. Such youths unfortunately abound, and unless they are made to consider the consequences of crime, they are led to imitate notorious felons, whom they regard as self-made heroes. It is right therefore that they should be asked to consider and reflect upon what the life of a felon is. A felon who has cut himself off from all decencies, all the affections, charities, and all the obligations of society is as helpless and degraded as a wild beast of the field. He has nowhere to lay his head, he has no-one to prepare for him the comforts of life, he suspects his friends, he dreads his enemies, he is in constant alarm lest his pursuers should reach him, and his only hope is that he might use his life in what he considers a glorious struggle for existence. That is the life of the outlaw or felon . . .'

Ned: 'An outlaw!'

Barry: 'The love of country, the love of order, the love of obedience to the law, have been set aside for reasons difficult to explain, and there is something extremely wrong in a country where a lawless band of men, you and your associates, are able to live 18 months disturbing society. And you have actually had the hardihood to confess to having stolen 200 horses even during your short life.'

Ned: 'Who proves that?'

Barry: 'More than one witness has testified that you made the statement on several occasions.'

Ned: 'That charge has never been proved against me, and it is held in English law that a man is innocent until he is found guilty.'

Barry: 'You are self-accused. I do not accuse you. That is your own statement.'

Ned: 'You have not heard me. If I had examined the witnesses, I could have brought it out differently.'

Barry: 'I am not accusing you. This statement has been made several times by the witnesses. You confessed it to them and you stand self-accused. It is also proved that you committed several attacks upon the banks, and you seem to have appropriated large sums of money — several thousands of pounds. It has also come within my knowledge that the country has expended about £50 000 in consequence of the acts of which you and your party have been guilty. Although we have such examples as Clarke, Gardiner, Melville, Morgan and Scott, who have all met ignominious deaths, still the effect has apparently not been to hinder others from following in their footsteps. I think that this is much to be deplored, and some steps must be taken to have society protected. Your unfortunate and miserable associates have met with deaths you might envy, but you are not afforded the opportunity.'

Ned: 'I don't think there is much proof that they did die that death.'

Barry: 'It would be well for those young men, who are so foolish as to consider that it is brave of a man to sacrifice the lives of his fellow creatures in carrying out his own wild ideas, to see that it is a life to be avoided by every possible means, and to reflect that the unfortunate termination of your life *is a miserable death*. It could hardly be believed that a man would sacrifice the life of his fellow creatures in this manner The idea is enough to make one shudder in thinking of it. The end of your companions was comparatively better than the death which awaits you.

'It is remarkable that, although New South Wales had joined Victoria in offering a large reward for the detection of the gang, no person was found to discover it. There seemed to be a spell cast over the people of this particular district, which I can only attribute either to sympathy with crime or dread of the consequences of doing their duty.

'In your case the law will be carried out by its officers. The gentlemen of the jury have done their duty. My duty will be to forward to the proper quarter the notes of your trial and to lay, as I am required to do, before the Executive all circumstances connected with the case, but I cannot hold out any hope to you that the sentence, which I am now about to pass, will be remitted. I desire to spare you any further pain, and I absolve myself from anything said willingly in any of my utterances that may have unnecessarily increased the agitation of your mind.

'I have now to pronounce your sentence. You will be taken from here to the place from whence you came, and thence on a day appointed by the Executive Council to a place of execution, and there you will be hanged by the neck until you be dead. May the Lord have mercy on your soul.'

Barry seemed to have had the last word, but Ned had one more thing to say to his judge, calmly and quietly. 'I will go a little further than that and say I will see you there, where I go.'

Barry's 'Remove the prisoner!' was probably uttered with a little more feeling than usual. But as the warders moved to obey the Puisne Judge, Ned raised his hand and stopped them, then turned and blew a kiss to Kate Lloyd, saying, 'Goodbye, you'll see me there . . .'

Ned turned and left the dock, 'appearing quite unconcerned'.

On the way back to gaol with a phalanx of warders, he kept his spirits up by a display of bravado:

He said that the last of the Kellys was not disposed of yet, and that it would take 40 000 policemen to get rid of them. He added that he would 'come back' to render assistance to his relatives, whatever that promise may mean.

It was harder to maintain this façade when he had to strip off his civilian clothes and, for the first time since his capture, put on convict clothing: dark woollen jacket and corduroy trousers of a special pattern, buttoned from cuff to waist on each side to accommodate the leg irons which a blacksmith now riveted on each ankle, joined by a chain with a central ring. A cord ran from this ring to a special belt, holding the chain off the ground when he walked.

He was taken to cell No. 38 in the old wing of the gaol — an outer compartment behind an ordinary prison door with an inner cell enclosed behind an iron grille. This was the Condemned Cell where Ned would be kept, truly 'like a wild beast' in his cage, constantly watched by a warder sitting outside the bars. Yet, after he was locked in this forbidding coop and given a dinner of 'ordinary prison fare', he was his old defiant self:

The prisoner engaged in the pastime of singing secular songs as he had done on other occasions since his reception in the establishment; and one of the warders reminded him that his conduct was hardly becoming in a man in his position.

Now that Ned seemed safely on his way to the gallows, he was allowed visitors more often — an indication that the fear of suicide had been an excuse and the isolation policy was meant to hamper his defence. The next day, Saturday, a contingent of friends and relatives were allowed to visit and talk to him through the iron grille. They were Maggie and Tom, Kate Lloyd, Joe Ryan, Dinny McAuliffe and his sister; and on Sunday, his mother, again with the bars between them. Each midday at the court-yard wall between the Supreme Court and the gaol, Ned's chains could be heard clinking as he took his hour's exercise.

The execution date was to be decided by the Executive Council, which did not consider the issue at its Monday meeting and would meet again on Wednesday (Tuesday was Melbourne Cup Day, on which 100 000 people watched the great race). Meanwhile, David and William Gaunson planned a public meeting for Friday followed by a grand march, four abreast, to Government House to plead for the Governor's intervention. By the Wednesday, petition forms for Ned's reprieve had been printed and were being distributed.

PETITION FOR REPRIEVE

To His Excellency the Governor-in-Council, -
Your humble PETITIONERS (having carefully
considered the circumstances of the case) respectfully pray
that the Life of the CONDEMNED man EDWARD KELLY
may be spared.
n.b. — This list is to be sent to Mr David Gaunson M.L.A.,
Solicitor for the Prisoner, so as to reach Melbourne on
Monday morning next, 8th November, 1880.

On that day, 3 November, Ned dictated a letter, a 'history' of his case, to the Governor. In similar vein to the Cameron and Jerilderie letters, he canvassed the Fitzpatrick incident and the events at Stringybark Creek, then pointed to discrepancies in McIntyre's evidence. It was a hurried note, dictated to a warder and signed with a cross then sent off in time for the Executive Council meeting. It ran the usual gamut of officials, arrived too late and was eventually forwarded to the Governor by Graham Berry. Judge Barry was at this meeting of the Executive Council. Having mis-directed the jury and refused to refer the case to the Full Court, he damned any chance of vice-regal mercy with a letter to the Governor:

The history of the prisoner during the last two years and the numerous criminal acts with which he admitted on several occasions to different people he was connected are sufficiently well known to render it unnec-essary for me to say any more than that the case was amply proved and that I see no reason whatever to recommend that the sentence should not be carried into execution.

This remained Barry's attitude and the Executive Council saw no rea-son to interfere with the course of justice. The execution was set for Thursday 11 November, eight days off. Told by Castieau, Ned 'appeared much cast down' but said simply, 'It is short.'

That same day the new hangman, Elijah Upjohn, was transferred from Pentridge to the Melbourne Gaol — a huge, forbidding Ballarat man, gaoled three months before for chicken stealing. His career of petty crime stretched back to Ned's days with Harry Power, when Upjohn had been gaoled for 'emptying a privy and carrying away the contents without a licence'.

Kate Kelly had been looking after the Kelly and Skilling children. She arrived by the Thursday afternoon train and visited her brother with Jim. Their parting was 'of a painful nature'.

The next morning, Friday 5 November, Ned dictated another letter to the Governor, this one largely devoted to Glenrowan. It is a strange document in which Ned outlines the 'cover' plan: halting the train, making hostages of 'the leaders of the police' then trading the life of 'the superintendent' for the release of Ellen, Skilling and Williamson. But, Ned claims, he changed his plan, describing how:

> I let a man go to stop the train about a mile below the ['Barracks' crossed out] Railway Station and opposite the Police Barracks and to tell them that we where in the Barracks. he had a double Barrel Fowling Piece and Cartridges and to fire as a signale for me if the Police got out and Surrounded the Barracks which I expected they would do as It was a most likely place for me to be as it was a strong brick building and they would only send a few men on to the platform to look after the Horses as they could not take them out without going to the Station and it was my intention then to take possession of the train Horses and every thing and returning along the line leaving the Police Surrounding the Barracks at Glenrowan while I had the train and robbed the banks along the line . . . the reason I differed from the ['first' interpolated] plan is *I wanted the man that Stopped the Train to have the reward as I heard it was to be done away with in three days* so you can see from the above it was not my intention of upsetting the Train for the Purpose of killing the Police . . . [my italics]

It is hard to take this 'plan' seriously. Apart from anything else, the mere giving of information — especially false information — would not qualify for the reward. The money could be paid only when the members of the Gang were captured or killed. It all seems an aberration of the moment, like the nonsense at Glenrowan about the informer Sullivan.

Ned goes on to raise unimportant details about whether Arthur or Kelly found his cap and rifle in the bush; and whether Kelly or Steele searched him and took his watch, seeking to show 'the contradictory statements put forward by the police', but his conclusion strikes home: 'I should have made a Statement of my whole Career but my time is So short on earth that I have to make the best of it to prepare myself for the other world.'

This letter would be intercepted by Graham Berry, held until the following Monday and read to the Executive Council before being given to the Governor. Overall it proved damaging. It was reported that Ned claimed to have sent Curnow to stop the train — an allegation the schoolteacher denied and which provided ammunition for the anti-Kelly press.

That night, while Guy Fawkes Day fireworks spluttered and crackled around the city and bonfires blazed, the public meeting was held in the Hippodrome, a roofless, high-walled sporting venue in Exhibition Street. Some 4000 men and women packed inside and another 2000 or 3000 gathered in the street. Melbourne's pressmen outdid one another in attempts to denigrate and dismiss this mass support for Ned. The *Argus* said that the women present were 'from Little Bourke Street and the vicinity', inferring that they were prostitutes. The *Telegraph* quoted an unnamed detective who said, 'he had never, in the whole of his experience . . . seen such a number of known vagabonds, thieves and persons who had been convicted, gathered in one place.' While it pointed out that 'the lower classes were largely represented', the same paper found it 'humiliating to have to admit that a great number of respectable working men were present'.

The *Bendigo Independent* went further than any of the Melbourne papers, revealing an underlying fear of this huge demonstration:

> In revolutions and on occasions when executions take place in Paris a new element appears in the mobs . . . male and female beasts — and these came out of their holes and were at the Kelly meeting, *and shocking the respectable classes, and enabling them to comprehend upon what a fearful volcano society stands.* [my italics]

As rockets lit the sky and an occasional firework burst in the arena, the Gaunson brothers, a young politician called Caulfield and the meeting's chairman, phrenologist and anti-hanging campaigner, Archibald Hamilton, addressed the huge, well-behaved audience, telling them that the night's planned procession had been called off but a deputation would meet the Governor at 10.30 the next morning. A resolution was passed, asking the Governor 'to favourably regard the prayers of this meeting — that the life of the prisoner may be spared'.

At the Town Hall next morning about 200 men and women gathered (predictably described as 'of the labouring classes', 'idle and seedy looking' and of 'a very nondescript character'). Supposedly because they were embarrassed by the poor quality of their crowd but actually because the Governor had specified 'a small deputation', the Gaunsons, Hamilton, Caulfield and Kate Kelly caught a cab to Government House and met the Governor in 'the yellow drawing room'. The Marquis of Normanby, a truly aristocratic man of rather stolid military bearing, listened to the 'prayers' of the Hippodrome meeting, received the resolution and gave a compassionate response, 'I should be deceiving you and acting a cruel part towards the unfortunate man now under sentence of death, if I were to hold out any hope of the mitigation of sentence.'

In an embarrassing gesture phrenologist Hamilton took Kate's hand and brought her forward, suggesting, 'It might have some effect if she went down on her knees before His Excellency and begged for mercy'.

'No. No,' Normanby protested, 'I have a painful duty to perform and I do not see that anything can be got by prolonging this interview.'

He withdrew and the deputation took their cab back towards the city to tell their dispirited supporters what had happened. Did the Governor's words strike home to any of them — David Gaunson in particular — that it was 'acting a cruel part' towards Ned to buoy him up with the hope of reprieve? This visit to Government House had marked David Gaunson's last public involvement in the reprieve campaign. He did not see Ned again and would decline to attend the execution. William Gaunson now took over his role.

Meanwhile, thousands more signatures were being scrawled on petition forms at several city hotels, the Exhibition Building and Flemington Racecourse, where the Governor would soon be driven in state to attend the last day of the spring meeting. At one of the signing venues, the Rainbow Hotel in Elizabeth Street, Jim Kelly, Wild and Tom drew a crowd of 2000, causing a gigantic crush in the bar as men tried to shake Jim's hand.

The next day was Sunday and church congregations were asked to sign. On the footpath outside St Francis' Church, where Red and Ellen had been married, Kate Kelly collected signatures. The *Age* sneered, 'A large number of weak-minded people, principally females, signed.' On Monday, three days before the execution date, completed petition forms were pouring into the Robert Burns Hotel, which had become the headquarters of the reprieve movement. Publican Daniel Buckley, 'said to have the largest beard ever seen in the city', was quick to deny suggestions that this had made his house 'the resort of persons of doubtful character', assuring a *Herald* reporter, 'There had been no row or disturbance . . . and if there had been, I would not allow it.'

Another deputation was formed at the Town Hall to ask the Governor for more time to collect signatures. With extreme snobbery the *Argus* reported that '200 people of both sexes turned out from the back slums of the city'. William Gaunson, Maggie, Jim and Kate set off on foot for Government House 'with the unwashed-looking mob at their heels'. Maggie had to turn back, troubled by a bad knee, but the rest pushed on, delayed by police at Princes Bridge and eventually halted at the gates of Government House. Captain le Patourel, the Governor's secretary, announced that the petitions could be received at the Treasury up to 2 p.m., when the Executive Council was due to meet. At 2 p.m. with a crowd of 'fully a thousand' outside the Treasury, William Gaunson, Caulfield, Kate and Maggie arrived to present le Patourel with 32 424 signatures. Later William told Graham Berry that, given a little more time, they could have obtained 50 000.

The Executive met at 3 p.m. and refused to reverse their previous decision; Ned Kelly would hang on Thursday. The huge crowd received the news in silence but, back at the Robert Burns, Jim Kelly called from the door that 'It was not all over yet!' and they burst into cheers.

Petitions continued to arrive, signatures continued to be collected, bringing the total claimed to 60 000. One sheaf of petition forms would reach Jerilderie too late. In this feverish atmosphere of hope, 14-year-old Grace Kelly arrived in Melbourne.

On the Tuesday, two days before the date set for the hanging, another mass meeting was called for 8 p.m. at the Supreme Court Reserve, followed by a march to Graham Berry's home in East Melbourne. Then, as handbills to advertise the event were being printed and distributed, there was a flash of new hope. Kate Kelly received a letter from one of the jurors saying that, if she and Gaunson called on him, he was prepared to make 'some curious revelations' and sign the petition for reprieve. If the jury's decision had not been genuinely unanimous, if there had been any coercion of this juror, the guilty verdict might be overthrown. Kate and Gaunson hurried to the man's home, but he denied any knowledge of the message. It had all been a cruel 'practical joke'.

Then Uncle Paddy Quinn arrived in the city and saw Ned with Maggie that afternoon. He was prepared to swear an affidavit that, before Stringybark, Constable Strahan had boasted of his intention to kill Ned. The plea of self-defence was revitalised with this evidence.

That night more than 1500 people gathered at the corner of La Trobe and Swanston Streets to attend the advertised meeting but a dozen police kept them back from the Supreme Court Reserve. A few hotheads called, 'Rush the ground!' and police reinforcements were called out — another seventy men commanded by Acting Chief Commissioner Nicolson. Two men were arrested (both discovered to be 'respectable parties') and the confrontation was interrupted by the dramatic arrival of a horse-drawn lorry escorted by several 'rough-looking persons' carrying blazing torches. William Gaunson and Caulfield, 'the boy politician', rode on the lorry with Maggie, Kate, Jim, Wild and several supporters, some of them also with torches. Blocked from entering the reserve, Gaunson led the crowd to a nearby vacant allotment, took a vote to request another meeting of the Executive Council and paraded by torchlight along the streets to the Treasury. Here Gaunson presented Graham Berry with Patrick Quinn's statement quoting the threat made by Strahan 'two or three days' before the police shootings: 'I'll shoot him [Ned Kelly] down like a dog. I'll carry two revolvers and one I'll place by his side and swear he had it on him when I shot him.'

Patrick Quinn came forward and asked Berry for a Royal Commission, assuring the Premier, 'if one were appointed something would come out of it'.

Berry handled the situation well, with due consideration of the 1500 men and women gathered below the Treasury building, the blazing torches casting restless shadows of revolution in this Parisian quarter of Melbourne. He denied that there had been any haste or irregularity in the trial (he called it 'a patient trial') or in the timing of the execution. He dismissed the petitions because 'whole pages of them were written in the same hand' recording every member of a family 'down to the young children'. As for the Patrick Quinn affidavit, it had not been properly sworn and should have been presented at the trial. He promised to raise the case again with the Executive Council the next day but 'could not hold out the slightest hope of any alteration'. The blazing torches were extinguished and the crowd silently broke up.

From his cell in the old wing, Ned had probably heard the near-riot at the neighbouring Supreme Court Reserve. The next morning, twenty-four hours before the time set for his hanging, he finished dictating to Warder William Buck a third letter to the governor which he had begun the day before. Again he deals with Stringybark and the difference between setting out to murder police and merely setting out to disarm them. He declares:

> Even to take the Police evidence all through & the Two Years Career of me and my companions will show that we were anything but blood-thirsty and likewise in the whole of our Career we never ill used or mal-treated women or child and always refrained from doing a cowardly act.

But he returns to the 'plan' at Glenrowan and the bizarre 'reward' strategy:

> I thought it might be wise to leave them surrounding their Police Barracks at Glenrowan, and get possession of their Train and Horses without an encounter, and get a civilian to Claim the reward so when the Police obtained their Horses they would have no entisement to follow me as the Reward would have been obtained so they would not interfere with me until such times as there was another Reward issued and if they did not give the Reward to the man that Claimed it no person would inform on me again.

Putting the best possible construction on this preposterous 'plan' of Ned's, he may have concocted it to divert attention from the true strategy and intention of the Glenrowan campaign and so protect those loyal followers who, knowingly or not, had prepared to join the Gang in Murder and High Treason. But this wasn't something dreamt up on the spur of the moment like the 'Sullivan' fable at Glenrowan. The decoy-siege and reward plan had been described on 5 November and, after five days, developed further in this letter. With the agitation for reprieve always in the background of his isolation during this last week, Ned had become torn between the certainty of his death and the seductive possibility of survival. In this cruel borderland his grip on reality had become tenuous, his condition described as 'a state of nervous unrest'. In spite of this, his plea throughout the three letters is not for mercy but for understanding.

At the end, as he finished dictating the additional details of the 'reward' plan and waited for the warder to write the last few words, the sad mirage faded and he went on to finish the letter, confronting the inevitability of death with dignity:

> I know now it is useless trespassing on your valuable time because [of] the expense the Government have been put to which was not my fault they will only be satisfied with my life, although I have been found guilty and Condemned to death on a charge of all men in the World I should be the last one to be guilty of. there is one wish in conclusion I would like you to grant me, that is the release of my Mother before my execution as detaining her in prison Could not make any difference to the government now, for the day will come when all men will be judged by their mercy and deeds and also if you would grant permission for my friends to have my body that they might bury it in Consecrated ground.

For the last time, Ned scratched a cross with his crippled right hand, identified by Buck as 'Edward Kelly his mark'. The strokes are unusually bold and firm.

The Executive Council met early, at midday, to forestall a deputation of women led by Maggie, Kate Lloyd and her mother. It considered Ned's case for the third time and, for the third time, 'unanimously decided that the law should take its course'. Ned would die at 10 tomorrow morning. On hearing the news, the waiting women 'completely broke down' and Maggie prepared to catch the afternoon train back to Glenrowan. She wanted to be with the children when Ned was hanged.

At Ned's request — because he wanted a portrait for his family — the gaol photographer, Charles Nettleton, took two photos, probably during his midday exercise. Standing in the shade against a bluestone wall, Ned posed for a full-length study. Conscious of his crippled right hand, he clenched it into a fist planted on his hip and masked his withered left arm by holding the cord attached to his leg irons. For a close-up, he stared out past the camera, long, dark hair carefully oiled and combed, his face fleshier and paler than in his outlaw days but still with a touch of fire in eyes slightly narrowed against the daylight, seeing far beyond the dusty yard and grimy bluestone.

That afternoon Ellen was brought to see her son. Traditionally she told him, 'Mind you die like a Kelly, son' — strange words from a mother like Ellen to a son such as Ned. It is more believable that she said, 'I mind you'll die like a Kelly, son.'

Jim, Kate and Grace were also allowed to make their last farewells to him. Even the *Telegraph* had to report that it was 'a most affecting scene', though later claiming that Jim declared, 'As long as he lived, Ned should never die — that, "he should be avenged".'

There were other visitors, unrecorded by the press, on Ned's last day. Gaol Governor Castieau brought his 13-year-old son Godfrey to meet the condemned man. It was an uncharacteristic gesture from Castieau, appreciated by Ned and acknowledged with a gesture of his own. He reached his hand through the bars, placed it on Godfrey's head and said, 'Son, I hope you grow up to be as fine a man as your father.' The meeting had an extraordinary impact on the boy, generating a lifelong fascination with Ned Kelly. Tall and good looking, he became an actor and, as Godfrey Cass, would play Ned in three films — the last time in 1923 when Cass was 57, yet still able to recapture the strange power of the man he had met so briefly.

The other visitors who escaped the eyes and ears of the press were Kate and Tom Lloyd. What passed between Ned and Kate in their short time together has never been spoken of, but Ned's farewell to Tom is recorded:

> Tom, near the head of the Rose River, line up the hill in front of you to the west and the rocks behind at the east and you'll find a place in the creek like a cattle crossing. Just as you come up out of the crossing you'll find a hollow stump and there's a good saddle in it.

Tom would always repeat his cousin's farewell with a smile, yet his eyes used to fill with tears.

On his last afternoon Ned was visited again by chaplain Donaghy and also by Dean O'Hea from Pentridge, here not as prison chaplain but as the priest who had baptised the infant son of Ellen and Red and the man who had helped send Ned out of Pentridge as a 19-year-old, determined to lead an honest life. O'Hea promised Ned he would be beside him on the scaffold in the morning — his minister from birth to death. The priests left him to enjoy his last meal, 'roast lamb, green peas and a bottle of claret'.

That night, while a crowd of 4000 gathered outside the Robert Burns Hotel to launch a last deputation to the Governor and the Treasury, Warder William Buck sat in the outer cell watching Ned behind the iron grille. As if this were any other night, perhaps mellowed by the claret, he spent some time 'singing hymns and songs, "The Sweet Bye and-bye" being apparently an especial favourite'. Eventually he stopped singing and Warder Buck matter-of-factly recorded the prisoner's last night on earth:

Kelly was sent to bed at half-past 1 a.m., and remained very restless up to half-past 2, when he slept well up to 5 o'clock. He awoke at 5 o'clock, got up, and went on his knees, and prayed till twenty minutes past 5, when he laid down again.

Ned rose at 8 and sang or hummed a few songs. At 8.45 the black-smith arrived to chisel out the rivets and remove his leg irons. With the irons Ned lost the special belt and went to his execution with 'a twisted blue handkerchief' holding up his corduroys. Soon after the arrival of Dean Donaghy at 9, warders escorted Ned out of the condemned cell and across a courtyard to the new wing of the gaol. Walking through the hospital garden, he remarked on the beauty of some flowers and passed the hospital handcart that was waiting to carry his body. In the new wing he was led to a light-well below a skylight and cupola at the meeting point of two cell blocks, then taken up an iron staircase to a railed, U-shaped gallery. Ned looked around and smiled. This was his destination.

Above the gallery opposite was an oregon beam with an inch-thick rope coiled around it. Below the beam, a large wooden trapdoor, 'the drop', was set in the floor, held shut by a bolt that would be jerked from its socket by a metal lever jutting upwards to waist height at one end.

Ned walked around past the gallows to a cell with an open door. He and Dean Donaghy entered, soon to be joined by Dean O'Hea with a priest carrying a tall, gilt cross and a boy to serve as an acolyte. Behind the closed cell door, Ned knelt and the last sacraments began.

Outside the huge iron-studded gate of the gaol a crowd of more than 5000 had gathered and 100 vehicles 'of all descriptions' were drawn up. The *Herald* noted,

The general sympathy which appeared to be felt for the condemned man was not confined to the lower orders alone, as the crowd which assem-bled around the gaol gates this morning testified ... Women — many of them young, well-dressed and apparently respectable — were there mix-ing with the others.

To the jaundiced eye of the *Telegraph* reporter the huge crowd was 'a mob of nondescript idlers, whose morbid and depraved tastes ... had led them from ... the pursuit of honest toil ... It must be acknowledged that the criminal and most depraved classes in the community predominated.'

New arrivals were closely studied to see if they could be members of the Kelly family or their friends. If this hope had brought the crowd here, they were disappointed. Jim, Kate, Grace, Wild and the Lloyds were all at the Robert Burns Hotel, waiting silently for the coming of 10 o'clock.

Perhaps by choice, Ellen was in the prison laundry, among the last of the female convicts who had not yet been transferred to Pentridge. She had long before earned the respect of fellow prisoners and the prison officers, and not one of them would ever breathe a word of how Ellen carried herself through this dark hour.

Approaching 10 o'clock, twenty-seven official witnesses gathered on the coconut matting covering the stone floor of the light well and looked up at the ritual in which the Sheriff, Colonel Rede, in his black uniform frock coat, presented his warrant to Castieau for 'the body of Edward Kelly'. Rede then crossed to the cell door and knocked. As it was opened Upjohn, the hangman, chicken thief and one time plunderer of dunnies, emerged from the compartment at the other end of the gallery and crossed to Ned's cell with a glance down at the witnesses. He was in his shirt sleeves, tall and powerful for his 60 years, with a stubble of white hair. He carried a broad strap and what looked like a small white cloth bag. As he went to pin Ned's arms behind his back with the strap (a normal procedure to stop the victim trying to save himself by grabbing the rope), Ned protested, 'There's no need to pinion me, I'll go forward quietly,' but, when told it was 'indispensable' he submitted, undoubtedly suffering pain as his wasted left arm was forced back and the strap buckled. Upjohn next unfolded the white execution hood and fitted it on Ned's head, doubled above his forehead like a nightcap. Then, preceded by the priest with the cross, the two deans reciting the sacrament of the dying and the young acolyte, Ned walked out on to the gallery.

As he stepped onto the drop, Ned said something. To the *Herald* man, it was 'Such is life', the words Beechworth's *Advertiser* attributed to him when told 'the hour of his death'. The *Argus* would claim that he said, moments later, 'Ah well, I suppose it has come to this.' Surprisingly, the hostile *Telegraph* might have come closest to the truth:

> On leaving the cell, and before stepping upon the drop, an expression, with a sigh, escaped Kelly's lips, which the warders and the Governor interpreted to this effect — 'Ah well, I suppose' — probably meaning to say he supposed this was the last of it, or this is what it had come to, but the expression was never concluded.

Ned walked calmly and steadily to the centre of the drop, though one witness thought he saw a slight shudder as Ned stopped under the rope.

Upjohn then fitted the noose over his victim's head and adjusted the massive slip-knot under his ear, with gaol surgeon Dr Edward Barker watching closely. This was Upjohn's first execution and correct placement of the knot was crucial for a quick death. A reporter noticed that Ned moved his head to make Upjohn's task easier. The knot was pulled down, slightly tighter and, as the hangman's hands went to the hood, Ned was seen to look up at the skylight above him. A last glimpse of sunlight before the hood was pulled down over his face. Upjohn moved to pull the lever. Just as Dr Barker stretched out his hand 'as if to adjust the rope', the trap crashed open and the body of Ned Kelly dropped 8 feet into immortality. The moment was proclaimed by a great howl of rage from the convicts in the cell block. It was four-and-a-half minutes past ten.

The echoes died, the priests continued their prayers, the strained hemp creaked as the body slowly revolved, the light catching 'a plain ring' on the right hand. Another shallow rope scar on the top of the beam recorded another death.

Reporter J. Middleton of the *Herald* stared at the hooded figure suspended 4 feet above the stone floor:

> There was for a second or two only the usual shudder that passes through the frame of a hanged man but then the
> LEGS WERE DRAWN UP
> for some distance, and fell suddenly again. This movement was repeated several times, but finally all motion ceased, and at the end of
> FOUR MINUTES ALL WAS OVER
> and Edward Kelly had gone to a higher tribunal to answer for his faults and crimes.

Middleton feared that Ned had taken all that time to die, but death had been 'absolutely instantaneous'. The flexing of his legs was caused by 'postmortem involuntary contraction of the extensor muscles'.

Outside, as the clock had struck ten, an unidentified woman dropped to her knees 'and offered audible prayers for the repose of Kelly's soul'.

In the Robert Burns Hotel there was a long silence, with the minutes ticking by, eventually broken by Jim Kelly when he trusted himself to speak. 'Ah well, the poor devil is out of his misery anyhow by this time.' Wild Wright muttered 'something about the police'.

Carefully avoiding any hint of the supernatural, a journalist outside the gaol recorded an odd detail:

> A singular coincidence attached to the execution was the sudden change in the weather which occurred just as the bell tolled the prisoner's death knell. The wind, which had been blowing from the northward all the morning, raising up clouds of dust over the people in the street,

suddenly dropped and veered around to the south. The cool change in the atmosphere seemed to be emblematical of the finish of the last act in the Kelly tragedy . . .

The last act had not quite finished. The body hung for the required half-hour before being taken down, pronounced dead, placed on the hand-cart and trundled out across the courtyard to the hospital dead-house. When the hood was removed, it was found that:

> Kelly's face presented a most life-like appearance. The features were undisfigured, and their expression was one of remarkable placidness [one man would speak of 'his smile in death'] while the eyes wore a bright expression.

Mr Maximilian Kreitmayer, proprietor of the waxworks in Bourke Street, shaved Ned's hair and beard and made a mould of his head for a death mask which would be on display at his establishment the following day. Then the body was at the mercy of science — a group of doctors and students. The head was sawn off and the brain removed — a point-less atrocity that has been common knowledge for many years. The brain would be given some spurious scientific value, preserved in a jar; the head, stripped of flesh, would be kept purely as a curio, supposedly as a paper weight on the table of some minor government official. But this was only the beginning.

> The students particularly went in heavily taking part of his body and generally examining every organ. It was a ghastly sight — indeed, hardly ever parallelled. I am told that portions of the corpse are now in nearly every 'curiosity' cabinet in Melbourne medical men's places. The skull was taken possession of by one gentleman, and it is probable that he may hereafter enlighten us upon the peculiarities of the great criminal's brain. The medical men call these things 'preparations' . . .

The headless, mutilated corpse was put in a rough, redgum coffin, covered with quicklime and buried in the gaol yard the following day, without any marking on the wall beside it. As one paper gloated, 'The body of the last Victorian bushranger was laid to rot in unconsecrated ground.' The monster was at last disposed of. It had all been properly done.

♣
___

23

LEGACY AND LEGEND

11 NOVEMBER 1880 –

Far from being 'the last act of the Kelly tragedy', Ned's death was the prologue to a complex saga that reaches to the present day, interweaving the stories of the ongoing Kelly rebellion and its outcome, the fate of the Kelly family and their friends, the impact of the outbreak on the police force and the steady advance of Ned Kelly into legend.

The threads of this tapestry were distinguishable within days of the execution. One night four men 'howled' and fired a shot outside the new Greta police station; a shot was fired at the Glenrowan barracks; Jim and Kate Kelly appeared in a bizarre stage presentation before Ned was even buried; the press started clamouring for an inquiry into the police conduct of the Kelly pursuit and, more disturbingly, their role in the genesis of the Outbreak; and Sir Redmond Barry had to suspend his official duties because of 'a boil or carbuncle', a symptom of the diabetes which, with 'congestion of the lungs', would kill him only twelve days after Ned's execution. Some people remembered Ned's words after Barry had sentenced him to hang, 'I will see you there, where I go,' and recalled Ned saying, 'The day will come when we will all have to go to a bigger court than this.'

A handsome statue of Sir Redmond would be erected outside his Public Library, prompting an irreverent observation by journalist Les Carlyon a century later:

> There are two other statues near Barry's; St George and the Dragon and a magnificent Joan of Arc. The pigeons and seagulls ignore these last two, but defecate profusely on the Barry statue. The thought is pure mischief but irresistible: are we seeing the evidence of some judgement in that higher court?

The *Age* was quite confident of the benefits that would spring from the hanging of Ned Kelly, who, in the paper's words, had 'plunged recklessly into war with society':

Kelly kept in prison would have expected pardon after a term of years, or would have been plotting to escape; would have been regarded as still conqueror over the law. Kelly in his grave is an impressive lesson of morality. The scores of young men who are just on the boundary line between respectability and crime ... cannot plead that they were not warned in letters of blood.

Beechworth's *Advertiser*, however, saw all too clearly that the hanging had only inflamed, 'in what is known as the KELLY country', an already explosive situation, reporting that 'some relatives and friends of the late outlaws ... talk openly of revenge'. While not wishing 'to create a public alarm', the paper urged:

An Act should be immediately passed empowering the Governor-in-Council not only to suspend the Habeas Corpus Act in a defined region, but to place it in a state of siege. No one within the boundaries should be allowed to carry or possess fire-arms without a certificate from a police magistrate and power ought to be given to billet police in suspected houses ... if a handful of ruffians commence a war of incendiarism and personal outrage, the public ought to be so armed as to make it a war of extermination.

The *Advertiser* advocated the death penalty for arson and any future attempt to wreck a train, concluding, 'Parliament ... cannot over-estimate the magnitude or importance of the situation.'

One man had no problem understanding the magnitude of the situation: Constable Robert Graham. He had accepted a posting to Greta after Senior Constable Kelly had flatly refused, considering it almost suicidal and calling Greta 'the worst place in the Colony'. With three constables, Leahy, Wallace and Macdonald, Graham had set up his station on 29 September on the first floor of Bridget O'Brien's Hotel. It was an extraordinary location. Graham was maintaining the Queen's peace directly above the bar where Kelly sympathisers spoke of vengeance and sedition. He had instructions from Nicolson, as Acting Chief Commissioner, that 'every offence against the law shall be instantly and strongly grappled with', yet he also had the support of Sadleir, who had handed over the bodies of Dan and Steve then carefully avoided a clash over the inquest. Sadleir's policy was to uphold the law in the Kelly Country while avoiding unnecessary confrontation. Graham was perfect for the job.

No one — including his family — knew why Robert Graham became a policeman. He was 36, tallish and brown-bearded. A gentle man, he was also a crack shot, a fine horseman and a capable bushman. His 11-year police career had been 'honest and unspectacular'. His transfer from Camperdown to the Kelly pursuit in November 1879 had interrupted a romance with Mary Kirk, daughter of a local blacksmith, and the two planned marriage as soon as the Kelly business was over. But

Graham impressed Sadleir at the siege of Glenrowan ('he behaved bravely and well') and earned from him the challenging Greta appointment. Now his marriage must be postponed until he could deal with the situation which threatened the peace of this tiny town and the whole north-east.

In spite of the tension Graham treated the locals tolerantly. A lad with too much grog under his belt and looking for trouble would be given a talking to, but when some young bucks from Wangaratta kicked up their heels in town, Graham and his men 'came down on them like a ton of bricks'. The young men of Greta realised that they were being treated with fairness, not weakness.

Graham yarned with the older men, often over a bottle of brandy he carried in a saddle bag on his regular sorties to familiarise himself with the district and its people. He wanted to find the underlying cause of the continuing unrest, something he believed lay deeper than a quest for revenge. It was Ned's uncle, Tom Lloyd, who gave him the key piece to this baffling jig-saw:

> The Kellys wanted ground, he said. Now, the sympathisers wanted land, and if they could be guaranteed access to that land, they would get rid of the few troublemakers and hotheads remaining in the district.

Graham passed on this advice to Sadleir, who was now better prepared for a critical meeting with 'one of the Kelly relatives, the prospective leader of the new gang . . . when matters looked most threatening':

> My interviewer was pretty frank, not to say impudent, at first. When he was reminded of what happened to the Kelly Gang and that, though a constable might be shot, the police went on for ever, he became more reasonable, and asked only that those of the Kelly circle who had taken up land should not be dispossessed. I was able to promise that *no-one who continued to obey the law would be interfered with, but that no further selections would be allowed to doubtful characters.* [my italics]

Sadleir was saying, in effect, that the black list was alive and well but would be applied with greater regard for a man's present conduct rather than his links with the Kellys.

As the year drew uneasily to its end the four constables had begun to gain acceptance in the town and Constable Wallace was establishing a special rapport with the widowed Bridget O'Brien. The new year seemed to promise better times, but in fact it would bring the threat of a full-blown Kelly rebellion, almost a year after Glenrowan.

All this time Maggie Skilling and Tom Lloyd had been the core of the Kelly family. Tom, in his new role as head of the household, was keen for peace and would show a readiness to co-operate with the police by helping to locate a police horse lost from Glenrowan.

Jim and Kate arrived back home in December after strange adventures. The night of Ned's execution they had appeared on the stage of the Apollo Hall above Bourke Street's Eastern Arcade, seated side by side in armchairs with Kate holding a bunch of flowers. The curious or the sympathetic paid 1 shilling admission and this sad exhibition was said to have taken 'a good deal of money' before it was closed down by police the following day — supposedly at the instigation of William Gaunson. The hall's licensee was told that 'if the exhibition were continued, the Chief Secretary would be moved to cancel the licence'. That night the Georgia Minstrels resumed their season at the Apollo while Jim headed home 'in order to bring down the Kelly horses with which an entertainment is to be given in the Hippodrome, with Jim and Kate Kelly as the riders'.

Wisely abandoning the idea of another Melbourne appearance, Jim and Kate took their horses to Sydney on the steamer *Katoomba*, accompanied by 'two agents', and by Saturday 22 November were arranging a 'Kelly Show' in that city. On the Tuesday night, in 'an old out-house up a lane in King Street', Jim appeared riding 'Ned Kelly's grey mare' with 'Ned Kelly's saddle' while Kate, 'in deep black' was mounted on her pony, Oliver Twist. For two nights, the show was 'well attended by sympathetic audiences' at 1 shilling a head. On the third night police blocked access to the lane and entrepreneurs Tomkins and Pringle faced the remarkable charge of Creating a Nuisance Through Allowing Relatives of an Executed Criminal to Exhibit Themselves.

◆

ONE EARLY SUMMER evening Constable Graham had ridden up from Greta through Kellys Gap when he saw a thoroughbred galloping across a paddock with a slip of a girl clinging to its bare back, her arms around its neck. Assuming the horse was bolting, he had started to give chase when he realised that the girl had complete control of the animal. He reined in and watched as she continued her wild ride over the hills. Robert Graham had almost met Kate Kelly. Kate didn't stay long at Eleven Mile Creek. On 17 December she passed through Melbourne, dogged by detectives, who reported that she was accompanying a publican to Adelaide to work as a barmaid — and act as a drawcard for his hotel.

Jim Kelly became the focus of police fears and sympathisers' hopes. Bigger and more hot-headed than Ned, he had the potential to be another dangerous figurehead. He met with Dick Hart and Paddy Byrne, the three young men 'almost like the ghosts of the Kelly Gang, uncertain who had summoned them or why'. Constable Armstrong, who had spoken to Jim for an hour and a half, reported him as saying:

> I will not enter the bush; I have got a good trade; I can earn £3 a week by making boots; and I am too fond of going to theatres, and taking girls in

the gardens at night, for the work; *but should I ever be interfered with by the police* I will not do as Ned has done; I will shoot every man and have satisfaction. [my italics]

Armstrong also spoke with Tom Lloyd and Dinny McAuliffe, reporting, 'They seem inclined to be most friendly with the police, *if the police will treat them in the same friendly way.*' [my italics] By early 1881 an uneasy peace was settling over the north-east, an armistice of mutual wariness.

In the second week of February Ellen was released from Melbourne Gaol with only eight months remission, a month less than normal on a three-year sentence. This was inexplicable treatment in view of her three-month imprisonment before trial and the trauma of her son's execution, quite apart from her unblemished prison record. By now, Kate was back home from Adelaide ('where her "season" was not a success') and came down to Melbourne with a sister, probably Grace, to meet her mother and travel with her back to the north-east. Did they get off the train at Glenrowan and see the ruins of the inn, with a rough shack thrown together against one of the chimneys as a home for Ann Jones and her children? Did Ellen stand on the platform where Dan's charred body had lain? There was a smell of burning eucalypt in the air, palls of dark smoke rising from distant ranges, angry bushfire light on the bleached grass slopes of the Bald Hill as summer came to a hellish end. Kate carried 'flower-plants and two cypresses in pots'. Asked what they were for, she said, 'To put on poor Danny's grave.'

The arrival at Eleven Mile Creek was commemorated by a photograph. There is a new bark roof on the house Ned had built for his mother and lace cafe curtains across the widows. A small, deciduous tree or shrub planted out the front is bare, killed or sent into an early autumn by this brutal February. Ellen sits on a kitchen chair in front of the verandah, smiling in the shadow of an unstylish hat, young Jack is close by her, little Ellen has a pet lamb with a ribbon around its neck and feeds it from a bottle while a surprisingly young-looking Grace pats the Kelly cattle dog, Faith. Kate, in her black 'Kelly Show' costume and hat, also sits on a bentwood chair, her arm protectively around toddler Alice who leans against her half-sister, unsure of the lady they say is her mother. To one side, in frock coat and top hat, stands the Reverend Gould, who had married Ellen to George King. No longer at Benalla, he has driven here to welcome her home.

Everyone is in their Sunday best, defying the mid-afternoon heat of that long-lost day to honour the occasion. There is an air of ordinariness over it all; an impression of peace and happier times to come.

By March Beechworth's *Advertiser*, which had trumpeted its dire warning four months earlier, could announce, somewhat prematurely: 'The Kelly business is all over, and the family have settled down quietly at Greta, and are likely to forget the past, and give us no more trouble.'

A board had been appointed three weeks after the destruction of the Gang to distribute the Kelly reward. It held its first meeting a week after Ned's execution and advertised in Sydney and Melbourne for claims, attracting ninety-two applications which were commented on by Nicolson or Sadleir then considered by the board. Between 8 March and 21 March 1881, only five witnesses were examined: former Chief Secretary Robert Ramsay and four Glenrowan eye witnesses — volunteer Charles Rawlins (whose evidence lent considerable support to his own application) and journalists Melvin, McWhirter and Allen (who had not lodged claims but probably should have). The board rejected twenty-four claimants — including Constable McIntyre, Ellen Sherritt and Anton Wick — and divided the £8000 between the rest.

Hare received the lion's share of £800. School teacher Curnow (already presented with a clock specially selected by Captain Standish), was awarded £550 and launched a campaign for more, which succeeded in April 1882 when the amount was increased to £1000. Senior Constable Kelly came next with £377 11 shillings and eightpence; Sergeant Steele with £290 13 shillings and ninepence; Constable Bracken, £275 13 shillings and ninepence; Superintendent Sadleir, £240 17 shillings and threepence; Stanhope O'Connor, £237 15 shillings. Railway Guard Jesse Dowsett was awarded an ungenerous £175 13 shillings and ninepence. The other applicants received diminishing amounts, generally related to the hour they had arrived at Glenrowan. A glaring exception was Detective Ward, who was not at the siege yet received £100 because of his 'connection with the employment of Aaron Sherritt'. The board's rationale was that Aaron had provided information which had resulted in his killing, which had led in turn to the siege at Glenrowan and the end of the Gang. Because Aaron's widow was already provided for with a pension, the money went to the man who had conspired to bring about her husband's murder. An even more glaring injustice was the treatment of the Aboriginal troopers. White constables in the first attack on the inn each received £137 11 shillings and eightpence; the black constables with them were awarded £50 each. Worse still, because, in the eyes of the board, *it would not be desirable to place any considerable sum of money in the hands of persons unable to use it*, their shares were paid to the governments of Victoria and Queensland, *to be dealt with at their discretion*. It appears that none of the Aborigines ever received a penny of his money.

Stirring up the ashes of Glenrowan and distributing the 'blood money' caused some resentment in the Kelly Country but it was a mere curtain raiser to the eruption of anger caused by the Royal Commission which trod on the heels of the Reward Board.

The demand for a police inquiry had first sounded early in the Gang's outlawry, then built to a crescendo immediately after Glenrowan and again after Ned's execution. The day after his trial Ned had 'expressed a hope . . . that the result of his execution might lead to an investigation into the whole conduct and management of the police.'

On 7 March 1881 the Marquis of Normanby, at the request of Graham Berry, issued Letters Patent appointing a Royal Commission. The first witness, Captain Standish, began his evidence on 23 March. By 20 September the Commission would hear sixty-six witnesses answering 17 874 questions to produce 682 closely printed foolscap pages of evidence. The chairman was Francis Longmore, enemy of Standish and the police since the days of the Harry Power pursuit. One of the Commission's seven members — and its most dutiful, apart from Longmore — was George Wilson Hall, the 'closet Kelly sympathiser', editor and newspaper proprietor, and now a member of parliament. The police were in for rough handling.

In Sadleir's words, 'Mr Longmore was eminently honest and conscientious, but he went relentlessly for scalps.' Sadleir was also 'disposed to think that this commission had all the faults of other like bodies that our short history has brought into being.' Rules of evidence were not followed, allegation had the weight of truth, hearsay could outweigh personal knowledge and opinion was permitted or encouraged.

The bumbling of the police pursuit was exposed and, while the Commissioners would state that 'no evidence has been adduced to support the allegation that either the outlaws or their friends were subjected to persecution or unnecessary annoyance by the police', the Commission's minutes would provide ample material to support such a view.

The washing of the force's dirty linen proved an unpleasant spectacle. Standish paraded his arrogance and pomposity, Brooke Smith his paranoia, and the unworkable triangle of Hare, Nicolson and Standish was exposed in bitchery from Standish and thundering indignation from Nicolson. Hare tried to sail through it all on a cloud of self-esteem, airily unconcerned with inconvenient facts and details. Longmore and his fellow commissioners watched the upper echelons of the Victoria Police self-destructing. The sittings were open to the press so the public could not only watch these displays of what the *Advertiser* called 'most ungentlemanlike and un-officerlike ill-feeling', but also hear some highly indiscreet revelations. In the first minutes of his evidence Standish saw fit to reveal that Brickey Williamson, in Pentridge, 'entirely corroborated every word of Fitzpatrick's evidence; and he gave me some considerable information, and volunteered to assist me in every kind of way'. There were immediate threats to kill Brickey on his release. There was also alarming evidence about the work of police spies, some of whom were easily identified, even if unnamed.

Within weeks the north-east was at explosion point again. The sympathisers careered around the district in search of traitors, and the police spies — many of them still employed by Sadleir — panicked. Sadleir told the Commission:

> It was inevitable that the agents should take fright at the disclosures by some of the witnesses. At the last there were two agents left. One of these came to me, rushing away from his farm. He had not a penny of money. There was £20 due to him for a reward, and the money was actually coming by post for him, yet he would not wait for it. The other [agent] came to me the following night in much the same state.

At this crisis point Sadleir received an order that all the equipment necessary for extended bush work — 'pack-saddles, tents, compasses etc' — was to be returned to the depot in Melbourne, making it virtually impossible to control areas of the district far from Benalla. Yet his request for new police stations at five potential north-eastern trouble spots had earlier been refused. 'Denied the means of carrying on the work, with safety to the public and credit to myself,' he applied to leave the district on 22 April.

Inspector Montfort took over at Benalla with a dozen reinforcements, and Stanhope O'Connor was sent up to take charge of black trackers. It all had an air of *déjà vu*, strengthened on 25 April by a telegram from Steele.

> Stolen last night from Acock's, Seven-mile Creek, two large pit saws, *supposed taken to construct armour out of*. Would be well to send trackers at once to Acock's near Glenrowan. Will have tracks, if any, preserved.
>
> *A. L. M. Steele*. [my italics]

Next day there was a report from Constable Graham, still operating precariously in Bridget O'Brien's hotel.

> A number of them were here yesterday drinking, viz: — Jack Quinn, Tom Lloyd Jun., Paddy McAuliffe, Tom McAuliffe, Jack McMonigal, and Jack Nolan; and *from their manner I am led to believe that another outbreak among them is imminent*. [my italics]

Constable Graham now slept with a loaded revolver under his pillow and he and his three troopers carried loaded Martini Henry carbines whenever they left their 'station', ready for the breaking of the storm. Then, the very day he wrote his report to Sadleir, a leading article appeared in the *Benalla Standard*, run by George Wilson Hall, whose sources of information among the sympathisers were more reliable than most.

There is not the slightest doubt but that the formation of another gang of bushrangers is being meditated in the Greta district ... the Kelly sympathizers have recently spoken openly to this effect ... some secret work is occupying their attention. *The sympathizers' rendezvous — Mrs Kelly's house — is seldom empty and ... the number of visitors to this domicile is very large.* Many threats of revenge have been made since the tragedy at Glenrowan, and grave fears are daily entertained of another outbreak. [my italics]

Father Thomas Egan of Wangaratta, a great horse lover and known friend of the Kelly family, often drank with the sympathisers at O'Brien's. Robert Graham approached him with an extraordinary request. Would the Father ride with him to Eleven Mile Creek? He wanted to meet Mrs Kelly.

Behind the lace cafe curtain of the house Ned Kelly had built, where it had all started three years before, Robert Graham, Father Egan and Ellen Kelly drank tea while Graham put his case. He pointed out that Ellen Kelly had lost two sons in conflict with the police, that her third son was in grave danger of becoming involved in an outbreak which could lead to further tragedy and loss of life. Would she help Graham prevent that tragedy? Use her influence with the sympathisers to convince them that this planned outbreak must end in disaster?

For a time there was no way of knowing if Graham's approach had been successful. Then, one afternoon, Jim Kelly drove his mother to O'Brien's Hotel and the sympathisers watched as they went upstairs to have tea with Constable Graham. On a Saturday soon after, Graham was seen riding beside the Kelly buggy in full uniform on the way to a race meeting, then spending the afternoon with the tall, bearded bushman and the small lady in black, showing for all to see — selector and squatter alike — that the bitterness of the past had gone. Nothing could change what had happened, but perhaps the wounds could heal as surely as the fire-blackened timber on the surrounding hills was shooting green from the autumn rains.

By the end of the year a suit of armour made from saw blades rusted in the bush near Greta. Robert Graham travelled to Camperdown, married his Mary Kirk on New Year's Eve and brought her back to Greta, to a new police station he had set up in a farmhouse. Their first child would be born there. Constable Wallace, who had fought at Glenrowan and toughed out the dark days at Greta with Graham, would leave the force and marry Bridget O'Brien. They would take over the Broken River Hotel in Benalla. Here, in April 1893, 'a little boy' would appear with Sergeant Kennedy's watch for return to his widow.

As soon as the threat of rebellion was over, Jim Kelly and Wild Wright rode up to the Riverina and stole two horses near Cootamundra. They brought them back to the Kelly Country but were tracked down and remanded to trial at Wagga, where Wild was discharged and Jim sentenced to five years on the roads.

Meanwhile *The Second Progress Report of the Royal Commission of Enquiry into the Circumstances of the Kelly Outbreak, the Present State and Organization of the Police Force etc*, was presented to both houses of Parliament 'by His Excellency's command!'

Standish, already retired, was criticised for 'his want of impartiality, temper, tract and judgement' which caused many problems among his officers. He would die within two years, mentally unstable, living at the Melbourne Club in genteel poverty. Hare and Nicolson were recommended for retirement. Both became police magistrates. The Commission blamed Sadleir for 'several errors of judgement' in the Kelly pursuit and found his leadership at Glenrowan 'not judicious or calculated to raise the police force in the estimation of the public'. He was recommended for demotion to the lowest level of superintendent. Brooke Smith, for his 'indolence and incompetence', was 'to be called on to retire'.

Detective Ward's murderous strategy to use Aaron Sherritt as bait was cloaked under 'active and efficient service'; a slap-on-the-wrist demotion of one grade was recommended because he had misled his superiors. Sergeant Steele's demented conduct at Glenrowan was ignored but, for failing to pursue the Gang on their way to the Warbys in the week after Stringybark, the Commission thought he should be demoted to Constable. (There was a huge outcry from the respectable folk of Wangaratta, with petitions and public meetings, and it didn't happen.) The four police in Aaron Sherritt's hut when he was killed were guilty of 'gross cowardice' and the dismissal of the remaining three was urged. (Armstrong had already resigned and was leaving for America.) The Commission recommended the immediate dismissal of the double agent James Wallace from the Education Department, and advised against the permanent appointment of Stanhope O'Connor to the Victoria Police.

The broader examination of the police force produced a number of recommendations which in some cases proved effective — as in the complete revamping of the detective force — and in other cases were totally ignored — as in a recommendation to do away with the impractical black 'bobby' helmet. It was not replaced until sixty-four years later.

There were two important developments. The new Acting Chief Commissioner, H. M. Chomley, was confirmed in his position, the first Chief Commissioner to have risen through the ranks. Regrettably this did not set a lasting pattern, but Chomley made his mark, laying the foundation for a new, revitalised force and restoring the morale that had eroded during the later years of the Standish regime. Perhaps most importantly, the 'Kelly Commission' created in the Victoria Police a tradition of public accountability and self-examination which exists to this day, helping to give the state what is arguably Australia's finest police force. This could be seen as Ned Kelly's most enduring legacy.

After three years Robert Graham asked for transfer from Greta — life was perhaps too comfortable for efficiency — and went on to complete a successful police career, twice honoured for rescues in the flooded Goulburn River, eventually retiring as an inspector with the nickname 'Honest Bob'. His impact on the people of Greta was symbolised for many years by Tom Lloyd wearing a pair of white police riding breeches given to him by Graham. Tom's son, Thomas Patrick, remembered his father in those breeches and recalled him saying, 'If there'd been more like Graham and less like Fitzpatrick, there never would have been a Kelly Outbreak.'

Thomas Patrick Lloyd, second cousin of Ned Kelly, would become a policeman.

Jim Kelly served slightly more than four years of his five-year sentence and came home to Greta at the beginning of 1886. Even then it was an event considered important enough to be the subject of a full-page memo by Superintendent Montfort, reporting: 'he states it is his intention to work at his trade, shoe making. He also states it is his intention to live honestly in future.' In spite of this, Montfort devoted half the page to a detailed description of Jim to be circulated throughout the north-east. The police fears were not groundless. For a time, to Ellen's concern, Jim showed signs of being 'restless'. The phase passed and he set up a bootmaker's shop on the highway at Winton (opposite Lindsay's store where Fitzpatrick had enjoyed his brandy and lemonade), sometimes worked as a drover and, from being an object of suspicion to many, eventually came to be 'universally loved and respected' in the district — a man who lived out a challenging destiny with dignity, his life devoted to the care of his mother, his half brothers and sisters and, later, a sister's children. He died a bachelor in 1946.

In 1888, while working at a station in New South Wales, Kate married blacksmith William Foster and settled in Forbes. The couple had five children, two of whom died in infancy.

Eight years after Kate's marriage in 1896, Maggie died of rheumatic gout, after bearing Tom ten children in thirteen years. Kate survived her sister by only two years, her death by drowning providing a field day for myth makers. In one account, 'milk fever' sets in after the birth of a daughter and she kills herself in a state of what we would call today postpartum psychosis. In another version, 'a Kelly play' visits Forbes and Kate suicides after seeing herself portrayed on stage. Kate had a drinking problem and often, when drunk, spoke of committing suicide, particularly after Maggie's death. She gave birth to a daughter, Catherine, in May of 1898 and before she was even out of bed her husband left home to take a job as 'a horse tailer' at Burrawang, a couple of hours ride from Forbes. He last saw Kate on 5 October when she was 'under the influence of drink', before he rode off. That afternoon Kate, still 'slightly under the influence of drink', asked a neighbour to write a note for her (its contents not revealed) and to look after her five-month-old baby 'as she wanted to go away for a couple of days'. Nine days later her decomposed body was found floating face downwards in a lagoon of the Lachlan River. The Forbes Coroner stated simply: 'That deceased Catherine Foster was found drowned in the lagoon on the Condobolin Road, on the 14th instant, but there was no evidence to show how deceased got into the water.' The stigma of suicide was avoided but a rumour of murder remained.

The Kelly family was notified and Jim drove 'a hooded buggy and pair' up to Forbes to bring Kate's children back. Though legend would have him make the return journey with the baby nestled in a pillow beside him on the buggy seat, little Catherine was also dead by the time he reached Forbes. Jim came back to Eleven Mile Creek with 9-year-old Fred, 8-year-old Gertrude and 3-year-old Maude.

Ellen and Jim raised the three children. Fred, 'the most handsome boy you could look at', joined the 1st A.I.F. and was mortally wounded at Pozières. His last words to an Anglican padre who bent over him were, 'Kiss me, Granny'.

Grace Kelly married Ned Griffiths. Ned's brother Tom moved into the Kelly homestead when Jim built a wattle-and-daub house for himself and his mother on a 640-acre selection he had taken out on a hillside near Kellys Gap. Here Ellen lived out her years, cared for by her son, looking out across the valley she had first seen on that trek from Avenel after Red's death. In her eighties she grew frailer, and her grandson-in-law, Doug Cavanagh, Gertrude's husband, made her a wheel-chair. A last photo of her was taken at 90 as she sat in it, fragile as a bird, a blanket around her lap, a white bonnet tied under her chin, perhaps trying to smile. An overcoated priest, Father Ryan of Benalla, stands protectively by her. In the background is Jim's wattle-and-daub where a log fire burns in the broad, galvanised-iron fireplace lined with clay. You feel that as soon as the photo is taken, Ellen will be grateful to be wheeled back inside. That year, 1922, Joseph Ashmead wrote of Ellen: 'sitting in her chair by the fire; she is cold, always cold. Her great age has made her blood thin and she loves to sit by the fire. Some day she will have her last sleep here.'

A grand-daughter provides a last glimpse of Ellen as she looked in a mirror and murmured. 'That poor old lady, she looks so sick'.

Ellen died peacefully at 2 a.m. on 27 March 1923, with Jim at her side. When he rode into Wangaratta and gave a report of her death to the local paper, it was under the name she had not used for 45 years, Mrs Ellen King. Asked for the names of any children, Jim said brusquely, 'We don't want anything like that,' and left. The member of staff he had spoken to was Sylvia Living, daughter of bank accountant Living of the Jerilderie hold-up, who was now manager of a Wangaratta bank. Recalling the incident, Sylvia told how her father often passed time with retired Sergeant Steele, talking about the Kelly years *as though it was terribly important to them.*

All this time the Kelly Outbreak had been drifting away into the past as an aberration — a last spasm of the bushranging era, interpreted as the actions of a group of criminals in pursuit of criminal gain, supported by people who stood to benefit from their crimes.

Nevertheless there was an indefinable appeal about the Kellys' exploits and they became the subject of the world's first-ever feature-length film, *The Story of the Kelly Gang*, 26 years after Ned's death.

In this raw, 'bushies and bobbies' tale, many factors which explain its appeal stand out. Perhaps most of all, it has a spectacular climax built around two powerful symbols: Ned Kelly in armour and the blazing hotel. Popular imagination combined the two and Ned emerged from the blazing hotel to wage his last fight. As late as 1990, a widely published historical writer could claim:

> The police . . . set fire to the inn in the hope of driving the gang out. During the fire Ned Kelly went outside in an attempt to work around the police lines but when he realised that there were police all around the building he emerged from the trees wearing his armour and began to fire at the police.

This tenacious myth implied that Ned had been forced out to battle with his enemies. It denied his courage, endurance and loyalty to his men. Yet the phrase 'Game as Ned Kelly' became a proud citation and persisted, unsupported by the myth.

◆

OUTSIDE THE TRADITIONS of Irish-Australians who clung to the image of Ned as a martyr in the fight against English misrule, the Ned Kelly of myth was a quintessentially Australian figure. This did no violence to his memory. So powerful was the claim of the land that his pride in his Irishness was almost overpowered by his recognition of himself as a 'native', a 'colonial' and a 'creole', even with the first dream of a republican rebellion in the Irish tradition described in the Jerilderie Letter as a 'colonial stratagem'. Irishmen have a rich store of imagery for traitors and policemen. It takes an Australian to look on a traitor as a black snake; or to see an overweight policeman as a goanna that has gorged itself fat and lazy on a dead bullock.

◆

FOR ALMOST fifty years after Ned Kelly's death, the literature was overwhelmingly anti-Kelly, but in folk songs and often wildly inaccurate oral traditions, a Robin-Hood-like figure survived: good-looking, brave, a fine horseman and bushman and a crack shot, devoted to his mother and sisters, a man who treated all women with courtesy, who stole from the rich to give to the poor, who dressed himself in his enemies' uniforms to outwit them. Most of all a man who stood against the police persecutors of his family and was driven to outlawry when he defended his sister against the advances of a drunken constable.

Such was Ned Kelly the myth — everything the frontier Australian wanted to be and doing many of the things the frontier Australian would have liked to do: take the banks and squatters down a peg or two; defy officious, semi-military police; and perhaps even kill them when the only other choice was to be killed. This mythic Ned Kelly has all the earmarks of a wish-fulfilment figure, like Robin Hood, who was built piece by piece through the centuries on the memory of little more than a name and an idea.

Yet the Ned Kelly of myth — with minor variations and as we have seen, inadequacies — was also the man who would emerge as the Ned Kelly of history. Perhaps he was the only real Robin Hood who has ever lived.

An embodiment of frontier ideals and dreams, he had appeared at a time when Victoria, and much of Australia, was poised between two ages and two worlds. Edward Henty, Victoria's first white settler, died in the year of Ned Kelly's outlawry. The very next year would see Melbourne's first night football match played under electric light. It was a time of bad seasons, plunging gold yields, bank failures and unemployment. At such a time people controlled by an underfinanced, demoralised and sometimes corrupt police force needed a hero, and Ned Kelly provided such a figure, not purely by chance. He and Joe Byrne cultivated an image of the highwayman hero — Dick Turpin with shadings of Michael Dwyer. (The earliest Kelly play, soon after Stringybark, was probably a hurried rework of an earlier highwayman hero script; a Staffordshire pottery figure of Ben Hall had been a repainted Dick Turpin.) Yet the Kellys grew beyond the archetype. If they had started their outlawry by playing gentleman bushrangers, they ended their twenty-month careers living far more complex roles. The figure who walked into legend from the dawn mists of Glenrowan was much more than a badly wounded bushranger in home-made armour and an oilskin coat. As Ned's first true biographer,

Max Brown, would put it in 1948, 'Ned Kelly summoned up such aspects of heroism, dormant in all but a few of us, that some say this man was approaching the stature of god or devil. So does the myth become greater than the reality to act upon reality.'

This was the towering shadow behind the highwayman hero of popular imagination. Those who feared and hated Ned Kelly, like those who saw him as a martyred hero, recognised that shadow as a reality, giving him a stature far beyond that of a mere bushranger.

◆

THE TIDE of the published word turned sharply in 1929 when J. J. Kenneally published his *Complete Inner History of the Kelly Gang and their Pursuers*, which combined deft use of Royal Commission evidence with oral tradition, much of it drawn from Tom Lloyd in the last years of his life. The book portrayed Ned Kelly as straight-out hero and the police, his persecutors, as straight-out villains. It remained in print for more than fifty years, during which the pro-Kelly tide swelled and a handful of anti-Kelly works were swept aside. More recent writing has done nothing to reverse the trend, in spite of one or two anti-Kelly tirades which now seem revisionist. Perhaps the most notable contribution, Dr John McQuilton's *The Kelly Outbreak*, came from a native of the northeast, descended from a Kelly sympathiser.

Today, as the Australian identity is being confused by complex forces, the significance of the Ned Kelly figure is also becoming obscured and confused. The move for an Australian republic might produce the same attention as the centenary of Ned's death in 1980 — when he was seen in terms of 1980 attitudes, values and politics. That year I said:

Ned Kelly has become a commodity to be packaged and promoted. A till to clink, a drum to thump or a banner to be waved. The Kelly helmet has become a piggy bank. Or a sort of national suggestion box — a receptacle for theories and causes and ambitions . . . and even neuroses. None of this, of course, is new. In 1980 it is simply more frenetic.

Ned Kelly will always be seen in the light of a particular time and place — like a mountain which changes appearance with the play of sunlight and cloud.

In the farthest corner of the continent from the Kelly Country, the Yarralin Aboriginal people of north-western Australia have taken Ned Kelly into their Dreaming. They tell how, when salt water covered the land, Ned Kelly and his angel friends came in a boat, made a river and caused the salt water to retreat. Another story relates that he came to Wave River Station and taught the Aborigines there how to make tea and damper, and that, 'although there was only one billy of tea and one little damper, everybody was fed'. This Dreamtime figure who evokes Jesus, Noah and Moses is also present in the age of European settlement. According to another Yarralin story, he kills four policemen at Wyndham and Captain Cook takes him back to England. There Ned's throat is cut, and he is buried. The sky darkens, there is a sound like thunder and Ned Kelly rises up into the sky. The white men are rigid with fear and in distant Darwin buildings tremble.

To the Aborigines Captain Cook and the English represent the theft of their land, the exploitation of their labour and the denial of their cultures. Ned Kelly opposes policemen who carry on the process initiated by Cook and is destroyed by them in the process. He therefore dies as a champion of the Aboriginal people — a white man who was a shaper of the black man's land. The Aborigines affirm that Captain Cook is long dead while Ned Kelly — because he is concerned with freedom, dignity and true justice — lives on.

Among European Australians even Ned's most starry-eyed supporters have never made comparable claims, but if we look beyond the surface of these Dreamtime stories, the Ned Kelly they portray is equally comprehensible to white Australians. Douglas Stewart, Robert Drewe, Sydney Nolan and Albert Tucker have created a Ned Kelly, in words and paint, of similar scope, power and timelessness. Ned speaks in blank verse or terse modern prose. He acts out his tragedy against a kaleidoscope of the Australian landscape, eternally black-armoured, nonhuman, anonymous, or — in Tucker's extraordinary image — he towers, head and shoulders above a ridge, a huge, horned and armoured god-figure, something to worship or destroy.

◆

BECAUSE Ned Kelly was what he was and did what he did, Australians will always speak and write about him in terms of their own gods or their own demons. This is the Kelly phenomenon, today as in 1880. This is perhaps Ned Kelly's tragedy, yet it is also his triumph and the seed of his immortality.

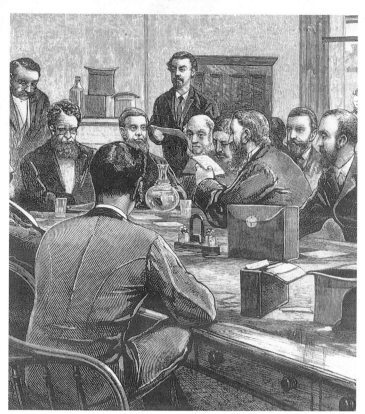

An early sitting of the Royal Commission from the *Sketcher*. From right, Nicolson, Standish and Hare, with bearded, bespectacled chairman Longmore at the head of the table and Stanhope O'Connor in the foreground. (*La Trobe Collection, State Library of Victoria*)

A photo of Ned taken for his family the day before his execution. He plants a fist on his hip to disguise a crippled right hand and masks his withered left arm by holding the cord attached to his leg irons.

Ned Kelly's half-brother, Jack Kelly (King), during his two years of service with the Western Australian Police (1906–08), a brief interlude in his colourful life as a trick rider, 'stockwhip champion of the world' and soldier in the First World War. (*Elsie Pettifer/Leigh Olver*)

Ellen Kelly in 1911 with two of her granddaughters, Lil and Alice Knight, daughters of Ellen Jnr. The hard years have left their mark but at 79 Ellen is still a forceful, resilient woman. The death of her grandson Fred in the First World War will be a cruel blow from which she never completely recovers. She will die in 1923, frail and wandering. *(Elsie Pettifer/Leigh Olver)*

A remarkable photograph celebrating Ellen Kelly's return home from prison in 1881. Ellen sits at right, her daughter Kate at left, outside the house Ned had built for her only four years earlier. The members of the group are identified on p.329.

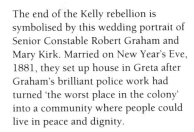

The end of the Kelly rebellion is symbolised by this wedding portrait of Senior Constable Robert Graham and Mary Kirk. Married on New Year's Eve, 1881, they set up house in Greta after Graham's brilliant police work had turned 'the worst place in the colony' into a community where people could live in peace and dignity.

SOME PEOPLE OF THE KELLY STORY

Armstrong, Const. Harry — in charge of police in Aaron Sherritt's hut when Aaron was killed.

Arthur, Const. James — prominent in Last Stand at Glenrowan.

Ashmead, Joseph — boyhood friend of Ned and Dan.

Babington, Sgt James — befriended Ned at Kyneton.

Barry, Ellen — married Aaron Sherritt, 1879. (Her mother, also Ellen.)

Barry, Sir Redmond — judge.

Berry, Graham — radical, sometime Premier of Victoria.

Bindon, Henry — barrister who defended Ned, 1880.

Bowman, John — barrister, sometime Crown Prosecutor, also defended Mrs Kelly and the Kelly sympathisers.

Bracken, Const. Hugh — at Glenrowan in 1880.

Brown, G. Wilson — school inspector.

Byrne family of Woolshed Valley — inc. **Joe**, Ned's best friend and member of Kelly Gang; his mother, **Margret**; brother, **Paddy**.

Byrne brothers of Moyhu, **Thomas** and **Andrew** — prominent graziers (no relation to Joe's family).

Carrington, Thomas — cartoonist and artist.

Castieau, John — governor of Melbourne Gaol, 1880.

Cherry, Martin — civilian mortally wounded by police fire at Glenrowan, 1880.

Chomley, Arthur — crown prosecutor at Ned's trial, 1880.

Curnow, Thomas — Glenrowan schoolteacher.

Delaney family — inc. **Patrick**, helped with Kelly armour; son **John** at Glenrowan.

Devine, Sr Const. George — in charge at Jerilderie, NSW.

Dixon, James — prominent Wangaratta merchant, key figure in town's financial disasters of 1874.

Dowsett, Jesse — railway guard, prominent in Last Stand at Glenrowan.

Dudley, Henry — prisoner of the Gang at Faithfulls Creek, Euroa.

Dwyer, Const. James — prominent in Last Stand at Glenrowan.

Elliott, William — school teacher at Jerilderie, chronicler of the hold-up.

Evans, Evan and **John** — prominent squatters.

Farrell, John — grazier son-in-law of James Whitty.

Fitzgerald, William — with his wife at Faithfulls Creek homestead, Euroa.

Fitzpatrick, Const. Alexander — at Benalla from 1877, sometime friend of Ned.

Flood, Const. Ernest — at Greta in 1872, arch enemy of Ned.

Frost, Bill — sometime lover of Ellen Kelly, sued by her for maintenance of their daughter.

Gascoigne, Const. Charles — prominent in siege of Glenrowan.

Gaunson, David — solicitor and MLA, with his brother William, took up Kelly cause.

Gibney, Dean Mathew — Catholic priest prominent in siege of Glenrowan.

Gloster, James — hawker, Kelly sympathiser and 'prisoner' at Faithfulls Creek, Euroa.

Gould, Ben — hawker and Kelly sympathiser.

Graham, Const. Robert — stationed at Greta in 1880, defused the continuing rebellion.

Gribble, Rev. John — Congregational Minister, Jerilderie.

Gunn, Alex — husband of Ned's sister, Anne.

Hall, Sr Const. Edward — at Greta in 1870, became Ned's enemy.

Hall, G. Wilson — newspaper editor and publisher, later MLA and member of the Kelly Royal Commission, sympathetic to the Kellys.

Hare, Supt Francis — sometime leader of Kelly pursuit, joint captor of Harry Power.

Hart family of Wangaratta — inc. Steve, Dan's best friend and member of Kelly Gang; his brother, Richard, prominent Kelly sympathiser; sister, Ettie, sometime girlfriend of Ned.

Jeffrey, Robert — prominent grazier/farmer, neighbour of James Whitty.

Johnston, Sr Const. Charles — prominent in Kelly pursuit and siege of Glenrowan.

Jones, Ann — publican of Glenrowan Inn, children included Jane (d. 1882) and Jack, (d. 1880) after being wounded in police siege.

Kelly, Sr Const. John — prominent at Last Stand, Glenrowan.

Kelly family — Red (d. 1866) and Ellen; their children, Mary Jane (d. 1851(?); Anne (d. 1872); Ned, Maggie, Jim, Dan, Kate, Grace. Also: Uncles Edward, Daniel and James; Aunts Anne and Mary.

Kennedy, Daniel — selector, former schoolteacher and police spy ('Diseased Stock Agent').

Kennedy, Sgt Michael — killed at Stringybark Creek, 1878.

Kennedy, Sr Det. D. — later Sub-insp. — pursuer of Gang and helped prepare prosecution case for Ned's trial.

Kershaw, James — Kelly sympathiser, married to Jane Graham, friend of Mrs Kelly.

King, George — Ellen Kelly's second husband (1874), father of Ellen, John and Alice.

Living, Edwin — bank accountant at Jerilderie, NSW.

Lloyd, Jack Sr — (d. 1877) married Ellen Kelly's sister, Catherine Quinn, family included Tom Lloyd Jr, leading Kelly sympathiser, and Jack Lloyd Jr(1).

Lloyd, Tom Sr — married Ellen Kelly's sister, Jane Quinn, family included Ned's beloved cousin Kate and Jack Lloyd Jr(2) d. 1879.

Lonigan, Const. Thomas — enemy of Ned, killed at Stringybark Creek, 1878.

Lowry, Allen — under various aliases, minor bushranger, friend of the Kellys at Avenel, later in Ned's horse-stealing gang.

McBean, Robert — prominent Benalla grazier and J.P.

Macdougall, Robert — Kelly prisoner at Faithfulls Creek, Euroa.

McAuliffe family — inc. Dennis, prominent sympathiser.

McDonnell, Patrick — Glenrowan publican and Kelly sympathiser.

McIntyre, Const. Thomas — survivor of police party to Stringybark Creek.

McMonigle, Jack — a friend from Ned's sawmill days, became a Kelly sympathiser.

Metcalf, George — prisoner at Glenrowan, died 1880, after being wounded in police siege.

Montfort, Sgt (later Sub-insp.) — took part in capture of Harry Power, in charge of N.E. District after destruction of Gang (sometimes confused with Const. Mountiford).

Nicholson, Dr John — of Benalla, treated Ned after capture.

Nicolas, Supt William — sometime in charge of Benalla District (often confused with Supt Nicolson).

Nicolson, Supt Charles — sometime

leader of Kelly pursuit, joint captor of Harry Power.

O'Connor, Sub-insp. Stanhope — in charge of Queensland Aboriginal Mounted Police party at Benalla.

O'Hea, Father (later Dean) — baptises Ned, present at his execution.

O'Loghlen, Sir Bryan — sometime Attorney-General and Acting Premier of Victoria.

Power, Harry (real name Johnstone) — bushranger, Ned's tutor.

Quinn family — **James** (d. 1869) and **Mary**, their children included **Patrick** (d. 1850), **Helen**, **Jack**, **James**, **Ellen** (Ned's mother), **Jane**, **Catherine** and **Margaret**.

Quinn, Patrick — confusingly with the same name as the Quinn's dead eldest son, married Margaret Quinn and became Ned's uncle.

Ramsay, Robert — Chief Secretary of Victoria at the time of Glenrowan.

Reardon family — prisoners at Glenrowan, inc. **James** (platelayer), his wife **Margaret**, children inc. **Michael**, seriously wounded in police siege, and baby **Bridget**.

Reynolds, Hillmorton — postmaster at Glenrowan, probably a Kelly sympathiser.

Richards, Probationary Const. Henry — at Jerilderie, NSW.

Ryan family — **Timothy** and **Helen** (Ellen Kelly's sister) children inc. prominent Kelly sympathisers, **Joe** and **Jack**.

Ryan, Dr (later **Sir**) **Charles** — a doctor who treated Ned after capture.

Sadleir, Supt John — in charge of N.E. District from 1878, prominent in siege of Glenrowan.

Scanlon, Const. Michael — killed at Stringybark Creek, 1878.

Scott, Robert — Bank Manager at Euroa.

Scott, Susy — wife of Robert.

Shelton, Dick — son of a prominent Avenel family, saved from drowning by Ned Kelly, 1865(?).

Sherritt family — including **Aaron**, prominent Kelly sympathiser and double agent, killed by Joe Byrne, 1880; his brother **Jack**, double agent, joined police at Glenrowan.

Skilling, (spelt in police records as 'Skillion') **Maggie** — Ned's sister, married to **Bill**, imprisoned from 1878.

Smith, Insp. Alexander Brooke — a paranoid pursuer of the Gang.

Smyth, Charles — a Crown Prosecutor at Ned's trial, 1880.

Standish, Capt. Frederick — Chief Commissioner of Police.

Stanistreet, John — stationmaster at Glenrowan.

Stanley, James — 'The Vagabond', famous journalist of the 1870s.

Steele, Sgt Arthur — in charge at Wangaratta from 1877.

Tarleton, John — bank manager at Jerilderie, NSW.

Upjohn, Elijah — petty criminal, appointed hangman, 1880.

Ward, Det. Michael — hated enemy of the Gang.

Whelan, Sgt James — in charge at Benalla.

Whitty family — inc. **James**, grazier/farmer of Moyhu, Ned's arch enemy; **James** (his nephew) also grazier/farmer; **Charles** (a cousin) boyhood friend of Ned, later a policeman.

Williamson, William 'Brickey' — friend of Ned and the Kelly family, imprisoned with Mrs Kelly and Bill Skilling from 1878.

Woodyard, 'Big Mick' — under various aliases, member of Ned's horse-stealing gang.

Wright, Isaiah ('Wild') — Ned's boxing opponent (1874) later a loyal friend and Kelly sympathiser, married Bridget, daughter of Jack Lloyd Sr, sister of Tom Jr.

Wyatt, Alfred — Police Magistrate at Benalla from 1877.

Zincke, William — Beechworth solicitor, later MLA, often defence counsel for Kelly family and friends.

ABBREVIATIONS

ADB	*Australian Dictionary of Biography*	n.d.	undated
ad.	advertisement	*op. cit.*	previously cited
Age	Melbourne *Age*	*O&M*	*Ovens and Murray Advertiser*
Argus	Melbourne *Argus*	OUP	Oxford University Press
AOT	Archives of Tasmania	p., pp.	page, pages
B.E.	*Benalla Ensign*	PG	Victoria *Police Gazette*
cf.	compare with	Q.	Question in Royal Commission of 1881
Commission	*Minutes of Evidence Taken Before Royal Commission on the Police Force of Victoria, 1881*	q.	quoted
		RC	Roman Catholic
Const.	Constable	Sgt	Sergeant
Det.	Detective	*Sketcher*	*Australasian Sketcher*
Det. Insp.	Detective Inspector	*SMH*	*Sydney Morning Herald*
DSA	Diseased Stock Agent	Sr Const.	Senior Constable
D.T.	Melbourne *Daily Telegraph*	Sub-insp.	Sub-inspector
et al.	and others	SUP	Sydney University Press
et seq.	and those following	Supt	Superintendent
Herald	Melbourne *Herald*	v.	versus
ibid.	the same source	*VGG*	*Victorian Government Gazette*
inc.	including	VPC	Victoria Police Correspondence
Insp.	Inspector	VPRO	Victorian Public Record Office
J.P.	Justice of the Peace	*W.D.*	*Wangaratta Dispatch*
MLA	Member of the Legislative Assembly	*W.T*	*Weekly Times*
		w.e.	week ending

Imperial–Metric Conversion Table

Length and Area
1 inch = 25.4 mm
1 foot = 30.5 cm
1 yard = 0.914 m
1 mile = 1.61 km
1 acre = 0.405 ha

Weight
1 ounce = 28 g
1 pound = 454 g
1 stone = 6.36 kg
1 hundredweight = 50.85 kg

Money
12 pence (d) = 1 shilling (s)
20 shillings = 1 pound (£)
1 guinea = £1 1 shilling

NOTES

1 SON OF RED, page 1

On 29.6.1880 Ned said that he was born on a 'little hill' at Beveridge. (Melbourne *Age* — hereafter *Age* — 29.6.1880.) At the time of his birth (see below) his father owned a farm on the lower slopes of Mount Fraser at Beveridge. ('The Big Hill' of Ned's childhood had become 'little' to a man reared among the ranges of the north-east.) A month later, travelling north by train and 'passing Donnybrook', he pointed out 'the spot where I first drew breath' (Melbourne *Argus* — hereafter *Argus* — 2.8.1880.) At this point the site on Mount Fraser was clearly visible.

Ned Kelly's birth was not registered, the record of his baptism has been lost. Kelly family tradition said Ned was born 'at the time of the Eureka Stockade', an event which occurred in December, 1854. (Paddy and Charlie Griffiths quoting Ned's brother, Jim, interview, 1963.) In registering the births of other Kelly children, Ned's mother and father gave Ned's age in years, *usually* consistent with a December 1854 birth.

In July 1870 Ned's mother recorded that Ned was 15½ — a birth date of *approximately* January 1855, again consistent with December 1854 (birth registration, Ellen Kelly, 13.5.1870). The most reliable record of his birth comes from school inspector G. Wilson Brown who, on 30 March 1865 at the Avenel Common School, noted Ned's age as 10 years and 3 months, confirming a date of December 1854. (G. Wilson Hall's notebooks, Victorian Public Record Office, hereafter, VPRO.) Ned had arrived at the school only two months before and his older sister, Anne, or his parents would have provided his correct age. Ned confused the issue on 28 December 1866, when he provided the information for his father's death certificate and gave his own age as 11½, suggesting he was born in June 1855. In large, poor families like the Kellys, birthdays were not an issue. It seems most likely that, in registering his father's death, Ned recalled that the last time he had heard his age mentioned, he was 11½ That was close enough for him on this traumatic day, even though he had probably just turned 12 (on this same occasion he was a year out with the age of his sister Kate).

Through the years, Ned steadily lost track of his birth date and by 1880, thought he was 'about twenty-eight' (*Age*, 29.6.1880), the age to be given on his Death Certificate (11.11.1880). School inspector Brown remains our most reliable witness.

Red Kelly buys 41-acre farm, Memorial Book 7, Folio 963, Titles Office, Melbourne. This is the first of his Beveridge land purchases, carefully documented by Keith McMenomy (notes provided to the author, 1981), who compared 'John Kelly' signatures on conveyancing documents with Red's signature on marriage and birth registrations. Subsequent research by the National Trust (Victoria) confused Red and a second John Kelly who was one of Beveridge's first landowners.

Red never speaks of the crime for which he was transported, 'Glenden Gordon' (Joseph Ashmead), *The Briars and Thorns — a True Story of the Kelly Gang*, unpublished quarto typescript, n.d. but 1922 (hereafter *Ashmead*), p.3. Ashmead knew Ned and Dan Kelly from the 1870s and befriended Mrs Kelly in 1883. His MS is a reliable source on

Kelly family lore. (I was given a copy of the typescript in 1966 by Ronald Davenport, whose sister had copied and edited Ashmead's MS shortly before its loss in the 1939 bushfires. In 1995 Peter Gillooly loaned me a handwritten copy of the original which carefully reproduced Ashmead's quaint spelling. While grateful for this insight and for the chance to check the text, I have followed Miss Davenport's edited version.)

Red's brother-in-law (Jack Lloyd) claims to have been transported, interview, Tom Lloyd Jr (Jack's grandson), 29.7.1969; Red as an activist, J.J. Kenneally, *The Complete Inner History of the Kelly Gang and their Pursuers*, Moe, Vic., 8th Edition, 1969 (hereafter *Kenneally*), p.17; newspaperman who had spoken with Mrs Kelly, G. Wilson Hall, *The Outlaws of the Wombat Ranges*, Mansfield, 1879, typescript copy in the La Trobe Collection, (hereafter *Mansfield Pamphlet*), pp.6–7; 'an agrarian outrage', *1881 Victoria Police Commission*, Second Progress Report (hereafter *Commission*, 2nd Progress Report), Section 1; 'gothic fantasy', 'The Australian Silverpen' (H. Glenny), *Jottings and Sketches at Home and Abroad*, Port Fairy, 1889 q. *Walkabout*, February, 1965, p.5 (my thanks to Bob Stagg for this reference).

I am indebted to a number of Irish researchers for their work on Ned's father, much of it presented in a 1988 Bicentennial project: Terry Cunningham of the Fethard Historical Society for pinpointing the site of the Kelly home in the townland of Clonbrogan, Moyglass (confirmed by maps of 1840 and Griffith's *Valuations* for 1850); Sean McSweeney of the Bru Boru Project, Cashel, who with Terry Cunningham located the files documenting Red's case in Dublin Castle; John Hassett of Ballysheehan for identifying James Cooney's holding; Australian Bob Reece, first Keith Cameron Professor of Australian History at University College, Dublin, who drew together much of this local research in a paper for the Australia and Ireland Conference at Ennis, County Clare, in which he suggested that Red was an informer; and Steven Ffeary-Smyrl of Dublin, who confirmed a link between Red Kelly and the arrest, later escape attempt and fatal shooting of Phillip Regan (interviews, 1993–94). Ffeary-Smyrl believes that Red's involvement may have gone beyond informing on his friend and that Red was an unnamed 'witness' who accompanied police when they caught Regan engaged in stock theft. See *Tipperary Star*, 27.8.1988 and Melbourne *Herald-Sun*, 29.10.1990.

The details of Red's transportation are drawn from his Convict Record, CON 33/15, Archives of Tasmania (hereafter AOT), and his Convict Indent, CON 4/11, AOT, with some additional material (surgeon's name, number of deaths) from Charles Bateson, *The Convict Ships*, Sydney, 1974, pp.364–5 & 392–3; English convict's view, Mark Jeffrey, *A Burglar's Life*, Hobart n.d., pp.55–6; Red's career in Van Diemens Land, Convict Record, *op. cit.*; 'places of tyranny and condemnation', Ned Kelly in an 8300-word letter written in 1879 (hereafter the 'Jerilderie Letter'). The original is privately owned, a copy is held by the VPRO. Punishment for informers, Robert Hughes, *The Fatal Shore*, London, 1987, p.539. A number of 'John Kellys' crossed to Port Phillip at the end of the 1840's. It is virtually impossible to identify Red.

Arrival of the Quinns, Register of Assisted Immigrants, Book 1, p.27, VPRO, passenger list, *The England*, arr. Port Phillip, 17.7.1841; Ellen's childhood, *Ashmead*, p.1; 'a great favourite', *ibid.*, p.2; Redmond Barry's billiards room court, Michael Cannon, *Old Melbourne Town*, Main Ridge, Vic., 1991, pp.62–3; the fortunes of the Quinns, largely from the Mansfield Pamphlet, pp.4–6, with some details from *Commission*, 2nd Progress Report, Section 1 (James sells firewood), and letter, Fred Hopkins, c.1932 (Ellen works at McNaughtons' saddlery), transcribed by the author in 1951 from the collection of the Melbourne saddler, Kinnear (hereafter the Kinnear papers) present whereabouts unknown; Ellen at Wallan, *Ashmead*, p.3; description of Red, *ibid.*; 'fencer and splitter' and the *poteen* scheme, Mansfield Pamphlet, p.7; Ellen's image of Red, *Ashmead*, p.3; 'took a drop too much', *ibid.*; the 'elopement', Mansfield Pamphlet, p.8; Ellen's pregnancy, R.C. baptisms, Kilmore, 1849–53, Mary Jane Kelly, baptised 30.(*sic*)2.1851, born, 25.2.1851. (Note that this is in a group of registrations transcribed in extract. It is possible that she was born on *January* 25 and baptised on the 30th. This would fit the sequence of entries); Red builds 'snug little hut', Mansfield Pamphlet, p.8; Patrick drowns, *ibid.*, p.4; 'Separation' festival, Cannon, *op. cit.*, pp.461–2; Red's and Ellen's marriage, R.C. Marriages, St Francis Church, 1849–53, 18.11.1850; birth of Mary Jane, baptism registration, *op. cit.*; 'first record of her death', birth registration of unnamed Kelly boy (Dan), 1.6.1861. (The idea that Mary Jane died in infancy may have been encouraged by the fact that the entry 'Mary Jane deceased', heads the list of the Kelly children and their ages. This meant of course that her birth — not necessarily her death — preceded that of the next child, Anne.)

Pretty Sally ascent, William Howitt, *Land, Labour and Gold or Two Years in Victoria*, London, 1855, SUP, facsimile edition, 1972, Vol. 1, p.311; goldrush leaves six women in Wangaratta, D.M. Whittaker, *Wangaratta*, Wangaratta, 1963, p.53 (my thanks to James Morey for this source); Red goes to Bendigo, Mansfield Pamphlet, p.8; goldfields life at Bendigo, Howitt, *op. cit.*, pp.372-82; Irish banner, *ibid.*, p.405, Englishman's version, *ibid.*, p.406; Red 'averse to quarrelling', Mansfield Pamphlet, p.7; earns enough to go home, and horse dealing, *ibid.*, p.8; Anne born November 1853 (baptism record St Francis, Melbourne, 31.1.1854); Timothy Ryan's land, Allotment 44, Township of Beveridge, 26.5.1853, Parish Map, Central Plans Office, Crown Land and Survey; Red's town block, Crown Grant; Allotment 6, Section 7, 27.10.1854.

Mrs Gorman as midwife at Ned's birth, *Euroa Gazette*, 28.1.1953; site of Gorman house, J.W. Payne, *The History of Beveridge*, Kilmore, 1974, p.19; and map between pp.8 & 9; Ned baptised by Father O'Hea, Melbourne *Daily Telegraph* (hereafter *D.T.*), 12.11.1880; wounded Lalor at land sale, Les Blake, *Peter Lalor, the man from Eureka*, Belmont, Vic., 1979, pp.114–15; main road 'stupidity', Howitt, *op. cit.*, p.303; 'crab holes' etc., *ibid.*, p.309; Red's mortgage, Memorial Book 26, Folio 832, 10.5.1855; 'vast numbers' of birds, Howitt, *op. cit.*, p.210; drink ruins storekeeper, Payne, *op. cit.*, p.21; 'drunkenness . . . reigns supreme', *ibid.*, p.22; Red sells the 41 acres, Memorial Book 60, Folio 491; sells half town block, Memorial Book 48, Folio 815; Margaret (Maggie) born, 15.6.1857 (baptism records, St Paul's Coburg, 11.8.1857); James Quinn's land, Mansfield Pamphlet, p.5, (Portions 38 & 39, Parish of Wallan).

Lloyd brothers reach Victoria, (on the *Blanche Moore*, 1842), *Victoria Police Gazette* (hereafter *PG*); Prisoners Released w.e. 23.3.1869 and 2.8.1869; descendants of Welsh horse dealer, interview, Tom Lloyd Jr, 26.10.1879; 'Young' Tom Lloyd born 5.11.1855 (son of Jack, but referred to in the Kelly period as 'Tom Lloyd Jr' because of his uncle having the same name).

Arrival of Red's brothers and sisters, Register of Assisted Migrants, Book 11, p.436, VPRO, *Maldon*, 28.7.1857; growth of the Whitty/Farrell clan: Bronwyn Binns, 'James Whitty and his Sphere of Influence', a monograph based on research material gathered by Bronwyn for this book (copy lodged with the La Trobe Library). We are grateful to Michael Whitty who shared his knowledge of the family (letters 27.1.1993 and 16.5.1993) and provided signposts for the above study. Whitty family's links with the Kellys, Michael Whitty letters, *op. cit.*

Red's new town block, Crown Grant Allotment 12, Section 6, 4.5.1858; view from Mount Fraser, Howitt, *op. cit.*, p.310; Beveridge's Catholic Church and school, Payne, *op. cit.*, p.81 (the building survives, privately owned); Red's 21 acres and town block, Memorial Book 82, Folio 806, 10.2.1859.

Red's house on this farmlet was the subject of a much-publicised inquiry by the Historic Buildings Council on 16.9.1992. See *John Kelly's House, Beveridge — a report to the*

Historic Buildings Council Classifications Committee, by Daniel Catrice and Megan McDougall, which includes public and institutional submissions to the inquiry. My description of the house is based on inspections with Keith McMenomy in 1964 and with Miles Lewis, an expert on vernacular timber buildings, in 1981 and 1992. Restoration of this much-abused structure is at last under way.

The well water, interview, Keith McMenomy with Patience Stewart, July 1964, James (Jim) Kelly born, 31.7.1859 (R.C. baptism records, St Paul's, Coburg); Daniel (Dan) Kelly born, 1.6.1861, and Catherine (Kate) Kelly, 12.7.1863, both registered, as were all subsequent Kelly children.

The Quinn/Lloyd/Kelly troubles with the law, listed, *Commission*, Appendix 10, p.699; Uncle James Kelly's trial, *Kilmore Examiner*, 23.4.1863; Uncle Edward Kelly's town block, Crown Grant, Allotment 13, Section 8, 23.10.1863; Ned at the Beveridge school and classmates, Fred Hopkins, Letter, Kinnear Papers, *op. cit.*; assessment of teacher, Tom Wall, G. Wilson Brown notebook, 6.5.1868, formerly, Ministry of Education Historical Collection. Ned's progress: accepted in Second Class the following year (see below); departure from Beveridge fixed by sale of the farm and house (to James Stewart) on 16.1.1864, Memorial Book 135, Folio 645.

The picture of Avenel is drawn from Amelia Jane Burgoyne, *Memories of Avenel*, Sydney, 1954 (hereafter *Burgoyne*), and H.G. Martindale, *New Crossing Place*, Melbourne, 1958 (hereafter *Martindale*). Squatter Lloyd Jones and the baronet stockman, *Burgoyne*, pp.28–9; 'character of a ducal park', *Martindale*, p.14; William Mutton background, death, *Burgoyne*, pp.14, 24; Red rents Mutton land, *ibid.*, p.38 (Kellys' arrival stated incorrectly as 1861); family's 'hard struggle' and Ellen in local tradition, *ibid.* p.38; neighbour Michael Kelly, *ibid.*; Morgans also on Mutton land, *Martindale*, p.73 (see also pp.178–9 for valuable notes on the Kelly stay at Avenel, including the status of the Morgans); The Avenel Common School, G. Wilson Brown notebooks, *op. cit.*; description of building and classroom, ibid., 30.3.1864; Irving boxes ears, carries 'a tawse', *ibid.*, 30.8.1863 (a visit pre-dating the arrival of the Kellys); Kellys 'well behaved', *Burgoyne*, p.38; Ned 'very quiet', interview, Pat Kelly (grand nephew of Joanna), 1991; maps in schoolroom, G. Wilson Brown, notebook, 30.3.1864; Campion, 'of gentlemanly education', *Burgoyne*, p.23; the Sheltons, *Martindale*, p.74; *Burgoyne*, p.23; *Victoria and its Metropolis*, Melbourne, 1888, Vol. 2, p.331. I am indebted to Shelton descendant, Geoff Richardson, who introduced me to his relatives, Mr and Mrs Bill Gee and Mrs Stan Shelton (interviews, 23.10.1973); Ian Shelton (interviews, 1993–94), provided valuable detail, including the story of the missing stallion.

Inspector's visit, G. Wilson Brown notebooks, *op. cit.*, 30.3.1864; James Quinn buys Glenmore, R.V. Billis and A.S. Kenyon, *Pastoral Pioneers of Port Phillip*, Melbourne, 1974, p.214; 'remote and lofty monarchy', Keith McMenomy, *Ned Kelly, The Authentic Illustrated Story*, South Yarra, 1984 (hereafter *McMenomy*) p.13; Ryans and 'colony' at Lake Rowan, Doug Morrissey, 'Ned Kelly and Horse and Cattle Stealing', *Victorian Historical Journal*, June 1995, p.33; the Lloyds move to the north-east, *Commission*, Q.3237–8, p.167. (Montfort, then a sergeant, claims that the arrival of the Lloyd brothers made the district 'a focus of crime'); Lloyds 'already under suspicion', see Montfort's comment, 'We were looking out for them for a very long time' (Q.3254, p.167); convicted and sentenced to five years, Appendix 10, p.699; G. Wilson Brown's inspection, notebooks, 30.3.1865.

Red's theft of Morgan calf, Frank Clune, *The Kelly Hunters*, Sydney, 1954 (hereafter *Clune*), pp.50, 342. Clune cites the Charge Book, Avenel Courthouse, and Occurrence Book, Avenel Police Station, neither of which is now available. Phillip Morgan 'a hungry old bugger', interview, Bill Gee, 28.10.1973. There is no record of Red's imprisonment nor of his fine being paid. The scenario of being allowed to work out his sentence at the Avenel lock-up while Ellen *tried* to raise the money, fits all available facts, including the eleven-week delay between the birth of Grace Kelly (10.8.1865) and the registration of the birth by Red on 30.10.1865.

All branches of the Shelton family preserve traditions of Dick Shelton's rescue by Ned. I have drawn largely from Mrs Stan Shelton, interview, 28.10.1973. The traditions describe Ned being given the 'sash of honour' which Mrs Shelton believed had come from the stock of a family drapery business. See also, *Kenneally*, p.151; Red's Drunk and Disorderly charge, Avenel Cause List Book (entries begin the month after Red's previous conviction), VPRS 287, Unit 2, VPRO, 12.12.1865 and 19.12.1865.

Bushranger Morgan 'petted, feted and elevated', *O & M*, 19.11.1864 q. Brenda Leitch, *The Fatal Dice*, Wangaratta, 1993, p.16; the death of Ben Hall, Edgar F. Penzig, *The Sandy Creek Bushranger*, Lane Cove, NSW, 1985, p.135 (coming from Penzig, a rabidly anti-bushranging historian, the picture of the police losing their heads is especially damning); Ben Hall obituary, *Kilmore Free Press*, 1.6.1865; butchering of Morgan's body, *ibid.*, 18.5.1865; Sgt Montfort's comment, *Whittaker, op. cit.*, p.159; dispatch of Morgan's head to Melbourne via coach, *ibid*, (for enduring memories along the route of 'that ghastly box ... well into the twentieth century', *Martindale*, p.47); for Lowry's career, arrest at Avenel, trial and imprisonment, *PG*, Prisoners Released w.e. 24.5.1864; *PG*, 25.8.1864, p.326; *PG*, 25.8.1866, p.3; *PG*, Prisoners Released w.e. 31.10.1870; for Lowry links with Kelly family, Report, Sr Const. Hall to Supt Nicolas, 17.11.1870, Kelly Papers, VPRO.

'Poisonous rotgut', north-eastern tradition, encountered by district historians Gary Dean and Nanette Green (interviews, 1993); a spirit served by mistake, *Ashmead*; p.4.

Red develops dropsy in November, see 'duration of last illness' on Death Certificate, below; 'Dr J.T. Heeley from Seymour', the certificate identifies a 'Doctor Healey' who saw Red 'seven days before death'. There was no doctor of that name (or any other name) at Avenel. For Heeley, a Sydney doctor in practice at Seymour, *Martindale*, p.129; Red dies, 27.12.1866; Ned registers death with Campion, 28.12.1866; details of burial on certificate; 'Ned Kelly, son of Red Kelly', Deposition, James Gloster, 9.8.1880, Prosecution Brief, Queen v. Edward Kelly, Kelly Papers, VPRO; the rifle inscribed 'Ned Kelly son of Red', a Snider Enfield Artillery Carbine originally issued to Queensland Aboriginal Mounted Police, is privately owned.

2 'THIS CRIMINAL BROOD' page 25

Akehurst kills digger, Raffaelo Carboni, *The Eureka Stockade*, Melbourne, 1855, pp.78–79; Ellen's court appearances, Cause List Book Avenel Petty Sessions 20.6.1865 to 28.7.1870, VPRS 287 Unit 2, VPRO; Anne Kelly case, 19.2.1867; Thomas Ford case, 28.5.1867; Michael Kelly loses mare, *PG* 6.6.1867, p.221; description of Ned, p.224; 'charged with horse stealing', *PG* Index, June 1867.

Descriptions Seven Mile and Eleven Mile Creeks, *Ashmead*, p.4; 'home of the solitary settler', *ibid.*, pp.7–8; the Greta bunyip, *Howitt*, pp.153–4, cf. S.E. Ellis, *A History of Greta*, Kilmore, 1972, p.24.

Description of Glenmore, the stockyard, etc. from Wilf Burrows of Whitfield who lived in the Quinn homestead from 1896 to 1905, interview, 2.3.1960; burning of the shanty,

Uncle James's trial, *Ovens and Murray Advertiser* (hereafter *O & M*), 21.4.1868; Ellen at 'the little house in Wangaratta' etc., *Ashmead*, p.4; Description of the house on Eleven Mile Creek, *O & M*, 22 and 30.10.1869, *Commission Q*. 1024, p.47. The Lands Department file on Ellen Kelly's land has disappeared. Rent rolls show that, from June 1869, Ellen paid fourteen six-monthly rents on Block 57A, Parish of Lurg, County of Delatite, and in 1880 solicitor David Gaunson confirmed that these payments had covered a seven-year lease under the Amending Land Act of 1865 (*Herald*, 19.10.1880). However, in 1869, a new Land Act had applied, demanding a three-year 'licence period' of occupancy before a lease could be granted. In June that year, Ned testified that he had lived at Eleven Mile Creek 'for about twelve months' (*O & M* 19.6.1869) — that is, the family had moved there in about June 1868. This indicates that there had been some two years of occupancy before this date under the terms of the 1865 Act. Showing a not unusual degree of flexibility, the Department granted the lease in 1869 under the 1865 Act, enabling the three-year occupancy to cover the 1869 'licence period' requirement. (For a valuable summary of Victorian land legislation see John McQuilton, *The Kelly Outbreak 1878–80*, Melbourne, 1979 (hereafter *McQuilton*), Appendix 1. I am also grateful to Michael Dalton for his thesis (B.A. Hons) 'Kellys, Cops and Cockies — a survey of the Social Milieu of Ned Kelly, Land Parish of Lurg, 1867–80', 1971).

Ned's unbranded 'pet' sheep on Myrrhee, *O & M*, 19.6.1869; the shearing life, Chapter 2, John Merritt, *The Making of the AWU*, OUP, 1986, see especially pp.35–8, 45 & 55; route of N.E. shearers, *Benalla Ensign* (hereafter *B.E.*), 21.10.1870; Ned shears regularly at Gnawarra, *Melbourne Herald* (hereafter *Herald*), 2.3.1879; romantic view of N.E. 'natives', Edwin Carton Booth, *Australia Illustrated*, London 1873, p.63.

Ellen Kelly as a sly grog seller, *O & M*, 4.5.1870; Standish as ditto, Paul de Serville, *Pounds and Pedigrees*, Melbourne 1991 (hereafter *de Serville*), p.48; Kellys live 'happily ... roughly', B.W. Cookson, *The Kelly Gang from Within — survivors of the tragedy interviewed*, serialised *Sydney Sun*, 27.8.1911 to 24.9.1911 (hereafter *Cookson*), 27.8.1911.

Johnstone (Power) escape reported, *PG*, 18.2.1869 (time given as noon). Harry describes his escape to journalist James Stanley ('The Vagabond'), *Argus*, 10.3.1877. His account tallies almost exactly with a report in the *Geelong Advertiser*, 21.6.1870. The widely repeated story of Harry escaping under a load of rubbish seems to be precisely that. For detail on Harry Power's background I am indebted to Kevin Passey and Gary Dean, *The Bushranger Harry Power, Tutor of Ned Kelly*, Wodonga 1991, and to the huge collection of unpublished Power material gathered by Allan Nixon. I am particularly grateful to Allan for sharing his exhaustive transcripts of Victoria Police Correspondence (hereafter VPC) of the Power years.

Harry's feet and boots, *PG*, 10.5.1870, p.109 & *Kyneton Guardian*, 30.4.1870; 'fearless rider' etc., *Argus*, 3.3.1877; 30 men held up in 24 hrs, Francis Hare, *Last of the Bushrangers*, London, 1892 (hereafter *Hare*), p.57; talks his way out of capture, *Kyneton Guardian*, 5.6.1869 and John Sadleir, *Reminiscences of a Victorian Police Officer*, Melbourne, 1913 (hereafter *Sadleir*), p.156; Harry's prayer answered, *Hare*, pp.73–4; Harry's version of how he become a bushranger, *Argus*, 10.3.1877; Tom Lloyd arrives home, *PG Prisoners Released*, w.e. 23.3.1869.

The Mount Battery incident described, *Hare*, p.94, *Sadleir*, pp.157–8 and *Mansfield Pamphlet*, p.18; the incident reported and dated, *O & M*, 29.5.1869. Harry's version is from *Hare*. Pursuit described, *Mansfield Independent*, 12.6.1869, *O & M*, 29.5.1869; spent bullet hits Harry's horse, *D.T.*, 5.7.1880; Ned 'thought Power would shoot him', *Hare*, pp.93–4; Rowe's description of Power's companion, *Mansfield Pamphlet*, p.18; young Lake suspected, *O & M*, 29.5.1869; Marriage, Annie Kelly and Alex Gunn, 9.4.1869; description Alex, *PG Prisoners Released*, w.e. 25.8.1873; loses selection, *VGG* 1869,

Vol. 1, p.288; Ned 'a splitter', *O & M*, 19.6.1969; Ellen's relationship with Frost, *B.E.*, 21.10.1871; (Frost's appearance, dress, based on description of Harry Power when he was mistaken for Frost. See Chapter 3); Uncle Jimmy robs a Chinese, *PG*, 13 and 27.7.1869, 3 and 24.8.1869; Jack Lloyd released, *PG Prisoners Released*, w.e. 2.8.1869; death of James Quinn, 22.8.1869 (registered 25.8.1869); squatters campaign against the Quinns, letters Evans to Badcock, 13.9.1869, and Standish to Badcock, 11.9.1869 (both private collection). Evans 'peacocking', *McQuilton* pp.28–30, 'dummying,' *ibid.* p.33 (part of a chapter, 'Selection: the Regional Failure', which vividly portrays the seed-bed of the squatter–selector conflict).
The Ah Fook case, *O & M*, 22 and 30.10.1869, *B.E.* 22.10.1869, Petty Sessions Benalla Cause List Book, 16, 19, 21 and 26.10.1869, VPRS 1874, Unit 4, VPRO; lock-up rations, *VGG*, 1869, Vol. 1, p.143; assessment of Whelan, *Sadleir*, pp.281–2.
Bill Frost shot, *PG*, 22.2.1870, pp.42–3; 1.3.1870, p.51.

3 POWER'S MATE, page 41

McBean's influence with Standish, *McQuilton*, pp.61 & 73; wife helps the Lloyds, *Ovens Spectator*, 8.6.1870; q. *Argus* Supplement, 11.6.1870; McBean and Dickens hold-ups, *PG*, 22.3.1870, pp.57 and 70; *B.E.*, 18.3.1870; *O & M*, 19.3.1870; 'Confound your impertinence' etc., *Ashmead* (a friend of McBean), pp.9 & 10.
Journalist Stanley's assessment of Harry, the high country rhapsody, *Argus*, 10.3.1877; 'wild bull mountains', *B.E.*, 1.4.1870; Longmore's attack on Standish, *O & M*, 24.5.1870; 'a niggard government' to blame, *B.E.*, 1.4.1870; the 'Moyhu poundkeeper' yarn, *O & M*, 10 and 17.5.1870. (There was no pound at Moyhu and, dubious as it is, the original story concerns 'a poundkeeper' who happens to be 'riding out' near Moyhu.)
Warrant for Jack Lloyd, *PG*, 12.4.1870, p.85; Balwoski hold-up, *PG*, 26.4.1870, p.95; hold-ups of Murray and Murray/O'Leary, *Kyneton Observer*, 28.4.1870; 'half caste' description of Ned, *PG*, 2.5.1870, pp.101–2; McBean urges increase in reward, *Sadleir*, pp.159–60; exchange between Standish and Chief Secretary, Chief Secretary's Correspondence, 27.4.1870 and 4.5.1870; £500 gazetted, *VGG*, 29.4.1870, p.672.
Benalla Ensign incriminates Ned, *B.E.*, 1.4.1870; Split with Harry, *Hare*, p.94; 'making free' with bread and butter, *PG*, 10.5.1870, p.101; Ned learns to smoke, *B.E.*, 6.5.1870; rides 160 miles in three days, *Kyneton Guardian*, 14.5.1870; 'a brown paper bushranger', George Morris, *Devil's River Country*, Mansfield n.d., p.38; arrest of Ned, *B.E.*, 6.5.1870 & 13.5.1870; 'worn, jaded . . . sick' and 'peculiarity of never washing', Standish to Winch, 7.5.1870, VPC P1607 (Nixon Transcripts); Hare and Nicolson on 'mysterious mission', telegram Standish to Nicolson, 9.5.1870, *O & M*, 14.5.1870; Nicolson for 'light duties' as PM? *Kyneton Observer*, 28.6.1870, q. *Bendigo Independent*; Nicolson joins the Power pursuit, *Commission*, Q.666, p.27; Hare chosen 'over the heads of . . . eleven senior officers', *Commission*, Q.16861, p.624, see also Q.16899, p.632 and Q.1592, pp.93–4.
Hare thinks Ned 'flash, ill-looking', *Hare*, p.93; Nicolson 'taken with his appearance', Hilary Lofting, *Bail Up! Ned Kelly, Bushranger*, Sydney, 1939, Vol. 2, p.171 (unidentified press clipping, apparently of 1878); Nicolson's 'skill and patience', *Sadleir*, p.207; Ned describes leaving Harry, *Hare*, pp.93–4; Standish circulates information drawn from Ned — to Winch, 11.5.1870; to Inspector General, Sydney, 12.5.1870; to Officer-in-charge,

Seymour, 12.5.1870; *VPC*, P1661–77 (Nixon Transcripts).

Jack Lloyd's release, *PG*, 17.5.1870, p.115; interview with Jack at Kilfera, affidavit Robert McBean q. *Commission*, Q.16861, p.624 (hereafter *McBean affidavit*) and *Sadleir*, p.160.

Ned's trial for McBean robbery, Petty Sessions Benalla Cause List Book, VPRS 1874, Unit 4, VPRO, 5.5.1870 and 12.5.1870; *B.E.*, 13.5.1870; manipulation of Murray and O'Leary, *Kyneton Guardian*, 14.5.1870 ('failed to identify Kelly'), and 18.5.1870 ('were not confronted with him').

Standish sees Ned at Richmond Police Depot, Standish diary, MS9502, La Trobe Library, entry for 15.5.1870; Standish's character and career, *ADB* entry by Stewart Legge, Vol. 6, pp.172–3, & *de Serville*, Chapter 2, a superb 35-page biography; gambles half his annual salary in a night, *ibid.*, p.69; provides naked women as dinner companions, *ibid.*, p.60.

Ned's arrival in Kyneton, 'by no means unprepossessing', *Kyneton Guardian*, 18.5.1870; Ned describes the 'watchbox', Nicolson's account of the Power capture, published in the *Argus* and *Age* in February, 1892 as a riposte to Hare's highly egocentric version in *The Last of the Bushrangers, op. cit.* and quoted verbatim, Charles White, *History of Australian Bushranging* (Lloyd O'Neil facsimile edition 1970), Vol. 2, pp.253–81 (hereafter *Nicolson*); Ned's first court appearance, *Kyneton Guardian*, 21.5.1870.

Jack Lloyd ready to 'point out' Harry's hideout, *McBean affidavit*; Standish and Hare letters to Nicolson, *Commission*, Q.16861, p.624; departure, *Hare*, p.58; Ned's second court appearance, *Kyneton Observer*, 28.5.1870. The expedition to capture Harry is described in great (and sometimes contradictory) detail in *Nicolson*, *Hare*, pp.58–71 (he manages to avoid mentioning Nicolson by name!), and in an official 'dispatch' (*Argus*, 9.6.1870 and Chiltern's *Federal Standard*, 13.6.1870). Harry's version, *Argus*, 3.3.1877. *Sadleir* (pp.160–2) tries for a balanced account but probably tips too far towards Hare. Harry Power confused the issue with a letter to the editor of Melbourne's *Evening Standard* (q. *Whittaker*, pp.161–2) claiming that Hare had tried to shoot him. Although Montfort 'would scarcely speak at all about the matter' (*Sadleir*, p.162), he eventually delivered a lecture in which he described the capture as accomplished entirely by Hare and himself with Nicolson as an onlooker (*Whittaker*, p.162). He was and remained Hare's man. My account has drawn from all these sources (with gleanings from the Royal Commission evidence of Hare, Nicolson and Montfort), leaning rather to Nicolson's version as, overall, the most reliable.

Ned's last court appearance, *Kyneton Observer*, 4.6.1870. The subsequent events at Kyneton are documented in a series of attachments to memo, Nicolson to Standish, 24.10.1870, VPRS 937, Unit 272, VPRO (hereafter Babington File). These are photocopies, the originals 'in the safe at PRO Laverton, Location Plan Press Dr.4'.

'Strange fantasy' that Ned disguised as blacktracker, *Melbourne Punch*, 9.6.1870. See also, *Argus*, supplement, 11.6.1870.

Hotel bill for 'Dan Kelly' and Babington memo to Inspector Disney (referred to Nicolson), Babington File.

Although Hare recorded that Jack Lloyd's reward was 'paid ... to a gentleman he named' (*Hare*, p.76), the role of Jimmy Quinn has caused some confusion (see John Molony, *I am Ned Kelly*, Ringwood, 1980 — hereafter *Molony* — p.53). In a letter to the Chief Secretary, 19.8.1870, Standish requests payment, with a marginal note, 'Jas Quinn £500' and on 1.9.1870 when Treasury declines payment because Jimmy is in custody, Standish notes, 'The *claimant* ... is not identical with the James Quinn within mentioned.' (my italic) VPRS 1189, Unit 502, VPRO.

Ned's letter to Babington — the only letter personally written by him yet discovered — is in the Babington File and was first published by John Lahey in the Melbourne *Age*, 23.11.1985.

Nicolson's 'proposal' for Ned to 'go to a station in New South Wales', Lofting, *op. cit.*, p.171, cf. Max Brown, *Australian Son,* Melbourne, 1948 (hereafter *Brown*), p.33.
Ned admits he was Power's mate and smiles, *O & M,* 21.12.1878.

4 THREE YEARS HARD, page 58

Greta police station opened, *PG,* 7.6.1870; for premises see Ellis, *op. cit.*, facing p.2; Hall wears out horses, *McQuilton*, p.81; 'specially selected' by Hare and Nicholson, *Commission*, Q.3208–9, p.166; Eldorado incident, *O & M,* 5, 6 & 18.1.1870; Cause List Petty Sessions Wangaratta, 2.1.1870 (page removed and held in police file); memo, Sub-insp. Dobson to Supt Wilson, 15.1.1870 (quoting P.M. Wills, Hall 'too hot tempered' etc.); Standish to Supt Wilson, 31.1.1870, all in VPRS 937, Unit 412, VPRO; see also anonymous letter, VPRS 937, Unit 411, VPRO; the Tighe case discussed in detail, Passey and Dean, *op. cit.*, pp.82–4; Hall again accused of perjury, *O & M,* 9.6.1870.

The stirrup iron fight, *O & M,* 1 & 3.9.1870; *B.E.*, 2.9.1870. The story emerges from evidence in three separate trials, James Quinn, Patrick Quinn and James Kenny; the police version, Criminal Offence Report, 26.8.1870; Hall to Supt Nicholas, 28.8.1870; Sub.-insp. Montfort to Nicholas, 27.8.1870; Arrests, Standish to Nicholas, 29.8.1870 (including annotations); all VPRS 937, Unit 49 VPRO.

The 1870 deluge, *O & M,* 1 & 3.11.1870; ground 'would bog a duck', Jerilderie Letter. The Gould/McCormick affair described by Ned briefly in a 3500-word letter written in 1878 to Donald Cameron, MLA (hereafter Cameron letter) copy in Kelly Papers, VPRO, more fully in Jerilderie Letter. For Tasmanian convict backgrounds of the McCormicks see CON 40/4 AOT (Conduct Register, Catherine Doherty or Dougherty); CON 15/1, AOT (arrival Catherine Doherty on '*Hope*'); CON 35/1, AOT, (Conduct Register, Michael Joyce); CON 33/38, AOT (Conduct Register, Jeremiah McCormick). Catherine Doherty married Joyce, a convict constable, in Hobart, 24.3.1845, yet she married Jeremiah McCormick at Beechworth, 25.8.1856 and described herself as 'spinster'. See also Death Certificates, Jeremiah McCormick 10.6.1889, and Catherine McCormack [sic] 2.7.1909.

The previously unknown convict background of Ben Gould, CON 33/102, AOT (Convict Record) and CON 14/42 AOT (Convict Indent). He was tried at Nottingham Assizes, 31.12.1846, arrived Tasmania 28.5.1851. After punitive stints at Norfolk Island and Port Arthur, received his Certificate of Freedom, 31.12.1853. For convict loathing of constables, Hughes, *op. cit.*, pp.383–4, citing Governor Arthur's intention to create 'mistrust and jealousy' by recruiting field police from convicts.

Ben Gould's account of the 'calf's testicles' note and Ned's clash with McCormick, *Kenneally*, *op. cit.*, p.22; McCormick's version, *O & M,* 12.11.1870; trial and sentence, *ibid.*; see Police Magistrate's notebooks, Wangaratta, 10.11.1870, VPRS 1503, Unit 4, VPRO, including Ned's version of the note's contents (quoted by Hall as though the statement had been made by Ned), and Ned's insistence that he neither wrote nor sent the note. *PG Prisoners Released*, w.e. 10.5.1871, and *Prison Register*, Folio 13096, specify that the sureties involved a provisional twelve-month sentence rather than a simple twelve-month bond.

Hall's reward, *PG,* 29.11.1870; 'chilling welcome' to Ned, *O & M,* 12.11.1870; description of flogging, *O & M*, 10.11.1870; prison description of Ned, Prison Register, *op. cit.*, and *PG* Prisoners Released, *op. cit.*

Death of Ellen Gunn, 28.3.1871. The date of Wild Wright's visit to the Eleven Mile is fixed by the evidence of James Murdoch (*O & M*, 2.5.1871); Wild 'mad as a tiger snake' etc., interview Albert Blanche, January 1948; incident with Dummy, interview Jack Walsh, January 1960; description of Wild, including dress, *PG*, 9.5.1871, Ned's description of the chestnut mare, Jerilderie Letter; postmaster calls her 'rather remarkable', *O & M*, 13.5.1871. Ned refers to the case briefly in Cameron letter and gives a detailed account in Jerilderie Letter. Mare found by Gunn and Williamson, *O & M*, 5.8.1871; Ned stays in Wangaratta 'several days', Jerilderie Letter. The date of Wild's arrival (see above) and Ned's return to Greta (see below) establish the stay as five nights and four days.

Hall describes the 20 April encounter with Ned on the bridge, *O & M*, 2.5.1871; Hall's account of the fight and aftermath — report, Hall to Supt Barclay, 22.4.1871, VPRS 937, Unit 413, VPRO; Ned's version, Jerilderie Letter; siege of police station, Hall to Insp. le P. Bookey, 14.8.1871; Hall's note to Montfort, with annotations of reinforcements, 20.4.1871; Dr Hester account for eight guineas, 22.4.1871; Dr McRea's comments to Standish, 15.5.1871, all VPRS 937, Unit 413, VPRO.

Ned 'would not split', *O & M*, 5.8.1871; would go back to prison 'before he would put anybody else into it', *O & M*, 2.5.1871.

Theft of postmaster's horse reported, *PG*, 25.4.1871, p.104. As noted, the entry is published five days after Hall's arrest of Ned and the theft is dated 3 April, a week after Ned's release from prison rather than the actual date of 16 March, 11 days *before* he left Beechworth Gaol. Wild pursued for 160 miles, at least four shots fired, *O & M*, 13.5.1871, Hall to Barclay, 2.5.1879. Standish's guarded comments on the arrest of Ned, Standish to Barclay, 25.4.1871 — both VPRS 937, Unit 413, VPRO.

Trials and sentences, *O & M*, 2, 6 & 13.5.1871 and 5.8.1871; Wild's sentence 'a curious paradox', McQuilton, *op. cit.*, p.81. Ned's scars, Prison Register, *op. cit.* We have yet to locate a record of Ned's time in Beechworth but his troublesome behaviour there is indicated by a loss of three months remission from his total sentence, with only seven days docked after transfer to Pentridge (Prison Register, *op. cit.*).

Hall replaced at Greta by Montgomery then Flood, *Commission*, Q.3214–3233, pp.166–7; Flood 'active', keeps clan 'continually under "pressure"' Q.3232–3, pp.166–7.

Birth of Ellen Kelly (Frost), 25.3.1870; Frost's presents etc., *B.E.*, 21.10.1871; Frost marries Bridget Cotter, 4.6.1871 (certificate includes professions etc.); maintenance case adjourned, 19.9.1871 and 3.10.1871; hearing and verdict, *O & M*, 21.10.1871; Furious riding, Benalla Petty Sessions Cause List Book, 23.10.1871, VPRS 1874, Unit 4, VPRO, *O & M*, 26.10.1871.

Death of Ellen Kelly (Frost), 28.1.1872; Flood's appearance etc., Record Sheet, Police Historical Unit (with some details provided by his strong resemblance to Const. McIntyre, see Chapter 9); Flood's marriage, 2.10.1870, birth of son, 11.7.1871; the police inquiry into the events of 2.1.1872, including Flood's note to Mrs Short, and the comments of Standish and Barclay, VPRS 937, Unit 414, VPRO. See *Molony*, p.72 for the first published account of the Flood/Annie relationship.

Birth of Anna Gunn Jr, 9.11.1872; death of Anna Sr, 11.11.1872; Flood charges Ellen and friend, *O & M*, 15 & 22.11.1872.

Description of George King, see Wm Williamson statement, 29.10.1878, *Commission*, Appendix 13, p.702, in which he describes 'Billy King' (Joe Byrne) and comments that he 'is like King who is married to Kelly's sister' [*sic*] — a slip by Williamson or Inspector Green who took his statement; see also *O & M*, 11.12.1877, description of 'George Stuckey' — an alias of King — 'about five feet ten inches in height, brown hair and whiskers'. The birth of Ellen's daughter by King on 3.10.1873, suggests that the relationship began in the summer of 1872–3. Jim Kelly and Tom Williams convicted of cattle stealing, *O & M*, 28.2.1873, 3.3.1873 and 18.4.1873.

Ned's transfer to Pentridge, Prison Register, *op. cit.*; joins train at Longwood, *Ashmead*, p.10; the picture of life in Pentridge is drawn from 'A Visit to Pentridge' by 'A BOHEMIAN', serialised in *O & M*, 27.11.1875, 4.12.1875 and 14.12.1875; 'Pentridge', reprinted from *The Spectator*, *O & M*, 18.12.1875; and 'A Month in Pentridge,' by 'The Vagabond' (James Stanley), serialised in the *Argus* in eight parts between 24.2.1877 and 23.6.1877.

Ned's transfers to the hulk *Sacramento* and the battery are dated in Prison Register, *op. cit.*, with details from *Weekly Summaries Hulks 1869–1884*, VPRS 10911, Unit 1, VPRO, and *Progress Report of Royal Commission on Penal and Prison Discipline, in Papers Presented to Parliament*, 1870, Vol. 2, pp.XII and XIV. The 'battery' was invariably identified as a second hulk until McMenomy's characteristically thorough research corrected the error.

Total confusion has been caused by the inclusion of Ned's Kyneton photograph on the Prison Register with the spurious date '12.1.74'. A second photograph of Ned in convict jacket *with a stubble* is dated '20.6.73'. Prisoners were allowed to grow their beards in the last three months of a sentence. Coupled with a note made in January that Ned would be released on 2 February, this suggests that the 'stubbled' photograph was taken on, or soon after Ned's return to Pentridge from the battery (credibly 24.1.1874) when it was discovered that he was eligible for six months remission.

Ned's allegation that Flood stole his horses, Jerilderie Letter; Flood 'assisting at' removal of horse, 6.12.1874 entry on Record Sheet, Police Historical Unit; the encounter at the hotel, *Commission*, Q.12609, p.455; Ned's 'alexandrite' eyes, Sir Charles Ryan, q. M.H. Ellis, 'The Legend of Ned Kelly', *Bulletin*, 31.12.1966.

5 A QUIET MAN, page 76

Ned as 'faller', for Saunders and Rule, Jerilderie Letter. (Ned dates his job from February 1873. Clearly he meant 1874.)

The date of the fight at Beechworth is established by an inscription on the photograph of Ned as a boxer, 'Ned Kelley [sic] August 8/1874'. The photograph was drawn to my attention by a friend and colleague, Johanna Parsons-Nicholls, in 1962, weeks after 'legendary spruiker' and showman Charlie Fredricksen had told me that Wild Wright spoke of being given 'the hiding of his life' in a fight with Ned Kelly at Beechworth.

Edward Rogers stages sports at the Imperial, *O & M*, 26.12.1876; as 'caterer for the public', *O & M*, 21.12.1878; hop and fruit garden, *O & M*, 6.3.1877; London Prize Ring rules, J.J. Farnol, *Epics of the Fancy*, London, 1928, with additional detail in 1979 notes from Merv Williams, former editor of the *Sporting Globe*; Wild 'rather given to ... assaults', *W.D.*, 23.9.1874; fight lasts 20 rounds, later inscription on the 'boxer' photograph in same hand, 'Fought Wild Wright 20 and Won'; Ned Kelly 'mad', typescript MS by Constable McIntyre, MS6342, La Trobe Library (hereafter *McIntyre Typescript*).

Ned works for Heach and Dockendorff, Jerilderie Letter, confirmed, *O & M*, 21.12.1878; 'gigantic failure' of 1874, *W.D.*, 25.12.1875; Dixon debts £20 000, *W.D.*, 10.6.1874; 'as much paper floating ...', *W.D.*, 20.5.1874; banks 'screwed me up ...', *W.D.*,

25.12.1875; suicide of Jackson Orr, inquest, *W.D.*, 27.5.1874; Heach and Dockendorff settle Dixon's affairs, *W.D.*, 10.6.1874, 15.7.1874 and 26.8.1874; 'fire sales', *W.D.*, 1.7.1874 and 23.9.1874.

Dockendorff refused selection, *W.D.*, 27.2.1874; timber lease, *VGG*, 12.2.1875. For help with research on the Killawarra mill I am grateful to Len and Lorna Schoer of Killawarra. Mill plant etc. and surplus timber, *W.D.*, 5.6.1875 and 9.6.1875; Ned's wages, Jerilderie Letter; workmates' description of Ned, *O & M*, 21.12.1878. For Walter Power's friendship with Ned I am indebted to the careful research of Walter's grand nephew, Laurie Power, who, in letters of 30.12.1992 and 18.1.1993, documented a number of interviews conducted between 1973 and 1984, including the reminiscences of Matt Power, grandson of Walter, who lived for a time with his grandparents (hereafter Power interviews).

The fight at the Killawarra races, *O & M*, 21.12.1878; the trip to Flynn's Creek, Power interviews, *op. cit.*, shanties every 4 or 5 miles, Richard Mackay, *Recollections of Early Gippsland Goldfields*, Traralgon, 1916, p.9. For 'Graham family lore' concerning Ned's time at Flynn's Creek I have drawn on Margot Fulton's careful documentation (letter and interview, 1994). Herself a Graham descendant, she cited Kathleen M. Huffer, *A History of Loy Yang 1844–1978*, Traralgon and District Historical Society, 1979, p.66, which records the tradition, while incorrectly dating the Grahams' arrival as 1878 — too late for Ned's Gippsland trip. Mrs Fulton provided documentation that Robert Graham had occupied the land since 1871, also survey maps showing the neighbouring Wright and Graham holdings.

John King born, 18.3.1875; 'no man could work harder', *O & M*, 13.11.1880; Ned as bullock driver, *O & M*, 21.12.1878; fencing Baileys' vineyard, local tradition (honoured by Baileys in 1986 when launching their latest Hermitage vintage). Ned breaks Ashmead horse, *Ashmead*, p.11; Police Regulation 183, *Regulations for the Guidance of the Constabulary of Victoria*, Melbourne 1877; Ned 'quelling unseemly rows … hounded down', *O & M*, 21.12.1878; works for John Evans, Mrs Evan Evans interviewed by Mary Jean Officer, 27.10.1963; Ned denies stealing horse and saddle (*Age* report, 13.11.1878), Cameron letter; builds granite house by Lake Winton, Louise Earp, 'The Kelly Story condensed from Mr Ashmead's (Sen. of Winton North) book (never printed) and from stories told me by Ned's contemporary J. McMonigle Sen. (died about middle 30s and his daughter Sarah McMonigle', unpublished quarto MS (hereafter *Earp*), pp.4, 5.

Saunders and Rule hire Ned as overseer, Jerilderie Letter; 'natural-born leader', *Earp*, p.4. The partners may have looked to Ned as an overseer after John Rule left the firm, notice, *W.D.*, 17.2.1875; mill and plant described, auction ad., *W.D.*, 5.6.1875; Ned's Beechworth portrait, *McMenomy*, p.57; Ingram's memories of Ned, *Kenneally*, p.13.

The Lydecker case is documented in the warrant issued by Robert Wood J.P. on 25.1.1876 (in private collection), in *PG*, 22.2.1876, and in reports of the trial, *O & M*, 5.8.1876 and *W.D.*, 5.8.1876.

Beechworth's falling gold yield, *Australasian Sketcher* (hereafter *Sketcher*), 3.12.1876; 'industry … collapsed', *W.D.*, 29.12.1875; dying towns and villages, *O & M*, 13.8.1874; 'arrest on request', *McQuilton*, p.61.

Jim Kelly free, *PG Prisoners Released*, w.e. 28.8.1876; encounter with Dan Kelly, *Ashmead*, p.8; Ned resolves the Lydecker case, *PG*, 9.8.1876, p.211; *O & M*, 5.8.1876 and *W.D.*, 5.8.1876 (quotes are from the *Dispatch* report).

Planned move to Gippsland, *Earp*, p.3; Dan's saddle stealing case, Benalla Petty Sessions Cause List Book, *op. cit.*, 29.10.1876. *Commission*, Q.15493, p.560; Jack McMonigle to take plant and set-up team to Gippsland, *Earp*, p.3; Oakley and Peter Martin, interview Louise Earp, 1962; see Ian Jones, *The Years Ned Kelly Went Straight*, June 1962, p.17;

the backgrounds of Joe Byrne and Aaron Sherritt, Ian Jones, *The Friendship that Destroyed Ned Kelly*, Melbourne, 1992 (hereafter, Jones, *Friendship*), Chapters 1 to 4, Joe and Aaron at Bullock Creek, pp.44–7; *Lorna Doone*, Ned's favourite book, Charlie and Paddy Griffiths quoting Grace Kelly, interview 1963; Ned, the wild bull and Lydecker, Jerilderie and Cameron Letters; Aaron and Joe for assault, Dan Kelly saddle case, both at Beechworth General Sessions, *O & M*, 1.3.1877 and 3.3.1877.

Ned describes the Moyhu Races confrontation with Whitty in both the Cameron and Jerilderie letters. (I have used passages from both in the quote from Ned.) In the Jerilderie Letter he places the encounter at the *Oxley Races*. This seems to be a slip of the tongue or pen rather than a correction to the earlier version. The Oxley Races were on 2 April. Whitty's conciliatory tone would have been very unlikely on this date, three weeks after Ned's and Tom's pound rescue described below. However, his response is perfectly credible at the *Moyhu* Races, a couple of weeks before the rescue. Details of the Moyhu meeting are from, *W.D.*, 3.3.1877; description of the storm from, *O & M*, 1.3.1877.

Outcome of Joe's and Aaron's trial, editorial comment, *O & M*, 3.3.1877.

'Some time after' encounter with Whitty, Cameron letter; again I have combined Ned's accounts, 'stealing a mob of calves ...', Cameron letter; 'I began to think ...', Jerilderie Letter; Ned describes 'Whitty and Burns' impounding, Cameron letter; six unfenced roads through Whitty Land, *O & M*, 2.5.1877; Dockers try to close roads, *W.D.*, 10.11.1877 'permanent wells' dry up, stock fed on saplings, *W.D.*, 17.2.1877; Heach impounding for Simpson, *O & M*, 7.4.1877; Heach's oat stack torched, *O & M*, 24.3.1877; Whitty's and Byrne's notice of impounding, *W.D.*, 17.2.1877; Ned protests on behalf of 'poor farmers', Jerilderie Letter; Ned's and Tom's horses impounded, *O & M*, 15.3.1877; their horses rescued, *O & M*, 17.3.1877.

6 'THE WHITTY LARCENY', page 91

'Perfect as any properly conducted business', Ward q. Cookson, *Sydney Sun*, 5.9.1911; Ned as 'head centre', *O & M*, 13.11.1880; 'only pair of draught horses ...', *W.D.*, 24.10.1877; Joe Thompson, bookmaker, *de Serville*, p.66 (thanks to Marian Matta for this reference); John Thompson, sparring partner, *O & M*, 17.1.1878; Ned's comments, Jerilderie Letter; had stolen 280 horses, q. by Gloster, *Argus*, 29.10.1880; horse stealing *modus operandi* described by Aaron Sherritt, *Hare*, pp.170–1; problem in NSW, *Commission*, Q.1041, p.47; Ned and Joe believable as young squatters, *Hare*, p.135; Nicolson's report, *Commission*, Q.1024–8, p.47; 'opinion' to Brooke Smith, Q.1028, p.47.

James Whitty takes possession of Myrrhee, April 1877, Billis and Kenyon; *op. cit.*, p.257; auction on 9.1.1877, see ad. *W.D.*, 2.1.1877, inc. description of the property. A fuller description of the house etc., auction ad., *B.E.*, 18.3.1870; Union Bank land described, ad., *O & M*, 22.12.1877; see also Whitty's and Byrnes's ad., *W.D.*, 17.2.1877. I am grateful to the present owner of Myrrhee, Michael Falkenberg, for sharing his knowledge of the property and showing us over the homestead on 31.10.1993, shortly before it was almost completely rebuilt. Death of Catherine Whitty, 3.4.1874; memorial window, *W.D.*, 3.3.1875.

Jim Kelly's arrest and trial, *Wagga Wagga Advertiser*, 30.6.1877; Nicolson entry in Crime Report

Book, *Commission*, Q.16222, p.590; Letter, Singleton, Q.1041, p.47.

The Myrrhee raid reported, *PG*, 26.9.1877, p.257; Ned's story of 'Farrell the policeman' taking George's horse, Jerilderie Letter. Here, Ned identifies the Farrell theft as a cause of the Myrrhee raid. In the Cameron Letter he makes it *the* cause. Michael Farrell left the force in April, 1875 (Record Sheet, Police Historical Unit).

Value of the eleven horses, original *PG* report, *op. cit.*; Howlong without bridge, *O & M*, 30.5.1878; without telegraph, *O & M*, 28.5.1878; Lowry scouts ahead, *O & M*, 22.12.1877. Ned's comments on disposal of the horses are from Jerilderie Letter. The complex story of the roles played by Petersen, Kennedy and the Baumgartens emerges from a series of police court and General Sessions trials reported in *O & M*, 22.11.1877, 11.12.1877, 13.12.1877, 22.12.1877, 2.3.1878, 5.3.1878 and 4.5.1878. For changing of the brands, *O & M*, 2.3.1878 and 11.12.1877.

Baumgartens 'well-to-do' etc., *Argus*, 10.8.1880, see also *Daily Telegraph* of same date. Links with Margerys and John Tanner, *McQuilton*, pp.71, 84; Baumgarten: 'brands were wrong', *O & M*, 22.11.1877; cheque presented by Lowry, *O & M*, 11.12.1877.

Fitzpatrick posted to Benalla, Police Muster Rolls, VPRS 55, Unit 7, VPRO; 'stalwart' and 'ride like a centaur', Cookson, *Sydney Sun*, 23.9.1911; Tom Lloyd's assessment, interview with Tom Lloyd Jr, 4.1.1964; Ned's description of Fitzpatrick is drawn from the Cameron and Jerilderie Letters; 'said we were good friends', Jerilderie Letter; Fitzpatrick's view of Ned, Cookson, *Sydney Sun*, 23.9.1911.

The bootshop brawl in Benalla following Ned's uncharacteristic drunkenness is described by Ned in Jerilderie Letter, also in an account to David Gaunson (reported, *Age*, 9.8.1880), in which he described his 'dazed' condition the next morning and the resulting suspicion that he had been drugged. Ned did not 'care about grog', *Commission*, Q. 17716, p.671. Fitzpatrick's claim that he treated Ned 'kindly', Cookson, *op. cit.*; Fitzpatrick suggests handcuffing Ned, *Clune*, p.123, possibly based on a missing report by Sergeant Whelan; Ned's apocryphal threat to Lonigan is contained in a highly inaccurate version of the brawl in, *Mansfield Pamphlet*, p.26; Ned's court appearance, fines, Benalla Petty Sessions Cause List Book *op. cit.*, 18.9.1877.

The 'mysterious fracas' at Goodmans', *O & M*, 20.11.1877; Goodman's 'fantastic tale' to police, *PG*, 3.10.1877, p.265; *Advertiser* tirade, *O & M*, 2.10.1877; Ned's protest, *O & M*, 21.12.1878; Ned's 'excruciating pain', *Age*, 9.8.1880; Fitzpatrick persuades him to surrender boys, *Commission*, Q.12873, p.465. See also, *PG*, 10.10.1877, p.271 and *O & M*, 13.10.1877. Dan's, Tom's and Jack's trial, *O & M*, 20.11.1877; Goodman perjury, Cameron letter and *O & M*, 20.11.1877; Solomon disappears, *PG*, 17.10.1877, p.275.

Meeting between Fitzpatrick and Kate, *Ashmead*, p.11; big haul of horses from Moyhu and Greta, *PG*, 17.10.1877, p.516. Legend surrounds the disappearance of George King. A granddaughter believes he went to Queensland and that he asked Ellen to accompany him (interview Elsie Pettifer, 22.5.1995).

Formation of the North-Eastern Stock Protection League, public meeting, *W.D.*, 24.10.1877; inaugural meeting advertised, *O & M*, 3.11.1877, and reported, office bearers listed, *O & M*, 22.11.1877; Whitty advertises reward, *W.D.*, 24.10.1877.

Lowry theft from Mark Whitty, *PG*, 27.6.1877, p.174; Pat Quinn informs on Lowry, *Commission*, Q.17691, p.669. The police investigation is described in the 'Baumgarten Case' trial reports cited above and documented in *PG* entries on, 21.11.1877 (arrests of the Baumgartens and Kennedy); 28.11.1877 (warrant and reward for Wild, already serving one month); 5.12.1877 (warrant for Lowry); 12.12.1877 (arrest of Lowry, warrant for Woodyard); 13.2.1878, (arrest of Woodyard). Woodyard theft from Jack Quinn, *PG*, 22.11.1876, p.301; horses killed, *PG*, 21.11.1877; Joe steals chestnut, *PG*, 17.4.1878 and 3.7.1878.

Sgt Steele takes charge of Wangaratta, *W.D.*, 15.11.1876; officer father, *O & M*, 11.6.1881;

'tweedy charm', interview, Sylvia Living, 1969; 'more side than a billiard ball', interview, Claude Brown, 1963; 'very dour man', interview, Father Walter Ebsworth, 1970; 'ring' of horse thieves, *W.D.*, 7.3.1877; Steele's window broken, *W.D.*, 14.3.1877.

Steve Hart described, 'bow-legged ... slow-speaking', *PG*, 5.3.1879; background from two nephews, Steve Hart (interview, 1957), and Tom Lloyd Jr (interview, 28.12.1979, including his mother's story of Steve tying the tail of Steele's horse to a fence). Steve's trial, re-arrest and convictions, *W.D.*, 25.7.1877, and *PG Prisoners Released*, w.e. 17.6.1878.

Steele and Detective Brown suspect Ned (and Dan), *Commission*, Q.8813, p.318; children warn of Steele's approach, Q.8832, p.319.

Ned builds new Kelly homestead, interview, Paddy and Charlie Griffiths, 1963; description based on inspection of the house in 1959 with Ron Shaw. The front wall had collapsed but there was still a hurricane lamp hanging from a tie beam, furniture in the rooms and pictures on the walls. The then owners, Charlie and Gwen Griffiths, were hospitable and helpful but feared that if there was any private attempt to preserve the house 'someone would throw a match into the paddock'. Over the next twenty years the building disappeared through natural decay and pilfering. All that now remains are two brick chimneys erected early this century.

Dan free, *PG Prisoners Released*, w.e. 21.1.1878; Ned sells horses, becomes 'rambling gambler', Jerilderie Letter; Hare paraphrases as 'a "wandering gamester"', *Hare*, p.154; seen as rhyming slang, *Clune*, note, p.348; Ned and Joe head for Wagga, see *PG*, 3.7.1878, p.189; backblocks of Darling, Michael Woodyard statement to Supt Winch, 1.11.1878, Kelly Papers, VPRO; warrant for Ned, *PG*, 20.3.1878, p.78; for Dan and Jack, *PG*, 10.4.1878, p.110; Ned's and Dan's warrants in Prosecution Brief, Kelly Papers, VPRO.

Jack Lloyd Jr tried and discharged, *O & M*, 30.5.1878.

7 THE FITZPATRICK MYSTERY, page 107

Fitzpatrick's illegitimate child at Meredith, VPRS 937, Unit 145; his pregnant fiancee, VPRS 937, Unit 144, both VPRO, q. *Molony* p.271. The colony's political crisis of 1878 is deftly sketched by Ernest Scott, *A Short History of Australia*, Melbourne, 1947, pp.267 & 273–7, with fascinating detail from the introductory section of Alfred Deakin, *The Crisis in Victorian Politics, 1879–1881*, edited by J.A. La Nauze and R.M. Crawford, Melbourne, 1957. The police force saved from disbandment, *Sadleir*, pp.179–81; 'the shadow of Black Wednesday', *ibid.*, p.183.

Fitzpatrick at Cashel, *Commission*, Q.5944, p.235; ordered to Greta, Telegram, Brooke Smith to Whelan, 11.4.1878; Kelly Papers, VPRO (incorrectly dated to 12 April in Whelan's Royal Commission evidence). Fitzpatrick's late return to Benalla and Healy's 'patrol' to Greta, Whelan endorsements to Brooke Smith telegram, *op. cit.*; warrants for Dan Kelly and Jack Lloyd, *PG*, 10.4.1878, p.110: Fitzpatrick had seen them at Cashel, Cookson, *Sydney Sun*, 5.9.1911; Whelan tells him 'to be careful', *Commission*, Q.12817, p.413; defends Fitzpatrick's action, Q.5951, p.236; Fitzpatrick's 2 a.m. return to Benalla, Q.5947, p.236.

Fitzpatrick's 'strange tale', Deposition, 17.5.1878, Prosecution Brief, Queen v. Ellen Kelly, *et al.*, Kelly Papers, VPRO; 'miss a man three times at a yard and a half', Jerilderie

Letter; Fitzpatrick on 'friendly terms' with Ned etc., *Commission*, Q.12871, p.465; Dr Nicholson's 'frequently quoted' evidence, *O & M*, 10.10.1878; sheet of bark with bullet mark removed, Fitzpatrick notes, 6.6.1878; Prosecution Brief, Kelly Papers, VPRO; Flood finds matching bullet mould, sworn undated statement, probably 16 May, *ibid.*; Joe Byrne mistaken for Skilling, Jones, *Friendship*, Notes, p.209; if one part of crown evidence false 'jury cannot believe the rest', *O & M*, 10.10.1878; Crown invitation to call Kate and Grace, undated note by Sergeant Whelan, Prosecution Brief, *op. cit.*; Tom Lloyd's version of Fitzpatrick incident, *Kenneally*, pp.34–5; Kenneally deletes Ned's version from the text of Cameron letter (covered by three dots on p.72); Mrs Kelly's admission that Ned present, Cookson, *Sydney Sun*, 28.8.1911; Ned's Jerilderie version, *Herald*, 14.2.1879; Jim's account, *Datas: The Memory Man by Himself*, London, n.d., but 1930, pp.170–1 (my thanks to Peter Arnold for this reference); interview with Kate, *Herald*, 7.2.1879; Jim tells relative that Ned shot Fitzpatrick, interview, Gwen Griffiths, 1961.

Kate Kelly's chestnut pony stolen, *PG*, 21.4.1879, p.129; Williamson's 'highly detailed account', Williamson to Inspector General of Penal Establishments, 6.8.1881, Kelly Papers, VPRO; Ned's witness (Joe Ryan) admits Ned was near Greta that day, *O & M*, 10.10.1878; Ned 'lets slip' that he was present, McIntyre Deposition, Prosecution Brief, Queen v. Edward Kelly, *op. cit.*; Ned admits that he shot *at* Fitzpatrick, McIntyre and Sr Const. Kelly, Depositions, *ibid.*

The bullet hole in Fitzpatrick's sleeve, Fitzpatrick to Officer in Charge, Beechworth, 24.5.1878; Kelly Papers, VPRO; Dr Nicholson confirms Fitzpatrick's story, Deposition, 17.5.1878; Prosecution Brief, Queen v. Ellen Kelly *et al.*, *ibid.*; the doctor's 'neglected comment' at the trial, *O & M*, 10.10.1878.

Whelan says Fitzpatrick left at 2 p.m., endorsement to Brooke Smith telegram, *op. cit.*; Skilling sees Fitzpatrick pass at about 5 p.m., Sr Const. Strahan to Supt. Police Benalla, 27.9.1878, Prosecution Brief, *op. cit.*; Williamson confirms that Fitzpatrick threatened to shoot Mrs Kelly, Letter to Inspector General, Penal Establishments, *op. cit.*; Ned says that, immediately before this, his mother 'was putting some fire on the oven', *Age*, 9.8.1880; 'She then took a spade etc.', Williamson's Statement, *op. cit.* Ned imagines Fitzpatrick 'a man against whom he had a special hatred', *O & M*, 10.9.1878. In an Editorial, 'The Greta Shooting Case', the editor of the *Advertiser* makes and reiterates the point that Ned mistook Fitzpatrick for 'someone else who had made himself particularly obnoxious to the Kelly family' and concedes, 'We quite believe that the shots which were fired were not intended for Fitzpatrick.' The references are clearly to Flood. Within a few months it would emerge that Flood's seduction of Annie was common knowledge in the district, *Herald*, 8.11.1878, Mansfield Pamphlet, p.28.

8 'THERE WOULD BE MURDER NOW', page 119

£100 reward for Ned, 29.4.1878, published in *VGG*, 3.5.1878, p.963; Ned tells Williamson, 'Fitzpatrick had promised to say nothing . . .', Williamson Deposition, *op. cit.*; movements of Ned, Dan and Joe, *ibid.*; 'Offenders will make for NSW . . . warrants will issue', Telegram, Whelan to Detective Police, 16.4.1878; Prosecution Brief, *op. cit.*; Movements of Steele etc., *Commission*, Q.8817–22, p.319; Deposition Sgt Steele,

17.4.1878; Prosecution Brief, *op. cit.*; Memo, Sr Const. Strahan to Supt Police, Beechworth, 27.9.1878, *ibid.*; Mrs Kelly hasn't seen Ned for four months, Strahan, *ibid.* 'I
know I've got a damn bad temper' etc., Steele, *Commission*, Q.9214, p.334; but for
Kate 'would have finished Fitzpatrick off', Q.9215, p.334; arrests of Williamson,
Skilling and Ellen Kelly, Steele Deposition, *op. cit.*; Strahan Memo, *op. cit.* and
Commission, Q.8822, p.319. It is popularly believed that Ellen Kelly was taken from
her bed with her baby and driven into Benalla 'before daylight on a bitterly cold morning' (*Kenneally*, p.36). Steele's evidence makes it clear that (a) she had not been to bed
and (b) was lodged at Greta overnight with Skilling and Williamson. See *Sketcher*,
11.5.1878 for arrival at Benalla lock-up 'during Wednesday afternoon'.

Ned and Joe head for the back blocks of the Darling, Woodyard Statement to Supt Winch,
op. cit., see also, *PG*, 3.7.1878, p.189; prisoners 'committed to stand trial on the
capital charge', *O & M*, 18.5.1878; snow around Beechworth, *O & M*, 30.4.1878; night
of hearing, Kate and Maggie bogged, rescued by police, *Commission*, Q.3039–40, p.160;
Ned's description of the police raids, Cameron and Jerilderie letters; Ellen Kelly bailed,
O & M, 16.6.1878; Recognisance of Bail taken before P.M. Foster, 31.5.1878;
Prosecution Brief, *op. cit.* Note that the document is dated some two weeks before the
Advertiser item which describes Mrs Kelly being admitted to bail 'a day or two' before.
The staunchly conservative, anti-Kelly *Advertiser* would be unlikely to misreport in
such a way. The two-week delay in Ellen's release seems inexplicable.

Steve Hart free, *PG Prisoners Released*, w.e. 17.6.1878; Steele reports visit to Hart selection,
Steve's 'short life' speech, *Commission*, Q.9133, p.331; Aaron Sherritt's attempt to decoy
Fitzpatrick into Kelly hands, Q.12925–9, p.467.

Calendar for Assizes 'heaviest and most serious ... for years', *O & M*, 8.10.1878; 166 jurors
on rolls, 140 summoned, *O & M*, 12.9.1878; Sir Redmond Barry's views on 'mistak-
en, misdirected lenity', *Report No. 2 of the Royal Commission on Penal and Prison
Discipline*, 1871, p.1; trial proceedings, *O & M*, 10.10.1878; Frank Harty 'would fight
up to my knees in blood' for Ned Kelly, Report, Fitzpatrick to Officer in Charge,
Beechworth, 22.5.1878, Prosecution Brief, *op. cit.*; Sentences and *Advertiser* comment,
O & M, 15.10.1878.

In 1929, J.J. Kenneally claimed that in sentencing Ellen, Barry declared, 'If your son Ned
were here I would make an example of him for the whole of Australia — I would give
him 15 years' (*Kenneally*, p.44). The only source yet discovered for this extraordinary
statement is G. Wilson Hall's *Mansfield Pamphlet* of 1879 in which, after describing
the sentencing of the Fitzpatrick prisoners, Hall continues, 'Furthermore, a reward of
£100 was offered for the apprehension of Ned Kelly, to whom it was intimated that
had he stood in the dock, he would have received a sentence of 21 years ...' (*Mansfield Pamphlet*, p.15). Hall seems to imply the '21-year' threat was 'intimated' during
the sentencing but the reference is doubly ambiguous through being linked with the
£100 reward proclaimed five months before.

'There would be murder now', quoted by Williamson, Statement to Insp. Green, 29.10.1878,
quoted by Green to Supt Winch, 30.10.1878, Kelly Papers, VPRO.

9 STRINGYBARK, page 125

Ned 'would rush through a hundred bayonets' to get Fitzpatrick, *O & M*, 21.12.1878; Wyatt
    newly appointed, *O & M*, 14.5.1878; his eccentricities, *Melbourne Bulletin*, q. *O & M*,
    30.10.1880; 'old English gentleman', Mrs Susy Scott, 'The Kellys at Euroa, Being Her
    Reminiscences', typescript, MS.A4143, Mitchell Library (hereafter *Mrs Scott Typescript*);
    Wyatt thinks Mrs Kelly's sentence 'very severe', *Commission*, Q.2275, p.131; propo-
    sition for Ned and Dan to surrender, Q.2327, p.133; Wyatt's response, Q.2275, p.131;
    offer 'probably' conveyed to Whelan, Q.2273, p.131.
'Sluice bores' etc. at Bullock Creek, Letter, Edward Kelly to the Governor of Victoria, 3.10.1878,
    Capital Case File, VPRO; 'good wages', Jerilderie Letter; Ned describes whisky still pro-
    ject, E. Kelly to Governor, *op. cit.*; at Bullock Creek in September of 1968, with my
    sons Darren and Angus, I found broken pieces of the cast iron pot from Ned's whisky
    still, brought to the surface by the rooting of feral pigs. A section of the rim (which
    still showed the mark of a sledge hammer) enabled me to calculate the pot's diam-
    eter. The location of the find, about 150 metres downstream from the hut site, tallied
    with Ned's description of the 'main distill' being 'further down the creek'. The hut
    described, *O & M*, 27.10.1878. Presence of 'door hinges' among the 'great variety' of
    articles around the hut suggest that the door 'of stiff slabs' (*ibid.*), armoured with iron
    from a ship's ballast tank (*Sadleir*, p.193), was newly built and demanded stronger
    hinges. The hut and its surroundings, including the bullet-scarred trees, were also
    described in a telegram from Sr Const. James to Pewtress, 24.11.1878 (hereafter James
    telegram). Note that James incorrectly sites the hut on Germans Creek, an adjoining
    tributary of Ryans Creek.
Ned's sawn-off carbine described, inc. 'shoot around the corner', Deposition, Edwin Living,
    10.8.1880, Prosecution Brief, Queen v. Edward Kelly, Kelly Papers, VPRO; 'shoot a
    kangaroo at 100 yards', McIntyre Deposition, 7.8.1880, *ibid.* For many years the car-
    bine was on display at the Melbourne Aquarium. When the building burnt down in
    1953, the weapon was taken to the Museum of Applied Science and disappeared. Dan's
    shotgun and Joe's and Steve's alleged weapons described, McIntyre Deposition, *ibid.*;
    three revolver bullets in target, *O & M*, 27.10.1878.
Ned believes that 'three parties of police . . . thirteen in number' are leaving to search for him-
    self and Dan, Letter, E. Kelly to Governor, *op. cit.*; Ned told of hobbled horses at Mans-
    field, *ibid.*; in Jerilderie Letter Ned described finding tracks of police horses 'between
    Table Top and The Bogs'; identified as site of Johnny Byrne's hut, interview, Jack Walsh,
    son-in-law of Johnny Byrne, January 1960. The Byrne hut was then in original con-
    dition (except that a ceiling of corrugated cardboard had replaced the earlier calico).
    The walls were still covered with newspaper — a new layer each year. Jack told me
    of Johnny's skill as a blacksmith and that he was related to Joe.
The departure of Kennedy's party was common knowledge in Mansfield by noon on 26
    October (*O & M*, 5.11.1878). Ned finds 'a different lot of tracks' between Emu Swamp
    and Bullock Creek (Cameron letter) heading for 'the shingle hut' on Stringybark Creek
    (Jerilderie Letter). For Ned standing guard, see McIntyre report to Pewtress, 28.10.1878;
    Prosecution Brief, *op. cit.*; ('he [Ned] wanted a sleep') and tracks 'on a rise near the
    hut', James Telegram, *op. cit.*; Ned and Dan spy on the police camp, 'long firearms .
    . . our doom was sealed', Jerilderie Letter. The Cameron letter fixes the date of the
    reconnaissance as 26 October, the presence of all four police establishes that it was
    before 6 a.m. when two left on patrol.

Tom Lloyd due, *Kenneally*, p.61; Wild Wright shearing on the Murray, *O & M*, 31.10.1878. For Ned 'as a rebel': he was never previously described as wearing his chinstrap under his nose or wearing a sash. The 'bright red sash' (*Sketcher*, 23.11.1878) he wore that day was never seen again. Both Ned and Joe, previously 'well dressed men' who passed as young squatters, appeared at Stringybark in the 'flash', rebellious guise of the Greta mob.

Description of the boys' approach to the police camp and my subsequent orientation of the gunfight are based on lengthy research and on fieldwork with my son, Darren, in October 1993, which identified the site, several hundred metres south of the accepted location (which is marked by 'The Kelly Tree') and on the opposite, eastern bank of the creek. This complex exercise was described in my paper, 'The Gunfight at Stringybark Creek — new evidence from a surviving witness', at the C.A.E. Kelly Seminar, Beechworth, on 13 November 1993. Basic sources are summarised in Jones, *Friendship, op. cit.*, note, p.211. For re-siting police camp to eastern bank, James Tomkins q. *Devils' River Country*, *op. cit.*, p.41; telegram, James to Pewtress, *op. cit.* and *Kenneally*, pp. 55, 57 & 59. Kenneally had Tom Lloyd as a guide for his fieldwork at Bullock and Stringybark Creeks in the 1920s. Bog to north of police camp site, James Tomkins, *op. cit.*; Ned 'recognises' Flood (McIntyre deposition, *op. cit.*), and Strahan (Jerilderie Letter).

Ward's information in May, *Commission*, Q.3042, p.161; Q.3121, p.163; Ward's plan for search, Q.3118, p.163; Sadleir corresponds with Kennedy, Q.1738, p.105; Kennedy's 'first memo' includes suggestion of depot at Stringybark, Q.1741, p.105; shared reward with Scanlon, *PG*, 2.12.1873; McIntyre 'zealous, conscientious', Q.1755, p.106; Lonigan's inclusion and new horse for Kennedy, Q.1742, p.106; horse's 'unusual traits', *Sadleir*, p.188; 'clerical error' in make-up of Greta party, Q.1742, p.106; Ward 'never had the remotest idea they would shoot', Q.3125, p.163; Ned: Lonigan 'the man who would shoot him', Jerilderie Letter; Strahan would shoot Ned down 'like a dog', Jerilderie Letter, cf. Letter, James to Sadleir, 24.6.1898; Sadleir Papers, La Trobe Library, q. *McQuilton*, p.99; Patrick Quinn statement, *Herald*, 10.11.1880; 'first blood, Lonigan', McIntyre Typescript, *op. cit.*; straps to carry dead bodies, Jones, *Friendship*, note, p.210; McIntyre on unusual armament and ammunition, *Age*, 12.8.1880; Kennedy borrows shotgun from vicar, *ibid.*; Spencer carbine from Snr Const. Kelly, *Commission*, Q.7978, p.299.

McIntyre described the killings at Stringybark Creek in reports of 27, 28 and 29.10.1878, in depositions at the three inquests, in statements and depositions for both trials of Ned Kelly in 1880, in several newspapers and magazine interviews, at the Royal Commission and in the McIntyre Typescript, *op. cit.* Major variations are indicated in the text. In his first report to Pewtress, 27.10.1878, McIntyre said, 'Constable Lonigan made a motion to draw his revolver which he was carrying immediately he did so he was shot by Edward Kelly' (Prosecution Brief, *op. cit.*). The day after, in a fuller report sent to Standish, he wrote, 'Const. Lonigan had his revolver on ran towards a tree at the same time placing his hand upon his revolver before he had gone two paces he was shot by Edward Kelly,' (*ibid.*). The *next* day, in a statement to Supt Sadleir, he said, 'Lonigan ... put his hands to his revolver, at the same time slipping down for cover behind the log on which he had been sitting. Lonigan had his head above the level of the log and was about to use his revolver when he was shot through the head' (*Sadleir*, p.187). On this one occasion he confirms Ned Kelly's account of the shooting of Lonigan (with the minor variation that Ned claimed Lonigan ran to cover behind a log 'six or seven yards' away). In every subsequent description, McIntyre has Lonigan shot while drawing, or trying to draw his revolver, and/or running towards cover. 'What a pity; what made the fool run?' *O & M*, 31.10.1878. McIntyre later amended this highly credible comment, to the unlikely, 'Dear, oh dear, what a pity that man tried to get away', Deposition, 7.8.1880 *op. cit*. The Gang, described by McIntyre, *PG*, 6.11.1878 (original and amended descriptions) with additional detail from *Sketcher*, 23.11.1878 and McIntyre Typescript, *op. cit*. Conversation with Ned, McIntyre Depositions, *op. cit*.; rumours of Flood and Annie, *Herald*, 8.11.1878, Mansfield Pamphlet, p.28; Ned on police armament, Jerilderie Letter.

Ned on shooting of Scanlon, Jerilderie Letter; Kennedy wounds Dan in shoulder, Stephens Deposition, 10.8.1880; Prosecution Brief, *op. cit*.; McIntyre claims Scanlon shot while kneeling, Deposition, 7.8.1880, *op. cit*.; 'Scanlon . . . endeavoured to get behind a tree . . .', McIntyre Deposition at Scanlon Inquest, 29.10.1880; 'I do not think I ever said Scanlon was shot whilst running for a tree. I was annoyed with reporters . . .', McIntyre q. *Age*, 9.8.1880; Joe fires fatal shot at Scanlon, Jones, *Friendship*, notes, pp.211–12.

Ned described his gunfight with Kennedy in both the Cameron and Jerilderie letters and in several conversations during his outlawry, some of which are documented in depositions for his trials — notably from James Gloster and George Stephens, both of which I have used for the closing stages of the encounter. (Stephens, a former policeman, was a particularly good witness. However, he confused the issue seriously on one point, claiming that Ned's first shot merely grazed Lonigan's head, and he sank back behind cover then emerged to be killed by a second shot. There *was* a graze on Lonigan's forehead but the doctor who performed the post-mortem subsequently expressed doubts that it was caused by a bullet [*Age*, 9.8.1880]. It seems likely that Stephens had unintentionally included a detail from Ned's account of the gunfight with Kennedy, especially as in one undated statement he speaks of Ned killing Lonigan 'with the contents of the other barrel'). Kennedy re-loading revolver, see McIntyre, Additional Statement, 22.7.1880. McIntyre quotes Ned saying that Kennedy fired 'about two rounds of his revolver' and interpolates '(12 shots)'. Ned: 'he must have dropped his revolver . . .', Stephens Deposition, *op. cit*.; Position of Kennedy's body, Deposition, Henry Sparrow, 1.11.1878, Kennedy Inquest, Prosecution Brief, *op. cit*.

The Perkins version of Kennedy's death, q. *Argus,* 13.12.1878, cf. *Herald*, 13.12.1878 and *Mansfield Pamphlet*, pp.33–5; Ned: 'The bravest man he had ever heard of', q. Aaron Sherritt, *Hare*, p.104; aftermath from Hall, *Mansfield Pamphlet*, p.34–5.

Joe takes Lonigan's and Scanlon's rings, Jones, *Friendship*, note, p.212; 'ugly claim' that Ned made the others fire into the bodies, *Sadleir*, p.189. See John Phillips, *The Trial of Ned Kelly*, Melbourne, 1987, p.82, for an expert examination of the evidence concerning this claim, including a persuasive argument that a bullet wound in Lonigan's thigh had been self-inflicted — presumably fired in a reflex action after Ned's bullet struck him. It is surprising that Dr Reynolds failed to notice powder burns, but his post-mortem reports on the three bodies are far from exhaustive — as when he describes only the final, fatal wound to Kennedy's chest (deposition, 1.11.1878, Kennedy Inquest, Prosecution Brief, *op. cit*.). See telegram, Pewtress to Standish, 31.11.1878, q. *O & M*, 2.11.1878, for Kennedy's head wounds; for wound under right arm, Dr Reynolds, interview, *O & M*, 2.11.1878.

Meeting with Tom Lloyd, *Kenneally*, p.61; Tom guards the Gang, *Sadleir*, p.193; tracks, James telegram, *op. cit*.; leave three rundown horses in paddock and fire the hut, *ibid*.; 'detritus', *O & M*, 27.10.1878; 'a good axe and other tools', James telegram, *op. cit*.

10 FUGITIVES, page 141

McIntyre's 'last glimpse of the doomed sergeant', McIntyre Deposition, 29.10.1878, Scanlon Inquest, *op. cit.*; 'great number of shots', McIntyre Deposition, 7.8.1880; Prosecution Brief, *op. cit.*; Joe fires one shot at McIntyre, George Stephens, Statement (undated, and incomplete), Kelly Papers, VPRO. The best account of McIntyre's journey to Mansfield, *O & M*, 31.10.1878, with some interesting detail in Hall's agonisingly wordy narrative, *Mansfield Pamphlet*, pp.35–9. 'Torn off the horse', McIntyre Deposition, 7.8.1880, *op. cit.*; Ned Byrne drives McIntyre into Mansfield, telegram, Sen. Const. Maud to Sadleir, 28.10.1878, Kelly Papers, VPRO; 'This is hell', *Commission*, Q.17647, p.667; 'earliest detailed account', Report to Sub-insp. Pewtress, *op. cit.*; '5.40 p.m.', annotation by Pewtress.

Pewtress, ex-London police, *Sadleir*, pp.279–80; 'unacquainted with bush work', *ibid.*, p.184. For a superb description of 'dark, wet journey' to retrieve the bodies, C.H. Chomley, *The True Story of the Kelly Gang of Bushrangers*, Melbourne, n.d., but 1940s, pp.14–16.

Meehan's panicky journey to Benalla, *Commission*, Q.17647, p.668 (Meehan, a delightful eccentric, records Sadleir telling him what a fool he had made of himself and asking, 'Meehan, would not it be better for you then, that you were shot ...?' Meehan comments drily, 'Of course I differed with him in that'), *Commission*, Q.17654, p.668.

The Gang's ride to Greta and the plan to rob a bank at Howlong, *Kenneally*, p.61; The best overall accounts of the Gang's remarkable journey to the Murray and back are, *Sadleir*, pp.193–6, and his Royal Commission evidence, Q.1858–65, p.111. The visits to the Pioneer Hotel and Coulson's store described by Detective Ward, *Commission*, Q.3148–66, p.164–5, with valuable detail from *Age*, 8.11.1878.

Sixteen-mile detour via Taylors Gap, telegram, Const. Bracken, 4.11.1878; Kelly Papers, VPRO; Gang signal for Aaron, *Commission*, Q.13157, p.475, Q.3162–4, p.165; Aaron guards the Gang in 'a magnificent cave', *Hare*, pp.140–1 and 168. This is now known as The Kelly Cave, an inaccessible and consequently unspoilt Kelly site. £800 reward, *VGG* Supplement, 28.10.1878; Nicolson put in charge, *Commission*, Q.6, p.1; 'authority to take any steps he thought proper ... incur any expenditure ...', Q.7, p.1; first of 79 men to N.E., Police Muster Rolls, VPRS 55, Unit 8, VPRO; extra armament, *Commission*, Appendix 7, p.697 — a valuable table which shows the manpower and weaponry distributed in the north-east between July 1878 and October 1880.

Beechworth fireball, *O & M*, 31.10.1878; 'the greatest flood', *Commission*, Q.354, p.15; encounters with Margery and Christian, Telegram, Det. Sgt D.S. Kennedy, 1.11.1878, q. *O & M*, 5.11.1878; see also, *O & M*, 7.11.1878 and Nicolson, *Commission*, Q.344–7, p.15; location of Rats Castle, *O & M*, 16.11.1878.

Visit to Baumgartens', Nicolson, *Commission*, Q.347, p.15; the Gang's narrow escape from Harkin–Kennedy party in floodwaters, *Sadleir*, p.194 cf. *Commission*, Q1865, p.111; make a fire to dry guns etc., *Hare*, p.108; punt sunk at Bungowannah, *Commission*, Q1865, p.111.

Reward to £2000, *VGG*, 30.10.1878, p.2777; bark stripper sees Gang at Sherritts, 'men and horses pretty well worn out', *Sadleir*, p.195; 'speechless state of drunkenness', *ibid*.

Gang 'pass through' Everton 'and call at certain places', Nicolson Commission, Q.354 & Q.356, pp.15 & 16. (Incorrectly, Nicolson has the Gang at Everton on the night of 3 November, perhaps meaning the early morning. It was late on the night of 2 November.) Mary Vandenberg's vivid account of the Gang's visit to the Victoria Hotel, and its aftermath, is from her daughter, Christina Vandenberg, interview, October 1960. For location of the Victoria, ad., *O & M*, 26.1.1878.

No crossing places on Ovens between Bright and Wangaratta, *Age*, 8.11.1878; Delaneys 'respectable people', *Commission*, Q.17309, p.653; Mrs Delaney's description of the Gang and their horses, Q.17415 (with material from Q.17403), p.656; Gang pass under One-Mile Creek bridge, 'break the bank' of the creek, cross wooden bridge towards Warbys, Q.17417, p.656; 'just at grey in the morning', Q.8856 p.321; members of the Gang all known to the Delaneys, Q.17314, p.653; Gang had earlier crossed bridge and ridden through Wangaratta, *Hare*, p.108.

11 PURSUERS?, page 150

Sadleir and the terrified carriers, *Sadleir*, p.186; Ward 'only with a little revolver' and 'hemmed in by the floods', *Commission*, Q.3148, p.164; Steele: 'undoubtedly the outlaws ... evidently Steve Hart ... piloted them under the bridge', Q.8856, pp.320–1; 'Report the matter to Mr Smith', *ibid.*; Steele's conduct 'highly censurable' etc., *Commission*, 2nd Progress Report, Recommendation 9; referring Const. Twomey to Brooke Smith seen as 'an attempt to evade responsibility', *ibid.*, Section VII.

Brooke Smith 'natty in his person', Q.16899, p.631; Ned's 'colourful invective', *Jerilderie Letter*; Brooke Smith's age, years of service, Q.17502, p.659; imprisoned for debt, *O & M*, 18.6.1870; 'Chronic state of marching orders', *O & M*, 7.10.1875; 'acting superintendent four times', *Commission*, Q.17559, p.661; thought it 'too dangerous' to keep notebooks, Q.17363, p.651; outlaws 'might get hold of' Nicolson's notebook, Q.17363, p.655; within a year, 'a wreck both in body and mind', Nicolson doubts Brooke Smith has the courage to suicide, Q.16233, p.591.

Brooke Smith 'said something about sending a telegram', Q.17443, p.657; Const. Twomey 'disgusted', *ibid.*; Brooke Smith leads party, some to Lake Rowan, rest to Yarrawonga, Q.12356–61, p.444.

The much-lampooned raid on the Sherritt House, five days after the Gang had been there, described, Jones, *Friendship*, Chapter 7, 'The Great Sebastopol Raid'. See, *Herald*, 7.11.1878, and *Argus*, 8.11.1878, for accounts by reporters who rode on the expedition. The crucial interview with Aaron Sherritt described by Sadleir (*Commission*, Q.1786–1813, pp.108–9), Nicolson (Q.405 & 405A, p.17), and Standish (Q.15775–7, pp.573–4, and Q.15873–9, p.577).

Brooke Smith heads for Lake Rowan too slowly, men complain, Q.17583, p.662; tracks in Timothy Ryan's stockyard, Q.12362–4, p.444; Sr Const. Johnson and Jim Dixon track horses to Warbys, Q.12365, p.444 and Q.12375, p.445; orchardist Brien tells Brooke Smith he gives the Kellys tea and oranges, Q.17578–9, p.662; the inspector's signal shot upsets the men, Q.17572, p.662; Ned and the Gang 'held their horses ... all night,' Q.12509, p.448.

Johnston 'picking up the tracks and fighting the outlaws', Q.12395, p.445; party find Scanlon's horse, Q.12397–404, p.445; Brooke Smith's 'Halt; form up ... proceed to Wangaratta', Q.12411, p.446.

To Taminick and Glenrowan, Q.12461, p.447; the warm trail of the white-faced chestnut, Q.12474–5, p.447.

The Gang split up, two near Greta, two towards Yarrawonga, Q.16894, p.629.

Nicolson: 'men ... dissatisfied', Inspector 'unfit for that work', Q.16896, p.631; Nicolson claims

Gang 100 miles away, organises expedition 'to soothe the men', Q.16899, p.632.

Platelayer sees two suspected Gang members gallop across line at Glenrowan, enter Warbys, Q.1875, p.112 and Q.16690, p.612. Sadleir's 'Appearances of the Kelly Gang' (*Commission*, Appendix 5), dates this report simply to Monday 11 November. However, this was the very day that Johnston and Dixon had tracked the three furtive riders from the previous Friday's train meeting at Glenrowan. Obviously, Monday's horsemen had galloped through the crossing into the Warbys after the party of police had returned to Wangaratta, placing the sighting in late afternoon or evening. Large-scale pursuit based on this sighting, *Commission*, Appendix 5, p.690; Sadleir: tracks lead into possible ambush, Q.1877, p.112; Johnston: 'into some thick scrub', Q.12477, p.447; Sadleir: trackers 'misleading us', into swamp, Q.1875, p.112; 'they would be first to be shot', Q.1878–80, p.112; Johnston: trackers reluctant to enter scrub, Q.12477, p.477.

Nicolson: tracks lead to 'dry swamp ... no scrub or other cover', Q.16899, p.632.

Sadleir: with good blacks, 'a very good show', Q.1880, p.112; Johnston: 'tracks of the outlaws ... given up', Q.12498, p.448; told he must obey orders, Q.12495, p.448; Nicolson: 'Johnston gave up the job', Q.16899, p.632; 'through some mistake of orders' (Q.1880, p.112), Steele and men leave without Nicolson, apparently ride past Gang, Q.16899, p.632; Nicolson has picnic lunch, orders Brooke Smith off pursuit, Q.415, p.18; Ned's description of the police picnic, could have shot Nicolson and Sadleir, Q.1880, p.112.

Johnston 'dissatisfied', applies for transfer, Q.12498, p.448; The Commission's 'judgement on the eight days', *Commission*, 2nd Progress Report, Section VII.

Nicolson successfully pulled the wool over the Royal Commission's eyes by glossing over the aborted pursuit and blurring together the Friday and Monday sightings, suggesting that the entire incident involved four-day-old tracks. It was late in the day — one of the Commission's last sittings — and Sadleir's evidence, corroborating Johnston's, had been delivered five months earlier. However, even then, the Commission had given the abandoned hunt less-than-rigorous scrutiny, forming, as it seemed to, a mere finale to the Brooke Smith debacle.

12 'THE COUNTRY BELONGS TO US', page 159

Felons Apprehension Act ('Outlawry Act'), *VGG*, 1.11.1878, p.2779; notices to surrender, *O & M*, 7.11.1878; Proclamation of Outlawry, *O & M*, 16.11.1878; 'a declaration of war', *Kenneally*, p.65.

Maggie baking bread for Gang, nightly rides on Whitefoot, spied on by police agent, *Commission*, Q.1887–1922, pp.112–3; 'ace of spies' identified as Donnelly, Donnelly to Sadleir, 11.11.1878, Kelly Papers, VPRO, q. *Molony*, p.278.

Oxley and Milawa banks' precautions against robbery, *O & M*, 16.11.1878; Euroa a 'sleepy hollow', Mrs Scott typescript, *op. cit.*

Ned's relatives in Euroa district, *ibid.*, Letter, Robert Scott, 20.12.1878, Kelly Papers, VPRO; *Argus*, 12.12.1878; *Age*, 16.12.1878; Ned had worked on Faithfuls Creek, *Herald*, 12.12.1878. The Faithfulls Creek homestead (invariably confused with the neighbouring Faithfulls Creek *run*) was actually an outstation of the Euroa run and part of the vast

Younghusband/Lyell conglomerate, see Robert Spreadborough and Hugh Anderson, *Victorian Squatters,* Ascot Vale, 1983, for ownership of runs and maps showing boundaries.

Ned's friends at Faithfulls Creek, *Herald,* 12.12.1878, in which two of the Gang's prisoners say the 'old station hands' knew the Kellys were nearby 'on the Sunday morning' and thought the affair 'a good performance'. For Andrew Morton, Report, Const. Hayes, 8.7.1880, Kelly Papers, VPRO, and Report, Const. Blade, 6.7.1880, *ibid.*; for John Carson, Report, Const. McGuirk, 8.7.1880, *ibid.*; for Ben Gould, Letter, Robert Scott (Euroa bank manager), 13.12.1878, *ibid.* and *Argus,* 16.12.1878. For hawker James Gloster's complicity, Report, Sen. Const. Gill, 13.10.1879, Kelly Papers, VPRO. Gill's compelling evidence was totally rejected by Standish (endorsement to report) enabling Gloster and his assistant to be called as Prosecution witnesses at Ned's trial. For involvement of Gloster's assistant, Beecroft, *O & M,* 14.12.1878; see Jones, *Friendship,* note, p.214, for assessment of Gloster and Beecroft evidence.

Parliamentarian Cameron's question re. the Kellys, *Herald,* 14.11.1878; 'shrewd comment' on 'political football', *McMenomy,* p.112; government copy of Ned's and Joe's letter (Cameron letter), Kelly Papers, VPRO. Neither of the two originals has yet been located.

Death of Bill Gouge, Kevin Passey, *In Search of Ned,* Albury, 1988, p.102. I have amended Bill's age to 12, as on his Death Certificate. Bill's father 'an old resident', Mrs Scott typescript, *op. cit.*; The Gang's horses, 'magnificent', *Herald,* 12.12.1878; 'very valuable ones ... far superior to anything in the district', *O & M,* 14.12.1878; for 'Mirth' and 'Music', Jones, *Friendship,* note, p.208; Music recently foaled, Telegram, Sgt Burland, 12.12.1878, Kelly Papers, VPRO; Music travels 65 miles in a day: Joe seen at Woolshed, 8.11.1878, *Commission,* Appendix 5, p.690, Joe's reconnaissance of Euroa with Ben Gould, Sunday, 8.11.1878, *Commission,* Q.15545, p.566. Here, Mr Graves MLA reveals that the Euroa publican, de Boos, saw Joe's body at Glenrowan and recognised him as the man, previously believed to be Steve Hart, who was at his hotel two days before the robbery.

The events at Faithfulls Creek on the Monday and Tuesday are documented in a saturation coverage by metropolitan and country papers, in statements gathered for Ned Kelly's trial two years later, in depositions taken at the Beechworth hearing and in the press coverage of evidence at that hearing and the subsequent trial. All these sources have been used in this account.

Bailing up the station, Fitzgerald statement of 20.9.1880, Stephens's deposition of 7.8.1880, his undated statement ('You're a damned good guesser') and another undated and incomplete statement by him, all, Kelly Papers, VPRO.

Macaulay's arrival, his undated statement to Police Magistrate Wyatt (Kelly Papers, VPRO); Gloster bailed up, Gloster and Beecroft depositions, 9.8.1880; Prosecution Brief, Queen v. E. Kelly, Kelly Papers, VPRO; see also *O & M,* and *Herald,* both 12.12.1878. Gloster (deposition, 9.8.1880, *op. cit.*) gives the best account of Ned's night with the prisoners in the store shed, including the offers of money.

For Joe writing fair copies of the letter and entertaining Mrs Fitzgerald, *Argus,* 14.12.1880, including two stamps for the letter and putting it in his pocket.

The complex breaking of the telegraph lines, *Age,* 13.12.1878; Ned: 'Here's nine traps!' Macaulay's undated statement to P.M. Wyatt, *op. cit.*

Ned bailing up the troublesome hunters, depositions by Dudley and Macdougall, 10.8.1880; Prosecution Brief, *op. cit.*; also *Age, Herald, Argus, O & M,* all 13.12.1878, with splendid colour from *Age,* 13.12.1878 ('I smell the pooder noo' — perhaps a little *too* colourful from an Englishman!). A delightful description of Dudley ('He is John Bull, sir.'), *Herald,* 11.8.1880, after the *Herald*'s excellent coverage (10.8.1880) of his evidence (and Macdougall's) at Beechworth, including 'a rather touchy customer' and his gun sold before it was taken by Ned.

The Gang's new clothes described, Det. Ward, Supplementary Report, 17.12.1878, Kelly Papers, VPRO; with the 'magenta tie' detail from memo, Sgt Purcell, 26.12.1880, *ibid.*

The hold-up of the bank, spirited coverage in Mrs Scott's typescript, *op. cit.*, and an interview with Robert Scott, *Argus*, 12.12.1878. Mrs Scott's slightly flirtatious 'chaffing' of Ned was described by her to Supt Hare (*Hare*, pp.126–7), and cleverly paraphrased in *Chomley*, p.77. Mrs Scott cites Chomley's paraphrase in her typescript and, like her, I have accepted it. Scott's *Argus* interview and Mrs Scott's typescript cover the jaunt back to Faithfulls Creek. Scott's near-reluctance to help the Prosecution case against Ned is highlighted by a bald, one-page deposition (10.8.1880) in the brief, a sharp contrast to the richly detailed, one-and-a-half-column *Argus* interview.

P.M. Wyatt describes his investigation of the broken telegraph lines and his encounter with Steve Hart, *Commission*, Q.2122–44, pp.122–4; Steve's 'old buffer with the sheet round his hat', *Seymour Express* q. *Herald*, 18.8.1880.

Gang watch Wyatt pick up the wires, Macaulay deposition, *op. cit.*; trick riding display, *Herald*, 13.12.1880; Dudley describes Ned's horsemanship, *Age*, 13.12.1878; Gang off 'in a perfect cloud of dust', *Herald*, 12.12.1878.

Ned had expected £10 000 – there was £20 000 at Alexandra, *Argus*, 13.12.1878; 'no attempt at violence' and 'perfect gentlemen', *Herald*, 12.12.1878; 'thank yous' and 'much obligeds', *W.T.*, 14.12.1878; 'played with the children', and 'would have bought . . . a drink', *Herald*, 12.12.1878; rave reviews, *Age*, 12.12.1878; *Argus*, 12 and 13.12.1878; *Herald*, 12.12.1878; Ned, 'a splendid specimen', *Herald*, 12.12.1878; 'The country belongs to us', *Argus*, 12.12.1878; Euroa guarded by 'solitary constable', *Herald*, 12.12.1878; '16 well-mounted troopers' at Mansfield, *Argus*, 14.12.1878; 'something radically wrong', *Argus*, 14.12.1878; 'outcry about police mismanagement', *O & M*, 12.12.1878; 'an awful disgrace', *Herald*, 12.12.1878.

Wyatt describes his encounter with Sadleir and Nicolson, *Commission*, Q.2162–66, p.125; the 'wild goose chase', Q.473–524, pp.20–2; Q.1996–2001, p.117; 'some strange evidence', Q.28, p.3; 'No pressing reason' for Sadleir and Nicolson to go to Albury, *Sadleir*, p.205; wires and insulators like bunch of flowers, *Commission*, Q.487, p.21.

'Glamour' of the robbery and Ned as model for bush policeman, *Herald*, 19.12.1878; Ned takes the premier's vacant chair, Carrington cartoon, Melbourne *Punch*, 19.12.1878.

13 STATE OF WAR, page 173

Garrison Artillery to N.E., *Argus*, 17.12.1878; police reinforcements, armament, *Commission*, Appendix 7, p.697; reward to £2500, *VGG*, 13.12.1878, p.3315; *PG*, 18.12.1878; '700 or 800 calico posters', *Argus*, 14.12.1878.

Nicolson's futile pursuit, Johnston fast asleep, *Commission*, Q.551, p.23; Nicolson 'heart-broken', Q.585, p.24; almost blind from ingrowing eyelashes (usually ascribed to 'blight'), *Argus*, 17.12.1878; Standish finds him 'quite knocked up', *Commission*, Q.15970, p.581; orders him back to Melbourne, sends for Hare, Q.25–6, p.2; Hare knows only what he has seen in papers, Q.1254, p.62; 'reliable reports', *Hare*, pp.139–40.

Gang meets 'the mock gang', interview, Tom Lloyd Jr, 9.7.1970; 'people ... flush with cash', *Herald*, 18.12.1878; drinks bought with 15 shillings in sixpences, *Herald*, 17.12.1878; Maggie shops with sovereigns, *Argus*, 16.12.1878; Mrs Byrne settles £65 bill, Cookson, *Sydney Sun*, 4.9.1911; Aaron Sherritt pays his debts, Jones, *Friendship*, p.91; Hawker Gloster, previously in debt, now has 'plenty of money', Report, Sen. Const. Gill, *op. cit.*

Standish moves to quash publication of Cameron letter, Telegram to Berry, 18.12.1878, Kelly Papers, VPRO; Sadleir's copy of letter received, *Herald*, 23.12.1878; *Argus* and *D.T.* derisive comments, 18.12.1878; *Herald*'s 'highly sympathetic summary', 18.12.1878, reprinted, *O & M*, 19.12.1878.

'80-odd members of the clan', P.M. Wyatt (who gives a precise '77'), *Commission*, Q.2351, p.134; spread of influence, Wyatt, Q.2352, p.134; Hare, Q.1393, p.76 (after starting to list towns and districts, Hare says, 'There is no part of the colony you can mention free from them'). For spread of 'tacit sympathisers', see Letter, Standish to Acting Chief Secretary, 4.5.1879, Kelly Papers, VPRO; 'unusually well-informed' Yea correspondent, *Herald*, 23.12.1878.

Arrest of Ben Gould, Ward's evidence, *Herald*, 14.12.1878; 'suffering a recovery', *Argus*, 16.12.1878; see also, *Age*, 16.12.1878 ('It was his tongue that got him in trouble'); Ward had arrested Joe and Aaron (Jones, *Friendship*, pp.36–7) and seduced Joe's sister, *Commission*, Q.14669, p.532; Joe 'would swing easily if he could shoot Ward .. .', *Age*, 13.11.1878.

'Broken heads and houses in flames', *Sketcher*, 28.12.1878; Standish collects names of sympathisers for arrest, *Commission*, Q.1266–8, p.63; Sadleir: 'unwise step', Q.2065, p.120; Hare: 'no evidence against those persons ...', Hare, p.194.

First sympathisers arrested, 'getting in the crops', *Herald*, 4.1.1879; 'Steve Hart' furphy, *Herald*, 3.1.1879; subsequent arrests, *Herald*, 5.1.1879 & 6.1.1879; Tom Lloyd Sr warns Gang with telegram, *Commission*, Q.1522, p.90; Jack Ryan arrested by mistake, Q.1269, p.63; Jack McMonigle's arrest, the 'worst blunder', wanted nothing to do with Gang, *Earp*, p.11; 'marched publicly up the Benalla platform', *ibid.*; 'uncomplimentary remarks', *Herald*, 6.1.1879; men of Garrison Corps in Beechworth Gaol, *O & M*, 7.1.1879; first sympathiser hearing in Beechworth Gaol, *O & M*, 14.1.1879.

Scene repeated weekly for next three-and-a-half months — see a valuable table of the sympathiser proceedings, *McQuilton*, p.114, showing the date of each man's arrest, the reason stated, the number of remands and date of release; Ned and the Gang pay for defence of sympathisers, *Commission*, Appendix 5, p.612, report of 31.7.1879; Sadleir calls police tactic 'unlawful', Q.2065, p.120.

Ward's early morning accident, *Herald*, 24.1.1879; Aaron visits him in hospital with 'plan', *Commission*, Q.13847, p.500; Aaron's meeting with Hare, Q.1270–3, p.63, and *Hare*, pp.140–1; parties 'head eastwards to intercept the Gang', *Commission*, Q.1274–6, pp.63–4; Murray 'now a shallow stream', *Sydney Morning Herald* q. *Herald*, 14.2.1879.

14 A LONG WEEKEND, page 181

The major source of this chapter is 'The Kelly Raid on Jerilderie' by 'One Who Was There' (William Elliott), originally serialised in 1913 in Elliott's *Jerilderie Herald* (successor to the *Gazette* of the Kelly period), and published as an appendix comprising more than half of the Rev. H.C. Lundy's *History of Jerilderie*, Jerilderie, 1958 (hereafter, *Lundy*).

Mrs Devine's dream is the first of several details from her reminiscences of the robbery recorded in interviews with her granddaughter, Mrs W.J. Corby, in 1969 and 1979 (hereafter, *Corby interviews*); Devine suffers 'severe rupture', *Herald*, 18.2.1879; exchange with the night caller, *Lundy*, pp.70–1; 'Move and I'll shoot you', Jerilderie Occurrence Book, Mitchell Library q. *McMenomy*, p.124; Ned and the bathwater, *Corby interviews*, *op. cit.*; exchange with Devine, *Lundy*, p.71.

Crossing the Murray and the ride to Jerilderie, Joe Byrne q. *Lundy*, p.67; interlude at Davidsons', *Herald*, 14.2.1879, and *Jerilderie Gazette* q. *Herald*, 18.2.1879; night 'excessively hot', the Rev. J.B. Gribble, 'A Day with Australian Bushrangers', *The Leisure Hour*, London, 1885 (hereafter, *Gribble*), p.193. This previously neglected account provides valuable insights into the later stages of the hold-up. I am grateful to Jim Mills for providing a copy.

'You'll have to do without Mass . . .', *ibid.*; Father Kiely thinks the Kellys are 'more police going to the border . . .', *Lundy*, pp.72–3; Ned 'narrowly' watches delivery of meat, *Gribble*, pp.193–4; weapons emptied, cleaned, re-loaded, *Herald*, 18.2.1879; uniformed Gang members introduced as 'constables about to be stationed here', *Hare*, p.144.

The 'photolithographed plan' and Joe's pun, *Riverina Herald* q. *D.T.*, 17.7.1880; Joe's Sunday night call on Mary the Larrikin, Jones, *Friendship*, note, p.217.

A government copy of the Jerilderie Letter is in Kelly Papers, VPRO. The original is privately owned and I was granted access to it in 1969 via Keith Harrison, to whom I owe an enormous debt. Like the Cameron letter, it was physically written by Joe, based on the original draft of the Cameron letter. See Jones, *Friendship*, pp.98–9, for two facsimile pages of the original in Joe's handwriting; Ned reads Mrs Devine 'several pages' of the letter, she remembers none of it two days later, *Herald*, 18.2.1879.

Ned 'resembled a military man', *Lundy*, p.110; Elliott's remarkable comments about Ned wishing to be 'at the head of a hundred followers . . . to upset the existing government' and perceptions of him as a 'Don Quixote . . . a bit of a fanatic . . . a dreamer . . .', *ibid.*, p.105.

The well-thumbed events of Monday 10 February are drawn largely from *Lundy*. The description of Living is from an interview with his daughter, Sylvia Living, in 1962. In some folklore, Living is so shocked by the hold-up (in one version, when he is surprised in his bath), that he develops a stammer. Sylvia insisted that her father had the slight impediment 'since childhood'. Living gave several press interviews at the time. His deposition, (7.8.1880, Prosecution Brief, *op. cit.*) is concerned largely with Ned's accounts of Stringybark.

The Ballarat man's picture of Ned looking 'horribly ferocious', and Gill's *Gazette* image of his eyes 'frenzy rolling' are both from, *Herald*, 18.2.1879; Elliott's account of the Rankin diversion and his recognition of it as 'bluff . . . from first to last', *Lundy*, p.84; Jefferson runs telegraph wires along a fence, *Argus*, 11.2.1879; Mrs Gill, Living and the letter, *Lundy*, p.86; *Herald*, 12.2.1879; the incident with Minnie the racehorse, *Lundy*, p.87, and interview with Henry Richards, 1929, q. Henry H. Neary, *The Kellys*, Lakemba, n.d., but 1940s, p.38.

The extraordinary exchange between Ned and Constable Richards in the Royal Mail, with its sub-text of respect for human dignity and courage, is recorded by Elliott, *Lundy*, pp.89–90; Elliott's perception of Ned's threat to kill Richards as 'another piece of bluff', *ibid.*, p.89.

For Ned's release of the prisoners, well before the Gang's departure, *Lundy*, p.90; Ned: 'I Like you Richards . . .', Neary, *op. cit.*, p.38.

Most of the last phase of the hold-up is drawn from Gribble's account. Writing six years later, he has refreshed his memory from newspaper clippings but provides a vivid and authoritative narrative which is most valuable in its picture of the Jerilderie townsfolk scoffing at his attempt to organise a posse (*Gribble*, p.195), a picture at odds with Elliott's spirited defence of them (*Lundy*, pp.118–20) against a biting attack on their courage by Supt Sadleir on p.208 of his *Recollections of a Victorian Police Officer*, published the same year that Elliott serialised his account in the local paper.

Mrs Devine 'didn't want her husband chasing Ned Kelly', Corby interviews, *op. cit.*; Ned takes the police horses for return to John Evans, Mrs Evan Evans interviewed by Mary Jean Officer, 27.10.1963; horses described, *New South Wales Police Gazette*, 19.2.1879; Gribble's encounters with Ned and Steve, *Gribble*, pp.195–7; 'Strangers' in Jerilderie, *Argus*, 14.2.1879; *Herald*, 19.2.1879; the Gang at Wunnamurra, *Lundy*, p.102; Rains four hours that night, *Argus*, 12.2.1879; 'The Man Who Shot Thunderbolt' in pursuit, *Herald*, 19.2.1879.

15 'LIKE A WANDERING WIND IN THE NIGHT', page 195

Police 'catalogue' hiding places, *Commission*, Appendix 5, p.691, report of 23.7.1879; Ned getting into Melbourne cab, Q.15514A–5, p.564; Steve at St Kilda, Detective Report, 17.9.1879, Kelly Papers, VPRO; Dan crosses Goulburn, interview, Mrs E. White, 18.1.1948 (my first documented piece of Kelly oral history, valuable for Mrs White's memory of 'a coat rolled up around a rifle slung over his shoulder' — the Kelly swag, cf. *Hare*, p.321); Joe steps over Hare, *ibid.*, pp.191–2; Gang at Emerald, *Herald*, 12.5.1879, Dandenong Police telegram, 11.5.1879, Kelly Papers, VPRO; Gang hides in fallen tree, *Hare*, p.231; Ned rides with police party, Ned Kelly to the Chief Secretary, January 1979, copy in Burke Museum, Beechworth; the battle of Sydney and Melbourne *Punch*, q. Adelaide's *Frearson's Weekly*, 29.3.1879 and 5.4.1879; Inter-colonial correspondence on reward q. White, *op. cit.*, pp.307–8; £8000 reward, *VGG*, 18.2.1879, p.397 and *PG*, 26.2.1879.

Jerilderie money smuggled south? *Lundy*, p.103; Jerilderie police horses in King Valley, *Herald*, 20.9.1897 (found in April, *Commission*, Q.11898, p.422), and interview, Mrs Evan Evans, *op. cit.*; yarns of crossing the Murray and the bank device, Dr W.H. Lang, *Australia*, London, n.d., but 1908, pp.228–9.

No more sympathiser remands without evidence, *O & M*, 21.1.1879; ultimatum from Bowman, Telegram, Bowman to O'Loghlen, 22.1.1879, Kelly Papers, VPRO; 'remands . . . in all cases . . .' endorsement by Standish, 23.1.1879, *ibid.*; Zincke and Bowman to the attack, *O & M*, 28.1.1879; Standish: 'I may have gone a little too far . . .', Letter, Standish to O'Loghlen, 9.1.1879, Kelly Papers, VPRO; Kate Kelly paying solicitors' fees, *Herald*, 27.1.1879; Wyatt: 'would give you fair play if I could', *Herald*, 8.2.1879 & 15.2.1879; Mary Miller letter and editorial, *Herald*, 27.1.1879; *habeas corpus* case in Melbourne, *Herald*, 17.2.1879; Joe Ryan breaks leg 'while larking', *Herald*, 25.2.1879.

Tom Lloyd and Bill Tanner on assaulting police, Interview, Tom Lloyd Jr, 28.12.1979; *Herald*, 12.3.1879 and *O & M*, 13.3.1879.

Ned's offer to Jem Mace, *Herald*, 18.3.1879; the Foley/Hicken fight, *Herald*, 20 and 21.3.1879. The tradition of Ned's and Joe's presence is highly credible, particularly as it emerged and endured when Ned's boxing prowess was not widely known. See J. Alex Allan,

Men and Manners in Australia, Melbourne, 1945, p.143. Allan was a keen student of
Australian boxing history and no admirer of the Kellys, but recorded the story.
'Even-handed' *Herald* summary of Jerilderie Letter, 15.2.1879.
The version of 'The Ballad of Kelly's Gang' quoted is from a manuscript copy in Joe Byrne's
handwriting transcribed in 1951 from the Kinnear papers, *op. cit.* Present whereabouts
of these documents is unknown. 'Hymns of Triumph' sung to 'clapping of hands and
stamping of feet', a demonstration by Albert Blanche, 1948; 'The Kellys Have Made
Another Escape', *Herald*, 18.2.1879; parody of 'Such Lies', Kelly Papers, VPRO;
caricatures etc., *Commission*, Q.15105, p.547; picture of coffin, *Argus*, 2.8.1880; 'Christmas in Kelly Land', *Commission*, Q.14744, p.534; G. Wilson Hall, *The Book of Keli*,
ed. Graham Jones and Judy Bassett, Wangaratta, 1985; sympathiser letter, *Herald*,
4.7.1879; *O & M*, 12.7.1879; 'imperishable idea of outlaw heroes', Jones, *Friendship*,
p.2.
'Penniless woman' (Mrs McAuliffe) buys side saddle etc., Report, Sgt Whelan, 19.10.1879,
Kelly Papers, VPRO; police 'threatening ... ransacking ... yelling ...', sympathiser let-
ter, *op. cit.*; Standish's grumpy report, Telegram, Standish to Attorney-General, 22.4.1879,
Kelly Papers, VPRO; last word by Royal Commission, 2nd Progress Report, Section X.
Description, Stanhope O'Connor, *Herald*, 11.3.1879; the Queensland Aboriginal Mounted
Police as 'cannibals', *Herald*, 4.3.1879; pay, term of service etc., *Herald*, 17.7.1880;
O'Connor called 'Marmie', *Commission*, Q.11994, p.427; calls his men 'troopers',
Q.11988-9, p.426; tracking ability, *Sadleir*, p.214; O'Connor's background, *Herald*,
4.3.1879; officers 'like brothers', *Commission*, Q.1320, p.72; O'Connor's secret mar-
riage, *Kenneally*, p.109; he has 'no authority ...', *Commission*, Q.6153-4, p.587; Hare
not interested in the Aboriginal troopers, *Sadleir*, pp.215-16; Hare's comment, *Hare*,
pp.227-8; Gang moves to hut in snow, *Argus*, 6 & 9.8.1880; *D.T.*, 9.8.1880;
Corporal Sambo dies of 'congestion of the lungs', *Commission*, Q.1079, p.49;
Standish snubs Aboriginal troopers at victory parade, Q.1624-9, p.592; Standish
'rusticating peacefully', *Commission*, 2nd Progress Report, Section X; 'discourteous' to
O'Connor, Letter, O'Connor to Graham Berry, 7.9.1880, *Commission*, Appendix 2, p.684.
Ward tells Hare that Aaron Sherritt would never betray Joe, *Hare*, p.158; Aaron thinks Ned
'superhuman', *Commission*, Q.1282, p.65; The first 'cave party' Jones, *Friendship*,
pp.112-23; Standish renegs on his arrangement with Aaron to spare Joe's life, Letter,
Standish to O'Loghlen, 9.1.1879, Kelly Papers, VPRO; Aaron's share of Jerilderie money
not delivered, Jones, *Friendship*, p.129; the 'complex squabble' involving Aaron, Mrs
Byrne and Maggie Skilling, *Herald*, 26.7.1879 & *O & M*, 29.7.1879.
Photo of 20 June search party, see photograph pages; Standish poses, *McMenomy*, p.111; his
one night on watch, *Commission*, Q.47, p.3; loses 'a stone weight', Q.16163, p.588;
waits anxiously for Hare's return, *Sadleir*, p.268; Standish on sympathiser problem,
Letter, Standish to Acting Chief Secretary, 4.5.1879, Kelly Papers, VPRO; 'remedial
measure', *ibid.*; sympathisers, 'labouring class ... described as farmers', *Argus*, 4.1.1879;
'large number of names' on black list, *Commission*, Q.3542, p.176; Bill Tanner's land
application refused, Q.3553, p.177; Whelan's reasons for names on black list, Memo,
Whelan to Sadleir, 8.10.1879, Kelly Papers, VPRO; Montfort on Jack Quinn,
Commission, Q.3529-30, p.176.
Hare breaks down, *Hare*, p.225; Standish winds down force, ends *carte blanche* expenditure,
Commission, Appendices 7 & 8, pp.697-8; Q.708-29, p.30; Nicolson's bitter sum-
mary of the Hare regime, Q.16901, p.633; his 'canny economy campaign', Q.713 &
Q.729, p.30.

16 A REPUBLIC, page 210

Civilian volunteers 'of the right sort' another feature of Nicolson's economy campaign, *Commission*, Q.713, p.30; 'impressive' precautions by Beechworth banks, Q.13854, p.501; discouraging reports via Jack Sherritt, Appendix 5, p.692 & Q.13855, p.501. Maggie and Tom buy ammunition: Tom's account, *Kenneally*, pp.116–17, cf. *Commission*, Q.8458–62, p.310, Detective Report, 16.6.1879, Kelly Papers, VPRO; Ned at the Sherritts, *Jones Friendship*, p.130, notes, p.200 and *Commission*, Q.13166–8, p.475.

'Overnight dashes of 60 and 70 miles', Q.47, p.4; 'iron plates on breast and head', R.D. Blackmore, *Lorna Doone*, OUP, Melbourne, 1949, p.10; Joe opposes idea of armour, *Commission*, Q.17786, p.674; materials for armour tested, *D.T.*, 6.8.1880; 'idle plough was to become a weapon', Jones, *Friendship*, p.154; James Wallace buying mouldboards, Report, Ward and Considine to Secretan, 22.12.1881, Kelly Papers, VPRO.

Garibaldi as guerilla and political symbol, *McQuilton*, p.169; Thomas Carrington's clubland background, de Serville, *op. cit.*, pp.361, 380; Carrington's cartoon, 'Our Rulers', see p.214.

It is easy to imagine that the reiterated cartoon images of Ned as a political figure — occupying the premier's chair, joining in a waltz of power with the *Age* and Berry — helped encourage his vision of himself as a leader capable of challenging England's right to impose her rule on the people of the north-east; and equally easy to imagine the guffaws of clubland becoming a trifle hollow as the Kelly spectre took shape and Carrington's 'joke' foreshadowed a genuine threat to the mock-English order of things in 1880 Melbourne.

My research on the 'shadowy republic' is sketched in Jones, *Friendship,* notes, pp.223–4. Key evidence came from Tom Lloyd Jr, whose father had told him of the 'exercise books containing records of meetings' in which Ned, Joe and key sympathisers developed their treasonable plans (interviews, 4.1.1964, 10.5.1964 and 29.7.1969).

Joe's alternate plan, *Commission*, Appendix 5, pp.693–4; Jack informs police, Q.15624–5, p.559; second 'cave party' set up, Q.13541, p.489; Joe and Aaron at Chinese store, Q.14973, p.542; Joe visits home while police are watching, Q.15028, p.544 (see Jones, *Friendship*, notes, pp.222–3); the clearest statement of Ward's plan to set up Aaron as bait, from Joe Byrne's mother, Q.13490, p.487; see also Nicolson's endorsement on Ward's claim to Kelly Reward Board, 20.8.1880, Kelly Papers, VPRO; and, Letter, Enoch Downes to Sadleir, 14.9.1880, *ibid.*; Nicolson distrusts Aaron 'in everything', *Commission*, Q.1480, p.82; Nicolson: Aaron 'did nothing' for police, Q.15115, p.548; Nicolson defies orders to sack Aaron, pays him 'out of his own pocket', Q.919–20, p.42.

For the strange career of 'Captain Moonlite' and his pathetic 'gang', Stephan Williams, *The Wantabadgery Bushrangers*, (modestly sub-titled, 'A Partial Study'), Popinjay Publications, 1991; Moonlite's homosexuality, Gary Wotherspoon, 'Moonlight and . . . Romance? the death-cell letters of Captain Moonlight (*sic*) and some of their implications', *Journal of the Royal Australian Historical Society*, Vol. 78, pts 3 and 4, pp.76–89 (which includes some particularly wobbly suggestions that Joe Byrne and Aaron Sherritt were homosexuals). I am grateful to Brian McDonald for both these references. Victoria Police watch the 'possum hunting picnic', Moonlite's offer to Ned, *Sadleir*, p.191; Jim Kelly's release, *New South Wales Police Gazette*, 21.1.1880; police worries of him joining the Gang, *Commission*, Q.12167, p.435; photos to stations along the Murray, 'Yarrawonga' print formerly in, Police File, 0.6650; Jim meets the Gang, the Royal Commission quotes a 'general impression' among police that he had joined them, Q.12167, p.435; Jim in discussions re. 'breaking up the Gang', and 'Ned committed to the rebellion', Interview, Tom Lloyd Jr, 26.10.1979; description of Darlinghurst Gaol gallows (now part of the Fashion School, East Sydney Tech.), *Town and Country Journal*, 24.1.1880, q. Williams, *op. cit.*, pp.209–10.

Saddle stolen from Aaron's wife, memo, Sadleir to Acting Chief Commissioner, 16.12.1880, Kelly Papers, VPRO; Nicolson incriminates Jack Sherritt, *Commission*, Q.16896, p.631; case contrived by Ward, Q.12184–7, p.435; allegations of Aaron's 'ugly and unbelievable' threat to Joe, see Jones, *Friendship*, pp.161–2, and notes, p.225; Aaron 'sentenced to death', *Kenneally*, p.124; Ned 'clings to an idea' that Aaron had been tortured by police, *Commission*, Q.12214, p.437; theft of mouldboards 'silly practical joke', *Ashmead*, p.21; first theft, *Commission*, Appendix 5, p.694 (included under report of 21 February, though the theft is dated to 22 March); investigation of the mouldboard thefts described, Q.750–54, p.33, including Nicolson's information (Q.751), 'the Kelly gang were the offenders'.

The making of Ned's prototype armour, Interviews, Tom Lloyd Jr, 4.1.1964, 26.10.1979. *Kenneally*, pp.113–16, draws on Tom Lloyd's account, but includes some inaccurate details — *all* mouldboards stolen, all four suits made by the same men on the same occasion, bulk of work carried out in the Kelly smithy and the unsupportable claim that only one helmet was made. The other three helmets were documented and two were photographed the day of Ned Kelly's capture (see photograph pages); Testing of the armour described, *Commission*, Q.755, p.33; inspiration from Scott novel, Prof. E.E. Morris in, *Cassell's Picturesque Australia*, 1889, Child and Henry facsimile, *Australia's First Century*, 1980, p.857, cf. *Herald*, 2.7.1880, which identifies the novel as *Ivanhoe*; makers of the armour: for Culph and Delaney, Letter, Montfort to Secretan, 8.7.1880 (also implicating Jim Brien of Wanganderry who 'could build a steamer almost without being seen'); for Straughair, Letter, Meade to Secretan, 31.5.1881, both Kelly Papers, VPRO; for Delaney, Culph, and Knight, Interviews, Jack Plant (February, 1964) and Bill Knowles (October, 1970); see *Argus*, 26.11.1880 in which John Delaney, a witness at Ann Jones's trial for harbouring the Gang, virtually admits that his father Patrick was involved in making the armour; 'carefully tailored misinformation', *Ashmead*, pp.21–2; 'stain of sap', *ibid.*, p.22; 'The armour business ... a sort of eternal guessing competition', Cookson, Sydney *Sun*, 12.9.1911.

Laurence O'Brien's death, *W.D.*, 7.10.1874; Daniel Kennedy as 'Denny', the DSA, see L.J. Pryor, 'The Diseased Stock Agent', *Victorian Historical Journal*, December 1990, pp.243–69, sadly, Pryor's last, meticulously researched contribution to knowledge of our past; petition against Kennedy, *W.D.*, 4.4.1878; dispute with McAuliffes, Pryor, *op. cit.*, p.250; DSA report to Nicolson, *Commission*, Q.2818, p.150; Sadleir: 'an impossibility', Q.2818, p.150; Nicolson told in May he is to be replaced, 'second attempt' to deprive him of credit, Q.16903, p.634; 'urgent representations', 2nd Progress Report, Section XIII.

For Aaron Sherritt with the fourteen police and Aboriginal troopers as 'Nicolson's clumsy incrimination of an informer', Jones, *Friendship*, pp.164–66; incident dooms Aaron, *Commission*, Q.15115, p.548; Q.7308, p.282; Q.11110, p.397, etc.

Hare takes over, seen by Ramsay as 'change of bowlers', Q.933, p.47; police stationed in Aaron's hut, Q.13860–1, pp.503–4; *Hare*, pp.233–4; Sadleir opposes plan, *Sadleir*, p.221; police in 'sort of uniform', Q.13810, p.499; Q.3637, p.180; no sentry to be posted, Q.12207, p.437; Q.14158, p.516; Q.16909, p.638, etc.; 'idea from the *Benalla Standard*', 31.10.1879; Hare, 'anxious they should do something, *Hare*, p.233; Hare: police to remain in Aaron's hut until discovered, Q.16579, p.606; enough 'to seal his doom', 2nd Progress Report, Section XIV; 'planted rumour' of blowing up Beechworth train, *Hare*, p.194.

Leonard Radic, the 'highly reputable witness' who described Ned's Declaration of the Republic of North-Eastern Victoria, was formerly a senior journalist on the Melbourne *Age*. In the winter of 1962 he saw a printed copy of the Declaration displayed at London's Public Records Office (interview, 1969). An intensive search in 1969, assisted by Barry Jones and Tony Richardson, failed to locate the document and the PRO denied its existence. Radic now believes that the item could have been loaned by a private collector and that either the PRO was protecting his anonymity or his identity was known only to the organiser of the display — who may have left in the intervening seven years (interview, 1992). For the handwritten copy, interview, Tom Lloyd Jr, 29.7.1969.

Arming for Glenrowan, see the author's 'Guns of the Kelly Story', *The Last Outlaw*, ed. Les Carlyon, Melbourne, 1980, pp.66–7; and, 'Six Kelly Guns at Glenrowan', *Caps and Flints* (magazine of the Antique and Historical Arms Collectors Guild of Victoria), Vol. 7, September 1980, p.139.

The Kelly strategy for Glenrowan emerges in its execution and in subsequent developments. For the Bank of New South Wales as a target, Interview, Ned, *Argus*, 2.7.1880; alleged alternative plan, Letter, E. Kelly to Governor of Victoria, 5.11.1880, Capital Case File, VPRO; 'another statement', 10.11.1880, *ibid*.

Tom Lloyd's version, *Kenneally*, p.125; Gang forbids use of 'stop' signal, interview with Stanistreet, Glenrowan stationmaster, *Argus*, 29.6.1880; goings-on at Glenrowan Inn, *Commission*, Q.765–7, p.33; Q771, p.34; Tom Lloyd in 'strange diversionary tactic,' *Commission*, Q.777, p.34, Appendix 5, p.695, report for 15.5.1880; 'horses being stolen', *Hare*, p.235; theft from the Ryans of Dookie, *PG*, 30.6.1880, p.171; 'Gang ... would astonish ... the whole world', *Hare*, p.235; 'do something good', Q.14112, p.514; 'this is a particular time', Q.5124, pp.213–14; watch parties on Kelly and Hart homes, *Hare*, pp.334–5; Hare receives DSA report, dismisses him, *Sadleir*, pp.221–2.

Hare: Kellys ride at full moon, Saturday, Sunday and Monday, 'those were their lucky days', *Commission*, Q.1615, p.99.

17 TO GLENROWAN, page 228

'At least ten horses', made up of the two Ryan horses — one found in McDonnell's stables, *Age*, 29.6.1880, the other 'about six miles from Benalla' the next day, *Age*, 1.7.1880 and *Commission*, Q.9767, p.353; a pack horse stolen from 'Mr Fitzsimmons of Greta', *Argus*, 30.6.1880; a horse which later died from a gunshot wound, stolen from Walter Griffiths, Griffiths to Sadleir, 27.7.1880, Kelly Papers, VPRO; three horses subsequently sold by the police, Whelan to Sadleir, 6.9.1880, *ibid*.; at least two actual Kelly horses among 'four of the outlaws' horses' shot and killed by police, Report, Steele to Sadleir, 6.7.1880, *ibid*.; and 'Ned Kelly's grey mare', see Chapter 20.

Lonigan's and Scanlon's saddles on packhorses, Montfort to Chief Commissioner, 21.7.1880, *ibid*.; 'the bomb', Report, Const. McHugh to Sadleir, 5.7.1880, *ibid*.; Ned: 'four stone weight of powder', *O & M*, 29.6.1880; armour and rockets in buggy, interview, Tom Lloyd Jr, 10.5.1964 and 28.12.1979; Gang dressed identically, long coats, 'flat' hats, Letter, Tom Cameron to his brother, 8.7.1880 (my thanks to Noel O'Shea for this source); short haircuts, drawings of Ned after capture and photos and drawings of Joe after his death; Ned's and Joe's clothing, *ibid.*, and press descriptions; Ned wears trooper's boots, *Herald*, 17.7.1880; 'sash of honour', *Kenneally*, p.151 (it is now displayed in the Benalla and District Historical Society's Museum).

Skull cap, see photograph pages; cap described in caption notes by Const. Robert Graham; Joe's rings and contents of his pockets, *D.T.*, 29.6.1880; Ned with 'young woman', *Age*, 1.7.1880; Harry Power's 'courtly' attitude to women, *Argus*, 10.3.1877; Ned's love for Kate Lloyd, interview, Tom Lloyd Jr, 10.5.1864; Kate was the unnamed 'fiancée' described by various reporters during Ned's Petty Sessions trial at Beechworth, *D.T.*, 10.8.1880; *Herald*, 11.8.1880 etc.; Kate's daughter, Mrs Winifred McLean, spoke of the cousins' 'devotion' to each other, but denied a romance, interviews, 1980 and 1991. Perhaps she was protecting this intensely personal facet of her mother's life; or perhaps Kate had never revealed to her the depth of the relationship.

'Other girls', Paddy and Charlie Griffiths, interview, 1963; Kate's 'classical beauty', see photograph pages; Kate's 'special costume', *Australian Pictorial Weekly*, 10.7.1880, p.33; Aaron: 'nothing', will turn Catholic, *Commission*, Q.13286–90, p.479; away for three hours, Q.3804–5, p.184; cave on far side of hill, *Argus*, 2.8.1880; no horses, *Commission*, Q.12162, p.435.

For the murder of Aaron, see Jones, *Friendship*, pp.175–7, notes, pp.227–8. The dialogue between Joe and Wick at the door is from an excellent report of Aaron's inquest in *Age*, 1.7.1880, including the detail of Aaron's head hitting the box-table and laughter at the inquest over police timidity; 'Councils-of-war', deposition, Henry Armstrong, 30.6.1880, inquest on Aaron Sherritt, VPRS 24, Unit 285/382, VPRO.

Ned and Steve wear body armour under oilskins, *Commission*, Q.7736–40, p.280; leave horses on hillside behind McDonnell's, Q.7770, p.280; Glenrowan, 'an insignificant collection of buildings', *Herald*, 28.6.1880; Ned and Steve wait for last train to pass, Letter, E. Kelly to Governor, 5.10.1880, Capital Case File, VPRO; try to break line, *Argus*, 29.6.1880; make noise bailing up labourers, Ned goes to inn, Detective Report, Eason to Sadleir, 26.7.1880, Kelly Papers, VPRO.

Ann Jones's background and the events at her Glenrowan Inn are documented in the MS, 'Minutes of Evidence of the Board appointed to inquire into claim made by Mrs Jones for compensation for destruction of the Glenrowan Hotel', 18.11.1881, with attached documents including an inventory of contents, insurance details and letters from Mrs Jones, all, VPRO (hereafter Jones Inquiry).

'Ten pounds in the hundred', Jones Inquiry, p.171; £6 block of land, *ibid.*, p.145; 'a pitiable shelter', *N.E. Ensign*, q. *D.T.*, 14.7.1880; 'very nicely furnished', Jones Inquiry, p.129; Ann Jones bed-ridden with neuralgia, *ibid.*, p.153; exchange with Ned, Letter, *Argus*, 5.12.1881; Kelly girls against her, Jones Inquiry, p.150; 'a traps' woman', *ibid.*, p.153; Ned believes Ward got her the licence, Letter, *Argus*, *op. cit.*; Ann Jones a friend of Sgt Kennedy, *Herald*, 25.11.1880; has photograph of him, Jones Inquiry, p.200; 'staggering with sickness', Jones Inquiry, p.154; Stanistreet bailed up, *Argus*, 29.6.1880; 'a lot' of police shot, *Commission*, Q.7607, p.276; Steve with Jane Jones, Jones Inquiry, pp.176–7; rails with sleepers still attached, *Argus*, 30.6.1880; Ned hesitates, accepts Mrs Jones's invitation to inn, Jones Inquiry, p.234. (In quoting Ned, witness Dennis Sullivan carefully corrected the transcript's 'you' to 'ye', a fascinating glimpse of the Irishness of Ned's speech.) Jack Jones left concertina on verandah, Jane plays it Sunday morning, Jones Inquiry, pp.157, 178; layout of Inn, *Commission*, Q.10554–69, p.379; description of bar, Jones Inquiry, pp.127, 131; 'best room' as armoury, *ibid.*, p.158; 'couple of lads' stable Kelly horses, *Commission*, Q.7770, p.280; 'totally different stories' from McDonnell's, *Herald*, 29.6.1880 (inc. 'Mrs Mac' in bed) and *W.T.*, 3.7.1880; James Kershaw as sympathiser, Const. Bracken to Sadleir, 6.7.1880 and Const. Barry to Sadleir, 4.7.1880 (with endorsements by Sgt Whelan), both Kelly Papers, VPRO; Glenrowan police party withdrawn, ill, previous day, *Commission*, Q.1477, p.81; Postmaster Reynolds 'would not tell' on Ned, Letter, 5.12.1881, Jones Inquiry (not to be confused with Ann Jones's letter to the *Argus* of the same date the next year); Reynolds 'as right as if ... locked up', *O & M*, 27.11.1880; prisoners laugh at hold-ups, Letter, 5.12.1882, Jones Inquiry.

Curnow described his experiences in a long letter to Standish which was released to the press and formed the basis of his reward application and his Royal Commission evidence, *Commission*, Q.17597, pp.663–6. I am indebted to L.J. Pryor's incisive, *Thomas Curnow*, privately published, Melbourne, 1986, part of an epic study of some 100 Kelly Country school teachers which was, sadly, uncompleted at the time of Len's death.

John Delaney had tried to join police two years before, *O & M*, 27.11.1880; Curnow. 'a ruse on Kelly's part', *Commission*, Q.17632–35, p.667; Joe: 'send the train and its occupants to hell', Q.17597, p.664; Curnow forming a plan, *ibid.*; 'what a splendid danger signal', *ibid.*

18 'IN THE VERY JAWS OF DEATH', page 240

Sixty-two prisoners, *Commission*, Q.7606, p.276; Jane Jones helps guard them, Q.10542, p.378 (see Jane's admission, Jones Inquiry, pp.177–8); she would warn Ned of any escape attempt, letter, Tom Cameron to his brother, 8.7.1880, *op. cit.*, Jane 'making free ... kissing them', *ibid.*; bail up a circus, *Commission*, Q.7769, p.280; kill a bullock, Jones Inquiry, p.135; 'fat dogs', *O & M*, 27.11.1880; 'the very jaws of death', *O & M*, 24.7.1880; 'six little demons', *Age*, 30.6.1880; 21 prisoners released, *Commission*, Q.7764, p.280; Curnow: 'with him heart and soul', Q.17597, p.665; Bracken describes his capture, *Argus*, 29.6.1880; 'someone from Benalla ... to try my pluck', *D.T.*, 29.6.1880; Ned shakes hands with son, *Argus*, 30.6.1880; 'Don't dream too loud', Argus, 29.6.1880; train danger signal 'like a cock crowing', *Commission*, Q.7761, p.280.

Hare learns of Aaron's death, 2.30 p.m., Q.1500–1, p.84; Standish advised 4.30 p.m., Q.77, p.6; Hare has 'two expert trackers', Q.1499–1500, p.84; train ready from mid-afternoon, Benalla Stationmaster, Clement Stephens, Claim to Kelly Reward Board, 10.12.1880, Kelly Papers, VPRO; train of special type for Beechworth trip, *W.T.*, 24.7.1880; Standish plans to send O'Connor and his men by 'an early train on Monday morning', *Hare*, p.243 (recording this, even Hare prefaced the detail with, 'Strange to say ...'); special Sunday night train 'on the initiative of Chief Secretary Ramsay', *ibid.* & *O & M*, 10.7.1880 (Ramsay 'would not allow it to remain until Monday'). 'Crack like a bullet', *Argus*, 29.6.1880; 'rattling pace', *D.T.*, 29.6.1880; carriage oscillates, *Argus*, 5.7.1880; at Benalla, 'new round of dithering', *Commission*, Q.1501, pp.84–5; Train at 40 m.p.h., 60 m.p.h. past Glenrowan, *Argus*, 1.7.1880; guard sees red light, changes hats (!), Archibald McPhee, undated statement, Claim to Kelly Reward Board, Kelly Papers, VPRO; two locomotives coupled together, *W.T.*, 24.7.1880; Hare positions his men on train, *Hare*, p.248.

'The Party', interview, Louise Earp, 1961; Jack Jones sings, Jones Inquiry, pp.162–3; Bracken's background, *Herald*, 1.7.1880; 'a decent fellow', *W.T.*, 3.7.1880; Ned chats with Bracken, joins in 'a set of quadrilles', *Argus*, 30.6.1880; Ned's 'vision for the northeast', Const. Bracken, claim to Kelly Reward Board, 5.1.1881, Kelly Papers, VPRO,

q. *McQuilton*, p.165; Ned 'a darling man', Ann Jones, Letter, 5.12.1882, Jones Inquiry; Ann Jones's 'red stuff dress', *O & M*, 27.11.1880; Ann Jones: treated 'like a bloody blackfellow', Jones Inquiry, p.249; 'revenge is sweet', her 'intimacy' with Ned and Joe, and, pleased if Gang 'stopped for a week', *O & M, op. cit.*

Key 'carelessly near the chimney', Bracken places it in cuff, *Argus*, 29 & 30.6.1880; 'feast of blood', *O & M*, 15.7.1880; Ned's warning to Reardon, Jones Inquiry, p.216; 'Sullivan' exchange, *ibid.*, pp.216–17; 'an honest man?', *Argus*, 30.6.1880; Kershaw helps with armour, Report, Const. Barry to Sadleir, 4.7.1880, Kelly Papers, VPRO; cf. *Commission*, Q.11312, p.402; Ned sees train halted in cutting, *D.T.*, 29.6.1880; arrival at Glenrowan, Rawlins, Hare and Mrs Stanistreet, *Kelly Reward Board, Report of the Board ... together with the Minutes of Evidence, Melbourne, 1880–81* (hereafter, *Reward Board*), Q.49, p.4; Bracken: 'Lie down ...', *Commission*, Q.10551, p.379; Joe's 'Bracken' pun, *Argus*, 30.6.1880; 'horses half-rearing and plunging ...', Q.1116, p.54; 'Over there . . .', *Argus*, 5.7.1880 (the first of several quotes from an unnamed *Australasian* writer ('One Who Went in the Special Train'), whose account was reprinted in the *Argus* and *Sketcher*. He is easily identified as Thomas Carrington); Ned recognises Hare, fires first shot, *Commission*, Q.16317, p.595; Hare weaving through revolving gate, Q.1503, p.86; 'Good gracious! I am hit ...', Q.7675, p.284; Ned's two wounds, *Reward Board*, Q.55–6, p.5 (evidence of Rawlins who testifies that Ned was first wounded by Gascoigne); 'Ned Kelly's voice!', *Commission*, Q.1506, p.87; Ned's wounds described, *Age*, 29.6.1880; 60 police bullets in first minute, *Age*, 5.7.1880, a particularly valuable resumé of the action; Jack Jones shot, 'hands in my ears ...', *Age*, 29.6.1880; Jack taken to Reardons' by McHugh, *Commission*, Q.7701–2, p.279; Jack dies 'soon after midnight', *O & M*, 1.7.1880 (see also *Argus*, 1.7.1880); wounding of George Metcalf, Detective Report, quoting Metcalf, Eason to Sadleir, 26.7.1880, Kelly Papers, VPRO, (see Chapter 20 for another version alleging he was shot by Ned). I am grateful to Ron White, a Metcalf descendant, for prompting my investigation of the case.

Wounding of Martin Cherry, see *O & M*, 14.8.1880, for an anonymous eye-witness account and a matching version in, *Ashmead*, p.26, where the witness is identified as Larkins. Quotes from *Ashmead*, except 'bullets ... like hail', (see Chapter 20 for a subsequently discredited police version blaming Ned for Cherry's fatal wound, which prompted Larkins to reveal the true story — with a claim that police had pressured him not to tell it).

Jack Lloyd fires the rockets, interview, Tom Lloyd Jr, 10.5.1964; rockets seen by Arthur and Gascoigne, Q.11190, p.399. (Soon after, Arthur sees a man leave the inn, conjectures that it was Ned.) Gang fires 40 or 50 shots, police 80 or 100, Q.7654–58, p.290; Ann Jones's demented wandering, Q.7378, p.284; Reardon family turned back, Q.10584–605, pp.379–80; 'remarkable exchange between Ned and Joe', affidavit, Const. Phillips, 16.9.1881, Q.17786, p.674; Joe 'perfectly reckless', *Age*, 29.6.1880; exchange of shots with Gascoigne, Report, Const. Gascoigne, undated, Kelly Papers, VPRO; and *Commission*, Q.9761–6, pp.352–3.

Ned's movements over the next few minutes are vital to an understanding of several subsequent incidents. Gascoigne says Ned's rifle was found (by Consts Kelly and Arthur) 'in the direction he went', (Q.9766, p.353). With the rifle was Ned's cap, 'full of blood ... and there was a pool of blood there' (Q.8163–4, p.303). Rawlins reported, 'His mare was there; he told me she was in those bushes ... he went to look for the mare and fell down' (*Reward Board*, Q.59–61, p.5).

Next morning, during the Last Stand, Ned rested 'between three trees growing thus' said Const. Phillips, sketching trees spreading in a fan shape (Report, Phillips to Sadleir, 2.7.1880, Kelly Papers, VPRO). Phillips's sketch matches a Thomas Carrington drawing of 'The Kelly Tree' (*Sketcher*, 24.9.1881). Arthur identifies this site as 'where we found the rifle and the cap' and describes Ned leaving it and turning downhill towards the station (*Commission*, Q.11163, p.398). Phillips saw Ned 'walk about 25 yards and fall' (Report, *op. cit.*). See photograph pages for police at the tree where Ned fell. In the background, about 25 yards away, is a small clump of trees matching Carrington's 'Kelly Tree'; Tom Lloyd's attempt to recover Ned's rifle, interview, Tom Lloyd Jr, 4.1.1964; Ned q. Sgt Steele, Report, 10.8.1880, Kelly Papers, VPRO; see Arthur interview, *Age*, 2.7.1880, for his belief that someone was nearby when he and Sen. Const. Kelly found the cap and rifle.

Ned meets the sympathisers, interview, Tom Lloyd Jr, 4.1.1964 (with contributions from Joe Griffiths and Les Tanner, 10.5.1964); see also *Ned Kelly, Man and Myth*, ed. Colin Cave, Melbourne, 1968, pp.172–3; and Jones, *Friendship*, notes, p.229, inc. Ned's 'I had plenty of mates in the neighbourhood ready to join us', *Commission*, Q.16137, p.595.

Hare, 'drunk as possible', *Commission*, Q.1514, p.89; 'catch me please', Q.1509, p.87; O'Connor believes prisoners in kitchen, Q.1150, p.55; Bracken sends telegrams, joins Steele's Wangaratta party, *Argus*, 29.6.1880 (he was one of the few principal players at Glenrowan not examined by the Royal Commission); Sadleir takes a rope, Q.16700, p.614; official arrival times of Wangaratta and Benalla parties challenged, Q.11423–31, pp.404–5 (my thanks to Marian Matta for prompting me to grapple with the shaky 'official' arrival times compiled by Sadleir, *Commission*, p.154.) Wangaratta party pass close by Ned, Const. Dwyer in, 'How We Captured Ned Kelly', in W.H. Fitchett, *Ned Kelly and his Gang*, Melbourne, n.d., but 1940s (hereafter *Fitchett*), p.59, confirmed by Steele in 'The Story of My Fight With Ned Kelly', *ibid.*, p.55; Margaret Reardon's escape, *Commission*, Q.10617–32, p.380; Const. Arthur confirms her account, admits threatening to shoot Steele, Q.11125–7, p.397; On 7.8.1964 I interviewed Mrs Reardon's 'baby', 84-year-old Mrs Bridget Griffiths, who was told by her mother that 'a bullet' had grazed the middle of her forehead, leaving 'a powder mark'. Interestingly, the 'shawl' she had been wrapped in was of the Irish type, 'a rug with a big, green check pattern'; Michael Reardon's wound, *Commission*, Q.10668, p.381, and, *Herald*, 1.7.1880.

Joe calls McAuliffes to help, Detective Report, Eason to Sadleir, 26.7.1880, Kelly Papers, VPRO; Ned's return to the inn, interview, Tom Lloyd Jr, 4.1.1964; Ned describes seeing Joe shot, *Commission*, Q.9483, p.3431; W.T., 3.7.1880. ('When I saw my best friend dead …'); O & M, 29.6.1880; ('His best and truest comrade was no more and the other two were cowards; and therefore he would leave them to their fate'). See assessment of evidence, Jones, *Friendship*, notes, p.229; Joe's last words, *Commission*, Q.1141–2, p.55; Ned: 'I'll challenge the lot', W.T., 3.7.1880.

Gascoigne sees Ned heading from inn towards 'barn', Report, undated, Kelly Papers, VPRO; *Commission*, Q.9769, p.353; 'his mare' (identified by Gascoigne as the Ryan bay recaptured the next day) escapes at 6 a.m., Q.9767, p.353.

Ned's three revolvers: see the author's 'Six Kelly Guns at Glenrowan', *Caps and Flints, op. cit.*, The Pocket Colt was picked up the following day by Constable Dwyer and authenticated by Steele in a letter of October 189(?) [rest of date indecipherable] shown to the author in 1962 by Miss Eileen Wandel, then custodian of the Public Library's Historical Collection. This weapon was stolen in 1976 while on display in the United States. Lonigan's Webley was found by Const. McHugh, bloodstained, bullet-damaged and loaded with 'cut-down' ammunition 'in the bush about a hundred yards from Jones' Hotel' (Report, Const. McHugh to Sadleir, 5.7.1880, Kelly Papers, VPRO; and, O & M, 24.7.1880). McHugh noted that the weapon was 'branded with kit No. 730'. There is a marginal note, 'Const. Lonigan's No.'. The revolver disappeared. Devine's Navy Colt was identified by its NSWG (New South Wales Gaols) marking. It was held by the Public Library for many years (and its barrel plugged by the police!) before being returned to descendants of railway guard Jesse Dowsett.

Several eye witnesses of the Last Stand described Ned wearing a 'cloak' (cf. Steele's description (Commission, Q.9034, p.327), 'wrapped in a . . . cloak . . . threw his cloak back . . .'). It was subsequently identified as 'a long, grey mackintosh' (*Argus*, 2.7.1880), and Carrington, in his famous, *Sketcher* engraving, 'Ned Kelly At Bay (3.7.1880), showed Ned wearing it as a coat. However, given the bulk of the body armour and the large shoulder pieces, it is doubtful that Ned ever put his arms through the sleeves, certainly not after Tom Lloyd had given his arm wounds some rudimentary attention. See *Sketcher*, 17.7.1880, for Ned with the coat draped over his shoulders during the dance in the inn.

19 THE LAST STAND, page 258

Ned Kelly's Last Stand is one of the most densely documented incidents in Australian history. Many of the principals made official reports, gave press interviews; submitted claims to the Reward Board; two gave evidence at Ned's police court hearing and Supreme Court trial; most appeared before the Royal Commission; a few wrote articles or books. All these sources have been used in researching this account, with due regard for the fact that the whole affair became highly politicised in the clamour for recognition, reward, face-saving and professional survival, further complicated by some bitter feuds, such as that between Const. Arthur and Sgt Steele.

The 'lattice-work' image of the inn is from Sadleir, *Commission*, Q.7485, p.286; Const. Arthur's account, Q.11160–11188, pp.398–9; and, Q.11261–283, pp.400–1; *Argus*, 2.7.1880 ('Constable McArthur's (*sic*) Narrative') and, *Age*, 2.7.1880; 'a tremendous size . . .', *Commission*, Q.11184, p.399; 'ghost of Hamlet's father', *Argus*, 5.7.1880; 'some unknown demon', *D.T.*, 29.6.1880; 'madman in the horrors', *Commission*, Q.11183, p.399; 'seemed to be crippled', Q.11162, p.398; 'the devil', Q.9034, pp.328–8; 'bunyip'?, *Herald*, 5.7.1880; 'good shots, boys', Report, Const. Phillips to Sadleir, 2.7.1880, Kelly Papers, VPRO; 'Ned only laughed', *ibid.*; Steele: 'It's a blackfellow', Q.11163, p.398; 'like blows from a man's fist', *Argus*, 29.6.1880; eyes hurt and blackened, by Arthur's shots, *Argus*, 2.7.1880; facial lacerations visible in press drawings of Ned after capture correspond to the indicated features of his helmet; 'in a trance', *D.T.*, 29.6.1880; 'seemed to be drunk', Q.10043, p.362; 'more dead than alive', Q.11188, p.399; Music approaches Ned, account by Dr Nicholson, *Argus*, 2.7.1880; 'loyal', cf. Ned's comment, 'his own grey mare would gallop up to him when he called her', *D.T.*, 30.6.1880; 'allowed it to pass', *Argus*, 2.7.1880; shooting of Music, Report, Const. Phillips to Sadleir, *op. cit.*, Steele to Sadleir, 6.7.1880, Const. Moore, Claim to Kelly Reward Board, 19.12.1880, all Kelly Papers, VPRO; unable to re-load etc., see Ned's comment after capture, 'I had plenty of ammunition, but it was no good to me.'

Bullet strikes Webley, *O & M*, 24.7.1880. The revolver's finder, Const. McHugh, theorised that the damage had occurred while the weapon was holstered but this is unlikely, given McHugh's evidence that when found it was 'covered with blood and had no case' (Report to Sadleir, 5.7.1880, *op. cit.*). A bullet hole in the matching holster (subsequently recovered from Jack Sherritt who was with Beechworth police) prompted McHugh's theory.

Steele runs from cover, clutches eye, *Commission*, Q.9034, pp.327–8; bullet hits Ned's hand, blood on tree, Report, Const. Healy, 16.12.1880, Kelly Papers, VPRO; wound on Ned's little finger matches damage on revolver grip, interview, Mrs Ray Brown, descendant of Jesse Dowsett, 1961; 'like a cracked bell', Jesse Dowsett, Report, to Traffic Manager, 2.7.1880, *La Trobe Library Journal*, April 1973, pp.60–1; Steele's 'few minutes of unclear vision', *Commission*, Q.9034, p.328; exchange of shots (and banter!) with Dowsett from Dowsett's Report to Traffic Manager, *op. cit.*, interviews, with *Age* and *Argus* (both 1.7.1880) and *Commission*, Q.10919, p.389; Music moves between Steele and Ned, Steele in *Fitchett*, *op. cit.*, p.52; Ned: 'fell from loss of blood', Const. Phillips, Claim to Kelly Reward Board, 20.12.1880, VPRO. Note that Dowsett saw Steele 'rush from the tree *behind* Kelly' (my italics), *Age*, 1.7.1880.

The Last Stand ends in a welter of conflicting evidence. Steele's version is discussed in the text. Rawlins, local grazier, was a Steele man and backed his story, as were Wangaratta clerk of courts, Marsden (though his evidence was surprisingly vague), and, of course, Constable Dwyer from Wangaratta. Sr Const. Kelly was vigorously anti-Steele and Dowsett supported Kelly's account, as did on-the-spot reporters Allen and McWhirter. When in doubt, I have looked to Dowsett as the most unbiased witness intimately involved in those chaotic few seconds covered by Steele, *Commission*, Q.9038–9, p.328; Kelly, Q.8242–7, p.305; Dwyer, Q.9454–64, pp.341–2; Dowsett, Q.10920–5, pp.389–90; Rawlins, Q.11740–50, pp.415–16; Marsden, Q.13995–14003, pp.509–10; Allen, Q.10753–65, pp.384–5; McWhirter, Q.10349–54, pp.372–3.

Steele's oath, prepares to shoot Ned, Q.10934, p.390; 'blow the outlaw's brain out', Q.10762, p.384; Dr Nicolson's description, *Argus*, 2.7.1880; 'more than 28 wounds': estimates of Ned's wounds varied wildly, first reports quoting everything from 'three' (*Herald*, 28.6.1880) to 'seventeen' (*D.T.*, 29.6.1880); at Beechworth in August, Dr O'Brien reported that Ned had 23 wounds 'in the lower extremities', *O & M*, 3.8.1880; widely reported wounds in arms and hands — even without the 'borderline' wounds to both groins — bring the total to above 28, ranging from the small punctures of shotgun pellets to the brutal .45–inch entry and exit wounds torn by Martini Henry bullets; 'wild ... wasted look', *Commission*, Q.10356, p.373.

There are various accounts of Ned pleading for his life, gleefully fastened on by Hare. 'Notwithstanding all Kelly's boasted pluck and bounce, how game he would die, &c., he was the only one who in any way showed the white feather. When the constables ran up to him after Steele had hold of him, *he begged for mercy, and asked them to spare his life*' [my italics], *Hare*, p.318; At the Royal Commission, almost a year later, Dowsett was unsure what Ned had said. 'That's enough: I have got my gruel' is from his Report to the Traffic Manager, *op. cit., four days after the event.*

Dwyer kicks Ned, 'war whoop', Q.10351, p.373; 'Take the man alive', Q.10934, p.390; Bracken protects Ned, Q.10762, p.384.

Steele's 'heroic spotlight': 'I told her to run on quickly', *Argus*, 29.6.1880; called on police not to fire, Steele's Claim to Kelly Reward Board, 6.7.1880, VPRO; had shot Joe Byrne, Q.14098, p.517; Steele's 'single-handed' capture, Q.9038–9, p.328; 'baldest re-arrangement of fact', Steele at Supreme Court q. *Herald*, 29.10.1880.

'Dan shouted with rage', *Herald*, 29.6.1880; 'very vicious shooting', *Sadleir*, p.234; Melvin: 'Keep watch!', *Commission*, Q.9473, p.342; Ned and armour taken to station, *Argus*, 2.7.1880; *Commission*, Q.8269–70, p.305, Q.9039, p.328; Dan at kitchen door, Q.9473, p.342; Dan hit in leg, *Herald*, 29.6.1880, cf. Dan's 'left knee was crippled', Q.9539, p.345; Ned faints 'once or twice', *Argus*, 5.7.1880; feet cold, *Argus*, 2.7.1880; 'gentle expression', *Sadleir*, p.238; 'every care and attention', Q.9482, p.343.

Call for surrender, *Argus*, 5.7.1880; prisoners 'like bees', Q.2829, p.150; armed reporters, Q.10825, p.369; 'polish off this lot', Reward Board, Q.85, p.6; Dan and Steve don't fire at police in open, *Commission*, Q.2832, p.150; 'like two condemned prisoners',

Argus, 5.7.1880; 'what will we do?', *Age*, 29.6.1880; Reardon's belief they would suicide, *Herald*, 30.6.1880; line repaired by 7 a.m., *Argus*, 1.7.1880; scene in Melbourne, *Argus*, 29.6.1880; news to London in 5 hrs, *O & M*, 2.9.1880; 90 000 words to Sydney, *Herald*, 29.6.1880.

'Constant galloping', *Commission*, Q.17626, p.665; help from 'Greta side', Reward Board, Q.144, p.9; attempt to drive off police horses; *ibid.*, Q.86, p.6; 'bad nest of them', *Commission*, Q.10038, p.362; 'their name was legion', *Hare*, p.318; 'about 30', *Illustrated London News*, 11.9.1880.

Dean Gibney gave various interviews and appeared before the Royal Commission. I have drawn material largely from an excellent interview in the *Sydney Evening News*, reprinted, *Herald*, 19.7.1880.

Sadleir: 'Keep your ground,' *Commission*, Q.2879, p.153; 'sudden rush ... might have been affected', *Sadleir*, p.236; had selected men he would lead, *ibid.*; Sadleir's field gun, *Herald*, 28.6.1880; electric lights and bonfires, *Argus*, 29.6.1880; Ramsay 'directs' Standish to attend, *ibid.*

Johnston told 'keep quiet', *Commission*, Q.7173, p.266; Maggie's outfit, *Argus*, 29.6.1880; ordered back at gunpoint, *Commission*, Q.9539, p.345; Johnston and the four men, *Sadleir*, p.237; Tom Lloyd and Dick Hart see Johnston, Interview, Tom Lloyd Jr, 4.1.1964; 'over a thousand spectators', *Herald*, 29.6.1880; Maggie and Sr Const. Kelly, *Commission*, Q.10405–6, p.374; Kate and Gibney, *Herald*, 19.7.1880; 'rattle of gunfire', *Argus*, 5.7.1880; Johnston walks 'quite coolly', *Commission*, Q.2866, p.152; match misses fire, *ibid.*; Gibney's second approach to Kate, *Herald*, 19.7.1880; *Commission*, 12301, p.441; 'blue tongue of flame', *D.T.*, 30.6.1880; 'failed to catch', Q.2866, p.152; Gibney: 'no time to lose', *Herald*, 19.7.1880; 'religious sign of the cross', Q.2866, p.152; 'great sheet of flame', *Sadleir*, p.237; 'cloud of fire and smoke', *Commission*, Q.2869, p.152; Wild thinks inn will 'tumble down', *Herald*, 26.7.1880; finding the bodies, *Herald*, 19.7.1880, and, *Commission*, Q.12314–21, p.442. Surprisingly, Gibney was never asked to describe the two men he saw in the back room, but in his Sydney interview offered that they were 'beardless boys', persuasive evidence that these were in fact Dan and Steve and not — according to the most plausible theories — a pair of 'swaggies' (cf. *Ashmead*, p.27) accidentally killed and placed with the armour. Dwyer's identification of Dan Kelly (*Argus*, 29.6.1880 and *Commission*, Q.9539–40, p.345) is also persuasive. He is not an ideal witness but his testimony is preferable to the 'evidence', produced from time to time this century, that Dan Kelly — and possibly Steve Hart — survived, went to Queensland, the Boer War etc., etc. None yet produced stands up to close examination. The almost inevitable conclusion from Gibney's evidence is that Dan and Steve suicided — a theory supported by Wild Wright (*Herald*, 26.7.1880) who believed they shot each other. There is *some* evidence that one was killed and the other suicided, none of it conclusive.

Constable about to shoot Joe's body, *Commission*, Q.12322–3, p.442 & *Herald*, *op. cit.*; 'Don't shoot', *ibid.*; Armstrong and Dwyer see Dan and Steve, rescue Joe's body, Armstrong, *Commission*, Q.12250–6, p.439; Dwyer, Q.9539–64, pp.345–6; Gibney, Q.12322–3, p.442. The testimony is contradictory, with confusion between front and back doors of the inn. If, as Gibney swore, he did not re-enter the burning inn after leaving by the back door, he could have seen Armstrong pointing his revolver at Joe's body (and placed his hand on the constable's arm, Q.12323, p.442) only if he had then gone around to the front, which would also explain the applause he received. But this means that both Dwyer and Armstrong were wrong in insisting that they entered by the back door. My account tries to reconcile the three versions.

Cherry's last words, his inquest, *Argus*, 1.7.1880; Carrington describes the bodies, *Argus*, 5.7.1880; 'striking sketch', see photograph pages; 'howled loudly and lustily', *Argus*,

5.7.1880; photograph of burnt body by Mrs Jones's table, see photograph pages; 'look what is coming', *Commission*, Q.9947, p.352; 'friends ... began to come up', Q.2876, p.153; 'people ... in hundreds', *Herald*, 29.6.1880; Maggie's call for vengeance, *ibid.*; railway blocked, *Commission*, Q.7, p.6; Sadleir's 'unexpected favour', Q.2875, p.153; magisterial order?, Q.2895, p.155; 'beneficial to public peace', Q.2899, p.156; Standish 'did not interfere', Q.2877, p.153, Standish: 'possible ... there was a misapprehension', Q.77, p.6; 'on Captain Standish's part', Q.2898, p.155; special six-man squad, *Herald*, 28.6.1880; 'Melbourne ... preferable', Telegram, Standish to Chief Secretary, 28.6.1880, Kelly Papers, VPRO.

20 'A DEAL OF ILL BLOOD STIRRING', page 274

McIntyre and Sen. Const. Kelly confront Ned, depositions, prosecution brief, *op. cit.*; 'Gale's story', *D.T.*, 30.6.1880; Grant and the coffins, *Argus*, 30.6.1880; brass fittings, *Herald*, 30.6.1880; 'astir at 6.30', *Regulations for ... Constabulary ...*, *op. cit.*; Joe photographed, see photograph pages for one of Burman's widely sold studies; Glenrowan souvenirs, inc. bloodstained leaves, *Herald*, 29.6.1880; 'a charred foot' and blood-soaked soil, *D.T.*, 2.7.1880; Reardon points out packhorse, *Commission*, Q.7770–2, pp.280–1, and, Report, Const. McHugh to Sadleir, 5.7.1880, Kelly Papers, VPRO; McHugh hides the drum, *ibid.*; 'rude infernal machine', *Herald*, 1.7.1880, and *O & M*, 24.7.1880; Kelly horses in stable, *Age*, 29.6.1880, *D.T. & Argus*, 30.6.1880; Joe's mare caught and photographed, *McMenomy*, p.198, a group clearly photographed on the evening of the siege. 'Ned's mare' found on way home, *Age*, 1.7.1880; grey 'pony *horse*', *PG*, 18.8.1880, p.223, described by Whelan as a 'mongrel', escaped etc., *O & M*, 22.7.1880; Steele denies existence of 'grey mare', *ibid.*; Carrington sketch of her, *Sketcher*, 17.1.1880; Reporter Allen searches for her, *Commission*, Q.10778, p.385; Commission asks about her, Q.10777 and Q.10779, p.385; 'Ned Kelly's grey mare' in 'Kelly Show', see Chapter 23.

Arrival of Grant and coffins, *Ashmead*, pp.27–8; journalists pose, *McMenomy*, pp.196–7; 'eye witness' stories of wake, *Herald*, 30.6.1880; 'everything went off quietly', *Herald*, 26.7.1880; 'Kate Lloyd will break her heart', *Herald*, 29.6.1880; Kate 'crying bitterly', and costume portrayed, *Australian Pictorial Weekly*, 10.7.1880, Queensberry Hill Press facsimile, 1982; had seen Joe, *Age*, 29.6.1880; 'appeared terribly agitated', *ibid.*; 'cried without restraint', *Argus*, 30.6.1880.

Dr Ryan's report on Ned, *Argus*, 30.6.1880; crowds behind Cup barriers, the drive to gaol, *Age*, 29.6.1880; *Herald*, 30.6.1880; *Argus* and *D.T.*, 30.6.1880; 'prisoner's reckless daring', *Argus*, 30.6.1880; to a water bed, *D.T.*, 30.6.1880; Father Aylward alerted by Gibney, *Herald*, 5.7.1880; Ellen's dream, *D.T.*, 30.6.1880; cries uncontrollably, *ibid.*; Governor's congratulatory telegram, Sadleir 'mad with jealousy', *Commission*, Q.11969, p.425; 'more diplomatic message', *PG*, 7.7.1880, p.171 (including praise for 'very proper prudence and caution', shown in the siege, clearly a sop to Sadleir). Threats, *W.T.*, 3.7.1880; Steele's greyhound poisoned, Bracken guarded, *D.T.*, 30.6.1880; Steele 'killed by Kate Kelly' furphy, Sadleir's telegram, *Herald*, 30.6.1880; Rawlins 'shot' forced to leave property, *O & M*, 12 & 17.7.1880; Tom asks for Joe's body, 'load is hard to bear', *Herald*, 30.6.1880; secret burial of Joe 'great disappointment', *ibid.*; Dick

Hart's defiance, *Age*, 1.7.1880; Dan's and Steve's inquest to go ahead, *ibid.*, and *Argus*, 1.7.1880; 'pitched battle' in Benalla, *Herald*, 1.7.1880; Wild and Mrs McDonnell, *Herald*, 30.6.1880; 30 mourners overnight at Maggie's, *O & M*, 3.7.1880; police ready to move on Greta, *Argus*, 1.7.1880; Coroner and clerk 'disinclined to undertake the duty', and police will have to fight for bodies, *ibid.*, *Age* and *D.T.*, 1.7.1880; 'fifty armed men', telegram, C. Stephens, to J. Anderson (Traffic Manager, Spencer Street) 11.30 a.m., 30.6.1880, Kelly Papers, VPRO; preparations for funeral, *O & M*, 3.7.1880; Crown Law Office intervenes, *Age*, 1.7.1880; 'game . . . not worth the candle', *Argus*, 1.7.1880; 'curious certificate', *D.T.*, 30.6.1880 and *Age*, 1.7.1880. Legends gathered around the burial of Dan and Steve, most popularly, that they were buried at Eleven Mile Creek and the Three Mile. The story in the *O & M*, 3.7.1880, the basis of my account, is detailed, authoritative and fits all available evidence. For presence of Jim, *Herald*, 1.7.1880; of Dick Hart, interview, Steve Hart, 1957; first soil on coffin, *ibid.*; wait 'a long time', *D.T.*, 1.7.1880.

'Tell her to be quiet, too', *W.T.*, 3.7.1880; description of this 'extraordinary reunion', *Herald*, 1.7.1880; quotes from Ned, *D.T.*, 1.7.1880; 'of a very affecting character', *Herald*, 1.7.1880; 'FIFTY SYMPATHISERS ARMED', *Herald*, 30.6.1880; 'a deal of ill blood stirring', *ibid.*; Kelly Country centres reinforced, *D.T.*, 1.7.1880; 'men wolves', *Age*, 29.6.1880; 'day of prayer', *Herald*, 2.7.1880; 'constabulary force requires reorganization', *Age*, 3.7.1880; 'searching inquiry', *Argus*, 10.7.1880; 'tone . . . has deteriorated', *O & M*, 24.7.1880; disillusionment from 'The Vagabond', *O & M*, 10.7.1880.

Sadleir releases claim that Ned Kelly had shot Martin Cherry, *Argus*, *Age* and *D.T.*, 2.7.1880; *O & M*, 3.7.1880 (while 'raging like a wild beast'). Piazzi claims Ned shot Metcalf, Detective Report, Eason to Sadleir, 26.7.1880, Kelly Papers, VPRO; Piazzi compensation claim, Letter, Standish to Chief Secretary, 26.8.1880, Kelly Papers, VPRO; (Piazzi, who suffered no wound or injury at Glenrowan, died only fifteen months later, on 26.9.1881.) Sadleir's version of Cherry's death 'generally discredited', *Age*, 3.7.1880; Larkins's story and police pressure on him, *Benalla Standard* q. *O & M*, 14.8.1880. Standish urges inquiry, Letter, Standish to Chief Secretary, 5.7.1880, q. *Commission*, Appendix 2, pp.682–3.

Maggie, Tom and Jim McElroy 'triumphantly escorted', *D.T.*, 6.7.1880.

21 A LAST FIGHT IN BEECHWORTH, page 286

George Metcalf dies in Melbourne, 15.10.1880. Despite claims that he had not been wounded by a police bullet, his board and lodging and medical bills were paid by the department (Nicolson to Chief Secretary, 9.12.1980, Kelly Papers, VPRO); Jane Jones dies 15.4.1882; Mrs McGuirk dies 25.8.1880; fear of Kelly sympathisers as cause of death, *Benalla Standard* q. *Herald*, 28.8.1880.

Standish's questions for Tarleton, Letter, Standish to Tarleton, 19.8.1880, Prosecution Brief, *op. cit.*; 'Missing Friends' entries, *PG*, 1.9.1880, seeking John Carson and William Fitzgerald from Faithfull's Creek; Ramsay refuses 100 applications to visit Ned, *Age*, 8.7.1880; Kate turned away, *Argus*, 7.7.1880; Maggie and Tom etc., followed, Report, Detective O'Donnell, 6 & 7.8.1880, Kelly Papers, VPRO; 'a monstrous tyranny', *Age*, 7.8.1880; affidavit on police attempt to stop family raising money on land, *Herald*,

15.10.1880 and *Age*, 16.10.1880; the *D.T.* and *Argus*, both 16.10.1880, omit reference to police.

Ned's nurse, a Collins Street financier, *D.T.*, 27.7.1880; Ned speaks with Zincke, *D.T.*, 29.7.1880 & *O & M*, 31.7.1880; description of Zincke and 'string ensemble', photos in Burke Museum, Beechworth; Zincke on his background, *Herald*, 19.7.1880; quotes from interview with Ned, *Age*, 5.8.1880; Zincke talks with Beechworth journalist, *O & M*, 31.7.1880; 'more like a priest ...', interview, Tom Lloyd Jr, 4.1.1964; Tom and Maggie return to Melbourne, *Argus*, 2.8.1880; hearing in hospital kitchen, *D.T.* and *Argus*, 2.8.1880; press engraving, *Sketcher*, 14.8.1880; Ned leaves gaol in 'stylish outfit', *D.T.* and *Argus*, 2.8.1880; *O & M*, 3.8.1880; 'impudent bearing', *Argus* 2.8.1880; 'mysterious special train', *ibid.* and *Herald*, 2.8.1880; 'will I ever be there again?', *Argus*, 2.8.1880; police smile, *O & M*, 3.8.1880; clash with Steele, *Argus* & *O & M*, *op. cit.*; arrival in Beechworth and hearing, *O & M*, 3.8.1880; Maggie again refused permission to see Ned, *Argus*, 5.8.1880; Maggie and Tom play politics, *D.T.*, 6.8.1880; speak with Gaunson, letter to Ned, his telegram to Gaunson etc., *Age*, 7.8.1880; Gaunson's meeting with Ned in Beechworth Gaol, *ibid.*

Gaunson's background, *ADB*, article by Geoffrey Serle, Vol. 4, p.238; see also article on Grant, by Geoffrey Bartlett, *ADB*, Vol. 4, p.283–4; 'warts-and-all portrait', Deakin, *op. cit.*, p.79; obituary in *Labor Call*, 7.1.1909; 'heads of the aristocrats', Deakin, *op. cit.*, p.15; 'unstable as water', *O & M*, 3.6.1880; Ned on 'full and fair trial', and 'kept here like a wild beast', *Age*, 7.8.1880.

'Many, mere girls', *ibid.*; Ned 'a hero of romance', *O & M*, 7.8.1880; Standish sits with Foster 'by courtesy', *Herald*, 6.8.1880; description of Ned's entrance, *D.T.*, 7.8.1880; Ned 'lame and maimed', *Argus*, 7.8.1880; Gaunson's plea for visitors and his clash with prosecution, *Age*, 7.8.1880. Consistently, the *Age* and the *Herald* recorded points scored by the defence, *generally* ignored or glossed over by the *Argus*, *D.T.*, and, to a lesser extent, the *O & M*. Yet, ironically, when Ned and Maggie at last exchanged a few words, the most effective coverage was from the latter papers — from the *D.T.* until Ned's last remark, 'there's one native that's no cur ...', which is from the *Argus*.

McIntyre describes Lonigan's death and 'how he caught at his revolver', *O & M*, 7.8.1880; Ned 'shoots' at boys, Interview, Roy Harvey, June, 1959.

Reading-back of McIntyre's evidence, *O & M*, 10.8.1880; Ned's portrait 'for legal purposes', *Illustrated Australian News*, 28.8.1880; 'gentleman with the brush and pencil', *Age*, 9.8.1880; 'appearance of a true brigand', *Herald*, 9.8.1880; engraving of Ashton's painting, *Illustrated Australian News, op. cit.*

Ned 'smiling', *Argus*, 9.8.1880; 'a cannon?', *Age*, 9.8.1880; unusual amount of ammunition, *Argus*, 12.8.1880; 'incapable ... as he fell on his knees', *O & M*, 12.8.1880; 'prisoner fired the shot', *Herald*, 11.8.1880; 'will not swear ...', *Age*, 9.8.1880; left Kennedy 'in the lurch', *Age*, 9.8.1880; 'two men firing at each other', *Herald*, 11.8.1880; McIntyre 'nearly hysterical', *Herald*, 9.8.1880; 'turn you inside out', *Age*, 9.8.1880.

Lonigan behind a log? 'that is only nonsense', *D.T.*, 9.8.1880; McIntyre's account three days after Stringybark, *Sadleir*, pp.187–8; For a clear indication that Sadleir is carefully transcribing from his original note of the conversation, see the use (and bracketed correction) of third person instead of first ... 'the horse moved towards him (McIntyre) ...' (p.188); Sadleir 'austere and dignified', Interview, Mrs Val Murray, 1974; Kennedy's ear chewed off by a wildcat, *Herald*, 12.8.1880.

Gaunson's interview with Ned for *Age* reporter, *Age*, 9.8.1880; 'the big language used in Parliament', '*O & M*, 17.8.1880. Kate Lloyd in court, *D.T.*, 10.8.1880; Stephens takes 'a mauling', *Herald*, 9.8.1880; Stephens helped Bracken watch Maggie's house, *Herald*, 10.8.1880; 'a general rule' to warn prisoners, *O & M*, 12.8.1880; Const. Kelly fired at 'innocent people?', and 'the police ... murdered Cherry', *Age*, 11.8.1880;

Foster: 'irrelevant', *ibid.*; Gaunson's closing remarks, *O & M*, 12.8.1880; Gaunson sings at charity concert, *O & M*, 14.8.1880 ('a good, though not powerful voice').

Decoy loco, *Herald*, 12.8.1880; Ned, in wagonette, met by escort, *O & M*, 14.8.1880; special equipment in van, *Herald*, 12.8.1880; 'there's a lot of colonials', *Age*, 13.8.1880; 'tears ... in his eyes', *Herald*, 13.8.1880; heavy snow on Buffalo, *O & M*, 17.8.1880; 'Engine No. 38' ploughs through sheep, *Herald*, 13.8.1880.

22 'THEY WILL ONLY BE SATISFIED WITH MY LIFE', page 300

Ned 'tired and depressed', *Age*, 14.8.1880; bullet removed from foot, continuing trouble with wounds, *ibid.* & *Herald*, 12.8.1880; arm and hand withering, *Herald*, 16.10.1880; 'premier bushranger ... sees what the end will be', *O & M*, 2.9.1880.

Civil servants being 'Black Wednesdayed', *Herald,* 23.8.1880; Payment of Members Bill, *O & M*, 7.10.1880; Yarra floods, *Herald*, 12.9.1880; first telephone pole, *Herald*, 18.9.1880; 1200 unemployed, 6 shillings a day, *Herald*, 12.8.1880; selectors live on 'boiled wheat and rabbits', *D.T.*, 20.9.1880; talk of 'riot and revolution', *Herald*, 23.8.1880; 'agrarian outrages', *O & M*, 14.8.1880; trial transferred to Melbourne, *Herald*, 18 and 22.9:1880; sympathy spreading, *D.T.*, 5.8.1880.

Maggie and Tom visit Skilling, *D.T.*, 20.10.1880, *O & M*, 21.10.1880. Kellys can't pay for defence, *Herald*, 13.10.1880; Molesworth and his fee, John Phillips, *The Trial of Ned Kelly*, Sydney, 1987, pp.26–7; 'Time-honoured tactic', *ibid.*, pp.29–30; Ned borrows William Gaunson's coat, Maggie Skilling and Kate Lloyd in court, *Herald*, 18.10.1880; Ned shaken by Bindon's late arrival, *ibid.*; for proceedings, see also, *Age, D.T.* & *Argus*, all 19.10.1880; 'very becoming', *Herald*, 18.10.1880.

Special arrangements to light court, *Herald*, 14.10.1880; Barry willing to sit until midnight, *Herald*, 28.10.1880; Bindon bumbles, Smyth indicates Ned on trial as enemy of society, *ibid.*; Tarleton's 'splendid summary' of defence, *Age*, 30.10.1880; Scott: 'not ... a single rude word', Ned winks, *Herald*, 29.10.1880; Barry confirms *Herald* story, *Argus*, 29.10.1880 (the *Herald* claim that Barry was prepared to sit until midnight had appeared in the early edition, covering only the morning's proceedings). Jury locked up in Supreme Court Hotel, *D.T.*, 29.10.1880.

City 'enveloped in dust', family and friends in court and Ned's appearance, *Herald,* 29.10.1880; Barry sustains Bindon's extraordinary objection to the Jerilderie Letter, *ibid.*; 'evidence for the prisoner ...', Roger Simpson, *The Trial of Ned Kelly*, Melbourne, 1977, p.34 (a television play by a gifted writer who had practised law for three years and first recognised the depth of Bindon's tragic blunder in opposing admission of the Jerilderie Letter as evidence. John Phillips examines the ramifications in Phillips, *op. cit.*, pp.58–61).

Bindon's attempt to have his objections referred to the Full Court, *Age*, 30.10.1880 ('transactions ... after the death of Lonigan' and Barry's response), *D.T.*, 30.10.1880 ('whole of the evidence ... was admissible'); 'the sole speech in defence', Robin Corfield, *The Trial of Ned Kelly*, unpublished typescript MS., 1960, n.p. (this third work of the same title is, again, a television play, comprising a carefully reconstructed transcript of the trial based on a *variorum* reading of all available press accounts); 'a number of things foreign ...', *Age*, 30.10.1880; ignore shooting of Kennedy etc., *ibid.*; 'unfortunate fracas', *ibid.*; 'shots fired by others at the same time', *O & M*, 2.10.1878; McIntyre's story, 'deliberate and careful preparation', *Age*, 30.10.1878 (a claim borne out by McIntyre's pencil draft of his evidence at Beechworth, Prosecution Brief, *op. cit.*); Lonigan 'met his death in a fusilade', Corfield, *op. cit.*; Barry's summing up 'in favour of the Prosecution', Phillips, *op. cit.*, p.94; 'a double protection' and, 'What right had four armed men ...?', *ibid.*; 'for the jury to decide whether the police were acting as ministers of justice ...', *ibid.*, p.87; 'Edward Kelly was not afforded a trial according to law', *ibid.*, p.94, an authoritative judgement which complements the 1967 opinion of Professor Louis Waller that, if competently defended, Ned Kelly *might* have escaped the charge of murdering Lonigan (Louis Waller, 'Regina v. Edward Kelly' in *Man and Myth, op. cit.*, pp.105–41, see also pp.152–3).

Jury retires for half an hour, *D.T.*, 30.10.1880; only Kate Lloyd and McAuliffe girl wait for verdict, *Argus*, 30.10.1880; 'the Anglo-Irish nightmare', *McQuilton*, note 78, p.229; 'too symmetrical for comfort', *de Serville, op. cit.*, pp.74–5; Ned's elbows on rail, *O & M*, 30.10.1880; Ned, 'calm and collected', *D.T.*, 30.10.1880; replies in 'mild undertones', *Argus*, 30.10.1878.

The extraordinary exchange between Ned and his judge was widely and selectively reported. I have gratefully used Robin Corfield's text (Corfield, *op. cit.*).

'Goodbye, you'll see me there', *D.T.*, 30.10.1880; 'appearing quite unconcerned', *O & M*, 30.10.1880; Ned's bravado to warders, *Herald*, 30.10.1880; Condemned Cell described, *Argus & D.T.*, both, 12.11.1880; 'ordinary prison fare' and 'singing secular songs', *Herald*, 30.10.1880; 'contingent' of Sunday visitors, *ibid.*; Ellen visits Ned, clinking of chains from daily exercise, *Herald*, 1.11.1880; text of reprieve petition form, Capital Case File, VPRO; Letter, E. Kelly to the Governor, 3.11.1880, *ibid.*; 'it is short', *D.T.*, 4.11.1880; Upjohn gaoled in August for chicken stealing, *O & M*, 20.11.1880; 'emptying a privy and carrying away the contents without a license', *PG Prisoners Released*, w.e. 17.1.1870; parting from Kate and Jim 'of a painful nature', *Herald*, 4.11.1880; Letter, E. Kelly to the Governor, 5.11.1880, Capital Case File, *op. cit.*; 'ammunition for the anti-Kelly press', *Herald*, 6.11.1880.

Mass meeting at Hippodrome, women 'from Little Bourke Street', *Age*, 6.11.1880; 'unnamed detective', *D.T.*, 6.11.1880; 'respectable working men', *ibid.*; 'upon what a fearful volcano society stands', *Bendigo Independent*, 9.11.1880; meeting's resolution, Capital Case File, *op. cit.*

Crowd at town hall, 'of the labouring classes', *Age*, 8.11.1880; 'idle and seedy looking' and 'very nondescript', *Argus*, 8.11.1880; interview with Marquis of Normanby, 'I should be deceiving you', *Age*, 8.11.1880. 'I have a painful duty ...,' *Argus*, 8.11.1880; Jim, Wild and Tom at Rainbow Hotel, *Herald*, 6.11.1880; 'weak minded people, mainly women' sign Kate's petition, *Age*, 8.11.1880; publican of the Robert Burns, Daniel Buckley, 'largest beard ... in the city', R.H. Cole Collection, La Trobe Library, City Index, Vol. 1, Pt 2, p.139; 'no row or disturbance', *Herald*, 9.11.1880; 200 from 'back slums of the city', *Argus*, 9.11.1880; deputation to Government House, 'unwashed ... mob', Maggie turns back etc., *Herald*, 8.11.1880; le Patourel presented with 32 424 signatures, more time, 50 000, *Argus*, 9.11.1880 (I have assumed that '500 000' is a misprint!); Executive firm, Jim: 'not done yet', *ibid.*

Petitions to Jerilderie, *Albury Banner*, 13.11.1880; meeting at Supreme Court Reserve, *Argus*, 10.11.1880; Nicolson leads seventy reinforcements, *D.T.*, 10.11.1880; two men arrested, both 'respectable parties', *Herald*, 10.11.1880; (they received six-month good behaviour bonds); 'rough looking persons' with torches, Patrick Quinn's statement, asks for Royal Commission, 'something would come out of it', Berry's response, *ibid.*; 'a patient trial', *D.T.*, 11.11.1880.

Letter, E. Kelly to the Governor, 10.11.1880, Capital Case File, *op. cit.*; Ned 'in a state of nervous unrest', *Age*, 10.11.1880; Executive Council meets early to avoid deputation of women, *Herald*, 10.11.1880; last photograph, see photograph pages; close-up, *McMenomy*, p.246; Ellen's words to Ned, *D.T.*, 11.11.1880, cf. *Hare*, p.319; Jim's, Kate's and Grace's farewells, *D.T.*, 11.11.1880; Jim: Ned will be revenged, *D.T.*, 12.11.1880; Ned meets Godfrey Castieau, Godfrey's later career, Mary Bateman, 'The Lincoln-Cass Films', *Cinema Papers*, June–July 1980, pp.170–2. My thanks to Castieau descendant Ian McKellar for this reference; Kate and Tom Lloyd visit, Interview, Tom Lloyd Jr, 4.1.1964; Ned's farewell to Tom, *ibid.*; Ned's last meal, *Ashmead*, p.29 (a detail undoubt-edly gleaned from Ellen Kelly, which prompted Ashmead, self-styled 'puritan', to find Biblical sanction, 'Give strong drink to him who is to perish'); Crowd of 4000 at Robert Burns Hotel, *D.T.*, 11.11.1880; Ned sings, 'Sweet Bye-and-bye' a favourite, *Bendigo Independent*, 12.11.1880; Warder Buck's matter-of-fact record of Ned's last night, *D.T.*, 12.11.1880.

Ned's execution received enormous coverage in city and country papers, that day and for days to come. I have sourced a few less-dog-eared details.

'A twisted blue handkerchief', *Bendigo Independent*, 12.11.1880 (a hostile paper which pro-vided many closely observed facets from an anonymous and as yet unidentified cor-respondent); Ned reaches gallery, smiles, *D.T.*, 12.11.1880; hot north wind, *Herald*, 11.11.1880; 100 vehicles 'of all descriptions' *ibid.*; 'apparently respectable' women, *ibid.*; 'criminal and depraved classes', *D.T.*, 12.11.1880; respect for Ellen, *Herald*, 30.6.1880; Upjohn in his shirt sleeves (a detail at odds with the well-known *Sketcher* engraving of 20.11.1880); 'I'll go quietly', *The Leader*, 13.11.1880; 'Such is life', *Herald*, 11.11.1880; 'when told the hour of his death', *O & M*, 13.11.1880; 'I suppose it has come to this', *Argus*, 12.11.1880; 'the expression was never concluded', *D.T.*, 11.11.1880; 'slight shudder', *D.T.*, 12.11.1880; Ned looks up at the skylight, *Bendigo Independent*, 12.11.1880; Dr Barker goes 'to adjust the rope', 'four-and-a-half minutes past ten', body 'slowly revolves' and 'plain ring' catching light, *ibid.*

Movement of Ned's legs, the scene at the Robert Burns and the 'singular coincidence' of the chill wind, *Herald*, 11.11.1880; woman offers 'audible prayers', *D.T.*, 12.11.1880; 'con-traction of the extensor muscles', *Bendigo Independent*, 12.11.1880; body hangs half an hour, *D.T.*, 12.11.1880; 'life-like appearance', *ibid.*; 'his smile in death', phrenol-ogist Hamilton in, *Herald*, 18.11.1880; Kreitmayer's death mask on display next day, *Herald*, 12.11.1880; medical mutilation of Ned's body, 'hardly ever parallelled', *Bendigo Independent*, 19.11.1880; 'laid to rot', *ibid.*, 12.11.1880.

23 LEGACY AND LEGEND, page 325

A 'howl' and shot outside Greta police station on 20.11.1880, *Argus* and *Herald*, 23.11.1880; same night, a shot at Glenrowan barracks, *Age*, 24.11.1880 and *Herald*, 25.11.1880; Jim and Kate in 'bizarre stage presentation', all Melbourne dailies, 12.11.1880; 'clam-our' for inquiry, predictably, led by the *Herald*, 12.11.1880 and 14.11.1880, with the *Argus* reporting the urging of 'some officers', 15.11.1880, and *D.T.*, 17.11.1880, not-ing Mr Graves MLA taking up the issue in Parliament. Sir Redmond Barry died on the morning of 23.11.1880, and that very evening the *Herald* linked his death with Ned's remarks at the trial. Les Carlyon's 'irreverent' comment, *The Last Outlaw*, *op. cit.*, p.58.

Death of Ned, 'an impressive lesson of morality', *Age*, 13.11.1880; hanging inflamed situation in north-east, suspend *habeas corpus*, etc., *O & M*, 25.11.1880; Greta, 'the worst place in the colony', *Commission*, Q8365 p.308; the four police stationed at Greta, Muster Rolls, VPRS 55, Unit 10, VPRO. The story of Robert Graham's work at Greta is sketched in the author's 'New View of Ned Kelly' in *Man and Myth, op. cit.*, pp.176–81. 'Nicolson: every offence ... grappled with', *O & M*, 27.11.1880; Graham's romance with Mary Kirk, letters, 17.3.1879 to 14.12.1881, extracts quoted, *Man and Myth, op. cit.*, pp.86–8, copies held by author; 'behaved bravely and well', Sadleir's endorsement on Graham's Record Sheet, 16.8.1880; Graham's policy with locals, interviews with Chauncey Graham, Mrs E. Smurthwaite and Mrs R. Fordyce, children of Robert Graham, 8.5.1963 (hereafter, Graham Interviews); Tom Lloyd Snr: 'the Kellys wanted ground', *Man and Myth, op. cit.*, p.178; 'no further selections to doubtful characters', *Sadleir*, p.239; Const. Wallace's 'special rapport' with Bridget O'Brien — they later married, Report, Det. Sgt. Ward to Insp. Kennedy, 22.12.1892, Kelly Papers, VPRO; Tom helps locate police horse, *Commission*, Q.12181, p.435.

Jim and Kate's 'strange adventures' — in the Apollo Hall, all Melbourne dailies, 12.11.1880; took 'a good deal of money', *O & M*, 13.11.1880; closed by police, at instigation of William Gaunson? *Bendigo Independent*, 16.11.1880; move to cancel licence, *Age*, 13.11.1880; Georgia Minstrels resume, *Argus*, 13.11.1880; Jim's and Kate's plans for the Hippodrome, *Bendigo Independent*, 16.11.1880; sail to Sydney, *Sydney Evening News* q. *Herald*, 23.11.1880; Kelly show 'up a lane in King Street', *O & M*, 25.11.1880; entrepreneurs face 'remarkable charge', *Herald*, 25.11.1880; Const. Graham sees Kate on 'bolting' horse, Graham Interviews, *op. cit.*; Kate on way to Adelaide, Detective Report, 21.12.1880, Kelly Papers, VPRO.

'Like ghosts of the Kelly Gang ...', *Man and Myth, op. cit.*, p.177; Jim: 'will not enter the bush ...', *Commission*, Q.1281, p.435; Tom and Dinny 'inclined to be most friendly', Q.1282, p.435.

Ellen freed, *PG Prisoners Released*, w.e. 14.2.1881; only eight months remission, cf. *Herald*, 30.6.1880, predicting nine months remission in view of her excellent conduct and attitude; Kate's Adelaide venture 'not a success', comes to Melbourne 'with a sister', flowers and cypresses for 'Danny's grave', *O & M*, 10.3.1881; homecoming photograph, see photograph pages, the group identified by two of Mrs Kelly's grandchildren, Mrs Alma Davies (interview, 1969) and Mrs Elsie Pettifer (interview, 1995), both daughters of Ellen Jr who is feeding a pet lamb in the photograph; 'the Kelly business is all over', *O & M*, 10.3.1881.

Reward Board rejects 24 claimants, Schedule A, p.IV, Reward Board; rewards allocated, Schedule B, p.V, *ibid.*; Curnow campaigns for more, an additional £450 (taking his total reward £200 above Hare's!) included in the 1882 estimates for the Chief Secretary's Department, L.J. Pryor, *Thomas Curnow, op. cit.*, pp.32–3; Board's rationale re. Ward, Report, p.III, Reward Board; comments re. Aboriginal troopers' and trackers' rewards, *ibid.* p.IV. The scandalous treatment of the Aborigines emerged in 1994 when descendants of the Queensland Aboriginal troopers announced that they were suing the Premier of Victoria for 40 million dollars. At the time of writing, the issue is unresolved (see *Age*, 23.8.1995).

Ned urges 'investigation into ... conduct and management of the police', *Herald*, 30.10.1880; Letters Patent for Royal Commission, *VGG*, 7.3.1881, p.743; Longmore 'went relentlessly for scalps' and 'all the faults of other like bodies', *Sadleir*, p.240; no evidence of 'persecution or unnecessary annoyance by the police', *Commission*, 2nd Progress Report; Standish exposes Williamson as informer, *Commission*, Q.3, p.1; threats to kill him, Q.9873, p.357 cf. Q.16716, p.617. Sgt Whelan was uncertain whether the threats were against Skilling or Williamson, but the context clearly identifies Williamson.

Sympathiser vendettas, agent defections, return of equipment for bush work and refusal to establish new stations in trouble spots, all covered by Sadleir in Q.16716, p.617; his application to leave the district, Q.9862, p.356; police reinforcements under Montfort, O'Connor to head blacktrackers, *ibid.*; pit saws stolen for armour, Q.9870, p.356; Const. Graham report, 'another outbreak ... imminent', *ibid.*; Graham sleeps with revolver under pillow, men carry loaded carbines, Graham Interviews, *op. cit.*; 'another gang of bushrangers ... sympathizers' rendezvous — Mrs Kelly's house', leading article, *Benalla Standard*, 26.4.1881 q. *Commission*, Q.9871, p.356; Graham approaches Father Egan, they visit Mrs Kelly, Graham Interviews, *op. cit.* (Father Walter Ebsworth, interviewed 1970, recalled hearing of 'the priest and the sergeant' who used to visit Mrs Kelly. Around Greta, Graham was referred to as 'sergeant'.) The visit to Mrs Kelly, the subsequent visit to O'Brien's Hotel by Mrs Kelly and Jim, Graham escorting them to the race meeting, Graham Interviews, *op. cit.*; saw blade armour rusting in the bush, interviews, Gwen Griffiths, 1960, Louise Earp, 1962, Ken Embling, 1961; Const. Graham marries Mary Kirk, 31.12.1881; refurbishing of 'Adams farm house' described in his letter of 14.12.1881, *op. cit.*; their 'first child born here', Chauncey Graham who, 80 years later, took part in the Graham Interviews. Const. Wallace and Mrs O'Brien marry, take over the Broken River Hotel, receive Kennedy's watch in 1893, Report, Det. Sgt Ward to Insp. Kennedy, *op. cit.*; Letter, Wallace to Chief Commissioner, 19.7.1892; Telegram, Wallace to Chief Commissioner, 22.4.1893, all Kelly Papers, VPRO. 'A little boy' delivers the watch, interview, Bridget Griffiths, 7.8.1964.

Jim and Wild steal horses in NSW, *New South Wales Police Gazette*, 3.8.1881, p.277; caught in Kelly Country, remanded to Wagga, *ibid.* 26.10.1881; Jim, 5 years, Wild discharged, *ibid., Return of Prisoners Tried*, 30.11.1881, p.428.

Standish slammed by Royal Commission, *Commission*, 2nd Progress Report, Recommendation 2; Nicolson and Hare, Recs. 3, 4 & 5; Sadleir, Rec. 6; Brooke Smith, Rec. 7; Det. Ward, Rec. 8; Sgt Steele, Rec. 9; police in Aaron Sherritt's hut, Rec. 10; Wallace, Rec. 13; O'Connor, 1st Progress Report, Rec. 1.

Robert Graham's subsequent career, Graham Interviews, *op. cit.*; Tom Lloyd in police breeches, interview, Tom Lloyd Jr, 4.1.1964; 'more like Graham and less like Fitzpatrick ...', *ibid.*; Jim Kelly released, *New South Wales Police Gazette*, 21.1.1886, p.28; Memo, Supt. Montfort to Officers-in-Charge, 30.1.1886, draft to Const. Reilly, held by descendants (my thanks to Joan Murphy for this reference); Jim 'restless', *McQuilton*, p.183 (in a characteristically thorough examination of the pacification of the Kelly Country so lightly sketched in the present work). Jim's subsequent life, interviews, Gwen Griffiths, 1960–80; 'universally loved and respected', interview, Louise Earp, 1962.

Kate Kelly marries William Foster at Forbes, 25.11.1888; Fred b. 1889; Gertrude b. 1890; Arthur b. & d. 1891; Maude b. 1893; Ruby b. & d. 1897; Catherine b. & d. 1898. Kate's life is summarised by her nephew, Edward Foster, in a letter to the *Forbes Advocate*, 21.10.1955. My gratitude to Noel O'Shea for the above material.

Maggie Skilling dies, 22.1.1896, (registered as Skillan). Tom recorded the marriage to Bill Skilling and only the two children of that marriage, not those he fathered himself.

My account of Kate's death is drawn from her inquest, reported in the *Forbes Gazette*, 18.10.1898. My thanks to Laurie Moore for providing a copy of this source. Jim's 'hooded buggy and pair', *Ashmead*, p.33; he reached Forbes after the death of baby Catherine, 15.12.1898. Kate's headstone, a landmark of the Forbes cemetery, was erected in 1910 'under the direction of relatives in Victoria and Mr McDougall [a former employer]', Letter, Edward Foster, *op. cit.*; Fred Foster, Kate's son, 'the most handsome boy you could look at', interview, Elsie Pettifer, 22.5.1995; Fred killed in action, 17.3.1916. His last words, *Ashmead*, p.49.

Ellen Kelly's wheelchair, interview, Jack Cavanagh (Kate's grandson) 1980. (As a tiny boy, Jack could remember great granny holding his hands and walking around with his feet on hers, saying, 'Oh Jacky, ye're a baist of the faild'.) The wheelchair photograph, Dagmar Balcarek, *Ellen Kelly*, Glenrowan, 1984, end paper.

'She is cold, always cold', *Ashmead*, p.44; a last glimpse, interview, Elsie Pettifer, *op. cit.*; Ellen Kelly dies, 27.3.1923; Jim reports death, interview, Sylvia Living, 1969; her father and Steele reminisce, *ibid.*

The development and nature of the Kelly myth have been examined in two interestingly contrasted works, Graham Seal, *Ned Kelly in Popular Tradition*, Melbourne, 1980, and Wendy Morgan, *Ned Kelly Reconstructed*, Melbourne, 1994. The 'tenacious myth' of Ned leaving the burning hotel, Peter Taylor, *The Atlas of Australian History*, French's Forest, 1990, p.41.

The printed word on Ned's life and times is given a compact and witty overview in *McQuilton*, Appendix 6, 'Kelly Literature, a Brief Review'.

'The stature of God or devil', *Australian Son*, *op. cit.*, p.13; 'Ned Kelly ... a commodity to be packaged and promoted ...', the author at the Centenary Wangaratta Kelly Seminar, November, 1980; Ned Kelly in the Yarralin Dreaming, Deborah Bird Rose, *Ned Kelly Died for our Sins*, the Charles Strong Memorial Lecture, 1988, drawn to my grateful attention by Dr Joyce Richardson. The European works I cite as capturing a similar 'scope, power and timelessness' are Douglas Stewart's verse play *Ned Kelly*, Robert Drewe's short novel, *Our Sunshine*, Sir Sydney Nolan's Kelly paintings and Albert Tucker's 'King Kelly and his Legions'. It is intriguing that Nolan's first Kelly paintings showed Ned masked with a handkerchief. The armoured Kelly figure seems to have been influenced by the iconographic 'Images of Modern Evil' created by his friend Albert Tucker.

INDEX